Southscapes

NEW DIRECTIONS IN SOUTHERN STUDIES

Thadious M. Davis

Southscapes

GEOGRAPHIES OF RACE, REGION,

& LITERATURE

UNIVERSITY OF NORTH CAROLINA PRESS CHAPEL HILL

This book was published with the assistance of the Fred W. Morrison Fund for Southern Studies of the University of North Carolina Press.

Designed by Michelle Coppedge. Set in Charter with Schmutz and Gotham display by Rebecca Evans. Manufactured in the United States of America. The paper in this book meets the guidelines for permanence and durability of the Committee on Production Guidelines for Book Longevity of the Council on Library Resources. The University of North Carolina Press has been a member of the Green Press Initiative since 2003.

Library of Congress Cataloging-in-Publication Data
Davis, Thadious M., 1944–
Southscapes : geographies of race, region, and literature / Thadious M. Davis.
p. cm. — (New directions in southern studies)
Includes bibliographical references and index.
ISBN 978-0-8078-3521-0 (cloth : alk. paper)
ISBN 978-1-4696-2195-1 (pbk. : alk. paper)
1. American literature—African American authors. 2. American literature—Southern States. 3. Geographical perception in literature. 4. African Americans—Race identity. 5. Place (Philosophy) in literature. I. Title.
PS153.N5D336 2011
810.9′896073075—dc23
2011024073

cloth   15 14 13 12 11   5 4 3 2 1
paper   18 17 16 15 14   5 4 3 2 1

THIS BOOK WAS DIGITALLY PRINTED.

Rita Dove poetry excerpt from "Mississippi" from *Grace Notes: Poems*, © 1983 W. W. Norton & Company, reprinted by permission of Rita Dove and W. W. Norton & Company.

Sybil Kein poetry excerpts from *Creole Journal: The Louisiana Poems*, © 1999 Lotus Press, reprinted by permission of Sybil Kein and Lotus Press; and *An American South*, © 1996 Michigan State University Press, reprinted by permission of Sybil Kein and Michigan State University Press.

Etheridge Knight poetry excerpts from "A Poem for Myself (Or Blues for a Mississippi Black Boy)" and "The Bones of My Father" from *Belly Song and Other Poems*, © 1973 Broadside Press, reprinted by permission of Janice Knight Mooney and Broadside Press; and from "The Idea of Ancestry," "Last Words of 'Slick' (or a self/sung eulogy)," "Once on a Night in the Delta: A Report from Hell," and "Television Speaks" from *The Essential Etheridge Knight*, © 1986 University of Pittsburgh Press, reprinted by permission of the University of Pittsburgh Press.

Yusef Komunyakaa poetry excerpts from "History Lesson" from *Magic City* (Wesleyan University Press, 1992), © 1992 Yusef Komunyakaa and reprinted by permission of Wesleyan University Press; and "Kosmos" from *Thieves of Paradise* (Wesleyan University Press, 1998), © 1998 Yusef Komunyakaa and reprinted by permission of Wesleyan University Press.

Harryette Mullen poetry excerpts from "Black Nikes" and "Exploring the Dark Content" from *Sleeping with the Dictionary*, © 2002 the Regents of the University of California; published by the University of California Press.

Brenda Marie Osbey poetry excerpts from *All Saints: New and Selected Poems* (Louisiana State University Press, 1997), © 1997 Brenda Marie Osbey and reprinted by permission of Brenda Marie Osbey and Louisiana State University Press; *Desperate Circumstance, Dangerous Woman: A Narrative Poem*, © 1991 Story Line Press, reprinted by permission of Brenda Marie Osbey; *Ceremony for Minneconjoux*, © 1983 University Press of Kentucky, reprinted by permission of Brenda Marie Osbey; and "Geography" and "House of Bones" from *In These Houses* (Wesleyan University Press, 1998), © 1998 Brenda Marie Osbey and reprinted by permission of Wesleyan University Press.

Sterling D. Plumpp poetry excerpts from *Blues: The Story Always Untold*, © 1989 Another Chicago Press, reprinted by permission of Sterling D. Plumpp.

Norman Shapiro translations of "Les Aveux" and "Vers Ecrits sur L'Album de Mademoiselle***" by Pierre Dalcour, "Souvenir du Bal" by Oscar-Charles Dugué, "Epigramme" by Armand Lanusse, and "Regrets d'une Vielle Mulâttress; ou, Désepoir de Sanite Fouéron" by Camille Thierry from *Creole Echoes: The Franco-phone Poetry of Nineteenth-Century Louisiana*, © 2004 Board of Trustees of the University of Illinois; used by permission of the translator and the University of Illinois Press.

Natasha Trethewey poetry excerpts from "Gesture of a Woman-in-Process," "Family Portrait," "Limen," "White Lies," "Floun-der," "Give and Take," "Microscope," and "History Lesson" from *Domestic Work*, © 2000 Natasha Trethewey; and "January 1912," "March 1911," and "March 1912" from *Bellocq's Ophelia*, © 2002 Natasha Trethewey. All reprinted by permission of The Permissions Company, Inc., on behalf of Graywolf Press, Minneapolis, Minn., www.graywolfpress.org. Excerpts from *Native Guard: Poems*, © 2006 Natasha Trethewey; reprinted by permission of Houghton Mifflin Harcourt Publishing Company. All rights reserved.

Margaret Walker poetry excerpt from "Jackson, Mississippi" from *This Is My Century: New and Collected Poems*, © 1989 University of Georgia Press; reprinted by permission of University of Georgia Press.

To the memory of

MAMIE LIVAUDAIS (14 July 1917–4 July 2010),

New Orleans neighbor who, after my loss of mother and grandmothers,

became my loving other mother, and who, in her nineties, became my

unfailing clairvoyant informant on the 2008 presidential election

Contents

Illustrations

Southscapes

A Map of the Territory

The map is not the territory.
—ALFRED KORZYBSKI, *Science and Sanity* (1933)

In "Entering the South," Lucille Clifton transmutes the stark geographic metaphor that often appears as the landscape of the South for African Americans.
The map she draws is a living one, alive in memory and in blood, but dead too
in the literal skin of animals and in the material body of the mother. Luxury,
beauty, and heritage combine into a familiar space; however, the familiar also
sustains and is sustained by death and destruction. The South Clifton maps is
not without the weight of a horrific past that continues on in hushed voices,
coiled rope, and dark blood.

> i have put on my mother's coat.
> it is warm and familiar
> as old fur
> and I can hear hushed voices
> through it. too many
> animals have died
> to make this. the sleeves
> coil down toward my hands
> like rope. i will wear it
> because she loved it
> but the blood from it pools
> on my shoulders
> heavy and dark and alive.[1]

Clifton's poem is a reminder of the allure of the South as a warm, luxuri-
ant familiar, but it is also a road map referencing the weight of the South
alive today in all of its complexity. Without ever naming "race" as an aspect
of the configuration of the South as a space, Clifton evokes the lynching of

black bodies and the ever-present oppressive danger enveloping the bodies and minds of black people. Clifton maps a "southscape," a geography of race and region.

My term "southscape" is intended to call attention to the South as a social, political, cultural, and economic construct but one with the geographic "fact of the land."[2] It references landscape in broad geographical-social contexts and mediated symbolic structures. As a concept, "southscape" has both subjective and objective elements, but primarily it acknowledges the connection between society and environment as a way of thinking about how raced human beings are impacted by the shape of the land, or what German geographers in the nineteenth century termed "*landschaft*."[3] My formulation of "southscape" engages, then, the natural environment and the social collective that shapes that environment out of its cultural beliefs, practices, and technologies.[4] This notion of a collective shaping carries with it an assumption of a power dynamic that can obscure how a society's practices or beliefs take shape.

Southscapes: Geographies of Race, Region, and Literature examines the political and power dynamics of the South. It is invested in understanding the persistent conceptual power of the South as a spatial object and ideological landscape where matters of race are simultaneously opaque and transparent. The examination focuses on placing African Americans at the center of current discourses on "The South" and "Southern Literature" as categories of critical inquiry, literary analysis, and theoretical positioning, but it is also committed to situating visibly black southern writers as central to any full analysis of writing within the southern region and its local and global contexts. It is intended to complement contemporary expansions of the boundaries mapping the American South and formulating the Global South. Attention to the local in this study, therefore, does not preclude today's dynamic global world but rather engages that world at individual points of accessibility where the connection between society and environment are legible. That legibility allows for the close reading and critical speculation in *Southscapes*.

As a concept, "southscape" is an effort to think about space, race, and society in the Deep South. It functions to expand "geographical imagination beyond the current limits," as Edward W. Soja has urged in deploying "Thirdspace" as a "flexible term that attempts to capture what is actually a constantly shifting and changing milieu of ideas, events, appearances, and meanings."[5] "Southscape" is, then, an attempt to expand the boundaries of regional discourse by coining a term that accepts Soja's underlying assessment of a spatial imaginary or Thirdspace, while also extending its conceptual frame to race matters. The result is an engagement with the politics of race, space, and representation.

Engaging racial-spacial representation as a political strategy in *Southscapes* derives from three sets of formulations that recognize the complexity of race within contemporary geographies. First, *Southscapes* attends conceptually to racial representation as "a political strategy for empowerment and articulation," as Homi Bhabha has suggested in thinking through "Third Space" as a means of avoiding a politics of polarity used to exclude minority subjects, particularly postcolonial subjects, from geographic discourses on the changing dynamic of late twentieth-century global spaces.[6] In linking politics, power, and articulation with race and space, "southscapes" utilizes Bhabha's negotiating of oppositions and opening spaces of translation in order to make political projects possible and accessible.[7]

Second, *Southscapes* locates a raced space of articulation or enunciation as "a place of struggle," which bell hooks forwards in positing a black southern subject as informing political alternatives to domination and marginalization. Understanding the production of space as a function of hegemony, hooks contributes a "politics of location" to discourses on identity and marginality. That effort she enunciates as moving beyond "the boundaries of domination" by focusing on her own radical standpoint, perspective, or position, as she puts it, "to change the way I speak and write, to incorporate in the manner of telling a sense of place, of not just who I am in the present but where I am coming from, the multiple voices within me."[8] This politics of location enables a connection in *Southscapes* between a spatial organization and racialized voices and, by means of that connection, a reformulation of marginalization and domination from an alternative perspective.

Third, *Southscapes* hinges upon the idea of political counternarrative as formulated by the Black Public Sphere Collective. The Collective defines its subject as "a transnational space whose violent birth and diasporic conditions of life provide a counternarrative to the exclusionary national narratives of Europe, the United States, the Caribbean, and Africa. Thus the black public sphere is one critical space where new democratic forms and emergent diasporic movements can enrich and question one another."[9] The Collective's identification of a black public sphere, a "critical social imaginary" in which "visionary politics" intersects with critical practice, suggests a way of approaching literary and racial representation within the South as a shared rather than exclusionary social space. The idea of space as interactive and constitutive and the formulation of a black public sphere as political counternarrative converge in the organizational focus of this study.

Southscapes thus uses multiple ways of thinking about a politics of race and space to focus on the production of texts that recognize the existence of race discrimination and racial injustice. While an understanding of fixity, rigidity, and separation informs the analysis of social landscapes and spatial regionality, the idea of space on the margins, in between, liminal, in flux, and interactive functions as an alternative way of enunciating and translating a productive space of alterity, otherness, and difference. Rather than merely representing the trauma or pain inflicted on black victims of segregation, *Southscapes* articulates how black writers from the Deep South use their spatial location to imagine, create, and define new and unproscribed subjectivities. In the process, they assert geographical claims and transgress regulatory boundaries that counter racial exclusion as a practice of power and privilege. The attention, then, to alterity and difference is not simply a static reaction to segregation as a constrictive stimulus but also a spatial practice that initiates the flow of ideas and empowerment of actions.

The Deep South states of Louisiana and Mississippi form the platform for the spatial, geographic, and aesthetic analysis. *Southscapes* originates in the spatial, in particular the spatial aesthetics and spatial economies that emerge out of segregation in Mississippi and Louisiana, and the implications of a spatial hermeneutics in southern African American writing from the mid-twentieth century to the present. Space is inextricable from social processes and the phenomena that occur in the specified South as place. Although social theory has often lacked the inclusion of space, in the last decades of the twentieth century, new geographers have advocated strongly for integrating space into the formulation of social theories because to separate spatial processes from social processes defies the logic of understanding that phenomena occur in a specified or given place.[10] A spatial, rather than chronological, organization of the manuscript emerges out of my exploration of an aesthetics of space and my attention to the social geography of black southern writers as an elastic social group with some aggregate aesthetic practices that can be parsed from a comparative reading of their work or a mapping of their relational space. Divided into six chapters, the book attends to Louisiana and Mississippi as two of the southern geographical spaces with the most fascinating connection between land, space, and social place, spaces in which social theory as a consideration of the everyday is most apparent in the outpouring of literature and where changes during the twentieth century are most marked. In focusing on these contiguous states, I also identify a metaphorical and symbolical basis for making the Deep South analytically and aesthetically accessible as a signpost of a larger geographical region. I do so without excluding the significance, individuality, distinctiveness, or specificity of other Deep South states, such as Alabama and Georgia.

I consider both the distant history of Louisiana and the near history of Mississippi to read the experience of raced bodies moving within a nexus of unstable contexts produced and actualized as space. Michel de Certeau formulates a definition of space as "composed of intersections of mobile elements. It is in a sense actuated by the ensemble of movements deployed within it. Space occurs as the effect produced by the operations that orient it, situate it, temporalize it, and make it function in a polyvalent unity of conflictual programs or contractual proximities."[11] This particular way of thinking about space is flexible, though Certeau insists that space is *a practiced place.*"[12] In explaining, however, he raises the issues of usage, context, and time that suggest the difficulty of application. Space, for Certeau, carries with it ambiguity because it is dependent upon and actualized by different transformative contexts. His thinking makes apparent that mobile elements intersect in the composition of space and that these constitutive elements do not maintain either stability or "univocity" but rather undergo transformations as contexts shift. His point allows for a reading of experience, or the relationship between spaces and movement, by concentrating on examining the actions of "historical *subjects*," in that "movement always seems to condition the production of a space and to associate it with a history."[13] The choice of Mississippi and Louisiana, then, has much to do with historical subjects, historical patterns, racial configurations, and racial politics that may be configured as regional models.

The analytical focus is on Mississippi and Louisiana as dominant, though asymmetrical, representations of historically persistent issues of justice. Social justice and racial justice specifically are central to the analysis of literary representations in this Deep South region.[14]

This focus is not a matter of abstract morality or fairness in the production or distribution of goods but rather a way of responding to the particularities of a concrete, material society. The centuries of racial injustice in the American South correspond to concerted efforts to cordon off black bodies from whites, and with that separation, to maintain a hierarchy of race-based power. The South, from the introduction of slavery in the seventeenth century through its abolition in the nineteenth century, has structured spheres of production that in turn organized social relations and created a language of spatial differentiation that depended upon race. These spheres of production identified not merely occupation or trade, but fundamentally place, and most often constructed race as well and with it, status. Though we rightly shy away from speaking today in essentialist terms, race was deemed an essential and irrefutable marker that determined place. In this sense, place is more than a way of identifying a stratum of society or a geographical location; it is, as Tim Cresswell insists, "a way of seeing, knowing and understanding the world."[15] While Certeau offers an elastic way of explaining place as "the order (of whatever kind) in accord with which elements are distributed in relationships of coexistence," his understanding of place as "an instantaneous configuration of positions . . . an indication of stability" may at once encompass race but also excuse the fixity of race as a place marker within a segregated society.[16] With attention to Louisiana during the colonial period and to Mississippi in the modern era, it becomes impossible to ignore the usages of race in the constitution of place and the demarcation of space.

Although racial configurations in the twenty-first-century South are no longer reducible to a black-white binary, the residue from the centuries of that bifurcated world persists in its ethnically and racially diverse regions. The old racial divide marks recent social relations. Just as slavery was the dominant subject of many U.S. historians and literary critics in the last half of the twentieth century, segregation may well be the dominant subject emerging in the first half of the twenty-first century. This return to another underexplored aspect of American social life, intellectual history, and cultural production may be necessary to move forward in understanding much of the dynamics impacting the world we live in today. Slavery and segregation come together in the contemporary efforts to formulate a new Southern Studies, which encompass both global contexts and local literatures.[17] Consequently, segregation as a powerful epistemological and ontological system dependent on the markings of spaces and the mapping of races underlies much of the conceptual frame for this study.

Within the regime of segregation, place is a spatial marker conveying quite specific meanings. Place is a powerful signifier of identity that cannot be overestimated, particularly in terms of the South with its specific history and sociology. No section of the United States has taken on so contested but persistent an identity or role in the creation of an image as the South. In *Our South: Geographic Fantasy and the Rise of National Literature* (2010), for example, Jennifer Rae Greeson reads the South as the projected geographic and deviant "Other," which remains central in literature to the evolving idea of the nation-state.[18] She tracks the formation of U.S. national literature out of an opposition to images of the American South by juxtaposing geography textbooks, travel writing, gothic fiction, and romance novels from the founding of the nation to 1905. Both in the creation of place and in the consumption of space, the region's people, whether as protagonists or antagonists, have participated in mythmaking out of the landscape, its occupants, and their sociocultural and geopolitical networks.[19] Blacks have to "know their place" and to "remain in their place." The white hegemonic understanding of the place occupied by black people, no matter their economic or class status, was always already measured and calibrated in relation to a standard of white superiority. Accordingly, the place of blacks, though not necessarily static, was by necessity lower and less than, narrower, contained, and limited. The clearly marked "place" for blacks was both subtly and brutally enforced. From the signs that read "For Colored" to those that said "Whites Only," signages created the iconography of separation and designation of the "subsurface" reduction of blacks into clearly marked areas corresponding to the psychology of race segregation and racism.

The assumption behind the visible markers of exclusion and separation was that blacks would accept the social constraints and act according to the dictates of assigned place. The reality, however, was that from the 1890s, when the "separate but equal" ruling in *Plessy v. Ferguson* accelerated racial segregation and its public markers, black people pushed back against all efforts to delimit and dictate their existence. It is as Gillian Rose suggested: "Space itself—and landscape and place likewise—far from being firm foundations for disciplinary expertise and power, are insecure, precarious, and fluctuating. They are destabilized both by the internal contradictions of the geographical desire to know and by the resistance of the marginalized victims of that desire."[20] An objective description of the southern region as place is not the primary work of literary artists and critics, both of whom seek to move beyond the merely physical aspects and render a felt experiential reality along with metaphorical or symbolic undergirding. Their constructions of place are political, connected to social ideology and social movements or to inscriptions of more abstract space. The South's geography, its space itself—"landscape and place," in Rose's sense—becomes for literary artists and critics a way of thinking about its movement into a certain modernity that involves the acknowledging of precarious foundations. The signs erected to segregate, or the representations of white ideology, achieve upon analysis not a hegemonic complacency as response but rather the contradiction of that intent, in that the signs became the ostentatious prompt for a necessary politics of solidifying racial identity in resistance and ultimately rebellion.[21]

Similarly, the spatial boundaries erected in the segregated South may be read as manifestations of a desire on the part of the dominant group in power to prevent blacks, or any minorities, from polluting their space. In reading geographic exclusion as a form of psychological distancing of self from the abject, those individuals who are projected as not pure or clean and who thus represent not just difference but deviancy and danger, David Sibley explores the connection between psychoanalytic theory (object relations theory in particular) and spatial processes. Utilizing the work of Julia Kristeva and Melanie Klein, Sibley in *Geographies of Exclusion* considered not only how spatial boundaries function to designate and shape social space by separating some people or groups from others but also how the role of the psyche functioned in the process of perceiving who belongs and who does not.[22] *Southscapes* traces the improbable reclamation of an identity that is not forged in the same historical communities that once linked African Americans in the South. In the postsegregation moment, instead of a return necessarily to a racially exclusive community of blacks, return migrants disperse throughout every identifiable space within the New South—into farming areas, megacities, suburban oases, small towns, manufacturing hubs, and even by choice not chance to all-black enclaves such as those ringing Atlanta, Georgia.

The creation of spaces to mark social relations and to segregate by racial difference produces hierarchies of power and privilege. Once the system of segregation in the twentieth century replaced the institution of slavery, hierarchical spaces of power may have been redefined but not eliminated. The South as a region and as a space historically allowed for the production of structures of power based on its slave economy and white racial hegemony. Louisiana, with its more complicated founding, settling, and colonization, may be considered in retrospect as a space that offered the potential for a different racial paradigm to develop in the nineteenth century. With its geographic proximity to the Caribbean Islands and Latin and South America, Louisiana early symbolized difference from the American mainland norm along with racial and linguistic mixtures unfamiliar in much of the rest of the American South. Throughout the twentieth century, however, the abiding tension in southern life involved maintaining the separation of the races, of black spaces of inferiority and subordination to white domination. Louisiana's distant history was not of sufficient power to enable a rejection of the prevailing racist paradigms or to encourage an alternative understanding of social geography. In attending to Louisiana as emblematic of the lost possibilities of early multiculturalism and multiracialism, *Southscapes* attempts to illuminate the aspects of region, race, and space that are constitutive of modernism, and thus it is a project emanating from an intersection with spatial constructions and racial constructions.

The primary readings are of texts by modern and postmodern major writers from Louisiana and Mississippi, but the general analytical work takes into account the multiple South(s) and the production of art in a variety of "southern" contexts, from *Les Cenelles* produced by *gens de couleur libre* in 1845 to the young writers of the twenty-first century. Both Natasha Trethewey and Anthony Walton, two of the writers included in Kevin Young's anthology *Giant Steps: The New Generation of African American Writers* (2000), for example, have connections to Mississippi as a site of memory and of inspiration. Their work argues for a not-yet-depleted reservoir of creativity in one of the most controversial of Deep South spaces. Walton reflects:

> By the time I went to homecoming at Ole Miss I had traversed Mississippi for several years, had renewed relationships with family and made new friends, had read volumes of books and documents, and had, through all of this, endured a steady darkening of my outlook. American history, and the future possibilities it implied, were becoming in my eyes a net of irony and sorrow from which I could not free myself. I was a young man, with a young man's taste for certainty and closure. But in sifting the complexities of Mississippi I found that each question I answered branched into three more, into infinitudes I could not grasp.[23]

Much of the work I undertake in *Southscapes* might well be summed up as "sifting the complexities" of Mississippi and Louisiana as intimate state-specific sites and diffusing out of their racial exclusion into the multiple South where discourses of race, space, and region allow for rethinking writing produced by southern African Americans.

Two primary writers from the Deep South—Richard Wright (Mississippi) and Ernest Gaines (Louisiana)—are central to this project because their creative work and their persistent attention to social geography allow for examination specifically of their regional location yet also for reflection generally on the diffusion of ideas across the larger southern region and through several generations of writers. A third primary writer central to this study is Alice Walker, a Georgia native whose tenure in Mississippi helps to account for the direction of her investment in framing the interconnections of race and region. Her work pioneers the shift of writers and critics toward a broader theorizing of southern space and place. In tracking Alice Walker's mobile sense of place and the linkages between new spatial locations and their relation to Mississippi, as well as to the racial segregation of her youth in Georgia, I suggest the ways in which geographical configurations and conceptions emanating from the U.S. South of the twentieth century have morphed into the space identified as the Global South in the twenty-first century. These three—Wright, Gaines, and Walker—are not only highly recognizable for their distinctive literary achievements, but they are also remarkably elastic in their relationships to the cultural and social worlds of the South and to the ways in which the social geography of the Deep South transmutes and transfigures in their creative writing and diffuses into the writings of new generations of black southern-identified writers, particularly Natasha Trethewey, Olympia Vernon, Shay Youngblood, Brenda Marie Osbey, and Randall Kenan, who form the main core for considering recent region-specific, spatial-racial narrative practices.

These and other African American writers in the post–civil rights era are "sifting the complexities" of space and place by bringing their attention to bear not merely on the past and its relationship to the present moment but also on place and its location in black subject formation. They recognize this period as both grounded by the temporal and unleashed by the spatial. While they do not deny that the South is polyglot, polycultural, and polycentric, they also understand that the South is a space imagined as a unitary place and exemplary locality, particularly one in which it is possible to chart within fiction and poetry and drama the construction of racial identity and racial writing. In part, theirs is a recognition of a rapid and perhaps unanticipated move into a postmodern existence by people of African descent, who, having survived the ravages of extended modern segregation and the violence of desegregation, emerged into a dispersal away from traditional sites of black communal experience. The new integrated, but often isolating, spaces offer little traditional means of coping with the persistent residue of segregation, yet they may in fact stimulate new transformative methods of becoming in the world.

There are two spatial configurations emerging from segregationist practices that are inextricably linked to the projection of blackness in the United States, or to the projection of the black body against the thing that will define it as black. The first is the Urban City, whose contextual orientation or place is always the city as center, though we understand that urban is not synonymous with city and that any discourse on the city with attention to a racialized black body invariably becomes elided with "the ghetto" as concept. The second is the Rural South, where space reemerges as important in unyoking the new modern stereotypes of blacks from the ground on which the black body can be made visible. In the South, the rural has long been the dominant physical expression of the region as a spatial configuration. In renegotiating the significance of the rural in keeping with the global prominence of the urban, the cityscape, it becomes increasingly clear that the rural has not been completely undermined as a signifier of the South. Importantly, however, contemporary writers of the South, such as Shay Youngblood and Brenda Marie Osbey, engage the urban of black subjects that is neither northern nor ghetto. The "in-placedness" of the black body is keyed into both urban and rural spaces, and while the two may indeed overlap, they may also connote distinct ideas that resonate throughout the texts I examine.

Experience for raced subjects occurs, then, within a place that may be rural or urban; nonetheless, the black body as a spatial parameter or boundary is particularly significant to *Southscapes*.[24] Adrienne Rich encouraged examinations of the body as inscribed with social values and as inscriptions of social mores when, in 1986, she identified "the geography closest in—the body" as the subject of geographical knowledge, which led to the body becoming one of the key sites in postmodern readings of place.[25] Locating the body as a geographic construct also forwarded reading the body as a sociopolitical structure. While feminist scholars working in a wide range of disciplinary fields have been both noticeable and persistent in interrogating the relationships between women, women's conditions, and space—whether bodily, global, or textual space—there has been little comparable attention to the body raced as black.[26] Taking my lead for a spatial hermeneutic from these multiple mappings of body, experience, and place, I examine the ways in which excision of certain bodies, in particular bodies raced as black, from places of coexistence within the segregated South ultimately results in two distinct spatial phenomena: one, exclusion, or the more noticeable isolation of blacks from specific places and experiences; and two, diffusion, or the less visible manifestation of the spread of black bodies throughout the delimited, contested spaces. Both spatial phenomena offer ways of thinking about specific texts by southern African Americans and about the interlocking figurations of ideas among those authors over time and the spreading of tropes among those texts across space.

Although I resist constructing a metanarrative out of my reading and interpretation of the South, an underlying thread is a conception of the South in the twentieth century as modern in the acceptance of space as a controlling factor in social theory (also relationships) and the South in the twenty-first century as postmodern, with the shifting or transformation beginning to occur in the 1980s and continuing through the end of the century. My formulation of "southscapes" as a spatial endeavor requires attention to historical transitions and representational modes, in particular regarding postmodernity, which has become so significant to U.S. theorists of space in their focus on American cities and the urban.[27] My study, however, is not a tracing of the complicated and contested evolution of modernism and postmodernism in the context of southern African American literary production. It does, nevertheless, place an understanding of the literary and aesthetic functioning of modernism and postmodernism as intrinsic to an examination of space and race, especially as race is constructed by social geography. My dating of southern modernity begins with the 1863 Emancipation Proclamation, the coming of freedom for those enslaved and the concomitant radical realignment of social structures and identities for all Americans. I represent the transition from modernity to postmodernity as beginning a century later in the period of legislative changes between the 1963 March on Washington, the Civil Rights Act of 1964, the Voting Rights Act of 1965, and the *Loving v. Virginia* ruling on interracial marriage in 1967. In the 1970s or the start of the post–civil rights era, the emergence of visible black artists, intellectuals, theorists, and philosophers to articulate the changing state of African American life and to deconstruct the controlling paradigms or powers enabled the iteration of postmodern blackness, as in the cultural analysis of bell hooks and Cornel West, which forwarded a politics of location. I use social theory to help make sense of everyday life and to assist in the analysis of literary texts both as geographic spaces and in relation to such spaces.

The South imagined and constructed as a largely rural space in the literary and figurative texts of the last quarter of the twentieth century would seem to be antithetical to the modern, especially as modernity has been linked so specifically to the city. However much representations of the rural have been used to assuage anxieties about the new, the urban, there has also been the undeniable fact of the persistence of the rural, of "country" in spatial, structural, and architectural terms, whether in interior design or acoustic music or pictorial images. The antagonism between the rural and the urban connected to the historical and spatial antagonism between blacks and whites, the struggle over occupying the same space, the segregated space in the public sphere held exclusively for "whites only," though such signs rarely had to exist because of the presumption that the best visible space would be reserved for whites and that blacks would automatically understand their exclusion from being physically or visibly present in such spaces.

This statement of modern and postmodern in relation to the South goes against the primary grain of thought by the white Southern Agrarians and literary critics, historians, and sociologists of the South, who argue in one way or another for the South as a premodern society, and not merely in the antebellum period. Their emphasis has been on the largely preindustrial, agricultural nature of the southern economy and social structure. But the closed system that was the South through much of the twentieth century, until the ferment of the civil rights movement in the 1960s and the fomenting changes into the 1970s, signified a modernity, almost hieroglyphic in its closed system of values, meanings, codes. At the same time, that South had begun transitioning to modernity when in the decades of the nineteenth century before the emancipation of enslaved people, it depended upon the spread of market capitalism, including the interstate traffic in slaves, as an expanding basis for accumulating wealth in new marketplaces, and that aggressive capitalism produced both the hierarchical social structure and the glaring economic and social inequities still apparent after the twentieth century. In addition to an economic modernity, the social narratives developed to enframe the closed South were embedded in a philosophical modernity. Stemming from the Enlightenment, modernity as an enterprise most often is marked by a search for rationality, foundations, and universal truths.[28] The privileging of a rational and knowing ego results in a modernist framing of social life and history.

The postmodern follows different strategies of cultural practices primarily connected to the temporal frame of capitalism and antagonistic as a discursive practice to the hegemony of the humanism characteristic of the Enlightenment. Infused in the postmodernist strategies is typically a radical break with the past, as theorists such as Fredric Jameson and Linda Hutcheon have explained. Jameson has drawn the distinction in terms of the "New" that Ezra Pound made familiar: "Modernism . . . thought compulsively about the New and tried to watch its coming into being . . . but the postmodern looks for breaks, for events rather than new worlds, for the telltale instant after which it is no longer the same . . . or, better still, for shifts and irrevocable changes in the representation of things and of the way they change."[29] In a different strategy, Jean-François Lyotard posited postmodernism as a term to describe "the condition of knowledge in the most highly developed societies. . . . The word is in current use on the American continent among sociologists and critics; it designates the state of our culture following the transformations which, since the end of the nineteenth century, have altered the game rules, for science, literature, and the arts."[30] Lyotard situated the transformations within "the crisis of narratives": the tension between what he termed "modern"—a self-created discourse of legitimation or philosophy that appeals to "some grand narrative, such as the dialectics of Spirit, the hermeneutics of meaning, the emancipation of the rational, or working subject, or the creation of wealth"—and what he defined as "postmodern"—"an incredulity toward metanarratives."[31] Whether a radical break or a transformation of knowledge, the "discontinuity between past and future trends (whether cultural, political-economic, or philosophical)" creates "the problem of *theorizing contemporaneity*, of making sense of the swirling maelstrom of contemporary life," so that postmodern thought may be seen as "a long overdue reassertion of the significance of space in social thought," perhaps even a "postmodern hyperspace," as Michael J. Dear suggests in representing the postmodern as "a stretching and reorganization of society's time-space fabric into dimensions we can so far only dimly perceive."[32] Dear, in his focus on the spatial, also echoes bell hooks and others in his finding that "the radical opening made possible by postmodernism is both invigorating and exasperating" because it has "legitimized a wide variety of different voices" even while calling attention to the increasing atomization of spaces.

Literary scholars now frequently align space with the production of narrative in postmodern discourse. Brian Jarvis, in *Postmodern Cartographies*, suggests from his examination of American fiction that geography itself is infused with narrative: "Given the structural inseparability of space/place/landscape and social relations there can be no geographical knowledge without historical narrative. In other words, all spaces contain stories and must be recognized as the site of an ongoing struggle over meaning and value."[33] Approaching space as a site of struggle over value and meaning necessarily involves engagement with the structures underpinning and driving narration itself. In positing narration alongside space in postmodern studies, Patricia Yaeger raises a series of interconnected issues:

> If ordinary space can be scripted as heterogeneous and multidimensional, refusing the simplicity of linear narrative, if local politics can be concealed or immersed in tropes of tragedy and romance . . . space has an additional political-psychological dimension. The physical world is also a site where unrequited desires, bizarre ideologies, and hidden productivities are encrypted, so that any narration of space must confront the dilemma of geographic enigmas head on, including the enigma of what gets forgotten or hidden, or lost in the comforts of ordinary space.[34]

Because the forgotten or the hidden, repressed, or disguised in narrative all too often will turn on issues of power, *Southscapes* utilizes this theorizing about postmodernism and narrative to explore the shifting sites of power in contemporary Deep South texts.

Southscapes is, in the sense of a space of possibility to articulate differences in the South's "time-space fabric," a mapping of modernity and postmodernity in the geographies of race and region. The very concepts of homelessness and alienation and uprootedness, for example, are standpoints and take their meanings against the backdrop of space and the relationship of the body to space. While homelessness, alienation, and uprootedness, so much a part of the modern ethos, may assume profoundly different meanings when home is an incarcerated space, threatful and destructive, as it very often was in the twentieth-century South for people of African ancestry, these concepts retain nonetheless an association with the modern and with modernist perspectives on the lives of black people, for whom home, belonging, and roots retain meaning. In *Ride out the Wilderness: Geography and Identity in Afro-American Literature* (1987), for example, Melvin Dixon places attempts to define self and to counter rootlessness or homelessness as central to understanding the key spaces recurrent in African American literary production. He identifies those geographical and mythical spaces as the wilderness, the underground, and the mountaintop and infers their relationship to modernist narratives. Because of his focus on African Americans, Dixon's work necessarily also contains an embedded, implied, but unstated relation to the South. While I am concerned, like Dixon, with the literature of African Americans, I am as well most interested in the ways in which the South as both literal and symbolic space produced social relations and constructed social identities or public expressions of power, whether in political institutions or domestic arenas. These concerns, rather than a focus similar to Dixon's on key tropes, inform my study. The social structures of segregation and inequality in the "separate but equal" era, for example, become a physical frame and a spatial lens through which creative writers could read their own modern condition and their cultural milieu.

Southscapes presses the social significance of space without the assumption of urban alienation or rural class conflict as the major tropes for thinking about southern spatial-racial matters since the 1970s. It follows Derek Gregory's view that "any standpoint is incomplete and situated, linked to power interest and refracted through various prisms of social position," and that "times and spaces are made by ordinary folk in everyday life, and that the outcomes are always contingent and never predetermined, even if . . . they are likewise never random or chaotic."[35] It values the work of Madhu Dubey in *Signs and Cities: Black Literary Postmodernism* (2003) in examining the "twinned inheritance of print culture and urban modernity" in African American texts that contribute to postmodern culture.[36] It nevertheless moves away from her underpinning tropes of the book and communities of print readerships as identified by Benedict Anderson in *Imagined Communities: Reflections on the Origins and Spread of Nationalism* (1983; 2006) and substitutes a spatial hermeneutics that takes both cities and rural communities as aspects of a multipronged postmodernism.

The postmodern in southern African American writing may reference neither literary nationalism nor traditional race-identity constructions, yet the impact of space on social relationships and on conceptions of societal location emerges with force and clarity. Harryette Mullen, for example, whose native Texas seems a distant land from the terrain of her avant-garde, postmodern language poetry, writes of the material consequences of social hierarchy within a spatial realm in "Black Nikes":

> We need quarters like King Tut needed a boat. A slave could row him
> from his crypt in Egypt full of loot. We've lived quietly among the stars,
> knowing money isn't what matters. We only bring enough to tip the shut-
> tle driver when we hitch a ride aboard a trailblazer of light. . . . This is a
> big ticket item, a thickety ride. Please page our home and visit our sigh on
> the wide world's ebb. . . . Time to throw down and take off on our launch.
> This flight will nail our proof of pudding. The thrill of victory is, we're
> exiting earth. We're leaving all this dirt.[37]

It is precisely the issue of "all this dirt" that in its multiple connotations maps the vexed terrain of social space in the postmodern era.

The spatial movement rather than the chronological template that Mullen uses in "Black Nikes" is an example of diffusion as the other side of exclusion. The creative space that Mullen occupies is one that emphasizes interlocking language and conceptual affinities that move through the space of the poem. Although racial segregation most dramatically calls up ideas of exclusion, spatial separation, and psychological repulsion, as theorized by David Sibley and Julia Kristeva among others, it also carries with it ideas of diffusion, what happens within the separated and bounded group in the spread of words, concepts, ideas, and practices that may flow in less-rigid formulaic patterns of association and connectivity, as suggested by Mullen's "Black Nikes." Diffusion is a countermanifestation of mandated racial and spatial separation in the regime of segregation.

Studies of diffusion in cultural geography have included how concepts, ideas, objects, or technologies spread over space and through time. Initially connected to the flow of cultural traits into new areas, diffusion developed through the Berkeley School of cultural geographers as a way to follow the pathway of a spreading phenomenon or to examine the impact of physical barriers. Under Carl Sauer, whose interest in culture led to a rejection of environmental determination and a turn toward cultural landscapes, the geographers at the University of California, Berkeley, connected their field studies to the relationship between people and the land and fostered their work in the diffusion of cultural traits and the evolution of cultural regions. Currently associated with innovation in systems of tracking the circulation of information through a population in a regional system, diffusion demonstrates that impediments to information flows function to catalyze innovation by transforming and multiplying the ways in which information can spread.[38] Although not a vibrant aspect of cultural geography today, diffusion as a spatial process is useful to *Southscapes* as an alternative to exclusion for articulating the spread and circulation of phenomena within the spaces occupied by segregated black populations.

In the diffusion model I am using to organize *Southscapes*, the referential in the spatial construction of African American texts and their concern with spaces of opportunity and production diffuse inside the very boundaries established by exclusion to reverberate among and between other black writers. While this is not to say that white writers or the nation-state prominent in some recent studies are ignored in *Southscapes*, it is to point to the overlooked: one result of the erection of racial boundaries is that we often do not observe the work that goes on inside those boundaries, as opposed to the work that pushes back against exclusion.[39] Thus, conceptions of resistance and trauma, while certainly important discursive and affective areas, are not central to this study, even though they may be figured into the interpretative conclusions. The fear of pollution or defilement that operates as a conscious or unconscious determinate of necessary separation may well produce psychoses on one side and abjection on the other; however, both products are reactions to and not generative, which is the aspect of power that I add to the discourse by focusing on a range of twentieth- and twenty-first-century writers of African and southern descent. Rather than reading African American writers as solely in a position of responding to segregation, I also read African American writers during the era of segregation and its aftermath as innovative creators of texts born of their spatial aesthetics and raced locations. Rather than taking up issues of national belonging or the racialization of whiteness, as Grace Elizabeth Hale does in *Making Whiteness: The Culture of Segregation in the South, 1840–1940*, *Southscapes* makes more apparent how blackness has served itself and within aesthetics that have too frequently been reduced to untroubled themes and uncomplicated affinities.[40] By turning to the creative arenas inside what is constituted as black space, I foreground not merely sites of danger or wounding for black people but simultaneously also sites of memory and imagination that together in a complex nexus produce racial art.

Each chapter of the book focuses on the literary representation of an embodied and material South that has since the nineteenth century been interconnected with the issue of race. The chapters center on the ways in which space and the concepts central to human geography and new geography illuminate the nature and constitution of regional and racial identity. Focusing on the social geography that makes exclusion and containment acceptable foregrounds the normalizing of restrictive social controls in order to produce a specific system of race-based identity and social relations in the South. Each chapter of *Southscapes* forges an interpretation of race and region that depends, intertextually and intersectionally, on spatial, historical, and social theory to think about the place of African Americans in the production of the literature of the American South. The emphasis on texts is not intended to elide the performative—or an African American contribution in music, dance, ritual, sound, linguistic, and spoken word—to modernity and postmodernity. Houston Baker's interpretation of the performance of the verbal in the modernism of the Harlem Renaissance, Paul Gilroy's observation of music in the formation of a Black Atlantic, and Joseph Roach's examination of Circum-Atlantic orature, or nonwritten performance—all groundbreaking in different ways—have contributed effectively to the current prominence of performance in considerations of work by African Americans representing alternative modes of artistic production that oppose a modernist insistence on written texts and to the proliferation of excellent new studies in their mold.

The order of the chapters is spatial rather than chronological in terms of both the sequential placement and the internal progression. The focus on Mississippi comes before Louisiana as a way of immediately tapping into the relational aspect between the issues of black return migration and southern racial identity in the first chapter. Each space in turn, Mississippi and Louisiana, has two chapters examining the spatial aesthetic; one chapter is general in engaging a variety of writers and the multiple ways of thinking about the geography of race and region they perform, and the other chapter is specific and tied to a major Mississippi and Louisiana writer, with a tracing of the diffusion of that writer's spatial practice into the work of a prominent writer from a different spatial location.

The first chapter, "Southscapes: Race, Region, and Reclamation," focuses on the claiming of the South by African Americans in theory (as in literary production) and in practice (as in actual physical movement). The chapter introduces the methodology deployed throughout *Southscapes*, first by centering on space as aesthetic and theory to enable discourses on race and region and second by focusing on segregation and division in social geography as well as in disciplines and scholarship. In establishing region as both space and place, I consider Mississippi and Louisiana as emblematic of place as process rather than enclosure. The two states, then, allow for the interlocutory interaction that may be used to represent the spatial-racial configuration of the larger southern region. In asserting a regional identification along with a racial one, African Americans have, since the 1980s, been leaving other parts of the nation, the North in particular, and moving back to the South in the process that is now known as "return migration." They have joined in the process also apparent in writings by African Americans from at least the 1970s onward. This process involves the recovery of a later modern black identity that is rooted in the South as grounded manifestation of the ever-desired formative "homeplace." Functioning counter to the exilic imagination and migratory identity often apparent in the displaced writers of color from the Caribbean, South America, Africa, and other parts of the world associated with formerly colonized peoples, black southerners by means of a spatial imagination locate themselves within a relationship to a "homeplace," no matter whether they classify themselves as émigrés or expatriates.[41]

My larger argument is twofold. First, African Americans who wish to have a regional identity as southern can and increasingly are claiming that right. Second, the traditional literature of the South has begun to acknowledge more fully the presence of blacks and other minority groups within its ranks, including the previously overlooked remaining southern Native American and Chinese populations or the growing newer communities of Latinos, Vietnamese, and South Asians. That acknowledgment has also extended to authors outside of a white-black binary who have long resided within the region—for example, Judith Ortiz Cofer (Puerto Rican in Georgia) and Marilou Awiakta (Eastern Band of Cherokee in Tennessee)—as well as to more recent writers, such as Roberto G. Fernández, Lan Cao, and Susan Choi, who place additional racial groups within their fictions of the South, just as Robert Olen Butler did with his narratives of the Vietnamese in Louisiana. In a subversion of the dominant "old" southern ideology, writers of color claim the very space that would negate their humanity and devalue their worth.

The first chapter is subdivided into two parts: "Reclaiming the South" and "Embodying Race and Region: Natasha Trethewey's Apertural Space." "Reclaiming the South" charts out the theories of space and the ideology of region undergirding this study. "Embodying Race and Region: Natasha Trethewey's Apertural Space" moves specifically to the spatial ground informing my primary reading of race and region and to the postmodern within the work of Natasha Trethewey, a Deep South author connected by birth, residency, and heritage to Mississippi and Louisiana, the two states I locate as contiguous social geographies and distinct sites of segregation.

The second chapter, "Poverty and Porches: Controversial Mississippi," follows from the contemporary construction of Mississippi central to Trethewey and turns back to the social conditions, poverty and its multiple manifestations, defining the public sphere for generations of black Mississippians. It excavates the personal, subjective constructions of space that functioned as a counterbalance to the official social narrative of black southern life. The writers Endesha Ida Mae Holland, Sterling Plumpp, and Etheridge Knight, among other Mississippians, are illustrative, along with Mira Nair's film, *Mississippi Masala* (1992). Divided into "Rural Landscapes of Communal Want" and "External Structures of Racial Memory: Olympia Vernon's Vision," the chapter juxtaposes the social configurations of segregated life in the South and the hierarchies of power inherent in physical spaces and imaginative work of black writers.

The third chapter, "Power and Profession: Richard Wright's Mississippi and Its Expatriate Legacies," examines the necessary movement out of and away from the segregated South for black writers of Wright's generation. It connects space to the historical power struggle for a mature, masculine subjectivity in decreasing economic and class resources and challenging social and regional locations that diminish the possibilities for individual self-awareness, racial actualization, and social agency. The three chapter divisions are "Cultural Geography and a Black Professional Writer," "Human Geography and New Black Subjectivities," and "Spatial Legacies and Shay Youngblood's Paris." The first two sections center on Richard Wright and the relationship between physical and psychological space associated with the South/North axis and with the liberatory northern migration. The third section takes up the contemporary transnational location of Shay Youngblood's fictional search for a space to become a writer by following the expatriate journey of Richard Wright and James Baldwin, but gendering and queering that space.

The fourth chapter, "Politics and Paysans: Multicultural Louisiana and the Space of the Créolité," turns to nineteenth- and early twentieth-century Louisiana as a microcosm of multiculturalism within the southern region that was not allowed to become the nation's dominant societal model or the social theory of space, primarily because of the fear of racial amalgamation and racial mongrelization. Divided into "Mutable Geographies," "Cultural Flows," and "Body Maps," the chapter examines the collision of the public sphere with subjective space and traces the fluid boundaries, identities, and movement of the cosmopolitan *gens de couleur libre* and their literary descendants, such as Sybil Kein and Brenda Marie Osbey, among the contemporary Louisiana *Créolité*.

The fifth chapter, "Parishes and Prisons: Ernest Gaines's Louisiana and Its North Carolina Kin Space," examines race, space, and representation in the fiction of a twentieth-century writer who chose to make his fiction out of his racial and cultural memories of the past in a specified and contained space that is largely unchanged yet simultaneously dynamic and volatile. The three sections of the chapter are "Plantations as Remembered Geographies," "Landscape as Prisonscape," and "Spatial Kin and Randall Kenan's North Carolina." In each section, I examine the ways in which narratives and people inhabit space. I focus on the metaphorical nexus of the plantation and the prison as architectural spaces delineating Ernest Gaines's Louisiana. His modern-day deployment of the plantation system follows the social organization and political economy of a racially segregated and class-bound population. The last section diffuses forward to Randall Kenan's mapping of a queered geography of black masculinity within the rural and domesticated landscape of a fictional North Carolina community. Kenan's fiction revises the dominant modernist sensibility at the center of Gaines's fiction and produces a postmodern spatial aesthetic within a comparable black space.

The sixth and final chapter, "Alice Walker Matters: The Fruits of Gendered Space," argues for a new geography of the South and the geographies of race and region. The two subdivisions of the chapter, "Reconstruction of Southern Racial Space" and "Geographies of the Black Female Body," point to the material expressions of the polarities of space in Walker's work, especially in the conjunction of her political and literary work. Her work, extending from the turbulent 1960s and now resolutely into the first decades of the twenty-first century, has made a critical intervention in the ways in which the South as a region can be represented and studied. It provides a concluding southscape for meditating on the spatial-racial nexus in the construction of region.

Walker's own conclusion to *The Way Forward Is with a Broken Heart* (2000) serves here as an opening for *Southscapes*: "And yet . . . the past doesn't exist. It cannot be sanctuary. Skin color has always been a tricky solace, more so now that the ozone has changed. . . . We have reached a place of deepest emptiness and sorrow. . . . We see that everything that is truly needed by the world is too large for individuals to give. We find we have only ourselves. Our experience. Our dreams. Our simple art. Our memories of better ways. Our knowledge that the world cannot be healed in the abstract. That healing begins where the wound was made."[42] The site of the wound becomes the space for healing, and for beginning this rethinking of the South.

chapter one

Southscapes

RACE, REGION, & RECLAMATION

I. RECLAIMING THE SOUTH

[W]ithin this dynamic simultaneity which is space, phenomena may be placed in
relationship to one another in such a way that new social effects are provoked. The spatial
organization of society, in other words, is integral to the production of the social, and
not merely its result. It is fully implicated in both history and politics.
—DOREEN MASSEY, *Space, Place, and Gender* (1994)

One of Marion Post Wolcott's most recognizable photographs bears the description: *Negro Going in Colored Entrance of Movie House on Saturday Afternoon, Belzoni, Mississippi Delta, Mississippi.*[1] The subject is a dramatic interplay of light and shadows, of sharp angles and flat surfaces, but more it is a stark reminder of segregation and the racial separation in public spaces practiced by law and custom in Mississippi and throughout the South well into the last decades of the twentieth century. The spatial separations, only partially imaginable from Wolcott's 1939 photograph, were accompanied by the injustices and inequities always already visible because of the proximity of black and white lives. Climbing the stairs to the colored entrance to the movie theater meant walking past "the entrance," or the main access point for whites that did not even have to carry a sign designating it as such. The indignity of seeing what could not be used, accessed, or enjoyed compounded the exaggerated sense of difference and undermined any sense of equality. As a visual representation of segregation, social and racial, the photograph marks both a material configuration of literal space (the stairs to the gallery that contains, holds, and separates blacks from whites) and a conceptual framing of abstract space (the distance between the races that the subject cannot traverse and for which there is no measure).

Negro Going in Colored Entrance of Movie House on Saturday Afternoon, Belzoni, Mississippi Delta, Mississippi. Segregation for black Mississippians belied "Good for Life" slogans. (Marion Post Wolcott, photographer, 1939; Farm Security Administration/ Office of War Information Collection, Library of Congress Prints and Photographs Division, Washington, D.C.)

Wolcott's photograph suggests the different planes within the frame from which a reading or interpretation of "region" as subject might begin. Region as a section of the nation is clearly at work in the largest general sense; Belzoni, Mississippi, represented in the photograph by the single man amid multiple planes or surfaces, is also standing for the southern region. Wolcott's vision inspired my approach to the South as a region in this book. I use Mississippi and her contiguous sister state Louisiana as representative of the larger southern region for initiating focused individual readings and suggestive expanded interpretations while acknowledging the difference of these two states, both from each other and from other southern states. Michel de Certeau complicates the definition of region while locating the term as a simple basic union, "the place where programs and actions interact. A 'region' is thus space created by an interaction. It follows that in the same place there are as many 'regions' as there are interactions or intersections of programs. And also that the determination of space is dual and operational, and, in a problematics of enunciation, related to an 'interlocutory' process."[2] Mississippi and Louisiana, then, assume the intricate spatial position of interlocutory in my approach to region.

Wolcott's photograph, however, serves another introductory purpose in "Reclaiming the South." It helps to underscore distinctions in geographical distances, or in actual spaces and theoretical spaces. Mike Crang and Nigel Thrift have made clear the "problem" that space has become in contemporary analysis: "Space is the everywhere of modern thought. It is the flesh that flatters the bones of theory. It is an all-purpose nostrum to be applied whenever things look sticky. It is an invocation which suggests that the writer is right on without her having to give too much away. It is flexibility as explanation: a term read and waiting in the wings to perform that song-and-dance act one more time."[3] In cautioning against rendering space too elastic, Crang and Thrift emphasize that "in all disciplines, space is a representational strategy": "For example in literary theory, space is often a kind of textual operator, used to shift registers. In anthropology, it is a means of questioning how communities are constituted in an increasingly cosmopolitan world. In media theory it tends to signify an aesthetic shift away from narrative—and temporal— modes of structuring primarily visual media. In geography and sociology, it is a means of questioning materiality."[4] In reading the Wolcott photograph, I am attempting to avoid having "space" become too elastic, but at the same time I want to suggest that applications using the lens of space may cross over and move between the disciplinary boundaries and their ways of "doing" space.

Segregation comes together with its precursor slavery in a space-time continuum useful for understanding the dynamics impacting our world today and for working toward sustaining a different future. In discussing the origins of his classic study *From Slavery to Freedom* (1947), the late John Hope Franklin talked about the need for the text in the 1940s and his writing it while teaching five classes at Durham's segregated North Carolina College. While pointing to the phenomenal success of the paperback edition in the 1960s, after the surge of civil rights activism created a larger demand for a comprehensive history of black people in the United States, Franklin remarked, "I haven't taught [black history] in thirty years. . . . I teach history of the South."[5]

His casual but pointed remark made, without embellishment, an important point about the segregated dimension not only of public space in the South but of intellectual space as well. Within a specific time frame, Franklin was laying claim to a space, pedagogical and intellectual, that historically depended upon the relationship between blacks and the South to characterize both race and region. His bringing of a temporal frame to bear on an articulation of space and its conception is a reminder that time boundaries are intricately connected to the exclusionary practices he defied in refusing to adhere to the separation of black experience from the experience of the South. Even during the era of segregation, Franklin would not designate racial experience as exclusively black or normalize regional experience as exclusively white. Social relations articulated within Franklin's statement "necessarily have a spatial form in their interaction with one another," as Doreen Massey has observed more generally about the social as also spatial.[6] In the postemancipation southern public sphere, the separation of racial groups into space-defined units unfolded as Jim Crow politics, racial segregation, or, simply put, black history and southern history. The history that Franklin was compelled to write and the statement about his teaching the history of the South converge in his articulation of social relations within space during a specific time.

The process of rethinking southern culture and region is much like Franklin's description of writing his book: "There was no original research. . . . It was a matter of organizing, reconstructing and conceptualizing."[7] This attention to a reclamation of "southernness" is, in a sense, descriptive; it identifies vital contemporary activity, suggests some underlying causes, and explains the activity as a response to particular needs: the recognition of the exclusion of a major aspect of self from the conception of identity and the determination to achieve redress by communal positionality within the landscape of the South. It also makes more visible an informing principle behind John Hope Franklin's statement and my larger project—the issue of racial justice. Racial justice is the informing desire that makes it necessary to revisit segregation as a practice and an ideology. Segregation is the social structure shaping Franklin's statement about his process, particularly "reconstructing and conceptualizing."

Segregation is also the social geography shaping this study, which looks from the perspective of those who, like Franklin, were relegated to separate social, political, and cultural spaces that by definition were also geographic and physical spaces. "Separate but equal" emanated from the 1896 decision in *Plessy v. Ferguson* that ruled that the spatial divisions between black and white in public conveyances, accommodations, buildings, institutions, and structures were legal. This judgment by the Supreme Court of the United States set the process for the segregationist practices and ideology pervading most of the twentieth century and leaving a legacy in the twenty-first.[8] Responding to what he termed the "epoch-making" effects of the court's *Plessy* decision, Charles W. Chesnutt observed in 1911: "The function of courts in the organization of modern society is to protect rights—to pass upon disputes between man and woman or between the individual and the State; and then, by their mandate, to set in motion the art of the executive to prevent or punish a wrong or to enforce a right. Obviously if this great power be not rightly exercised, if it be swayed by prejudice or class interest, justice will not be done."[9] Chesnutt's point was precisely that justice was not done, and that the struggle for rights after *Plessy*, essentially the battle against legal segregation, was a struggle for justice and for remedies to the denial of rights and privileges under law.

David Sibley has read the human landscape as a landscape of exclusion. To explain marginalization and the spatial separation of some social groups, Sibley describes these processes as social constructions rooted in psychology as much as in geography. He proposes Self versus Other as a way to apprehend how, in the process of identity formation in childhood, individuals may accept and sublimate stereotypes of the Other as not merely different but as deviant, which in adulthood can contribute to fears of being defiled or violated by the encroaching Other. Focusing on the relationship between spatiality and subjectivity, Sibley demonstrates how stereotypes serve in the production of landscapes of exclusion. His attention to social and spatial exclusion is particularly helpful in thinking about segregation as a practice and policy because it demonstrates how spatial exclusion functions to maintain social boundaries.

Sibley draws the connection between exclusionary processes and boundaries of self: "Experience of the world in childhood also involves the confirmation of the boundaries of the self and situating the self in the social world through the sorting of people and things into 'good' and 'bad' categories. 'Good' and 'bad' enter the unconscious and, in the process of socialization, they are projected onto others who become the objects of fears and desires."[10] The multiple stereotypes of black bodies promulgated in white southern society rendered black people vulnerable to the projections marking them as threats and pollutants who would defile the purity of both white spaces and white bodies. More than a means of drawing personal boundary lines or zones of preference, these projected stereotypes entered into the public sphere in terms of legal mandates, official sanctions, and social practices, all of which resulted in protections for "white only" exclusive zones that had the power both to define racial blackness and to effect civic punishment for being black. The exercise of such extensive social, political, and economic power over black people and their everyday lives within the culture of segregation, and the resultant landscape of exclusion, made and continues to make the struggle for justice and equality a slow, arduous process, particularly because the underlying beliefs or psychoses have little basis in rationality or actuality.

Exclusion is, thus, one of the ways not only of understanding the divisions apparent in the modern South but also of managing racial difference within that South. The historical presence of blacks in the actual or imagined landscape of the South has forwarded more than one idea of the region based on stereotypes of blacks in its social structure. The last decades of the twentieth century, however, witnessed the linkage of the region to more sophisticated media images of a primarily white "Sunbelt" by downplaying the presence of blacks and of racial and ethnic minorities. That obscuring of a black presence simultaneously asserted changed conditions in the region and denied one significant aspect of those changes: the post–civil rights political and social progress of black southerners. Natural disasters and economic downturns in the twenty-first century, however, have adversely impacted the selling of a Sunbelt South and left vulnerable populations particularly visible both in their underclass status and in their racial identities.

Though some sociologists of the South choose to write only about white southerners in isolation from matters of race by referring to them as an ethnic group, that tendency implies an attempt to define the region and its culture without one of the major components. The matter of race is undermined, dismissed as somehow applicable only to blacks and inapplicable to new considerations of the region. Defining white southerners as an ethnic group is plausible only if ethnicity is one of the markers of identity rather than a way of eliding the obvious issue of "white" as a racial category particularly prominent in the construction of identity in the South. In point of fact, the concept of race in defining the region has not merely meant the historical presence of blacks in the American South, or of Native Americans in the region, but the presence of whites, in particular Anglo-Saxons, in much of the region, who defined race in terms of difference from their majority group rather than ever needing to discuss or examine race as a self-defining factor. "Not white" or "non-white," or even distinctions on the basis of polar opposites such as "colored" or "black," did not directly address the matter of "white." Importantly however, what these "not" definitions achieved was an acceptance of self-definition and self-individuation on the basis of exclusion. They also helped to perpetuate a binary mode of thinking and writing about the South as a region, so that the notion of two exclusive and oppositional groups permeated discourses on the southern region and southern writing.

The tendency toward exclusion, then, did not remain applicable only to individuals but became one of the primary ways of defining the region and its culture, not only for cultural insiders but for outsiders as well. (Though "slavery" and "slave-based economy" historically provided one primary means for cultural outsiders to define the region and for cultural insiders to justify both self-perception and social order.) There was a presumption of racial affinity, commonality in the dominant views of the human geography of the South as a region. Diversity was not an issue, but difference was. The result has been curious: whites in the South became simply "southerners" without a racial designation, but blacks in the South became simply "blacks" without a regional designation. Increasingly, this disjuncture is being recognized as one of the unarticulated legacies of Jim Crow racial segregation and racial domination.

There are still manifestations of this phenomenon today, as suggested by John Hope Franklin's reference to teaching the history of the South as opposed to the history of blacks long after he began teaching in integrated elite universities, or more particularly by the labeling of those scholars who study slaves as working in the field of black history and culture, whereas those who study owners work in the field of southern history and culture; similarly, those who study the roots of blues and jazz work in black musicology, while those who study the roots of country and bluegrass work in southern musicology. The stratification in scholarship has largely gone ignored but not completely unnoticed. Reviews of the forward-thinking collection *Look Away! The U.S. South in New World Studies* (2004), edited by Jon Smith and Deborah Cohn, cite its excellent comparative focus but observe the virtual absence of inclusion of a black southern cultural and literary presence.[11]

More invidious is the carefully reasoned, nonpartisan scholarly work appearing after the civil rights movement and especially during the last decades of the twentieth century that reexamines the idea of the South by emphasizing memory and the process of remembering as crucial to understanding the region, but which suffers itself from a severe lapse of memory. Such scholarship is frequently among the best written about the South, and it can earn a very fine reputation without any serious consideration, let alone mention, of nonwhite southerners. For example, Richard Gray in *Writing the South: Ideas of an American Region* (1986) states: "The main aim of this book is to make some small contribution to this study of the Southern argument, the various ways in which people from below the Mason-Dixon line have tried to forge the uncreated conscience of their region."[12] He then adds, "it [meaning his 300-plus-page book] offers no more than a series of notes towards a definition of the Southern idea."[13] Perhaps the statement is anticipatory of questions about the study; if not, it ought to be, because in the entire book there is only one mention of a black writer, as far as I can determine, and that one is simply a listing of Charles Chesnutt's name, along with George Washington Cable's, as an example of an interest in "the idea of the 'tragic mulatto'" that predates William Faulkner's.[14]

While I am not suggesting that any representation of the South be mimetic and reproduce a particularized image of the South, I do see the exclusionary representation as a function both of racial blindness and of a discrete discourse that naturalizes the existence of a white racial category and elides the existence of a black one, and that consequently produces a self-perpetuating discourse that is seemingly racially unmarked but normalized from the perspective of white. Thus, if the discourse has traditionally had no articulation of blacks or self-consciousness of whites as raced or racialized, then the resultant representation of the South will be devoid of any attention to blacks. The construction of the South without multiple racial valences is not bipartisan but an investment in white racial hegemony. Ruth Frankenberg has suggested that "'white' is as much as anything else an economic and political category maintained over time by a changing set of exclusionary practices, both legislative and customary."[15] Grace Elizabeth Hale has furthered the examination and maintained: "Central to the meaning of whiteness is a broad, collective American silence. The denial of white as a racial identity, the denial that whiteness has a history, allows the quiet, the blankness, to stand as the norm. This erasure enables many to fuse their absence of racial being with the nation, making whiteness their unspoken but deepest sense of what it means to be an American. And despite, and paradoxically because of, their treasured and cultivated distinctiveness, southern whites are central to this nationalism of denial."[16]

Although Gray does make a few perfunctory nods to "the institution of slavery" and "the image of the Negro in Southern writing," he appears here not only as an example of the continued omission of black southerners, but also as an example of the more serious misreading of the culture and its artifacts that explains the omission. Gray ends his discussion of Walker Percy with the following: "Perhaps the last word should be given to Percy's black characters, however, since blacks occupy the margins of his stories, just as they do in traditional Southern writing."[17] My intent in citing this assertion is to present it as a type of persistent conception that still necessitates the descriptive work of thinking through the spatial claims by which black writers undermine and deny the ontology at work in their erasure from anything except the margins of southern writing.

Lest the assumption be made that only white men have been exclusionary in their thinking and writing about the South, I should point out that Anne Goodwyn Jones, in *Tomorrow Is Another Day: The Woman Writer in the South, 1859–1936* (1980), does not even address by a nod to the temporal period under examination the problematic of her construction of "the woman writer" as white and her total exclusion of black women writers. Often issues of gender have been disconnected from issues of race, or race has been normalized as white, or presented in what Roland Barthes termed "the voice of nature," with the resultant disappearance of race from discourses otherwise politically conscious and concerned about social and cultural inequities.[18] Jones, like Gray and Richard King, constructs her paradigm so as to exclude women of color and any attention to gender that would entail race. Fortunately, Jones and an ever-enlarging contingent of white scholars with the South as their subject have, since the beginning of the 1990s and the emergence of a widespread acceptance of African American literary topics and the mainstreaming of Frederick Douglass, Harriet Jacobs, Zora Neale Hurston, and Alice Walker, turned their attention to black writers as part of the southern panoply. Linda Tate, for example, in *A Southern Weave of Women: Fiction of the Contemporary South* (1994), understands that since the 1980s, a new generation of women writers, black and white, concerned with race and class and gender have reconfigured the representational landscape of the South and transformed the world of southern literature. Patricia Yaeger argues further in *Dirt and Desire: Reconstructing Southern Women's Writing, 1930–1990* (2000) that "deregionalizing" black writers "skews our reading of southern literature and skewers the complex racial texture of women's writing coming out of the South."[19] And Jones herself has coedited with Susan V. Donaldson *Haunted Bodies: Gender and Southern Texts* (1998), a collection of essays with a slightly more pronounced attention to issues of race.

My concern here is less with white critics taking up black subjects or forcing black writers into preexisting white racial paradigms than with what has been gradually occurring in the region and in the literature in the last decades of the twentieth century and into the beginning of the twenty-first. These exclusions are paradigmatic because it is precisely from the once-segregated base of the South that African Americans have launched their claims to identity as citizens and subjects. The spatial basis for their efforts is especially noteworthy because whether or not there has been a verbal accompaniment to their efforts, there has been a clear bodily articulation of a dynamic with new social effects and an inherent understanding of "Third Space" that, as

Bhabha suggests, is a political liminality rupturing fixed binary, polarized, and hierarchical structures such as those associated with racial segregation in the South.

By the end of the 1980s, it became increasingly problematic and difficult to conceptualize and analyze southern culture as "White Only." In large measure, this shift was due to the visibility of black authors writing about the South. What has occurred since then is an expansion of the definition of southern culture based upon an insistence that race and region are inextricable in defining a southern self, society, or culture. And this change includes an understanding of how whites are not "raceless" despite the naturalization of whiteness in their majority worldview. There has been change, or perhaps more accurately augmentation and amalgamation, which, in several of its less-detected forms, is the focus of my observations here. It may even be that the former notice of blacks on the margins of southern writing is in very small measure an implicit suggestion of measured attention to the work of "the other," which in itself is a slight change from exclusion and perhaps begins a gesture toward a recognition of existence. In his last essay before his death in 1981, "No More Monoliths, Please: Continuities in the Multi-Souths," C. Hugh Holman called for a greater recognition of "a profoundly pluralistic world"; he remarked the work of critical theory, feminist studies, and black studies for "casting fresh illumination on southern literary culture."[20] Observing the change brought about by the inclusion of black writers into assessments of southern culture, Holman welcomed "these new and vital forces": "It is not merely that we are at last looking at slave narratives, giving Frederick Douglass his long overdue place in southern letters, and examining Charles Chesnutt as an artist rather than a curiosity. A number of writers of great importance are entering the canon—such as Ralph Ellison, Richard Wright, Ernest Gaines, Ishmael Reed. When they enter, they greatly increase the meaning of southern culture, enrich the themes of southern writing, introduce new experiences of their own, and give new perspectives by which to judge the old."[21] Despite its seeming suggestion that all of the black writers are men, Holman's call for recognition of variety in southern culture, for change in attitudes, was not an isolated position in the 1980s, when women's studies, black studies (including black women's studies), and emergent theoretical and cultural studies were compiling scholarly records and research to challenge and subvert old paradigms about "the South." Holman's understanding of a necessary reformulation rather than an addition in thinking about the literature and culture of the South functions against the grain of some assumptions that any focus on race and gender would be merely an effort to force different writers or groups into a preexisting and invented formula for the South and its literary culture.[22] The important aspect here is that there is no "master narrative" of the South into which new groups will merely append their stories. Instead, the very discourse of the South is contested. Holman's repetition of "new" is more to the point than perhaps he realized.

The more pronounced evidence of change from practices or ideologies of exclusion has appeared in the work of numerous historians beginning especially in the late 1970s and 1980s with texts such as Joel Williamson's *Crucible of Race: Black-White Relations in the American South since Emancipation* (1984), John Blassingame's *Slave Testimony: Two Centuries of Letters, Speeches, Interviews, and Autobiographies* (1977), Deborah Gray White's *Ar'n't I a Woman: Female Slaves in the Plantation South* (1985), and Angela Y. Davis's *Women, Race, and Class* (1983). "To provide a soul to legitimate the presence of our bodies upon this American earth is what we 'thinking' southerners are all about and have been since 1865," Williamson concludes metaphorically about the assimilative intent of his own work and that of those he calls the "numerous rest."[23] While Williamson connects the place of the South and the space of Americanness to group intent developing since the Civil War, Sterling Plumpp understands the space of change as the individual taming irregularity:

And I write
transformations. Changes
the blues
stitched in my tie.
And I
cry through my pen
til pulses of the page be
come regular[.][24]

Plumpp's focus on the "I" and on the pen and page, with "blues" and crying as expressive discourses, is an articulation of transformation that is not an effort merely to join in a post-1865 chorus of right thinkers. It is a more radical effort to introduce a different narrative, perhaps running parallel to, or crossing intersectionally, the old.

Evidence of movement toward a more expansive reading and representation of "southern" culture in the 1980s is *The History of Southern Literature* (1986), edited by Louis D. Rubin Jr. and an impressive grouping of senior editors who replaced the vacant space caused by the relegation of black writers to places outside of southern literature with inclusion of black southern writers in the literary landscape of the region. The literary history contains six essays specifically on black writers, as well as incorporations of southern black writers into other essays, all of which caused at least one reviewer discomfort about this new "over-emphasis" on black writers.

In popular culture, one short-lived enterprise worth observing is *Southern Magazine*, which situated "southern" as ethnicity *and* racial, and both of these markers of identity as constructed by social culture and practices. In the premiere issue, "The South and Welcome to It" (October 1986), the editors featured essays by Willie Morris ("Yes, the South Exists"), Harry Crews ("Mourns for Mules"), Al Green ("The Southern Soul"), Rosemary Daniel ("The Southern Body"), and so on. The inclusion of black soul singer Green certainly helped to establish *Southern Magazine*'s larger vision of the culture; however, the cover announcement of "Live Ghosts: A Tear-Out Performance from a Southern Storyteller" was even more revelatory because the article, William Hedgepeth's "Art of the Southern Storyteller," features black and white storytellers, and the tear-out performance is a recording of a black woman, Jackie Torrence, telling "The Bell Witch." The editors did not feel compelled to label Torrence anything other than "southern" on the cover. Each subsequent issue of *Southern Magazine* continued this expansive view of the region and its people right up to its demise, so that by the 1990s *Southern Magazine* became a collector's item. Imbricated in the construction of a raced regional identity are the politics of race, racial discourse, and racial representation, all of which the journal managed to foreground. The history of the literature and the magazine of popular culture are part of what can be called an integrationist move largely initiated by the very faction Joel Williamson described as the "thinking southerners," who moved toward justice from a raced position as white southerners with a conscience and perhaps also the "soul" Williamson included.

Less prominent but highly visible, however, during this period was the claiming of a regional identity in addition to a racial one in the work of a number of creative artists who are black and southern. For example, Samm-Art Williams staked his claim to regional identity in his play *Home* (1979), which chronicles the return migration of a black North Carolinian from the urban North to the rural South. *Home* enjoyed a New York revival in 2008–9 with little change to the original version. It represented the attachment linking people and place, or a way of seeing "worlds of meaning and experience" coming together in the desire for connection. As Tim Cresswell states in considering place as a way of understanding: "To think of an area of the world as a rich and complicated interplay of people and the environment—as a place—is to free us from thinking of it as fact and figures."[25] Such thinking, for example, would move away from the numbers associated with Africans taken from their homes on the continent, separated from their people and customs, or the count of those who survived the Middle Passage only to be enslaved in places throughout the Western Hemisphere on so many plantations and farms and toward the interaction of people with social space that could be both actual and imagined. In part, creative texts such as *Home* functioned to collapse the distinction between real and imagined space.

The focus on return and the South as home is a reversal of the movement most prominent for three quarters of the twentieth century. While anthropologists and sociologists may see the increasingly frequent pattern of black return migration as flight from the hardships of urban life, I suggest that it is also a claim to a culture and to a region that, though fraught with difficulty and the memory of pain, provides a major grounding for identity, particularly when in the absence of a distinct racial binary it has become harder to formulate identity within the nexus of community. This return to the South is, as well, a new form of subversion—a preconscious political activity or a subconscious counteraction to the racially and culturally homogenous construction of the "Sunbelt" as a way of occluding black presence in the South.

The claim was particularly evident in the publication of journals with such titles as *Black Arts South* and *Callaloo: A Tri-Annual Black South Journal* that emanated from the region, and also in the counterdistinction of names for more long-standing cultural organizations such as "Free Southern Theater" that assumed race while specifying region. Recently in New Orleans, Junebug Productions, under the direction of John O'Neal, launched a workshop for the Free Southern Theater Institute designed to assist young people through "monologues, spoken word, and movement" to "confront and share challenges they face post-Katrina and explore how race and racism shape their lives and identities."[26] And *Callaloo*, which moved from Southern University in Baton Rouge to the University of Virginia in Charlottesville and now is published at Texas A&M University in College Station, has transformed over time into the premier journal with a diasporic and global attention to black cultural production. It is now *Callaloo: A Journal of African Diaspora Arts and Letters*, with the masthead noting: "Founded in 1976, Baton Rouge, Louisiana." Even when institutions fold, new ones taking their places represent a general assumption of diversity and the existence of difference within the South. With those recognitions has come a fresh perspective on the region as a shared cultural space and as connected to the cultures and populations south of Florida, Louisiana, and Texas. That perspective works against the once-prevalent myopia and exclusiveness that functioned in conjunction with nationalism and imperialism to maintain hegemony, power, and exceptionalism.

Counterbalancing the homogenous appeals of a new white southern "Sunbelt" was the prominent turning to historical fiction as a specific mode of expressive production by a number of black writers. The novel of blacks in the nineteenth- or early twentieth-century South emerged as a dominant form in the 1980s. It encompassed a displacement of the distance between real and imagined space. It was, however, no nostalgic turning back to a time when there were "good old days"; it was gut-wrenching revisioning of specifics long obscured by synoptic cultural patterning. A major example is Toni Morrison's novel *Beloved* (1987); however, in citing this novel, I do not mean to suggest, as one of my students did recently, that all black people in the United States are "southerners." Morrison is a midwesterner who until 1998 had never even visited her father's southern birthplace, Cartersville, Georgia, yet she reaches backward in time and into the South to claim a history, to explain a legacy, and to understand what I call "the regionality of the black self." In a radio interview, she called it the process of "appropriating and reclaiming" to counter racial discourse, which she describes in *Playing in the Dark: Whiteness and the Literary Imagination* as "a way of referring to and disguising forces, events, classes, expressions of social decay and economic division far more threatening to the body politic than biological 'race' ever was."[27] She has persisted in this view in her collected essays, *What Moves at the Margin: Selected Nonfiction* (2008), which takes its title and epigraph from her 1993 Nobel lecture: "Tell us what the world has been to you in the dark places and in the light. . . . Tell us what it is to be a woman so that we may know what it is to be a man. What moves at the margin. What it is to have no home in this place. To be set adrift from the one you knew. What it is to live at the edge of a town that cannot bear your company."[28]

Morrison's iteration of being cut off from "home," of not belonging, of living in the space of exclusion, is in effect a way not only of addressing the condition but also of beginning a necessary redress that punctuated the 1980s and that persists in the twenty-first century. For instance, Natasha Trethewey, a writer born some thirty years after Morrison, revealed in 2004: "Being born in a place that is my home yet not my home . . . was infuriating. I am a native daughter, and yet I am a kind of outsider. . . . I am a non-daughter of the place that I was born, that is my home, and so I wanted to try to restore the narratives that have been overlooked, erased, or buried because another narrative has been inscribed upon the landscape with the naming of the roads and buildings and monuments."[29] Morrison's effort, then, is not an isolated one.

A similar effort began to appear with increasing frequency in the 1980s, from the writing of Californian Sherley Anne Williams in *Dessa Rose* (1986), Illinois-born Leon Forrest in *Two Wings to Veil My Face* (1983), and Pennsylvanian David Bradley in *The Chaneysville Incident* (1981) to Gloria Naylor (a New Yorker with roots in Mississippi and a room of her own on St. Helena Island, South Carolina) in *Mama Day* (1988) and J. California Cooper in *The Wake of the Wind* (1998). These works are by black outsiders to the region, who are nonetheless intimately involved in the process of writing not personal or individual history but communal and public history at the very moment when a form of dispersal different from the migrations earlier in the twentieth century was occurring. Much like the social scientists and humanists who, though not natives, take the region as their subject matter, these creative writers have functioned in the vanguard of evaluative work, of trying to reconfigure the possibilities of a communal space, a racial home, that has its basis in the familiar, in the historical place setting most associated with people of African descent in the United States, but that, simultaneously, gestures toward a configuration of space that has only been possible imaginatively.

The conclusions of these works all emphasize the recognition of place (the South and all of its meanings for blacks) as a major aspect of identity and the reunion of blacks positioned communally to face a new day. The last words of Williams's epilogue are: *"Mother, brother, sister, husband, friends . . . my own girlhood all I ever had was the remembrance of a daddy's smile. Oh, we have paid for our children's place in the world, again and again . . ."*[30] Her words reference space and all its implications, geographical, psychical, social. At the end of Morrison's narrative, Paul D thinks: "Only this woman Sethe could have left him his manhood like that. He wants to put his story next to hers." Touching her face and holding her fingers, he says, "'Sethe . . . me and you, we got more yesterday than anybody. We need some kind of tomorrow.'"[31] His concept of tomorrow includes not just the temporal but the spatial, in part because the past in the text has already been space-defined (the plantation, the house, the river, the six-mile woman, etc.). Forrest concludes with Nathaniel "unleas[ing] his soul" at Great-Momma Sweetie Reed's "bedside altar": "Commanding him to silence, cursing, praying, denouncing, rendering up counter-memoirs, phrases from scriptures, spirituals, then only gestures; the gestures of sign language, and homemade ones spun up from the grievousness of her soul's captivity in a windstorm. . . . Only grief-stricken gestures, as her soul chased and chastened his words, long and deep into the night and unto the dawning light of the new day."[32] These endings all utilize the cathartic power of telling about the black experience in the South and the healing power of uniting with another's story in order to weave a necessary future within the narrative space of fictional texts.

Narrative space is where the social is constituted anew for black writers. The geographies of race and of region come together within the telling of the individual but simultaneously communal story in the observation of a place connection in the forging of an identity. Despite efforts to isolate blacks in material and narrative spaces that would restrict their possibilities for full creative living, these writers chose to constitute a black space through which the transmission and diffusion of their ideas could occur.

I maintain that the 1980s marked a decided shift among African American writers who considered "history" and the past and its relationship to the present moment by examining space, place, and location. In a sense, this period is both grounded by the temporal and unleashed by the spatial. In part, it is a recognition of a rapid and perhaps unanticipated move into a postmodern existence by people of African decent, who, having survived the ravages of extended modern segregation and the violence of desegregation, emerged into a dispersal away from traditional sites of black communal experience and into integrated but often isolating spaces that offer little means of coping with the residue of segregation. If, in the 1960s and 1970s during the civil rights movement and the concomitant black arts movement with its Black Power revolt, blacks turned their spatial attention to Africa, often configured as Mother Africa, for the inspiration to struggle against a segregationist regime for rights, justice, and equality, then in the 1980s blacks could become self-reflexive and consider not merely the limitations and violations of their citizenship within the United States or the material and symbolic Africa as a lost point of origin, but also how they could, within the spatial construct of freedom, enact rights and achieve justice. No longer needed was a recovery or acceptance of historical "fact" or historical location because narrative space opened up a new political comprehension instead.

The turn to historical formations, then, may be read as a turn to place matters as a site of relational identity, rather than as a return to slavery as a site of memory. In this sense, the move to a place-specific ground or to a claiming of land, to the South whether rural or urban, may be considered as a mode of constructing subjectivity. This move is not framed as an act of resistance to enslavement nor a potent healing of the trauma of slavery, though both resistance and healing may be significant for some writers. A claiming of the spatial ground of the South, then, is not a framing of a narrative of integration into the social network of white southerners from which blacks had been excluded on the basis of race. More than a reclamation of an abject black body, it is an exertion of power over the very spatial configurations that could coerce an identity. In creative expressions of a power of authority over the land, or the staking of a claim of ownership rights, black writers during the 1970s and 1980s who produced "historical" fictions exercised their agency in creating black identities and actuated those identities in a world most often associated with "nature."

What these writers were doing with historical fiction form is a developmental and transformative outgrowth of the racially and culturally necessary work undertaken by Arna Bontemps, who pioneered a race- and region-specific historical fiction. Bontemps indeed recovered events as sites of memory in two important historical novels on black rebellions during enslavement: *Black Thunder: Gabriel's Revolt, Virginia 1800* (1936), based on an actual though failed insurrection that Gabriel Prosser planned to free enslaved blacks and capture Richmond; and *Drums at Dusk* (1939), based on the successful black revolution on Saint-Domingue that lead to the founding of Haiti. His work became one starting point for the historical fictions in the 1970s and 1980s. Yet identifying Bontemps's place in relation to development during this period is not to assume, as critic Michael Kreyling does, that there is ever a metanarrative to uncover and thus to upset or unsettle older narratives; or assume, as does novelist Alice Randall in writing *The Wind Done Gone*, that the narrative of Margaret Mitchell's *Gone with the Wind* can be dislodged from its place in the cultural and human geography of the South by a new narrative, a "parody," from the perspective of Scarlett O'Hara's imagined black half sister.[33]

Beginning in the 1960s, black southerners such as Margaret Walker Alexander in *Jubilee* (1966), Ernest Gaines in *The Autobiography of Miss Jane Pittman* (1971), and Alice Walker in *The Color Purple* (1982) have all claimed the region as their own. With that claim, they created a cosmopolitan narrative space in which to explore the complexity of modern life through the lens of an African American past that is rooted in the South, necessarily replete with slavery and segregation. These texts were the harbingers of what would develop in the 1980s. Though they chose a particular individual as a vehicle for grounding their narratives of identity formation, these authors also envisioned a public acknowledgment of a communal history woven together in a landscape of interconnected lives. Walker's Celie says at the very end of *The Color Purple*: "I feel a little peculiar round the children. For one thing, they grown. And I see they think me and Nettie and Shug and Albert and Samuel and Harpo and Sofia and Jack and Odessa real old and don't know much what going on. But I don't think us feel old at all. And us so happy. Matter of fact, I think this the youngest us ever felt."[34] Reunion reverses the emotional depressions that weigh down the spirit; the result is a buoying upward that Celie equates with youth. She makes her observation from the front porch, the spatial location that allows access to a multiplicity of references to both individual awareness and subjectivity and to community, including the African context of her long-lost sister and children. The litany of names reiterates the reunion of the black southern family and the African diasporic community as well as of their stories, once scattered in letters and in fragments of memory. The signal rejuvenations in spatial arrangements recuperate time and mark the beginning of a new era in a transformed place with transformed people.

Nonetheless, the problematic at stake, and not transparently so, is that the reunion of black diasporic bodies within the South of porch culture is a representation of a modern moment already past when Walker produces her novel. The modernist story of survival and overcoming the trauma of separation from Africa, of dislocation in the South and dispersal throughout the Western Hemisphere, builds upon shared racial experience that by the 1980s was being destabilized by changed social and environmental circumstances. That period marks a turning point toward a recognizable postmodernity that Walker begins to acknowledge in texts in which decentered subjects occupy the foreground of the narratives and evoke hostile critical responses for the very departure from master narratives or universalized stories of black life. The shift beginning in the 1980s is gradually toward an understanding that individuals who are decentered "invent their own radical subjective politics, and the production of identity (and place) becomes fragmentary, deeply conflicted and frequently contradictory."[35] The transnational made over into a narrative of conjoined and transformed blacks in the space between inside and outside, the porch, and in the space connecting past and present, the South, is a modern narrative that can be difficult to sustain given the divergent populations of black people who, beginning in the 1980s, have no common narrative in which all can participate and stake identity claims. bell hooks puts the issue plainly: "Postmodern culture with its decentered subject can be the space where ties are severed or it can provide the occasion for new and varied forms of bonding. To some extent, ruptures, surfaces, contextuality, and a host of other happenings create gaps that make space for oppositional practices."[36] She sees the issue as providing opportunity for a political reformation of the subject on the same ground that functions as the breaks between, the gaps interrupting ties of connection, or what Homi Bhabha and Edward Soja have termed Third Space.

The Color Purple reminds me that the intentional connection of race and region that resulted in an expanded definition of both southern culture and southern space is not merely reflex. It is an initiative that was hard to sustain or perhaps even unsustainable in the changed climate of U.S. life for black people after the 1970s. This aspect of a landscape of division that was not the understood and familiar segregationist binary world was insufficiently observed in the flurry of heated criticism over Walker's novel and the film version or in the ensuing debate between black men and women over the right to determine how the race should be portrayed in fiction. (That question was the subject of a symposium proposed by W. E. B. Du Bois in *Crisis*, February 1926, and posed again by Henry Louis Gates Jr. in *Black American Literature Forum*, Spring-Summer 1987 and Fall 1987, when the issue of racial representation once again became a major issue for black people.) The struggle was as well over who has the "right" to define space—whether the domestic space of black southern life or the rural South or the bodies of black women or even Africa as a transnational location—and ultimately over the representation of "blackness" and all of its attendant aspects. Moreover, the blacks represented were not all of a piece: not all were born in the United States, and not all had their formative experiences within the United States. The new reality underscored in the process was that there was no longer either agreement or the common ground on which agreement could easily be forged. Racial binaries of production and consumption gave way, and the result was unsettling. Put in the terms bell hooks has suggested, the struggle over representation around *The Color Purple*, novel and film, constituted "a space . . . there for critical exchange. It is exciting to think, write, talk about, and create art that reflects passionate engagement with popular culture, because this may very well be 'the' central future location of resistance struggle, a meeting place where new and radical happenings can occur."[37] In *The Same River Twice: Honoring the Difficult* (1996), Walker rehearses her responses to the controversies surrounding her novel and Steven Spielberg's film, and she fully addresses the complexities of competing claims to either belonging or not belonging in particular locations. Using the language of folk aphorism, she makes clear that because river waters flow constantly, a place in the river will not remain the same. In exploring the contested terrain that her novel and the subsequent film represented and provoked, she suggests, in a vein similar to hooks, that the experience provided a new place for critical exchange.

Overlooked too often in the Walker criticism is her fictional examination of racial and regional identity, along with gender identity, and her portrayal of a contemporary need to reinstate a black southern experience into cultural

and historical contexts despite the reality of pain that a truthful reinstate-
ment necessarily bears. Walker was seeking a continuation of a communal
racial identity, but one with a new flexibility to accommodate new under-
standings of gender roles and intraracial oppression. She was locating the
black woman's body within discourse, what Michel de Certeau terms "enun-
ciative focalizations."[38] As a means of redressing the exclusionary practices
that have resulted in a limited notion of southern culture, Walker insisted
in *The Color Purple*, as in her two earlier novels, *The Third Life of Grange Copeland* (1970) and *Meridian* (1976), on writing blacks back into the shaping
of an idea of southern culture, on the situating of blacks into the regionality
of the South, but with a difference. This process, seen intermittently in her
subsequent novels as well as in her poems and stories (particularly the much-
anthologized "Everyday Use") and in her essays (especially "In Search of Our
Mothers' Gardens"), then telescopes a way of preserving black subjectivity in
a rapidly changing world. "No one," Walker has concluded, "could wish for a
more advantageous heritage than that bequeathed to the black writer in the
South: a compassion for the earth, a trust in humanity beyond our knowledge
of evil, and an abiding love of justice. We inherit a great responsibility . . . for
we must give voice to centuries not only of silent bitterness and hate but also
of neighborly kindness and sustaining love."[39] She articulates a sensibility not
often considered in treatments of blacks and the South, specifically a sensibility with an emphasis on compassion, trust, love, and justice gleaned from
the experience of being black in the South of oppressive power and a sensibility valued as the necessary way forward. The exercise of power by whites
who controlled southern space and thus black southerners that Walker acknowledges is a conception of geographical space and power articulated by
Michel Foucault in *Power/Knowledge*: "A whole history remains to be written
of spaces—which would at the same time be the history of powers."[40] Walker's concept, however, turns on the ability of blacks to seize control of how
they respond to and write their spatial-racial experience under controlling
powers.

Looking back at the 1980s as a decided shift toward space, place, and location, I would claim that perhaps at no other time has there been so visible an evidence or manifestation of historical imagination in a specified
cultural context among black creative writers and their critics as well. Beginning in the 1980s, retrieval projects directed attention to historical texts
that had been lost: Henry Louis Gates Jr.'s collection *The Classic Slave Narratives* (1987), Jean Fagin Yellin's edition of *Incidents in the Life of a Slave Girl*
(1986), William Andrews's collection *Sisters of the Spirit: Three Black Women's*

Autobiographies of the Nineteenth Century (1986), and Mary Helen Washington's critical anthology *Invented Lives: Narratives of Black Women, 1860–1960* (1987). In the aftermath, the 1990s witnessed a continuation and expansion that extended into the new century with a slowed pace of retrieval. Was this general activity evidence of a perverse love affair between blacks and the old South? Obviously not; it suggests that something else was at work that may be related to a space-time shifting that was being accommodated in the ways of representing identity and location in the world but that almost imperceptibly registered the shift from a modern to a postmodern positionality for black people in the United States.

Bernice Johnson Reagon advises: "If, in moving through your life, you find yourself lost, go back to the last place where you knew who you were, and what you were doing, and start again from there."[41] Her astute comment, uttered initially during a Sweet Honey in the Rock concert in Durham, North Carolina, early in the 1980s and later written expressly for anthropologist Carol Stack as an epigraph for *Call to Home: African Americans Reclaim the Rural South*, goes directly to the issue of self-identity located within and constituted out of a known place.[42] Reagon's notion of return, an embodied relocation different from the Freudian return of the repressed, is invested in place as a key to the identity, self-knowledge, and well-being of a person. Her words seem prophetic, particularly in conjunction with one fascinating example of location and place involving Alex Haley, but not in terms of his historical reconstruction in *Roots: The Saga of an American Family* (1976).[43]

Before his death in 1992, Haley bought and refurbished a 120-acre antebellum farm in East Tennessee, where he staked his claim not merely as a black man but as a southerner. Perhaps *Roots* and its television spin-offs, *Roots: The Second Generation* and *Henning, Tennessee*, took hold of him to the extent that he could no longer resist the pull of region in shaping an identity. Haley, however, was not about a quiet, unpublicized relocation; he announced his move to Norris, Tennessee, and the opening of his manor house and "gentleman's farm" with a week-long party to which he invited 250 guests from around the world.[44] He also opened the fête to newspaper and magazine reporters. Here was a private black self functioning in concert with a very sophisticated public self. Haley's performance as a black descendant of enslaved people turned owner of the manor house constitutes new history in the making: a redefinition of identity and meaning that hinges upon the intersection of race and region, upon the claiming of place and space, upon the inversion of traditional paradigms of power, and upon the determination that the activity does not go unnoticed.

In the face of increasing dispersion out of the familiar spaces of modern black life, Haley's creation of his Tennessee place suggests a point Linda McDowell makes in thinking about spatial locations and politics: "Places are made through power relations which construct the rules which define boundaries. These boundaries are both social and spatial—they define who belongs to a place and who may be excluded, as well as the location or site of the experience."[45] Haley asserted an authority over the very concept of farm/plantation and the cultural force it represented. In the process, he determined that those who "belonged" would be constituted out of those who historically would have been the excluded.

In the aftermath of Haley's phenomenal success with *Roots*, it became increasingly clear that African Americans were shaping a contramodern identity out of the individual and communal, the personal and societal, the communal and cultural, and upon the very landscapes that had denied them meaning and subjectivity. Noticeably in relation to the narrative concerns here, Haley purchased land, property, a farm and a house with the money earned from the telling of the story of the capture and subsequent enslavement and sale of his African ancestor Kunta Kinte. With the flowering of genealogical searches in Africa and the South occupying a greater and larger portion of the black population, there is no mistaking the search for a way to claim a repressed, suppressed, and alienated part of the self that coincides with racial identity and is tied to the conceptualization of "roots"—the land and identity formation—space and a way of thinking about self. Haley formed a connection between diasporic geographies previously only dreamed about or imagined, and he made those geographies not merely central but a lived reality of the connective links between African Americans and Africans, between the landscape of the Americas and the land mass of the African continent. In a sense, he transformed the past and its unattainable temporality into the space of the present and the geographies of the future.

Toni Morrison's *Song of Solomon* (1977) appeared the year after the publication of *Roots*. In this groundbreaking fiction, Pilate Dead travels about the South not only with a bag of ancestral bones, which is most often noticed in readings of the text, but also with a geography book, which Melvin Dixon astutely points out in his treatment of *Song of Solomon*.[46] As part of Morrison's mapping of the South, Pilate's geography book is significant for its representation of a value assigned to a way of knowing the external world and reading the ontological. The geography of mobility and freedom evident in Morrison's Pilate suggests a connection Patricia J. Williams made in *Open House* between mobility and modernity: "We want to escape the world, the world escapes us. . . . America was founded on the ability to escape the status of serf; we are committed to the notion that it is possible and desirable to step out of one's place in a given society, go where one wishes and be governed by nothing but individual ability and free will."[47] Yet, for African Americans with a knowledge of the difference between serf and slave, while escape may well be a motivation, there is also the attempt to find a location that reorientates a life away from dislocation and toward a stopping place, "a simulacra of home," where, as Williams puts it, "we are known but that we have never known, a place where the static is less a prison then an idealized source of peace."[48] Pilate carries the geography book as a reminder and map of possible locations.

What Morrison, Haley, Williams, and a host of black writers have recognized about the pleasure and the pain of recuperating the history of a people displaced from their African origins and in search of what Williams calls "the simulacra of home," Harryette Mullen has expressed succinctly in her poem "Exploring the Dark Content":

This dream is not a map.
A poem is not the territory.

The dreamer reclines in a barbershop
carpeted with Afro turf.
In the dark some soul yells.

It hurts to walk barefoot
on cowrie shells.[49]

Mullen points to the pain in the act of return that is also a retrieval of space and spatial connection over time and fractured heritages, though the fractures remain in place, unmoved even if reimagined. Punctuating the dream of a return to the stolen and lost past, to Africa as ancestral homeplace mapped from safe utilitarian places made to correspond to the map of discovery, is the voice of a reality, the incongruous truth of what lies beyond the symbol of the territory. While the modernist dream is constituted in historical consciousness, the subjective postmodern acknowledgment, as Mullen demonstrates, is of the inability to either arrest or inhabit the past.

The retrieval of space and with it subjective formation is at the center of efforts to build public monuments and living museums to the lost and painful past. African heritage sites, slave forts and villages, and U.S. sites of enslavement all link to the act of reclaiming that is simultaneously also an act of invention, evident with Haley's creation of a new plantation as an extension of his black southern identity. Inspired by Haley, one extended family of North

Carolinian blacks traced their ancestry back to a particular plantation, Somerset Place, and held a reunion in 1986 at the plantation their ancestors built during the 1830s. The genealogist of the family, Dorothy Spruill Redford, discovered twenty-one families all descended from those enslaved on Somerset Place. Though they lacked a sophisticated mechanism for explaining the necessity of returning to, of all places, the white plantation or of the meaning of that particular return, they were nonetheless affirming unequivocally their sense of connection to the public image of the region, of themselves as black southerners with a share in the monuments of white southerners. As with Haley, their private need functioned along with their concerted manipulation of public images and measured media campaign to attract attention.

Historian Nell Irvin Painter, covering the first Somerset Homecoming for a local newspaper, pointed out that the participants concentrated on family not slavery, but "slavery was obviously the ghost of the feast" and "the central public theme."[50] The organizer, Redford, as family spokesperson, said: "For me this homecoming is a healing . . . and I will leave feeling whole and more complete as a human being, as will all who attend."[51] Although Redford and her kin found it necessary in spoken comments to obliterate the more painful reality of their common racial and regional past in favor of their celebratory homecoming, current successes, and material acquisitions, they were moved by an unarticulated belief that their presence made a statement about their conjoined participation in restructuring and reconceptionalizing a southern culture that could no longer omit their existence and significance. Both Redford and Painter spoke to the movement away from thinking of place, the plantation home, as a site of nostalgia; neither retreated from the fact of slavery as the ghost of pain, fragmentation, and dehumanization on public display within a public space that is not bounded or unproblematical.

The highly publicized reunion at Somerset resulted in Redford's book documenting that first gathering on the plantation grounds. Her *Somerset Homecoming: Recovering a Lost Heritage* (1988), written with Michael D'Orso, carried an introduction by Alex Haley in which he commented of Redford's narrative: "[I]t's all our stories." Haley, who attended the Somerset Homecoming, saw "the scores of families, all returned to the soil of their ancestors, resurrecting the spirit of their kin who came before" as "connections . . . the thread that ran back through the generations and will must surely run ahead into the future."[52] Redford went even further than Haley by stating that she believed interest in the Somerset event was the result of an interest in life, as opposed to slavery's concern with death: "we were finding our roots here, connecting with family, celebrating strength and survival."[53] She suggested that unlike the reporter from New York who expected tears and pain, "[m]any of the more than a hundred newspaper, radio and television reporters who arrived were Southerners. This was homecoming for them, too. And it was something wholesome, something to be proud of. This wasn't the kind of story they'd come to expect from the South."[54]

Redford was so right when she remarked that many of the reporters were also southerners, white southerners, experiencing a homecoming. Since the publicized event at Somerset, there has been a trickle of explorations by white southerners of their pasts in relation to slavery. *Slaves in the Family*, for example, is Edward Ball's carefully researched examination of slavery on the South Carolina plantations owned by his family. He documented the lives of the enslaved people who built the Ball family's plantations and their wealth through two centuries. In an interview, Ball recounted why he, a successful New York journalist, returned to Charleston and the plantations of South Carolina and what investigating his past meant to him: "The Balls lived side-by-side with black families for six generations . . . but I never knew much about the slaves, even though on the plantations black people far outnumbered the white. What were their names? How did they live? Who were their loved ones?"[55] The gap in his family's stories of their plantation life and the silent piece of their history emerged for Ball in the recognition of slaves in all gaps and silences. The shared environment with its necessary but unacknowledged interactions of differently raced bodies in the plantation culture of slavery became a way for Ball to realize all the implications of his privilege and his family's wealth and status. Like Alex Haley, Ball traced the slaves owned by his family back to West Africa and, remarkably, filled in aspects of the long-obscured history of enslavement on the African continent. Like Dorothy Redford, Ball returned to Limerick, one of the Ball plantations, accompanied by Thomas Martin, a seventh-generation descendent of Priscilla, who in 1756 was purchased from African traders in Sierra Leone and enslaved at Limerick. Both men believe that, despite the misgivings of their families about excavating a painful past, their return to Limerick was a pilgrimage to "hallowed ground" where together they can make "a gesture toward reconciliation."[56]

In 1998, the same year that Ball received a National Book Award for *Slaves in the Family*, the North Carolina Humanities Council honored Redford for "work that goes to the very heart and soul of understanding slavery, work in words and in organizing and in preservation that enhance our nation's sense of self-understanding"; in his keynote address on the occasion, the writer Randall Kenan said, "By honoring Ms. Spruill Redford's extraordinary work, the North Carolina Humanities Council joins in this exciting time of recovery and remembrance, where, step by step, by fits and starts, we grapple more seriously and honestly and completely with the obscured and forgotten history of African Americans and of Americans of all hues."[57]

For the organizers of the Somerset Homecoming, as Painter reported, the "reunion represented a nonjudgmental acknowledgment of the historical attachment of several generations to a certain place," but she wondered whether they were encouraging a "fantasy," one that collapses time and lives historically and "reduces every black person into no more than a descendant of slaves, and . . . elevates every white person into a descendant of planters," particularly "in these days of rampant backward-glancing and pining after the good old days when the South's lower classes stayed in their places."[58] Painter's judgment would resurface a decade later in critiques of the heritage plantation tours and living history sites of enslavement in the South. Perhaps, however, the point of Somerset Homecoming and the similar events in southern locations that followed is more in keeping with Julius Lester's affirmation in *Do Lord Remember Me* (1984), which opens with a character's writing himself into a time and place (*"The Reverend Joshua Smith, Sr. was born November 5, 1900 in Ouchitta, Mississippi"*) and ends with his gathering all of his past and future together "at the very edge of that moment coming on like the morning star giving a benediction to the night, he began."[59] Reclamation ultimately is also a means of creative invention in which "history" and "fiction" necessarily intersect, interact, and fuse.

The issue is important in terms of the black families' seeking so openly to validate their "homeplace," to authenticate their ancestors' lives and labor at Somerset, and thereby to transform plantation myth and ideology that would deny the roles of the "Baums, Bennetts, Blunts, Cabarruses, Dickensons, Honeyblues, Lees, Sawyers, Spruills, Treadwells, and Trotters"[60] in building Somerset Plantation and would insert in their places the white Josiah Collins family, which owned the land, the slaves, and the house. However, it is also important in terms of the other related activities I have described here: the prominence of the historical novel form among black writers, the purchase of an old Tennessee estate by Alex Haley, and so on. Despite all of the implicit convolutions of historical, psychological, and familial baggage, these developments manifest an insistent regionality of black selves, a grassroots redefinition, and signs of a public claim to the South that cannot be ignored. This latter may be the key to why these more recent activities may make a larger difference in expanding conceptions and perceptions of the region. It is based upon an intrinsic awareness that cultural products are manufactured, and upon a determination to manipulate that reality at long last for their own private well-being and public benefit. It is as well another way of comprehending the spatial dimension of social organization and of its transforming power.

Somerset Homecoming was the precursor of twenty-first-century designations of public spaces commemorating those individuals who were enslaved. It announced a change that prompted wider acknowledgment of the usually unmarked sites of enslavement and of slavery's benefits to grand estates, such as Jefferson's Monticello in Virginia, and to public buildings of the new republic, such as the first White House in Philadelphia. These became better known as structures that were built by slave labor and in which enslaved people worked, served, and suffered. These new sites, living history museums replete with heritage tours, have since the 1980s moved from the ignored background of consciousness by people of African American descent to another aspect of destination, vacations, and tourism that convey the recuperation of the past and carry added aspect of reasserting racial identity.[61] This latter, the body as both spatial marker and identity marker, is one of the more obvious legacies of Somerset Homecoming, though it is just beginning to receive critical attention. This new form of tourism, however, is obviously problematic. It also cannot begin to forge an overall cohesiveness of community and purpose in the current postmodern moment, despite the fact that these new sites, marking the existence of black people in history and inserting black bodies into a new narrative of nation, indeed function to represent individual strands of a narrative of modern black subjectivity that wards off a postmodern, decentered subject position. This form of experiencing the past in a virtual reality existing parallel to or even surrounding the present moment is ultimately also *not* history, but only the newly constituted *unreal*, virtual real, that can, and most likely will, become a new narrative space in the future. Natasha Trethewey, in "Pilgrimage—Vicksburg, Mississippi," contemplates what the brochure in her room in one of the restored southern antebellum mansions calls *"living history"* and understands the problematics of the space marked *"Prissy's Room"* and its relationship to a black body: "A window frames / the river's crawl; toward the Gulf. In my dream, / the ghost of history lies down beside me, / rolls over, pins me beneath a heavy arm."[62]

The room bearing Prissy's name is home for neither Prissy in the past nor the speaker in the poem; it is, as Williams observed of every attempt to locate a life toward "a simulacra of home," that which never was and cannot be recovered. Trethewey's reflection allows the room to flow through the window into the river and toward the open space of the Gulf of Mexico, but both Prissy and the narrator remain closed in, pinned down not only by "dead" history but also by the narrator's own "living" dream as well.

During the civil rights era, few observers of race and region would have predicted this grassroots effort to validate identity by claiming and reconstituting the recalcitrant region. It has, of course, antecedents, not merely in the ritual of hundreds of black family reunions and homecomings held annually from Virginia to Texas (often around "Juneteenth," the June 19 celebration of word of emancipation reaching enslaved people in Texas) or in the group political activism of the 1960s, but also in the individual self-assertions of other black southerners, some of whom are prominent and others not. The well-known Mississippian Richard Wright and the less-well-known Georgian Frank Yerby may have become expatriates, but these two modern writers provide another extension of my point. After thirteen years in France and at the end of his life, Wright returned in *The Long Dream* (1958) to the South as the shaping factor in the maturation of his black protagonist, Fishbelly, and concomitantly returned to his own relationship with the South—which he reiterated in 1958, two years before his death, by labeling himself a "southerner" who "knew what the subject matter down there was" and "accepted that subject matter as valid."[63] Much of Wright's writing constitutes what I term "bridging," explored in a later chapter, which involves Wright's ways of connecting his interior and exterior spaces while also resolving his formative relation to the South in the context of subsequent spatial locations.

Yerby, the most prolific of black novelists from the South, returned to his early racial explorations of blacks after decades of writing popular, historical fiction mainly set in the South but almost totally excluding major black characters. In his fiction, the South was raced as white. Taking its impetus from the civil rights movement and the reemphasis on the past history of black southerners, his fiction in the 1970s and 1980s begins to consider blacks in the context of region and under slavery, as for example in his two novels *The Dahomean* (1971) and *A Darkness at Ingraham's Crest: A Tale of Slaveholding* (1979). Toward the end of his life, Yerby donated his papers to Paine College, the small black institution in his hometown of Augusta, Georgia, from which he graduated in 1937 and received an honorary degree in 1977. That gesture would have been most uncharacteristic for Yerby before the 1970s, when he was an expatriate writer seeking freedom from oppressive racism though not necessarily eschewing a racial identity.[64] His escape from the racial oppression of the American South resulted in his occupying race-neutral places. Because of his experience of segregation in the United States, Yerby understood race as constituted and maintained out of the occupancy of space. Living the expatriate life in Spain without the patrolling of racial boundaries and spatial designations to confine or define blacks, he no longer had to live as a person "raced" as black and different. To congregate and affiliate with other African Americans would, however, convert the space into one making race visible, unavoidable, and ultimately detrimental to normalcy. In other words, the very occupancy of a space by black bodies "blackens" that space and converts it and any occupants or residents within it to an identity racialized as black.[65]

Yerby occupies an important place in any reading of African American writers coming to terms with southern space and in how critics have read African Americans in relation to the South. Yerby mined the spatial configuration of the plantation for his fiction, which is now often characterized as historical romance, though when he began writing his dramatic narratives in the 1930s, they were in the vein of Margaret Mitchell's *Gone with the Wind* (1936) and Stark Young's *So Red the Rose* (1934). In *The Foxes of Harrow* (1946), his best-known novel, Yerby dramatized a nineteenth-century plantation culture with romance and Louisiana at its center. An immediate best seller, the novel became the template for many of the additional thirty-two historical fictions he would publish from the 1940s to the 1980s. In 1947, when Twentieth-Century Fox brought out a major motion picture version of the novel with Rex Harrison and Maureen O'Hara in starring roles, Yerby's financial success was assured, though he expressed disappointment with the film adaptation because, as he put it, "nobody, absolutely *nobody* who has read the novel has liked the picture."[66] Despite Yerby's reservations, the film was important in that it reintroduced in the late 1940s the big-screen versions of Louisiana plantation life and paved the way for his continued production of sprawling narratives of antebellum adventure and violence that placed a bold and flawed hero and a beautiful but equally flawed heroine in a historical landscape rife with traumatic and tumultuous social events. This formula, which Yerby himself labeled the "Costume Novel" in a 1959 article for *Harper's Magazine*, often had Louisiana as the setting; see, for instance, *The Vixens* (1947), *Benton's Row* (1954), *The Serpent and the Staff* (1958), and *The Girl from Storyville* (1972).

The only U.S. author of African descent to consistently land on the annual best-seller lists throughout the 1950s, Yerby did not hide his race, and he was not ignored by the black press. On the publication of *The Saracen Blade* in 1952, *Jet* magazine published a full-page photo of Yerby with the caption "Frank Yerby: Seven Novels in Seven Years" and identified Yerby as a Georgia-born Fisk University graduate.[67] In 1954 *Time* magazine featured the then-thirty-eight-year old author in "The Golden Corn: He Writes to Please," an article that in an off-putting way makes much of Yerby's race. The anonymous journalist begins the piece with an eye-catching sentence: "Frank Garvin Yerby, 38, probably makes more money from books than any novelist now writing in the U.S."[68] After pointing to the success of the sales of Yerby's novels and his estimated $1 million in earnings, not including movie or magazine rights, the *Time* writer moves in for heavy hitting: "The really intriguing item in this success story is that Yerby is a Negro—a Negro whose stuff is just as terrible (and entertaining) as any white author's." Were this racial point not clear enough, the writer continues: "Few of the Southern housewives who buy Yerby's slick melodramas of sex, sadism and violence, know that their favorite author is a Negro. Nothing in his stories of strutting white aristocrats, swooning heiresses and yassuhing darkies would declare it, and jacket blurbs, noting that the Georgia-born author formerly taught at Florida A&M and Louisiana's Southern University, leave it to the reader to know that these are Negro Colleges." The article drips sarcasm, even labeling Yerby's unpublished novel "a Richard Wrighteous novel." However, it is Yerby's affluent lifestyle that gets attention: "Twelve years ago he was a foundryman in a Detroit war plant. Today Yerby lives on the French Riviera with his tiny, light-skinned wife Flora and their four children. When he is not whipping out profitable prose in his villa garden in Cimiez, Nice, Author Yerby goes skin-diving in the Mediterranean, skiing in the Alps or whizzing off in his Jaguar XK 120 to attend sports-car races."[69] Clearly, Yerby's known race was the focus of the writer's attention—that and the money a "Negro" had managed to make from writing.

Despite dismissive treatment in the white press, Yerby was well known as a successful black author, a storyteller. After his move to France in 1952 and then to Spain in 1955, Yerby continued his string of best-selling and well-publicized novels. Eventually in the 1960s and 1970s, with the changed racial climate in the United States, he explored issues from the perspectives of blacks that had been noticeably absent from his representations of the historical Deep South. Yerby's career lasted over forty years, much of it with many of his thirty-two novels on the best-seller lists. That Fisk University, where he studied under James Weldon Johnson and received a master's in English, awarded Yerby an honorary degree in 1976 and anticipated by one year Paine College's honor suggests that by the 1970s Yerby was being honored in a homecoming at his two black alma maters for the regionality of his black self. It is perhaps not a coincident that honoring Yerby occurred at precisely the moment when African American novelists were participating in a turn toward African American history and the American South and away from the black urban fiction dominating much of the 1950s and 1960s.

In the preface to *Call to Home*, Carol Stack remarks that the phenomenon of return migration caught scholars by surprise: "We had been led to believe that the great migrations that formed the modern states were one-way, permanent movements. People's footsteps, it seemed, were facing one way, as if they had stopped cold in their tracks somewhere out there in the urban diaspora. We had also assumed that people in the modern world, once torn from their roots, never look back."[70] Stack suggests that "the resolve to return home is not primarily an economic decision but rather a powerful blend of motives; bad times back home can pull as well as push. People feel an obligation to their kin or even a sense of mission to redeem a lost community . . . or simply a breathing space, a refuge from the maelstrom. For all of us, in good times and bad, the image of home is multilayered, and the notion of returning is unsettling."[71]

Call to Home is brilliantly evocative. It "takes seriously the imaginative, performative, and political aspects of a process that social scientists usually see as a one-dimensional response to economic [conditions]," as Jacquelyn Dowd Hall observes: "The stories told by these return migrants contribute to a powerful literary tradition, a tradition of writing about the South as a longed for—yet vexed and dangerous—home. Such stories are actions. They send people moving across the country, confounding our expectations about migration and modernity. They influence not just individual lives but the unfolding of entire communities."[72] And they open up new discourses on place and person, on region and race, on space and class.

Return migration became one of the "hot" topics at the end of the twentieth century, and not merely in terms of the rural South of Stack's subjects. In May 2004 the Brookings Institution Center on Urban and Metropolitan Policy released its findings, "The New Great Migration: Black Americans' Return to the South, 1965–2000." The report, authored by William H. Frey, a demographer at the University of Michigan, analyzed migration data from the past four decennial censuses at regional, state, and metropolitan-area levels and found that the "South scored net gains of black migrants from all three of the other regions of the U.S. during the late 1990s," when metropolitan areas in the South, particularly Atlanta, led in attracting black migrants. In addition to highlighting the South's net gains as reversing a thirty-five-year trend in out-migration, Frey emphasized two other major findings: "Southern metropolitan areas, particularly Atlanta, led the way in attracting black migrants in the late 1990s"; and "College-educated individuals led the new migration into the South" from 1995 to 2000.[73]

On 5 April 1998, during the height of the returns, Nashville's *Tennessean* newspaper carried five related stories on America's changing race picture.

In one story, "Links to the Past Draw Blacks Back to the South," David Judson stated that although "reverse migration is part of a broader movement of people from the North to the South and western Sunbelt states," the population shift of black people specifically involves a move to the South. Judson quoted demographer Frey's observation that "African Americans are moving to the South and not to states such as Arizona or New Mexico. California actually is losing blacks, with more than half those leaving the state each year moving to the South." Judson also reported that these findings hold true for the larger South; as one return migrant to historic Selma, Alabama, Michael Hayes, put it, "We're all coming home."[74] Southern cities like Atlanta, Dallas, Charlotte, Raleigh-Durham, Memphis, and Columbia were all magnets; the primary exception to the trend was New Orleans, which since 1965 has consistently lost black residents.[75] The pull factors now outweigh the push factors that caused the Great Migration in the first half of the twentieth century. African American returnees from the North and West, according to demographers, exceeded 2 million in 2000.

The United States in the twenty-first century, Judson concluded, "is expected to be increasingly Hispanic in the Southwest, Asian in the West, and African American in the South, and less white everywhere." But the South would continue to attract residents from all racial groups and is currently experiencing a growth in both Asian and Hispanic populations. Tennessee is also accounting for an increase in Native Americans, some of whom are reversing the flow of the Trail of Tears, with Western Cherokees returning to join groups of the Eastern Band of Cherokees. Another reporter, Deborah Mathis, tracking the census figures and observing the flow of people to the South for her article "America's Race Picture Changing," concluded: "By all accounts the American South will be the nation's most populous region in the next century."[76] Return migration already accounts for a large part of that growth. Between the mid-1970s and 1990, the South regained half a million African Americans from the urban belts in the North and West, but between 1995 and 2000, Georgia alone gained 129,749 blacks in return migration and the South netted a gain of 680,131 blacks.[77]

The 6 April 1998 issue of *Jet* magazine had as its cover story "Why Blacks Are Returning to the South," which pointed out a major shift after nearly fifty years of "Great Migration" movement in search of better lives free from racial hostility and economic deprivation. In the short span from 1990 to 1996, the South experienced 65 percent of the nation's black population growth because it offered greater economic opportunity, political leadership, and family ties.[78] Former Atlanta mayor Bill Campbell pointed out the two-prong appeal of the South. "Most African Americans have roots in the South," he explained. "There we've always had a connection, either our fathers, mothers, grandparents, aunts or uncles. So it's natural to have an affinity for the region." In addition, "African Americans see more opportunities available in the South politically, economically, spiritually—all a part of the new South, and Atlanta is the capital of the new South." Campbell continued: "If you're an African American looking to start a business, go to college or find a place to raise a family, it's very difficult not to return to the South, Atlanta, in particular."[79] Discounting Campbell's promotion of his city, his rationale is precisely what is being voiced by return migrants themselves, who are in fact moving to Atlanta for all the reasons he mentioned. The Brookings Institution's study concluded, however, with an admission of improved racial conditions as a factor:

> Both economic and cultural factors help account for this long-term reversal of the 'Great Migration.' The economic ascendency of Southeastern states, such as Georgia, Florida, Virginia, and the Carolinas, made them primary destinations for black migrants to the region in recent decades. Texas, too, stands for its continued appeal to black migrants. Improvements in the racial climate in these states over the past three decades helped create momentum for the return south, as many black Americans sought to strengthen ties to kin and to communities from which they and their forebears departed long ago.[80]

There is a gender-specific aspect of return migration that is perhaps being slighted in favor of the more political and entrepreneurial: women are coming home. There are now several generations of women returning to home and to the South, and, in addition to the claim and pull of cities like Atlanta, the rural South is just as strong a magnet for returning women as the urban areas. The Promised Land in the industrial North has become the Rust Belt, and the South, with all of its hardscrabble rural areas filled with kin and memories, with privation and pain, has become the return destination. Women come home with children, women return home alone, women lead and families follow. Not all is peace or prosperity. Grinding poverty can batter a family as much as an abusive parent. While the gendered stories collected from women interviewees for her ethnography project, *Call to Home*, suggest a reimagining of the domestic, home, and belonging in relation to modernity and the South, Carol Stack does caution that: "Obviously the new Old South isn't the old Old South, but distrust, fear, and hostility persist." Eula Grant, one of the return migrants to rural North Carolina, says, "You definitely can go home again.

You can go back. But you don't start from where you left. To fit in, you have to create another place in that place you left behind."[81] Her words resonate with the unruly possibilities inherent in the call of home: "What people are seeking is not so much the place they left behind as a place they feel they can change, a place in which their lives and strivings will make a difference—a place in which to create a home."[82] This practical assessment of motive is neither idealized nor romanticized. The American South as "home" is clearly much more complicated and filled with more complexity for black people than any notion of simply creating another place in the left-behind place.

One of the more visible returns "home" by an African American writer since Haley is that of Ernest Gaines, who, with his wife Dianne, has built a primary residence on the same Louisiana plantation where he was born and raised. The house named *La maison entre les champs et la rivière* is on False River in Oscar, Louisiana, where generations of Gaines's family worked the land.[83] Gaines has purchased and moved the church building that was also the plantation school for Cherie Quarters on River Lake Plantation during his youth. It now has a place of honor behind his new house "as a shrine for the people who once received instruction in the ways of the spirit and the ways of the world within its walls."[84] With his return to his family site, Gaines has been able to rewrite the plantation tradition. He has not only spent more time tending the plantation graveyard but also organized the Mount Zion River Lake Cemetery Association, which annually on "*Les Tous Saintes* or *Le Toussaint* (All Saints Day)" brings family and friends to "work together to honor the dead by cleaning their resting places and offering them a gift of communion with the living."[85] According to Reggie Scott Young, Gaines is driven as a man and as a writer by "the preservation of the little piece of Louisiana that he identifies as home, and he has worked just as hard to preserve it in his later years as he did as a much younger man."[86]

No matter how ill-formed, incongruous, incompletely conceived, or inadequately understood, all of these gestures of racial bonding with region signify somehow that the choice of regional identity along with a racial one is being made (just as it has been made, if not always acknowledged, in the past) and, perhaps more significantly for the process of expanding the limits of definition, the choice is being proclaimed for public consumption. In words and in actions, a complex but felt truth about the necessary intersection of race and region is being articulated, and with skillful marketing strategies that could rival those that keep and protect the image of the Old South. While proponents of the Black Arts Movement insisted that "the revolution will not be televised," they were swimming against the tide of the significance of new media. The result is that now too few know their names or their achievements, though fortunately there is a new recovery effort under way to correct what has been erased or obscured in a literary landscape. What grassroots people and creative writers know and tell us today is that any revolution had better be televised—recorded, transcribed, disseminated, played, and replayed. Given the available new digital technologies, including cell-phone cameras especially, the expectation is that all revolutions will be televised. Place and its residents become "real" to outsiders and nonresidents very much as a result of twenty-first-century "reality" broadcasts, just as mid-twentieth-century television made geographical knowledge possible and, with images of a world hitherto invisible, questioned indifference to justice on a world stage. As Etheridge Knight slyly observed in juxtaposing South African riots and Massachusetts vacationers:

Television speaks:
"Blacks
die on Soweto Streets!"
On Cape Cod, indolents
Buy "burgers" and sticky sweets![87]

The space imagined in the camera lens constitutes the exploratory process central to the following southscapes.

II. EMBODYING RACE AND REGION: NATASHA TRETHEWEY'S APERTURAL SPACE

The question of the conceptionalization of place also links in again to the issue of dualisms. For, as with space, so with place certain formulations of the concept are embedded in concatenations of linked and interplaying dichotomies which in turn are related, both in their general form and in their specific connotational content, to gender.
—DOREEN MASSEY, *Space, Place, and Gender*

Natasha Trethewey's poems reimagine the reclamation of the South by black writers from the 1970s and 1980s and their transition to representations of a southern homeplace. Referencing a spatial-racial location that extends the work produced in the history-conscious, place-aware texts by Margaret Walker, Alice Walker, Toni Morrison, Leon Forrest, and others, Trethewey stakes out her claim of "native daughter" status without resorting to narratives of uncontested space or to illusions of unequivocal acceptance. Calling the South at once "my home yet not my home," she understands that her conflicted dual relationship to that South has much to do with her racial designation and with her connection to the absences and erasures of black contribution to southern cultural life and historical spaces.[88]

Trethewey's poetry forms a direct link to the spatial world of the Deep South, Mississippi, and Louisiana, simultaneously places in which the past too often has produced untenable allocations in the present, and sites in which memory offers malleable interpretations for the future. Whether she locates her temporal lines of vision in the Old South or the new, Trethewey confronts segregation in a specific South as the space of indignity suffered by black men and women in their everyday existence as well as the space of injury experienced intimately within her own being and in her immediate family. That South is also the home she claims and reclaims in a repetitious act of reconstituting nonbelonging and exclusion. Thus, she offers not only one of the strongest visible instances of the continuing significance of grappling with the racial claims of southern identity for African American writers, but also a prominent body of work situated as postmodern within the context of a Deep South that is both urban and rural.

The personal in Trethewey's poetry pervades the cultural space and frames two ongoing arguments: the one for public acceptance of embodied difference, represented by the mistreatment in the South of a black and white mixed-race body; and the other for social justice for abused women, represented by an embedded discourse on physical abuse inflicted on a mother and a wife and by a surface tracing of a survivor's grief, guilt, and mourning. Intertwining the maternal body with the distaff, Trethewey displaces the opposition between real and imagined space and creates a melding of poet into a gendered subjectivity that is at once autobiographical and fictional. Her three books of poetry, *Domestic Work* (2000), *Bellocq's Ophelia* (2002), and *Native Guard* (2007), canvas the Deep South through time for signs of the inner lives of black people living in a divided world under the segregationist regime created and sustained by whites, for whom the division meant power and control. In her collections of poetry, Trethewey pulls up from memory actual events and people who took shape because of the Mississippi and Louisiana social geography in which they were located, yet the images and narratives she presents are postmodern and not the familiar stories of the past.

Locating herself both within and seeing through an apertural space, Trethewey configures a mechanical reproduction as central to her access to subjectivity and to creativity. The split in her location is not only an imaging of the segregationist social structure shaping her early life but also a mirroring of her racial and familial construction. On the one hand, the apertural space sites a desire for the continuance of a modernist epistemology, but on the other hand, the apertural space allows for envisioning a postmodern ontology. Often it is a photograph, the end product of mechanical technology and human skill, that functions as the site of memory and of the regionality of a black subjectivity. The 1957 photograph of the young woman in a Chicago lab "distilling / light from volatile darkness" becomes a vague memory in "Give and Take" of the old woman, an émigré returned home to Mississippi and the Dixie White House nursing home.[89] The only photograph of a soon-separated mother, father, and child is taken by a legless photographer observed in "Family Portrait" "bother[ing] / the space for knees, shins, scratching air / as—years later—I'd itch for what's not there" (*Domestic Work*, 30). Two photographs taken forty years apart on the same beach with identical "hands on flowered hips" poses remember segregation of the outdoor, natural world and bear witness to history: a beachscape changed from the grandmother's photograph "on a narrow plot / of sand marked *colored*" to the granddaughter's photograph "on a wide strip of Mississippi beach" in "1970, two years after they opened / the rest of this beach to us" ("History Lesson," *Domestic Work*, 45). In the connected Gulf Coast landscape where Mississippi and Louisiana share cultural flows, Trethewey finds inspiration for a body of work enmeshed in the history of place and race and achieved in the visual and spatial language of photography. As Rita Dove put it in her introduction to *Domestic Work*, "Trethewey eschews the Polaroid instant, choosing to render the unsuspecting yearnings and tremulous hopes that accompany our most private thoughts—reclaiming for us that interior life where the true self flourishes and to which we return in solitary reverie, for strength."[90]

Dove's mention of the Polaroid instant is an important reminder that the visual and aural (sight and sound) are inextricably linked to African American modernisms. The painting, the daguerreotype, the photograph, later the photoplay or film, all become technologies of display and visualization for documenting the formerly erased and invisible, unseen black subject in the moving, surging passages out of enslavement, just as the song—the spiritual, the blues, the gospel, the jazz vocalizations and mechanical reproductions in recordings—also become the technologies of the heard. The recorded music is an extension perhaps of Houston Baker's conception of deformation of mastery and mastery of form regarding orality, speech, and forms of discursive expression in African American cultural production.[91] All of these become self-images, markers of cultural engagement and, importantly, spaces of preservation that often also serve as projections of racial empowerment and social agency, of signification, of movement in terms of progress, as well as of passage over time and the debilitating past of African Americans in the U.S. context. In Trethewey's apertural space, however, the stance toward scripted narratives is more of a smashup, and more in line with what Terry Eagleton terms postmodernist "irreverent pastiche," though perhaps less playful than the riot of mashed-together images in Harryette Mullen's poetry. Trethewey may not use the Polaroid instant, but she does use the camera's technology of display, distancing, and documentation as a central aspect of her creative work.

In *Bellocq's Ophelia*, Trethewey experiments specifically with the camera as a way of coming into a subjective focus that is the antithesis of silence. The mixed-raced writer of letters and diaries, Ophelia works in a New Orleans brothel, where she practices the art of stillness and silence in staged *tableaux vivant*.[92] She advances from entrapment as immobile object that was first dictated to please her white father in Mississippi and then required by the New Orleans photographer E. J. Bellocq as well as the male gaze of the patrons in the red-light Storyville district.[93] Initially, this Ophelia considers "forgetting" a desired freedom that lies outside the reaches of people of her race: "I want freedom from memory. / I could be somebody else, born again, / free in the white space of forgetting."[94] Recognition of "the white space of forgetting" and its difference from memory-shaped, raced space marks the desire for transformation, because in a race-defined world, only secure, comfortable, free subjects can live unencumbered by memory. Trethewey utilizes the foundational thinking of bell hooks, who, in articulating a politics of black feminist location, observed: "Thinking again about space and location, I heard the statement 'our struggle is also a struggle of memory against forgetting'; a politicalization of memory that distinguishes nostalgia, that longing for something to be as once it was, a kind of useless act, from that remembering that serves to illuminate and transform the present."[95] In making her point clear, hooks traces her development: "I have needed to remember, as part of a self-critical process where one pauses to reconsider choices and location, tracing my journey from small town Southern black life, from folk traditions, and church experience to cities, to university, to neighborhoods that are not racially segregated, to places where I see for the first time independent cinema, where I read critical theory, where I write theory. Along that trajectory, I vividly recall efforts to silence my coming to voice. In my public present I was able to tell stories, to share memories."[96]

"Remembering that serves to illuminate and transform the present" is applicable to what Trethewey accomplishes in *Bellocq's Ophelia*. Ophelia moves from being a model for the photographer to buying her own camera, a Kodak, and becoming a photographer who understands the varied uses of the camera to manipulate and conceal as much as capture and reveal: "I've learned the camera well—the danger / of it, the half-truths it can tell, but also the way it fastens us to our pasts, makes grand / the unadorned moment" ("December 1911," 30). For her, the camera is a way ultimately of remembering: "I would like one day; if you would / permit me, to take your photograph, fix / an image of you for my table / to accompany what is left in my head" ("December 1911," 30).

The work both of the poem and of the photograph throughout the collection challenges the confines of a photographer's lens and reconstitutes the racial contours of memory and forgetting. Similar to what hooks identifies as "the need to remember, as part of a self-critical process where one pauses to reconsider choices and location," Trethewey produces a trajectory of remembering as an act of recovery of voice, movement, and sight; as Ophelia reflects, "I see, / too the way the camera can dissect / the body, render it reflecting light / or gathering darkness" ("September 1911," 27). Trethewey juxtaposes the position of the black female body in relation to memory with the white body and forgetting in a way that is suggestive of the concluding remark Jessica Adams makes in the chapter "Plantations without Slaves" in *Wounds of Returning: Race, Memory, and Property on the Postslavery Plantation* (2007): "It turns out that what is wrong with 'us' [whites] is intimately connected to the fact that remembering through forgetting is never a comfortable process, and the results it achieves can be terrifying."[97] For Trethewey's Ophelia, however, her own eye becomes her camera accessing memory: "The first time I tried this shot / I thought of my mother shrinking against / the horizon—so distracted, I looked into / a capped lens, saw only my own clear eye" ("[Self] Portrait—March 1912," 46).

Replacing the camera in a move reminiscent of Dos Passos's camera eye, Trethewey locates the poet persona within the space of the page as an encompassing knowledge site, enabled by focus and frame to isolate and magnify her subject and to move backward in time. She manipulates an apertural space so that it is sometimes a slit, torn or sliced with the violence of a blade, as in poems venturing into the abuse a mother suffered. At other times, the apertural space is a gap between the inside and the outside of structures or relationships. It is the disjunctive space between a daughter's love and trauma, or the resistance measured in the space between a white photographer and black women refusing to be passive objects of his camera. At still other times, the apertural space is the hole through which the liminal is made possible.

It is the means of accessing a mixed-race woman in the Storyville district of New Orleans and her transformation in front of a camera, or tracing the black Native Guards shot by Confederate soldiers and refused burial by Union officers. But no matter the configuration, the apertural space remains constant in Trethewey's process and art.

Each of Trethewey's collections, then, utilizes the photograph as a space of entrance into the lives of southern black people, into an interiority possible only from the poet's creative perspective. In addition, the architectural process of bridging that Richard Wright used in his writing is also visible in Trethewey's focus on connecting her own inner life and the shape of her emotional or creative reality to the external world and to the material spaces found there. In one poem, her persona muses on "*travel*, no place / so distant that I couldn't dream my self / there" ("January 1912," *Bellocq's Ophelia*, 31). Places on a globe—Africa, Atlanta, Massachusetts, New York—are linked by reading *American Highways and Byways* and looking at its pictures. Touching a globe, she "imagined the line between us, words / we post to bridge what seems to me, / now an impossible distance" ("January 1912," 32). Trethewey's bridge work is not just in terms of words and geography; it also involves the camera and photography. Her placement of the embodied subject within identifiable sites of separation and segregation link her to similar aspects within Wright's work evocative of his Mississippi heritage and to related concepts within Ernest Gaines's chains of memory encasing midcentury Louisiana life. Like them, she understands a positionality within a moment and a place recognizable for its racial inequities, but she moves resolutely against fixity and entrapment in racist structures. Yet Trethewey differs notably from Wright in her insistence on memory and the historical past and its intersection with the subjective present, and from Gaines in her imagining of breaking free of ties of history and stepping through fragments without emerging whole.

In "Southern Gothic" (*Native Guard*), the very body of the poetic persona merges with a time past and in a material space that connects her to her parents as they once were: "I have lain down into 1970, into the bed / my parents will share for only a few more years."[98] But the poem is also dependent upon the poet's apertural positioning, watching and seeing her child self and her young parents seeking refuge from a threatening racist milieu:

. . . I have come home
from the schoolyard with the words that shadow us
in this small Southern town—*peckerwood* and *nigger*
lover, *half-breed* and *zebra*—words that take shape

outside us. We're huddled on the tiny island of bed, quiet
in the language of blood: the house, unsteady
on its cinderblock haunches, sinking deeper
into the muck of ancestry. (40)

"Southern Gothic" ends with an awareness of a burdensome past, mired home and ancestry, but also of the cameralike projection of the family trio made visible in their conjoined difference: "Oil lamps flicker / around us— our shadows, dark glyphs on the wall, / bigger and stranger than we are" (40).

Like "Southern Gothic," Trethewey's poems are haunted by the ghosts of places. They hide stories in ordinary words or everyday objects that have "hollow places in which a past sleeps," and, as Michel de Certeau claims, those places that are "haunted by many different spirits . . . are the only ones people can live in."[99] Trethewey inhabits these haunted places in her poems, but they are fractured histories often floating up from her childhood and often necessitating a photographic image to allow for a temporary adhesion.

In thinking about the work of photography, Roland Barthes reflects on the inability of photography to "signify (aim at a generality) except by assuming a mask," which, following Italo Calvino, is "what makes a face into the product of a society and its history."[100] In poems such as "Southern Gothic," the poet functioning in apertural space opens the viewer precisely to the act of signifying that does not stand outside of meaning. Yet the segregated racial and spatial order lacks meaning within a house and family "sinking deeper / into the muck of ancestry." The gap between the poet and the mask of a child self is slight, with a decided tendency to hone in on some aspect of the child's occupation of space for the production of meaning for the whole. In fact, this process is connected to Trethewey's identification and use of Barthes's concept of the *punctum* as her starting point in viewing a photograph and then beginning the imaginative process of making new pictures. She defines Barthes's *punctum* in her work as "the thing in the photograph that draws you outside the frame. That would be the moment that allowed me to enter the realm of the imagination."[101] Barthes appropriates the term *punctum* from the Latin to designate "this wound, this prick, this mark made by a pointed instrument," or that "element which rises from the scene, shoots out of it like an arrow, and pierces me."[102] Presenting *punctum* as also incorporating the idea of a punctuation mark, Barthes calls it a "sting, speck, cut, little hole—and also a cast of the dice."[103] His choice of words to explain his selection of *punctum* as a means of discussing the photograph seems related to my concept of apertural space, that opening, hole, slit, or cut at work in my reading Trethewey's poetry. The pain implicated in the idea of *punctum* as a cut extends beyond a visual field to an affective realm in which loss and separation are part of the experience. Barthes meditates on photography in *Camera Lucida* and on his own grief over the death of his mother and his longing for her in order to fill the void left by her absence. Trethewey, too, implements photography as a spatial practice allowing her entry into aspects of presence that otherwise are fractured and fragmented by the loss of her mother.

A native of Gulfport, Mississippi, Trethewey shares her personal history as a mixed-race modern daughter of a black mother and a white father who, as she writes in "Miscegenation," "broke two laws of Mississippi; / they went to Ohio to marry, returned to Mississippi" (*Native Guard*, 36). This social history pervades her poetry with a racial eye that strains against the boundaries and the absurdities of racism and racial segregation. It allows her specific access though with limited knowledge to a familial and sectional history, but it also provides her with the autobiographical impulse, as she has said, for poems "in which I have sought to rewrite a story that I had been part of, that I had experienced . . . as a child, as someone who was powerless to affect the outcome of the story at that moment. Through the process of my very particular and selective language, I find that I can take charge of narratives that I was not in control of at the time."[104] Extending this observation, she acknowledges that poetry is her means of seeing a way to make order in her own family and to make sense of the personal histories that emerge from the places she and her interracial family occupied in Mississippi. For all her images and words directed at taking charge of those familial narratives, they remain "disorderly" pieces that prick and wound without necessarily adhering or healing.

At the same time, Trethewey's social history enables her attention to the body as a signifying project and inscription site. Transgressive and fluid, the body in Trethewey's work is related to Peter Brooks's understanding of the body through the lens of psychoanalysis "as at once a cultural construct and its other, something outside of language that language struggles to mark and to be embodied in."[105] While Brooks is most interested in the body defined by its sexuality, Trethewey is instead invested in the body defined by its raciality. That raced subjectivity often carries an injunction to remain silent about abuse or trauma. According to Patricia J. Williams, black people have suffered from an

> inability to grasp or heal those most painful bits of our history. The impenetrability of that past creates a portal for ghosts, if ghosts are a way of representing what we do not know. . . . I think a legacy of violence

against and among one's people . . . always engenders a certain preparation for death, a magnification of life by planting lots of yourselves in
many difference guises and forms. I am a this, not a that. I am here, not
there. You live life as though you are writing your own obituary—so
that other will know, so that no one will ever mistake you for "just" a
this or a that.[106]

For Trethewey, it is the speaking out to break a history of silence by "planting" a raced body in multiple places and in many different times past so that
there is neither mistaking that body's complex geography nor reducing it to
simplistic stasis.

Trethewey's poems of childhood in Mississippi and Louisiana evoke the
complexity of being "both" black and white when the social structure expects
"one" racial designation. In "Flounder," words the child hears while fishing
with her aunt—*"You 'bout as white as your dad, / and you gone stay like that"*—
reverberate in the fish caught,

> that wiggled and tried to fight back.
> *A flounder*, she said, *you can tell*
> *'cause one of its sides is black.*
> *The other side is white. . . .*
> I stood there watching that fish flip-flop,
> switch sides with every jump. (*Domestic Work*, 35–36; Trethewey's italics)

The useless fighting back becomes the watched and helpless flipping from
black to white, which then becomes in "White Lies" the "growing up / light-
bright, near-white, / high-yellow, red-boned / in a black place" in which either
telling or not telling white people details in order to be identified within their
racial group results in:

> But I paid for it every time
> Mama found out.
> She laid her hands on me,
> then washed out my mouth
> with Ivory soap. *This*
> *is to purify*, she said,
> *and cleanse your lying tongue.*
> Believing her, I swallowed suds
> thinking they'd work
> from the inside out. (*Domestic Work*, 37; Trethewey's italics)

Laying on of hands can be read as the religious ritual of casting out evil or sin to make way for grace and goodness or as a way of describing a beating as punishment, so that duality and ambiguity cohere in the physical scene enacted and in the expectation of transformation. This seeing of the body that the poet does through a lens poised to expose the dislocation in a segregated space of identity occurs with ordinary objects, Ivory soap or a fish, or a microscope to examine hair texture in a scientific experiment to undo the "puzzle of shifting shapes—Africa, Europe, / and the Americas" and the racial and bodily images produced in the *World Book Encyclopedia* under "Races of Man" ("Microscope," *Domestic Work*, 38). The body thus represented performs different social identities and has its own geography, which, as Linda McDowell observes, is "affected by and reflected in embodied practices and lived social relations."[107]

Primarily gendered and connected to a woman's body, Trethewey's methodology evokes photography and the work of the camera, in which the aperture is the hole, gap, or split that limits the amount of light passing through a lens. As a space, the aperture connotes absence that allows for presence. An apertural space marks all of Trethewey's poetry, much of it exploring what she terms "the landscape of her body," the maternal body in "What Is Evidence." In "3. Flood," the third section of "Scenes from a Documentary History of Mississippi," Trethewey provides a glimpse into her practice and the ideology underlining it:

> . . . the opening
> in the sight of a rifle; the camera's lens;
> the muddy cleft between barge and dry land—
> all of it aperture, the captured moment's
> chasm in time. (*Native Guard*, 23)

The conscious linking of the poet's eye with the opening, with the camera lens, with aperture, allows for a view of the violence done *by* the gun but also *to* the eye seeing through the aperture. The apertural space may be read as process and product in the context of Trethewey's "all." It gives a name to her description of her methodology: "I have tried to see something of the lives of people that history and public memory often forget. . . . [T]he lens opens wide at the beginning, then gradually narrows and becomes more privately focused by the book's end."[108]

Native Guard, winner of the Pulitzer Prize, demonstrates the work of embodying race and region within a text arguing for a reclaiming of the South by blacks. Beginning with the poem "Theories of Time and Space," Trethewey muses: "You can get there from here, though / there's no going home. / Every-where you go will be somewhere / you've never been" (I). The space and time that the poems explore involve the black Native Guards formed in Louisiana who were called into service in the Civil War, but into her treatment of this specific southern place and time Trethewey threads her own autobiograph-ical space, with its roots in that Louisiana past but more immediate anteced-ents in the life and early death of the poet's mother, to whose memory she dedicates *Native Guard*. The epigraph is from Charles Wright's "Meditation on Form and Measure": "Memory is a cemetery / I've visited once or twice, white / ubiquitous and the set-aside / Everywhere under foot."[109] It telescopes a dual focus on the dead, near kin and distant ancestors, and the places where the dead remain. In the repository spaces of memory within and cemetery without, Trethewey begins her movement back though time and space. She names her places on the literal map: Mississippi's Highway 49; Gulfport's pier; and Ship Island. These lead to the buried "tome of memory" that the poet will take with her on her journey into the "terrain of the past." "Theories of Time and Space" ends with a familiar symbol in Trethewey's canon, the photograph: "On the dock / where you board the boat for Ship Island / some-one will take your picture: / the photograph—who you were—will be waiting when you return" (*Native Guard*, I). This usage of the photograph provides both a way of seeing ahead to changes wrought by experience and of look-ing back at past formations of self; it is Trethewey's agile double subjectivity made plain by means of her vision of the camera and the work of the photo-graphic space.

The first section of *Native Guard* contains poems establishing the move-ment into her mother's realm following her mother's journey from 1959—when as a teenager she leaves Mississippi for California, where she will meet her own father—to her early death at the hands of a husband. That journey, however, is intertwined with the shared journey of the daughter and mother, as seen from the daughter's limited but discerning perspective. A traditional hymn announces the spiritual and metaphoric journey of the dead, the mother and the child evoked in the first part of *Native Guard*: "I'm going there to meet my mother / She said she'd meet me when I come / I'm only going over Jordan / I'm only going over home." The homeplace, familiar and comforting though outside of and antithetical to the material and worldly, provides the site for reunion and satisfies the longing and desire for the lost maternal. The emotional ache palpable in all of the poems in the first part of *Native Guard* situates desire for reconnection and completeness within the emptiness and wound of loss: "I'm too late, / again, another space emptied by loss. / Tomorrow, the bowl I have yet to fill" ("After Your Death," 13). In this sense, I read an expansion of the now-familiar term "survivor discourse" to refer not only to the literal victims of abuse but also to those left behind and affected emotionally and psychically by witnessing its physical effect on the body of another. Minrose Gwin, in *The Woman in the Red Dress*, expanded the conception of survivor discourse to apply beyond a literal or factual case of rape, incest, or sexual abuse in order to explore in literary texts "questions about how and under what circumstances such discourse can emerge and mutate."[110] Gwin's analysis of the articulations and complications in the discourse of sexual abuse suggests the possibility enacted here of utilizing the space of survivor discourse in a wider application.

The survivor discourse in this expanded sense is at work in the poem "Monument" (43), where there is an analogy between the sight of ants in the present moment making a hill at the front steps ("I watch them emerge and—/like everything I've forgotten—disappear—/into the subterranean—a world/made by displacement") and the memory of ants: "At my mother's grave, ants streamed in/and out like arteries." At that grave, which had been hard to locate ("In the cemetery/last June, I circled, lost—/weeds and grass grown up all around—/the landscape blurred and waving"), the ants in their industry signified the daughter's neglect:

> I've tried not to begrudge them
> their industry, this reminder of what
> I haven't done. Even now,
> the mound is a blister on my heart,
> a red and humming swarm.

That the ants work the soil from below and include particles of the decomposed body in order to make their "tiny hill rising/above her untended plot" is what the daughter cannot begrudge, but it is in fact what leaves her contemplating displacement and inaction. This aspect and application of survivor discourse may be said in some measure to diffuse through the work of multiple contemporary African American writers as they struggle with representing the natural and unnatural world of the postmodern South.

In Trethewey's sonnet "What Is Evidence" (11), the negations yield the material body disappearing each day under its wounds:

> Not the fleeting bruises she'd cover
> with makeup, a dark patch as if imprint
> of a scope she's pressed her eye too close to,

looking for a way out, not the quiver
in the voice she'd steady, leaning
into a pot of bones on the stove. Not
the teeth she wore in place of her own.

This "landscape of her body," though secreted, is read by the child, who knows intimately the "thin bones / settling a bit each day" and the marks on a battered body in pain. Each takes a toll on the daughter who survives to mourn in her own pain, the abstraction, the slowly fading temporal disappearance of the materiality of "mother," whose grave marker like her name becomes "abstract as history." Impersonal and fading, the pieces mark the most personal of relationships, between mother and daughter, subject to the changed circumstances of the body as evidence.

What makes the poems recounting the mother's too early death doubly moving is the elision of the space between the mother and the daughter: "I watch / each small town pass before my window / until the light goes, and the reflection / of my mother's face appears" ("The Southern Crescent," 6); "Why / the tired face of a woman, suffering, / made luminous by the camera's eye?" ("Photograph: Ice Storm, 1971," 10); "I was asleep while you were dying. / It's as if you slipped through some rift, a hollow / I make between my slumber and my waking" ("Myth," 14). The camera's eye is the apertural space allowing the poet to see suffering on the other side but also to imagine the very opening through which the dying mother slips. It is as well the consciously manipulated gap that can displace the opposition between mother and daughter, real and imagined.

The poems in *Native Guard* attend to the troubled memory and the space of the mother within it. "Gathering," for example, names memory seen both through a natural landscape and within the domestic as "our minds' dark pantry" (49). In "Saturday Matinee," the mother's image coalesces out of double-edged secrets: of the sounds of abuse heard from a girl's room ("my mother whispers / resistance, my stepfather's voice louder / than the static of an old seventy-eight"); and the desire for another mother, a white mother ("Lana Turner glides on screen, / the camera finding her in glowing white, golden haired among the crowd"). The camera's glittering images of an always-smiling mother from *Imitation of Life* compete with "the run-down mama, her blues— / dark circles around the eyes, / that weary step and *hush-baby* tone," all combined with "the dull smack, / the stumbling for balance, the clutter of voices" to make the mother's reality plainly visible and unobscured by the camera or the television (40). Here the portrait emerges of two raced bodies suffering, one physically and the other emotionally; neither of these particular black bodies in pain has the power to change the circumstances, and that inability, that helplessness, is a dominant articulation in the survivor discourse marking much of Trethewey's poetry.

It is difficult to resist reading the mother in Trethewey's poems as emblematic of the South, racialized as black and abused yet offering a homespace to shape the daughter's subjectivity. This reading deepens in the second part of *Native Guard* that begins with Nina Simone's warning "Everybody knows about Mississippi" from her 1964 protest song "Mississippi Goddam." Structured to move from a place in which the personal intersects with the public, this part of the collection divides into three components. In the first, "Pilgrimage—Vicksburg, Mississippi," "Scenes from a Documentary History of Mississippi," "Native Guard," and "Again, the Fields—After Winslow Homer," Trethewey duplicates the movement of the whole by beginning with a contemporary trip to Vicksburg. Located at the confluence of the Mississippi and Yazoo Rivers and the site of a major Civil War battle, Vicksburg is alive with mementos of 1863—the landscape, the flowers, the battlefields, the cemeteries, the mansions, the museum all signify the past and its oppressive presence: "This whole city is a grave. Every spring—/Pilgrimage—the living come to mingle/with the dead, brush against their cold shoulders/in the long hallways" (19–20). That entry to the past is through physical presence, the literal sharing of antebellum space, but immediately in the next poem, "Scenes from a Documentary History of Mississippi," a four-part sequence, Trethewey returns to the photograph as the point of entry from the public to the private: "From every corner of the photograph, flags wave down/the main street in Vicksburg" ("1. King Cotton, 1907," 21). From the pageantry of celebration of "*Cotton, America's King*" with "negro [sic] children rid[ing] the bales, clothes stiff with starch./From up high, in the photograph, they wave flags down/for the President who will walk through the arch, bound/for the future, his back to us" (21), the poet locates in black space the coming disaster and indifference to black children and black people in general.

From the infestation by boll weevils and the flood of 1927 to the segregation of the Greenwood Public Library, the poems emphasize both time-space compressions and the discrepancies over time of black life within Mississippi's public and civic life by using the camera and photographs. "3. Flood" (23) has at its center a photograph showing National Guardsmen on the levee with rifles pointed at a group of black refugees from the 1927 flood in order to block them from safe passageway to higher ground. All of the conjoined public and private places in the poems lead back to the central narrative of the Louisiana Native Guard in the crucial period between 1862 and 1865 and to the poet's need to remember the heroism and the cruelty possible in human beings who are subject and object of a racial regime. The epigraph from Frederick Douglass's 1871 "Address at the Grave of the Unknown Dead" emphasizes the tension between forgetting and remembering readily apparent in much of Trethewey's work: "If this war is to be forgotten, I ask in the name of all things sacred what shall men remember?" From this beginning in Arlington National Cemetery in the nineteenth century, the poems connect the recent death and the long dead, mother and kin to soldiers and forebears, through the apertural space, which sees the recorded as writing, as snapshots fluidly accessing moments in the experience of the black men in the Guard as immediate and continuous as opposed to a formal photograph freezing their experiences in time. Trethewey states that she wanted "to make poems that stand as monuments to our overlooked past," but moreover she "tried to build in words—degrees—a monument to the life of my mother" and thus divided the book into "document, monument, and testament."[111] The dead form the connective tissue, a fabric woven out of the images and the processes of imagining that gather in racial memory and produce within the public the embedded dual memorials.

What is brilliant about Trethewey's act of civic memorializing and national remembering of men and war, of social relations and public acts, is the framing within the maternal body that is not the figurative body of the nation-state but the "real" body of a mother whose death and loss are the subject of a daughter's mourning and memory. That death is not the result of an institution, of segregation as a political practice, yet it is the loss of a black woman's body within a social structure that has accommodated itself to devaluing that kind of bodily configuration, no matter its relational ties. The twinned bodies of women both frame and contextualize the Native Guards, not feminizing them but making their story the condition of the raced story of the mother-daughter and the subject of the aesthetic production of the daughter-mother. Rather than following the modernist trope of a master narrative of analogy as a formal mode of connection between the stories, Trethewey adheres to a postmodernist narrative of impossible reunion (either of the racist men of the Blue and Gray armies or of the Louisiana Native Guards with freedom and recognition or of the poet herself with the Fugitives and Whitman or of the mother and her daughter).

In the ten parts of the section "Native Guard," dates from late 1862 to 1865 anchor the diary format of the poetry and provide a guide to the momentous historical shifts in which the men participated and discourses of masculinity and nation emerged. Here Trethewey enters again into the subject position of the mixed-raced "southerner" who historically has represented the sins of the father against the body of the black woman and her offspring, but in her treatment "Native Guard" stands for the civic and national sins of the Confederate and federal governments in racist collusion against an abused and neglected citizenry. The first entry, "November 1862," reaffirms the necessity of not forgetting and of recording the personal experience of enslavement of a thirty-three-year-old man born at harvest time in Louisiana's Ascension Parish (25):

> Truth be told, I do not want to forget
> anything of my former life: the landscape's
> song of bondage—dirge in the river's throat
> where it churns into the Gulf, wind in trees
> choked with vines. I thought to carry with me
> want of freedom though I had been freed,
> remembrance not constant recollection.

As in all of the larger volume, Native Guard, the burden of not forgetting and of remembrance is racial, and landscape is visibly situated as integral to the work of the poem in remembering this South and slavery, in which human beings become subordinate objects, such as the men of the Guard being not "infantry" but "supply units" performing "nigger work" ("December 1862," 25). The journal writer, whom Trethewey imagines as Francis E. Dumas, a Louisiana Creole of Color born to a mulatto mother and a white father, views the intersections of his new "free" life with "history"—"berth upon a ship called the Northern Star / and I'm delivered into a new life, / Fort Massachusetts: a great irony—both path and destination of freedom / I'd not dared to travel"—and the lessons of the natural world: "I can look out / upon the Gulf and see the surf breaking, / tossing the ships, the great gunboats bobbing / on the water. And are we not the same, / slaves in the hands of the master, destiny?" ("January 1863," 26). Dumas at once references Alexandre Dumas *père*, the celebrated Afro-Creole French novelist whose lineage was in Saint-Domingue (Haiti), and the Afro-Creole Louisiana journalists who during the middle of the century in New Orleans produced political newspapers and broadsides; in the dual references, Trethewey encodes the Atlantic slave trade as economic circulation of capital and production of mix-raced bodies. The apertural space allows for both the specific material landscape of the Gulf and the physical body of those enslaved to merge together into view as a way of envisioning how the workings of destiny move things and humans, objects and subjects, similarly. It is a manifestation of what Trethewey terms her interest in "hidden landscapes."[112] It is as well an emblematic statement of the enduring presence of Louisiana Creoles of Color in the literary imagination and as a historical claim on a heritage of belonging to a South and of visibility in that South.

The narrative unfolding in the journal is that of black men, free in name but working much as they did as slaves, with the added duty of guarding the Confederate prisoners. The journalist "Dumas" writes letters for those illiterate Confederates who can only make an *X* to sign their names: "Still, they are wary of a negro writing, taking down letters. . . . / I suspect they fear / I'll listen, put something else down in ink" ("February 1863," 27). The incongruities of their lives become clear when in "April 1863," they bury their dead, who in retreating from Pascagoula, were killed by "white solders in blue firing upon us / as if we were the enemy." But the indignity of being shot by Union soldiers is compounded by the commanding colonel's words: "*an unfortunate incident; . . . / their names shall deck the page of history.*" The irony of their position and its inherent tragedy does not end with one incident. At Port Hudson, when "colored troops" fell dead in the battle, the Union commander "General Banks was heard to say *I have / no dead there*, and left them, unclaimed." ("June 1863," 28). Yet, the black men, already starving and nearly dead, continue to enlist and: "Dying, / they plead for what we do not have to give" (29).

"Dumas" contrasts his life under a "fair master," who may well be his own father and who taught him to read and write: "I was a man- / servant, if not a man" who "studied natural things—all manner / of plants, birds I draw now in my book: wren, willet, egret, loon. Tending the gardens, I thought only to study living things, thought / never to know so much about the dead" ("August 1864," 29). Instead, his job is to tend graves on Ship Island and record the deaths for families back at home, but the knowledge that began with illiteracy is now expanded into "things which must be accounted for," including the treatment of the black men in the Native Guard: "[S]laughter under the white flag of surrender— / black massacre at Fort Pillow" ("1865," 29). However, what also has to be taken into account is the very erasure of the meaning of the Native Guard, black men of the slaveholding South fighting for the emancipation of black people and the abolition of slavery. Their location within the space of belonging was a matter of pride and inspiration; however, that space was easily undermined by the simple changing of their name to "the Corps d' Afrique," which as the journal writer observes: "[W]ords that take the *native* / from our claim; mossback and freedman—exiles / in their own homeland" (29). The not-belonging, the exiles at home, the exclusion is the echo that runs through the poems as Trethewey traces the dissolution of a promise and a plan. In her very tracing of the historical and the imagined record, she reclaims the Native Guard as men, as free, and as black soldiers in the fight for their and their nation's freedom. That process achieves social justice for them in the longer lens of righteous action and thought.

The third part of *Native Guard* concludes with eleven poems interlocked with the two opening sections and following an epigraph from Walt Whitman: "O magnet-South! O glistening perfumed South! my South! / O quick mettle, rich blood, impulse and love! Good and evil! / O all dear to me!" This many-faceted magnetic South of the poet Whitman is the South the poet Trethewey claims and names in the poems that follow. Place becomes saturated with "inward-turning histories" that Certeau suggests are enigmatic "symbolizations encysted in the pain and pleasure of the body."[113] "Pastoral" opens the section with a sonnet's knowingness about the manipulations of the rural, the South, race, writing, and photography (35). The poet occupies the apertural space and sees a dream of the poet's posing for a photograph in urban Atlanta with the Fugitive Poets but against a false "photographer's backdrop— / a lush pasture, green, full of soft-eyed cows / lowing, a chant that sounds like *no, no.*" The Fugitives' rural iconography is made obsolete by the sound of bulldozers building more of the city. Robert Penn Warren orchestrates the group into position, and the dream turns into nightmare: "*Say 'race,'* the photographer croons. I'm in / blackface again when the flash freezes us. *My father's white,* I tell them, *and rural. You don't hate the South?* they ask. *You don't hate it?*" Things are not what they seem. The camera in this South will not capture the truth of either blackface or a white father, and belonging to this coterie of racially white poets necessitates the speech act articulating paternity (white) and authenticity (rural), both of which can only evoke Faulkner's race-haunted Quentin Compson at the end of *Absalom, Absalom!* deteriorating in obsessive affect and emotional distress.

The next seven poems all retrace the history of the poet, her father, and her mother as an interracial family unit in Mississippi; "Miscegenation," "My Mother Dreams Another Country," "Southern History," "Blond," "Southern Gothic," "Incident," and "Providence" in a variety of poetic forms chronicle the impact of racism on the biracial child and on the parents whose marriage cannot withstand the racism of the region, from the bold statements of hatred, as when the Ku Klux Klan burns a cross in the family's yard ("Incident"), to quiet reinterpretations of history, such as a teacher's reading from a textbook about happy, well-cared-for slaves ("Southern History"). "Blond," however, displays the child's response to a racially segregated world in which white is valued and black denigrated as the desire for blond hair, which carries another valence: "And with my skin color, / like a good tan—an even mix of my parents'—/ I could have passed for white" (39). The awareness circulating through the poem, however, is that the Christmas gifts of blond wig and blond ballerina doll and pink sequined tutu were a "primer for a Mississippi childhood," in the era before a positive black consciousness would have questioned those early choices. For that time and place and the child's psychology, the scene of the bewigged child is a "whirl of possibility," emblematic of the might-have-been, viewed by the child now grown but captured then in a photograph taken by her mother with her father on the edge of the frame.

The last three poems ("Monument," "Elegy for the Native Guards," and "South") reiterate the major tropes of the volume: the death of the mother, the memory of the Native Guards, the poet's present-day location in the South. "Elegy for the Native Guards" directly confronts Allen Tate's "Ode to the Confederate Dead." The dead of Tate's poem are honored with tombs and headstones, with memory and monuments; they are celebrated and memorialized in southern history and literature, whereas the Native Guards have no names carved on plaques, no "monument to their legacy," no grave markers ("all the crude headstones—water-lost"). Into the loss and erasure, Trethewey's poem figures a word monument to the Native Guards on Ship Island, now split in two by an act of nature, analogous to the split between the ways of honoring the white soldiers and of ignoring the black guards. Hurricane Camille left only the unfinished fort, which the poem exposes as "half open to the sky, / the elements—wind, rain—God's deliberate eye" (44). The "Elegy" is both monument and reckoning.

The final poem, "South," speaks of return to a land of dualities and complexities, a "tangle / of understory—a dialectic of dark / and light" (45). This South has a natural landscape of trees, pines, magnolia, mangrove, live oak, gulf weed, palms, and palmettos, signaling at once victory and defeat. The repetition of "I returned" punctures the landscape with the litany of emotion and of what is within both the sight line and the insight of the poet ("I returned to a stand of pine"; "I returned / to a field of cotton hallowed ground—/ as slave legend goes—each boll / holding the ghosts of generations"; "I returned to a country battlefield / where colored troops fought and died." The final use of return shifts from past to present tense and concludes on the material body and being of the poet: "I return / to Mississippi, state that made a crime / of me—mulatto, half-breed—native / in my native land, this place they'll bury me" (46). Just as the poet reclaimed the Louisiana Native Guards and restored their abandoned place to historical record and to Mississippi, so too, in the concluding stanza, the poet restores her own physical self to the contemporary record and stakes her claim to Mississippi on the very contradictions of her legal existence.

chapter two

Poverty & Porches

CONTROVERSIAL MISSISSIPPI

I. RURAL LANDSCAPES OF COMMUNAL WANT

Citation thus appears to be the ultimate weapon of making people believe. Because it plays on what the other is assumed to believe, it is the means by which the "real" is instituted. To cite the other on their behalf is hence to make credible the simulacra produced in a particular place.
—MICHEL DE CERTEAU, *The Practice of Everyday Life* (1984)

"If South is a perspective as well as a direction, then the Mississippi Delta may well be the most southern place on earth," Endesha Ida Mae Holland writes in the prologue to *From the Mississippi Delta: A Memoir* (1997).[1] Her return to Greenwood, Mississippi, for a celebration of her achievement in arts and letters after her devastating early years in the Delta's harsh racial climate forms a link to the conception of black reclaiming of a southern regional identity and to the process of coming to terms with the impact and legacy of segregation.

Holland, much like Natasha Trethewey and the black writers crafting work in the 1970s and 1980s, represents in imaginative output the social configurations of segregated life in the South and understands from her lived experiences the hierarchies of power inherent in physical spaces. Her conception of the South as "a perspective" and "a direction" argues for a mapping of Mississippi and the Delta specifically as the quintessential southern place. Her citing of "South" and "southern" aligns Mississippi with Trethewey's representation of Mississippi as emblematic of the racial-spatial complexities troubling her location of a black southern subject position. Holland, like Trethewey after her and Anne Moody before her in *Coming of Age in Mississippi* (1968), responds to the strictures of black life in segregated Mississippi in autobiographical writings. Just as blacks in the new historical fiction of the 1970s and 1980s reclaimed the South as a space for reconstituting a modern identity in a time of change and transition, and just as Trethewey grappled with Mississippi as a home but not a home in a postmodern understanding of a decentered subjectivity, so Holland and a coterie of writers from the civil rights and post–civil rights eras return to the experiential landscape of Mississippi for the ground of their artistic production. Rather than allowing their often desperate conditions to isolate and exclude them from the possibilities of living fully as human beings, they function from within a black defined space to create and to spread their narratives as testimony to their existence. Their Mississippi black space constitutes what I call a "bluescape" because of its actualizing in visual imagery the private and public landscape of pain and pleasure associated with the blues music that originated in the Mississippi Delta.

Remembering the arrival of voter registration workers, Student Nonviolent Coordinating Committee (SNCC) volunteers, and others attempting to transform a stagnant and backwards South and its inhabitants, Holland tells a painfully honest story of her own personal movement from making do and accepting less into political consciousness and activity. Raped as a child by a white man who presumed the act was his right, Holland rebelled against the social norms that accepted conventions of racial violation in her community, but not initially as a political activist. She turned to prostitution. The SNCC workers recognized her potential, and through their efforts she recognized her own ability to change and foster change. Holland faced enormous resistance from both a fearful black community and an angry white one in Greenwood, her town in the Delta, but the most devastating act was the firebombing of her family home and her mother's agonizing death from the fire. Holland's narrative is a bluescape in which the segregated world produced a remarkable opportunity for her personal redemption and social formation as activist-writer.

For Holland and for generations of black southerners, the social conditions—poverty and its multiple manifestations—define not only their public sphere but also their personal, subjective constructions of space that functioned as a counterbalance to the official social narrative of black life. Memory becomes testimony and a way of asserting a place on a contested social ground. Their South is an inhibiting space linked to a landscape of desire and want during the era of segregation. Yet, as Michel de Certeau maintains, "What the map cuts up, the story cuts across."[2] In Holland's generation and those that immediately precede and follow, there is probably no escaping Mississippi as emblematic of the recalcitrant, repressive, and racist South during the period between 1954 and 1970. However, these same generations of black southerners deprived of the rights and privileges of citizenship and impoverished in ways barely imaginable have within their imaginative work exposed the social configurations of segregated life and even opposed the hierarchies of power inherent in physical spaces in the modern South. They have used a defined spatial Mississippi to fuel their writing and as a basis for maintaining a connection not only with their own creativity but with a network of other writers who share a similar impetus for their creativity. No matter their actual place of residency, they reside in a creative communal relationship to Mississippi, and to a Mississippi configured primarily as a twentieth-century entity, because, as Trethewey notices in her poetic efforts to find, document, and assert the history of African Americans in the nineteenth century and the early twentieth century, so much of that history has been obscured, erased, and distorted that the effort results in frustration and ultimately in fiction concocted out of slender threads, faded photographs, and disembodied memories.

The narratives of this diffused "community" cut across the mapped space and enunciate their Mississippi as a "practiced place" with inscriptions on the body.[3] What is often left unexplored is the way in which the material landscape and the physical conditions it engendered leave marks on both the body and the psyche of black people that then translate into new articulations that are not merely "memories" or the residue of memory. The body itself carries with and within it unhealed wounds, those inflicted on the mental subsurfaces, and scars, the outward signs of surface healing. However, the body itself becomes an articulation that surpasses and supercedes what wounds or scars may signify. What the story cuts across is an unanticipated black space of articulation rather than a narrative of trauma.

Years later, in recollecting that place, Holland states: "'South.' It doesn't come easy on my tongue like I thought it would. Fingers trace lines of red and black on a map. 'Here, right here,' you say. But it's neither here nor there. If only I could make you understand that geography can never map my heart."[4] It is not so difficult to understand after reading Holland's story that "South" is a complex nexus of interior and exterior spaces of the heart and head, of experiences and people taking shape because of, and not despite, a landscape. For her and others of her generation, Mississippi's literal "geography," whether social or political, is ultimately not the way to map the space she occupies.

Holland's story counters the aims of segregation in Mississippi. It dramatizes both the grinding poverty of ordinary black people and the deprivations in health, education, and well-being that the Mississippi poor suffered under a segregationist regime. However, it is in its details that Holland's story takes on a larger signification; that is, the contest for public space and visibility by black Mississippians. One of Holland's plays is entitled *The Autobiography of a Parader without a Permit* (1984). It alludes to the "crime" of public visibility by blacks, who were to be the unseen laborers occupying the backstreets, entering the back doors, living across the tracks. This aspect of life under segregation leads to demands from a white social order for silence and subservience and to expectation of obedience and compliance in every aspect of public conduct, including the smallest movements or the slightest of gestures. An equally rigid marking of spatial boundaries formalizes the hierarchical mapping of relations and interactions, and with it the exclusionary drawing of lines of demarcation for "white only" spaces. The outdoors and all public places then become "place" that is the most problematic for interactions between blacks and whites, because by its very nature the out-of-doors and the in-public cannot be so completely policed and controlled so as to prevent all infractions or to render black bodies invisible. The expectation of obsequious behavior and servile countenance fed false assumptions about human beings and their sense of self-worth. Routinely, whites inflated their sense of their own power and immunity to standards of decency and morality and deflated any estimate of black humanity, though ironically often fully expecting black workers to care for their bodies in the most intimate of ways—wet nursing babies, bathing the elderly, cooking for families. Control by public intimidation accompanied control of economic resources already scarce in the nation's poorest state.

The spatial architecture of the South has been marked by two interlocked configurations: the porch and the fields. Both are part of the built environment, though the porch bears the more obvious connection to a human-made environment. Fields, however, while a participant in the natural world of the outdoors, are constructed, tilled, planted, and cultivated as work-specific sites of production. Like the porch, the field functions dually as inhibiting or enabling. While laborers might well communicate via work songs in the fields, they have little time for socializing. The porch, the public extension of the private domestic space, signifies the right of ownership and occupancy and access to public visibility. The porch is as well a transitional space. It is neither inside nor outside; it is a social sphere with access to nature but not of nature. It allows for social relationships between and among people and is a stage or platform for their performances of interaction and exchanges.

Porches and what has come to be termed "porch talk" both designate a place in which the space itself fosters and promotes a cultural activity, one which for some observers of the South is a defining phenomenon.[5] Zora Neale

Hurston and Ernest Gaines provide primary examples of the social function of the porch and its relationship to communal storytelling and to gender and age hierarchies. Using Florida and Alabama as her models for representation in her short stories and novels, Hurston marked the porch as contested space, whether for bragging rights in "lying" or storytelling or for participation in the exchanges. In *Their Eyes Were Watching God* (1937), Janie Crawford battles gender conventions to participate in verbal exchanges with the men congregated on the porch. She comes into an empowering self-consciousness of equality when she trades words with the men on the porch and "bests" her husband when he intervenes. Whether in terms of an all-black town in which men dominated the porch as an extension of their public sphere so that gender equality was the main issue of contestation, or in terms of visible black-white segregated spaces so that racial occupancy was the point contested, the porch functions in Hurston's work to underscore the in-placedness of the ideology and politics of segregation.

Gaines uses the porch in his Louisiana settings to evoke a harmonious space for the coming together of residents on the plantation where he grew up under segregation: "I came from a place where people sat around and chewed sugarcane and roasted sweet potatoes and peanuts in the ashes and sat on ditch banks and told tales and sat on porches and went into the swamps and went into the fields—that's what I came from."[6] The porch was an integral part of a social existence that was, he recalls, "limited to the quarters as our living place. Just about everything we did was limited to the quarters."[7] The porch, however, was expansive as a public sphere, a place for communal gathering, interaction, and talking: "Sometimes they would sew on quilts and mattresses while they talked; other times they would shell peas and beans while they talked. Sometimes they would just sit smoking pipes, chewing pompee, or drinking coffee while they talked."[8] His accounts all evoke the communal sharing and exchanging of the adults; children were not excluded from the space, despite being relegated to observing and listening—in other words, to becoming apprentices to the practices and customs of porch talk.

One of the aspects of social control of black sharecroppers in Mississippi was the lack of porch space on their shacks. The absence of the porch meant a limited possibility for congregating, and the lack of a social space for gathering undermined the possibility of uniting for sharing grievances and thereby of building an aware, alert political community. Isolated out of sight or in workplaces under surveillance, black Mississippians had fewer opportunities to congregate and organize outside of religious services and juke joints, the two extremes for escaping the everyday repressions.

In *Back of the Big House* (1993), Jon Michael Vlach made a significant intervention in our knowledge of the southern built environment by attending to the architecture of plantation slavery and to the spaces made by enslaved people.[9] He revised the dominant image of the architectural spaces of the South as Tara, the plantation house in Margaret Mitchell's *Gone with the Wind* (1936), and nothing else. Increasingly, the role of African Americans not merely as agrarian laborers but also as master builders who designed and produced numerous familiar icons of southern architecture, from the iron work of the New Orleans French Quarter to the ubiquitous southern porch, has been incorporated into the written record of southern cultural achievement. Labeled a creolized space with origins in several cultures, particularly African diaspora culture, the porch also is part of the discourses of memory articulated as vernacular architecture. Vlach's archive of photographs, however, makes clear that porch space was not typically a part of the dwellings of Mississippi blacks—neither during enslavement nor during tenancy.

In 1995 Mick Gidley looked over the cultural and literary work being produced in U.S. contexts and rightly concluded: "'Landscape' has moved of late to the centre(s) of various symbolic structures—that is, a term signifying not simply external terrain but the interplay *between* human perceptions, ideological structures and the external terrain—it provides a sophisticated means of probing a variety of phenomena."[10] Gidley's understanding of landscape as a complex reference for the space of interaction in which ideas, perceptions, and terrain meet corresponds to Mississippi as Holland explains it: a raced space of blatant inequities and injustice.

White Mississippians perceived a different Mississippi. Bordered by Tennessee, Alabama, Louisiana, and Arkansas, with the Mississippi River coursing down its western side and the Gulf of Mexico lying at its southern tip, their Mississippi is a beautiful landscape with a once-prosperous economy. From the 1830s through the 1850s, cotton flourished and with it plantation society, as Mississippi became a leading producer of cotton at a time when the Gulf states grew 75 percent of all cotton grown in the United States. In 1860, the eve of the Civil War, Mississippi was the fifth-wealthiest state in America, a wealth largely based on the $218 million estimated value of its slave population, which at that time comprised 55.2 percent of the state's population. In 1865, at the end of the Civil War, Mississippi's fortune was completely reversed. It ranked last among all the states in wealth, and it has remained in that position to the present day. Because its prosperity had depended upon slave labor for the production of cotton in a one-crop economy, the emancipation of slaves sounded the death knell for Mississippi's prosperity. The end of enslavement and the great fluctuations in the cotton market proved devastating not only in economic terms, but also in social and political terms. The state has continued to be mired in poverty and has remained the most rural and undeveloped of all southern states. During the Depression, the state treasury went bankrupt in 1932, when the per capita annual income in Mississippi was $126. Whites blamed Mississippi's reversal of fortune on the loss of slave labor and the defeat of their sovereignty during the Civil War, but forgotten is the glaring fact that in 1817, the year it became a state, Mississippi was an isolated frontier, what the media might today present as the "Wild West," and two-thirds of the land belonged to Native Americans—the Choctaws, Chickasaws, Algonquins, Natchez, Pascagoulas, and Yazoos, to name the most dominant tribes—who were effectively displaced from their lands by "treaties" and worse.

Greenwood, much like other towns in the state, had remained the same for generations of black Mississippians; and contrary to national expectations but in keeping with Mississippi's poverty, progress in the twentieth century was all but invisible. Emancipation from slavery did not change dramatically the everyday living conditions of farm workers sharecropping in the Delta, who in fact continued in a new type of economic bondage for their supposedly free labor, and it did not change their perception of the landscape they inhabited. But the civil rights movement did.

The Greenwood that witnessed Holland's maturation as a rights activist was also the site of the Mississippi headquarters of SNCC, which had in the early 1960s almost two dozen ongoing projects in the state of Mississippi. Barbara Ransby, in *Ella Baker and the Black Freedom Movement: A Radical Democratic Vision* (2003), describes the Greenwood project as being the one best reflecting Ella Baker's own conception of organizing. Ransby locates SNCC's Sam Block in the midst of what was a Delta town of "lucrative cotton plantations . . . thriving while white vigilantes carried out ruthless repression."[11] Block, a native of Cleveland, Mississippi, built relationships with local residents, "trying to identify local militants, and earning people's trust through his dogged perseverance, thus following Baker's edict that activists meet people where they are. . . . He not only talked to people about SNCC, voting rights, segregation; he also listened to the locals talk about their fears, concerns, and aspirations."[12] From small meetings with participants merely singing freedom songs, the gatherings progressed to discussions of politics. From there it was a short step to increased political activity, voter registration drives, recruitment efforts, and mass meetings.

Block's patient strategy paid off in producing leaders out of Greenwood's

Day Laborers Picking Cotton, Near Clarksdale, Miss. Families of sharecroppers picked cotton in Mississippi but barely maintained subsistence. (Marion Post Wolcott, photographer, 1939; Farm Security Administration/Office of War Information Color Photographs, Library of Congress Prints and Photographs Division, Washington, D.C.)

own black population—Laura McGhee and June Johnson—but also in convincing the ordinary black working-class individuals, such as Endesha Ida Mae Holland, to join in political action. With their commitment, Greenwood became "a vital center of movement activity throughout the 1960s."[13] Eventually, the grassroots activity in Greenwood and neighboring Sunflower County's Ruleville, with its phenomenal rights worker Fannie Lou Hamer, led to heightened awareness of the human cost of segregationist structures and the necessity of struggle for change throughout the Mississippi Delta as well as the rest of the state. These in turn led to the production of artwork attempting to articulate the two driving aspects of rights activity: the literal place and the material body. Thus the body of Hamer with the sounds emanating from it becomes iconic in representing Mississippi as the epitomized place of black deprivation and black resistance. "More than any other individual," John Dittmer concludes in *Local People: The Struggle for Civil Rights in Mississippi* (1994), "Mrs. Hamer had come to symbolize the black struggle in Mississippi."[14] Holland in her plays and autobiographical writing reconstitutes

POVERTY & PORCHES

her own body and her home place within the context of Fannie Lou Hamer as the known, the transformed, and the powerful black woman emerging out of rural and small-town segregated life in the Mississippi Delta.

In 1991 the Off-Broadway production of Holland's *From the Mississippi Delta* opened at the Circle in the Square Downtown. The play had a long history before claiming a major spotlight in New York City with financial backing from Oprah Winfrey. In the 1980s, while a student at the University of Minnesota, Holland began writing plays about her life as a victim of child rape by a white man who saw his act as an economic exchange because he paid her for "helping out" in his house, and about her later turning to prostitution as rebellion against the bleak, impoverished environment in which she lived. Holland received her undergraduate degree in African American Studies in 1979. By the time she was awarded a master's in American Studies, she had written not only her autobiographical thesis, *The Autobiography of a Parader without a Permit*, but also at least six plays: *Second Doctor Lady, Requiem for a Snake*, and *The Reconstruction of Dossie Ree Hemphill* (all circa 1980); and *Miss Ida B. Wells, Fanny Lou*, and *Prairie Woman* (all circa 1984). Primarily written within a brief temporal frame, Holland's plays took their impetus from her early life in Mississippi. The spatial and temporal template allowed her to rethink her life before the advent of the civil rights movement in her small town and to reconstruct the story of her transformation. Occupying a central place within Holland's work was her mother, a midwife, who was killed in the firebombing of her house, presumably by the Ku Klux Klan in retaliation for her daughter's participation in movement activities. *Second Doctor Lady*, the play based on her life, won the 1981 Lorraine Hansberry Award for best play and was staged by the Negro Ensemble Company. When Holland earned a Ph.D. in American Studies from Minnesota in 1986, she had revised *Second Doctor Lady* into *From the Mississippi Delta*.

Holland's writing recognized that social acts take place within a material landscape that has a social past. It locates the action almost consistently within Greenwood and its Mississippi environs and within the still-accessible history of segregated life in Mississippi. The specific catalysis for Holland's drive was the death of her mother. Death connects the desire to live more fully, without oppression, with the need to transform place. The space of the coffin and the memory of the entombed dead conjoin to stimulate a movement out of the mental and physical containment of abject black life under the segregationist regime in Mississippi for Holland, but also eventually for a nation of black citizens who had begun to forge a new claim to the protections the Constitution assures its citizenry. Following the public display of Emmett

Till's beaten and disfigured body nearly a decade before Holland joined the struggle in Greenwood, blacks across the nation began to focus on Mississippi as the epitome of their lack of protections and rights.

Emmett Till's "lynching" in 1955 functioned to rivet the attention of modern African Americans to one reality of repression and power exercised over black bodies not merely in Mississippi but across a nation legally maintaining segregation. Importantly, the public attention to Till's death catapulted African Americans into black creative self-expression and artistic subjectivity. The response both in the South and the North to Till's murder introduced into the public sphere a wider consciousness of the social organization and resources existing within a segregated and marginalized racial group, and that consciousness in turn resulted in texts attending to how people produce social practices sustaining them within the boundaries erected for racial segregation.

Although Holland's mother was not technically a victim of lynching, the calculated burning of her inside her own house adheres to the vicious intimidation of and retaliation against blacks associated with lynching. One unfortunate historical fact is that lynching and its related violence formed one of the aspects of the human geography of Mississippi. Between 1883 and 1959, 538 blacks were lynched in Mississippi, according to the Tuskegee Institute reports on lynching in the United States. The unabated recurrence of lynching in Mississippi during the first half of the twentieth century helps to explain why the state has remained the poster child for violence against blacks. Mississippi, though obviously not the only site of lynching presented in the popular 2000 exhibition of lynching ephemera collected by James Allen, stands as the sign already both filled with meaning and waiting to receive meaning. This historical space that Mississippi occupied in stories of lynching looms large and is not mythical. The atrocities depicted in Allen's book *Without Sanctuary: Lynching Photography in America* (2000), which displayed over 100 photographs from actual lynchings, were all too familiar to black Mississippians.[15] Since the end of the 1990s and through the first decade of the new century, a number of books on lynching in America have appeared, including an anthology of readings, *Witnessing Lynching: American Writers Respond* (2003), edited by Anne P. Rice, and a major critical study, *A Spectacular Secret: Lynching in American Life and Literature* (2006), by Jacqueline Goldsby. At the same time, with the new century has come new indictments of Klansmen and white Mississippians accused of murdering civil rights workers in the 1960s. And importantly, too, there is the continued significance of the Emmett Till murder case to creative writers and to African Americans who will not allow the Chicago youth's death to go unmemorialized.[16]

The contest for public space for black Mississippians in particular and black Americans in general came into national consciousness with the murder of Till in 1955. His "lynching" occurred during a pivotal moment in the long century of struggle for black civil rights and in modern African American awareness of the extent of the brutalization of blacks and black bodies under the repressive segregation of Mississippi. Just as the 1850s had witnessed a wave of repression in law and custom in a Mississippi attempting to stave off the abolition of slavery, so too the 1950s ushered in a period of extremist actions against blacks in Mississippi to waylay legal challenges to segregation. If the period leading up to the Civil War encompassed some of the harshest repressive measures and strategies against enslaved people at the very moment when the institution could no longer survive in a democratic and free society, then the period following the Second World War proved to be comparable in terms of the brutality of the social practices exerted to counter the increasingly successful challenges to racial segregation. When the Supreme Court handed down *Brown v. Board of Education* on 17 May 1954, the response in Mississippi to what was dubbed "Black Monday" was immediate and decisive: the founding of the White Citizens Council on 11 July 1954 to fight integration.[17] Initiated by the leading white citizens of towns across the state, the Citizens Councils functioned in conjunction with the Ku Klux Klan to leverage the response of ordinary working-class whites and poor whites to the *Brown* decision: an explosive anger against uppity blacks who would try to get out of their place. A year after *Brown*, Emmett Till supposedly got out of his "place" and suffered the consequences at the hands of two Mississippians from the poor white class. On the basis of an alleged violation of a social restriction against "bothering" a white woman, the fourteen-year-old Till met a horrifying death at the hands of two white men after an almost unimaginable night of being beaten, tortured, shot in the head, tied with barbed wire, weighted by a cotton gin fan, and drowned.

Till's mother, Mamie Till Bradley, refused to accept a private burial with a closed coffin for the battered body of her son. A Chicago resident, she cooperated with the black news media—the nationally circulated newspaper the *Chicago Defender*; the Johnson Company magazine publications *Jet* and *Ebony*; and the official organ of the National Association for the Advancement of Colored People (NAACP), *The Crisis* magazine—in order to "make the whole world see" the marks of white racist brutality upon the body of her son.[18] The image of Till's body in the coffin moved the talk and work of civil rights to a new level. The space of the coffin magnified the dehumanization of all black bodies under segregation. As the horror of the relations embodied in the space of the coffin spread through civic, political, social, religious, and personal arenas, the ever-present threat of violence and death in the everyday living of black men, women, and children came fully into a public consciousness, and with clarity and outrage at the ordinariness of the events that led to the body in the coffin.

During the summer of 1955, the Chicago-reared youth Emmett Till was visiting his mother's relatives in Mississippi when he was kidnapped and murdered—beaten, shot, and dumped naked and alive into the Tallahatchie River with a seventy-four-pound fan tied to his torso with barbed wire. His alleged offense was either whistling at or making an inappropriate remark to a white woman tending a store. The boys who were with him on 24 August 1955 in the Money, Mississippi, store where the incident occurred knew immediately that there would be a violent retribution, but Till did not anticipate that his playful behavior could have such dire consequences. When recovered on 31 August, his body was almost impossible to identify as that of the fourteen-year-old Chicago youth, so badly was it beaten and disfigured. Mamie Till Bradley remembered years later the state of Emmett's body: "[T]he right eye was lying on his cheek. His tongue had been choked out by the weight of the fan, parts of both ears were missing. The back of the head was practically separated from the face area. The mouth was wide open. You could only see two of the three remaining teeth."[19] Bradley's grief turned on the extent of the abuse her son had suffered. Outraged, she would not let Emmett's lynching go unnoticed. Not only did she resist having him buried in Mississippi and in a closed coffin, but she also agreed to have photographs taken of the boy's disfigured body in an open casket.[20]

The nationwide dissemination of the photograph of Emmett Till in death made it impossible to ignore the violence done to a black body by whites claiming racial superiority and thus immunity for their actions. It was a turning point in the use of media to reformulate public opinion. The Chicago funeral for Emmett Till with approximately 10,000 people attending and viewing the body over a four-day period made national news. What the public display of Till's battered corpse and the public spectacle of black mourners signified was not merely the right to an open casket for a black body but the right to open public space for black people. Citing the death of Emmett Till and referencing the image of his brutalized body became the new language to signify the treatment of black people under segregation and the place Mississippi held as the most vicious site of that treatment. From the end of the nineteenth century, with the Supreme Court's ruling on public accommodations in *Plessy v. Ferguson*, separate and *unequal* had effectively become the law driving blacks out of any visible space in trains, hotels, schools, churches, restaurants, and even cemeteries; but with the publicity surrounding Till's murder, a new public visibility for black bodies themselves as public spaces emerged. Converting the abused black body into a public memorial and monument, nevertheless, would prove to be a double-edged sword in the last quarter of the twentieth century.

The trial of Roy Bryant, the husband of the alleged victim in the Till case, and his half brother, J. W. Milam, however, proved that it was indeed possible to acquit the perpetrators of the Till lynching and to deny even that the body was that of Emmett Till. The men were acquitted after only sixty-seven minutes of jury deliberation. Once freed, the two openly acknowledged their guilt and proclaimed defenses of their actions in the pages of the nationally circulated *Look* magazine. Milam insisted: "'I'm no bully; I never hurt a nigger in my life. I like niggers—in their place—I know how to work 'em.'" But he said that Emmett Till was "hopeless," unafraid, "never hollered," and kept saying that he was as good as they were, that he had white women, and that his grandmother was a white woman. Milam stated that he "stood there in that shed [where they had taken Till to beat him] and listened to that nigger throw that poison at me, and I just made up my mind." Milam repeated his exact words to Emmett Till: "'Chicago boy,' I said, 'I'm tired of 'em sending your kind down here to stir up trouble. Goddamn you, I'm going to make an example of you—just so everybody can know how me and my folks stand.'"[21] Milam spoke freely about his intentions to the journalist William Bradford Huie, who had paid the men to tell their story: "I just decided it was time to put a few people on notice. As long as I live and can do anything about it, niggers are gonna stay in their place. Niggers ain't gonna vote where I live. If they did, they'd control the government. They ain't gonna go to school with my kids. And when a nigger gets close to mentioning sex with a white woman, he's tired o' livin'. I'm likely to kill him."[22]

Milam and Bryant celebrated not merely what they had done to Till but what they were capable of doing to all uppity blacks who forgot their place. The raw language and uncensored ideology evidenced in Milam's confession may have been shocking to some whites, but for many white Mississippians it was the public admission of guilt that was surprising and not the words or the ideas.[23] The articulation of motive depended upon citation, the referencing of beliefs sanctioned by the white population of Mississippi; voting rights, integrated school, and interracial sex, specifically black men with white women, were at the shared core of a hegemonic view of "keeping blacks in their place." Milam's rationale was, thus, the familiar, acceptable reality produced out of the assumption that white power produces an uncontested reality. The confession of guilt in public without masks or veils, however, broke with an implied decorum in managing, dominating, and subjugating blacks; that decorum meant keeping the potential of violence and devastation as an anonymous and amorphous form unattached to specific white bodies but assumed to be resident in all whites, particularly white men.

Emboldened by the 1954 *Brown v. Board of Education* decision and angered by the verdict in the Till case, blacks in Mississippi and across the nation began a renewed and determined struggle against the existing classification of people and division of space. For the next decade, roughly from 1955 through 1964 and 1965, when two Civil Rights Acts passed the U.S. Congress, blacks fought against the racist ideology and its legal mandates. The Till lynching became a catalyst for making the black abused body visible, for negating anonymity for black victims of race crimes, for claiming public dissemination of visual representations of racist brutality, and for moving a local "incident" into a national shame. By 1961, with the memory of Emmett Till's battered body still fresh, Bob Moses of SNCC would without hesitation label the rabid racism in Mississippi the "heart of the iceberg" affecting all America. The involvement of youth, black and white, fueled the next phase of activism, especially the challenging of voter restrictions. Their determination to fight the brutalities of segregation in Mississippi and throughout the South that the Till lynching spawned would continue into the mid-1960s with activist civil rights workers from the newer SNCC, the Congress of Racial Equality (CORE), and from the stalwart NAACP. Endesha Ida Mae Holland, Anne Moody, and other young blacks born and reared in Mississippi joined in this phase of struggle and later conjoined in turning to it as inspiration for their creative writing. Elizabeth Alexander has assessed the prominence of Till another way: "For black writers of a certain age and, perhaps, of a certain region, a certain proximity to southern roots, Emmett Till's story is the touchstone, a rite of passage that indoctrinated these young people into understanding the vulnerability of their own black bodies coming of age and in the way in which their fate was interchangeable with that of Till."[24]

Published during the height of the civil rights movement in Mississippi, Moody's *Coming of Age in Mississippi* is a valuable illustration of how ordinary Mississippians came to understand the significance of their lives in a larger public, civic context and how they turned their life experiences on the battleground of discrimination into creative self-expression. Moody's memoir is one of the most reproduced and quoted documents from the era, in part because the author, who was born poor, black, and female in 1940 to sharecroppers near Centerville, Mississippi, incorporates some of the most momentous events occurring in that volatile period: the murder of Emmett Till, the killing of Medgar Evers, the Woolworth lunch-counter sit-ins, the voter registration drives of CORE, the organization work of SNCC and the NAACP, and the March on Washington. Unlike Holland, who in order to come to life writing required many years of separation from Mississippi and her active phases of civil rights work, Moody constructs the narrative of her radicalization and involvement while the movement is still active in the 1960s, though after she has already begun to be disillusioned with its direction and progress. Although she readily admits that she did not see herself initially as a writer but rather as "an activist" in the movement, Moody developed such a clear and compelling narrative that *Coming of Age in Mississippi* now epitomizes the political awaking, idealism, and activism of southern black youths from the 1950s through the 1960s. It is with Till's murder that she recognizes the sad true face of the "Evil Spirit" behind rumors of violent deaths: "Up until his death, I had heard of Negroes found floating in a river or dead somewhere with their bodies riddled with bullets. But I didn't know the mystery behind these killings then."[25]

In Moody's account of coming to self-consciousness with learning of the murder of Till, two domestic spaces, one black and one white but both kitchens, represent her frustrated quest for knowledge of her racial condition. One of the two, the kitchen of her white employer, sets the stage for her fearful understanding that she could be killed simply for being black. The other, her mother's kitchen, establishes that trying to acquire knowledge about the conditions of blacks in Mississippi also ignites fear of repercussions from whites. For Moody, the kitchen, whether in her white employer's house or in her own mother's house, represents the vulnerability of not knowing. It is the space that dramatizes her subordination to two sets of authority figures, a white employer and a black mother, both of whom display anger that magnifies her sense of ignorance, her determination to know and thereby to move into full consciousness of herself and the segregated world she occupies.

Working as a maid for a Mrs. Burke, whom she calls "one of the meanest white women in town," Moody has her innocence-shattering experience in her employer's kitchen after hearing from her male classmates that a fourteen-year-old boy had been killed in Greenwood. Denied an explanation by her mother, she instead receives the warning: "'You go on to work before you is late. And don't let on like you know anything about that boy being killed before Miss Burke them. Just do your work like you don't know nothing.... That boy's a lot better off in heaven than he is here'" (105). Mrs. Burke, however, wastes no time unraveling the mystery and instilling fear: "'Essie, did you hear about that fourteen-year-old boy who was killed in Green-wood? . . . He was killed because he got out of his place with a white woman. A boy from Mississippi would have known better than that. This boy was from Chicago. Negroes up North have no respect for people. They think they can get away with anything.'" Mrs. Burke asks: "'How old are you, Essie?'" When she responds, "'Fourteen, I will be fifteen soon though,'" she gives Mrs. Burke her opening: "'See, that boy was just fourteen too. It's a shame he had to die so soon.' She was red in the face, she looked as if she was on fire" (107). Essie continues to reflect on the incident: "I went home shaking like a leaf on a tree. For the first time out of all her trying, Mrs. Burke had made me feel like rotten garbage. Many times she had tried to instill fear within me and subdue me and had given up. But when she talked about Emmett Till there was some-thing in her voice that sent chills and fear all over me" (107).

Moody's words recounting this moment have reverberated through al-most every account of Mississippi during the civil rights era: "Before Emmett Till's murder, I had known the fear of hunger, hell, and the Devil. But now there was a new fear known to me—the fear of being killed just because I was black. This was the worst of my fears. I knew once I got food, the fear of starving to death would leave. I also was told that if I were a good girl, I wouldn't have to fear the Devil or hell. But I didn't know what one had to do or not do as a Negro not to be killed. Probably just being a Negro period was enough, I thought" (107). Moody does discover the information that she needs to know regarding the NAACP and the civil rights activities countering the horrors of black deaths in Mississippi from her homeroom teacher, Mrs. Rice, who cannot answer the questions within the school for fear of losing her job but does so over the dinner table in her home, which provides the needed sustenance Moody sought from knowledge: "I spent about five hours with her. Within that time, I digested a good meal and accumulated a whole new pool of knowledge about Negroes being butchered and slaughtered by whites in the South. After Mrs. Rice had told me all this, I felt like the lowest animal on earth. At least when other animals (hogs, cows, etc.) were killed by man, they were used for food. But when man was butchered or killed by man, in the case of Negroes by whites, they were left lying on a road or found floating in a river or something" (109). Despite precautions, the retaliation against Mrs. Rice did happen, as Moody reveals in concluding this poignant chapter: "At the end of that year she was fired. I never found out why. I have never seen her since then" (109). The complexity of racial positions and interactions in Mississippi and the abrupt interjections of violence as retaliation for blacks entering into knowledge come through in Moody and other writers who lived through and remembered this period.

Alice Walker, for example, drew on her experience of living in Mississippi to produce one of her stories incorporating black participation in the Vietnam war as a way to demonstrate the continued racial oppression and retaliation possible in a closed society determined to maintain the ethics of Jim Crow. Her brief sketch, "Petunias" in *You Can't Keep a Good Woman Down* (1981), envisions a son returning from Vietnam with the ingredients to make bombs: "'Let's make a big noise in Tranquil, Mississippi, he said.'"[26] Indeed, the noise made was that of the explosion of his mother's house. But the noise with which Walker fills the last of the sketch is emotional outrage: "We have always lived in Tranquil. My daddy's grandmama was a slave on the Tearslee Plantation. They dug up her grave when I started agitating in the Movement. One morning I found her dust dumped over the verbena bed, a splintery leg bone had fell among my petunias."[27] Similar to the firebombing of Endesha Ida Mae Holland's mother's house to retaliate against the daughter for her movement work, the disturbing of the grave of the long-dead foremother serves as a warning to activists that they are known, they and their families are vincible, and no violation of their persons is off limits. Burning down the house and emptying out the grave are two interconnected ways of violating space. The ironic play on "Tranquil, Mississippi," links together several acts that signify anything but tranquility. Destroying the home, the domestic space, of not merely the individual but of the family drives the victims out into even more vulnerable public space and reduces them to homelessness. Uprooting the dead from their graves unearths the bones and dust of the ancestors and exposes those remains to unrest and disrespect and implicates them in instilling fear of both death and rootlessness into the living.

Richard Wright in an earlier generation aptly described that Mississippi of white racism and black deprivation when he wrote of segregation in "The Man Who Killed a Shadow" as "a world split in two, a white one and a black one, the white one being separated from the black one by a million of psychological miles."[28] The racial separation translated into a psychological distance measured in spatial terms allows for the enormity of segregation in an ordinary worldview. In placing Wright in relation to Mississippi, Margaret Walker focused on the "psychic wound of racism" affecting all those who spent a substantial portion of their lives in the state. Although not a native of the state, she included herself, as she was a resident of Jackson, Mississippi, from the 1940s until her death. Walker wrote of Wright's suffering "all of his life from that psychic wound of racism": "I used to wonder when I read his first books from whence came all the violence and the horror. Years of study and research taught me. They came out of his deep-seated anger, neurotic anger and realistic anger against the system of segregation and the violent white racism he experienced here in Mississippi."[29] Not only does Margaret Walker come to understand Wright's anger in response to the damage done by segregation and racism, but she also writes about her own efforts to live within those debilitating conditions, as is the case in "Jackson, Mississippi," from her collection of poems *This Is My Century* (1989):

> City of tense and stricken faces
> City of closed doors and ketchup-splattered floors,
> City of barbed wire stockades,
> And ranting voices of demagogues,
> City of squealers and profane voices,
> Hauling my people in garbage trucks,
> Fenced in by new white police billies,
> Fist cuffs and red-necked brothers of Hate Legions
> Straining their leashed and fiercely hungry dogs;
>
> . . . .
>
> City of stooges and flunkeys, pimps and prostitutes,
> Barflies and railroad-station freaks;
> City with southern sun beating down raw fire
> On heads of blaring jukes,
> And light-drenched streets puddled with the promise
> Of a brand-new tomorrow
> I give you my heart, Southern City[.][30]

The polarities of being a part of the South as a black person in the South of racist segregation are readily apparent and perhaps too easily reconciled by someone of Walker's sensibilities, but for the most part, it has been exceedingly difficult for black writers to reconcile the history and heritage with the positive aesthetic and creative energies that Walker locates as part of a black southern subjectivity.

The long era of segregation that Richard Wright experienced in the early decades of the twentieth century and that Margaret Walker referenced predominates in the literature produced by black Mississippians in the last half of the twentieth century. It is the Mississippi in psychological if not material terms experienced by African American writers who rose to prominence in the twentieth century. It is what the writers knew and understood whether or not they resided in Mississippi. Their lived experience shaped by the color line with its oppressive social system and by the color hierarchy with its attendant rigid codes of conduct informed their creative writing and diffused through black space. Though one would think that with the public outcry over the murder of Emmett Till, much would have changed and changed rapidly in the last half of the century, so much has remained the same, at least from the perspective of creative writers who find their inspiration not in a changed and transformed society but in the memory of the treatment of blacks in Mississippi and within their own bodily identification as black in the systemic racism of the larger nation-state. Wright, Margaret Walker, John A. Williams, Etheridge Knight, Endesha Ida Mae Holland, and Sterling Plumpp, in successive generations, are all impacted by the experiential reality of segregation and its crushing control of black Mississippians. While Anthony Walton, Natasha Trethewey, Olympia Vernon, and a contemporary generation of writers with Mississippi connections by birth or lineage occupy a different temporal and locational space in the twenty-first century, they too write with traces of Wright's divided black and white worlds. Walton, writing in the late 1990s, is blunt in his assessment: "There is something different about Mississippi, something almost unspeakably primal and vicious; something savage unleashed there that has yet to come to rest. Of the forty martyrs whose name are inscribed in the national Civil Rights Memorial in Montgomery, Alabama, nineteen were killed in Mississippi. How is it that half who died did so in one state?"[31]

Sterling Plumpp ventures possible answers in his volume of poems *Blues: The Story Always Untold* (1989). His "Mississippi Griot" links his social history and autobiography to the mythic bluesman persona, "Mississippi griot, Mississippi son":

> He
> bent strings and my grandfather's
> fields were flooded and I
> stood out
> on a
> red
> clay hill/looking at
> the pain.
> I used to feel. The blues
> he played built the levee

as the river with
in him ran down
through my eyes and my pen
trembled like Lucille does
when B. B.'s tender fingers
stroke her hair in tongues.
The
delta rolled out
beneath his shadow
and he sang shacks
along the perimeters of debts.[32]

Plumpp calls up the poverty and the danger of Mississippi, past and present in the singing of "shacks / along the perimeters of debts":

He
takes Emmett Till's decomposing body
from the river in
side him. Lifts it
with the fork of his cries
to a corner
in my skull. And I
scream terrors of multitudes.
Every bone
from nameless black victims interred in the
river
recite their identities
in pulses breathing. (13–14)

The body of Emmett Till, for Plumpp and other black writers such as Yusef Komunyakaa in "History Lesson" (*Magic City*), is the holy relic that helped to enrage and engender rights activism, and it is that body that metamorphoses into all of the Mississippi victims of racism. But the river is also place; the grave is resting and hiding place. Mutilated and lynched bodies secreted in the river come out to the accompaniment of screams that resonate in the music of the blues. What Plumpp does from the outset of *Blues* and "Mississippi Griot" is to write the history of the creation of the blues in the Mississippi Delta and how within that intertwined space, the music and the land, lives the bodies of actual people.

Mississippi's blues music is almost inseparable from southern black culture in that both take shape from the structures inherent within and the discourses emanating from the segregationist practices of Jim Crow. Those practices as Plumpp outlines in the mythic blues narrative persist over time, though their manifestations change over time. Out of these divided spaces, the cultural limitations of segregation that include conscription and containment, blues emerged as a configuration of pain associated with survival not unlike the spirituals from an earlier period. For Plumpp, the icons of blues, Robert Johnson and Bessie Smith, are emblematic of the place ordinary blacks occupy in Mississippi. Johnson, who supposedly made a deal with the devil in order to produce his music, is the most famous and mythical of the legendary Delta musicians. He is the figure prominent in the discourse of the crossroads constructed by Houston A. Baker Jr. to indicate that black identity functions intersectionally. Plumpp, in "Robert Johnson" (129–30), writes in that persona:

Feasts
on worries my grand
father prayed nightly.
Crunches
on the penitentiary of my for
got
ten miles of / feelings /
and I
wake
up mumbling at the cross
roads / my head
hung
down and I. Crying
poison / whips
hissed-screamed
in my past.

Crossroads imagery combines with lineage and penitentiary to emphasize the "windows/painted / with blood in my soul" and the constant movement the brutality of Mississippi required:

. . . I
Crawl a thousand
steps
for his voice.

Hell
hounds on my trail
Hell
hounds on my trail. (130)

At the same time, these very icons configure the efforts to seize public space
in an exercise of creativity and imagination. Plumpp writes in "Bessie Smith"
(36):

She
calls the hurt to an open
wound in
side her and it siphons
their pain into epics . . .
. . . She
calls
diasporic exile
to tenements in bosoms of her words.

The work of the blues is as well a claim on visibility and prominence for
black bodies, often men as representative of the race. In the late twentieth
century and early twenty-first century, similar claims can also be seen in the
southern rappers having their say on the "dirty South," which Riché Richardson examines in "Gangstas and Playas in the Dirty South." In that concluding
chapter of her study *Black Masculinity and the U.S. South: From Uncle Tom
to Gangsta* (2007), Richardson explains: "In rap, 'Dirty South' attempts to
unsettle the persisting view of black southerners as romantic in the African
American context by underscoring the struggles and stresses of black life in
the contemporary South, a site that has often been imagined as a retreat from
and alternative to the violence and crime in the inner city."[33] The struggle
for economic possibility that Richardson emphasizes in the emergence of
southern rap and hip-hop entrepreneurs, especially from Atlanta and New
Orleans, translates also into the extravagant public display of wealth and material goods, which in turn is linked to obvious expressions of masculinity but
linked as well to the less-often remarked claiming of public space within the
very arenas in which it had been denied to blacks, men and women, under
segregation.

For African American Mississippians of an earlier generation, the discourse
of visibility is not so different. The persona in Etheridge Knight's "Last Words

by 'Slick' (or a self/sung eulogy)" wants to have a funeral and burial worth seeing and remembering:

> Take me out to my pink cadillac
> Prop me up / under the steering wheel,
> Tow me out to a real high hill,
> Dig a hole—twenty feet long and twenty feet wide,
> Place a giant joint of reefer / weed by my side;
> Then leave me *alone*—
> And let me drive to hell in style!³⁴

Visibility for black men from Mississippi, however, often has little of Slick's audacity and takes on instead a more conventional form of pride in family and in relational identity despite the dehumanizing nature of their home place. Etheridge Knight's best-known poem, "The Idea of Ancestry," opens with family portraits:

> Taped to the wall of my cell are 47 pictures: 47 black
> faces: my father, mother, grandmothers (1 dead), grand-
> fathers (both dead), brothers, sisters, uncles, aunts,
> cousins (1st & 2nd), nieces, and nephews. They stare
> across the space at me sprawling on my bunk. I know
> their dark eyes, they know mine. I know their style,
> they know mine. I am all of them, they are all of me;
> they are farmers, I am a thief, I am me, they are thee.³⁵

From within the confined and restricted space of his prison cell, Knight speaks expansively of connections spanning generations, of his "father's mother, who is 93 / and keeps the Family Bible" and of how "[e]ach fall the graves of my grandfathers call me, the brown / hills and red gullies of mississippi [*sic*] send out their electric / messages, galvanizing my genes." The hills and gullies of his native state and their colors brown (his skin) and red (his blood) are bodily forces motiving the core of the man. The toll of race violence, however, has forced him far from home and from the lives of his ancestors:

> This yr there is a gray stone wall damming my stream, and when
> the falling leaves stir my genes, I pace my cell or flop on my bunk
> and stare at 47 black faces across the space. I am all of them,
> they are all of me, I am me, they are thee, and I have no children
> to float in the space between.³⁶

The imprisoned and incarcerated black man can speak of ancestors but knows how little progress has been made from them to him, yet the pictorial representation of family anchors a sense of belonging in the world. Prison as home place becomes a part of the Mississippi remembered, and of the visibility of familial remembrance, but also of the futility of his being able to fill "across space" and "the space between."

Knight refuses in the post–civil rights era to find comfort in small victories over the containment imposed by the racial structures in Mississippi. His 1981 poem "Once on a Night in the Delta: A Report from Hell" is dedicated to Sterling Brown, the creator of Slim Greer, who was amazingly resilient under the pressures of Jim Crow:

> The poor live on both / sides / of the tracks
> In this town peopled by Blacks.
> Tho the bloods / now / pack pistols
> And rap on two-way radios,
> And the homes of a few are spacious and new,
> With sunken patios;
> Tho the dice are / shot / thru a leather horn and
> The whiskey burns my belly in the early morning
>
> We still shuffle in lines, like coffles of slaves:
> Stamps for food—the welfare rolls and the voting polls.
> We frown. Our eyes dark caves
>
> Of mourning.—So I'd like to repeat to you, Sir Brown—
> Fromaway / down / here—
> Mississippi is *still* hell, Sir Brown—
> For me and ol' Slim Greer.[37]

Knight's Mississippi, with its new spacious homes, still has residents with "eyes dark caves of mourning." It remains not just an echo of "Slim in Hell" and Brown's encapsulating myth and ethnopoetics, but as well the experiential space Nina Simone sang about in her signature protest piece from the 1960s, "Mississippi Goddam." The changing same that Knight observes in "Once on a Night in the Delta: A Report from Hell" is the result of some interventions in the economic and political systems in the South, but the power structure exerting control, exacting the "shuffle in lines, like coffles of slaves," remains in place in perhaps even more frightening ways than in the 1960s, the period of overt racist violence in Mississippi.

The incarceral landscape that Knight draws in poetry out of his own material condition and experiential understanding of Mississippi is evocative too of the symbolic imprisoning world Ernest Gaines delineates in his Louisiana fiction. From different locations across genres and across state lines, these two writers acknowledge the spaces of danger within the very social structures in which black men function. The incarceral space gives a structure to the formation of memories and to the creative process. In "A Poem for Myself (Or Blues for a Mississippi Black Boy)" (*Belly Song and Other Poems*), for instance, Knight links his life to the blues form and to Richard Wright's autobiographical text as a way of making himself visible:

> I was born in Mississippi;
> I walked barefooted thru the mud.
> Born black in Mississippi,
> Walked barefooted thru the mud
> But, when I reached the age of twelve
> I left that place for good.
> My daddy chopped cotton
> And he drank his liquor straight.
> Said my daddy chopped cotton
> And he drank his liquor straight,
> When I left that Sunday morning
> He was leaning on the barnyard gate.
> I left my momma standing
> With the sun shining in her eyes
>
> . . . .
>
> And I headed North
> As straight as the Wild Goose Flies.[38]

Knight's blues persona traverses the big cities of the North but discovers after all:

> I'm still the same old black boy with the same old blues.
> Going back to Mississippi
> This time for good
> Going back to Mississippi
> This time to stay for good—
> Gonna be free in Mississippi
> Or dead in the Mississippi mud. (50)

The ideal may be return and the claiming of place and home, but the reality is most likely that he will be dead rather than free in Mississippi, as the last poem in Knight's *Belly Song*, "The Bones of My Father," suggests in its conclusion (56).

> Our steps have been shaped by the cages
> that kept us. We glide sideways
> like crabs across the sand.
> We perch on green lilies, we search
> beneath white rocks. . . .
> THERE ARE NO DRY BONES HERE
>
> The skull of my father
> grins at the Mississippi moon
> from the bottom
> of the Tallahatchie.

The reference points are all there, with the Tallahatchie signifying once again the death of Emmett Till and the place where his body was recovered. In a sense, the work of remembering and making black people, especially men, visible in these creative texts is what Cornel West remarks: "The search of black space (home), black place (roots), black face (name) is a flight from the visceral effects of white supremacy."[39] The result, perhaps ironically, is a creative bluescape that reverberates in the production of black artists over time.

In *Seems Like Murder Here: Southern Violence and the Blues Tradition* (2002), Adam Gussow examines the blues tradition in relation to lynching. He posits that because lynching is a visual and existential challenge to black life, blues subjects confront their own bodies in varying modes of identification with and against the lynched body. The struggle, according to Gussow, is either to embrace or to possess the abjection figured in lynching: "If lynching inflicts soul murder on those potentially subject to it by destroying an exemplary black body, then embrace undoes soul murder by reclaiming that body with a resolute tenderness it extends toward other cherished bodies. *Possession*, by contrast, is a kind of failed rationality; the subject's helpless collapse into, rather than an embrace of, the abject."[40] In essence, the blues subject gives in to the nightmare of past lynching victims and anticipates the violence that will inevitably become reality. These then become the dominant modes of literary representation of lynching and a recurrent touchstone in representations of Mississippi's repressive racial strategies during the civil rights movement.

The events of Mississippi's past racial struggles are not yet resolved, in part because of the enduring bank of images of lynching among blacks and in part because of civic and legal indifference to pursuing perpetrators of racial violence. Periodically throughout the 1990s and into the first decade of the twenty-first century, trials occurred for those who were accused of perpetrating crimes against blacks during the days of civil rights activism. Most recently, the Emmett Till Unresolved Civil Rights Crime Act, a 2007 bill sponsored in the House of Representatives (HR 923) by John G. Lewis, Democrat from Georgia, was passed into law on 7 October 2008. The legislation enables the pursuit of cases now decades old and supports an annual fund of $11.5 million to investigate civil rights crimes and also a fund for a Community Relations Service within the Department of Justice to help local communities solve civil rights crimes. Under the Emmett Till Unresolved Civil Rights Crime Act, the Department of Justice will be required to report annually to Congress on the progress in solving crimes committed during the civil rights era. Testifying before Congress, Myrlie Evers Williams, widow of Medgar Evers, and Rita Schwerner Bender, widow of Michael Schwerner, made clear the necessity of prosecution, even belated or delayed prosecution, of those who perpetrated the violence during the 1960s and 1970s. They were recalling two of the many vicious occurrences in Mississippi that have, like the lynching of Emmett Till, not been forgotten.

In Mississippi, the rise of civil rights activism had been met with forceful resistance from the renewed Klan organization, the White Knights of the Mississippi Ku Klux Klan, who instigated the assassination of Medgar Evers on 12 June 1963 for his decade-long struggle against Jim Crow in Mississippi; during Freedom Summer (1964), the Klan perpetrated the murders of three voter-rights volunteers: Andrew Goodman and Michael Schwerner, white youths from New York, and James Cheney, a black native of Meridian, Mississippi, on 21 June 1964.[41] The bloody year between the death of Evers and the deaths of Goodman, Schwerner, and Cheney witnessed volunteers from across the nation arriving in Mississippi to effect social justice by changing the status of blacks in Mississippi, only 6.7 percent of whom were registered to vote.[42]

The lingering effects of the Till murder and the farcical trial of his killers as backdrop for exploring the attitudes of white Mississippians toward race is the subject of Paul Hendrickson's *Sons of Mississippi: A Story of Race and Its Legacy* (2003). Hendrickson begins with a 1962 *Life* magazine photograph of seven white Mississippi sheriffs gleefully posing with a billy club in preparation for preventing James Meredith from entering the campus of the University of Mississippi. The explicit racism of the photograph reveals a familiar Mississippi story, but Hendrickson goes beyond identifying each of the seven men and their location within the prevailing racial climate and views of the 1960s. In a work of investigative journalism, he tracks their descendants, their sons and grandsons, in order to ascertain whether they continued in the ideology of their fathers and how they understood their Mississippi heritage. The result is at once a sad commentary on the persistence of racism and a hopeful revelation of the possibility of transformation. In his epilogue, Hendrickson meditates on the racism connecting the treatment of Meredith back to the killing of Till and on the memory of both hauntingly intertwined into the present. "Perhaps it's remarkable only to an outsider, one who'll never be a Southerner, that the ghosts of Emmett Till seem everywhere in Mississippi," he observes before concluding: "On judgment day, all the slain bodies from all the fevered and silted Mississippi waters will rise as one."[43] Hendrickson is one of the few to delve so deeply into the personal and familial legacies of Emmett Till and James Meredith for white Mississippians.

In *"Stony the Road" to Change: Black Mississippians and the Culture of Social Relations* (2005), Marilyn M. Thomas-Houston undertook an ethnographical study in Oxford, Mississippi, Lafayette County, to understand why by the late twentieth century, the civil rights movement had not made a significant impact on the everyday lives of blacks in residence there. She observed that the place in which James Meredith integrated with the support of 20,000 federal troops—the University of Mississippi—appeared to be unchanged by the dynamic work of the movement. In Oxford, the home of the University of Mississippi, she observed: "The antebellum and postbellum homes that graced tree-lined streets symbolized more than a former way of life; they appeared to be symbols of the present conditions of servitude that did not reflect the changes brought about by the movement."[44] Thomas-Houston reports that some residents of Oxford and Lafayette County call it "the place the Civil Rights Movement left behind."[45] One of her major conclusions is that "despite its centrality to radical civil rights activity widely publicized in the national and international press, closer inspection reveals a virtual lack of participation by local residents."[46]

For many, however, Oxford remains the home of William Faulkner, whose presence looms large over the town and the university, and the era of civil rights activism is not how Faulkner is situated within public memory. In fact, his fiction from the 1920s through the 1940s may be the most place identified of all creative writing by Mississippians. Plumpp dedicates "Official" to William Faulkner and situates the poem in the triangulated spaces: Oxford of Faulkner's lived experience; Oxford's fictional clone—Faulkner's Jefferson; and Oxford's University of Mississippi campus. The reminder in the poem is that while Faulkner was honored with a postage stamp, no "living witness" will receive an honor because

> The pen
> would
> get too up
> pity. Claim blood
> stains.
> As signs.
> Wanna
> circulate among truths
> nailed down. (*Blues: The Story Always Untold*, 135)

Plumpp shows that while a faithful Dilsey lives still in Faulkner's fiction to signify the existence of black folks, in Oxford and on the grounds of the university, blacks

> rake leaves and
> pick up paper a
> cross hallowed lyceums.
> Where Meredith
> wrote a chapter
> with his spirit[.] (136)

The reference to the black man who integrated the campus but paid for it with a toll on his very interiority allows for an acknowledgment of the civil rights struggles that have perhaps not been fully resolved. Blacks still dutifully tend the grounds but remain outside the lecture halls of the university. Plumpp concludes "Official": "There / are no sanctuaries / here / for / memory" (136). Public racial memory collides with the formulation of public memory of both Faulkner and the university.

Rather than reading a historical continuity with the past and with a sameness in the hierarchies of race and class power in the exterior buildings and streets of Oxford, Natasha Trethewey turns to one of Faulkner's characters from *Light in August* to help mark her relationship to the state. In the poem "Miscegenation," she identifies Joe Christmas, who "was born in winter, like Jesus, given his name / for the day he was left at the orphanage, his race unknown in Mississippi."[47] For her own birth and naming, she repeats what she knows: "My father was reading *War and Peace* when he gave me my name. / I was born near Easter, 1966, in Mississippi." Knowing separates her from Faulkner and his Joe Christmas but it also links her to both author and character: "I know more than Joe Christmas did. Natasha is a Russian name—/though I'm not; it means *Christmas child*, even in Mississippi." To be a "*Christmas child*" in Mississippi is to be like Joe Christmas, an ambiguously raced person in a state expecting racial certainty. For the poet, as for the mother married to a white man and awaiting the birth of her child and worrying over the names the child might be called—"mongrel," or worse— "Mississippi is a dark backdrop bearing down/on the windows of her room" ("My Mother Dreams Another Country," *Native Guard*, 37).

In his journey through Mississippi, Anthony Walton spends a few uneasy days in Oxford, observing the continued separation of whites and blacks:

> Contemporary Mississippians refuse . . . to "recognize" each other, to acknowledge their commonality. The state's tragic history is testimony to what this refusal has wrought. And it is now likely that members of the two racial groups are permanent strangers, doomed to gape and stare but not see, blind to each other as siblings, humans, Americans.
>
> "The past," Faulkner said, "isn't dead. It isn't even past yet." He understood, in a way that seems profoundly foreign to Americans, that a person is infinitely more than what happens to him or her, the specific events and places of one lifetime. Men and women are also the product, or prisoner, of all the things that happened and were thought generation upon generation before their births. Freeing oneself from this psychic and cultural web can take superhuman effort; few manage to do so.[48]

Walton, like many contemporary observers, worries over trying to fathom the meaning of Mississippi and the disjuncture observed in the lives of those who remain trapped by that history and heritage, which for many is not Faulkner's *Absalom, Absalom!* to which Walton refers but instead a cultural media loop repeatedly playing scenes from Margaret Mitchell's *Gone with the Wind* interspersed with a few from Harper Lee's *To Kill a Mockingbird*, neither of which locates its drama in Mississippi. No matter the literal sites, for some Mississippians, these visual, moving-picture images determine the static narratives they hold of race and their state.

For most black Mississippians, there is no antidote to modern dislocation and fragmentation. In "The Place of the Past in the American Landscape," David Lowenthal remarks that for Americans in the decades after nationhood, "To renounce the past meant especially to reject parental influence. The generation gap was a cherished freedom. . . . The democratic urge, observed Tocqueville, makes men forget their ancestors and lets them 'imagine that their whole destiny is in their own hands.'"[49] What black Mississippians know, even without the historical record of nationhood, is that while they may be able to retain their imaginations, they by no means have their destinies in their own hands. Too many, like the bluesmen of Robert Johnson's generation and the poets of Etheridge Knight's, have found themselves set adrift from the too-complicated home and roots in Mississippi.

In the Mira Nair film *Mississippi Masala* (1992), homelessness and rootlessness coincide in unexpected places within a near-present. The film represents the enduring but ever-changing interconnection between spaces and oppression, and it envisions the expanding racial diversification of the Deep South. The racial and ethnic makeup of late twentieth-century Mississippi stands out dramatically in contrast to the past. Set in Greenwood, Mississippi, the same Delta town that was home to Endesha Ida Mae Holland, the film represents a more progressive place than the repressive dangerous environment of the first half of the twentieth century. The time period is 1990, and Demetrius ("D-Money") recognizes that changes have occurred as he tells Mina: "This is a new Mississippi. I like it here." Denzel Washington as Demetrius, an African American with a carpet-cleaning business in his native Greenwood, and Sarita Choudbury as Mina, an East Indian displaced from her birthplace not in India but in Uganda, provide the interaction between two different cultures and histories now coexisting but not intermingling in the state of Mississippi.[50] Mina calls herself a "mixed Masala," in reference to her being Indian but never having experienced India. In response, Demetrius says, "You just like us. We from Africa but we never been there either."

John Young, writing in *Video Magazine*, calls the film a "tart look at clashing cultures" with "'Stick to your own kind' [as] the implicitly racist philosophy on both sides."[51] While in the film there are no vestiges of the atrocities chronicled in "Mississippi Goddam," Nina Simone's hard-hitting sixties protest song, there is the paternalistic racism represented by Demetrius's obtaining a bank loan for his business only through the auspices of the white owners of the restaurant where his father still works as a waiter, and the immediate drying up of his clientele once his romance across race lines becomes public knowledge.[52] Young's notion of the "clashing of cultures" is evident in more than the cultures of the African Americans and the South Asians. There is also the intracultural clash of the structures of power both within the traditional Greenwood community and within the émigré South Asian community. The old white economic hierarchy clashes with the new entrepreneurial black working class but under a veneer of civility, and the East Indians use their color, money, and status beliefs against one of their own nonconforming families.

What is realistic about Mina and Demetrius's cross-cultural coming together is the element of their separate loneliness and need. Both are working-
class and do manual labor with few opportunities for release outside of family
gatherings. Whereas Demetrius's family sees him as a success in business but
failed in romance (his former girlfriend has left him for a career as a singer),
Mina's extended family, the South Asians who own businesses and property,
view her as an extension of her failed father, a lawyer who no longer practices law but clerks at the Monte Cristo Motel where the family lives. Demetrius is defined by the boundaries of race etiquette within the community,
while Mina is defined by the space of the motel in which she lives and works.
Classed and raced differently and yet the same, the two share a personal location. Mina's cleaning of motel rooms and Demetrius's cleaning of carpets
emphasize the labor of their bodies in specific sites, the body itself as trapped
within localized regimens of work that are socially constructed and inescapable for individuals of the lower classes.

The scene in which Demetrius and Mina escape from their ordinary,
everyday lives and head for the Gulf Coast provides a fresh vision of the diversity, geographical and cultural, that always has been Mississippi. The different space, with its carnival-like atmosphere of rides and games and fun
and anonymity, is juxtaposed to the drudgelike, fishbowl hypervisibility of
their workaday lives. Yet, intruding upon the simple, idealistic interlude is the
voice of one South Asian, who cannot conceive of cross-racial cultural interaction despite being displaced from India and living in a new diaspora. The
brief escape from a constrictive place foreshadows the conclusion in which
Demetrius and Mina leave Mississippi together to make a life for themselves
elsewhere, possibly in California, where one of the characters has already
gone. While there is no fairy-tale ending, the strategy of having Demetrius
and Mina set off together defies the old racial taboos so staunchly in place in
Mississippi and much of the South.

The backstory of Mina's parents and their forced departure from Uganda
under Idi Amin provides the broad global thematic of place and race that ultimately prevails. The film opens in Kampala, Uganda, on 7 November 1972,
with Mina's father, Jaymani ("Jay"), arrested and deported. As he puts it:
"After thirty-four years it all came down to the color of my skin." Expelled
from Uganda because of their race as East Indians, Mina's parents leave their
home and possessions behind, but Jay also leaves behind his homeplace,
homeland, and his African friend, who tells him that "Africa is for Africans,
Black Africans," that he is not African even though he has spent his life in
Africa. The bitter separation from the place that he loves and from the friend

whom he saw as a brother renders Jay moody and unstable, obsessed with suing the Ugandan government for the restoration of his property, which has become symbolic of his life, his happiness, and his contentment. His forced exile resonates with the fates of numerous black Mississippians who over much of the twentieth century found themselves having to flee the state. This is an analogy that the filmmaker barely acknowledges. Jay pursues his suit and letter writing over the course of five years—from 1985, when the Ugandan government changes, to 1990, the film's present.

Reduced in Mississippi to living in a motel, where his daughter cleans rooms, Jay is no longer practicing law or functioning as the breadwinner in the family. His wife, Kinnu, runs a liquor store to support the family. The close-knit Indian community, some of whom are wealthy or well-off, see Jay as a failure and Mina as undesirable, both because of the family's lost status and because of Mina's dark skin. The issue of skin as an aspect of identity within the émigré community echoes the color of skin as a designation of place within the white-black southern community. The old binary no longer holds, but in its place is a related permutation. *Mississippi Masala* is a reminder of how strongly and discernibly the geographical imagination works on the individual. It is the pull of home, the repelling of the foreign, the dream of utopia, but it is also the certainty of change, seasonal or cyclical, that complicates and destabilizes any conception of home, the familiar, the utopic. In the new immigrants and their global movement of capital and of bodies, and their interaction with commerce and the old resident populations, Mississippi witnesses the new postcolonial and its diasporic people.

A fascinating aspect of Mira Nair's film is the detailing of South Asians who have not only laid claim to the motel business in Mississippi but also reinvented their cultural practices in the American South. Nair establishes the motel—intricately connected to the highway, the icon of American mobility and travel throughout much of the twentieth century—as owned and operated in the American South by a quintessential outsider to the culture and to the place, not the familiar "Negro" but instead South Asians. They form a new cartel transforming the space into a triangulated, contested new apparition of the American dream. That this phenomenon should take place in the state most associated with the "Old South" and its singularity of identity is amazing.

Writing about the contemporary South in *This Land, This South: An Environmental History* (1983), Albert E. Cowdrey observes: "The changes in the metaphorical landscapes of culture have been mirrored in the physical landscape, where forms, more than ever before, are shaped by superabounding human power. Cotton fields have changed to pastures or to woods; marshes to soybean fields or rolling Gulf; wild land to neon strips. A generation after World War II, healthier, more prosperous, and more numerous southerners confront common American dilemmas without altogether shifting the burden of a peculiar past."[53] Cowdrey's conception of change is so optimistic as to appear utopic. His "landscape of culture" functions with the space of the material world that would not necessarily be recognized in the still hardscrabble Mississippi. The last two decades of the twentieth century did in fact witness a pronounced seedbed of changes in the literature in, of, and/or about the "multi-South," now so "multi" that Robert Olen Butler's writing on the Vietnamese in Louisiana is no more a curiosity than Ernest Gaines's Cajuns and Creoles or Judith Ortiz Cofer's narratives of Puerto Ricans in Georgia. In the process of these changes, "Southern Literature," for which white Mississippi writers had become midcentury exemplars, has been undergoing transformations. Slowly and perhaps imperceptibly, the tenets defining and codifying fiction, poetry, and drama under the familiar rubric have been loosening and dissipating. Ellen Douglas, writing out of Mississippi, moves her representation of people beyond the visibly white world that mainly preoccupied Eudora Welty in her best-known novels. The breaking down of barriers, symbolically located in the breaking up of the institution of segregation, the Jim Crowism that divided and defined the pre-1960s South, has produced a less walled-off, less isolated region in which people of color from Mexico, Puerto Rico, Latin and South America, Cuba and the Caribbean Islands, India, Vietnam, South and Southeastern Asia, and postcolonial Africa could figure and could, in fact, exist in less problematical circumstances than prior to the felling of the color bars that visibly separated blacks and whites and, by extension, virtually sealed the region from entry by other people of color who would in effect be subject to the same restrictive covenants as black people of African descent.

The once-ignored southern Native Americans, for example, are separating their race and ethnicity away from the old racial binary. Eastern Band Cherokee writer Marilou Awiakta Bonham grew up in Oak Ridge, Tennessee, where scientists conducted nuclear experiments in splitting the atom. Today, she self-identifies as an Indian, as a woman of color, and as a southerner. In her poem "An Indian Walks in Me," Awiakta writes:

> Long before I learned the
> universal turn of atoms, I heard
> the Spirit's song that binds us
> all as one. And no more

will I follow any rule
that splits my soul.
My Cherokee left me no sign
except in hair and cheek
and this firm step of mind
that seeks the whole
in strength and peace.[54]

When Alice Walker included "Motheroot," a poem by Awiakta, as epigraph to *In Search of Our Mothers' Gardens* (1983), she slid across the black-white racial binary characterizing the literature associated with the South; and in that early recognition of Awiakta's work in what we now know as ecofeminism, she in effect located both herself and Awiakta within a larger progressive configuration of southern space. The material body Awiakta makes visible and the symbolic landscape she depicts—where ancient meets recent Appalachia—suggests Cowdrey's recognition that "changes in the metaphorical landscapes of culture have been mirrored in the physical landscape, where forms . . . are shaped by . . . human power."[55] For Awiakta, home is where mountain and atom meet, at the center of what Yi-Fu Tuan calls "an astronomically determined spatial system. . . . Home is the focal point of a cosmic structure."[56] Home, however, may not be where the body itself is centered. And in Awiakta's neighboring Mississippi, as Mira Nair projects in her film, South Asians have filtered into that selfsame Mississippi Delta region that gave birth to the blues and discovered there what Ralph Ellison termed "that same pleasure, that same pain."

At the end of her narrative, Endesha Ida Mae Holland recounts her triumphant return to Greenwood, to the Mississippi Delta:

> The first thing that struck me was how much the landscape had changed. Not the tabletop land or levees or trees or the rippling heat—those would go on forever—but the people. In 1990, Mississippi had over 825 elected black officials—more than any other state in the Union. Machines had replaced the endless lines of sharecroppers and day laborers picking cotton or hoeing weeds; backbreaking labor for subsistence pay had become a thing of the past. Nearing Greenwood, I saw a Wal-Mart store and roadside video rentals along the highway where a generation ago, I had turned tricks among the farmers.[57]

The landscape of change is one in which stories signal economic progress and black elected officials signify political empowerment. For "Cat," the girl that Holland had been in Greenwood, the homecoming is triumphant not merely because she has earned a doctoral degree and become a teacher and a playwright, but especially because the work she had started with SNCC and voter registration in Greenwood, that dangerous work that had culminated in the firebombing of her house and the death of mother, has come to fruition. There is a measured sense of justice. The landscape may still be pockmarked with rural poverty, but some very tangible marks of difference are legible. They are written on the new space Holland constitutes, and constitutes along with a raced "community" of modern Mississippi authors.

II. EXTERNAL STRUCTURES OF RACIAL MEMORY: OLYMPIA VERNON'S VISION

> To cite is . . . to give reality to the simulacrum produced by a power, by making people believe that others believe in it, but without providing any believable object.
> —MICHEL DE CERTEAU, *The Practice of Everyday Life*

Rita Dove begins her poem "Mississippi" with a reference to primordial times and space reconfigured as the New World:

In the beginning was the dark
moan and creak, a sidewheel
moving through. Thicker
then, scent of lilac,
scent of thyme; slight hairs
on a wrist lying down in a sweat.
We were falling down
river, carnal
slippage and shadow melt.
We were standing on the deck
of the New World, before maps:
tepid seizure of a breeze
and the spirit hissing away.[58]

In the southscape created in Dove's poem is a world before maps yet mapped with the bodies of those whose doom into slavery is impending. This is the prestory that persists and cuts across the lines of all maps drawn between Africa and the New World.

This second part of the chapter follows the movement across the lines of the map into the space of Olympia Vernon's postmodern fiction, which at once roots itself in the specificity of Mississippi as a spatial and psychological configuration and shatters the very concept of boundaries that would hold the fiction in place. Unlike Endesha Ida Mae Holland, who despite the pain experienced in Greenwood, Mississippi, returns insistently to that place as the subject matter of her writing, and unlike Richard Wright, who moved as far away as possible from the Mississippi of his youth but could not resist its pervading presence in his writing, Vernon occupies a Mississippi landscape as home—mysterious, volatile, and contested. From this uneasy rootedness in an unstable place, her novels exist in relational diffusion through what I term "fugue space," the unmapped evoking the hyperreal and signifying a heightened state of consciousness in which actions occur at sharp angles from the normal and a polyphonic thematic in which voices narrate contrapuntal stories of bodies struggling, futilely, to recover racial history and social memory. In the intersections, whether of people, events, or ideologies, memory may serve as testimony, but the objective, Vernon suggests, is to cut across while bringing together the specifically local or the regionally identified with its coordinates in the wider world or globally produced space.

Mississippi functions as a crucible of a landscape of racial memory. For black Deep South residents, it is difficult to escape the shadow of pain that Mississippi's bluescape has cast over much of the twentieth century, when the charge was to transform the racial landscape and bring relief finally, and perhaps a small measure of justice too. Modernist creative writers, however, taking their inspiration from the dominant strokes of the visible, tell a complicated story of more failures to bring about change than of successes. Self-described as "a black person, a black male, a colored man, a Negro, and certainly sometimes in Mississippi, a nigger," Anthony Walton begins his journey into Mississippi from the largest geographical perspective:

> If you look on a globe, or a good world map, between North and South America and between the Atlantic and the Pacific, you will see the Gulf of Mexico. Then, locating the city of New Orleans at the northern edge of this body of water, you can trace the ninetieth meridian north toward Memphis. The line you trace, between the thirtieth and thirty-fifth parallels, will roughly bisect the twentieth state in the Union, the poorest by most measures, a jurisdiction of eighty-two counties and 47,716 square miles, home to something over two million citizens.[59]

Walton's intent is to map Mississippi in terms of its geographic coordinates, but these include more than the recognizable points on a globe: "As your finger slides you'll pass place-names like McComb, Poplarville and Natchez,

Philadelphia, Clarksdale and Vicksburg, each name searing a scream in the minds and memories of people like me, black Americans. Mississippi can be considered one of the most prominent scars on the map of this country. When you trace the ninetieth meridian from New Orleans to Memphis you're fingering a scar."[60] Mississippi as a scar on the map, as a place to be traced like a scar on a wounded body, is one of the ways of forcing attention to the exploration Walton makes as he crosses the Mississippi River at Natchez and enters into a place that for him was his "heritage and background" but also a "tangle of contradictions and illusions."[61]

Contradictions and illusions are readily apparent in placing Harnett Kane's description from *Natchez on the Mississippi* (1945) next to Walton's: "In its surging passage below Memphis toward the Gulf of Mexico, the Mississippi . . . comes to a high, sunsplashed hill. . . . To the East, bordering the state of Mississippi, rise two hundred feet of red-brown bluff, crowned by vines of wild grape, magnificent magnolias and the sweep of oak. The river itself seems to change here. As if reluctant to leave, it makes a wide crescent of lake-like tranquility; then it turns again to glide, silver and yellow, into the distance."[62] The description calls up images of a state that Willie Morris later saw as "the most haunting landscape in the United States."[63] Indeed, the Works Progress Administration writers of *Mississippi, A Guide to the Magnolia State* (1938) pictured Natchez as a "pastoral terrain," and Oxford as "cloistered behind . . . cedar, magnolia, and oak trees," "like a sensitive plant" in "a dreamy lethargy," "static and preoccupied"; and they envisioned Jackson "spreading along a high bluff," "an unconsolidated city of breadth and space . . . with more than seven thousand crape myrtle trees."[64]

These guidebook perspectives capture place as essence rather than backdrop to human experience, or as the known space of social relations as Walton does. They function much like the way in which Roland Barthes describes "The Blue Guide," the Hachette World Travel Guides, as a way to direct the eyes of the traveler only to a narrow spectrum of sights and to train the traveler to appreciate certain landscapes, such as mountains and high grounds. The focus on travel as cultural appreciation leads to the mythologizing of selected monuments, parts of the built environment with particular histories that are deemed significant and worthy of study. In the essay that is connected to the larger argument of *Mythologies* (1986), Barthes envisioned landscape as a form of communication, as another aspect of the system of signs that can be used to forward and consolidate ideology. In "The Blue Guide," he suggests that the travel guide is "an agent of blindness" because its function is to obscure some aspects of landscape and to magnify others by concentrat-

POVERTY & PORCHES

ing attention and observation so as to create a sense of cultural continuity or stability, and in the process blinds the traveler to the multifaceted aspects of history and social life. Part of the blindness, however, is also the effort to adhere to the sight lines of a single narrative that disallows fragmentation, irregularities, or eccentricities.

For the creative writer, landscape and place become part of the material culture grounding physical relations and psychological dramas of human beings. Perspective becomes, as Wright states in "Blueprint for Negro Writing" (1937), "that fixed point in intellectual space where a writer stands to view the struggles, hopes, and sufferings of his people. . . . At best, perspective is a preconscious assumption, something which a writer takes for granted, something which he wins through his living."[65] For Wright, as for the contemporary Walton, there is no disassociation of landscape, place, and people, or of their interactions in history and memory, but the associations serve a specific purpose. For example, as hard-hitting and unflinching as Wright is on the brutal impact of segregation on black lives, he delivers in *Black Boy* a virtual catalogue of the sensual pleasures of boyhood in the physical geography of a Mississippi encoded with its own language, and a catalogue intended to demonstrate the aesthetic apotheosis of the boy Richard out of the ordinary space and into the realm of writer:

> Each event spoke with a cryptic tongue. And the moments of living slowly revealed their coded meanings. There was the wonder I felt when I first saw a brace of mountainlike, spotted, black-and-white horses clopping down a dusty road through clouds of powdered clay.
>
> There was the delight I caught in seeing long straight rows of red and green vegetables stretching away in the sun to the bright horizon.
>
> There was the faint, cool kiss of sensuality when dew came on to my cheeks and shins as I ran down the wet green garden paths in the early morning.
>
> There was the vague sense of the infinite as I looked down upon the yellow, dreaming waters of the Mississippi River from the verdant bluffs of Natchez.
>
> There were the echoes of nostalgia I heard in the crying strings of wild geese winging south against a bleak, autumn sky.
>
> There was the tantalizing melancholy in the tingling scent of burning hickory wood.
>
> There was the teasing and impossible desire to imitate the petty pride of sparrows wallowing and flouncing in the red dust of country roads.[66]

The Mississippi landscape becomes a performance space for the enactment of Richard's will and his ideas, of his becoming an artist of words. Sensual delight and apprehension of the infinite together with nostalgia and melancholy mark his positioning of his own body in relation to geographical and natural touchstones that bring life to the landscape.

This catalogue continues for another page in Wright's text. In amassing the catalogue, Wright follows the same pattern of melding with and transforming the exterior and interior world of the observer, whose participation and performance structure both environmental nature and human nature. Some of the items continue the layering of affect and sensation, as for instance in the enormity of the universe often unavailable from the perspective of city streets: "And there was the quiet terror that suffused my senses when vast hazes of gold washed earthward from star-heavy skies on silent nights"; or the not-so-pleasant reality of rural farming life: "There was the speechless astonishment of seeing a hog stabbed through the heart, dipped into boiling water, scraped, split open, gutted, and strung up gaping and bloody."[67] Taken as a whole, Wright's visual, sensual catalogue is an inescapable aspect of maturity in relation to bodily awareness of a spatial location within a specified landscape. In this outside world, there is only the freedom to take stock, to see, to appreciate, and to record with all the senses of the body and all the emotions of the sensate being, the existence of this world as experienced.

Not by mistake or accident is reciprocity impossible. There are no reciprocal acts within this out-of-doors that can validate the existence of the black body. Such catalogues of the visual appear twice in *Black Boy*, yet the main discourse in the autobiography is the cruelty of the Mississippi world; its narrowness on the parts of African Americans and its racism on the parts of the Anglo- and Euro-Americans propel Richard to leave the South if he is to have a chance for living fully and developing into the writer he longs to become. Nevertheless, the cataloguing of the pleasures and the surprises of the landscape occupy two major sections of the text. They constitute homages to the Mississippi land, but they also reveal the writer Richard is capable of becoming. Sensation as a source of knowledge is self-contained and hermeneutic. In holding the land within his senses and constructing it within his imagination, Wright refuses to relinquish it back in time or place to those who would relegate him to the margins and bar him from access to power over meaning. Holding ground imaginatively by means of sensation is a form of exercising power, of seizing power, and of understanding power. It is a way of making the modern out of the very aspects of cultural vision that should, but does not, askew mappings privileging transcendent power.

The exercise of power over the dual and contradictory space that Mississippi is for blacks is the work in which Wright engaged and for which he created a map for his successors to follow. The map that he drew of his father's body figured as the embodiment of the Mississippi landscape is one of his most powerful. Like the scar that Walton fingers on the map when he touches Mississippi, Wright figures his estranged father as the blight produced out of the Mississippi environment. An indigent sharecropper whose own father had been a slave, Wright's father, Nathan, appears fixed on a Mississippi plantation and seen through the lens of a twenty-five-year separation: "[A] sharecropper, clad in ragged overalls, holding a muddy hoe in his gnarled, veined hands . . . his body bent, his eyes glazed with dim recollection. . . . From the white landowners above him there had not been handed to him a chance to learn the meaning of loyalty, of sentiment, or tradition" (*Black Boy*, 42–43). Oppressed by whites, deprived of learning, mired in poverty, and broken in body and spirit, the father stands in for the Mississippi landscape.

The portrait is emblematic of Wright's perception of the South: dehumanized and dehumanizing. It is no celebration of values from the past because Wright dramatizes and exaggerates their absence in a victimized father who abandoned his family. In a few words, he calls up images of the caste system and the poverty of rural blacks, as well as the legacy of slavery and the reality of tenant farming. He emphasizes, too, the missing links in familial relationships and racial heritage, the wedge of humiliation and shame between generations, and he reveals the damaging effects of the physical and psychological environment of racism upon the personality and humanity of blacks. This image of the toll of an oppressive society and the compromises of accommodationist living on the material and psychological body is one that Wright consciously chose to represent ordinary blacks of the South, and chose repeatedly, though in some variations. The social and experiential reality of Mississippi life is paradigmatic in his father's existence, so that exacting justice cannot occur within the context of the land. Neither can the son expect or demand justice from the ignorant, neglectful, and aged father for whom change is no longer possible within the affective frame the son establishes. Justice or its potential can only come from escaping the reality of the father's life and place.

Wright's fictional work, then, may be read as characteristically an attempt to flee that reality, which even when absent from a particular text is understood as causal because spatial constrictions in other environments replicate the father and the Mississippi of his actual and imagined experience. This assumption of fleeing or flight as resolution appears most often as the process of becoming, perhaps Wright's primary modernist theme, which is formed in opposition to the social processes of a South that would restrict potential and deny being. Much like the instinctive knowledge of Robert Johnson and the Mississippi bluesmen in valuing mobility as a freeing space, an antidote to debilitating white domination, Wright's movement in space carries with it the resultant value of freedom within the process itself and the implied possibility of psychological growth and emotional maturity in occupying a different place.

The deep context of the South, then, is more than ephemeral features on a map. "In the history of a place," Anne Whiston Spirn believes, "the deep contexts are constraints that successive human generations must readdress." Spirn explains: "Traditions, values, and policies may change, but deep context remains key to the history and future of a place—why it was settled, its initial location, its transportation routes, its economic development, health and safety of its residents."[68] The constraints that blacks confront in Mississippi have conditioned their responses to cultural geography and influenced their sense of how to effect justice for the deep structure that continues to inform and, somehow against all reason, to inspire.

For Wright, Mississippi is obviously not as idyllic as the writers of the WPA Mississippi guide would have us believe. "The relationship between reality and the artistic image," he contends, "is not always direct and simple. The imaginative conception of an historical period will not be a carbon copy of reality. Image and emotion possess a logic of their own. A vulgarized simplicity constitutes the greatest danger in tracing the reciprocal interplay between the writer and his environment."[69] Wright's words are cautionary here. There is a delicate balance of personal experience, social history, culture, and imagination. And as he pointed out in "How 'Bigger' Was Born," "an imaginative novel represents the merging of two extremes; it is an intensely intimate expression on the part of a consciousness couched in terms of the most objective and commonly known events. . . . [The author's] imagination is a kind of community medium of exchange . . . a kind of self-generating cement which glue[s] facts together, and his emotions [are] a kind of dark and obscure designer of those facts."[70] The South, specifically Mississippi of the writer's formative years, would appear to function as "the self-generating cement" of his imagination. Moreover, it would also seem that the emotional nexus formed out of conditioning and responses to the immediacy of regional complexities would combine with individual predilections and racial affect to shape those ostensible "facts," those images and perspectives with which the creative imagination works.

Wright emphasizes imagination in his formulations (objective and known events) but not memory, though he points to emotion. The Mississippi of his creative reality, rather than being a mimetic guidebook landscape, corresponds in part to "the raw materials of the imagination [that] can be seen as arising not only as responses to social processes," according to Vytautas Kavolis in "Literature and the Dialects of Modernization," "but also as developing in response to the specific economic, political, communal stratification of particular societies."[71] The "economic, political, communal stratification" so glaring in the figurations of black life in Mississippi inevitably make up the points on the map of imagination, or as Wright himself put it in a 1944 letter to Antonio Frasconi, as "the crying claims of a world which it is our lot to see only too poignantly and too briefly." "It is imperative," he wrote to Frasconi, "that we artists seek and find a simpler, a more elementary, a more personal guide to the truth of experience and events than those contained in the mandates of frenzied politicians; and I say that we Shall find it where artists have always found it: In the visions which our eyes create out of the insistent welter of reality, and out of the surging feelings which those visions evoke in our own hearts."[72]

As a twenty-first-century fiction writer, Olympia Vernon *seems* in tune with the conceptual framework Wright articulated because her visions as a creative artist are central to her writing and her spatial ground is dependent upon the South of history, fiction, and memory. An African American Deep South "border culture" author, Vernon was born in Bogalusa, Louisiana, the same small city where the poet Yusef Komunyakaa was born. She grew up in the interconnected space of two southern cultures, Louisiana and Mississippi. Her childhood homes were in Mount Hermon, Louisiana, and Osyka, Mississippi; she graduated from South Pike High School in Magnolia, Mississippi, but her college degree is from Southeastern Louisiana University (1999 B.A. in criminal justice) and her master's is from Louisiana State University (2002 M.F.A. in creative writing). Vernon occupies and even straddles a dual Mississippi-Louisiana landscape, and unlike Wright, she seeks to disrupt the familiar definition of political in representations of black people rooted in a locality that exudes race politics. Vernon's postmodern, however, is not a reduction to a vernacular culture as a replacement for a highly technical community that Dubey observed in reading a crisis of representation in Toni Morrison's 1970s writing on the South.

All three of Vernon's novels, instead, refuse to resort to either a nostalgia for an intact cultural community or a residue of colloquial language. They are set in rural and small-town Mississippi with the cities of Jackson and New Orleans as constitutive, contributing, and accessible places, but they are also set within the space that encompasses the new geography of interconnected and interactive grids of power, economics, and politics. Racial memory grounded in Mississippi or Louisiana is and is not within the realms of intersecting networks of possibility. In *Eden* (2003), *Logic* (2004), and *A Killing in This Town* (2006), Vernon constructs a Mississippi that in thematics might be linked to the modernist writings that emerged in the first half of the twentieth century, but in style, these texts are postmodern. Each narrative refuses to tell an expected story of familiar Mississippi blacks and does not tap into an archive of expected images. At the same time, just as Marilyn Thomas-Houston found a conflicted legacy of civil rights reform and Anthony Walton observed a static assumption of a racial hierarchy in Mississippi, so too does Vernon recognize in her novels that the uneven distribution of resources and opportunity, including education, has resulted in a population of disadvantaged rural and small-town blacks who enter urban life at intervals of need. There is a reservoir of racial memory that is almost unattainable and illegible for contemporary subject formation.

All three of Vernon's texts produce a fugue space that traps hypnotic beauty and harsh circumstances in an almost unbearable struggle for control of the senses. The sensate being overwhelmed that Wright articulated in his catalogues of the rural Mississippi world is antecedent to Vernon's representation of knowledge appropriation by means of sensory experience. What I label "fugue state" in Vernon is in line with Elizabeth Alexander's general statement about African American literature, in which she identifies a dream space as "the great hopeful space of African American creativity."[73] In that black interior space, Alexander believes that black writers will be able to escape hegemonic constructions of what constitutes their "real" and to counter imposed realities that have "limited expectations and definitions of what black is, isn't, and should be."[74]

Vernon's experimental writing suggests the very escape that Alexander imagines possible. At stake is the material body that in each of the novels is intricately connected to the landscape and "natural" world in which it is located. In that space, Vernon explores not the divisions between the living and the dead but the connective tissue, the fiber that is literal and real but also magical and mysterious. Unlike the varieties of the postmodern that Madhu Dubey identifies as a recent southern aesthetic from the examples of fiction of the 1970s and 1980s, Toni Morrison's *Song of Solomon* (1977), and Gloria Naylor's *Mama Day* (1988), Vernon's postmodern establishes a fusion between possible South environments—cities such as Jackson, Mississippi, or New Orleans, Louisiana, and small towns in the formerly rural.[75] Dubey reads the earlier fictions of Morrison and Naylor as using the magical and the mysterious as a means of establishing a black community vital in its folk residual culture. Vernon's work makes no effort to recreate a grounded black folk community through connections to storytelling and orality. Unlike science fiction, speculative fiction, or fantasy writers, Vernon projects an anti-realism in her texts, but she redefines what "real" can mean in new spaces of knowledge. That knowledge is suggestive of Jean-François Lyotard's observation that "postmodern knowledge is not simply a tool of the authorities; it refines our sensitivity to differences and reinforces our ability to tolerate the incommensurable. Its principle is . . . the inventor's paralogy."[76]

Black writers, Melvin Dixon maintains, break down "arbitrary barriers to black settlement in the United States" and in the process reinvent racial identity in their "quests to change the land where they were forced to live into a home they could claim"; Dixon suggests that African American texts show "how images of journeys, conquered space, imagined havens, and places of refuge have produced not only a deliverance from slavery to freedom, but, more important, a transformation from rootlessness to rootedness for both the author and protagonist."[77] Vernon's body of work may be read as claiming the Mississippi landscape, in all of its dualism and contradictions, as roots. From this uneasy rootedness in an unstable place, her novels veer off into not merely "conquered space, imagined havens, and places of refuge" but into largely unhinged and unmapped spaces that are frightening in their evocation of some lurking surreality. I term it a "fugue space" in order to signify both the heightened state of consciousness in which actions occur at sharp angles from the normal and the polyphonic thematic in which voices narrate contrapuntal stories of bodies struggling to recover dream and memory—racial, social, communal, personal.

In an interview, Vernon said that all of her writing comes from "angels": "Only god knows where Eden emerged. I was not in this land, but another one of dying women and floating stars and there emerged Eden."[78] The resultant first-person novel won the 2004 Richard and Hinda Rosenthal Foundation Award from the American Academy of Arts and Letters and was nominated for a Pulitzer Prize. Throughout her commentary on her writing, Vernon mentions that God guides her and that the writing is a gift. She described Logic, the child protagonist of her second novel, as "an innocent child, a lamb born into the world where lambs are called to be slaughtered. Interesting about the lamb; it will go to whoever calls it without question. It will go to its own death without question. I've never heard of an animal with such faith."[79]

Logic is a narrative of secrets, driven by the absence of access to public space. It is not a narrative of isolation in rural spaces and instead depends on the presence of both town and urban spaces. The Harris family is in crisis, as is the neighboring family, a prostitute and her children, whose poverty is hidden by their surroundings. Logic Harris, like Maddy Dangerfield of *Eden*, occupies the strange space in the interior of an adolescent girl. After falling from a tree, Logic is locked inside her own world; it is an instance of a fugue space that Vernon constructs of the heightened awareness of events but limited ability to articulate meaning:

> She was thirteen now, but she had not learned the stability of time, how things were to be put in order. She lived in a place where time did not exist; she dreamed, on many occasions, of death and believed it came in threes. This is the memory that lived within her: three spirits into the Ultimate one, the number of days at a time that she'd stopped eating, the pointed invisible lines of the triangle, the alphabets of YOU—those which she added to herself, her vocabulary with a distinction that required no urgency, as it is passed through her lungs—a slow rising of the tongue, as if a baby had slept there unmoved.[80]

The triangulated place in which Logic lives is both the dream space and its memory that she describes, but it is also the material and relational of her situated life. It is the actual triangular house built by her father. Described as a mathematician of sorts, David Harris uses exactness to hold himself and a reality in place: "He picked up his gun and looked out into the heat: the wooden boards of the house were rotting from the inside. He had built this triangular house with what was left of his hands; he was sort of a mathematician. He had set each board perfectly into the map of the house, except the one that lay unevenly on the rooftop; he had found it on the side of the road. A metal hook had been hammered into it, a chain looped through the center. Steel" (8). The calculating mathematics that David Harris uses for perfecting "the map of the house" is undone by the happenstance of a found object, foreign and ominous, a hook and a chain, intersecting and interrupting the plane, or the "logic" of science as a space for rational action.

The triangular place is also the relationship Logic has with her parents. She is sexually abused by her father, who rapes her on a metal operating table, and ignored by her mother, Too, who is herself ignored by the husband whom she desires but whose sexual identity is so conflicted he cannot bring himself to have sexual relations with his wife. David sees Too as "molecular": "Everything that went into her mouth was broken into tiny pieces—the bones in her face fragile, the empty breasts, as if there was no fat beneath her nipples to push her self-esteem forward. Open your mouth and record the distance between air and lung, and you will notice an invisible line wrapped so tightly around the bones in Too Harris's throat that the transparency of the distance itself will cause you to suffocate" (7). This false sense of clarity of thinking emerges as well in his daughter's descriptions of herself: "Her body was emaciate; she felt she had a pyramid in her bones. The straight, invisible line that connected her nipples, the perfect navel in the center of her stomach, creating the image of a measurement that was equal on all sides—she had inherited the genes of her father the mathematician" (11). The relational triangle of the Harris family is fixed in points but unbalanced in the nature of interaction. With her representation of "science" and the spaces of the body and house all made mechanistic and equational, Vernon accomplishes a postmodern in which knowledge itself hides, obscures, and defies reason.

The narrative line is not linear. It unfolds not only from Logic's perspective and her interiority but also from her father's and her mother's. All three are damaged, though in different ways. In the background are stories of male rape, sexual abuse of male prisoners, and men from Mississippi seeking other men in the free space identified as New Orleans: "There was a time when he had drunk among men, until he had begun to notice how quickly they deteriorated before him: the explosion of one man's liver, another with a set of broken molars from when he had fallen under a streetlight in New Orleans, the tattooing of a name that he had been called his entire life: sissy" (60). These impinge somehow upon David's mechanical grip on reality and on his sense of his own body: "David Harris was loading his pistol when the sun began to burn. He paused for a moment, the light coming toward him. My God, he could have run right now and caught it, his hands and body and full self trapped by it. But he knew, down there where words turn to jelly, that he had nowhere to put it" (7). Sexual behavior constitutes a network of interactions that strain the social and familial fabric. The specter of emasculation haunting David intersects with Too, who has held a pillow over her daughter to suffocate her and who responds "as if she did not exist at all in this unbehaved environment" (12). Left to her own resources, Logic at thirteen tries to deal with the condition she terms "the butterflies" floating inside her. Celesta, the life-sized doll her father had given her after her fall, is her surrogate sufferer; both exist in silence and alternative realities that are barely legible except by means of a system of signs for interpretation. The doll, however, haunts David's nightmares and Too's waking moments: "Too herself had felt the doll was human. Logic would be in one part of the house and Too would be putting her nightgown on her dresser. It was Too who held Celesta in her hands and searched for a beating heart. A pulse. Then she would leave her in the corner never lifting Celesta's dress to search for the ripped clitoris" (85). Neither parent can escape the sight of Celesta's gouged eyes and taped mouth.

A boy, called simply the Tall One or "the tallest" to distinguish him from the other children of a neighborhood prostitute, takes the central character, Logic, on a trip to the "other side." This space turns out to be the public spaces of the town, where they both live but cannot experience openly. In the town, the tallest teaches her the social decorum expected of blacks—drinking from the water fountain marked with a C—and that "there was loneliness in the world" (201). Vernon uses the socially restrictive practices of racial segregation, however, to configure a resultant and equally material set of affective and psychological restrictions put in place to make the spatial world inside the boundaries of black life legible. The secrets the two children harbor—the tallest's attraction to cross-dressing in his mother's clothes and his attempt to help her abort the fetus and Logic's sexual violation by her father—are connected to the kind of secret lives and hidden and obscure placements within which blacks in Valsin County, Mississippi, are expected to exist. The deformation of the social space deforms the possibilities for reading one's own bodily space. The boy thinks of himself as the son of an elephant: "He had long tried to figure out who he was, what he wanted from the Eves of his life. He was an experiment. Everyone was an experiment waiting to sprout on a grand hip of discovery" (17). His gender confusion occurred early: "He could not figure out whether he was more inclined to be a man or the thought of having a woman in his genes: he had to choose" (69). The tallest creates his "circus-of-me" and dresses as he pleases in women's clothing and shoes, and he talks to God when he makes his choice.

Vernon builds the narrative exquisitely on language and insight, their absence and presence. The secrets, however, dominate the people and the places: "Secrets lie dormant in Mississippi. You never know the full truth about anything. There is what your folks choose to tell you and what you discover. One or the other is poisonous, vain" (173). Constructing wire wings from hangers and placing lamb's wool on them, Logic flies in the final sequence from the roof and dies trying to reach heaven with her secrets. She has shot and killed her father with the same pistol that he prizes as a sign of his manhood, and she leaves behind a message for her mother of the location of heaven.

A Killing in This Town, Vernon's 2006 novel, makes a powerful move backwards into the Mississippi that generations of blacks fled in order to live, but it also initiates a fresh narrative of the "localized" workings of labor and capital in the new global economy. Bullock, Mississippi, the setting of the dramatic text, is the kind of small southern town that still carries the imprint of a rigid racial hierarchy, with the local Klan members at the top of the social order and the black townspeople at the bottom. The visceral descriptions of the violence done to bodies in the ritual "calling out" of a black man to be dragged to his death behind a horse when a white boy turns thirteen are chilling. Vernon imagines the horrific way in which an entire society, black and white, can accommodate itself to the utmost form of cruelty and brutality.

The greatest threat to the whole town, its black and white citizenry, is the threat posed by the factory. Here Vernon translates into a local setting the way in which contemporary factory workers in Mississippi, but resembling all those "proletariarized" in ever-expanding global centers of production, find themselves at risk from the very work they are doing and by the environment in which they work. Vernon's "killing" in her title and in the town is literal and dual in its allusion. It is not only a reference to rituals of lynching as horrific and visceral as they are in the text, but it is also an indictment of institutionalized and systemic poisoning of the laborers at the town's plant. The Pauer Plant on one symbolic level embodies the poisonous ritual of hatred infecting the town that can thus allow it to accept the calling out of black men for killing as a rite of passage for white boys. On another symbolic plane, however, the Pauer Plant represents the noxious, automated, and mechanical culture of capital production and consumption that poisons entire labor forces, slowly, either with the seeping residue of its waste material or with the encompassing model of its indifference to human life. The wordplay on "power" and vernacular pronunciation shifts the discourse to a level of the reflexive, the parodic and ironic suffusing the narrative without reducing the tone to humor. Vernon makes the local a spatial platform for a discourse on the global. Her Pauer Plant thus operates "simultaneously" in its spatial configuration of interactions and in correspondence with Doreen Massey's observation that "'space' is created out of vast intricacies, the incredible complexities of the interlocking and the non-interlocking, and the networks of relations at every scale from the global to the local. What makes a particular view of these social relations specifically spatial is their simultaneity."[81]

The more observable aspect of *A Killing in This Town* will, of course, place it in a network of literary relations. Maud Casey, for example, reviewing

A Killing in This Town for the *New York Times,* links it to the "spooky vignettes of Sherwood Anderson's 'Winesburg, Ohio' and the lyric stories about Hancock County, Ga., in Jean Toomer's 'Cane.'"[82] But she also notices that in the background of the ritual killings are echoes of Emmett Till's mutilated body in the descriptions of Curtis Willow's body after being dragged along a road until parts disintegrate and the whole is misfigured. That Vernon may also have had in mind the horrific 1998 dragging death of James Byrd in Jasper, Texas, places both the past and the near present in a network of relations in her fictional narrative of lynching as ritual and rite of passage. It is the scenario, too, that Yusef Komunyakaa interacts with in "History Lesson":

> She told me
> How a white woman in The Terrace
> Said that she shot a man who tried to rape her,
> How their car lights crawled sage fields
> Midnight to daybreak, how a young black boxer
> Was running & punching the air at sunrise,
> How they tarred & feathered him & dragged the corpse
> Behind a Model T through the Mill Quarters,
> How they dumped the prizefighter on his mother's doorstep,
> How two days later three boys
> Found a white man dead under the trestle
> In blackface, the woman's bullet
> In his chest, his head on a clump of sedge.[83]

The subject matter of lynching and dragging a black man for a crime he did not commit seems closest to the familiar modernist and antiracist narratives of southern life, and perhaps not coincidentally *A Killing in This Town* won the 2007 Ernest J. Gaines Award for Literary Excellence. (The prize, given by the Baton Rouge Area Foundation, is $10,000 and a commemorative sculpture by Robert Moreland.)

Vernon's fugue text, however, is other than familiar ground or known outcome. The perspective in the novel shifts among many characters: Earl Thomas, a black pastor who will be the next black victim; his wife, who prepares herself for the inevitable; the widow of Curtis Willow, the last victim; Adam Pickens, who is about to turn thirteen; his father, Hoover Pickens, a Klansman; Salem and Hurry Bullock, men with "the lineage of power" that is "leaked within their blood"[84] in the town bearing their name and the other major Klansmen; Lenora Bullock, the seamstress who makes the Klan robes;

and a clerk who sells the fabric for the robes and who probably killed her husband, a Klansman. These perspectives interact to form a network that is not intended to suggest the "communal" but rather simultaneity, which then translates into a coexistence of power grids and intersections marked by "a horrible stench of laughter" and "the profound slope of malignancy" (18). The narrative doubles back and turns upon itself, repeatedly reviving, retelling, and intersecting parts of Curtis Willow's calling out. The cutting through the power grid iterates the placement of the Pauer Plant at the major points of narrative and symbolic intersection.

Gill Mender, once the thirteen-year-old boy responsible for Curtis Willow's dragging death, returns from a self-imposed entombment in his parents' house. His own guilt for the past and his understanding of the damage done to him as a boy by the act he committed enables him to try to effect change and end the violent ritual of entering into white manhood. Breaking the cycle though standing within ritual, Gill tries to reach Adam before another calling out; yet in the shifting fugue space of the multiple narratives, the ritual lives in the small town and in the diseased lungs of rural Mississippians. Adam's stance in the end is represented as "extraordinary, nude . . . an announcement to the constitution of men who'd deemed him the naked proprietor of a killing in this town" (246). Earl Thomas, who carried the message about the disease infecting the bodies of the workers at the Pauer Plant, has not been forgiven or forgotten for changing the white workers' lives with the padlocking of the plant. He emerges into a new space on a train heading north but bound "collectively to the invisible fabric of servitude" (244). The configuring of social relations is by means of sets of infected bodies, physically and psychically. The sound of infected breathing is both literal, the ravages of disease, and metaphoric, the calling out of black men. Words and breath, in life and in death, converge in a maelstrom that is a representation of a spatial geography mapped in rituals of destruction and transits of catastrophe.

Writing about geography well before the current resurgence of interest in the discipline, Lucien Febvre stated: "Some human geography is perhaps nothing but history revivified at its sources, rejuvenated in its methods, and happily revolutionized in its subject."[85] In 1925, when Febvre made that statement, he could not have imagined the kind of human geography that would emerge in the vision of Olympia Vernon, whose first novel perhaps best represents her perception of a place-based, geographically inspired creativity.

Maddy Dangerfield, the teenaged protagonist of *Eden*, narrates a strange tale of the fugue space between life and death in Pyke County, Mississippi. The narrative begins in mystery:

One Sunday morning, during Bible study, I took a tube of Aunt Pip's fire-engine-red lipstick and drew a naked lady over the first page of Genesis. Her chest was as flat as a man's, her face blank and clear. The language was loose around me, as I remember the sound of Mama's voice and the question that came along with it, the one that counted: "Don't you know that blood and milk is the same?" She shook me between her words. "They can't sit out long before the world get wind o' 'em and the next thing you know they caught in the tubes and the devil come out and you end up titty sick; 'cause he be red, red like this here mess you done made."[86]

There is no explanation of the mother's words, and neither is there a rationale for the drawing. The inexplicable becomes the expected from the opening paragraph and through the symbolism of "Genesis" and in the language infused with the religion of the mother and her parablelike utterances. The overlapping of the biblical page and the woman's body establishes a dual focus on words and interpretation, on scripts for and inscriptions on the body. Making blood and milk equivalent without a map to trace the lines between makes deciphering the relational referents difficult. Much of the text points toward recovering the "memory" that enabled the drawing and that will provide the explanation of it. That recovery is as well the construction of Maddy's subjectivity. Maddy describes herself as "a child of opinion. Every thought created within me, from birth, was like this one bright star, circling the kitchen of my mania, my depression. In this area of consciousness, my house of bereavement, I wondered where Aunt Pip's missing breast was, if it was labeled beside Willie's brain" (140). Consciousness of loss, whether of her Aunt's breast removed in a mastectomy or her schoolmate Willie's missing pieces following head surgery, places her in a hyperstate of relational self-awareness.

Throughout the narrative, Vernon uses language that is difficult to pin down either in its references or inferences. Maddy describes her mother as "made of a glass vase. Her throat was sharp and fragile, her lips clear, smooth. She picked up a porcelain paragraph filled with the words of *Jesus*" (6). The language comes from a place in the imagination of the girl Maddy, who reads the encyclopedia and depends upon it for the workings of things but depends on her mother for reading the body as a language. Her mother has a birthmark on her forehead in the shape of a tornado: "It was a red stirring of her soul. She always pulled it back before the storm to witness its color change in the mirror" (3). The inscriptions on her body, however, are not so easily read, and Maddy's mother herself evidences a need to explore the folds of her fat for meaning and to move furniture in an effort to dislodge the disturbances in her thoughts.

Maddy's parents, Faye and Chevrolet Dangerfield, have a difficult marriage because of the illiterate Chevrolet's alcoholism. Faye's mother had chopped off his arm "with an ax because he smelled like thievery" (5). The now-dead grandmother leaves her smell in the house, and also her way of thinking about people. Maddy remembers: "Grandma always said that an object in a woman's hands was the way she chose to lose a headache. She said this, that women who did not use their words caught a headache of the mind and spirit. If a woman was too weak to use her voice, her vocabulary got trapped in her temples and formed a blood clot. And with this came the disaster of silence" (6). The words may or may not apply to Faye, who works as a maid, cleaning toilets to support her alcoholic, gambler husband, whose lack of an arm becomes symptomatic of his overall inability to support his family, perform dignified work, love his wife, and read more than labels on liquor bottles. Faye's voice is trapped in religion and secrets, as well as in her desperation to hold on to the husband for whom she has given up her dignity.

Maddy knowingly contrasts her weak father with the town's white men, who

> worked just hard enough to call themselves men and went home and laid across their flatironed sheets with their long legs propped up on the bed rail, chatting and kissing the cleanliness from their white wives. A black man didn't have time to be gentle with his woman. He had enough stress already. Staying alive was stressful. Got to work and having to call a white man "mister" was stressful. Waking up with that black skin and that nappy black head that showed no roots, those rough black hands that they couldn't do nothing about, was enough stress to break him, no matter how much man he thought he was. (88)

Chevrolet faces the added stigma of being the brother of a man who was castrated and sent to prison for raping a white woman, so that in addition to his one arm, his gambling, his drinking, and his illiteracy, he is a man stripped of any semblance of pride but struggles to prove his manhood to his wife and daughter. The traditional structures of racial dominance are most in evidence in the exploitation of Chevrolet and Faye as laborers—she as a maid and he as a handyman. Both are forced to perform their menial jobs under the most demeaning of circumstances and the exacting eyes of critical whites. That Faye uses her hard-earned money to pay Chevrolet's gambling debts to a man named Jesus adds to the family's crisis and diminishes her in the eyes of her daughter and the community.

Public shaming haunts the family. The entire community knows that Faye discovered her husband's affair with her sister Pip. This shame is connected to Maddy's drawing, which leaves the religious churchgoers convinced that she was not a normal fourteen-year-old—and not because she drew a naked woman, but because she drew one with no breasts and with a lipstick that belonged to her sinful aunt. Public shaming is linked in unexplained ways back in time to the lynching of Justice Bates and imprisonment of "Uncle Sugar," Paul Ray Dangerfield, for the rape of Laurel Pillar, a white woman with whom Sugar may have been having an affair. The unknown third black man involved in the alleged rape is part of the mystery, as is the quietly threatening rural landscape: "'Mama says that if you cut down all the trees in Mississippi, you'll find Negroes from here to kingdom come,' I said" (74). The response from Landy Collins, the visiting son of a New Orleans casket maker, expands the area where a lynching can happen: "'Not just Mississippi. . . . Anywhere you find a tree, there's a Negro hanging from it. You might not see him, but he's there" (74). The rape, the lynching, and its impact remain in the realm of flashes of insight or blurred visions that neither clarify nor resolve.

After drawing the naked woman, Maddy is sent in disgrace from her house to care for her dying aunt, Pip, a woman who is herself living in disgrace in an isolated house. The familial relations over generations become apparent in the houses as the social structures rivaling the Owsley Sanctified Church, where Maddy commits her sin and where her mother goes to Jesus and is saved, and the pool hall, where her father loses his money to the hustler Jesus. Pip's house on Commitment Road had belonged to Big Mama, Maddy's great-grandmother, and stands in marked opposition to Faye and Chevrolet's house, which was owned by Maddy's grandmother. That closed-off house with its contents inherited from the avenging grandmother bore the mark of blood from the chopping off of Chevrolet's arm and the stain of Chevrolet's betrayal. On Commitment Road, however, "Aunt Pip's house was surrounded by magnolias. The petals were open, wide. The yellow parts had fallen onto the white, and they lay exposed like a woman's vagina at birth. Commitment Road was only a few miles from town, but there was a peace about it. It was safe to cry there. It was silently trapped by the earth" (37). The house on Commitment Road has a correspondence with nature, even when the natural world holds rabid dogs and hanging trees and mourning women. The only neighboring house on Commitment Road belongs to the widow of Justice Bates, the man hanged for rape. Pip counts her as her only friend and calls her by the nickname "Fat." Although Pip is dying of breast cancer, she and Maddy create a communion with the outdoor natural world from the porch, which is their shared space of reflection and remembrance.

On Commitment Road, Maddy functions in a fugue space in which she sees that breast cancer has taken the lives of her grandmother and great-grandmother and that the disease will take Pip as well. She sees her own body reflected in theirs. Her self-recognition and subject formation depend upon locating herself within and identifying with multiple bodies, the women in her social history, including Fat. In longing for knowledge of the body, her own and her women kin, Maddy experiences the special congruence between herself and her aunt. She shaves her head in transforming her body with its breasts not yet formed to mirror that of her dying aunt. In this space, she "remembers" her own birth and the mother's milk that fed her coming from the breast of her aunt and not her mother:

> I was the baby in my dreams—the blood from the tubes of my mother's stomach suffocating me like a green lizard trapped in the space of a mason jar. I was part of the world now. The milk of a whore's breast was in my mouth, and I needed to see, for my own mother's sake, the wrath that God had put upon a mistress. Because she had prayed for the saved breast, not the unsaved one, never knowing that I would soon be old enough to smell the milk of Aunt Pip's breast on a tube of fire-engine-red-lipstick—that which she had lain on a flat bed of porcelain, the words of *Jesus* calling me to it. (252)

The milk of a woman's body becomes the sign for multiple and simultaneous aspects that lead toward the death from breast cancer at the center of life that Maddy witnesses and remembers. Mississippi's race relations, for example, are figured in the image of the black woman as wet nurse for a white child but with embedded aspects of the poison of racial domination and exploitation of women:

> We were approaching the house of Mr. Diamond, the postman. His lips were yet pursed. Big Mama's nipple had once been in his mouth. One winter day, his mother went to beast-feed him and discovered that her milk was frozen. She carried his pale body in her arms, crying. Big Mama stuck her hand beneath her own warm breast and opened his tiny mouth. She fed him so much that he became used to the brown breast, not the white one. Much later, after the milk of his mother's nipple had thawed out, he cried himself into a frenzy when she went to feed him. She put

him back in Big Mama's arms, until the large Negro breast swallowed him. For this act of saving his life, he was grateful. But this was in no way to neglect the fact that the milk in her breasts was spawn from the penis of a white man. She was feeding Mr. Diamond the milk of a rapist. (50)

Maddy recounts the story of her great-grandmother's contact with a white child and her rape by a white man, but also implicitly how these two acts are connected in that white boy now an adult trusted by everyone black "because he was the only white man who touched them," but when Maddy entered his presence, she has a different response: "[H]e gave me a look that stirred the blood in my heart" (51). Without a logical explanation of how she could possibly know, Maddy alone sees Diamond for both a rapist and a murderer, leaving the victimized white woman Laurel and the brutalized black boy Willie unavenged and unappeased. The black man castrated and imprisoned for the rape is not vindicated, and the spirit of the black man lynched for the rape will not rest any easier because of Maddy's knowing. The unresolved becomes a part of the everyday of life in Pyke County.

In a surreal night sequence tracing the ritual preparation of Pip's body for death, Vernon places Maddy and Fat as guardians and helpmeets. Maddy thinks: "I did not know where she was. It was far beyond me. I was still green. Green like the land of Eden where the flesh is confused, where green is so beautiful that nobody noticed it. . . . We ate of a measured place where our lives were limited and unbalanced in human understanding. Not knowing that there was no understanding in human language. Only greenness and death" (261). Together, in the place "unbalanced in human understanding," they wash Pip and carry her into the outdoors, where the women spirits await ("I could not see the faces of the women. I did not know them, only their missing parts. And the cancer that had eaten away at them" [263]). Fat tells the dead woman that they are going to New Orleans, where they were known and welcomed. Fat's tree, where her husband died, falls, and she ignites it and Pip's coffin before jumping into the flames. In the end, Maddy understands still only vaguely what she had foreseen: "There, circling them both, was the bearer of footsteps: the naked lady whom I had drawn on the first page of Genesis, her chest as flat as a man's, her face black and clear, beautiful" (264).

The last words of the novel are "I was lost in the land of Eden" (272). They mirror the place reference in the opening to Genesis and thus stress the spatial terrain of Vernon's text as larger than the state of Mississippi, as mythical and consuming. Between Genesis and Eden lies the coming of age and the coming to a moment of knowledge about the world that is not Eden, is not the unpolluted or innocent. The fugue space that exists half way between waking and sleeping is the world Maddy inhabits. It is a world of pain, cancerous malignancies, surreal perception, erotic and poetic incantations of a different rural South. At the same time, in this magic-laced, religious-drenched world are fire-engine-red lipsticks and a girl's drawing that she cannot explain until, at the death of her aunt, she sees precisely the naked, breastless woman she drew. The coming-of-age is in conjunction with the crossing over. The two move together within the same space and within a bodily connection that links Maddy's birth to both her mother and to her aunt Pip. At the same time, the space that Maddy and Pip share is death, not life. The dual emergence into life and passing into death is extended into the representation of the generations of black women in Maddy's family.

From Maddy's one-armed father to the one-breast aunt and the castrated uncle, the damaged body is the subject explored, exposed, and left as it is with no rational explanation and no narrative to argue for its appropriate place. The effort to attain knowledge of the past and to ameliorate its impact on the lives and deaths in the community is short-circuited. The narrative displaces the conventional male-dominated tropes of lynching, rape, emasculation, and incarceration from the center and, while not dislodging them from a hold on the reality of Mississippi life, subordinates them to images of women in circles of care and of denial regarding the diseases affecting women's bodies, sexually transmitted diseases, cancer (particularly breast cancer), and disability. In the face of these, the familial disloyalties and infidelities, the racial traumas and insults, all recede, and only Maddy's empowered seeing remains encrypting the enigmatic space of both landscape and bodyscape. Vernon's creations invested in a limitless fugue space, then, remember pastness, argue with history, merge that history with fiction, intersect with power, and distribute justice on a plane that Richard Wright would not recognize as the terrain of the black professional writer.

chapter three

Power & Profession

RICHARD WRIGHT'S MISSISSIPPI
& ITS EXPATRIATE LEGACIES

I. CULTURAL GEOGRAPHY AND A BLACK PROFESSIONAL WRITER

*The mind learns to grapple with spatial relations long after the body has mastered them in
performance. But the mind, once on its exploratory path, creates large and complex spatial
schemata that exceed by far what an individual can encompass through direct experience.
With the help of the mind, human spatial ability . . . rises above that of all other species.*

—YI-FU TUAN, *Space and Place* (1977)

In a speech presented on 2 June 1939, Langston Hughes told the Third Annual
Writers' Congress: "It is hard for a Negro to become a professional writer.
Magazine offices, daily newspapers, publishers' offices are tightly closed to
us in America."[1] This assessment by the major black writer in America at the
end of the 1930s came as no surprise to other black writers who, inspired
by the cultural awakening of the New Negro Renaissance in the mid-1920s,
had attempted to support themselves by writing. Arna Bontemps, Zora Neale
Hurston, Jessie Fauset, Countee Cullen, Claude McKay, Hughes himself, and
their compatriots soon had discovered not only that the "vogue" for racial
materials was amazingly brief, but also that the opportunities for black employment in the world of letters were largely absent. The writers understood
that their exclusion was due to racism; for example, in an effort to erase the
difficulty of a black presence in a white office setting, Fauset offered an out for
any publisher interested in hiring her: "[I]f the question of color should come
up I could of course work at home."[2]

Hughes made his observation about the difficulty of becoming a professional writer at a critical juncture in the nation's cultural history, when the
decade-long economic pressures precipitated by the stock market crash of
1929 had nearly decimated the developing ranks of black writers, yet after the

institutional process for assisting writers, the Federal Writers' Project of the Works Progress Administration, had been initiated. Though Hughes never participated in the Writers' Project, he delivered his speech to a Carnegie Hall audience that included a young black writer from Mississippi who did: Richard Nathaniel Wright.

Wright, in recounting his early life in Mississippi, would write: "I had no hope of becoming a professional man."[3] Mississippi was the geographical no-man's-land for blacks of Wright's generation, despite the fact that many of them had the desire to write. In addressing the Federal Writers' Project and its ability to alter the hopes of a black man from Mississippi, I call attention to the way in which institutional space intersects with geographical space to reconfigure, modify, or create social conditions that in turn make possible new social, political, or cultural action. The several generations of black writers who ground their productions in the real and imagined space "Mississippi" would owe much to Wright directly and to the Federal Writers' Project indirectly.

Shortly after President Franklin D. Roosevelt established the Works Progress Administration (WPA) in May 1935 as a means to provide Depression-era Americans with jobs on building projects throughout the nation, the Federal Arts Project instituted its programs to put artists, musicians, writers, librarians, and teachers to work in their fields of expertise and to reduce their numbers on the relief rolls. When activated at the state level, the Federal Arts Project of the WPA included a variety of programs, including a Theater Project and a Writers' Project. What the Federal Writers' Project (FWP) as an institution enabled was the circumstance within a reconfigured spatial location by which Wright and others who were raced "Negro" in the 1930s could develop vocational ambitions and personal desires and become members of the writing profession. For Wright and those others, the FWP provided a movement into a public sphere that might otherwise have remained closed to them.

Two years before the Writers' Congress, Wright had arrived in New York from Chicago, where he had begun a writing career with the encouragement of the John Reed Club and, importantly, in 1935 with employment in the Illinois FWP. Ralph Ellison, whom Wright mentored at the end of the 1930s, has observed that "[t]hrough his cultural and political activities in Chicago [Wright] made a dialectical leap into a sense of his broadest possibilities, as a man and as artist."[4] Margaret Walker, who worked with Wright on the Illinois Writers' Project and in the South Side Writers' Workshop, has recalled that Wright's employment allowed him to move through his "various stages of conception, organization, and realization" and his "first scissors and paste job."[5] Essentially, the Project allowed Wright to conceive of himself as a professional writer, or as Nelson Algren, another FWP writer, has put it: Wright was the "writer whom the Illinois Project helped the most. . . . He was alert to its advantages and more diligent than most of us. It gave him the time to write."[6] Not only did he write his first novel, published after his death as *Lawd Today*, but he also completed the stories for his first book, *Uncle Tom's Children*, and his first major essay, "Blueprint for Negro Writing," which assumes as part of its premise that blacks can be both artists and professionals. "Writing has its professional autonomy," Wright concluded in that essay. "[I]t should complement other professions."[7]

The national, international, and transnational spaces ever apparent in Richard Wright's search for a space to be a black man in the twentieth century are touchstones for the consideration of the intersection between race and place manifested in the power struggle Wright undertook to create a mature, masculine subjectivity in times both of decreasing economic and class resources and of challenging social and regional locations that functioned to diminish the possibilities for individual self-awareness, racial actualization, and social agency. The physical and psychological space associated with the South/North axis and with the liberatory northern migration is typically figured as central to Wright's becoming a writer and his development as a writer; however, one aspect of his early years in Chicago and New York has received noticeably less attention. Wright's own drive to find a space not simply for an expressive black masculinity but for becoming a modern writer finds a counter drive in the formation of the Federal Writers' Project of the WPA to foster and employ writers during the Great Depression. The FWP became a way for Wright and other black writers to imagine their own lives as professionals, as practitioners of a vocation, despite their dislocation from the South and concomitant dispersal throughout the national landscape and the foreign places more hospitable to racialized subjects. In the WPA, a long list of individuals racialized as black—for example, Wright, Margaret Walker, Shirley Graham, Ralph Ellison, Frank Yerby, Theodore Ward, Frank Marshall Davis, Arna Bontemps, and Sterling Brown—could imagine themselves as writers and develop their craft within a cadre of practicing professional writers. The social, intellectual, artistic, and political space provided by the WPA enabled a young southern black man to become the writer Richard Wright and to inhabit the space he envisioned for himself in a writing career.

The segregated world of Mississippi in particular and the South in general could not accommodate a black youth like Richard Wright with ambitions to become a writer. The divided social space blacks lived within fractured their

Secondhand Clothing Stores and Pawn Shops on Beale Street, Memphis, Tennessee. The sign "Hotel Clark, The Best Service for Colored Only" in segregated Memphis referenced the black spaces for limited commercial and social empowerment within larger zones of exclusion that Richard Wright experienced on his way north. (Marion Post Wolcott, photographer, 1939; Farm Security Administration/Office of War Information Collection, Library of Congress Prints and Photographs Division, Washington, D.C.).

visions of potential and functioned to delimit their desires. While the very cultural geography of Mississippi dictated a narrow social sphere for blacks, the lack of any conception of blacks' earning a living by writing exacerbated the situation for someone of Wright's talents. Despite his poverty-ridden childhood, Wright was a precocious Deep South youth who had been spinning yarns to entertain his schoolmates and crafting stories to read aloud to them, including "Hell's Voodoo Half Acre," his first story. While within the private sphere of his race-defined social world, Wright might well have continued to write creatively, he would have been unable to pursue writing as his vocation. And he could not have earned a living as a creative writer of African descent in rigidly segregated Mississippi. His departure for Memphis and from there for Chicago enabled him to experience a place with institutions (libraries, writing classes, writers' clubs, publishing outlets) that both fostered and sustained writers.

While much attention has been paid to the role of the urban Chicago Communist Party and its various organs in developing Wright's creative ability, less notice has been given to the FWP in Chicago and its nurturing of his ambition to write. In fact, his decision to forego the safety of a job in the U.S. Postal Service was informed by his broader understanding of the possibilities for earning a living by writing developed during his tenure with the Writers' Project. Importantly, in May 1937, when Wright left Chicago for New York, he was not only already committed to writing as more than an avocation pursued in his spare time, but he also anticipated the continuation of his association with the New York WPA as a paid writer on the FWP.

The two major Wright biographies, Michel Fabre's *The Unfinished Quest of Richard Wright* (1973) and Hazel Rowley's *Richard Wright: The Life and Times* (2001), both present the facts of Wright's employment with the FWP, but neither attends to the larger implications of that employment for Wright and his development as a writer. Critical work on Wright in the context of his Chicago period outside of a focus on the John Reed Club and the Communist Party has been lagging, but Rosemary Hathaway's "Native Geography: Richard Wright's Work for the Federal Writers' Project in Chicago" not only addresses connections between Wright's assignments for the project and his fiction but also includes a reproduction of "A Survey of Amusement Facilities of District #35," a manuscript Wright wrote during his tenure with the FWP in Illinois and while he was residing in District 35, a deteriorating section of Chicago's Black Belt in the 1930s.[8]

When the Writers' Congress met in 1939, Wright was affiliated with the New York FWP and its *American Stuff* collection even though he had already achieved the publishing success that had eluded him in Chicago. The first of his published books, *Uncle Tom's Children*, a 1938 collection of four novellas, had resulted from his winning the 1938 *Story* magazine contest for WPA writers, some 500 of whom had entered. The Writers' Project had worked for him and for other blacks as well to become artists. Wright's prize-winning story "Fire and Cloud" earned him a contract from Harper for the publication of *Uncle Tom's Children*, and that book in turn brought him recognition as a serious, talented author. Though he found initial success within a year of his arrival in New York, Wright continued with the Writers' Project through the writing and publication of *Native Son* (1940). By then, he viewed the project as an access route to the literary and publishing world in New York.

Native Son, the novel that was to ensure Wright's place as a major black author, brought him immediate financial success because of its selection by the Book-of-the-Month Club. The powerful novel of a black youth in Chicago's ghetto eclipsed even the work of the acknowledged dean of black writers, Langston Hughes, whose autobiography, *The Big Sea*, appeared with less fanfare that same year. Wright's publisher, recognizing that the critical reception accorded *Native Son* gave its author national visibility and marketability, brought out a new edition of *Uncle Tom's Children* with an added story, "Bright and Morning Star," and an introductory autobiographical essay, "The Ethics of Living Jim Crow," which was, according to Sterling Brown, WPA national editor for Negro affairs (1936–40), "one of the finest pieces in *American Stuff*," the FWP's anthology of creative writings. These interconnections between the WPA's Federal Writers' Project and the phenomenal development of Wright's career, while not unknown, have not been linked directly to the progress that Wright made as a writer. "The Ethics of Living Jim Crow" from *American Stuff*, for example, was also the kernel of Wright's autobiographical work *American Hunger*, the first part of which was published five years later as *Black Boy*, a title Wright arrived at after his editors and publishers divided his "Record of Childhood and Youth" from the longer work. The essay's publication in the FWP collection signaled the process of bridging, or of building, as Wright put it, "a bridge of words between me and that world outside."[9] The architecture of the bridge is one of the ways of approaching Wright's construction of his fiction, and the span in the building process may be read as the WPA.

At the same time, an interrogation of the texts Wright produced during this phase of his career also reveals the relationships between race, racial conditions, and space (whether bodily, global, or textual). He focused specifically on the social geography in his native Mississippi that made exclusion and containment acceptable. In effect, Wright pointed to a normalizing of restrictive legal practices and social controls that produced a specific system of race-based identity and social relations in the United States, in particular in the American South, and in an exacerbated and cruelly exaggerated form, in Mississippi. What he demonstrated in those texts produced during his tenure with the WPA was how regulatory boundaries delimit not merely access to space but also subject formation and agency. Geographical and spatial claims are implicit in the transgression of legal and social attempts at racial exclusion and similar practices of power and privilege evidenced in *Native Son* and his short stories set in Mississippi, as well as in his autobiographical texts, *Black Boy* and *American Hunger*.

"The FWP had limited value for professional writers," Monty Noam Penkower observes in his thoughtful 1977 study, *The Federal Writers' Project: A Study in Government Patronage of the Arts*.[10] Penkower may well be right in drawing his conclusion about white creative writers because, as he points out, few of the literary projects came to fruition, and no permanent writers' bureau resulted. However, with regard to black writers, Penkower's observation misses the mark, even though it contains the term that perhaps best characterizes the main and lasting value of the FWP for the black writer: "professional." A generation of blacks became "professional" writers largely due to their work experiences with the FWP and their social experiences with writers involved in the project.

Although the label "professional writer" applied to a few black writers before the decade of the 1930s, not until then did it have a literal meaning for many aspiring black writers. Both survivors and heirs of the Harlem or "New Negro" Renaissance of the 1920s came to the Writers' Project from diverse and varied backgrounds; some, such as Sterling A. Brown, Zora Neale Hurston, Claude McKay, and Arna Bontemps, were already published authors who had earned reputations as participants in the Renaissance, while others, such as Ralph Ellison, Margaret Walker, Willard Motley, Theodore Ward, Frank Yerby, Ted Poston, and Wright himself, virtually began their literary careers during their tenure with the FWP. All of them, however, expanded their vision of the possibilities for earning a living by writing, for reaching wider audiences with their work, for practicing their crafts, for researching their subject matter (particularly folk sources), and for interacting with other writers.

It may seen odd to designate these black writers of the 1930s as an initial group of black professional writers, especially when the Harlem Renaissance writers of the 1920s actually achieved greater popularity and visibility than any black writers before them. Indeed, the Renaissance writers enjoyed a wider access to more varied publishing outlets both within and outside the black community, as well as in small private and large commercial ventures. They published in *Crisis, The Messenger*, and *Opportunity*, the official organs, respectively, of the NAACP, the Brotherhood of Sleeping Car Porters, and the Urban League; in *Fire!!!* and *Harlem*, short-lived independent magazines; and in *Survey Graphic*, the *Atlantic Monthly*, and *Forum*. Many shared the dream and enthusiasm of Bontemps, who arrived in New York from Los Angeles, as he said, "to find the job I wanted, to hear the music of my taste, to see serious plays, and to become a writer."[11] Few, however, considered writing their profession. Countee Cullen, for example, was a schoolteacher, as were Bontemps and Jessie Fauset. McKay and Wallace Thurman did manage to work as editors, but Rudolph Fisher was a medical doctor, Georgia Douglas Johnson a government worker, and Nella Larsen a librarian. Others, such as Hughes and Hurston, were primarily students who earned a living by performing a variety of short-term jobs.

When the Depression hit and, as Hughes put it, "the Negro was no longer in vogue," most of the surviving Renaissance writers retreated from Harlem to anywhere they could find employment. Georgia Douglas Johnson, who participated in the Renaissance from her home base in Washington, D.C., had eloquently articulated their common plight in June 1927, when she wrote an autobiographical sketch for *Opportunity* magazine's "Contest Spotlight": "I write because I love to write. . . . If I might ask of some fairy godmother special favors, one would sure to be for a clearing space, elbow room in which to think and write and live beyond the reach of the Wolf's fingers. . . . [M]uch that we do and write about comes just because of the daily struggle for bread and breath." By the mid-1930s, when, out of economic necessity, the coterie of Renaissance writers had scattered, Johnson's assessment had even greater valence for blacks who wanted to write, who dreamed of writing.

In Chicago, Richard Wright and others from his South Side Writers' Workshop became affiliated with the WPA. Although Wright wanted to write and had begun writing stories and poems before he left the South in 1927, his ambition was to get a position with the Chicago post office as the start of a secure career as a civil servant. His literary activity with the John Reed Club in 1932–33 and with the Communist Party had, of course, fueled his desire to write and to publish; nevertheless, before his first appointment with the Federal Writers' Project in 1935, he had seriously considered neither the possibility of writing full-time nor the idea of writing as a primary vocation. The urban space in which he found himself functioned in many social ways as an extension of the South; however, community interdependence fostered by the WPA represented an answer to the southern landscape of segregation and an access route to social justice within a new structure of power. One of the points Phoebe Cutler makes in *The Public Landscape of the New Deal* (1986) speaks to the overarching conception of American society that informed the WPA and FWP: "A cohesive, integrated society was sought, in which land patterns could promote a wholesome combination of work, play, and education. In the 1930s Americans still viewed the landscape, along with church and family, as a force in character formation. Recreation enjoyed the moral hegemony that conservation still retains. This idealism imbued the landscape."[12] Importantly for writers and artists, "the era romanticized not the place but the purpose of the place."[13] Art became linked to recreation in the work of character formation.

Wright was not alone among the black Chicago writers in viewing writing as therapeutic, perhaps even a psychological necessity, though not as an occupation. Of itself, writing constituted an "elsewhere" from the everyday, even when the details of that everyday found their way transformed into the writing. Margaret Walker recalled that when she was first introduced to Wright by Langston Hughes on 16 February 1936, neither she nor he had "published one significant piece of imaginative prose."[14] His work on the Illinois Writers' Project directed by Louis Wirth soon changed that. Walker, who had graduated from Northwestern in 1935, found herself still unemployed in the early months of 1936, but like Wright, she was searching for a way to remain in Chicago, where, as she says, she "hoped to meet other writers, learn something more about writing, and perhaps publish some of [her] poetry."[15] Her opportunity came on 13 March 1936, when she received a notice to report to the Wells Street office of the WPA Writers' Project; her salary was $85 a month, though a year later it was increased to $94. The opportunity was both to remain in the city and survive the ravages of want during the Depression and to pursue the desired work, writing, as a practice and as a way of being in the world. In almost utopic achievement of place, Walker joined the ranks of salaried WPA writers. As a junior writer, Walker reported to the project office for semiweekly assignments, and there she continued her friendship with Wright, who introduced her to Bontemps and Brown and brought her into the South Side Writers' Workshop. This period marked the beginning of Walker's sense of herself as a professional writer, though her career was in its apprenticeship stage and none of her work had been published.[16]

Although Wright's initial employment with the WPA began in 1935 before Walker's, he had been transferred out to the Theater Project in January 1936. That stint was short-lived, and though it generated Wright's interest in theater, it also increased his investment in realistic representations of racism and the treatment of blacks in the South. When he relocated back to the Writers' Project in July 1936 after publishing his short story "Big Boy Leaves Home" in *New Caravan* (January 1936), his position became that of supervisor with a salary of $125 a month because he had not only himself but also his mother and brother to support, and he had already published poems in *Left Front*, *The Anvil*, and *New Masses*. Wright's job required weekly writing assignments based on field research in the city, and even with supervisory duties, Wright had not only new materials but also free time for his writing. Though not free of either segregation or racism, Chicago, as a major metropolis and then the second-largest city in the United States, provided opportunities unimaginable in Mississippi, even in its quasi-urban areas, Jackson and Natchez.

Wright, Walker, Katherine Dunham, Frank Marshall Davis, Theodore Ward, Frank Yerby, and Arna Bontemps were only a few of the black writers who were on the WPA and who worked on the Illinois Writers' Project. All of them had connections to the South. It is important, however, to keep in perspective the relatively small number of blacks who were enrolled in the FWP nationwide. In February 1937, Sterling Brown's office reported that the number was 106, or a mere 2 percent of the total number of writers on the FWP; during the duration of the FWP, the number of blacks had been as low as 80 and never rose above 150.[17] Fortunately, Wright was among the 2 percent, and indeed he went on to become the most successful black writer of his generation. But in Chicago, he had been like the others, struggling to earn a living and affirmed in his vocation by the very existence of the FWP. "Every story is a travel story—a spatial practice," Michel de Certeau states.[18] For Wright, the story is his movement into an organization that made possible a different identity. Occupying the position of paid writer who could support his mother and brother meant a reorientation for Wright with which not even the John Reed Club or the South Side Writers' Workshop could compete.

In 1936 Brown's appointment as national editor of Negro affairs for the FWP marked a major turning point not only in the usually acknowledged impact that the project would have on studies of blacks in America but also on the professional careers of black creative writers. Brown's editorial position came about as the direct result of Director Henry Alsberg's decision to promote both the hiring of blacks and the inclusion of black sociocultural history in the state projects. Alsberg, however, was responding to influential blacks such as Ralph Bunche, Walter White, Robert Weaver, William Hastie, and John P. Davis, who individually and collectively through their organizations recognized that a knowledgeable black person should be appointed to the national FWP office in order to ensure that black history, culture, and literature would be included in the project's undertakings. Brown himself was a poet and critic, educated at Williams College and Harvard but completely grounded in the folklore and folk traditions of black America. Under his creative leadership from 1936 to 1940, the FWP began a massive program of researching and writing the history of blacks in America, which was Brown's idea for redressing the sparse treatment of blacks in individual state guides. It was a realignment of the American narrative and a struggle to assert power as part of racial equity and justice.

Brown, along with his editorial staff, had managed to prevent the state guides in progress from neglecting or excluding black material as had the six New England guidebooks that were completed before his tenure with the Project. Although, as Jerre Mangione observes in *The Dream and the Deal: The Federal Writers' Project, 1935–1943* (1973), the "honest and accurate . . . coverage given to the subject in these books represented, in effect, the first objective description of the Negro's participation in American life," that coverage still was not extensive enough.[19] Brown believed that comprehensive studies could reveal the Negro "as an integral part of American life," and so he instituted and directed field projects in which black writers researched black history, culture, and folklife within the contexts of their relationship to the larger American experience.[20] Brown's vision and directive authorized the creative work of collecting, recording, assembling, and narrativizing black life in ways hitherto unimaginable.

In terms of tangible publications resulting from Brown's research and editorial program, only *The Negro in Virginia* (1940), a study now considered a classic in the field, appeared in print. Supervised by Roscoe E. Lewis at Hampton Institute, the Virginia project was an all-black unit of the Virginia Writers' Project, whose state director, Eudora Ramsay Richardson, followed the lead of Brown and Alsberg in encouraging the research and production of what they hoped would be, and what indeed became, a model book. Despite the fact that other comparable publications did not materialize, the program was crucial to the development of black professional writers because two of its major research collection projects were in Illinois and New York, where large concentrations of blacks lived and where a number of young blacks found employment through the WPA.

Because of Henry Alsberg's assistance, Richard Wright was able to transfer to the New York Writers' Project. His initial assignment was on the New York City Guide, but he was soon placed with Willard Maas, Claude McKay, Harry Kemp, and Maxwell Bodenheim on the *American Stuff* project, an anthology that allowed the writers "to work at home on their own material, with the sole stipulation that they report to the Project office once a week with evidence of their work." The move and the continuation with the Project proved fortuitous because, though all the fiction manuscripts he had sent out from Chicago had been turned down by publishers, Wright's first manuscript submission in New York, "Fire and Cloud," initiated his success as a published author.

The New York City that Wright encountered as part of his migration and developmental process offered the opportunity for a new subjectivity. Migration east allowed for a redefinition of self in a new space, yet at the same time it came with the security of a ready-made organizational base that promoted writing as work and as career. Economic and vocational choices were easier to make given the system of support and acknowledgment institutionalized within the FWP.

Ralph Ellison, in "Remembering Richard Wright," an essay about his early days in New York and the beginning of his friendship with Wright, points to the FWP as "most important to the continuing development of Afro-American artists" and as providing "the possibility for a broader Afro-American freedom."[21] His statement suggests the concept that space equals freedom, an idea theorized later in the geographical work of Yi-Fu Tuan. Ellison clarifies his point by reflecting on his personal condition at the time he became involved with the "Living Lore" folklore FWP in New York. He states:

> Wright himself worked on both the Chicago and the New York Federal Writers' Project, and I could not have become a writer at the time I began had I not been able to earn my board and keep by doing research for the New York project. Through Wright's encouragement, I had become serious about writing, but before going on the project I sometimes slept in the public park below City College because I had neither job nor money. But my personal affairs aside, the WPA provided an important surge to Afro-American cultural activity. The result was not a "renaissance," but there was a resuscitation and transformation of that very vital artistic impulse that is abiding among Afro-Americans. . . . Afro-American cultural style is an abiding aspect of our culture, and the economic disaster which brought the WPA gave it an accelerated release and allowed many Negroes to achieve their identities as artists.[22]

From a personal perspective, Ellison recognized that the FWP made it possible for blacks to become writers and professionals during a bleak period in the national economy that was for those lowest on the socioeconomic scale even bleaker. Ellison's own words ("the WPA . . . allowed many Negroes to achieve their identities as artists") help to make the main point that I have stressed: that blacks not only found employment with the FWP but also began to conceive of themselves as professional writers whose vocation could be solely that of writer. This discovery and the shift in subjectivity mark the beginning of a class of blacks labeling themselves writers/authors and earning their living as writers. Importantly, too, it is a shift to an assumption of social significance and power within a space previously closed to blacks.

What Ellison expresses is the large impact of the FWP on "cultural activity" and the personal impact of Richard Wright as mentor on him, but what Ellison may not have known is the comparable role Sterling Brown played in Wright's own work, not through intimate contact but by citation and through his vision for the Writers' Project. Two points about Brown's collection and research projects on blacks in America relate directly to Wright's development as a writer. One is that the work done in Chicago, much of it still unpublished and housed in the Vivian G. Harsh Collection of the Chicago Public Library and in the Abraham Lincoln Presidential Library in Springfield, Illinois, formed the ideological framework for one of Wright's major essays on black writing and writers, "Blueprint for Negro Writing," which appeared in *New Challenge* in the fall of 1937 and which restates the premise that Brown had for the project: "There is a culture . . . of the Negro which is his and has been addressed to him; a culture which has . . . helped to clarify his consciousness and create emotional attitudes which are conducive to action. This culture has stemmed mainly from two sources: (1) the Negro church; and (2) the folklore of the Negro people" (54). Although "Blueprint" is more typically linked to the influence of Communism on Wright, it is even more a reformulation of Brown's general tenets for the FWP's Negro studies, as the section on "Social Consciousness and Responsibility" makes clear in its opening: "The Negro writer who seeks to function within his race as a purposeful agent has a serious responsibility. In order to do justice to his subject matter, in order to depict Negro life in all of its manifold and intricate relationships, a deep, informed, and complex consciousness is necessary; a consciousness which draws for its strength upon the fluid lore of a great people, and molds this lore with the concepts that move and direct the forces of history today" (54). It seems doubtful that without Brown's guidance, statements, and vision, Wright would have come so early to these conclusions about the black writer and black folklife and lore. And by extension, neither would Ellison and others of the black writers have come so directly at the start of their careers to so intense an appreciation of and commitment to the materials of black folklife had they not had the experience of working not simply with the FWP, but specifically with the studies of blacks conceived and planned by Brown.

Wright's work in the new edition of *Uncle Tom's Children* owed a debt to Sterling Brown's *Southern Road* (1932) and his signature poem in dialect, "Odyssey of Big Boy." Though born in Washington, D.C., Brown had spent six years living and teaching in the South during the 1920s, when he developed into a successful and well-published poet using folk forms and expressive speech most closely associated with southern black life.[23] Brown's Big Boy provides a model for Wright's "Big Boy Leaves Home" and Bigger Thomas in *Native Son*, as well as a bridge spanning the South that Wright had left behind and the South that he could construct in fiction and expose in narrative exploring the imbalances of power.

The second of these two connected points is that for many years after the FWP ended, black writers, whether or not they had been employed by it, made use of the cultural materials researched for the incomplete Negro studies projects. Examples include Gilbert Osofsky's *Harlem: The Making of a Ghetto, Negro New York 1890–1930* (1966), Roi Ottley and William J. Weatherby's *The Negro in New York: An Informal Social History, 1626–1940* (1969), and Sterling Brown, Arthur Davis, and Ulysses Lee's *Negro Caravan* (1941). And that usage continues today, with researchers availing themselves of the materials at the Schomburg Collection of the New York Public Library and, to a lesser extent, those in Chicago's Harsh Collection. Among the earliest scholarly works to utilize the FWP collection projects, Horace Cayton and St. Clair Drake's *Black Metropolis: A Study of Negro Life in a Northern City* (1945) seems especially pertinent here because Richard Wright wrote the introduction, in which he included yet another statement reiterating the position of the Negro in American life charted by Brown for the Federal Writers' Project: "Both the political Left and the political Right try to exchange the Negro problem into something they can control, thereby denying the humanity of the Negro, excluding his unique and historical position in American Life."[24] Thus, as Sterling Brown intimated, the WPA created a political and social space that allowed a racially restricted group of individuals an opportunity to step out into a public life, a public sphere, free to declare themselves without apology as writers.

By the time Wright produced the hard-hitting introduction for *Black Metropolis*, he had already begun to plan his departure for Europe. Changes in his location within the United States had allowed him to develop into a best-selling author, but his movement out of Mississippi to the North of Chicago and New York was ultimately not enough to counter the racism ingrained in the society. His second marriage across racial lines to Ellen Poplowitz (often referred to as "Ellen Poplar") would have been even more unimaginable in Mississippi than his becoming a writer, but that marriage, while tolerated in some but not all areas of New York City, was vulnerable to racist attacks that were consistent with and more virulent than those on his writing. Wright would take his wife and daughter to Paris, where he hoped to find the ideal space to be both a black man and a professional writer. Paris would, however, turn out to be an "Island of Hallucination," as Wright, a disillusioned expatriate, would entitle his draft of a long novel written near the end of his life. Doreen Massey's suggestion that to "keep moving" is a "gender-disturbing message," both in terms of space and identity, may also have valency as "race-disturbing."[25] The relationship to race appears plausible given Massey's explanation: "The challenge [to keep moving] is to achieve this whilst at the same time recognizing one's necessary locatedness and embeddedness/embodiedness, and taking responsibility for it."[26] Wright's movement from

Mississippi to Memphis to Chicago to New York to Paris, as well as his imagining of a yet further move to London toward the end of his life, seems very much in keeping with an effort to disturb his racialization, even within France, where he ultimately felt pursued and victimized precisely because of his race—that designation as a black man from the United States that he could not escape.

In a sense, the narrative of mobility, initiated in Wright's telling of his inner life's story in *Black Boy* and *American Hunger*, intimately connected his desire to write, to build his bridge of words from his interior space to the larger external world of blacks, is also the desire for location and place, for the stability against the constraints manifested in the materiality of segregated Mississippi. Whatever psychic wounds Wright sustained in an emasculating South could for a time be soothed by both physical movement and written production. The two autobiographical books narrate, develop, and may be read as a cultural story of the creation of the black professional writer in a field long unavailable to even the most serious black authors. Wright portrays in those narratives how his inclinations, temperament, and intelligence all combined to make him suited for no other role in life and how his Mississippi childhood forced him into an agile and determined search for a place that could fully accommodate and nurture his ambition and vocation.

In her introductory note to *Black Boy*, Dorothy Canfield Fisher called Wright "that rarely gifted American author." Those concluding words may well have been the most significant marker of Wright's achievement in the autobiographical work: his acceptance as author, an American author.[27] Though Fisher was, no doubt, responding to Wright's style and technique in *Black Boy*, she may have also recognized in the text a site of power over the creation of a unique black self as artist and the quest for authorship as profession.

II. HUMAN GEOGRAPHY AND NEW BLACK SUBJECTIVITIES

Spatial ability becomes spatial knowledge when movements
and changes of location can be envisaged.
—YI-FU TUAN, *Space and Place*

Richard Wright refused to consider altering the exceptionalism and individualism concluding *Black Boy*. His resistance to Dorothy Canfield Fisher's repeated suggestion that he alter the conclusion of *Black Boy* to encompass a specific sighting of Americanism—the American flag, she offered as a possibility—reiterates his conception of the work and his objective embedded in the final chapter, mainly in the last five pages, which he added after the manuscript had been divided. Those pages formed the logical, articulated outcome of his rebirth and transformation into an artist-writer glimpsing a vague light in an otherwise dark present. While Fisher would have a symbol of the nation draw Wright's black boy into the fabric of the myth of inclusion and opportunity, she did not recognize what he understood only too well: the grand myths, metaphors, and symbols of the nation were constructed by excluding the complexity of race and racial conditions for blacks, particularly blacks living under Jim Crow in the Deep South. He wanted a narrative removed from the civic but nonetheless political in the sense of the master narratives of high modernist writers, their determined formation of a critical and creative consciousness that would, he believed, produce empowering and lasting art.

Wright's project was not invested in connecting his story to the utopian impulses fueling constructions of the American nation. His desire for connection was in part a drive to heal the schism between his interior and exterior, his consciousness of being in the world and of how that world was constituted. That desire articulated as action I term "bridging," deriving it from a spatial and architectural concept that Wright introduced in his autobiographical text: "I picked up a pencil and held it over a sheet of white paper. . . . I wanted to try to build a bridge of words between me and that world outside, that world which was so distant and elusive that it seemed unreal."[28] A bridge in Wright's usage is a structure designed to span opposite spaces, to provide passage over obstacles, to join separate parts, to form a connection between circuits. Bridging as a noun in general usage refers, of course, to the supporting braces between beams that not only reinforce but also distribute stress. These definitions all point to the constructedness of a bridge and bridging, constructed and perceived as such in form and function.

Although bridge and bridging are spatial, building, and architectural terms, they are related to the practice of articulation that Brent Hayes Edwards frames in terms of diaspora and internationalism as "a process of linking or connecting across gaps" and of joining the structural and the discursive.[29] Edwards utilizes Stuart Hall's "Race, Articulation, and Societies Structured in Dominance" to ground articulation in Marx's theory of capitalist production and to locate articulation as a way to "consider relations of 'difference within unity,' non-naturalizable patterns of linkage between disparate societal elements."[30] Hall, following Althusser and Laclau, theorizes articulation as a complex structure in "that the mechanisms which connect dissimilar features must be shown. . . . It also means—since the combination is a structure (an articulated combination) and not a random association—that there will be structured relations between its parts, i.e., relations of dominance and subordination."[31] What interests Hall and Edwards is that "societies structured in dominance" are as well "the ground of cultural resistance," in which ideology becomes "the key site of *struggle* over competing articulations."[32]

In the published *Black Boy* and the longer manuscript version, *American Hunger*, Wright maps his own creation as artist. He locates himself as a structure of articulation between competing cultural claims and powers—for example, white southern domination and black familial authority. He etches in a traceable form his movement out of the deforming southern environment that is both white and black and into an outside world potentially providing the space for the reformation of his physical and psychical life. The bridge of articulation between aspects is verbal expression and discourse. When he discovers that the geographic suppression of desire that marked his life in the segregated South does not abate in the oppressive North, he reconfigures the bridge necessary to move him intellectually, emotionally, and psychically forward. Unequal structures of power persist. Race and skin color continue to translate into denial of opportunity or masculinity in new geographic spaces, but given the already acquired knowledge of racism and the bridging to mediate the effects, Wright represents the mechanism of his survival and his triumph figured ultimately in the production and publication of the text itself. Although he maps both the North and the South as regions of the United States inhospitable to a black man who imagines a profession as a writer, the North does offer the created spaces, educational and political, in which a black person can learn the craft and practice the art of writing. The northern city, while not the imagined utopia in the migratory process, nonetheless results in the formation of a new subjectivity, still mobile and in process but inviolately black. Migration enables a perspective for redefining of self in the context of new spatial geographies, not merely of built and natural environments but primarily of the institutional and organizational structures.

The end result of the dialogue with self about society and individuality articulated in *Black Boy* is that the artist is born, but the man of letters, the professional author, is made. It is the script of modernist narratives of development and actualization. In the cumulative process of bridging, Wright creates his subjectivity, which becomes the larger, more significant landscape displacing the looming southern spatial configurations. The basic confrontation of the book is repeatedly with self, not with others. There is a retreat into self that is characterized by embryonic existential ideology, the repetition of the frozen or paralyzed Richard, unable to move, to act, or even to feel, but always free to think, to rationalize, and especially to imagine. In citing how he comes to bring his mental states into harmony with a functioning material body, Wright develops his most radical positions. That process is a virtual map of Richard's ontological and epistemological difference from the material places in his past.

Toward the end of *Black Boy*, the persona Richard states: "And it was out of these novels and stories and articles, out of the emotional impact of imaginative constructions of heroic or tragic deed, that I felt touching my face a tinge of warmth from an unseen light; and in my leaving I was groping toward that invisible light, always trying to keep my face so set and turned that I would not lose the hope of its faint promise, using it as a justification for my action" (283). Leaving the South, he understands Light as space within which to actualize his desire to become a writer. That understanding recurs in his reflections on his decision to leave the South. "Groping toward that invisible light" becomes his metaphor for moving in the direction charted by his desire and his ambition. Both in *Black Boy*, which first appeared as a Book-of-the-Month-Club selection, and in *American Hunger*, which was planned as a follow-up publication entitled "The Horror and the Glory," Wright's embedded thematic concerns were the recreation of his life as the making of a literary artist and the establishing of himself as a professional writer, a black man of letters. In a sense, *Black Boy* is the writing backward to instantiate the position achieved through his becoming a professional writer.

The epigraph he chose for *Black Boy* is from the book of Job: "They meet with darkness in the daytime / And they grope at noonday as in the night." Light, dark, and groping connect the epigraph to the thematic of Wright's own text. Immediately the association would seem to rest with the black suffering inhabitants of the segregated, violently oppressive American South depicted in the book; Wright had considered "Southern Night" a fitting title for the first half of his autobiography once the Chicago portion had been split off from it. The usual reading, then, of *Black Boy* as an archetypal portrait of growing up in the segregated South of the 1910s and 1920s is appropriate. However, importantly, the association is also emblematical of Wright's own efforts and those of black people to become artists and authors. More generally, the book fills a previously blank area in African American letters: the psychological portrait of the making of a black artist. The adversities in the face of an overwhelming drive for success, the unavailability of the prerequisite books and reading materials to develop the intellect and provide literary models, or the inability to overcome racist practices in the publishing and writing trades—

these may be another frame of reference for Wright's epigraph. Desire forges the consciousness of movement through space and time, with the days and nights being demarcated but undifferentiated by light. Darkness oppresses and limits the possibilities for charting the movement out of and beyond the dark.

Like Job in his transforming crisis of learning through suffering, Wright transforms and learns through reconstituting his experience. The inversions of normalcy and the expected, explicit in the use of daylight, darkness, and night, insert from the outset of the book a possibility of a return to normalcy and to the expected or usual outcome—if the "they" of the epigraph were allowed to develop and exist in a naturally "right" or correctly functioning universe. To extend the idea another way, if black youths were allowed to develop their mental capacities more normally during their formative years, and if black writers were allowed to follow a more typical sequence of events for able, competent writers, then they, too, would be able to function in their primary identity as artists without the necessity of perverting occupation into jobs or vocation into avocation. Wright's suffering in *Black Boy* teaches him to trust not in external gods but in the internal genius of inspiration that leads to an enlarged concept of what the black writer might be. He renders a Joblike description of the process of purifying his life through trials and his building in blind faith a vehicle for negotiating the encroaching deluge.

Read through the lens of the book of Job, *Black Boy* becomes an account of the developmental transformation of a youth into an artist, one destined to become an artist. It presents a singular portrait of the emergence of an artist keenly aware of his culture and his alienation in the vein of James Joyce's *Portrait of the Artist as a Young Man* (1918) and other works in the modernist *künstlerroman* genre, which Wright discovered during his early days in Chicago. It is an argument for Wright's own authenticity as a writer. In writing the two-part "autobiography," Wright was not interested in telling the chronological events of his life; as we now know from his literary biographers, particularly Fabre and Rowley, and surviving relatives and friends, many of his biographical details are fabricated. In *Black Boy*, as in *American Hunger*, he drops the social mask of the artist as fiction writer and unfolds the shaping personality behind the fiction. The process is circuitous, because though the boy Richard is transformed and his personality is renewed, the psychical and imaginative personality remains what it was in the opening of the work, when the four-year-old Richard sets fire to his house by lighting straw under "the long fluffy white curtain" he had been forbidden to touch. He is beaten into unconsciousness for his act; his mother "lashed [him] so hard and long that

[he] lost consciousness . . . beaten out of [his] senses" (13). "My body seemed on fire," he remembered, "my mother had come close to killing me" (13). The symbolic act of burning, a trial by fire, frees Richard from the constrictions of the body from the beginning or from his earliest memory of an encounter with social, cultural, and familial forces. This burning of the house and the burning of the body distance him from both the home, with its domesticating influences, and the maternal, with its controlling authority.

Later in the narrative, he acknowledges his experiential perspective and the emotion coloring his experience. He reiterates the image of fire and burning in regard to the city that, as he puts it, "had lifted me in its burning arms and borne me toward alien and undreamed-of shores of knowing" (43). But prior to that knowing, he remains under a stricture of voicelessness or silence that necessitates his literal and figurative burning of his environment. "Experience," according to Yi-Fu Tuan, "is the overcoming of perils. . . . To experience in the active sense requires that one venture forth into the unfamiliar and experiment with the elusive and the uncertain."[33] What Wright's protagonist Richard terms "knowing" is "experience" in the sense of apprehending and interacting with the unknown, the unfamiliar, and the uncertain. This knowing for Richard is made manifest in articulation and citation.

The doctor attending his illness "ordered that [he] be kept quiet, that [his] very life depended upon it" (13). That order is comparable to and an extension of the one issued by his mother in the opening paragraph of the book: "All morning my mother had been scolding me, telling me to keep still, warning me that I must make no noise." This initial demand of silence precipitates Richard's burning of the curtains, as well as his desire to find a voice even if he must burn in the process. Richard learns; he comes to an awareness of the experience with fire and with expression that allows him to know, as well as to construct, his own reality. Desire counters the strictures of silence, and experience allows him to overcome the silencing mechanisms of his family and his society.

Donald B. Gibson argues persuasively from a close analysis of the first chapter that Wright's intention is to reveal his essential character, that of the strong-willed individualist capable of defying parental authority at any cost:

> Each section of the first chapter reveals another facet of Wright's parents' failing him or his assuming himself functions originally belonging to them. The point is that failing to find the necessary support and sustaining function in adults or in a community, he had to rely upon himself—to cultivate those qualities in himself, to become self-reliant,

a strong individualist. That is why in the book Wright differs from every other black person who appears in that world. And that is why he is able to resist efforts on the parts of black and white alike to make him conform to an inimical scheme of values.[34]

Initially, however, Wright is not overtly in rebellion against social norms and cultural mores; he merely wishes to be free to play and shout. The desire for bodily freedom and mobility dictates his behavior. He slips almost casually into tests of will and body that soon cause him to see himself in a rebellious relationship with his society in addition to his parents and family. The space he comes to occupy, physically and psychically, is sealed off and isolated from relatives and from the environment they inhabit. His self-made social geography has already begun to remove him from the contagions they experience.

From the age of four and the ritual burning of his environment, Richard remains inviolately unassimilated into his surroundings. Though after that incident he suppresses his impulse to destroy his physical domicile, he does not hesitate to sever his connection to home as it exists for him. He does not suppress his desire to achieve difference, to turn away from acculturation and assimilation into the daily activities of his home and family, and his society by extension. While "place" may ordinarily be associated with security and "space" with freedom, for Richard there is no security in "place" or its corollary "home."[35] Distancing himself from his "place" within the family and community, and thus from any possibility of "security," he becomes a self-conscious observer, disembodied from the ordinary ties to cultural values and meaning. In the process, he emerges free to assess his culture without the baggage of emotional intimacy with others. For example, he observes of his father: "[H]ow completely his soul was imprisoned by the slow flow of the seasons, . . . how fastened were his memories to a crude and raw past, how chained were his actions and emotions to the direct, animalistic impulses of his withering body" (43). He rejects the worn-down farmer who is his father, and he rejects with his father's material body all parental authority over him. Thus, it is not surprising that he concludes, "we were forever strangers, speaking a different language, living on vastly distant planes of reality" (42). The incarceral nature of his father's existence repulses him; imprisoned in the rote work of sharecropping and in the reductive urges of the body, Wright's father recedes into a place distinctly different from all that Wright himself represents.

Wright mediates his own "plane of reality," the experience and meaning of nature and the physical world, with a consciousness of his difference from his family in the temporal. In these moments of full cognizance of and complete identification with the space he inhabits, he reads the codes and pronounces himself a person of superior intellect distinct from the animal his father had become. Yet he apprehends the messages directly through his senses: "Each event spoke with a cryptic tongue. And the moments of living slowly revealed their coded meanings" (14). In so doing, he accentuates his own positionality, his ontology and epistemology, in relation to his father's.

In rejecting assimilation as a black man in the white-dominated South, he rejects by extension the occupational options into which he would be channeled: delivery boy, janitor, and sharecropper. The reality of economic necessity is not a deterrent to his rejection; instead, it compels him to seek beyond any immediate, and grossly inadequate, short-term employment or solution. In choosing to disobey the parental and societal order to keep silent and to relinquish speech for an inexplicable and untenable "social" good, Wright wrests from authority figures in his culture the right to his own voice and his own determination to tell. After writing a short story or mood piece relating the suicide of an Indian girl, he is compelled to say: "My environment contained nothing more alien than writing or the desire to express one's self in writing" (133). Yet, he is empowered to speak and to write by his own hard-won authority, or will, and to speak against the society's explanation of itself and of him. In the final analysis, he will not be contained in spirit, mind, voice, or body by the repressive strategies for sheer animal-level survival accepted by southern blacks (represented by his parents and relatives), or demanded by southern whites (represented by his various employers), or expected by organized groups (represented by religious denominations in the South and the Communist Party in the North).

By the end of *American Hunger*, Wright has rejected all external social and political referents for meaning and value. What is left open and available to him as a deliberate choice for self-direction and self-definition is art. As he plainly states: "I would hurl words into this darkness and wait for an echo, and if an echo sounded, no matter how faintly, I would send other words to tell, to march, to fight, to create a sense of the hunger for life that gnaws in us all, to keep alive in our hearts a sense of the inexpressibly human" (135). Words hurled into "this darkness," this place that has the contours of the South he has represented, are both sound and light constituting a sensory bridge connecting Wright and others to their humanity. A wordsmith, Wright forges both hunger and satiety in the process.

Wright's implicit juxtaposition of the South that he knew and the North that he envisioned leads him to configure both regions as mythical spaces.

Yi-Fu Tuan distinguished two kinds of mythical spaces: "In the one, mythical space is a fuzzy area of defective knowledge surrounding the empirically known; it frames pragmatic space. In the other it is the spatial component of a world view, a conception of localized values within which people carry on their practical activities."[36] In countering the known South with the unknown North, Wright constructed a "mythical geography" for Chicago as the North that bears little direct relationship to the everyday reality of Chicago. Once he leaves the South for Chicago, however, Wright reimagines the city through a group or social context in which there is a successive expansion of perception and knowledge.

In reviewing *American Hunger* for the *Chicago Tribune Book World*, Alden Whitman noticed that "[t]he rationale for the 1945 biography is . . . cloudy. It is unusual for anyone to sum up his life at the age of 37, which Wright was that year."[37] If Whitman were to place the writing of the autobiography into the context of being Wright's only slightly veiled attempt to insist upon his status as an artist and a professional, then he would have at least one possible motivation for the work. Wright's assumption of voice in his autobiography is a recognition of his entering into subjectivity. The space he occupies by the age of thirty-seven is precisely the desired and imagined space constructed in the autobiography.

Wright's technical strategy for achieving his ends is the process of spatial and psychological distancing from the putative ecosystem in both his own family and his environment. The body and mind together form a unit determined to counter the "ecology of knowledge" forged out of an understanding of the dynamic space-time context.[38] He separates himself from one after another of the entrapments of ordinary life: parents, grandmother, sibling, teachers, ministers, God, religion, sex and marriage, pleasures and vices, racial solidarity, political ideology—and the list drawn from his specifically remembered incidents could go on. He becomes accustomed "to change, to movement, to making many adjustments," because, as he states in *Black Boy*, "life had trapped me in a realm of emotional rejection; I had not embraced insurgency through an open choice" (282). The social structures of a segregated Jim Crow society aim to confine and silence blacks, but Wright, in embracing "insurgency," fights against the defining structure and its spatial configurations.

At the same time, the design of the text reveals an embracing of the life of the mind, of the intellect that is self-centered and self-absorbed but observant of others and of their activities. "At the age of twelve" he claims to have "had an attitude toward life that was to endure":

It made me want to dive coldly to the heart of every question and lay it open to the core of suffering I knew I would find there. It made me love burrowing into psychology, into realistic and naturalistic fiction and art, into those whirlpools of politics that had the power to claim the whole of men's souls. It directed my loyalties to the side of men in rebellion; it made me love talk that sought answers to questions that could help nobody, that could only keep alive in me that enthralling sense of wonder and awe in the face and the drama of human feeling which is hidden by the eternal drama of life. (112)

In the tension between distancing and embracing, the articulate and literate subjectivity emerges. That subjectivity is both philosophical and intellectual; in its passion for the mental and manual process of composition and creation, this new subjectivity defies the social space allotted for blacks under the narrow divisions of segregation.

W. E. B. Du Bois stated in his review of *Black Boy* for the *New York Herald Tribune*: "After this sordid picture [of black life] we gradually come upon the solution. The hero is interested in himself, is self-centered to the exclusion of everything else. The suffering of others is put down simply as a measure of his own suffering and resentment." Although Du Bois speculates that Wright's "actual record" may in fact be "a creative picture and a warning," he dismisses it nonetheless as a work that "misses its possible effectiveness because it is a work of art so patently and terribly overdrawn."[39] The problem is that Du Bois reads the surface of the text where the outline appears to be a literal record of external life and interaction. In so doing, he misses the insistent, intelligible, and visible subsurface that plaintively lays bare Wright's desire to be, and to be seen as, an artist-writer. In conveying his subjective identity, Wright is insistent in mapping his physical and psychological body in the landscape of privation and want, and given the social history of Mississippi in matters of race, he has an ideal landscape upon which to trace his formation.

What diversity of self Wright displays is displaced by the urgency of his battles against conformity, given the intensity of the oppression of individuality in his particular southern and later northern environments. So that in response, the more apparent emphasis would seem to be an overstatement of the primacy of self, or the self-centeredness of the hero that Du Bois observes, and that he would also have found in *American Hunger*, which continues in this same mode of development, had he been alive upon its appearance in book form in 1977.

On the surface, Wright told a story of poverty and abuse not only that white America needed to hear, but that he himself needed to articulate about his past. While he renders an ambivalent account of blood relatives, racial community, and southern environment, he presents no ambivalence about writing, reading, literacy, and art. "It had been my accidental reading of fiction and literary criticism," he reports, "that had evoked in me vague glimpses of life's possibilities" (*Black Boy*, 383). His immediate and practical models were Theodore Dreiser, Sinclair Lewis, and especially H. L. Mencken, all white professional writers. His more distant and inspirational models were not only those blacks from Frederick Douglass on who had become literate and used their literacy as the stepping-stone to personal emancipation from slavery in their authorship of autobiographical narratives, but also those blacks from Nat Turner on who had fought physical battles with their environments to become racial heroes in the struggle for individual achievement. One of those who had insinuated himself in both of these groups was the boxer Jack Johnson, to whom Ralph Ellison compared Wright: "In him we had for the first time a Negro American writer as randy, as courageous, and as irrepressible as Jack Johnson . . . one of the most admired underground heroes" ("Remembering Richard Wright," 215). Wright, however, mentions neither the Douglasses nor the Johnsons; he concentrates instead on the Menckens and the Lewises. As citation, they had achieved in precisely the medium Wright claimed as his own intellectual right.

Houston A. Baker correctly remarks the impact of these white writers on the young Wright:

> The fuel consumed by Wright is the work of H. L. Mencken, Sinclair Lewis, Theodore Dreiser, whose relationship to the quotidian, to "everyday reality," is less mediated by beautifying literary conventions than the work of their contemporaries. But it would not have mattered whether Wright fueled his hunger with Flaubert or Frank Norris, because he was not in search of literary *lights*. . . . The search presented in *Black Boy* is a quest for a correlative, an articulated set of relationships that will make sense of desire. It is not an expedition in discovery of literary, or "artistic," mastery.[40]

As Baker points out, Wright's turning to Mencken, Lewis, and Dreiser was an articulation of a relational identity, or what I would call his bridging, his construction of a bridge between his innermost desire and the objective correlative manifested in the writers he names.

There is, however, an added dimension to Wright's choice of writers offered as his stimuli: they are those writers who by the 1930s, when he was at work on the autobiography, were the most prominent professional men of letters in America. While he may well have selected them for their ability as artists to make sense of a recognizable everyday reality, he also suggests that it was not their messages that enthralled him. Mencken in this regard is particularly relevant because he was not a fictionist but was one of the undisputed major professional writers in America. And the specific book that Wright mentions is *Prejudices*, which awed him because of the passionate way that Mencken "talked" about Anatole France, Joseph Conrad, "Sinclair Lewis, Sherwood Anderson, Dostoevsky, George Moore, Gustave Flaubert, Maupassant, Tolstoy, Frank Harris, Mark Twain, Thomas Hardy, Arnold Bennett, Stephen Crane, Zola, Norris, Gorky, Bergson, Ibsen, Balzac, Bernard Shaw, Dumas, Poe, Thomas Mann, O. Henry, Dreiser, H. G. Wells, Gogol, T. S. Eliot, Gide, Baudelaire, Edgar Lee Masters, Stendal, Turgenev, Huneker, Nietzsche," to use Wright's own list (*Black Boy*, 272). Mencken, then, was a writer, but he was also a man of letters, cosmopolitan in his intellectual interests and reflecting as much in his book of essays.

Wright's response to Mencken is direct: "I had once tried to write, had once reveled in feeling, had let my crude imagination roam, but the impulse to dream had been slowly beaten out of me by experience. Now it surged up again and I hungered for books, new ways of looking and seeing. It was not a matter of believing or disbelieving what I read, but of feeling something new, of being affected by something that made the look of the world different" (*Black Boy*, 272–73). The desire to become a writer was rekindled and intensified after it had been "beaten out" of his existence by the "experience" of his familial, racial, and social place in the southern bifurcated and divided world, which forbade black boys to dream. Importantly, as Wright concluded about his reading, "The plots and stories in the novels did not interest me so much as the point of view revealed" (273). One aspect of his interest in point of view was the enlarged perspective that it offered on life itself, "new ways of looking and seeing"; however, another was the increased light that it shed on the more nebulous process of writing itself.

There is no circumstantial evidence to account for the personality that Richard is from the age of four to nineteen, when *Black Boy* ends, or during his twenties, when *American Hunger* takes place. Indeed, he is a miracle, ultimately a creative genius who no friend or enemy can fully comprehend. He is the consummate hunger artist, devouring and destroying all so that his life might be fed: "All my life I had been full of a hunger for a new way to live" (*American Hunger*, 135). Wright foregrounds the connecting incidents of family, education, employment, and the codes of the white South in the first volume, and the Communist Party and codes of urban Chicago in the second, but these are all background for his telling the story of becoming an artist. The necessary foreground implicitly and insistently present throughout is the matter of his vision and art, and the interlocking of the two by means of his feelings. Ironically, however, he freezes his emotions in relationships with people—even those he presumes, intellectually, to love, such as his mother, about whom he says: "That night I ceased to react to my mother; my feelings were frozen. I merely waited upon her, knowing that she was suffering" (111). When he does so, the person becomes symbol ("My mother's suffering grew into a symbol in my mind") and becomes, concomitantly, the matter of his art. Abdul JanMohamed in *The Death-Bound Subject: Richard Wright's Archeology of Death* (2005) argues that "matricidal desires in *Black Boy* . . . [rely] on the unconscious logic of the death-dream-work, those desires manifest themselves only via figurative disguise that includes a fundamental 'racial' displacement from his 'black' mother to his 'white' grandmother."[41] In his analysis of Wright as a "death-bound-subject," JanMohamed charts the mother's influence on that subject formation.

Wright, however, is by the writing of *Black Boy* neither the subject nor the object of social death; instead he has emerged in life as the professional author par excellence. Unique and self-reliant or self-dependent, the author of achievement and distinction can disassociate the person that he is from what any reader may have expected him to become. But at the same time, he can lay claim to what he is by virtue of how he writes about what was. Zora Neale Hurston opens her negative review of Wright's *Uncle Tom's Children* with the observation: "This is a book about hatreds."[42] Yet she also makes a significant point that is applicable to both *Black Boy* and *American Hunger*: "What is new in . . . Mr. Wright's book is the wish-fulfillment theme." Mainly wrongheaded about Wright, Hurston instinctively seizes upon wish fulfillment that, along with the notion of being and becoming, is diffused through all of Wright's work but is central to his autobiographies as spaces of desire.

Throughout two autobiographies, Wright does indeed set up a series of straw men and women, customs and conventions, institutions and organizations whose primary objective is to knock Richard down, level his ambition, and trample his desires. These are straw figures of his imagination, even though they may have some basic correspondence with material bodies or embodied actualities. They are drawn as caricatures of the varied segments of the society, family, and culture, and they are conjured from Richard's controlling desire for self-divination. Each of the figures is, of course, defeated, so that Richard can rise up after each confrontation renewed out of the blood agony of almost defeat. His phoenixlike ascendancy over all adversaries ultimately marks him with the power of light over darkness, of superiority over inferiority, of fulfillment over failure. Moreover, his astute observations of the implications of his confrontations (including what was at stake in each one) make him uniquely suited to the task of telling the record of his youth that literally offers a personal, objectified version of a society. This larger social vision of connection and complexity between frightened, subservient blacks and cruel, brutalizing whites becomes a testimony to his fitness as teller-artist-writer.

The embattled, solitary, desiring, and determined Richard emerges ultimately triumphant through a series of oppositions that posit the culture and its arbitrators against authorship and literature: impoverishment (cultural, familial, racial)—nourishment (books and words); negation (societal)—affirmation (literature); violence (cultural)—solace or comfort (books and intellect); want, need (physical, emotional, religious, or spiritual)—necessity, satisfaction or gratification (in reading and writing); powerlessness (including the societal and familial mandate against fighting)—power (specifically fighting with words); silence—communication; chaos (family life and southern racism)—order (literacy and literature); dislocation (familial homelessness, social rootlessness)—place (traditions of literature and authorship); discontinuity (home and family life, parental breakdown, illness)—continuity (life of mind and literature); authority (paternal/maternal, patriarchal/matriarchal, white racial southern)—authority (self and words). Pitted against the negative, entrapping, situational, emotional, and environmental contexts are the positive, psychological contexts: Richard's individualized awareness of transition, change, and his undeterred commitment to transformation, transcendency, to the power of the word and the creator of the word.

An assessment by Ralph Ellison puts into perspective precisely the emphasis that Wright himself placed upon his autobiographies, his carefully structured simultaneous telling of his desire to become a writer and of his actualization of that desire. Ellison has observed that "there were good Negro writers before Wright arrived on the scene . . . but it seems to me that Richard Wright wanted more and dared more. . . . But at least Wright wanted and demanded as much as any novelist, any artist, should want: He wanted to be tested in terms of his talent, and not in terms of his race or his Mississippi upbringing. Rather, he had the feeling that his vision of American life, and his ability to project it eloquently, justified his being considered among the best of American writers."[43]

Wright claimed in *Black Boy* and *American Hunger* authority over his life, but primarily over his art. He basically said to his audiences that his fiction was no accident of reciting one's lived experience, but that it was the different ordering, analysis, and synthesis of a creative imagination. At the same time that he claimed autonomy as a creative writer through the disengagement from social and cultural institutions in the autobiographies, he rendered the creative act and the creative will, along with their independence. And he claimed as well a place in a literary community that he defined, though he knew better, as a mainly white club of acknowledged professional writers, which unlike the black writers from Chicago's South Side Writers' Workshop or those at New York's *New Challenge* magazine included nationally recognized writer-editors, such as Mencken, and a Nobel Laureate, Lewis, though Lewis was the only judge of the six for the *Story Magazine* contest to vote against Wright's winning manuscript, "Uncle Tom's Children." Perhaps because of, rather than in spite of, Wright's particular maturation in the white-dominated South and his initiation into publishing through the white-majority John Reed Club, he aligned himself with a tradition in which the main frame of reference for the artist and professional writer included few if any blacks.

Toward the end of *American Hunger*, as the procession of party members heads toward the Chicago Loop, Richard reveals: "I remembered the stories I had written, the stories in which I had assigned a role of honor and glory to the Communist party and I was glad that they were down in black and white, were finished. For I knew in my heart that I would never be able to write that way again, would never be able to feel with that simple sharpness about life, would never again express such passionate hope, would never again make so total a commitment of faith" (133). His disillusionment with organizational strictures in the northern urban setting, much like the socially and legally sanctioned segregation in the rural South, is plain, but in an oddly unsettling sense, so is his acquiescence to a majority opinion, the majority outside of the party, and his commitment to making it as a writer at the expense of any personal ideology. Memory and recollection conjoin to create a solution to ending the autobiography; both reflect backward not simply to the events of that day, when the procession of marchers and workers and party members forcibly prevented him from joining them and moved ahead without him, but also to the narrative that ends *Black Boy*. Necessarily, given the bridging process that Wright created in *Black Boy*, the words he chooses to express his disillusionment with the Communist Party replicate those emotions and perceptions summoned earlier and put into play the sites of memory that would both characterize and rationalize Wright's successive moves through the material and known world.

The projection from Mississippi to Illinois to New York can be traced as repetition that paradoxically cannot be duplicated. Each space presents the same and yet different antagonists with identifiable markers traceable back to preceding incidents. Racism, enacted differently but perceived similarly, remains constant in the shifting environment. A disillusioned Wright can move from New York to France, but once there, when the extenuating circumstances begin to impede his writing, he cannot catapult himself into a new place; for example, England will not approve his residency visa, and similarly the newly emerging African nations are too vulnerable to U.S. Cold War politics, and therefore he cannot find a new landscape in which to actuate his desires. France becomes the end point on the map of transformation and migration. Once the reality of his inability to actuate a new space for either his professional or personal life descends, Wright seemingly settles into despair, with back looking replacing the bridging and future-directed movement from his interiority to the externality of his literal world.

In *Black Boy*, Richard's discipline is achievement, which, in its enviable distinction of self separated from and elevated above others, discounts the necessity of love or hate or pity or fear. In the discipline of achievement without emotion, the randomness of experience is ordered, so much so that it is honed to intricate literary patterns of meaning that both establish and destroy the authority of the adversary. Quite clearly, selective memory is at work in Wright's shaping of the autobiography. In fact, when he was searching for a suitable subtitle, he considered "A Record of Remembrance, Childhood and Adolescence" to be the most descriptive, though he also found it clumsy. Edward Aswell at the publishing company Harper took care of the awkwardness by eliminating "Remembrance," a word that in my reading is not only appropriate but a key to Wright's strategy. The text itself serves as a memorial to Wright's own elaboration of desire.

Melvin Dixon, in *Ride out the Wilderness*, suggests that Wright, much like Ellison and Amiri Baraka (LeRoi Jones) or Zora Neale Hurston, Alice Walker, and Gayl Jones, "expands the parameters of cultural mobility previously restricted by gender, race, sexual exploitation, or the artistic struggle to create meaning out of chaos, which may be simply another word for wilderness."[44] In a section of his book entitled "Richard Wright: 'The Landless upon the Land,'" Dixon undergirds his analysis with Wright's 1935 poem "Between the World and Me," which he believes "introduced [Wright] to a literal wilderness that yielded a theme potent enough to preoccupy him through his career: the poet's alienation from the world around him."[45] Dixon links Wright to fugitive slaves in calling Wright's departure from the South an "escape": "It is no accident that Wright would stake his emergence as a writer upon his escape from the social status and 'place' prescribed for him. . . . His search for a literary voice, however, drew him back to the land that had alienated him; his song in a strange land required exile and return. The imaginative geography in his fiction reflects not only what he calls his 'self-achieved literacy,' but also his self-created space."[46] The emphasis on "self" and some other expressive aspect, literary or space, in Dixon's iteration is another mode of accessing the bridging central to Wright's process.

In extending his analysis of the landscapes of Wright's imaginative geography, Dixon contends: "His expatriation reflected the ultimate act of ownership: only a native son can disown a native land. A better understanding of this movement in Wright's fiction as well as his invention of spaces for refuge and regeneration is provided by examining those key scenes in his work, especially, 'The Man Who Lived Underground,' that shape his long and often tortuous attempt to locate self and home in the 'wider' orbit of his prose."[47] While Dixon's contention that Wright's expatriation is in fact an act of ownership of his native land is intriguing, his more consequential claim is that Wright invented "spaces for refuge and regeneration" within his writing. That recognition of Wright's writing itself as a space for protecting aspects of self and for modeling his subjectivity functions to reiterate the generative bridge work performed in *Black Boy* and *American Hunger*.

At the end of an essay treating Wright's correspondence, Edward Margolies asks: "Who was Wright? Did he really know himself? Poet, novelist, playwright, communist, existentialist, 'international,' revolutionary nationalist—but really always alone. His letters tell us that from the start he wanted to write for films, for radio; that he wanted to be a photographer, an actor, a war correspondent like Hemingway whom he envied; and toward the end of his life, he wanted to be editor of a crime magazine. Did he know really what he wanted?"[48] One answer is embedded in the very "facts" from Wright's letters and in the multiplicity of terms that Margolies uses to pose his question. That answer, simply put, is that Richard Wright wanted to be, and was, a professional writer, an artist sustaining himself by working within the aesthetic and practical realm of his chosen profession in all of its intersectional articulations. He was the artist-author that *Black Boy* and *American Hunger* unequivocally declared him to be.

III. SPATIAL LEGACIES AND SHAY YOUNGBLOOD'S PARIS

The experience of space and time is largely subconscious. We have a sense of space
because we can move, and of time because . . . we undergo recurrent phases of tension and
ease. The movement that gives us a sense of space is itself the resolution of tension.
—YI-FU TUAN, *Space and Place*

The determination to become a professional writer at the end of the twentieth century and the beginning of the twenty-first bears but little relation to
Wright's efforts, as does the relative absence of blacks earning a living by writing that characterized Langston Hughes's address to the Writers' Congress in
1939. Shay Youngblood entered university in a different era for prospective
writers and ultimately received a master's degree that would distinguish her
as an educated artist in ways that Wright would not have imagined possible.
Yet her movement over time and space in order to find the expressive opportunity in the physical geography she occupies aligns with Wright's own
movement in search of the place that would allow him to become a writer,
a professional in the field of letters. The fruits of Wright's becoming diffuse
not merely through writers who shared a relational identity with Mississippi,
but also discursively through black southerners who envision another kind of
spatial connection with Wright.

Youngblood, like Wright, moved outside of the U.S. context and into France
in order to chart the positive impact of spatial location on a writer raced
African American in the late twentieth century. She has said of her objectives: "I am interested in transformation, sparked by generational influence,
how traditions are passed on in different cultures, how an individual's actions
can create global, political, and social changes. I write as a call to action using
theatre as a verb."[49] In her writing, she seeks space in which to articulate and
act out the potent drama of those changes. Along with the regional identification of southerner, Youngblood adds queer and aligns her writerly orientation with James Baldwin's and his preoccupation with the South. While her
sojourn in France would not result in permanent expatriation, it does become
the subject of *Black Girl in Paris* (2000), which plays directly upon Wright's
relocation to France and his emergence as a model and artistic forefather for
Youngblood's protagonist, and presumably for Youngblood herself.

Youngblood's diasporic mobility suggests the contemporary corollary to
Wright's. She wrote her first published short story, "In a House of Wooden
Monkeys," which was selected by Gloria Naylor for her collection *Children
of the Night: The Best Short Stories by Black Writers, 1967 to the Present* (1997)

while serving in the Peace Corps as an agricultural information officer in Dominica (1981). Youngblood has also been a live-in au pair and an artist's model in Paris, work that informs her laundry list of survivalist jobs for her character Eden. In addition to her writing projects over the past several decades, she has also been a teacher of creative writing and of black women's literature and, most recently, a painter, a creative process that began with a writer's block following 9/11. Her circumnavigation of the Black Atlantic calls attention to late-capitalism and time-space compression. Wright's dream of becoming a professional writer and earning a living in the writing profession is increasingly more difficult to achieve, even for someone of Youngblood's training and talent, given the economics of national and global markets and the speed of production of new books and numbers of new authors.

Although Youngblood sets out the expatriate's discourse familiar from an earlier era, contemporary writers such as Rita Dove, Randall Kenan, Tina McElroy Ansa, Pearl Cleage, Elizabeth Brown Guillory, Yusef Komunyakaa, Sybil Kein, Natasha Trethewey, Gerald Barrax, Linda Beatrice Brown, Lenard Moore, Kevin Young, and Brenda Marie Osbey have found that they can have careers as writers and choose or not choose to live in the South, to self-identify or not as southern writers. Wright's long exile in France has become in the case of these writers not a viable model for how to be a writer. Several of these writers, for instance Osbey, have lived in Europe, but increasingly those stays are not permanent but part of youthful exploits and adventures, of self-discovery and global identification, of study abroad and educational exchanges and not at all a way of life. The experience of Europe by an Osbey or Youngblood, nonetheless, raises issues connected to space and gender and not merely to expatriatism or internationalism. As Katherine McKittrick points out: "That black women allow their particular surroundings to speak, and to be heard, reorients existing spatial practices, asking us to think not only about the 'where' of politics but how the production of space is not a silent process."[50]

For Youngblood, the spatial legacies of the expatriate generation inspired the format and the structure of her novel *A Black Girl in Paris*. Paying direct homage to Baldwin because of both his intricate connection to France and his overt attention to homosexuality, Youngblood maps her fiction as a literal search for Baldwin and a symbolic quest to become a writer. In the evolution of her protagonist, Eden, from a young woman living in the segregated South and limited in that space by the very structures of racial apartheid to a writer discovering in France her subject matter and her place within the expatriate community of artists, Youngblood rewrites Richard Wright's biographical narrative, retaining the connection to the segregated South but dispensing with the sojourn in the American North, Chicago and New York. Her fictional "Eden" becomes the bodily site of transformation into artist and the desired utopia for spatial relevancy.

According to Elizabeth Grosz, "The body and its environment . . . produce each other as forms of the hyperreal, as modes of simulation which have overtaken and transformed whatever reality each may have had into the image of the other: the city is made and made over into the simulacrum of the body, and the body, in its turn is transformed, 'citified,' urbanized as a distinctively metropolitan body."[51] Eden's transformation begins with her departure for Paris when she cuts her hair and becomes the androgynous face in the mirror. The act is in preparation for entering the city of Baldwin, Wright, and Langston Hughes, as that city has become the site of both liberation and cosmopolitanism, but it is also a site of memory. The city's function, when conflated with Eden's search and objective to relive the experiences of Wright, Baldwin, and Hughes, becomes commemorative. Its very spaces reference a culturally produced expatriate masculinity. Although gender and sexuality matter in the representation of Eden's Paris, Youngblood does not dismantle the master narrative already set in motion by the lives and writings of her antecedents. She performs a simple insertion and creative substitution through the materiality of the city and the overlapping structures of labor, leisure, and mobility.

While on the surface seemingly a continuation of Wright's modernist master narrative, Youngblood's text instead may be read as a postmodern spatial accumulation of fictional images linked to a transcribed and represented series of captured memorabilia and maps, arrested in photographic realism. Her method involves the occupying of space and constructing subjectivity by what might be called "pictorial tourism." Pictures of places on an urban map constitute the narrative points of interest. The process depends on the primacy of surface, of images, of visuality, the visual in drawings and photographs, in an effort to constitute the "real" within the realm of the imagined. The reproduction technology of the modern age is required to complete Youngblood's text, because pictorial images appear before the start of each chapter. These reproductions force a recognition of the interdependency of words and images in the text, and simultaneously they construct the "reality" of the text. These "real" objects represent the past that is being made present in the narrative. They also preserve the past as memory and preserve too the relationship between Eden's specific cultural past and her emerging social identity.

Objects function to authorize, authenticate, and legitimate Eden's narrative and to transmit visually her story as a history to a present generation of

readers and as a history connected to the known histories of the black expatriate writers before her. Using the surface of the page as a canvas for a
visual representation of images that are drawn, painted, or photographed,
Youngblood extends the range of verbal description and verbal pictures. Realistic, but also evoking the surreal, or a magnifying of some unnamed and
symbolic but as yet unidentifiable aspect of the ordinary, the images function
like pictograms or hieroglyphs in creating a pictorial representation of data or
relationships, concepts or ideas.

Space as the dimension for the wide range of social engagements represented in Youngblood's text is central to a reading of pictorial tourism as narrative method. "If time unfolds as change," Doreen Massey posits, "then space
unfolds as interaction. In that sense space is the *social* dimension. Not in the
sense of exclusively human sociability, but in the sense of engagement within
a multiplicity. It is the sphere of continuous production and reconfiguration
of heterogeneity in all its forms—diversity, subordination, conflicting interests."[52] Youngblood's method is spatial in its production, reconfiguration,
and imaging of interaction figured by means of Eden's social encounters in
the American South and in France, in constructed and built environments,
and with people from the United States, France and much of Europe, Britain,
Senegal and other African nations, and the Caribbean Islands, a world of relational spaces captured in pictures. The interactions, however, do not change
the material circumstances or the cultural identities and remain in the realm
of pictorial tourism, even when the process involves the production of a collage of images. Massey's warning seems pertinent: "Space is a collage of the
static."[53]

Pictionary is a game that comes to mind as a way of locating Youngblood's
pictorial tourism because it depends upon both the verbal and the visual
united in a search for legibility. The directions for the game require a picturist
but not a talent for drawing, an empathetic ability to image and communicate, but in restricted circumstances. At once low-tech in terms of equipment
needed and highly evolved in terms of the words put into play, Pictionary
became popular in the mid-1980s with a generation of young partygoers for
whom Scrabble was out of synch with the new omnipresent world of images
from television, print photojournalism, and Polaroid or other personal cameras with the availability of easy photo processing.

Just as a travel guide would incorporate pictures and maps into its verbal
descriptions without carrying a list of illustrations, yet would be dependent
upon those pictures and maps to complete the guide, so too Youngblood's
narrative includes at the beginning of each chapter photographs, maps, ticket

stubs, metro cards, etc., that are not identified in any list of inclusions yet function as an integral part of the text. Collages of visual aspects linked together seemingly at random but artfully arranged evoke a relationship to the adjacent chapter title and first page. They collapse the rigidity of forms and experiment with collage as a formal technique of narrative. Youngblood uses the artifacts (visas, stamps, metro tickets, etc.) from an actual sojourn in Paris as sites of memory, Nora's *lieux de mémoire*, to mark the material culture of her subject and to divide her fiction into sections that map her movement in France.

A photograph of a Paris skyline that includes the Louvre, a postal cancellation marked "Paris Louvre CTC" and the encircled date "10 9 86," an "*Entrée Plein Tarif*" for thirty-nine francs for "*Réunion des Musée Nationaux*," and a "Historical Plan of the Louvre" make up the opening collage. The grouping appears opposite the start of the first chapter, entitled "museum guide." (All of the chapter titles are in lowercase, which in effect both reduces them all to the same level and negates their singular significance.) The design functions so that pictures, words, and numbers are legible and balanced against the verbal image on the opposing page. The map of the Louvre occupies the dominant place in the middle of the images and mirrors in spatial placement the opening paragraph:

> *Paris, September 1986. Early morning. She is lying on her back in a hard little bed with her eyes closed, dreaming in French.* **Langston was here.** *There is a black girl in Paris lying in a bed on the fifth floor of a hotel in the Latin Quarter. Her eyes are closed against the soft pink dawn. Delicate maps of light line her face, tattoo the palms of her hands, the insides of her thighs, the soles of her feet.* **Jimmy was here.** *She sleeps while small, feminine hands plant a bomb under the seat of a train headed toward the city of Lyon.*[54]

The opening is as visual as the collage preceding it. The second paragraph shifts voice from the third to the first person and adds the explanatory context for Langston and Jimmy and for the notion of "a black girl in Paris":

> James Baldwin, Langston Hughes, Richard Wright, Gabriel García Márquez and Milan Kundera all lived in Paris as if it had been part of their training for greatness. When artists and writers spoke of Paris in their memoirs and letters home it was with reverence. Those who have been and those who still dream mention the quality of the light, the taste of the wine, the *joie de vivre*, the pleasures of the senses, a

kind of freedom to be anonymous and also new. I wanted that kind of life even though I was a woman and did not yet think of myself as a writer. *I was a map-maker.* (1–2; Youngblood's italics)

Each of the subsequent collages of images beginning the chapters includes a map, a reproduction of a plan of the exterior spaces and interior places of tourism (Montmartre, Cimetière Montparnasse, Versailles, Champs Élysées, École des Beaux-Arts). These maps combine with photographs of French francs and iconic scenes (Eiffel Tower, Arc de Triomphe, the Seine, outdoor café, etc.), or pictures of ephemera (postage stamps, admission tickets, train and metro tickets).

Indirectly, Paris for Eden, the twenty-six-year-old protagonist and first-person narrator, becomes the point of possibility not yet available for full subject formation in the newly integrated but still racially problematical South adhering to a flawed historicized memory of domestic and subservient blacks. Set in 1986, the period I call the major transition and change for black Americans, *Black Girl in Paris* occurs at the moment when the set and fixed narratives of black individual and communal identity are becoming less applicable as blacks are dispersed throughout integrated educational environments and professional workplaces. It is in effect an effort on the part of Youngblood to go back and recapture some of the lost underpinnings of identity no longer accessible in a changed world. The epigraph from Toni Morrison's *Beloved* suggests as much: "If you go there in the place where it was, it will happen again; it will be there for you waiting."

Eden's development as a writer is straightforward: "I made up stories and acted out the little dramas for my parents, playing all the parts myself. I wrote sad poems about orphans, and I moved through my life taking pictures with a toy camera, recording things in my mind, writing them down between the lines of other books" (20). Given a typewriter at thirteen, she wrote a novel in fourteen days: "I wrote all the stories I knew and made up new ones" (20). It was her reading of Langston Hughes's autobiography, *The Big Sea*, that convinced her to be a writer and go to Paris. Eden's "little-girl dream" is simple: "'When I go to Paris I will leave behind the little orphan girl and all I will take with me is her body and some of her clothes. I'll make maps so other people can get there too, adventurers like me'" (21).

Michel de Certeau distinguishes between "map" and "itinerary." The map "colonizes space; it eliminates little by little the pictural figurations of the practices that produced it."[55] A map is constituted of "abstract places." A map "is a 'theater' (as one used to call atlases) in which the same system of projection nevertheless juxtaposes two very different elements: the data furnished by a tradition (Ptolemy's *Geography*, for instance) and those that came from navigation (portulans, for example). The map thus collates on the same plane heterogeneous places, some *received* from a tradition and other *produced* by observation."[56]

The term "map" recurs throughout *Black Girl in Paris* and *Soul Kiss* (1997), Youngblood's first novel. Encoded in literal movement, "maps" allow for the experience of defining place and orienting values in the everyday. Map is a key term in Youngblood's critical and creative vocabulary. "Before I left home," Eden remembers, "I cut my hair close to my scalp so I could be a free woman with free thoughts, open to all possibilities. I was making a map of the world" (3). The map for her is an articulation of desire, to move, to access, to navigate. It is not a destination but the process toward the "abstract places" Certeau identifies. The end objective is never fixed, but rather a location or orientation of the body.

Black Girl in Paris echoes the title of Wright's *Black Boy*. Youngblood's narrative models itself both on the driving desire Wright expressed for propelling himself into becoming a writer in his autobiographical text and on the spatial adventures encountered in various jobs and failed employment deployed to structure his movement into the only logical work—writing—that could satisfy his psychological and material hunger. Even though the plotline of *Black Girl in Paris* evokes a search for a sighting of James Baldwin as literary progenitor, it is the long-dead Richard Wright who pervades the text as a black person who not only wrote of the development of his consciousness of the power of words and writing to effect lives, but who also became that writer whom he himself had envisioned. The novel follows Carlene Hatcher Polite in utilizing transnationality and subjectivity as markers of identity for the emergent black woman artist.[57] Like Wright and Baldwin, Youngblood is invested in the subject formation of a black, U.S. national whose citizenship is delimited by both race (racism) and class. Eden announces: "My name is Eden, and I'm not afraid of anything anymore. Like my literary godfathers who came to Paris before me, I intend to live a life in which being black won't hold me back" (4). Before her departure for Paris, however, Eden is also constructed as a particularly southern young woman.

Eden's inspiration for her trip to Paris is rooted in her identity as southern and queer. Her earliest years were filled with the explosive violence whites perpetrated when blacks sought equal rights. Born in Birmingham, Alabama, she remembers when the city was "Bombingham," and when "the four little girls were killed by a segregationist's bomb at church one Sunday morning in 1963" (5). After her parents lived through eighteen bombings in six years, the family moved to Georgia, though Eden remained afraid of being blown up: "I slept at the foot of my parents' bed until I was eleven years old, when my mother convinced me that the four little girls were by now colored angels and would watch over me as I slept. But I didn't sleep much, and for most of my childhood I woke up each morning tired from so much running in my dreams—from faceless men in starched white sheets, from policemen with dogs, from firemen with water hoses" (5). Remembered anxieties about atrocities committed against black children constitute a major platform for Eden's construction of identity. The violence against blacks in the American South continues in memory and in pictures for Eden and influences her thinking about the "unfreedom" of black life, especially her own, in the United States. Ironically, the very memory of "Bombingham" makes it possible for Eden to endure the bombings that are rampant in France upon her arrival, and that memory forms a connecting image of the ravages of terror on an emotional and psychic landscape.

The immediate impetus for going to Paris is linked in part to the existence of a buried and unfulfilled life. After college, Eden works in a southern residence, Villa Luisa, the Dimple mansion, built by a Simon Dimple, "the richest black man born into slavery" (21) and the son of a white plantation owner. The Italian mansion is furnished with French and English antiques and European art because its last owner, Simon's son Mason Dimple, "hated anything too black and too African" (24). The house is a memorial to his family, who made a fortune from his Plantation Restaurant. Simon built the "White Only" restaurant with his wife, Daisy, a French-speaking octoroon from Louisiana, who with her brothers passed as white to buy the land and hire laborers. True to its name, the Plantation Restaurant evoked the "good old days" of old-fashioned food and an imagined and unreal southern past when blacks were happy to serve "with a grin and a shuffle" and to be subservient to whites. In this work at the Plantation Restaurant, black women dressed like Aunt Jemima and black men served in white uniforms, though with a nod to Uncle Ben. That was the key to the restaurant's success: "The novelty of whites being served in the manner of their ancestors by a wait staff that reminded them of the good old days" (25). Class intersects with race in the Dimple history. The production of capital by raced bodies extends the exploitation of black labor into a public sphere of constructed nostalgia and desire (queer desire).

Eden's regional identification functions to magnify her gendered, racial, and sexual identities—their intersectionality and fluidity in Eden's subject formation. Within this section of the narrative, Youngblood evokes the problematical reconstruction of history, but moreover, the effect of selective forgetting and remembering. Villa Luisa has been turned into a museum or a memorial to a dead man, though ultimately its function is, as Pierre Nora concludes about history, "to annihilate what has in reality taken place," which for Dimple involved his unfulfilled dreams and suppressed loves. Dimple, a gay man who could not within his social and cultural milieu admit and live his sexual identity openly, becomes a monument to a capitalist dream of success and wealth. The disjuncture between the material wealth Dimple inherited and that surrounded him externally and the impoverished existence of repression and isolation that marked his lived experience moves Eden into an awareness of her "orphan" state and her loneliness. She reads Dimple's conflicted sexual identity in conjunction with her own. She recalls that as a thirteen-year-old, she experienced "make-out" sex, "touching games" with both her childhood friend, Rosaleen, and with Rosaleen's older brother, Anthony, and that she desired both. With Rosaleen's loss to an early pregnancy, the death of the child, and Rosaleen's banishment to a distant city, Eden believes she will never know love again. Functioning outside the heteronormative boundaries of desire, Eden hides her experience and displaces her needs onto the hidden and secret narrative of Dimple.

Eden calls Villa Luisa "the house of dead things" (21). Hired to help the director of the museum that the mansion has become and to catalogue the family's collections, she senses before she uncovers its secrets that the house entombed its residents. The director, Dr. Edgar Bernard, a married but lonely man, has dedicated his life to preserving the memory of Mason Dimple, who sent him to Yale and made him his secretary and traveling companion. The secret Eden discovers in Dimple's hidden notebook and love letters is that Bernard was also Mason Dimple's lover. The couple spent their happiest and freest days in Europe, where they celebrated their love. That discovery and a tearful statement of encouragement from Bernard ("'Don't take only what life gives you, reach out and take what you want,'" [33]) propel Eden into actualizing her dream.

The deformation inherent within the existence of Villa Luisa as a way of (re)organizing the past is counterbalanced by the other aspect of Eden's desire to experience Paris: the memory of her Aunt Victorine, a woman free within her self. Aunt Vic, who takes Eden "on the first Saturday morning of each month for blessings at the Church of Modern Miracles," has urged her to seek the City of Light, where "black people are free. . . . Free to live where you wanted, work where you were qualified and love who you wanted. At least that was the rumor that she had heard" (16). Aunt Vic encouraged dreams of Paris: "From the first time she showed me on a map she drew with a broken pencil on her kitchen wall and told me that black people were free in Paris" (16). A place of freedom from the racism blacks experience in the United States is the utopic space Aunt Vic imagines and bestows on her "daughter" Eden, who has already been an artist in the making, a child singer-dancer in a juke joint: "I would sing songs I heard on Aunt Vic's record player. Aunt Vic taught me how to lift the hem of my dress and dance at the end of the song like Josephine Baker and the French can-can dancers who looked so glamorous in the photographs she showed me. The audience would throw handfuls of change and crumbled dollar bills at my dancing feet. . . . If Mama hadn't found out when I was thirteen, I might have become a star on the dirt-floor circuit" (18). By thirteen, nevertheless, Eden is fully imagining herself doing the can-can in Paris like Josephine Baker, who was for Eden "a symbol of complete freedom" (20).

The important function Aunt Vic served was to free the girl's imagination. She not only told stories of her old life as a dancer in Chicago, but she also "showed pictures" (20). These dual images inspire Eden to dream, especially of Paris: "I made maps in my mind that would lead to other worlds" (18). This strategy is a way of instituting living memory and of breaking out of the linear and spatial organization of an identification with a regional history and with "in-placedness" for black bodies. It is also a way of foregrounding the "inner geography" functioning within the text. Within this map of remembering, Eden sets out the collapsed boundaries between the spaces of emancipation familiar to Aunt Vic and the global capitalism figured on the bodies of transgressive black women like Baker who disrupt the old but cannot overcome the divisions implicit in class, place, race, and space.

The landscape of the South has become something very different from the local that Wright represented in his fictions of rural Mississippi. Youngblood's "dirt-floor circuit," enmeshed with references to the political and social economy of Paris in the 1920s and 1930s, creates a black public space corresponding to a platform of social capital and economic empowerment that is cognizant of the global. It is not merely a space of incarceral mandates from a white power structure for policing unruly or improperly socialized blacks. It is instead a space that, while still circumscribed by the remnants of a white-supremacist past, nonetheless admits the slight possibility of black development. It is also a space that, by means of the lives of Dr. Bernard and Aunt Vic and their real and imagined interconnections with Europe, functions in conjunction with a wider globalism against fixity and stasis, which Eden believes better accommodates difference, supports stepping out of place, and encourages dreams.

Importantly, too, Paris, the urban international cityscape, is not the one that Baldwin found in freeing himself from the constricted spaces of New York. While France still signifies freedom, it no longer constitutes an idealized, race-free, post-Fordism zone. It is both a discursive space and a set of economic power relations. Africans get deported. Bombs explode in political confrontations. Terror exists and is not contained by authorities or expectations. Alternative communities exist on the edge of society, in alternate places mainly hidden, vulnerable, unstable, unsafe, and insecure. Oppression continues in the marketplace. Expatriatism for Eden is constituted in economic realities, work and subsistence labor.[58] The network of workers she encounters is part of what Linda McDowell has analyzed as part of gender discrimination in a dual or segmented labor market, which is a secondary sector, predominantly composed of women, with low wages, poor work conditions, no job security, and few if any opportunities for advancement.[59] Eden and those she encounters in her effort to survive are primarily those who are perpetually foreign or different enough that they too experience the city as a migratory, shifting, and transporting space.

Whereas Eden's literary forebears had necessarily to leave for Europe because of racial discrimination and racial oppression, she is not compelled to leave the country in order to become a writer. That she does so is, in part, due to her sense of nostalgia for the way in which the careers of Wright and Baldwin took shape. Eden's nostalgia may be read in conjunction with Houston A. Baker's usage of nostalgia as "homesickness" in "Critical Memory and the Black Public Sphere." This homesickness is for a space of belonging that she has yet to experience. "I needed a map to help me find love and language," Eden muses, "and since one didn't exist, I'd have to invent one following the trails and signs left by other travelers. I didn't know what I wanted to be but I knew I wanted to be the kind of woman who was bold, took chances and had adventures" (3). In other words, a woman who could appropriate the history of black male expatriate writers, sashay across the City of Light, and find her own way. She conjoins and conflates "love and language," just as she conjoins sexuality and writing. She can define herself and her vocation by knowing that movement itself contains the logic, the map, necessary to define home, and ultimately belonging and place—or, at the opposite end, homelessness.

Eden's maps may be read according to Denis Cosgrove's conception of the map as "both the spatial embodiment of knowledge and a stimulus to further cognitive engagements" (2). Chapter titles duplicate and announce the "work" and relational identities Eden executes in Paris. They are supplemented by the pictorial collages of maps and memorabilia as prefix to each chapter. Her work identities are not exclusive, though they are successive. As museum guide, traveling companion, artist's model, au pair, poet's helper, lover, English teacher, thief (Eden's occupations in France that function as chapter titles and her epistemology of Paris and her inner geography), Eden works her map of adventures and becomes a witness, a *flâneur*, walking around Paris and observing the inhabitants of stories she concocts while being a spectator to her own movement through space. She first becomes in Paris an "ordinary practitioner of the city," as Certeau terms walkers experiencing the city from "down below": "These practitioners make use of spaces that cannot be seen."[60] In a landscape of internationals, students, musicians, artists, expatriates, émigrés, illegals, and workers of every stripe, Eden learns the city from below, on foot much of the time and with few financial resources despite the jobs she obtains. "Paris at night, on foot, is beautiful," Eden observes, "even if you are cold, hungry and tired. Everywhere I looked, something interesting caught my eye" (191). Her city is both magical and brutal, especially with the onslaught of terror and violence, the bombings, the demonstrations against apartheid and student unrest.

Moving through the city on foot, Eden finds beauty not only in the urban space but also in her own body. The suggestion Certeau makes that the "act of walking is to the urban system what the speech act is to language"[61] seems connected to Eden's way of experiencing Paris, her "spatial acting-out of language." She performs the city by means of the words she reconstitutes from and out of the movements of her expatriate forebears, and she remains a tourist. For her there is no process of translation in the sense that Stuart Hall describes in "Cultural Identity and Diaspora," in which native-born and émigré populations come together both to accept their differences and to embrace the change that their translated identities bring to the culture as a whole.[62] As a tourist in posed pictures, Eden remains the "American" who is not assimilating into Paris but touring Paris in the process of retracing the footsteps of those other Americans as they performed expatriatism.

Because Baldwin, Wright, Hughes, and the other writers of that generation have already created a mythical space in the magical city Paris, Eden cannot sustain anything like a concrete *real* place. All is referencing, citation, allusion. Her social practice, different from theirs, and separated from theirs by temporal conditions and human geography, cannot be meshed with theirs. Her social experience is nonetheless both a search for Baldwin and also for "place," that is, belonging. Eden attempts to make the black expatriates of an earlier generation, her "tradition" by occupying the same space they once inhabited. By the end of the novel, it becomes apparent that Eden cannot inhabit their Paris. Eden's Paris is discursive, what Certeau calls "verbalized, dreamed, or walked": "To walk is to lack a place. It is the indefinite process of being absent and in search of a proper. The moving about that the city multiplies and concentrates makes the city itself an immense social experience of lacking a place—an experience that is, to be sure, broken up into countless tiny deportations (displacements and walks), compensated for by the relationships and interconnections of these exoduses that intertwine and create an urban fabric, and placed under the sign of what ought to be, ultimately, the place but is only a name, a City."[63]

Eden can gesture toward Baldwin and his practice, but tracing his steps is ultimately futile. Her difference from Baldwin and her different temporal location, neither of which is fully recognized, make it impossible for Eden to accomplish the recovery of Baldwin (and with it, the experiences of Wright, Hughes, and others) or to achieve her ambition to become a writer through his (and their) experiences. Put another way, in terms of spatial politics, Eden is unable to decipher "the ways in which identities and places are being transformed and reconnected, positioning people with new patterns, or geometries, of inclusion and exclusion."[64] Simultaneously, Eden is both open to her experiences on the streets of Paris and closed to the implications they have on her desire to become a writer.

Finding James Baldwin does not finally become Eden's route to writing. After traveling to the area of St. Paul de Vence in hopes of meeting Baldwin, Eden discovers that he is in Paris after all, but moreover, that he does not hold "some kind of secret about love and life and writing" (231). The apotheosis is not unexpected given the images that accumulate around her observations and experiences in Paris: "I wrote down the things I was most afraid of: the maps of desire. Ving. The taste of need. Lucienne" (231). Using the gold pen given to her by Dr. Edgar Bernard when she departed Villa Luisa, Eden began what she had not yet done in Paris: "[B]etween my tears words began to bloom on the page, one after the other. Words crowded each other, trying to lead me out of despair. I was exuberant. The maps I'd made were guides to my interior. I remembered all the places I'd been, all the things I'd seen, and I caught them in my imagination. Jimmy was with me and Langston too. I understood where I had been, where I was going, to make sense of the world that had led me to the small room on the edge of the abyss" (231).

Ving, the New Orleans–born white musician, and Luce (Lucienne Marie-

Claire Héloise Rousseau), born in Barbados to a French mother who disappeared, become the two poles of desire for Eden. The two function to undermine some of the masculine elements in the construction of Eden in the city as shadowing Wright and Baldwin. Gender relations, however, seem removed ultimately from the context of aesthetic production. Existing in an in-between space does not emerge as an option for the subjectivity that Youngblood develops for Eden. Both heterosexual power and masculine hegemony are reconstituted and reaffirmed at the end. Neither Luce, who is ill, nor Eden, who is fearful, can imagine a way to remain together, so extreme is their poverty and so limited their options. Ving, androgynous and a cross-dresser when a young boy and sexually abused by his mother, is there unambiguously figured at the end, even when the writing comes mixed in dream and reality:

> In my dream someone was building a house underwater. I awoke to the sound of hammering. Someone was beating on the door. When I opened it Ving was standing there, as handsome as his music. I clung to him, kissing his face and neck.
> *Truly beloved.*
> This was not a dream. I had discovered something that no one could take away from me. I had found a path on my interior map and learned to follow it. There was power in the pen. . . . I didn't need Jimmy to tell me that. (232)

Yet, in the way in which the boundaries dissolve between the search for Baldwin and the onset of writing, Eden has served an apprenticeship to her mentor(s) without intimate contact, and "apprentice" is the one job description and work designation that does not appear as a chapter heading. The mentors whose aesthetic experience she desires and whose life experiences she appropriates may have stood outside conventional patriarchal structures; nevertheless, there is no escaping the fact that they represent an existing power structure and hierarchy from which Eden is excluded.

The final chapter, "witness," however, returns to James Baldwin figured in the quest for literary forebears and for permission to write. Eden spots a frail, aging, and weak Baldwin from across Boulevard St-Germain: "Baldwin raised his hand and waved in my direction as if he had read my mind. Do you think I can do it too? Then he nodded and I thought I saw his lips moving over the words. *Yes, soul sister, you can do anything*" (235). The apocryphal meeting that almost did not happen occurs on Eden's last day in Paris and from a remove, but it results in something more tangible than the imagined words. A waiter rescues something from Baldwin's table and offers it to Eden, whom he understands is a friend of the American: "The waiter handed me a map of London. . . . When I opened the map I realized that what I held in my hand was a treasure. Words were scrawled across the lines of the map like directions. They were so small and wild I could barely make them out, but it was as if he was speaking to me" (236). The words on the map conclude Eden's search and her stay in Paris:

> One word at a time
> story by story
> mile by mile
> let the sound of the voices carry you the distance
> welcome.

Baldwin's scribbled words on a map of another city, London and not Paris, both transpose the spatial structure of the text to a different plane of readability and transform the function of the map to articulate his relationship to Eden as one of the improbable possible. The subject formation modeled in *Black Girl in Paris* and charted in Baldwin's message goes against the unbridled individualism and conscious difference that constituted Richard's formation in *Black Boy*. It unsettles what might constitute an expatriate black experience gendered differently from Wright and Baldwin, but in the passing of power from a fading Baldwin to an emerging Eden, it retains a deference to their way of being an artist of words.

In her first novel, *Soul Kiss*, Youngblood also organized her subject by means of mobility and mappings that chart the maturation and the queering of Mariah, the young protagonist, as a "southerner" newly constituted in a changed relation to stasis and fixity of place or gender. An extraordinary coming-of-age story, *Soul Kiss* displays the complicated textures of late twentieth-century lives and narrates a transformative reality and beauty beyond the natural confines of any complacency with things as they are or are supposed to be. The opening sentence sets a poetic tone for the entire text, and with that tone the place of textuality and sensuality in the developmental processes of Mariah:

> The first evening Mama doesn't come back, I make a sandwich with leaves from her good-bye letter. I want to eat her words. I stare at the message written on the stiff yellowed paper as if the shaky scrawl would stand up and speak to me. *Mama loves you. Wait here for me.* I want her to take back the part about waiting. After crushing the paper into two small balls I flatten them with my fist, then stuff them into the envelop my aunt

Faith gave me after Mama had gone. I feel weak as water and stone cold as I set with my legs dangling over the edge of the thick mattress on the high iron-frame bed, reading by the dim lamplight.[65]

Mariah's love for her mother is refracted through her love for words, taught to her by her mother who devised word games to entertain and bond with her daughter. Her mother, thus, arms Mariah for life with the gifts of orality and textuality. Because of its celebration of language as an intricate part of development and maturation and its insistence on the specificity of place, *Soul Kiss* can be connected to a long line of major texts in African American and southern literature. The novel received critical acclaim for its lyrical intelligence, its confident subjectivity, its nuanced eroticism, and not the least for its beautiful writing, its "exquisite, loving attention to language and story," as novelist Tina McElroy Ansa put it.[66]

Home in *Soul Kiss* is fluid, and movement is part of the migratory experience and people of all races and ethnicities. Marked by displacement and rupture, the narrative begins on a military base in Kansas, relocates to a town in Georgia, and, after a bus trip across the United States to Los Angeles, takes in the multiethnic California scene before concluding back in Georgia. Mariah's mother, Coral, a nurse on a military base, leaves her daughter with her relatives in Georgia and never returns for her, but her quirky maternal nurturing gives her daughter a tactile, aural, visual, and oral facility that stamps her life and makes her amazingly resistant to destruction from relocation and displacement. Matisse, Mariah's father, is Joe El Jr., a painter who never married her mother but loves her long after their several intense weeks together end and accepts his daughter into his home in California as a way of honoring his relationship with Coral and constructing a form of family for Mariah. In each new place, there is a clustering around the familiar, maps of similar people with similar needs, though not necessarily similar backgrounds. Clarence Mondale equated the "pull of the familiar in the inner life of the individual migrant" to the "pull of gravity in the physical world."[67] *Soul Kiss*, like the later work of Alice Walker, moves "southern" writing into a larger twenty-first-century, transnational, cross-cultural, and diasporic space in which people have global connections and global dreams.

"Alone in my room that night," Mariah ends her story, "I write down the last word my mother gave me. *Water*. I lift the edge of the paper to my lips and I drink it off the page, swallow it in two long syllables until it meets the place that is burning as brightly as day. . . . I am light as a page in a blank book. I feel empty but somehow whole. . . . The sun comes out and the grass is green again and the taste of water is sweet. I write poems and draw maps of language" (206). The conclusion of this first novel underlines the premise of Youngblood's second. Denis Cosgrove observed that "the mapping's record is not confined to the archival; it includes the remembered, the imagined, the contemplated. The world figured through mapping may thus be material or immaterial, actual or desired, whole or part, in various ways experienced, remembered or projected. . . . Acts of mapping are creative, sometimes anxious, moments in coming to knowledge of the world."[68] The acts of mapping in both of Youngblood's novels interconnect the remembered and the imagined.

Youngblood explores homoerotic desire and the discovery of its unarticulated boundaries when she writes about the erotic attraction between young girls, between mother and daughter, or between father and daughter in *Soul Kiss*, yet she explodes notions of "deviant" sexual behavior by normalizing her protagonist's dressing in her father's clothes while masturbating to his pornography as actions of utter loneliness and aloneness, not of sexual desire. The point, however, is not to shock or incite, but rather to consider the erotic as a factor in the maturation and development of social beings and social relations. For instance, as a young girl, Mariah names her cello Rosemary, and the music she makes becomes an extension of her body as well as of her interconnectedness with people. The cello communicates directly with what Marlene Nourbese Philip names "the space between" as a way of identifying a distinctly gendered female space.[69] For Mariah, it is through this space that she redefines herself as a subject. Put another way, with the erotic interaction with male clothing, pornography, words, and music in Mariah's development, Youngblood produces a black queer female sexuality. The child of atypical parents with truncated emotional connections, Mariah forms a fluid nonheteronormative identity for herself accessed by means of music embodied by the tactile surface and shape of the cello and images articulated as graphic, sexual, and pornographic. Evelynn Hammonds, in thinking through black queer female sexualities, observes that they do not correspond to simple identities: "Rather they represent discursive and material terrains where there exists the possibility for the active production of speech, desire, and agency."[70]

A destruction of space, the collapse of the Twin Towers in New York City on 9/11, propelled Youngblood into a different configuration of creative expression. Since then, she has moved into a compression of her verbal articulation because she found it difficult to express herself in words on paper. A writer's block caused a redirection of her creativity. She turned to a different formal medium, painting on canvas and paper. Words became secondary to the images drawn in one clearly delineated and confined space. With the material destruction of the Twin Towers came a closing off of the infinitude of written language and a concomitant turning away from the writing of fiction and drama. The searing images of the destruction of space, however, moved Youngblood to a visceral containment in visual art, to drawing and painting within already determined boundaries. Sample titles include "queer crossing the bridge of sighs"; "Mississippi Madonna"; "let the cry come out"; "Under the Pink"; "dream 1: touch me / there are roses under my cypress"; and "facing facts: here is my broken body."[71] The words appear within the frames compressed as part of the image. On her website (shayyoungblood.com), she has posted the following statement of her praxis:

> [A]fter 9/11 language became an obstacle for me. I couldn't find words to express my grief, horror or rage at what I had witnessed. It is still difficult to write about the dangerous and uncertain times we live in now. Since 2002 I have found a new expression in painting. I create multi-layered, textured narratives that explore inner landscapes, the concept of the duality of home, fear versus faith, transgressive transformation and multiple identities. Drawing on my dreams, personal narratives, scenes from my written work and current events I use architectural forms, quilt patterns and sacred images to define the space on canvas. I use pens and sharp objects to write on the layered surfaces, scratching and erasing, adding and taking away, to reveal the stories underneath. The images surprise me and yet when they are done I can see that I have told myself another story.

Youngblood's analysis is fascinating because it details her turn to "architectural forms, quilt patterns, and sacred images," in a sense to established structures within the specified worlds of design and building, of domestic and sacred artwork. Within these already mapped worlds there are exact and exacting technologies, ontologies, and epistemologies, which require compliance with dexterity on the part of the artist.

This turning to the strictures of these maps in a time of crisis, "grief, horror or rage," and with it to a necessary compression of words into a contained space, reminds me of Richard Wright at the end of his life in Paris turning to pictorial images in haiku for expression. Under constant surveillance and repeated attacks from the United States and its various agents, Wright's world narrowed and with it his ability to maintain his standard of living. His previous responses to spatial restriction and bodily constraints had been movement and relocation in order to obtain a new measure of freedom. In his final period in Paris, however, he was trapped and immobile. Because his visa was denied, he was unable to leave France for England, where his wife and daughters had relocated. He continued with his fiction, but even his most supportive editor cautioned that the materials he proposed exploring in two novels seemed less than promising.

During this period of anxiety, combined with the stress of illness, Wright turned to the compressed emotion contained within an equally compressed space in the haiku. He wrote some 4,000 in the eighteen months before his death on 28 November 1960. In several of the haiku published in *New Letters*, he speaks to the pressures and threats from which bodily action cannot free itself. In another, he iterates the lingering sickness with which he suffered in his last months and figures death in the ill body's absence from the sickbed while leaving its trace on the pillow. In still others, he contemplates the natural world in relation to his feelings, particularly of loss, loneliness, and emptiness.[72] In a number of the haiku, references to autumn, the season of Wright's birth, signal transition into aloneness, isolation, and erasure; Wright also infuses autumn in some poems with allusions to his mother, who died in January 1959.[73]

Hazel Rowley states that Wright was "possessed" by haiku: "A form of meditation, they gave Wright a modicum of inner peace in the worst period of despair and self-doubt he had ever known."[74] But there may be another way of framing Wright's turn to haiku—that is, as a form of the spatial. Within the rigid formal demands and the spatial exactness of the three-line Japanese haiku, Wright found a map to chart, discipline, and concentrate mobility and creativity. The structured production then would result in as much a control over space and spatial location of subjectivity as an expression of ordering the emotional nexus and psychological matrix out of control in his material life. His crisis, like Youngblood's post-9/11 crisis of representation, led to formal spatial compression, to a reduction of narration and mobility of form into the very essence of confinement that necessitated his previous struggles and search for external spaces different from the constrictions of southern life.

chapter four

Politics & Paysans

MULTICULTURAL LOUISIANA
& THE SPACE OF THE CRÉOLITÉ

I. MUTABLE GEOGRAPHIES

The space in which we live, which draws us out of ourselves, in which the erosion of our
lives, our time and our history occurs, the space that claws and knaws at us, is also, in itself,
a heterogeneous space. In other words, we do not live in a kind of void, inside of which we
could place individuals and things. We do not live inside a void that could be colored with
diverse shades of light, we live inside a set of relations that delineates sites which are
irreducible to one another and absolutely not superimposable on one another.
—MICHEL FOUCAULT, "Of Other Spaces" (1986)

Any space occupied by people of African descent in the United States is contested. Escape to other places inevitably becomes marred by the floating signifiers of U.S. racial-spatial ideology, as Richard Wright discovered in the mid-twentieth century. Retracing Wright's footsteps, Shay Youngblood mapped the problematic of spaces outside the United States for people of the African diaspora. By the end of the twentieth century, Youngblood's Paris had changed over time and was at once the place of Richard Wright's expatriate refuge and the place of bombings that linked it to Birmingham and another rights struggle by people of color.

History repeats in the clashes and the narratives of contested space; however, the stories across time and space are not precisely the same. They repeat differently as landscapes and as bodies, and with, Youngblood suggested, the burdens of desire and need circulating through the construction of the two. In *Black Girl in Paris*, Eden, the narrator from the American South, understands desire and need as place-specific but attenuated as Creole space and disaporic body. Along with Ving, Louisiana-born musician, and Luce, mixed-race Barbadian cosmopolitan, Eden flows between spaces and through histories in an effort to create anew. Success is not assured.

The very identification of black people with geographical space results in a transformation to "raced" space with all of the intact markers of racism. Within the regulatory boundaries of raced space, black people experience both containment in narrow spatial parameters and exclusion from larger social practices. This practice, termed the spacialization of race, isolates blacks within structures of disorder, decay, and crime, most often identified simply as "the ghetto."[1] This "racial geography" results from practices of power and of privilege inscribed in law and custom, but which historically and socially have mandated a one-dimensional narrative of U.S. space and black bodies within that geographical configuration.[2] The struggle blacks then face is not merely to transgress the fixed boundaries and the resultant social conditions but also to construct the subjective ground that is heterogeneous, fluid, and counterhegemonic.[3] Fluidity and heterogeneity especially become the measures of potential success to which raced writers who constituted new spaces out of their "experience" of Mississippi might attest. Houston Baker observes, "all fixed points are problematical": "Fixity is a function of power. Those who maintain place, who decide what takes place and dictate what has taken place, are power brokers of the traditional. The 'placeless,' by contrast, are translators of the nontraditional. Rather than fixed in the order of cunning Grecian urns, their lineage is fluid, nomadic, transitional."[4]

Nowhere has the struggle of African Americans against fixity been more visible or vicious than in the U.S. South. Baker's observation of the "fluid, nomadic, transitional" is central to my thinking about the movement of blacks in the American South, both in temporal and spatial terms. For example, especially immediately following emancipation, black bodies flowed into freedom by searching, often futilely, to reconnect severed families and to establish places of becoming new; or during the Great Migration, when the outward flow from the South launched an often nomadic search for jobs, opportunity, and safety. This chapter takes up the promise and the failure of Louisiana as an alternative space for modeling a more expansive and less binary construction of race within the United States from the nineteenth century onward, a construction that would acknowledge the fluidity of racial designations and of raced bodies without necessarily resorting to nomadism in terms of location or periodicity in terms of time. It considers the multiracial and multilingual Creoles, Louisiana people of color and their cultural production, as a lost opportunity for developing not only more fluid populations but less segregated fields of study and scholarship within a contemporary United

States. If black Mississippi-identified writers arguably concentrate primarily on the twentieth century of rights-embattled Mississippi for constructing within their segregated boundaries of exclusion a new space constituted out of their racial connection and unlimited creativity, then race-identified Louisiana writers configure as a necessary subject and inheritance of their identity as artists the late eighteenth- and nineteenth-century history of Louisiana's Creoles of Color.

Slavery structured spheres of production and power. Owners of property, human movables, had the power to organize social relations and differentiate on the basis of race. In the Deep South, the plantation, with its spatial distinctions the fields, the quarters, the big house with parlors, porches, and outbuildings—kitchens and cabins—emerged as the primary organizational structure: economic, cultural, social, including class and status, as well as race and caste. Constituted in its race-baiting politics as the "Solid South" over the greater part of the twentieth century, the South in its present twenty-first-century configuration may be read as polymorphous and polyglot, yet it continues to call up a space imagined as a unitary place and a racial dynamic marked by fixity and rigidity, lines and divisions, boundaries and binaries.

In no time since the civil rights movement had the racial division been more pronounced than in the aftermath of Hurricane Katrina in 2005, when the desperation of poor black New Orleanians made visible the racial dynamics of segregation and its legacies of deprivation and discrimination. Repeatedly observers of those stranded citizens and their city called up images of island nation-states and ("black") Third World countries. Comparing the modern South to the Caribbean and Middle East in terms of a persistent exoticism that colors how it is perceived, Adrienne Rich reminds us: "When we allow a piece of the world to remain exotic in our imaginations, we dehumanize its people and collaborate in our own ignorance."[5] That dehumanization of black southerners was all too evident after Hurricane Katrina, when black residents of New Orleans were not only left behind in the flood and abandoned in untenable public structures but also demonized and slandered in the grossest of stereotypical labels. Since Hurricane Katrina, Louisiana has become the central focus for discourses on race and poverty, civic responsibility and governmental neglect.[6] Yet Louisiana, and New Orleans in particular, did not always present the face of black poverty, entrapment, and despair. In fact, and despite admitted contradictions, Louisiana, like the South today for which it may be read as emblematic, retains a power to command attention and analysis in the present surge of new studies of American regions coinciding with the rise in studies of the Global South, transnationalism, and postcolonialism.[7] It offers for *Southscapes* a Third Space from which to consider the political and cultural possibilities of flows and fluidity.

Within that spatial and cultural geography, the emerging central subject of fascination or romanticization is Louisiana, and in particular New Orleans, the principal city and capital of the southern part of the old Louisiana Territory. Read as "foreign" in relation to the South, Louisiana does not negate the primary discourses on the South as a region but instead produces a narrative that has aspects of sameness but, importantly, of difference. Its complex history and European, African, and Antillean heritage connect it to contemporary discourses on *Créolité* and circum-Atlantic politics, aesthetics, and culture, as well as on postcolonialism and transnationalism. In *Cities of the Dead*, Joseph Roach represents New Orleans as "a circum-Caribbean cosmopolis with old family fortunes and colonial architecture . . . through which the commerce of the nation's regions and the world's nations passed."[8] His emphasis on "family fortunes," however, may belie the tumultuous mixedness of hierarchies of wealth and power, race and heritage within New Orleans.

Cross-cultural formation as an area of analysis and interrogation has been transforming readings of the U.S. South, but not enough has been done to examine the historical cultural formations in Louisiana for the lost possibility of a multicultural, rather than melting-pot, conception of the United States as a nation. "*Mezcla de razas*," or the mix of races marking Louisiana from its colonial period through the middle of the twentieth century—or before Castro and the Cuban revolution that precipitated the rise of Miami as the major U.S. port instead of New Orleans in relation to the islands and South America— was very much a part of the flow of cultures and of ethnic- and race-marked bodies. In the introduction to "Franco-Americans and African-Americans" in *Creole New Orleans: Race and Americanization* (1992), their edited collection of essays, Arnold R. Hirsch and Joseph Logsdon make a relevant point:

> The pattern of race relations in New Orleans generally strikes American scholars as being either an exception to or an exotic variant of behavior found elsewhere in the United States. As a result, social scientists have not discovered much relevance in it for those living in more "typical" environs. Yet if we expand our vision beyond our national borders, New Orleans may be seen not as an exceptional case to be ignored but as a significant counterpoint against which to measure the rest of a deviant North America. Almost all of the New World's slave societies, whatever the origins of their colonizers, developed three-tiered, multiracial social structures in which a class of marginal status and frequently mixed origin

was inserted between blacks and whites. In its early years, New Orleans replicated that broader history while the rest of the United States (with a few notable exceptions) constructed a rigid, two-tiered structure that drew a single unyielding line between the white and nonwhite.[9]

Hirsch and Logsdon consider New Orleans, and Louisiana by extension, as "an intellectual hinge" that functioned to connect the "interracial systems that appeared in the Western Hemisphere," because "New Orleans was culturally, demographically, and economically part of the French and Spanish empires during its formative years, [and] it was legally and institutionally part of the United States during the nineteenth and twentieth centuries."[10] The point Hirsch and Logsdon emphasize is the locational position of New Orleans, its in-betweenness but also its connectedness to two different ways of approaching racial space and raced bodies. For them, this location provides a way of understanding the uniqueness of New Orleans in "issues of ethnogenesis" and in processes of assimilation. For this chapter of *Southscapes*, New Orleans and Louisiana are place markers of possibility, a liminal space perhaps, but clearly a configuration that represents a now-lost opportunity for an emerging United States to forge both a more varied identity as a nation-state and to interact more equitably with a wider array of nations and people, races and ethnicities, customs and languages—in effect, Louisiana as a potential model for formulating a multiracial, multicultural, and multilingual society much more in keeping with what we envision today as transnational and global.

In the past few decades, studies of Louisiana's Cajuns and Creoles have flourished. Much of this work has operated from a starting point of exclusiveness: the various ethnic and racial groups have been treated as isolated entities with barely a nod to the interrelatedness of Louisiana's peoples and cultures.[11] The exclusiveness of the scholarship has been especially noticeable in regard to Louisiana's people of color. Until the last decades of the twentieth century, African Americans of French descent in the state were virtually ignored; their existence was acknowledged only in a curt nod to one group of their nineteenth-century forebears, particularly *les gens de couleur libre*. For far too long, however, Louisiana studies largely overlooked African-Creole and African-French people and their culture, but American and African American Studies have not been models of inclusiveness in terms of these "different" people of African descent in the United States. While James Oliver Horton's 1993 *Free People of Color: Inside the African American Community* barely mentions the existence of Louisiana's free people of color, despite the fact that les gens de couleur libre have been the most identifiable free people of color within the North American U.S. context, several texts since the mid-1990s began to redress the oversight. Kimberly S. Hanger's *Bounded Lives, Bounded Places: Free Black Society in Colonial New Orleans, 1769–1803* (1997) and Judith Kelleher Schafer's *Slavery, the Civil Law, and the Supreme Court of Louisiana* (1994) forwarded awareness of the legal and social structures that made les gens de couleur libre possible under French and Spanish governing systems. Carl A. Brasseaux, Keith P. Fontenot, and Claude F. Oubre in *Creoles of Color in the Bayou Country* (1994) and James H. Dorman in the edited collection *Creoles of Color of the Gulf South* (1996), for example, entered into the previously ignored territory with a determination to clarify and correct: "Unwilling or unable to grapple with the complexity of south Louisiana's polyglot population, many popular writers either restrict the scope of their work to only one segment of the society . . . or attempt to simplify the problem of ethnic and racial diversity by dealing in broad, often inaccurate generalizations."[12]

There have been earlier efforts in the twentieth century to tell the story of the moment when Louisiana held the potential for a different societal model within the North American context. They are primarily efforts at retention and remembrance of the unique history of Louisiana's people of color and their contributions to the culture of the state. Alice Dunbar-Nelson's "People of Color in Louisiana," a 1916 essay by a native New Orleanian now as famous for her recovered diary and marriage to Paul Laurence Dunbar as for her two collections of Louisiana tales and stories, marks a major transition in the publication of texts on Louisiana's Afro-French and Afro-Creole populations.[13] Following the major work of Rodolphe Desdunes, whose *Nos Hommes, Notre Histoire* (1911) was published in French, Dunbar-Nelson sought to make more accessible the history of people of color in Louisiana. Generations of scholars would owe a major debt to Charles Barthélemy Rousseve for his pioneering studies *The Negro in Louisiana: Aspects of His History and His Literature* (1937) and *The Negro in New Orleans* (1969), which enabled the work of historians in the 1970s: John W. Blassingame's *Black New Orleans, 1860–1880* (1973) and H. E. Sterkx's *The Free Negro in Ante-bellum Louisiana* (1972).

Between 1924 and 1954, Edward Larocque Tinker, an amateur historian and man of letters, wrote a number of books on New Orleans and French and Creole Louisiana, the best known being his 1953 *Creole City: Its Past and Its People*, which incorporated materials from his previous monographs and articles. Tinker preserved in popular form much of the anecdotal social and cultural history of New Orleans, and in an egalitarian, if sometimes condescending, manner, he included significant commentary on and descriptions of Creoles of Color, their history, customs, literature, and language. Tinker, for example, published *Toucoutou* (1928), a novel based on the 1858 court case *Anastasie Desarzant v. Pierre Lablanc and Eglantine Desmazillier*, in which a woman sued a neighbor for slander for accusing her of passing for white; and *Les Cenelles: Afro-French Poetry in Louisiana* (1930), a book on the nineteenth-century poetry collection published by les gens de couleur libres in 1845. Tinker's materials in English utilized Desdunes's *Nos Hommes, Notre Histoire* for much of the inclusions on Creoles of Color and race, particularly for information about the poems and the satirical song Joseph Beaumont, free man of color, wrote while following the Toucoutou case.[14] Tinker's greatest contribution to the preservation of the writings of Creoles of Color is his *Les Écrits des Langue Française en Louisiane au XIXe Siècle* (1932).

Perhaps the most noteworthy effort to preserve the history of Creoles of Color occurred in the post-Depression era under the auspices of the Federal Writers' Project. Marcus Christian, a poet and contributing editor for the *Louisiana Weekly* (an African American newspaper published in New Orleans), headed the "Negro unit" of the FWP for a large-scale "history of the Negro in Louisiana." As was the case with Richard Wright and the African Americans working as writers for the WPA in Chicago and New York, Christian had the opportunity to do research and writing for pay as part of the Writers' Project, but unlike his northern counterparts, he could not sustain himself as a publishing creative writer in the South (as was also the case with Zora Neale Hurston working in Florida for the WPA). While Christian was able to escape the devastating fate Wright had foreseen for talented black men in the South, he was only able to survive within the segregated South as something less than the writer he dreamed of becoming in his youth. In his later years, few in New Orleans recognized him as a writer. Although he contributed to anthologies edited by Sterling Brown (*The Negro Caravan* [1941]) and Arna Bontemps (*The Poetry of the Negro* [1949]), his volume of poetry, *High Ground*, did not appear until 1958. Violet Harrington Bryan counts 1,175 unpublished poems in the Marcus B. Christian Collection at the University of New Orleans.[15] Nevertheless, between 1936 and 1946, the FWP's "Negro" unit in Louisiana under his direction collected an extensive amount of materials. Similar to the information gathered by "Negro" units in other states, the Louisiana materials were virtually ignored and neither incorporated into the state history nor published as a separate history. Christian preserved the collected materials in his personal archives. Similar to Bontemps, the Harlem Renaissance writer descended from Louisiana Creoles, Christian turned to work as a librarian to earn a living. Later using the resources from the collection, he began to draft a work entitled "History" that is rich in incident and details regarding les gens de couleur libres from the records of the eighteenth and nineteenth centuries.

These acts of recovery and correction by Christian, Alice Dunbar-Nelson, and Rodolphe Desdunes may be reassessed today as a way of rethinking creolization, not in terms of Brazil or South America, Trinidad or the Caribbean, Cuba or Haiti or Saint-Domingue, but in terms of Louisiana as the northernmost point of the Caribbean where the influence of the British and English-speaking world almost did not take hold, not even after the Louisiana Purchase in 1803 or after the Civil War and Reconstruction. Black bodies in Louisiana represented the collision of the public sphere with subjective space. Whether Anglo or Creole, they were part of a multiracial and multiethnic society, which included Native Americans, Cajuns (descendants of the French Acadians), and Creoles (descendants of the French and Spanish settlers and émigrés), whose conjoined tenancy on the farms and plantations, on the rivers and bayous, in the towns and cities of Louisiana takes shape around specific spatial designations and the mores they fostered. They also provide access to reclaiming and reframing Louisiana as a multicultural society juxtaposed to the monolinguistic and binary structure promulgated in the United States. Marcus Christian, in particular, focused on the processes of cultural mixing within the formation of New Orleans and its Creoles of Color. His unpublished work in the mid-twentieth century forms an arch with the publications of two Cubans, Alejo Carpentier and Fernando Ortiz, who appear frequently in the discourses of *métissage* and *mestizaje* and hybridity. (Slavery legally ended in Cuba in 1880 but effectively not until 1886.) Carpentier and Ortiz are typically cited for their identification of the Americas as "a continent of symbioses, mutations, vibrations, mixings." The concept of Creoleness for Carpentier was part of the recognition of the newness of the Americas, a "consciousness of being a new thing, a symbiosis."[16]

Édouard Glissant, from Martinique, has in both his fiction and criticism forwarded the idea of creolization pioneered by the Cubans. The point of Glissant's work that is of interest here is the idea of the poetics of relations, the fluidity of people and cultures in the Americas, his notion that there is "a completely new dimension that permits each and every one of us to be both here and elsewhere, rooted and exposed, lost in the mountains and at liberty under the sea, harmoniously at rest and restlessly wandering."[17] In a world that is "creolizing," to use Glissant's term, the idea of static regions or of a fixity of identity is no longer possible. His "Antillanité" as a descriptor for Caribbean identity attempted to move critical attention away from a primary focus on African ancestry and toward a more broad-based and mixed cultural heritage. With his often obscuring prose, Glissant is not always an eloquent spokesperson for his ideas. That has been left to an emergent group of scholars from the French Caribbean, Cuba, and the United States, who assert the model of race in the Caribbean as decentering the black-white polarized and oppositional racial designations in the United States.[18]

In 1989 Jean Bernabé, Patrick Chamoiseau, and Raphaël Confiant followed their fellow Martinican Glissant with the manifesto *Éloge de la Créolité* and the formulation of Créolité, a concept that engaged more fully the Creole linguistic, cultural, and racial roots of the Caribbean in processes of métissage, of mixedness, that is: "an interactive and transactional aggregate of Caribbean, European, African, Asian, and Levantive cultural elements, united on the same soil by the yoke of history."[19] They theorized a term first introduced in 1975 by Hector Poullet to defend the French Caribbean *départements de outre mer*, overseas departments of France, against negative comments by French officials, but they aligned their project against *Négritude*, which Aimé Césaire, Léon Damas, and Léopold Senghor had espoused in the 1930s as a way of linking blacks of the diaspora to Africa and to one another and of rejecting French colonial domination. In distancing Créolité from Négritude, the Martinicans also distanced themselves from false universality and monolingualism, though they celebrated the use of Creole in creative writing and scholarly discourse.

In a sense, Créolité is a recognition of a postmodern heterogeneity that refuses a reduction to the homogeneous in terms of history, race, language, or culture; however, this very insistence on heterogeneity has led to the misconception that particularly in rejecting Négritude's foundational idea of African heritage as the primary identity claim of diasporic people, Créolité rejected race. Shireen Lewis offers a rebuttal to such misreadings as part of her thoughtful analysis in *Race, Culture, and Identity: Francophone, West African, and Caribbean Literature and Theory from Négritude to Créolité* (2006), as she states directly from the outset of her study: "'Creole' identity does not translate into a 'raceless' identity or 'racelessness.' As with *Négritude*, race is still implicated within *Créolité*."[20] As an effort to counter the disparagement and disappearance of Creole in the Caribbean context, Créolité recognized the more complex origins, heritages, and cultures of diasporic people, who were positioned as constituting a dynamic, open, and diverse new culture that should be viewed from the interior rather than from the exterior of either Africa or Europe.

Créolité collided not only with Négritude in its rethinking of Creoleness at the center of and interior to identity, but also with later Caribbean formulations of culture and identity. Although not represented as a displacement of other possible paradigms, it contained inherent contradictions and confusions, which led to numerous critiques. Writers Maryse Condé and Derek Walcott, for example, criticized the seeming idealization of a folk outside of recent history and its provincialism in elevating Martinique above other creolized spaces. The concept has even been at odds with Glissant's own emphasis on hybridity and on openness to the larger world in his notion of "Relation," though Stuart Hall argues that Créolité, like Négritude, is still relevant because neither the black/white binary nor the essentializing of blackness has yet been displaced in cultural politics.[21]

In using Créolité in this study, I am deploying a locational positionality evident in Glissant, Bernabé, Chamoiseau, and Confiant as they delineated a disaporic space that was hybrid, multiracial, multicultural, diverse, and plural. Rather than either the "contact zones" of Mary Louise Pratt or the "imagined communities" of Benedict Anderson, with his emphasis on print culture in the formation of nationalism, or the "crossings" of Carolyn Vellenga Berman, I would like to posit the concept of more mutable geographies and of cultural flows and body mappings in Louisiana that defy and complicate the assertions of binary racial categories in the U.S. context.[22] At the same time, I am not overlooking the problematic or controversial aspects of Créolité as a way of rethinking history and culture, but it serves as a useful shorthand to identify the conceptions of language, culture, and race connecting historic Louisiana to contemporary notions of creolization.

Creoles of Color in colonial Louisiana embody the concept of flow and confluences. Just as "geographic racial, national, and linguistic heterogeneity," the characteristics that, according to Suzanne Bost, "empowered the [Caribbean] islands' challenge to imperialist domination" and "support postcolonial theories with a history of effective political resistance,"[23] so too are these same characteristics of heterogeneity configured and actualized within colonial Louisiana. Bost suggests that commentators on race in the Caribbean context may too "often idealize the Caribbean (reifying the racial mixture that was produced in conquest and violation) and oversimplifying the complexity of U.S. race relations."[24] Her observations are astute, but her specific examination of mixed-raced identities begins in the Americas of the 1850s, so that her temporal template excludes the earlier Louisiana gens de couleur, who have been too often overlooked in the simplification of the complex history of race relations and the conscious decisions made about racial classifications within the United States.

Because of the attention focused on Louisiana, Mississippi, and the Gulf

Coast following Hurricane Katrina, there has been a renewed interest in exploring the entirety of the history of that region as a spatial entity different from much of the rest of the nation and with enduring legacies of the cost of that difference. Books, such as Michael Eric Dyson's *Come Hell or High Water: Hurricane Katrina and the Color of Disaster* (2006), helped to chronicle both the plight of the displaced and the failures of civic responsibility exacerbating and extending the traumatic suffering of people in the storm's path. New Orleans and Katrina have almost become expected reference points for current scholarship on blacks in the United States; for example, Richard Iton concludes his 2008 study *In Search of the Black Fantastic: Politics and Popular Culture in the Post–Civil Rights Era* with a brief epilogue, "Space Is the Place," deploying the image of New Orleans in the wake of Katrina. Ned Sublette's *The World That Made New Orleans: From Spanish Silver to Congo Square* (2008) and Shirley Elizabeth Thompson's *Exiles at Home: The Struggle to Become American in Creole New Orleans* (2009) are among the most recent studies attending specifically to New Orleans and its Creole cultures.

Emerging in the eighteenth century out of the coming together of a mélange of people from France, Spain, Africa, and the Americas, Creoles of Color produced colonial identities that shifted and transformed with the languages, laws, and expectations of the governments controlling the Louisiana Territory and the physical geography of lower Louisiana, in which waterways, rivers, bayous, inlets, and rigolettes shaped the flow of commerce, trade, and emigration. In a fluid society, marked by relational and subjective politics of identity, mixing and mixtures brought pluralism and relativism. Defined over time by phenotype, color, and place, Creoles of Color were not a "cross between" groups of people. In fact, they rarely seem contained within the definitions more typically applied to them. An authoritative effort reads: "Ranging in appearance from mulattos to northern European whites, the Creoles of Color constitute a Caribbean phenomenon in the United States."[25] Perhaps the history of their formation accounts for the broad, slippery definitions.

In 1776, when Louisiana was under Spanish rule with Bernardo de Galvez as the governor, the Court of Madrid allowed the introduction of Africans into Louisiana by French vessels from whatever ports they might come, and thus, the decree opened migration from the West Indies. However, the linkage between Creoles of Color or gens de couleur and free blacks in Louisiana began a hundred years before West Indian migration into the Louisiana colony. Free blacks are recorded in Louisiana records in 1724, twelve years after the first recorded importation of slaves. Bartolomé de las Casas, a Spaniard who became a Dominican missionary to Native Americans, had asked as early as 1517 that the slavery of Africans be substituted for that of Indians in the Spanish colonies, and although Charles V initially refused his request, it was not long before the Spanish began to traffic in slaves and employ other nations to do so.[26] In 1712 France granted Anthony Crozat the right to send a ship to Africa once a year for the specific purpose of buying Africans for the large Louisiana Territory.[27] John Law's Company of the Indies brought 500 Africans from Guinea in 1719.[28] Subsequently, "the slave population began to lighten in color, and increase out of all proportion due to the importation and natural breeding among themselves. La Harpe comments in 1724 upon the astonishing diminution of the white population and the astounding increase of the colored population."[29] The policing of boundaries separating races proved problematical and difficult in Louisiana, particularly during the early settlement. A mixed-race, enslaved and free, people were already in evidence by 1724, when Bienville passed the Louisiana *Code Noir*.

Based on a 1685 edict that instituted regulations for slave labor and racial interaction in the French Caribbean possessions (the Antilles), the Code Noir was the first law regulating slavery in Louisiana. It "established the Catholic Church in Louisiana, ordered the expulsion of Jews, and provided that slaves should be instructed in the Catholic faith and married under its laws. It also provided minimum food and clothing allowances and granted neglected slaves the right to complain to the public prosecutor should their maintenance be substandard."[30] In addition to forbidding the separation by sale of young children from their mothers, the Code Noir restricted slaves from owning property, either through their labor or by inheritance, and whites from marrying or living in concubinage with blacks or mulattoes, whether slave or free. The Code Noir was, as well, "the only comprehensive legislation which applied to the whole population, both black and white . . . affecting social, religious, and property relationships between all classes."[31] Over the next fifty years, however, it would prove increasingly difficult to regulate social relations between blacks and whites in Louisiana and almost impossible to maintain absolutism in terms of either race or ethnicity.

By 1766, three years after Louisiana became a Spanish possession, Acadians were complaining that "Negroes were freedmen while they were slaves."[32] What had occurred was the modification of French codes with *Las Siete Partidas*, which was a digest of Spanish and Roman law, both of which held that "slavery was contrary to natural law and reason": "The *Partidas* directed the judicial sale of slaves who proved cruel treatment by their owners. Under the *Partidas*, slaveholders could manumit their slaves without government permission and without proof of meritorious acts. Most significantly, slaves . . .

had the right of self-purchase, or *coartación*. This important right enabled slaves to petition to have themselves appraised and to purchase themselves from even unwilling masters or mistresses at their judicially appraised market value."[33]

The Spanish law of seven parts had originated in the thirteenth century, and while it did maintain the existence of slavery, it acknowledged the humanity of the enslaved and considered freedom to be the ideal state of human beings, and it "promoted stability through paternalism and family formation."[34] Though harsh in its treatment of slave crimes, Spanish law allowed more access to emancipation, as slaves could not only purchase themselves (*coartación*) but also sue in court for their freedom and obtain an appraisal of their worth. The space for movement within the law allowed for social movement by people of African descent, both slave and free. In 1801, when Spain secretly traded Louisiana back to France, Spanish law was so ensconced that it remained in effect even though France reenacted the 1724 Code Noir in the twenty days between its taking over the territory and selling it to the United States. The enactment was a futile attempt to regulate a territory that, based on petitions, appellate cases, and legal documents, had allowed racial identity in Louisiana, and New Orleans in particular, to become "malleable and subjective."[35]

From 1803 through the first four decades of the nineteenth century, Spanish law regarding slavery remained in effect in Louisiana. In the three years between 1803 and 1806, *coartación* continued with the self-purchase or manumission of some 200 enslaved people, so that Judith Kelleher Schafer concludes: "Louisianians, including the notaries who processed the legal papers granting freedom, believed Spanish slave law to continue to be in effect in the new American possession until repealed and replaced by the new American territorial government or the federal government of the United States."[36] Schafer cites as an example the 1806 *Paul v. Succession of Carrière* case in which the new superior court of the Territory of Orleans declared Spanish law, rather than French law, to be in effect in the territory "unless it conflicted with American law."[37] The supremacy of Spanish law and its treatment of enslaved people created not only a class of free people within a slave economic system but also a class of property-owning people of color with the material capacity to purchase freedom for other blacks or to buy land to increase their own wealth. With stable family units encouraged among all people of color, the resultant society marked Louisiana as a space of uncertainty in relation to much of the legal fixity on race in other places in the United States with a dependency on slavery. Sibley terms such spaces "zones of ambiguity" in which there is the ever-present danger of undermining expected order or authority.[38]

After the Louisiana Purchase, however, and before statehood in 1812, the administrative Territory of Orleans government did attempt to force the territory into conformity with legislation regulating slaves and free blacks in much of the South and particularly Virginia, where the Gabriel Prosser rebellion precipitated stricter laws to regulate slaves and to separate them from free blacks who, it was feared, would instigate slave revolts. The fear of slave revolts increased dramatically after the long and hard-fought civil war in Saint Domingue ended with the establishment of the new independent nation of Haiti on 1 January 1804. With a free-black population of 1,335 in 1803 (out of a total population of 8,050, which included 2,775 slaves), New Orleans epitomized a "high degree of social and economic fluidity": "a Latin European religious ethic, an unbalanced sex ratio, and a shortage of skilled laborers and soldiers contributed to the city's fluid milieu and opened the way to freedom. Colonial policies designed to build a more rigid social order fueled the racial flux."[39] New laws in 1807 prohibited free black men from entering the Louisiana Territory and restricted manumission, and already in 1805, free blacks in New Orleans had their mobility challenged by a city ordinance requiring them to have a residency permit for which they needed legal proof of being free.

Despite these efforts, Sister Dorothea Olga McCants states that in 1810, "7,585 free persons of color [lived] among the 76,500" residents of the Territory of Orleans.[40] Moreover, according to Caryn Cossé Bell, between 1810 and 1830, "large numbers of free blacks migrated into the region from North and South. . . . Lured by the prospect of economic opportunity during the decades of economic expansion following the War of 1812, the majority of free black immigrants entered Louisiana clandestinely by way of the state's extensive networks of waterways."[41] As would be expected in a territory and later a state that had undergone so many changes in governing systems, Louisiana's laws and enforcement regarding enslavement and freedom, racial and legal identity could hardly keep pace with the transformations and overlapping but often contradictory rulings based on Spanish and French civil codes as well as American (British Common Law) codes. In other words, the fixity, exclusions, and certainty expected in the states regarding matters of race and place often could not be maintained in Louisiana.

The 1844 case of Sally Miller is an example of two conjoined aspects of racial matters in Louisiana. The first is that well after statehood and the primacy of American law, an enslaved person in Louisiana could sue for manumission and bring a suit against a white person. The second aspect is related to the tangled history of defining race in Louisiana, especially when appearance did not conform to the typical script and when race could be presumed on the basis of status. Sally, a slave, was working in a New Orleans café when she was recognized as Salomé Muller, the lost daughter of a German immigrant family who arrived with an influx of German and Irish immigrants in the 1840s and 1850s.[42] Sally Miller then began a lawsuit for her freedom, which claimed that her family was indentured to John Miller but that upon her father's death, Miller changed her status from redemptioner, bound to work but as white not enslaved, to slave and illegally sold her to the café owner Louis Belmonti. Belmonti responded that Sally's real name was Mary and that he had purchased her legally, and he produced a bill for sale from John Miller for $700 dated 9 July 1838. Miller responded that Sally Miller was a slave of African descent named Bridget whom Anthony Williams of Mobile left in his possession to sell in 1822. He produced three documents showing his receipt for $100 in advance on the sale, the sale of Bridget to his mother for $350 in 1823, and finally his purchase in 1835 of Bridget with the three children she had by then for the same amount of $350.[43] Whether as Sally, Mary, or Bridget, the enslaved woman had passed through a number of identities and places.

Sally Miller's case raised all the unavoidable but difficult questions about identity and status in Louisiana. Blacks were slaves and whites were free, but mulattoes could also be presumed free. The opposite reasoning also held regarding enslavement: slaves were black, the condition of enslavement defining their race rather than their race defining their condition. In Sally Miller's case, her physical appearance was that of a white woman, so the accepted descriptive of an enslaved person as African descended could not so easily be applied. The courts in Louisiana maintained slavery's connection to color, so that legal rulings about bondage were made on the basis of skin color. In an 1810 case, the Superior Court of the Territory of Orleans had ruled: "Persons of color are presumed free—Negroes otherwise."[44] The several rulings and reversals in the Miller case reveal just how unsettled race was even after the Louisiana Purchase. In *Miller v. Belmonti* (1844), the ruling was in favor of the claims that Sally Miller was a slave and not Salomé Muller. However, in *Miller v. Belmonti* (1845) the Louisiana Supreme Court declared Sally Miller free based on her appearance and her support by or comportment with friends who were white. In the 1848 *John F. Miller v. Sally Miller* case—against the overwhelming evidence of the existence of another Salomé Muller and her sister Dorothea in another part of Louisiana when Sally Miller, then Bridget, appeared in the Miller household—the court ruled against Miller's claims of fraud by Sally Miller, who could then maintain her free, white identity as Salomé Muller.

The ruling was basically that once a slave was declared free, that freedom could not be revoked by another and lower court, so that even if Sally Miller was actually a slave once named Bridget, she had been legally declared Salomé Muller, a free white woman, and could not then be reenslaved. Sally Miller dramatized the capricious efforts to identify slaves by their color and the futility of biological definitions of race. Not surprisingly, almost immediately after the case first appeared in newspaper accounts, African American writers advocating the abolition of slavery—for example William Wells Brown in his novel *Clotel* (1853) and William Craft in his narrative of escape from slavery—began to use Sally Miller/Salomé Muller's enslavement in their struggle for abolition.

Efforts to regulate people of color during the territorial period did not erase Louisiana's position as a zone of ambiguity and a geography of exoticism in comparison with other slaveholding southern states. In *The Repeating Island: The Caribbean and the Postmodern Perspective* (1992), Antonio Benítez-Rojo includes a segment on "The 'other' Caribbean city," in which he looks specifically at the issue of race within spaces he terms "fetal, minuscule nodules of turbulence."[45] These areas, which Benítez-Rojo calls "Negro quarters," are mainly the yard, or "solar," and the dockside, or "muelle." He describes both as "a variegated social cell, a dense melting pot that cooks together several religions and beliefs, new words and dance steps, unforeseen dishes and musical styles."[46] This "nodule of turbulence" produces, according to Benítez-Rojo, a racial and ethnic admixture in which "the Negro race usually dominates, but one almost always finds representatives of other ethnicities and hybrids or every sort."[47] Benítez-Rojo's representation of "the 'other' Caribbean city" might well apply specifically to the city of New Orleans, especially in the period between the revolutions in the islands and 1795, when the Spanish in the Treaty of San Lorenzo opened the port to commerce with the Americans. The flow of intercultural mores and customs defined the area as exotic in comparison to the developing U.S. nation-state.

New Orleans viewed as a Caribbean city seems closer to both past and present actualities than the conception of New Orleans as "America's European Masterpiece," as Helen Taylor has more recently labeled it.[48] To call attention only to the European heritage of the city is to miss its significant connection to the Caribbean and even more noticeably to Africa and the African diaspora, which is increasingly the direction of twenty-first-century scholarship. That was precisely the connection Thomas Marc Fiehrer made in a little-noticed

1979 essay, "The African Presence in Colonial Louisiana: An Essay on the Continuity of Caribbean Culture." Commissioned as a scholarly *public* document, Fiehrer's essay appeared in *Louisiana's Black Heritage*, a volume that was published by the Louisiana State Museum at a cost of $17,000 but did not receive wide circulation, although the intent was "to promote and advise the public on the historical development of Louisiana."[49]

In a chapter entitled "The Mouth of a New Empire: New Orleans in the Transamerican Print Trade," Kirsten Silva Gruesz locates New Orleans as one of the cosmopolitan exile centers for Latino writing. She names New Orleans the "Capital of the (Other) Nineteenth Century." The city "became a significant locus of Hispanophone literary activity for the Caribbean and more generally for the Americas. . . . Antebellum New Orleans seemed, to its wide range of Hispanophone visitors and permanent residents, a model space in which heterogeneous interests could functionally coexist, whereas New York . . . increasingly came to signify for them an insuperably strange one."[50] Like New York in 1850, however, 40 percent of the population of New Orleans was foreign-born. Because of its Spanish speakers and public architecture from its three decades as a colony of Spain and its immigrants from Cuba and Santo Domingo, New Orleans during the 1840s and 1850s was a comfortable and familiar place for a sizeable number of expatriates from Latin America and the Caribbean. The city had a physical resemblance to Port of Spain in Trinidad and Havana in Cuba, as well as to a number of old cities in Mexico. Gruesz remarks its similarity to Havana as "a nexus of trade in goods and slaves, smuggling, piracy, capital ventures, in- and out-migration, troop movements, filibustering adventurers, and travel between the eastern United States and points southward. Midcentury New Orleans was, fundamentally, a Caribbean city, strategically positioned within the transportation and communications system of the Gulf of Mexico's half-moon, linked to Cuba, Puerto Rico, Santo Domingo, and Mexico's Gulf Coast and Yucatán."[51]

Louisiana has been a borderland of American culture. This "fact" has entered into the consciousness of much of the nation following the devastation of New Orleans and the surrounding area in the aftermath of Hurricane Katrina, which hit the Gulf Coast on 29 August 2005. The images broadcast from the region suggested the poorer island cultures south of Louisiana, Haiti in particular, rather than any part of the United States. If today we position Texas and California as states signifying and making visible the borderland of mestizo culture that marks the late twentieth-century and early twenty-first-century United States and Mexico, Louisiana from the seventeenth century through the twentieth represented the permeable cultural boundaries and

631 Dauphine St., New Orleans, Orleans County, Louisiana. Houses and shops with ironwork balconies and louvered doors in the French and Spanish Old Quarter mark New Orleans as a Caribbean City related to Port-au-Prince, Haiti; Port of Spain, Trinidad; and Havana, Cuba. (Frances Benjamin Johnston, photographer, 1937–38; Carnegie Survey of the Architecture of the South, Library of Congress Prints and Photographs Division, Washington, D.C.)

melding of the racial, linguistic, culinary, artistic aspects of several cultures: African, Spanish, French, Haitian, Dominican, Cuban, Italian, German, and Irish, with a dash of eastern European mixed in. Not an island culture, though isolated from major U.S. centers of culture, Louisiana faced south especially because its ports from the colonial Biloxi to New Orleans were points of commercial exchange and body flows. In introducing his edited collection *Louisiana Culture from the Colonial Era to Katrina* (2008), John Lowe positions the essays as "break[ing] the old molds of traditional regionalism, but without disavowing the myriad southern aspects of Louisiana and its cultures. Yes, the Mississippi is the South's greatest waterway, but it is also its essential link to the Gulf of Mexico and the Caribbean, the Panama Canal and the Pacific, the Western Hemisphere and world trade."[52] His point is expanded further to "make a central case for Louisiana as a hub and generator of a new cultural configuration, but one with a rich, hybrid, and varied past."[53] Lowe's geographic and cultural mapping of Louisiana iterates the current efforts to move away from the fixity of regional studies and into the broader fluidity of culture and commerce.

Food and music are a means of documenting the existence and the pervasiveness of Afro-Creole culture, and the culinary and musical arts function as a metaphor for the inextricable "mixedness" of Creole individual and national identity. In a sense, food and music cultures of Creole Louisiana remind us that both mixed identity and the possibility of sustaining ethnic and racial mixture have survived despite the concerted effort within the United States to shape a binary culture held for the most part as separate and unequal. They are a reminder as well of an often overlooked point regarding the "race" of Creoles: race is only one marker of identity. Ethnicity is another, and within the matrix of ethnicity, Creoleness takes on a different register. In language, in customs, in food culture, in culinary arts, and in literature and music, ethnic Louisiana Creoles resemble one another even when their designated, and often arbitrary, races do not. But within that ethnicity, race is clearly constructed and fluid and needed "patrolling" from the early nineteenth century until into the mid-twentieth century. In fact, as Kimberly Hanger points out, "[a] person's racial designation depended on who recorded it, what purpose it served, when it was recorded, and what physical characteristics were considered more relevant."[54]

French and Spanish records in Louisiana courthouses from the colonial period are detailed. They provide the basis for the modern discoveries of the ethnicity and place of origin of the Africans brought to Louisiana.[55] These records also show that over time, race in Louisiana was neither static nor transparent; that it saw successive waves of immigrants from France, Spain, Portugal, Cuba, Saint-Domingue, Haiti, Brazil, Mexico, and the American states and territories; and it sustained its growth with slave labor from Africa and the European colonies. Not even the three-tiered caste system maintained stable distinctions among the racial groups, and well after 1803 (the Louisiana Purchase) and 1812 (admittance as a state in the Union), the race binary in place in the United States had not yet displaced the old patterns in New Orleans.

The Catholic Church contributed to the instability of racial distinctions. In fact, as Caryn Cossé Bell points out, "[u]ntil the 1830s, the city's liberal religious culture helped to delay the imposition of a sharply defined, two-tiered racial hierarchy."[56] Church clerics and Père Antoine, Antonio de Sedella, a Capuchin friar at the St. Louis Church, still performed "marriages of conscience" between members of different races and registered marriages, baptisms, and deaths that could be used effectively in civil lawsuits.[57] In a study of nineteenth-century court cases involving racial identity claims, Ariela Gross concludes that of all the states, Louisiana heard more cases and was the one in which it was "easiest to prove one's whiteness."[58] Many of these could base their claims on the records maintained by the church and by the French and Spanish systems of record keeping. Where the practices of the Catholic Church have mattered the most or left one of the richest resources is in its system of record keeping. Records of marriages and baptisms from St. Louis Church, the St. Louis Cathedral in the center of the Vieux Carré, have proved invaluable in tracing the social relations among the races in New Orleans and the movement from one racial designation to another. Although during the height of the struggle over school desegregation, the records were removed from the city and made difficult for researchers to obtain, they are now readily available with the generous assistance of church officials.[59]

Paul Gilroy, in conceptualizing the "Black Atlantic" as a social space, focused attention squarely on the interlocked social and spatial relations manifested in black migration and diasporic practices.[60] He proposed an approach that would impact analysis of the modern world while also producing "an explicitly transnational and intercultural perspective": "The fractal patterns of cultural and political exchange and transformation that we try and specify through manifestly inadequate theoretical terms like creolisation and syncretism indicate how both ethnicities and political cultures have been made anew in ways that are significant not simply for the peoples of the Caribbean but for Europe, for Africa, . . . and of course, for black America."[61] Given his paradigm and examples, Gilroy might well have included a reference to

New Orleans and to Louisiana's people of color, as his conclusion on Martin Delany's *Blake* would suggest:

> *Blake* is useful to this chapter's ["The Black Atlantic as a Counterculture of Modernity"] argument against ethnic absolutisms because its affirmation of the intercultural and transnational is more than enough to move discussions of black political culture beyond the binary opposition between national and diaspora perspectives. The suggestive way that it locates the black Atlantic world in a webbed network, between the local and the global, challenges the coherence of all narrow nationalist perspectives and points to the spurious invocation of ethnic particularity to enforce them and to ensure the tidy flow of cultural output into neat, symmetrical units.[62]

But Gilroy is uncritical in differentiating among the component parts of the "webbed network" and in celebrating migration and diaspora as preferable to nationalist perspectives, and as a result, he uses a primarily masculinist (with the exception of Toni Morrison and mentions of Zora Neale Hurston) and mainly mainstream, United States–based sequence of black texts and music to forward his argument, which would have been well served by the inclusion of Louisiana and indeed obviously more of the Caribbean, Cuba, and Haiti.

While Chris Bongie in *Islands and Exiles: The Creole Identities of Post/Colonial Literature* (1998) does an admirable analysis of the writers south of the U.S. borders (Glissant and Carpentier, for instance), for the United States he turns, as Glissant himself does, to William Faulkner's *Absalom, Absalom!* because there is a lack of recognition of the relationship between Louisiana's writers from the earliest period to the present as writing out of the same nexus or matrix of experience that impacted the Martiniqueans or Cubans or the Caribbean writers. The turn to Faulkner happens not merely out of a lack of understanding or knowledge of the writers of the U.S. Deep South, in particular those whose works and spaces influenced Faulkner's turn to cultural mixtures in *Absalom* and his early stories, but also out of a reliance on modernist narratives, especially novels, which tell in whatever form stories that can provide access to a formulation of ideas about the past and about the ideological and social concerns under examination. What the Island critics miss is that Haiti is connected to Louisiana in Faulkner's representation, and Eulalie is inextricably bound to Charles Bon's New Orleans "wife" and their *plaçage* relationship. The Louisiana connection is through the imagined Creoles of Color.

The "ethics of flow" that Deleuze and Guattari recognized in their analysis of the nomadic obtains in the case of Louisiana and New Orleans well into the middle of the twentieth century. On a direct line with Mérida, the capital of the Yucatán, an axis with Havana and Kingston, New Orleans is 1,200 miles from Haiti. The Gulf of Mexico and the Caribbean Sea form waterways of connection and flow with the bayous and rigolettes of the southern Louisiana coast. Recent excursions into Mexico's African heritage, called "The Third Root," have resulted in the uncovering of numerous links between specific Mexican states and Louisiana.[63] These are providing new evidence of racial and cultural mixtures in Louisiana. But the distances between New Orleans and Paris or Madrid are equally important for the aspects of movement and flow that are central to situating Creoles of Color within their larger milieu.

Louisiana has had a transnational identity with association with the nations south of its borders and waterways. The area bounded by the Gulf of Mexico and the Mississippi River had become a thriving mixture of French, Spanish, African, and Native American cultures in the early nineteenth century. The distinctive mixtures of ethnic, racial, and cultural groups gave the state a special flavor. In particular, the Creoles (descendants of the original French, African, and Spanish settlers) and the Cajuns (descendants of the French Acadian settlers of the 1760s) made lower Louisiana different in language, religion, customs, foods, and traditions. With a multiracial, mixed-race, and biracial population, which is also an ethnic cauldron of possible mixtures, hybridity marks the region. Instead of an English-speaking majority, as was the case in the rest of the nation, Louisiana had a French-speaking majority, a Spanish-speaking minority, and a Creole-speaking minority. Creole, a patois or combination of French, some Spanish, English, and African languages, had come into popular usage as early as the seventeenth century as a means of communicating between the French and the Africans and the Native Americans. By the early nineteenth century, Creole was commonly used throughout Louisiana by French, Spanish, and English speakers, as well as by German and Italian immigrants to the area, despite the fact that many educated individuals also spoke the language of European France. In 1758, for example, La Page Du Pratz's *Histoire De La Louisiane*, written in French, contained written examples of the Creole language. Importantly, because of French and Creole, lower Louisiana seemed to have more in common with France, a nation over 4,000 miles away, than with its near neighbor, the English-speaking United States.

Louisiana evidenced a plurality of racial identities made possible by racial amalgamation. The argument for multiplicity, for biracial and multiracial identities and recognition, has been largely suppressed and ignored in contemporary Louisiana, though it is one of the primary places where the literal and visual landscape holds all the tenets for the argument. Slavery was, of course, equally oppressive in Louisiana as in the rest of the slaveholding states; however, because of the development of lower Louisiana around ports and into town and urban areas early in its history, and also because of the pervasiveness of miscegenation with the resulting mulatto population, Francophone Louisiana had a higher concentration of urbanized blacks and of free people of color who engaged in trades and professions, received training and education, and held property and possessions. The urban areas, in particular the major seaport city of New Orleans, provided a density and an anonymity for blacks that was not possible in largely rural areas with large farms and plantations where slaves worked in the fields.

The black population in the city of New Orleans was more varied and its patterns of life more complex than in any other city in the United States, as John Blassingame has shown. In the period just before the Civil War, people of color, both slave and free, numbered 25,432 in 1860, and in 1880, just after the end of Reconstruction, that population had increased to 57,617; the white population numbered 144,601 in 1860 and 158,859 in 1880. The first free blacks appeared in New Orleans in the 1720s, forty years before the Acadians began to relocate in south Louisiana, and by 1860, the eve of the Civil War, they had increased in number to 10,939, or over two-fifths of the entire black population of the city. A majority of them were the manumitted children of white men; others had earned freedom by fighting in the colonial French or Spanish militia; still others gained freedom by rendering meritorious or faithful service to their owners and by being purchased by relatives. At the time of the Louisiana Purchase, the lower territory comprising the area that would later become the state had some 20,000 Native Americans, according to Vernon Valentine Palmer, who divides the remaining population into three categories: 26,000 whites, 23,500 black slaves, and 4,000 free persons of color.[64] In New Orleans, the 1805 census, the first after the Louisiana Purchase, lists "3551 whites, 1566 free people of color, 3105 slaves and 253 'others,' or a total of 8475 persons."[65] According to Blassingame, "Hundreds of other free (blacks) came from Maine, Massachusetts, New York, Ohio, and Pennsylvania, or from Haiti during the revolution on that island. In fact, the most distinctive feature of the free (black) population was the large number of foreign-born blacks. For example, in 1850 there were 889 (blacks) who had been born in Germany, England, France, Mexico, Spain, the West Indies, or several other countries."[66] Among free people of color, the ratio of skilled to unskilled laborers was "considerably higher than among the Irish and German immigrants," as Robert Reinders has found. The 1850 census listed some 1,792 free males engaged in fifty-four different occupations, and only 9.9 percent of them were in unskilled laboring jobs. The more prestigious jobs included teachers, doctors, architects, scientists, inventors, engineers, bookbinders, jewelers, artists, merchants, musicians, real estate brokers, money lenders, and general merchandising or import agents. But as Blassingame observes, "The strongest economic base . . . rested on ownership of real property. By 1850 [blacks] held $2,214,020 in real estate, with much of it in the city center."[67] The per capita wealth of blacks in New Orleans by 1880 was $40, as compared with $7 per capita in Savannah, Georgia, in the same year.

"New people," a term historian Joel Williamson adopted from Charles Chesnutt's novel *The House behind the Cedars* and used to described "mulattoes" in the United States, seems quite appropriate here. According to Williamson, "Mulattoes in America are a new people, new not just in the surface way of a new physical type, but new in the vital way of constituting a new culture that is both African and European, each transformed in America and married to one another."[68] While Williamson's term articulates the intervention in descriptives for "American" raced bodies, it does not address issues of modernity implicit in the configuration of new Creole bodies. Yet between the 1840s and the 1870s, when discourses of modernity were clustering around narrative and its capacity to express cultural production and institutions and formations of the new, Louisiana Creoles of Color were struggling to find ways to change their investment in political romanticism and bring the new identities resulting from the modern ruptures and transformations accompanying the successive nations governing their home region and their bodies.

II. CULTURAL FLOWS

There are also, probably in every culture, in every civilization, real places—places that do exist and that are formed in the very founding of society—which are something like counter-sites, a kind of effectively enacted utopia in which the real sites, all the other real sites that can be found within the culture, are simultaneously represented, contested, and inverted.
—MICHEL FOUCAULT, "Of Other Spaces"

Cultural movement and body movement coincide in the nineteenth-century Creoles of Color. The artists and professionals in particular who come to prominence all are part of the material flows between Louisiana and Europe, the West Indies, and South America. Their primary destination was France, where they found familiar social practices as well as a common spoken language. They carried with them the habits of Louisiana and bodies marked by their status as "new people." Creoleness was both legible and unreadable within the space of European culture. In a sense, their identities were already relational and mutable, but in France they became even more fluid.

The educated class of blacks in Louisiana until after the Civil War was the largely French-speaking free people of color. They inclined toward France for the opportunities that culture afforded. Many were not only educated there but remained there to live rather than return to Louisiana's more restricted provincial environment. Not until the founding of three universities during Reconstruction, Leland (1869), New Orleans (1873), and Straight (1869), did English-speaking blacks have the opportunity for higher learning and cultural resources.[69]

Charles Lucièn Lambert *père* (ca. 1828–96) and Lucièn-Léon Guillaume Lambert *fils* (1858–1945), New Orleans Creoles of Color, with another father and son, Edmond Dédé (1827–1901) and Edouard Dédé, were highly regarded as composers and musicians in New Orleans, Bordeaux, and Paris. Lambert and his half brother, Sidney (1838–ca. 1910), were musicians and composers who came from a family of musicians; both their father, Charles Richard Lambert, and Lucièn's son, Lucièn-Léon-Guillaume Lambert, were composers, teachers, and arrangers.[70] Edmond Dédé was a violin prodigy born in New Orleans to parents who arrived in Louisiana from the French West Indies in 1809; his father held the position of bandmaster with a local militia and taught Edmond to play his first instrument, the clarinet. In the twenty-first century, the Lamberts and Dédés have been acknowledged as "Creole Romantic" musical dynasties of New Orleans who contributed to the development of "the cross cultural musical language that served as a link between European concert music, ragtime, and jazz."[71]

Lambert and Dédé are representative of the artists who as Creoles of Color enjoyed ties to Louisiana and to France, but also the Antilles. Their movement through different social spaces and across national boundaries is comparable to that of the Creole poets during both an earlier and later period. These Louisiana Creoles of Color enjoyed international careers and retained places within the Louisiana social structure even when they spent most of their professional lives abroad. Much of the music they produced was called classical concert music, but it included music for dance and theater, as there was less of a "separation between popular and art music." Sidney Lambert had a music career in both Portugal and France; he died in Paris around 1909–10. The Lamberts as youths in New Orleans played music at the Théâtre d' Orléans, where Lucièn knew Louis Moreau Gottschalk, a Creole who was

arguably the most successful composer of those émigrés having musical careers in France.[72] Around 1853 Charles-Lucièn Lambert moved to Paris, where
he studied at Conservatoire de Musique and was successful in having his
compositions published. His son Lucièn-Léon Guillaume was born to Charles-
Lucièn's French wife in 1858. The family eventually moved to Brazil in the
1860s, where Lucièn *père* opened a music store and taught piano in Rio. He
became a member of the Brazilian National Institute of Music and died in Rio
in 1896; his son studied in France, where he published his compositions and
arrangements in Paris (1892–1911) and in Porto, Portugal (1912). Lester Sullivan suggests that Lucièn *père* was the first professional teacher of the Brazilian composer Ernesto Nazareth, who may have learned not only a love for
Chopin but also "an inclination toward the *style pianola* which coupled with
Gottschalk's pioneering use of American color in his compositions, suggests a
line of influence from Lambert *père* and Gottschalk to Nazareth and thence to
Heritor Villa-Lobos and even Darius Milhaud."[73]

The connections among the Louisiana Creole musicians were multiple and
crossed race lines. Lucièn *père* and Lucièn *fils* performed together in Rio with
their virtuoso contemporary from New Orleans Louis Moreau Gottschalk in
his 1869 appearance in which he had thirty-one pianists play simultaneously
in concert. Charles-Lucièn Lambert and Sidney Lambert were the sons of
Charles Richard Lambert, Edmond Dédé's early music teacher. Edmond Dédé
(1827–1903) also studied the violin with Ludovico Gabici, an Italian composer
who was the orchestra leader at the St. Charles Theater in New Orleans.

Dédé underscores the postcolonial and transnational explicit in considering the movement of these Creole musicians. He, like Charles Lucièn, was
born after Thomas Jefferson negotiated the 1803 Louisiana Purchase from
Napoleon for $15 million. That acquisition doubled the size of the new nation
and, importantly, gave the Americans control of the Mississippi River from its
source to its outlet. Napoleon Bonaparte's commentary on the sale is revealing: "The acquisition of these new lands firmly establishes the might of the
United States; and by this sale I have bequeathed to England a naval rival that
sooner or later will humble her pride."[74]

Edmond Dédé came into his majority not only well after New Orleans was
acquired by the United States but also well after Louisiana had become a
state. Yet, his movement throughout his adulthood was south and east. He
spent the period between 1848 and 1851 in Mexico, where other Creoles of
Color settled following the Mexican War. Recent histories of people of African
descent in Mexico are just beginning to demonstrate the fluid migration connections between Louisiana and Mexico in the middle of the nineteenth cen-

tury. Forced by illness to return to family in New Orleans, Dédé continued to compose music there until his 1857 departure for France, where he was admitted to the Conservatoire de Musique in Paris. Later, he directed the Grand Théâtre orchestra in Bordeaux, and subsequently was the orchestra conductor at Théâtre de l'Alcaza and the Folies Bordelaise.[75] Although he spent most of his career working in France, mainly in Bordeaux and Paris, Dédé continued a special relationship with New Orleans. A popular composer, violinist, and conductor, he returned to Louisiana several times during his career. His music was well known in New Orleans, where it was part of the culture of "genteel sheet music" that continued in popularity well after the Civil War. In August 1865, his *Le Palmier* overture was performed by a black orchestra in New Orleans.[76] When Dédé returned to New Orleans in 1893, he gave concerts from his most recent compositions published in Paris and introduced new works as well during this period.[77]

These musicians in a sense functioned in a developmental period when the distinctions between ethnic groups rivaled those between racial groups and when, in the performative arts, high and low culture often met. However, for them Paris was the matrix of the modern. There they aspired to achieve in their respective fields, and there they understood themselves not in the context of the old but rather of the new. Using Louisiana and a grouping of artists and musicians and *litteratures*, I would make several interconnected claims. It would seem that a Louisiana postcoloniality occurs much earlier than during the period between 1803 and 1812, when Louisiana was purchased and became a state. The period is marked by rapid and successive changes in the government of Louisiana and in the ways in which its residents identified themselves and their allegiances. The subsequent decades up to and including the 1860s saw the acceleration of the wealth, mobility, and education of a distinct class of Creoles of Color whose accomplishments reached unprecedented heights just as the Civil War approached.

The United States as a new nation-state and emerging imperial power (in large part on the basis of acquiring Louisiana) mainly rejected possible contributions by the Louisiana Creoles, and specifically the Creoles of Color. The movement of Edmond Dédé, Charles-Lucièn Lambert, and the Creoles of their generation, as well as that of their sons in the next generation, was much more fluid and constant or intermittent than is concluded about the colonial subjects from the Americas and specifically the West Indian islands whose movement is charted from the margins to the centers of culture, which are the cities of Europe and England where they remained. Because of its geographical location and relationship to Mexico, Brazil, South America,

Haiti, Cuba, the French and Spanish West Indies, and so forth, New Orleans remained culturally connected to regions south of it rather than to the North American geography and nation to which it belonged.

The idea of keeping the black body in place, so prevalent within U.S. racial politics and especially within the U.S. South, encounters two primary difficulties with Louisiana Creoles of Color. First, because of their mixed-race status, Creoles of Color were often undistinguishable from "white" Creoles of French and Spanish descent, particularly because of the Moorish infusion into Spain's native population. Second, because of their spatial mobility, Creoles of Color moved freely between the islands, Cuba, Haiti, Mexico, Brazil, and nations south of Louisiana and between Louisiana and Europe, not merely France and Spain but Portugal as well. The Lamberts, for example, spent time as musicians in Portugal. Often, as was the case with the dramatist Victor Séjour, Creoles of Color had relatives by blood or by marriage in far-flung places, particularly in Haiti and Cuba, as well as in Europe.

Compounding the difficulty of keeping Creoles of Color in their place was the spread of market capitalism and with it the social transformations that destabilized traditional space-time configurations, often collapsing the distinctions that had made for a marked and noticeable hegemony. However, rootlessness and homelessness seem to play an insignificant role in the identity formation of Creoles of Color. Alienation seems to occur most frequently with the loss of language rather than with the loss of other connections to spaces. Noticeably, it is language fluency that helped to enable their movement and flow into and through a variety of spaces in Europe and South America, as well as the islands, Cuba and Haiti in particular.

While the free people of color formed a third racial grouping with a legal definition and thus a higher-class position in antebellum Louisiana that largely patterned itself upon the model of French Creole society and therefore became one indication of the state's difference in terms of the treatment of blacks, the slave population contributed more significantly to Louisiana's distinctive culture. Because of the French laissez-faire attitude toward Louisiana slaves, especially in the urban and port areas, African slaves maintained aspects of their music and religion. Voodoo, the mixing of indigenous animist religions and Catholicism, was practiced openly. Charms and fetishes, potions and powders issued from the voodoo priests and priestesses not only into the black population but into the white one as well. Marie LaVeau, the most famous of the voodoo queens, had a large following of blacks and whites who took her predictions and workings seriously. Importantly, however, it is the dances (the Calinda and the Bamboula) and music associated with the voodoo ceremonies that still survive today. Dancing and drumming and singing in Congo Square, where the ceremonies were held, led to the distinctive music, now known as the New Orleans sound, that in the nineteenth century became the music of the Carnivals and Mardi Gras and other festivals in Louisiana and in the early twentieth century gave birth to jazz music.[78]

I incorporate the history of Louisiana Creoles and Creoles of Color here to signal the lack of stability in definitions and place. The idea of "place" in particular becomes most slippery in the convention of *plaçage*, the practice of "placing" women Creoles of Color with Creole men, specifically wealthy and white men of European extraction, but rarely those of "American" background. The idea of placing the women, establishing them by contract for financial security with a "protector" who provided a house and money, in and of itself involves a destabilizing of the marriage contracts within the Catholic Church, and it also undermines racial separation by making a recognized space within the community for interracial liaisons and mixed-race offspring.[79] Partly a struggle for recognition and difference and partly an assertion of modern enterprise and mores, plaçage was responsible for the high percentage of property ownership by free people of color in Louisiana and in the U.S. census of 1850. In the Faubourg Marigny in 1840, for example, free women of color owned 40 percent of the property, much of it resulting from plaçage financial arrangements.[80]

The fluidity of social relations within plaçage and within the mutable identity of the *placée* created a mobile population of free people who were not easily contained within the racial stratification. This practice, though now frequently mistakenly equated with prostitution, produced the large number of property owners among Creoles of Color and also produced the wealth that made containment of these raced bodies difficult. The plaçage was the semilegal, quasi-institutionalized arrangements between *femmes du couleur libres* and white Creole males in which the men provided a house and support in exchange for exclusive rights to sexual favors. Plaçage, or "*marriage de la main gauche*" ("left-handed marriage"), as the practice was called among Creoles, has rarely received a full treatment, especially one that takes into account the perspective of women Creoles of Color and the financial and political aspects of their arrangements.[81] Most often in scholarship today, the placée, the woman in the plaçage relationship, is represented as a victim of a sexual bartering resembling the selling of women slaves at public auction. While this comparison is viable to an extent, it renders an observation from the outside, from the largely white, and reformist, perspective that exposes the evils of slavery and its aftermath in terms of the violence done to women's bodies and to family structure. However, as is often the case, "victimhood" does not fully explain the economic motive from the perspective of women of color who, suffering from the very economic restrictions placed on blacks and on women that prevented them from undertaking a range of work options that would be deemed "respectable," find a way to sustain themselves and their families, and to do so within the highly acceptable "accumulation of wealth" that marked the rise of prosperity in the new capitalist regime emerging alongside the slave-based economy. The moralist view condemns the practice and aligns it with prostitution without observing that the structures it imposed on its very practices created a quasilegal overlay and an approximation of marriage sanctions. At stake is property and the clear uncontested accumulation of property and inheritance of property.

One white Creole, Charles-Oscar Dugué (1821–72) who was educated in Paris at the College St. Louis and worked as a journalist in New Orleans, wrote both plays and poetry evoking the visible landscape and cultural practices of the diverse people of Louisiana, including native Choctaws. His 1843 *"Souvenir du Bal"* ("Memory of the Ball"), with its repeated references to *"noir"* in the context of a sensual beauty whose body is seductive (eye, shoulder, mouth, bosom, waist all tempting) in dance at the ball but must be resisted, suggests the Creole balls designed to produce plaçage relationships. The last stanza is graphic:

> Still that black velvet, wherein is enlaced,
> In elegant caress, her comely waist,
> Slips lovingly betwixt my trembling fingers;
> And still—though powerless, I try my best—
> This angel-demon flames and chills my breast.[82]

Armand Lanusse, Creole of Color, however, takes a different strategy in his poem *"Epigramme"* from *Les Cenelles*:

> "Madame will not renounce the Devil," said
> A pastor to a zealous pietist,
> Who, every New Year, brought her sins, outspread
> Before him in a never-ending list,
> "I would," said she, "indeed renounce him. But
> Before grace sparks my soul, tell me I can . . .
> To rid all need for future sinning . . ." "What? . . ."
> *"Place* my daughter with a rich white man!"[83]

While these poets, particularly Creoles of Color, cast aspersion on the practice and practitioners of plaçage, they could not escape the reality of its force, economic and social, within their community. Neither could they escape the reality that many of the men in their class were the products of the practice or had family privilege because of the financial security resulting from plaçage. What they resented, however, was that "amalgamation," or sex across the color line in antebellum New Orleans, while not uncommon, was more likely to occur between women of color and white men, who were protected by their race and status under the law, whereas men of color were most likely to be prosecuted for having sex with white women.[84]

In the aftermath of the Civil War and Reconstruction, the effects of plaçage and race mixing were evident in the general population of Louisiana, as Blassingame notes: "miscegenation had been going on for so long that more people of both the 'white' and 'Negro' populations in New Orleans and Louisiana had more ancestors in the other race than did the residents of any other city or state in America. In fact, the population was so mixed that it was virtually impossible in many cases to assign individuals to either group."[85] Indeed, in concluding *White by Definition: Social Classification in Creole Louisiana* (1997), Virginia Domínguez states: "Despite the serious attempts by many New Orleanians to delimit the boundaries around the group with which they identify, the common jockeying for position means that there are no fixed boundaries around any groups and that it may be stretching the point to speak of groups in the context of southern Louisiana." Domínguez makes clear that even with policing efforts, racial boundaries were not rigid, but her point is more extensive: "And if boundaries are as fluid as much of the evidence suggests, then there can be no significant difference in ideas, beliefs, or expectations held by individuals in these overlapping sectors. If there are groups at all, it is . . . not because of cultural differentiation."[86] Her argument is for the sameness of culture and fluidity of identity markers among all the "Creole" people of southern Louisiana.

Place clearly was a signifier of identity for Creoles of Color, but precisely because they lived so much within a place of flux, they also seemed highly conscious of the fluidity of identity. Michel Fabre, in "New Orleans Creole Expatriates in France: Romance and Reality," details the culture of Creoles of Color in nineteenth-century France, in particular the careers of Victor Rillieux, an engineer; Camille Thierry, a poet; Victor Séjour, a dramatist; and Edmond Dédé, a composer. Fabre maintains that "France was often claimed by New Orleans Creoles of Color as a spiritual home to which they felt they belonged culturally."[87] In his representation of a multifaceted segment of the Creole expatriates, Fabre charts not only their lives in France but also the increasing climate of hostility in Louisiana that led to their eventual departure for France. Movement toward France, and Europe more generally, for those departing their native Louisiana was similar to their interaction with Haiti and Cuba in that it came as a result of both cultural and familial ties. Séjour, for example, was a French-speaking son of New Orleans, his mother's birthplace, but he had a close connection with Haiti, where his father was born. The elder Séjour returned to his birthplace and family home in Saint-Marc, Haiti, several times during his son's childhood.[88] Camille Thierry, though born in New Orleans, was the son of a French father from Bordeaux and as a result considered France as much a homeland as Louisiana.

For many of the Creoles of Color, place is important, but place itself is broadly based on language and customs and not contained within one geographical location. Rather than leading to detachment and displacement, this fluidity of place in the matrix of identity produced a cosmopolitan and worldly self-identification, and not coincidentally relational identities to place by conscious choice. They were mobile without being either nomadic or transitional, as Houston Baker remarked of African American life during later periods. Propelling Creoles of Color toward Europe was the pull of higher education and cultural experience unavailable in New Orleans. Diaspora as a concept applies to the space occupied by Thierry and these writers, but so does a postcoloniality that encouraged their gravitation to the nation-states producing their New World societies.

Generally well educated for individuals coming from a provincial place and culturally refined, free people of color were often Creoles who attended schools in Europe or in the American North: "About 2,000 . . . attended schools in Paris and in the North and West during the antebellum period."[89] Two of the prominent physicians, Louis Charles Roundanez and Alexandre Chaumette, received their training in Paris. As a result of their education and tastes, literary societies flowered among the free people of color. In 1843, for example, *L'Album Littéraire, Journal des Jeunes Gens, Amateurs de la Litterature* made its first appearance; it was the first recorded literary publication by Louisiana free people of color.[90] The little review, originally a monthly, presented stories, poems, fables, and articles; only four issues now survive.[91] The contributors, Armand Lanusse, Joanni Questy, Camille Thierry, Mirtil-Ferdinand Liotau, and Michel Saint-Pierre, had a radical purpose, despite the fact that they were forbidden by law to address slavery. Their struggle for expression as writers carries with it a struggle over both meaning and value epitomized by space and the social relations produced within their specific geographical and historical region.[92]

The contributors to *L'Album Littéraire* later participated in the publication of *Les Cenelles* (1845), a better-known anthology of the works of seventeen Creole poets written in French. With references to Alphonse de Lamartine, Victor Hugo, Pierre-Jean de Béranger, Félicité de Lamennais, and Alexandre Dumas, the poets linked their work to the more political of the French romantics and to the liberal issues of justice and progress.[93] In his preface to *Les Cenelles*, Armand Lanusse singled out Hugo and Dumas as "sublime geniuses" who could provide models for aspiring writers. Dumas is *"de l'immortel Dumas,"* which is an especially significant acknowledgment of a racial as well as the more obvious aesthetic and cultural kinship since Dumas was the celebrated French writer of known African descent.[94]

Taking their title from the small, berrylike fruit of the thorny hawthorn bush, the contributors may also have been forging an allusion to the hawthorn's dual production of a white and a pink flower as a way of incorporating their mixed-race identity. Desdunes offers the possible explanation that the small size of the berry "reflected the modesty of its authors" in their volume.[95] Elaborately printed and 215 pages in length with eighty-five poems, *Les Cenelles* was not a "modest offering." It was a substantial volume, though it was not as overtly political as *L'Album Littéraire*. Armand Lanusse was the principal editor and publisher of this first collection of poetry by writers of African descent in the United States. Because it was written in French, *Les Cenelles* was, until after the culture wars, often overlooked in literary histories of the United States and in accounts of African American literature, despite the fact that Edward Maceo Coleman, a professor of history at Morgan State in Baltimore, published *Creole Voices: Poems in French by Free Men of Color* in 1945, on the 100th anniversary of the appearance of *Les Cenelles*. However, only Coleman's preface and the foreword by H. Carrington Lancaster, a Romance languages professor at Johns Hopkins, were in English. Werner Sollors suggests that the neglect of writing such as *Les Cenelles* is a direct consequence of the "Creole" position of the writers both because it "defied an easy *national* location in an age in which literary history was imagined foremost to be the history of national literatures," and because it was "a *racially ambiguous* term in an era in which the color line was drawn more and more sharply."[96] Perhaps Sollors is correct in his speculations.

Camille Thierry, who produced fourteen poems for *Les Cenelles*, was quite visibly located within a Creole culture of people who were multilingual and multiracial. He and the educator and writer Michel Séligny, who founded Sainte-Barbe Academy in New Orleans, were highly respected in the Creole community for their erudition and publications.[97] Thierry's poems are considered to be at the front rank of all Francophone poetry published during this period, yet he wrote not only in French but also in Louisiana Creole, so that he clearly attempted to reach those who were not among an educated elite. An example is "An Old Mulatress's Lament; or Sanite Fuéron's Despair," written in the Creole language and translated into vernacular poetry in English:

Listen! Way back, Santo Domingo,
Black girls, them be like jewels! Just so!
White men, them pester us, them cling, oh!
Follow us everywhere we go.
    Them live with us,
    No fight, no fuss.
Love us like goddesses, worship, embrace!
    Them never cheap,
    Them pockets, deep:
Give what men want, them give us run of place! . . .
    Time change, us poor. Now you know what?
    Before, them trat us fine, each one . . .
    Soon, white brat laugh at us, make fun,
        Go call us trash and slut![98]

Toward the end of his life, Thierry published *Les Vagabondes* (1874) in Paris, where he resided following the Civil War and emancipation, when free people of color no longer had a legal status in Louisiana. Like his earlier work in the 1840s, the poems were in French and based on three figures from his childhood in New Orleans. He had returned to Bordeaux, the home his father had left to migrate to New Orleans. The colony had provided his father with the opportunity to become a successful businessman, and with a share of his father's fortune, Camille Thierry was able to live on both sides of the Atlantic in relative security. The details available about Creoles of Color who emigrated to France, however, have recurrent references to economics and capital and to reversals of fortune. Thierry, for example, arrived in France with great wealth but, through the mismanagement of funds by his agents in New Orleans, lost everything. He died a year after the publication of *Les Vagabondes*.

Pierre Dalcour, who contributed twelve poems to *Les Cenelles*, was born in New Orleans (1813) of free Creole parents Pedro Dalcour and Eulalie Allain, but his father sent him as a child to France for education. Although he returned to New Orleans as an adult, Dalcour did not remain in Louisiana because of the restrictions imposed on even free blacks in a slave society. He did, however, return to New Orleans for visits. He wrote the poems published in *Les Cenelles* during one of his trips to New Orleans from Paris, where he was involved in literary activities though not publishing his poetry. Lanusse favored Dalcour's poems enough to begin and end *Les Cenelles* with them. Dalcour's romantic poems stand out for their references to color and Creoleness. In *"Les Aveux"* ("Declaration"), he addresses a "Creole" (*"ô ma créole"*) directly in one stanza:

> The glance, more than the voice, can tell
> How deep the lover's sentiments:
> To say "I love you," Creole belle,
> Greater the glance's eloquence.
> So, mute my voice remains, although
> Many my loving, soulful sighs:
> What my lips dare not tell you, oh!
> Can you not see it in my eyes?[99]

"Lines Written in the Album of Mademoiselle ***" contains a clear connection of skin color and beauty: "[T]he star that twinkles high in heaven's expanse, / The moonlight, gentle, in the darkening skies, / Are not so sweet to look on as a glance / From your brown-lidded eyes."[100] Dalcour, like Thierry, seemed to write easily about Creoles and to move, with more ease than is usually attributed to Creoles of Color, between France and Louisiana.

Many of the poems of *Les Cenelles* were intended as lyrics—for example, Mirtil-Ferdinand Liotau's *"A un ami Qui M'Accusait de Plagiat"* or Thierry's *"Regrets d'une Vieille Mulâttress; ou, Désepoir de Sanite Fouéron."* The musical annotations were not provided, although the names of the melodies to which the poems were set were included. This grouping of poems then might be considered to function within "zones of ambiguity," in which lies uncertainty.[101] The differences between lyrics and voice and between words and the sound of words may now be impossible to ascertain.

The poets turn most often to natural landscapes. Nature for these cosmopolitan poets may obviously be read as affect and symbolic. The most accessible natural landscapes would encompass water, movement, and flow, and not without some signifier of danger. The Mississippi River and the lakes and bayous, while potentially threatening, also harbored the maroons who moved in and out of New Orleans, doing business and commerce with residents of the city. The attempt at permanence or stability on shifting ground is undermined by the undecipherable and illegible movement over water or on the bayous that can be watery graves or moving foundations. The bayou becomes the trope of impermanency, which nonetheless is represented in terms of the physical and seductive beauty masking the threat of death and destruction. The bayou is the natural counterpart to the representation of the plantation as a built environment of confinement.

Recent critiques point to the lack of protest in the poetry published in *Les Cenelles* and the affect of French romanticism without the political content, but Caryn Cossé Bell, in *Revolution, Romanticism, and the Afro-Creole Protest Tradition*, has rightly read the layered social criticism in the collection. I want to suggest that following Bell, closer attention to the poems and poets in context and in relation to their referents may yield more ways to reconstruct the political content of *Les Cenelles*. One way, for instance, is to examine one of the primary contributing poets, "B. (VALCOUR.)" as listed in the table of contents, who contributed eleven poems. Only three of the seventeen contributors have more inclusions: the editor, Armand Lanusse, with eighteen poems; Camille Thierry, with fourteen poems; and Pierre Dalcour, with twelve poems.

The poet listed in *Les Cenelles* as "B. (VALCOUR.)" and as the contributor of eleven poems ("*Table*," 211), among them several with specific references to blackness and race, was identified in Rodolphe Desdunes's 1911 *Nos Hommes et Notre Histoire* as "B. Valcour." Desdunes described the writer in terms of internal references in the poem, although he does claim that B. Valcour was a native of New Orleans. Scholars, such as Coleman, following Desdunes, identify the poet as "B. Valcour," as do subsequent references as in M. Lynn Weiss's introduction and notes to *Creole Echoes: The Francophone Poetry of Nineteenth-Century Louisiana* (2004; poems translated by Norman R. Shapiro). In her 1973 translation of Desdunes, Sister Dorothea Olga McCants comments in a note to Desdunes's description of "Valcour": "The dates of Valcour's birth and death are unknown. . . . No trace can be found of Valcour's first name. In *Les Cenelles*, to which he contributed eleven poems, he signs himself Valcour B + + +."[102] She does not comment on the discrepancy between her notation of "Valcour B + + +" and Desdunes's text (B. Valcour) and instead accepts that Valcour is the poet's last name. Régine Latortue and Gleason R. W. Adams, however, in *Les Cenelles: A Collection of Poems by Creole Writers of the Early Nineteenth Century* (1979), begin their "Biographical Sketches of the Poets" with "*Valcour B*" and note that the poet signs his name in *Les Cenelles* "Valcour B ***" and that Edward Larocque Tinker, in *Les Écrits de Langue Francaise en Louisiane au XIXe Siècle*, also identifies the poet in that way. While citing the biographical and critical material from Desdunes, they nonetheless observe that both Desdunes and Coleman refer to the poet as "B. Valcour."

As alphabetized in the "*Table*" and as signed after the first poem, "Valcour" is the first name of the poet, but that correction may not provide a full reading of the name. Noticeably, the signature "Valcour B + + +" appears only at the end of the first poem; all subsequent poems bear the signature "Valcour." I suggest that, like Joanni Questy, Valcour may have been using only his first name in the collection. All of Joanni Questy's poems in *Les Cenelles* bear the single signature "Joanni." In the *"Table,"* he is alphabetized under "J" for "Joanni," with no other name given. Desdunes writes with familiarity about Joanni Questy, even mentioning that he was a teacher of French and Spanish: "All of the children knew him as Mr. Joanni [Mr. Johnny]."[103] The difference between Desdunes's entry for Valcour and his entry for Joanni is striking. He obviously knew the details of Joanni's life, work, and place in New Orleans, while he has no information about Valcour other than what he could glean from his poetry. Desdunes admits to knowing little about Valcour and speculates from the internal references and the 1828 date of his poem to his teacher that he was born in New Orleans around 1800, which he calculates would make him one of the oldest of the contributors to *Les Cenelles*.[104] This observation leads to my reading regarding the identity of "Valcour."

I believe that "Valcour" is in fact a nom de plume in place to hide the actual identity of the poet. I draw this conclusion based not only on the matter of the listing of the name and Desdunes's lack of information but also from the name itself. There is no listing in the 1840s New Orleans city directories of "Valcour" as a surname. The name, however, can be traced to a literary text familiar to the *Les Cenelles* poets. "Valcour" is a character in Marquis de Sade's *Aline and Valcour or, The Philosophical Novel,* published in 1795 in the wake of the French Revolution but written while Sade was imprisoned in the Bastille. By 1815 the book was banned in France for its sexually graphic content. While it is a romantic tale of two lovers, it is also an epistolary, philosophical disquisition full of double lives and secrets, and "The Story of Valcour," the fifth letter in the text, contains much of the Marquis de Sade's own autobiography. Valcour is a poor but well-born youth who, though raised in the palace of a prince, is not accepted as a suitor for Aline. Indeed, his story reveals that he is impetuous and fiery, and he has abandoned another woman, Adélaïde, who loved him and received his promise. Aline's father objects to the union and is cruel in keeping them apart, but her mother accepts the lovers with kindness and affection. Sade's novel also places an African kingdom in a contrapuntal relation to a South Pacific island; the former is as brutal as Aline's father, while the latter is a utopia ruled by a Zamé, a philosopher. This work of Sade is a chronicle of his political shift to identify with the "citizens" of the revolution and away from the aristocracy of his birth. The political content suggests a connection to both a philosophy of freedom and a call to revolution.

B. (Valcour), the contributor to *Les Cenelles*, uses the epistolary format in his poetic tribute to the teacher Constant Lépouzé, "Epitre à. Constant Lépouzé."[105] He indicates that he was a student of French and Latin, which would have made him familiar with the work of Marquis de Sade. He may well have had a political motive for concealing his identity, and when read in that light, his poems take on more of an edge than they initially appear to have. Latortue and Adams observe that in "Louisiana Laborer" (*"L'Ouvrier Louisianais"*), Valcour "professes a love for his country and a pride in his origin which is not frequently expressed in the poems in *Les Cenelles*."[106] In that poem, he refers to the "Misunderstood sons of New Orleans" and aligns the poet with the sentiment: "Despite her many faults I love her still / Faithful to my land I want to remain." Dedicated to *"Mon Ami Armand Lanusse,"* the poem is a song in the style of Béranger (*"Imité de Béranger"*).[107] Valcour's eleven poems in the volume incorporate references to Virgil, Horace, and Lamartine, but also issues of color that have not been recognized as racial allusion. In "For Hermina," for example, Valcour concludes each of the three stanzas with the words "Far from Hermina, dark becomes my day," that have been read as a lover's despair over his absence from his beloved but may also be read as alluding to Hermina's race.

Valcour as a pseudonym, however, may serve a larger political agenda. Derived from Sade's text written during his imprisonment in the Bastille, it veils the references to the French Revolution even while aligning the poet with that political revolution. The linkage to *"la belle France,"* as Edward Maceo Coleman reminds us in his preface to *Creole Voices*, "was to the Creole the land of liberty" and not simply of "beauty, and cultural refinement."[108] Shirley Elizabeth Thompson entitles her discussion of *Les Cenelles* "Race and a Logical Harmonics of Place," in which she states: "Traditionally, birthright has included most prominently the claim to territory and has bestowed upon its bearer the responsibility of defining and refining that territory and defending it against encroachment. Demonstrating historical grounds for ownership and developing a cultural aesthetic of place are strategies that reinforce title and, when skillfully interwoven, ascribe meaning to particular places."[109] The poets of *Les Cenelles* may well have been locating themselves in relationship to their Louisiana, New Orleans in particular, which by 1845 was becoming increasingly "Americanized" with much harsher attitudes and practices toward free people of color and enslaved people alike. More importantly, I would argue, they were situating themselves by language and reference to France and to the social and political identity of "Citizen" in the French definition of the term.

Composed primarily by the Marquis de Lafayette, the "Declaration of the Rights of Man and of the Citizen" was adopted by the French National Constituent Assembly on 26 August 1789. It guaranteed the equality of all people under the law and all citizens specific rights. The seventeen articles begin with the two carrying the most weight for the citizen: (1) "Men are born and remain free and equal in rights. Social distinction may be founded only upon the general good"; and (2) "The aim of all political association is the preservation of the natural and imprescriptible rights of man. These rights are liberty, property, security, and resistance to oppression." Additional items in the list of rights would also be significant for the Creole writers; for instance, number 11 states: "The free communication of ideas and opinions is one of the most precious rights of man. Every citizen may, accordingly, speak, write, and print with freedom, but shall be responsible for such abuses of this freedom as shall be defined by law." The initial duo of rights, however, are the major ones because they contrast not with the words of the American Constitution but with the Creoles' sense of identification with its execution in a slave state and a larger slave nation. That "Valcour" has not been identified by those scholars examining *Les Cenelles* may well be because he instituted with his very naming a sequence of references to the French Revolution and the rights of citizens. Placing B. (Valcour) or Valcour B*** in this larger diasporic relation to the French Revolution is also to situate the poet and all the poets of *Les Cenelles* in a space of oppositional and radical politics that bell hooks described in considering her own choice of a spatial location as a political activist. Her formulation is suggestive in rethinking what might have constituted a radical spatial location for Valcour in his very signage. Marginality offers a "position and a place of resistance" that, according to hooks, "is crucial for oppressed, exploited, colonized people" because it is "a central location for the production of a counter-hegemonic discourse that is not just found in words but in habits of being and the way one lives . . . a site one stays in, clings to even, because it nourishes one's capacity to resist. It offers the possibility of radical perspectives from which to see and create, to imagine alternatives, new worlds."[110] Whether or not a strong argument can be made for Valcour choosing a space within *Les Cenelles* to sign himself cryptically and symbolically as one resisting oppression and envisioning an alternative new world signified by the French Revolution and its connection to the American Revolution, his naming does appear unequivocally as a space of difference and his poem as a site of political consciousness.

The female counterparts of the *Les Cenelles* poets appear to be nonexistent. Yet a native New Orleanian, Madame Louisa R. Lamotte, founded a literary magazine, *Revue*, which she edited and published in France, where she was educated. Madame Lamotte taught for forty years at the College of Young Women at Abbeville in France and became the school's directress. The French government awarded her magazine the *"Palmes Academiques"* (1881) for academic merit. Though she returned to Louisiana, where she died in 1907, she left hardly a trace of her literary activity in the land of her birth.[111] Similarly, Virginie Girodeau, who wrote for the French theater, is almost unknown in Louisiana, where she was born. She was a stage performer reputed to be excellent in Renaissance tragedies. Desdunes observes that "she left an enviable reputation as a tragedienne."[112] Madame Girodeau appears to have studied under one of the most famous professors in France, Perennès, but little is known about her life and career, except for a record of her friendship with one of the prominent poets of color, Armand Lanusse, the editor of *Les Cenelles*.

Predictable historical factors contributed to the absence of published writings by Louisiana women of color. Women, no matter their racial designation, generally were not encouraged to become "professional" writers either of performances for the theater or of poetry for reading audiences. The general belief was that women of a certain class should remain in more sheltered spheres, and the expectation was that when educated in convent schools, they would devote their abilities to the family so that any verse or drawing-room dramas or musical interludes they created would be for the benefit of family and friends in the very social world that Creoles created. Furthermore, the Catholic Church encouraged women to perform charitable services within their community and to devote themselves to assisting the clergy in feeding the hungry and clothing the poor.

The two overlapping areas into which free women of color directed their talents were religion and education. Often the two were combined in the founding of religious schools and the teaching of children. Henriette Delille, a Creole woman of color, followed this path. In 1842 she and another free woman of color, Juliette Gaudin, founded Les Soeurs de la Sainte Famille (the Sisters of the Holy Family), a still extant order of Catholic nuns who educated girls at St. Mary's Academy, initially located in the New Orleans Vieux Carré in a space once known, ironically, as the Orleans Ballroom and devoted to the balls that brought together Creole women and their protectors under plaçage arrangements.[113] Nevertheless, both religion, particularly the Catholic faith, and education, specifically the lack of schooling, functioned to prevent Creole women from participating extensively in the higher arts of poetry and creative writing.

In the generation after emancipation, a mixed-raced woman from New Orleans, the daughter of a woman born a slave in Opelousas, Louisiana, would emerge as a published author of considerable talent. Alice Ruth Moore produced a collection of stories and sketches in English, *Violet, and Other Tales* (1895). Four years later, she married the leading African American writer of the time, Paul Laurence Dunbar, just as her second book of stories, *The Goodness of St. Rocque, and Other Stories* (1898), appeared. When these books were published in the last decade of the nineteenth century, they were not received as the momentous occasions they actually were. Hardly any notice was made of the fact that Alice Ruth Moore (later Dunbar-Nelson), a New Orleans native, was one of the first Louisiana women of color to publish books in English and to explore Creole society, even though Louisiana's people of color had a long history of literary work.

Violets and Other Tales and *The Goodness of St. Rocque* emerged out of the Créolité contained within a stratified and race-assertive Louisiana in the late nineteenth century, when the Americans had finally won out over the surviving Creole elite in terms of instituting laws mandating segregation and having those legal restrictions upheld by the U.S. Supreme Court in *Plessy v. Ferguson*. Despite the changed legal climate, the spirit that sustained Creoles of Color throughout their existence in Louisiana was not crushed, as Desdunes pointed out in revisiting the strategic activities of the *Comité des Citoyens* (Citizens' Committee) formed in 1890, "when a return to exaggerated fanaticism about caste or segregation once again alarmed the black people"[114] and incited their willed refusal to submit to oppressive power: "Absolute submission augments the oppressor's power and creates doubt about the feelings of the oppressed."[115] It is in this spirit of resistance to oppression that Alice Dunbar-Nelson's two collections emerged.

Her early "Louisiana" work was the writing of a multicultural subjectivity, a racially plural subjectivity. Her training at Straight University brought her into contact with students from other parts of the state and teachers from other regions. Within that milieu, she came to understand the actual and imagined communities of culture within the physical geography of Louisiana in the decades both before and after. Nevertheless, taking her cue from the popularity of local color stories by Grace King and Kate Chopin and from the readymade audiences for quaint tales set in exotic Louisiana, Dunbar-Nelson made little overt use of race and the issues of racial oppression and discrimination. She was not unconcerned about race matters, as Gloria Thompson Hull has suggested in her reading Dunbar-Nelson's short fiction, but she followed an acceptable marketing pattern of naturalizing whites, albeit Creoles of Spanish and French descent, and in the process she also obscured her own racial identity as a woman of color in her seeming affinity with the white Creole characters in her texts.[116] In stories such as "Little Miss Sophie," with a Creole of Color placée rejected for a white bride, and "Sister Josepha," with a young novice who is uncertain of her racial identity, Dunbar-Nelson writes about race matters in Louisiana, but indirectly so. She takes the literal body as a contested space. She positions her characters in such a way that they become racially ambiguous or indeterminate, but rather than in-betweenness or outsiderness becoming a material prison, in Dunbar-Nelson's fiction it is signified as fluidity and can become the access to freedom from the typical or prevailing societal norms and customs, though it can also lead to an acceptance of the hegemony of place, as when Sister Josepha retreats behind the doors of a race-neutral convent because of her anxiety about not knowing her racial place in the outside world. In addition to the subtle bodily descriptions ("yellow woman," "brown hands," "dusky-eyed") that Hull mentions as clues to Dunbar-Nelson's handling of race, Violet Harrington Bryan points out that she also uses recognizable names of streets and neighborhoods in New Orleans to signal race.[117]

New Orleans for Dunbar-Nelson was a city place of streets, houses, churches, convents, schools, and neighborhoods, which she utilized in lacing her narrative plots with the symbolic overlay of the urban geography and its dramatic addition to the often slight or lightly sketched thematic cores. While the shrine of St. Rocque and the St. Louis Cathedral are clearly marked as landmark social spaces, she moves her sense of the city outwards from the religious and domestic spaces expected in stories by women at the turn of the century. Dunbar-Nelson also envisioned the city as a marketplace reflecting the vibrant life of the city as reflected in the open air, its shops open to the streets, vendors moving through the city, and outdoor market stands and stalls. She utilizes walking in the city as a way of bringing characters into contact with the diversity of the urban space.

Much like Charles Chesnutt at the turn of the century writing about his native North Carolina, Dunbar-Nelson concentrates on a mixed-race society, in her case a Creole society, which she celebrated and questioned. While Chesnutt could openly confront the struggle for contested space within a North Carolina where Reconstruction and its aftermath had fostered pitched battles that blacks invariably lost, Dunbar-Nelson was unable to write without veils about the Louisiana she knew. A mixed-race woman whose father was most likely a white Louisianian who never married her mother, she knew intimately the race and class restrictions in Louisiana, but she also knew firsthand the opportunities for mobility in the decades following her birth in 1875.[118] She recognized the problem of the caste of color in "Brass Ankles Speaks," in which skin color determined social class, so that in the New Orleans of her youth, the lighter the complexion, the higher would be the individual's status.[119] She nonetheless worked later in life to promote knowledge of the multicultural Louisiana that she had experienced as a child and young adult. She wrote in 1917, for instance: "There is no State in the Union, hardly any spot of like size on the globe, where the man of color has lived so intensely, made so much progress, been of such historical importance, and yet about which so comparatively little is known."[120] Given the poverty of her early years, she may well have exaggerated the positive in her attention to people of color in Louisiana, yet in some measure her assessment is accurate.

While writing at the turn of the century in Louisiana, Alice Dunbar-Nelson surely could not imagine creating her Creole stories and directly confronting racial issues at the same time. Influenced by the spatial configurations of the city, the blocks and pavements and banquettes teeming with people of many different accents and colors and customs, she pushed the short story form to express the vibrancy and the complexity that lay beneath the colorful figures; but following the accepted models of white local-color writers, such as the progressive George Washington Cable or the reactionary Grace King, she could not overtly change the script for racial expression or gender discourse. She nonetheless was subversive and resistant to the definitions of Creole that did not include people of color. At her death in 1935, Alice Dunbar-Nelson was remembered as a black journalist, the widow of Paul Laurence Dunbar, and an activist race woman living in the North.[121] She had outlived her connections to the Creole community of New Orleans that had provided her with creative inspiration for her two collections of sketches and stories. She would perhaps be amused to know that at the turn into the twenty-first century, Louisiana's own state university press would publish a volume entitled *Creole: The History and Legacy of Louisiana's Free People of Color*, edited by Sybil Kein, the nom de plume of Consuela Moore, one of her descendants.[122] Alice Ruth Moore Dunbar-Nelson's "People of Color in Louisiana" is included as the lead essay in the volume, and it may be read in conjunction with the collision of the public sphere with subjective space. What she created within her essay was a way of expanding her contemporary landscape, modern but hemmed in by the legal stranglehold of the *Plessy v. Ferguson* decision and also by the literal economic deprivation that marked much of her life and the lives of many Creoles of Color. In linking herself and Louisiana people of color to the achievements of their forebears, she pushed back the boundaries that contained blacks from the end of the nineteenth century and connected their lives to those that had preceded them. While literal kinship was not the intent of her essay, figurative connection with familial traces like a residue allowed her to transform a rights-challenged people into the inheritors of rights and of achievement.

Carolyn Senter, in "Creole Poets on the Verge of a Nation," explores one of the last major periods of productivity for nineteenth-century Creole writers, 1865–67, when the New Orleans newspaper *Creole of Color* published selections of poems in French by Creole writers. In the aftermath of the Civil War and emancipation, the privileging of les gens de couleur libres was as obsolete as slavery, and Creoles of Color sought to redefine themselves and their place within a vastly different society. Senter's essay advances the discourse on Creole writing by moving away from the 1840s prewar collection *Les Cenelles* and by taking on the politics of nationality. Senter rightly observes that the most recent translation of *Les Cenelles* by Regine Latortue and Gleason Adams attempts to place the Creole contributors within the language of mix-raced bodies in the U.S. context: "Trapped between the races, between classes, and between cultures, the Louisiana Creoles could not or would not confront the problems and conflicts that blacks, no matter how elevated, experienced."[123] Senter suggests that the real difficulty is attempting to place the work of these Creoles "in a genre that depends upon the fixity of such categories. Indeed, the definition of 'Creole' precisely elides such fixity. The very existence of the group and its cultural production challenged the binary divisions that underlay American social, cultural, and—at that time—legal and political institutions."[124] Senter raises valid and pertinent points because the reality of the world occupied by Creoles of Color throughout most of the nineteenth century was in almost constant flux rather than fixed in binary oppositions.

The challenging of the binary divisions in American life was not restricted to the mere bodily existence of Creoles of Color. Significantly, from the 1860s though the 1890s, Creoles of Color challenged each encroachment on their rights as citizens. They challenged the new segregationist policies and fought the evaporation of the privileges they had attained before the Americanization of Louisiana. What they could not fight, however, was the inability of the United States from the end of the nineteenth century through much of the twentieth to understand the cosmopolitan makeup of people of color, and in particular the Creoles of Color, whose ancestry linked them to multiple and mutual geographies that may have offered in a crucial time in the nation's modern history what David Harvey identifies as a cosmopolitan ethic of justice, fairness, and reason.[125]

POLITICS & PAYSANS

Without a societal basis for the acceptance of the descendants of les gens des couleur libre and the descendants of enslaved people of color, the eighteenth- and nineteenth-century heritage of a property-owning, educated citizenry with African ancestry devolved into efforts to preserve an elite based on skin color. Ultimately, Creoles of Color, despite the wide range of skin shade within their ranks, segregated themselves from other people of African descent, especially those who were dark skinned. Taking their lead especially in the aftermath of the failed effort on the part of Homer Plessy and the Comité des Citoyens to challenge the increasingly restrictive "race" laws regulating access to public space, Creoles of Color attempted to insulate themselves from the insults and threats of the new racism.[126] The name they selected for the committee refers back to the French "Declaration of the Rights of Man and of the Citizen," *de Citoyen*. In the late nineteenth century and at the turn of the twentieth century, the Seventh Ward of the city of New Orleans became the primary area in which Creoles of Color lived and attempted to escape in their home and social life the degradation they could not escape in much of their work and employment.

The self-othering of twentieth-century Creoles of Color, however, did not preserve intact a unique culture but instead created fault lines within an increasingly segregated community. An aura of suspicion surrounded Creoles of Color during the desegregation activities of the 1960s, even though several of the most prominent attorneys leading the struggle were Creoles of Color. A. P. Tureaud, for example, was an attorney actively leading the battle to desegregate New Orleans schools after the Supreme Court outlawed "separate but equal" in its 1954 *Brown v. Board of Education* decision. In the aftermath of the 1960s civil rights movement, the privileging of skin color and other visible signs of proximity to "whiteness" lessened, and with that lessening came a loosening of the reigns of color solidarity among lighter-skinned Creoles of Color.

How might the United States have looked if the cultural flow of the Creoles of Color had permeated its boundaries in the nineteenth century? We are unable to know. However, we may be able to construct an image of the possibility by rehearsing several of the debates around U.S. canon formation and multiculturalism in the 1980s. While a move to multiculturalism would suggest occupying a space outside of the web of transnational discourse, the Creoles of Color in their diasporic relationship to Créolité would complicate that assumption.

Gregory Jay, in *America the Scrivener*, speaks to the issue of American literary history as "a discipline with changing boundaries."[127] In deploying

Melville's "Bartleby, the Scrivener," he interrogates an "ideology of literary historiography in which the nation represents itself to itself as a writing subject, a single consciousness expressing its history and self-understanding."[128]

Jay does not claim a new metanarrative for American literary history; instead, he asserts: "[I]n the course of writing this book I have become convinced that we should abandon such stories and the nationalist agenda that they inevitably reinforce."[129] He concludes his section on African American literary history with the following:

> The study of African-American culture can mobilize the difference of race to undo the limits of history, ideology, and rhetoric. The African-American experience of slavery and oppression dictates that we cannot neglect factoring in material conditions into the history of ideas and literature (on either side of the hyphen); moral and ethical considerations likewise motivate the interpretive process, while also demanding a different relation between the reading subject and the speaking subject than had once obtained under the sway of aesthetic humanism. The difference of race continually prompts a reminder of one's own construction by a limited rather than total history.[130]

Though Jay's location of slavery within African American rather than American or U.S. experience suggests the difficulty of letting go of the paradigms within American literary history, his critique of a singular writing subject as national consciousness is insightful. Whether we wish to admit it or not, writing literary history depends on the familiar whose boundaries are typically fixed in ideology, just as perhaps satisfying literature may well depend on a process of defamiliarization or crossing a boundary that excites our expectations.

One legacy of 1960s and 1970s political and social activism was, indeed, a rise by the mid-1980s of visible minorities and women as a class into a broader spectrum of cultural participation and production; nevertheless, intersections of concerns and objectives were still rare. Today, however, there is an overt conjunction of concerns among various racial and ethnic groups that, while differently articulated, are nonetheless represented as evidence of a growing consciousness of difference and diversity. We trouble the interpretation of "multicultural," but we do not negate its existence or the urgency of attending to its manifestations in how we conceptualize ourselves and any conjoined future. Within the academy, of course, we "out" essentialism, interrogate cultural nationalism, and resist single conceptual categories for delineating identity or textuality. We have come to accept, though not without some unease, an awareness of our own multiple subject positions, the intersectionality of identity, and with that self-awareness, a wider acceptance of the multiplicity of coexistent cultures has inevitably resulted. Yet, the persistent problematic adheres around minority issues, raced bodies and their creative and scholarly production.

In *The Location of Culture* (1994), Homi Bhabha deploys the term "Border Lives: The Art of the Present" as a trope for our "need to think beyond narratives of originary and initial subjectivities and to focus on those moments or processes that are produced in the articulation of cultural differences":

> These "in-between" spaces provide the terrain for elaborating strategies of selfhood—single or communal—that initiate new signs of identity, and innovative sites of collaboration, and contestation, in the act of defining the idea of a society itself.
>
> It is in the emergence of the interstices—the overlap and displacement of domains of difference—that the intersubjective and collective experience of *nationness*, community, interest, or cultural value are negotiated.[131]

Bhabha addresses the emergence of a social articulation of difference in the fluid intersection of the subjective and the collective, and he opens up a space for an expanded discourse on multiculturalism as a desire on the parts of communities for recognition of their cultural presence. While his formulation of "nationness" may require further elaboration, his articulation of a "third space" functions appropriately in this discourse; that is, "the given grounds of opposition and . . . a space of translation: a place of hybridity . . . where the construction of a political object that is new, *neither the one nor the other*, properly alienates our political expectations, and changes . . . the very forms of our recognition of the moment of politics."[132]

"Multiculturalism," however, became bracketed, a contested term in the United States at precisely the moment when theoreticians like Bhabha escalated their intercultural work. Debates on multiculturalism were most often linked to those bounded areas around political correctness and issues of inclusion and exclusion from a recognized cultural canon. Curricular change, perhaps more so than any other manifestation of these debates, was the most publicized, and as well the most politicized when such changes directly correlated with the recognition of racism and sexism in many of the traditional icons of Western education.

The conjoined question Henry Louis Gates Jr. asks in "Trading on the Margin: Notes on the Culture of Criticism" is: "What is multiculturalism, and why are they saying such terrible things about it?"[133] His interlocking what-why play on popular culture mediates the seriousness of the question. Gates provides several examples of the "terrible" things being said to malign multiculturalism: "We've been told [multiculturalism] threatens to fragment American culture into a warren of ethnic enclaves, each separate and inviolate. We've been told that it menaces the Western tradition of literature and the arts. We've been told it aims to politicize the school curriculum, replacing honest historical scholarship with a 'feel good' syllabus designed solely to bolster the self-esteem of minorities."[134] His own response to these misreadings does not deny that the fragmentation of American society by ethnicity, class, gender, and race (which he pointedly omits) fostered the multicultural initiative, but he simply asserts: "Common sense says that you don't bracket 90 percent of the world's cultural heritage if you really want to learn about the world."[135] But prior to the intervention that multiculturalists made in the 1980s, much of the world's cultural heritage was indeed bracketed or worse in the average school curriculum.[136]

Loose Canons: Notes on the Culture Wars (1992), Gates's collection of essays containing "Trading on the Margins," would hardly have received serious consideration for publication during the 1980s, and most likely no Oxford University Press editor would have persisted in trying to obtain the manuscript, as Gates tells us was the case with *Loose Canons*. But much did change in the movement from the eighties to the nineties; more accurately, people changed or renegotiated their sense of relational and national identity, so that their location enlarged and their claimed space expanded into a global world.

Since then, we have increasingly absorbed "borders," "borderlands," and "border crossings," or, as Bhabha does of "border lives," taken our cue from contemporary Chicana/o interrogation of space and nationality. Gloria Anzaldúa's definition of "borderland" as a place where "two or more cultures edge each other, where people of different races occupy the same territory," has provided the terminology to name a cultural phenomenon and has become part of our cultural awareness of sites of struggle and of cooperation.[137] We now acknowledge the fluidity of a nation-state's borders as much more permeable and unmarked than ever before. People and cultures are moving, shifting, migrating, and expanding the nation-state's boundaries in ways that are not always easily understood. Hortense Spillers proclaimed the phenomenon in "Who Cuts the Border? Some Readings on 'America,'" her introduction to *Comparative American Identities: Race, Sex, and Nationality in the Modern Text* (1991): "The ways and means of negotiating borders and centers virtually constitute a new area studies in the liberal arts curriculum in the U.S. today." Paul Gilroy in *The Black Atlantic: Modernity and Double Consciousness* (1993) addresses "the continuing lure of ethnic absolutisms in cultural criticism produced both by blacks and by whites" by arguing that "black America's histories of cultural and political debate and organisation" may be read as having challenged and renounced "the easy claims of African-American exceptionalism in favour of a global, coalitional politics in which anti-imperialism and anti-racism might be seen to interact if not to fuse."[138]

No longer parochial or even national, cultural theorists such as Spillers and Gilroy crossed borders in elaborating and revising what cultural recognition signifies. In the discourses of cultural studies, marginalized communities move from the margins and challenge both their own marginalization and the very concept of center. In the process of challenging hegemony, Gilroy, for instance, not only exposes oppressive structures but also refigures the power dynamic, so that "transnational and intercultural" replace "national" and "cultural" as significations of a more complex perspective of history and culture. This move repositions "multicultural" as well, so that the concept is not in danger of becoming a "pluralism" that, as Gates has suggested, the Left finds objectionable because it "fails to be adequately emancipatory" and "leaves oppressive structures intact."[139] Intercultural, however, bears with it in the U.S. context the concept of integration, which in its relationship to assimilation deprives minority cultures of visibility and suggests some of the negative implications of the "melting pot" ideology. These moves are all in various ways references to contested space where "minority" people and cultures become visible and declare a presence that cannot be ignored. The problem arises in part because the hegemonic view has been of space as rigid, fixed, and hierarchical or other than fluid, interactive, and constitutive.

My focus here on multiculturalism is to recall a claim on public space. In 1995 the Black Public Sphere Collective responded to Jürgen Habermas's *The Structural Transformation of the Public Sphere* by defining its project as spatial—"a transnational space whose violent birth and diasporic conditions of life provide a counternarrative to the exclusionary national narratives of Europe, the United States, the Caribbean, and Africa. Thus the black public sphere is one critical space where new democratic forms and emergent diasporic movements can enrich and question one another."[140] Within this "critical social imaginary," as the Black Public Sphere Collective identified itself, was a significant awareness of politics, a "visionary politics" intersecting with critical practice, or put another way, the political taking shape and direction from vernacular practices within a shared social space.[141]

In the opening decades of the twenty-first century, the absolutism of nationalism has been called into question by our larger understanding of the multicultural stemming from the 1990s and by our concomitant desire to avoid collapsing competing microcultures into a macronarrative of culture. Discourses of imperialism significantly call attention to the practices of the federal state in its nationalistic, expansionist phases, yet they pay less attention to the unequal spaces occupied by different segments of the citizenry, and with those differentials in space come differences in power and the ability to impact federal practices. While "American exceptionalism" should be debunked, I wonder how past lapses in knowledge and failures of recognition can be ameliorated without some recourse to recovery and display, and to specificity of language and place, no matter how fluid.

Ronald Takaki concludes his *A Different Mirror: A History of Multicultural America* (1993) with this observation: "America's dilemma has been our resistance to ourselves—our denial of our immensely varied selves. But we have nothing to fear but our fear of our own diversity. . . . To get along with each other, however, requires self-recognition as well as self-acceptance."[142]

Takaki suggests that bringing our "rich cultural diversity" to visibility is to accept ourselves. He may be right, but my nagging suspicion is that he has fully apprehended neither the magnitude of the effort for cultural visibility on a spatial ground, whether creative or scholarly, nor the strength of resistance to self-knowledge and self-acceptance that both the hegemonic structures of power and the dominant ideologies of institutionalized hierarchies represent. Self-recognition and self-acceptance have most typically led to self-empowerment, which is perhaps the first step toward not simply "getting along" but toward "acting together." And perhaps it is conjoined political action that is the most feared, and forgotten, possible outcome of a multicultural consciousness.

III. BODY MAPS

The heterotopia begins to function at full capacity when men arrive at a sort of absolute break with their traditional time. This situation shows us that the cemetery is indeed a highly heterotopic place since, for the individual, the cemetery begins with this strange heterochrony, the loss of life, and with this quasi-eternity in which her permanent lot is dissolution and disappearance. —MICHEL FOUCAULT, "Of Other Spaces"

Could the early Creoles of Color in Louisiana have provided a model for a U.S. society not built on racial binaries? Possibly so. However, what becomes so clear in retrospect is the ferocity of racial prejudice from the highest to the lowest places in the United States, particularly following the failure of Reconstruction that made the resistance to the binary standard of race and substitution of alternative models of race impossible. While Creoles of Color were determined to challenge racial restrictions and with them all narrow conceptions of racial designations, they were increasingly denied the rights and privileges of citizens and placed within official boundaries that negated their options for self-definition and movement. Not surprisingly, New Orleans is the place that launched perhaps the most famous racial definition case, Homer (*Homère*) Plessy's legal suit in the 1890s to be accorded all the rights and privileges of a white citizen—not because all citizens were entitled to equal treatment under law, but because he was ⅞ white and ⅛ black, which meant that visually he projected an image of a white person or, for all matters of specularity, was white. Plessy was a Creole of Color who, in a political alliance with other men of color, resisted the changes that had narrowed their freedom and fluidity. Plessy's black heritage was hidden behind skin color, hair texture, and facial features that projected only whiteness, but his connection to that heritage remained a defining fact of his subjective identity. He challenged the notion that whiteness was fixed, transparent, and definable and that blackness was visible and immutable.

The decision of the U.S. Supreme Court, however, was that black people could be legally cordoned off, segregated, and separated from whites and from any claims on the protections of citizenship and equal rights under law. In effect, *Plessy v. Ferguson* nullified the Fourteenth Amendment.[143]

Casual passing occurred frequently in New Orleans throughout the first decades of the twentieth century by Creoles of Color, because the 1896 *Plessy* ruling maintained the legitimacy of separate public facilities and institutions for nonwhite citizens and upheld the Louisiana Separate Car Law mandating racial segregation in railroad cars. The decision, based on an acceptance of a simple binary opposition of white/black in matters of race, presumed that defining race was a straightforward matter. *Plessy v. Ferguson*, interpreted, meant that American citizens with even the smallest fraction of an African heritage would continue, through the remainder of the nineteenth century and through most of the twentieth, to function within a legally segregated and unequal environment designed to keep them in degradation and servitude. Gradually, by the rise of the modern civil rights movement, Creoles of Color became less visible; they had crossed the color line, migrated west to California, or left for the urban centers of the North. Census records and state registries reveal the decline in numbers of people with Creole surnames as segregation diminished their opportunities and rights.

Given the history of lower Louisiana from the colonial period through the tenures of the French and Spanish, it is not surprising that racial designation became an obsessive official objective in the twentieth century, when white privilege was a premium. New Orleans is the place where Naomi Drake, as supervisor and deputy registrar of the Bureau of Vital Statistics from 1949 until her dismissal in 1965, held up, reissued, and revised racial designations on countless birth and death certificates by "race-flagging," checking individuals against a "race list" kept by Vital Records and conducting genealogical record research to determine whether a person could be listed as "colored." Virginia Domínguez researched Drake's gatekeeping and found evidence that "between 1960 and 1965 a minimum of 4,000 applications for certified copies of birth certificates and a minimum of 1,100 applications for death certificates were held in abeyance by the bureau under Naomi Drake," and presumably over disputes regarding racial designations.[144] When Drake was finally dismissed in 1965, there had been "thirty-eight dockets of petitions for writs of mandamus filed against the Bureau of Vital Statistics, the City of New Orleans, the State Board of Health, and individuals who served as registrars of vital statistics under Drake,"[145] who remained to the end of her tenure an indefatigable searcher for the real, imagined, or constructed black body in the New Orleans woodpile. Drake's legacy continued at least until the late 1970s, when her successor confirmed that two full-time clerks still had the job of handling race-designation cases (some 6,000 man-hours in 1976 alone) and that "between sixty and a hundred surnames were regularly flagged by the bureau and checked in a special file room against fairly extensive genealogies kept by the bureau on the many branches of these families."[146] Moreover, an estimated 250 names of "white" families with partially black ancestry were also kept as part of the bureau's race-flagging files.[147] All of this after 1970, when Louisiana passed Legislative Act 46 under the title "Designation of race by public officials," which stated: "In signifying race, a person having one thirty-second or less of Negro blood shall not be deemed, described or designated by any public official in the state of Louisiana as 'colored,' a 'mulatto,' a 'black,' a 'negro,' a 'griffe,' an 'Afro-American,' a 'quadroon,' a 'mestizo,' a 'colored person,' or 'a person of color.'"[148] Policing blackness and the location of black bodies was paramount to maintaining a white racial identity when increasingly historians and genealogists were uncovering more about the fluidity of race in colonial and postcolonial Louisiana. When the revised *New Orleans City Guide*, compiled by the Federal Writers' Project of the Works Progress Administration, appeared in 1952, the section titled "Racial Distribution" announced: "The melting pot has been simmering in New Orleans for over two centuries, and the present-day Orleanian is a composite of many different racial elements. Intermarriage has broken down distinctions and destroyed the boundaries of racial sections."[149]

The goings-on over racial identity in Louisiana achieved high visibility over a well-publicized case from the early 1980s. Susie Guillory Phipps received national attention when in 1982 she sued to be declared white on her birth certificate, arguing that she had lived her life as a white person—attended white schools, married a white man, lived in a white neighborhood, and socialized with whites—but the state responded that her great-great-great-great-grandmother Margarita was black and enslaved but freed by her owner Jean Gregoire Guillory. Moreover, the state's attorneys produced two large boxes of exhibits and depositions tracing Susie Guillory Phipps's family back to 1762 and showing that besides Margarita, others of her ancestors were recorded as mulattoes, quadroons, and octoroons.[150] Anthony Barthelemy, in "Light, Bright, and Damn *Near* White: Race, the Politics of Genealogy, and the Strange Case of Susie Guillory," examines the constructedness of race in Louisiana by looking at the Louisiana statute for determining race and at the challenge to that law brought by Guillory, who had been socially constructed as "white" but whose birth record said "colored." In effect, Barthelemy exposes the absurdity of the five-generations test for the racial designation "white" and also the gendered distinctions inherent in and apparent in the law and several antecedent court cases, which suggest that even in terms of the strictures of racial designations, white men have the added power of patriarchal position to make their cases for the race of their offspring. The Susie Guillory case brings up echoes of Toucoutou, the 1858 case of Anastasie Desarzant, who, like Guillory, went to court to protect her claim of whiteness and who, also like Guillory, lost her case and became publically and legally black.[151]

One triumph Susie Guillory Phipps had, however, was the 1983 repeal of the 1970 statute defining race just after her case achieved prominence and the absurdity of the 1/32 rule became apparent; for example, Munro Edmundson, an anthropologist, claimed in court testimony that all African Americans average 25 percent white genes and that whites average 5 percent black genes, so that by using the 1/32 rule, "the entire native-born population of Louisiana would be considered black."[152] The racial landscape of Louisiana had spiraled into an even more confusing but more static space by the 1960s and 1970s, when the modern civil rights movement achieved legal victories that challenged the old boundaries and their mores.

With such a prominent and strident modern history of race in Louisiana, the legacy of the past and the possibility inherent within the society of Creoles of Color have become increasingly appealing, particularly as simultaneously transnational and postcolonial discourses have dislodged national paradigms from a stranglehold on how to image people in relation to social and political cultures. The creolization of the old Louisiana Territory has replaced a focus on its Americanization, and the cultural, racial, and linguistic diversity historically evident there has become a source of new ways of thinking about the United States in relation to the West Indies and Latin and South America, as well as to France, Spain, and Portugal, as opposed to a strictly British or Anglophone conceptual referential. While this work necessarily involves primarily back glancing and back looking, with or without nostalgia and regret, it may ultimately participate in the transformation of the future since it is already involved in a different translation of the present. Importantly, however, a focus on the emerging condition of modernity within the situation of Creoles of Color can also be fruitful, that is, a focus on the development of the individual rather than on the individual in relationship to a political state, nation, or government.

Although today the list of writers creating out of a Louisiana context is long and distinguished, one of the contemporary poets is emblematic of the multiple possibilities for functioning in a reciprocal relation to Louisiana's racial history and social geography, especially as configured by New Orleans. In her poetry, Brenda Marie Osbey forges identifications with a heterotopic Louisiana. The cemetery as "heterotopia function[ing] at full capacity" that Foucault describes as beginning "when men arrive at a sort of absolute break with traditional time" is central to Osbey's production of New Orleans and its cities of the dead. Death that undergirds Foucault's spatial explanation of the cemetery's beginning with the loss of life, "with this quasi-eternity in which her permanent lot is dissolution and disappearance,"[153] is central to her construction of space. Osbey winds her way backwards in time and space with a consciousness of the process and the outcome. For her, the issue is one of the authentic as an architectural site. Selective knowledge of a past is part of the cultural logic of her New Orleans as an architectonic space. Historical memory for her is a way to get at the structures of the past.

In her four volumes of poetry published in the 1980s and 1990s, Osbey commemorates those whose lives, deaths, and spirits map the terrain and the culture of Louisiana, particularly urban New Orleans. *Ceremony for Minneconjoux* (1983), *Desperate Circumstance, Dangerous Woman* (1991), *In These Houses* (1988), and *All Saints: New and Selected Poems* (1997) all envision a particular location structured through a time-space perspective. Throughout these volumes, Osbey invests in architectonics, in the designed and structural aspects of the built environment. In her "Invocation" to *All Saints*, the human infusion inside the architectural structures making up the city limn a narrative of the interaction of past and present:

> The slave ancestors who lie beneath the swamps, inside the
> brick of which our
> homes, our streets, our churches are made;
> who wrought iron into the vèvès that hold together the Old
> City and its attachments;
> personal gods and ancestors; musicians and street dancers;
> Hoodoo saints and their little Catholic cousins . . .
> our saints continue to live among us.[154]

Osbey insists on experience within a place and on the human body as the subject of geographical knowledge of place, but more than that she focuses on the built environment, the brick tombs of the cemetery that are connected to the living city, its streets, houses, and churches. The map Osbey draws is one of attached artifacts, lives and buildings, gods and saints living among the performers, the entertainers evoking attachments to "home" and to death and the work of the slave ancestors. The intricate place with its weave of living and dead sustains itself with the invocation to the ancestral dead "to continue to live among us" and never leave, but also with invitations to the newly dead to come "home" to the community that will feed them and to all the still living soon to be counted among the dead.

In "Of Other Spaces," Foucault focuses on the cemetery as a "strange heterotopia": "[T]he cemetery is certainly a place unlike ordinary cultural spaces. It is a space that is however connected with all the sites of the city-state or society . . . since each individual, each family has relatives in a cemetery."[155] In New Orleans, cemeteries defy the shift in the nineteenth century to bury outside the center of the city, though they continue to be regarded as "cities of the dead." The comparison is to the design of cities, rising tombs and "streets" or paved walkways laying out the way to raised white graves and mausoleums. The centrality, however, of the cemetery to the ideology of New Orleans as space reverberates throughout Osbey's poetry, which imagines the architectonics of a space contiguous between the living and the dead. The dual city, the city of the living and its embedded double the city of the dead, constitutes a platform for performance in all of Osbey's poems. Melvin Dixon has demonstrated how black writers utilized verbal performances in narratives to produce performances of narratives. By focusing on protagonists in black narratives, Dixon observed how they "enlarge their range of verbal invention by turning figures of the landscape into settings for the performance of identity."[156] The concept of physical settings for the performance of identity is especially applicable to the architectonic platform for performing racial, regional, and gendered identity in Osbey's poetry.

The first section of *All Saints*, "Live among Your Dead, Whom You Have Every Right to Love," focuses on the structures by which the living remember the dead. The seven poems move between mourning poems for the recently departed, the foreign dead in the transatlantic African world, and the familial dead in the factories of the American South. Osbey constructs an elegy that in its various separate poems speaks to the spatial connections among the dead and the living left to mourn them. Throughout, the references are to the multiple Souths that black bodies have experienced. The poem "Desire and Private Griefs" lists the spaces that can contain memory and emotion:

> i stand across a banquet hall from him
> a desk
> a room
> the gravesite of someone i cared too little for in life.
> he will not look into my face.
> (the damp.
> the quiet.)
> i take him home[.][157]

The mixture of grief with the affective in built spaces is analogous to the grave, the burying of the dead. The "home" is the domestic space and the grave space, both communal in a way not usually contemplated. The persona concludes:

> death changes some things:
> the way you feel about your mother
> the path you take to get to a cousin's house
> the greetings you give out
> at casual meetings and such
> the kind of woman you call on to stand for your dead
> —a genuine sorrow drawn across her face—
> you trust her to grieve for you
> without interfering in your fate.[158]

Isolated, "alone / carrying the heavy silences / of the dead," the lack of language makes the poem do the work for connecting and communicating.

"In the Faubourg," the second section of Osbey's volume, takes an area of the city as its locus of meaning. The emphasis on a city district allows for the layering of the history of the place with the stories of people. The poem "Faubourg" begins with establishing the borders of the space:

the faubourg is a city within the larger city
and the women walk in pairs and clusters
moving along the slave-bricked streets
wearing print dresses
carrying parcels
on their hips or heads.[159]

In this district, long associated with the houses of placées and with Creoles of Color, the poet enters an architectural space that resonates with slavery but with the economics of survival by women as well, especially in the work and the associations they could not avoid. "The Seven Sisters of New Orleans" (spiritualist mothers), "Incognita: Woman in Blue," and "Elvena" all function in the communal history being recalled in the Faubourg Marigny. Elvena's house is emblematic of the lives of the women and of the "conju" working back through time to conjure their stories:

there is a house down on old roman street
all the women pass through
one stands outside the gate
bare feet
broad skirts gathered loosely
about her hips,
have you lost anything today?
tell me, neighbor
what have you lost today?[160]

The porchless houses in the Creole Faubourg sit close to the banquette, the sidewalk, where passersby are in close contact. This collapsing of space signals both an intimacy with the outside world and a "gated" existence that is duplicated in the construction and placement of tombs in the New Orleans cemeteries, especially the St. Louis Cemetery in the Marigny where Marie Laveau, the most famous of the voodoo women, is buried. The shapes of the tombs mirroring those of the houses and the paved walkways between grave sites imitate the streets of the city's old Faubourgs.

Osbey concludes *All Saints* with a section entitled "Ex Votos," offerings in which historical figures (Mother Catherine, St. Martin de Porres, Sor Juana, Lúis Congo, St. Expedite, Juan San Malo) from the colonial past and its mélange of spiritualists, Catholic saints (actual and false), maroon rebels, and slave executioners are left by the poet to concretize the Creole place and attitude that began to emerge in eighteenth-century New Orleans. In delving backward with prayerful attention to hoodoo or Catholicism or spiritualism from Africa, Spain, France, Peru, and Haiti, Osbey fashions the mixedness that became the Creole city of New Orleans and its creolized people. In a sense, she constructs the identity of the urban residents by means of a long line of contradictory practices and mores, the impulse toward freedom evidenced by San Malo and the maroon community of escaped slaves living in near proximity to and trading with the city residents, enslaved and free, or toward repression, witnessed in Lúis Congo and his faithful conduct as free-black enforcer of slave punishment. The contradictory building blocks, the red bricks made by slave ancestors referenced in the invocation and infusing every part of the cityscape—these all converge into "Suicide City," the final long poem. In one of the stanzas, Osbey writes:

meditation is an urban preoccupation.
country people poke fun, they laugh.
here in the city
we all go mad together and simply refuse to tell.
we are so superior
we meditate.[161]

Her rendering of the cityscape is neither nostalgic nor romantic, but contrapuntal to the outside, the countryside, despite its attention to the city, which retains its association with the dead and with the distinctive cemeteries, the cities of the dead.

Named poet laureate of Louisiana in 2005 not long before the destruction of New Orleans after Hurricane Katrina, Osbey seems invested in locating the city within realms that are both real and imaginary. She seeks to make the boundaries fluid and malleable between these realms. In her essay "I Want to Die in New Orleans," Osbey states:

By the time I die I expect to have done a considerable amount of all-around living. And that is how I want to be remembered—as a woman who lived. And had the good sense to go home when it was over. Home to the only place in this country where people understand the importance of dying *well*. Where cemeteries are as prominent as office towers. Where the dead get equal time with the living, and in many cases, are still much better treated. . . . Where the dead walk and talk among the living as before, only now with an authority they never possessed in life.[162]

As richly colloquial as a Zora Neale Hurston sharing her anecdotes and collected wisdom from the folk, Osbey details the urban lore that gives shape and structure to her New Orleans and its citizens. Her appearance in the 2008 film documentary *Faubourg Tremé: The Untold Story of Black New Orleans* adds a voice of intimate knowledge punctuated with an affective urgency that infuses the screen with the living presence of a communal space that was and is "The Tremé."[163] Writing in 1993 about Osbey's first collection of poetry, Violet Harrington Bryan astutely observes: "The mission of the poet as historian/geographer is to trace the cultural terrain of a place and a people."[164]

Unlike Ernest Gaines's attachment to the past that reconfigures it as meshing with the present, Osbey seizes the past as an opportunity to reclaim and rewrite history. The residents of her historical New Orleans may be restricted by the race codes in which they live, but they inhabit their places in three dimension, in full access to all aspects of their own subjectivity. The architectonic design consistently figures people in relation to spaces, identity constructed by positioning within structures, whether secular or religious.

Osbey deploys New Orleans as a landscape of the past. In *Ceremony for Minneconjoux*, she focuses on the interiority of black women who have lived in the city. In a ritual-obsessed poetry, Osbey writes monologues in the Louisiana vernacular of women remembering and telling their stories. In an early review, Lorenzo Thomas compared Osbey's poetic strategy to that of major American poets Melvin Tolson in *Gallery of Harlem Portraits* and Edgar Lee Masters in *Spoon River Anthology* and praised her strength as "direct, honest utterance and the imagery inherent in the vernacular of ordinary people. Because Osbey has an ear for both the nuances of black speech and the clear diction of contemporary American poetry, the result is marvelous."[165] The "marvelous" also has a root in uncompromising attention to the spatial and architectural design in which Osbey draws her women and creates their voices. An astute critic, Thomas observed the facets of Osbey's achievement without identifying the specificity of her New Orleans landscape that calls up the analogy to poets who utilized space as the locus of meaning for their collections.

The title poem engages myth and history and madness that lurks within the very structures that evolve out of black (and Native American, in this poem) lives within a race-defined world:

it was years back you know
down bayou la fouche
she named her daughter
minneconjoux
so that people would not mistake
her indian blood.[166]

Mixed-race lives are complicated not only by the external society and its expectations of oneness but also by the very practices and traditions that stem from within the culture and the consciousness. The sad narrative poem ends with an isolation from all but the inauthentic and unreal:

i am minneconjoux
i live in the house on st. claude st.
to connect myself
to the used thing
i keep on my bureau
at mardi gras time
i stand on the walk-way
and watch the indians
dancing off dumaine.[167]

St. Claude and Dumaine as street locations in the Creole of Color–dominated Marigny signal the inability to move beyond the Mardi Gras Indian masquerades and into a life where all parts of an identity can be valued.

Osbey's second collection, *In These Houses*, is divided into three sets of spaces: "Houses of the Swift Easy Women"; "House of the Mercies"; and "House of Bones." These represent the communal, personal, and spiritual histories conjured in Osbey's poems evoking New Orleans life, history, and environment. The house is the architectonic space that is in Osbey's work at once domestic and public, private and communal. As an element connecting the past with the present, the house becomes the design allowing for entrance into and escape from the divisions marking black life, particularly the lives of black women. In "Geography," the persona is all knowing of the places, maps, and where they lead: "this body has done / its share of the journey."[168] The poem begins in knowledge:

the geography i am learning
has me place myself
at simultaneous points
of celebration

and all you see and hear in me
is these women
walking in the middle of the road
with hoodoo in their hands.[169]

The mysterious work of hoodoo and the "place no one chooses/is the land
i tarry in," the persona observes as "this map leads you to a desert-place."
Traveling of this sort has been done before by those who have gone ahead,
but for the poet, the objective is to reacquaint the world with this geography
and this mode of travel. The poem is the penultimate in the volume. "House
of Bones" follows it with the directive:

once you find this place
this is what you must do:
begin building
your hands behind your back
begin building
from scraps of living.[170]

This work is "building the structure/the years have torn down," and it is
ultimately

this . . . house
i have carried inside me
this is the house
made of artifact and gut
this is the house
all my bones have come from[.][171]

The body as house and the work of rebuilding in death become the trope
referenced like hoodoo and conjuring throughout Osbey's reclaiming of a
communal memory, one which can only stem from a Louisiana or a Haiti or
a Cuba or a Brazil or any of the culturally connected points in the African
diaspora.

Desperate Circumstance, Dangerous Woman, Osbey's third volume, is a
single poem divided into twelve chapters that reference the familiar territory
of the woman's body, the city space, the slave past, and the vodoun's work.
The central figure is Marie Crying Eagle, whose entanglement with her lover
Percy requires the advice of a family friend, Ms. Regina, a conjurer. Osbey
seeps these poems in the myth and magic associated with an exotic New
Orleans. She constructs a contemporary local color paradigm for moving in

and out of abjection, servitude, and freedom. The Faubourg Marigny is the structural site and the historical backdrop, which includes the maroon community that figures in much of Osbey's poetry. The reclaiming of a unique site extends over the entire New Orleans public space, constructed by both actual hands and vodoun's conjuring.

This collection with Marie Crying Eagle at the center produces the Louisiana that is a space of eroticism and a landscape of exoticism and that locates itself with a stronghold in popular culture. When Kasie Lemmons made *Eve's Bayou* (1997), she set her film in an exotic and erotic Louisiana of the early 1960s, when *Brown v. Board of Education* (1954) had not yet made any significant inroads into segregated Louisiana life. Lemmons, one of the few black women filmmakers, wrote the screenplay and directed the film.[172] The haunting bayou locale provides a fitting setting for the secrets and passions hidden within the Creole community, particularly within the family of Louis Batiste (Samuel L. Jackson), a physician, and his wife, Roz (Lynn Whitfield). Part of the impact of the film is its representation of Creoles of Color, beginning with their music making and dancing to zydeco and continuing through their connections to the world of voodoo and the supernatural. The mysteries at the center of Lemmons's film are dependent on the frailties of human beings: Louis's weakness for beautiful women; his daughter's possessive idealization of her father; his sister's fear of love. The film's powerful opening line ("The summer I killed my father, I was ten years old") introduces both memory and story as the province of a young girl, Eve Batiste (Jurnee Smollett), who narrates the mysteries embedded in her family's history. However, all of the mysteries are exacerbated by the isolated, shifting space in which the Batiste family resides. The bayou country is a swampy waterway overrun by undergrowth and overgrowth, which provides the geographical metaphor for the family, its interactions, and its relationships. Lemmons probes an isolated Creole community immured on the edge of a bayou and constricted by a heritage shaped by that racial and spatial geography, and she suggests that the destructive incestuous nature of that world contributes to its failure to emerge as a leader in the contemporary New South. Haunted by death and immured in a threatening landscape, the film calls up images of Brenda Marie Obsey's melancholy representations of the ghosts of a way of life that overvalued romantic love and fell victim to patriarchal power.

If the Créolité movement is intended today to move away from notions of culture defined by space and toward a notion of "the space of culture defined by elective diversity," then the message from the historical Louisiana Creoles of Color is much more complex than any configuration of a mosaic of identities. The Creoles of Louisiana, no matter their racial designation, continue to spur the imagination of creative artists. Barbara Hambly writes historical mysteries in which the protagonist, Benjamin January, is a gen de couleur libre, a surgeon, and a musician living in New Orleans of the early nineteenth century.[173] She introduced Ben Janvier in *A Free Man of Color* and placed him within a varied family and community of free people: a sister who is a light-skinned plaçée; another who is a dark-skinned vodoun priestess and a follower of Marie Laveau; and a mother who was once a slave and after an plaçage relationship becomes a woman of property (and pretensions). In a series of novels with Ben as a murder-solving detective, Hambly provides a vision of friendships across race and class lines and between different groups. She gives Ben a close musician friend who is European, educated, and non-Creole and another helpful but less intimate friend who is an unrefined American lawman from Kentucky. In the process of staging New Orleans as a specific cosmopolitan place, she recreates French and Spanish architecture, masked balls, opera and theater companies, plaçage relationships, girls' schools, voodoo religion, summer epidemics, city banquettes, wharves workers, open marketplaces, and slave traders—all evocative of the city in the first half of the nineteenth century. At the same time, Hambly does not shy away from the racism embedded in that culture. Ben is freer in France than in Louisiana, but even there, his profession as a surgeon is not without discrimination. And in one of the novels, *Days of the Dead* (2003), Ben and his wife travel to Mexico to free a friend falsely accused of murder. Within that setting, Hambly makes clear the transnational dimension of Ben Janvier's life and establishes a way of understanding his diasporaic placement in the western hemispheric context.

If the music of the "Creole Romantics," the Lamberts and the Dédés, and the poetry of *Les Cenelles* may be considered to set the tone for a reflexive discourse on space and the lost opportunity for a multicultural model for the United States, then the work of contemporary New Orleans poet and composer Sybil Kein (a.k.a. Consuela Moore), with the musicians in her family, including her brothers and her daughter, may be said to affirm the healthy presence and renewed potential of Créolité in Louisiana. Kein often performs (vocals, guitar, percussion) with her brother Raymond K. Moore (classical guitar, banjo, harmonica) as the Creole Troubadours. In music CDs such as *Creole Ballads & Zydeco* (1996), *Maw-Maw's Creole Lullaby* (1997), and *Creole Classique* (2000), she has recorded the songs and poetry of the early generations of Louisiana Creoles, both the so-called Creole Classique and the folk renderings.[174]

Sybil Kein occupies the space of a contemporary Louisiana Creole who writes in Creole, French, and English. For her, the question of authenticity is important. Like the Antilles writers who formulated Créolité, she insists on the importance of the language and cultural practices of Creoles, and not merely as part of African survivals but as new formations in a new world setting. She preserves the Creole history, language, customs, and literature in belle lettres, songs, stories, games, recipes, and more. These are acts of preservation. Kein's work is creating a collective memory of a culture that she feared was dying and in danger of being lost. Her writing, creative and scholarly, is shaped by personal memory and social memory of growing up Creole. A child of the 1940s whose identity was shaped by the geographical landscape and the locational culture of her homeplace, Kein self-identifies as African American but has insisted also on being "Creole" and recovering the Creole language in the poetry and prose and songs she produced throughout the 1960s and 1970s. Mary Morton believes that "the importance of Kein's poetry cannot be overestimated, not for the art alone, but for the artistic preservation of Creole history—creating voices of truth that deny the distortions, sentimentalized or not, of the 'tragic mulatto' themes found in literature."[175]

Kein's book of poetry *Gumbo People*, first published in 1981, was reissued in an expanded edition in 1999. Her elegant poems in Creole and English, for example "*Après le Bal du Cordon Bleu*," "*L' Énfante perdue*," "*Rêve érotique d'une quarteronne*," "*Ti Malice*," and "Zelime," appear in her 1996 collection, *An American South*. Only in the 1980s and 1990s did Kein begin to receive attention as a southern woman writer of color who complicates conventional notions of race, of language, and of region and whose aesthetic and creative traditions do not adhere to a traditional black-white binary. That positionality links her to the Creole artists of the past.

Kein's essay "The Use of Louisiana Creole in Southern Literature" initiates a challenging discourse on self-naming and identification in terms of the application of the term "Creole," while explicating the place of Creole patois in the literature of the U.S. South.[176] Her informative tracing of the appearance of approximately eighty Creole songs and of Afro-French fables in Creole sets the stage for her discussion of usage of the language in fiction as a means of class and status definition. Kein's *Sérénade Créole*, a cassette of songs, and its companion text, *Des Gardénias et Roses*, demonstrate the Spanish influence on Louisiana Creole music and poetry. Optimistic and upbeat despite a knowledge of the downward spiral in the history of Creoles of Color, Kein points to surviving contemporary Creole people "of mixed ethnic makeup who adhere to their inherited rituals, language, [and] social customs and who are native to the state. Most have strong French and/or Spanish heredity. Many are descendants of a variety of ethnic peoples, including but not limited to those of European, African, Jewish, Caribbean, Native American and Asian populations."[177] While she insists upon the mixed-race/ethnicity of Creoles and on their survival in today's world, Kein also laments that over 95 percent of the present generations of Creoles she mentions in her writings "have had to leave Louisiana to achieve and to have their gifts appreciated":

> On the other hand, Louisiana, this American South, which gave rise to the free people of color and their descendants, despite its problems, has the natural beauty, the enticement of rituals such as Mardi Gras which link it to other cultures, and the possibility of change through a mutual understanding and acknowledgment of the perils of the past. This type of American South, fortified with a true sense of history and infused with the souls and minds of the many who clearly would *not* choke the future with outdated or inhumane ideas, this South, may one day rise again.[178]

Kein's sense of the possibility inherent within Creoles of Color, their traditions, and their purpose as a gateway to a changed American South is in line with my reading of the potential lost for an early multicultural and multilingual American society that was lost with an Americanization and homogenization of Louisiana's diverse cultural groups, and in particular the Creoles of Color. Although since Hurricane Katrina in 2005 and the displacement of many of the remaining Creoles of Color from New Orleans, and from the Seventh Ward in particular, Kein's hope for a different future for Creoles in the South may never become a reality. She herself has now relocated to Asheville, North Carolina, where she has completed a mass and continues to work on music composition but still plans to return to New Orleans.

Shortly before Katrina hit New Orleans, Kein completed *Bonjour Créole! Éh La Bas! Learn to Speak Louisiana French Creole: An Introduction*.[179] That compilation complements her *Maw-Maw's Creole ABC Book: Pour les Petites for Children*.[180] The two books function to draw beginners into the Creole language and into the process of saving it for the next generations. Kein makes every effort to ground the language firmly into a print culture in addition to an oral one. She recognizes that the dissemination and preservation of Louisiana Creole will not depend upon the old tradition of passing a language down through its speakers, because as the surviving speakers are displaced to parts of the nation in which there are no vibrant communities of Creoles of Color, they will have few opportunities to speak the language and even fewer to safeguard it for the next generation. Kein understands what Yi-Fu Tuan has postulated: "Speech binds. Human beings know for sure that they live in the same world when they apply the same words to the same things—when they speak alike."[181] Language, as Tuan points out, is the aspect of culture that differentiates one group from another, but language is as well the medium for internal group cohesion, which in the past was often "a feeling of oneness and sameness that depended on the existence of a closed world, beyond which lay an incomprehensible Other."[182] While Kein's efforts are in the direction of preserving and expanding, they also invariably involve a stabilizing of identity and a confirmation of self and of belonging. In the twenty-first century, the balance has always to be struck between the isolating and exclusionary possibilities inherent in the reclamation of any lost language, particularly one that may still carry a separatist and exclusive rather than democratizing move in popular perception.

In a series of books creating an American South different from the one most often depicted in U.S. literature, Sybil Kein has herself reinvigorated the Creole language in current usage and represented the history of Creoles of Color. She negotiates the pitfalls and wards off exclusion by her acts of translation of language and cultural signs. She writes in "From the French Market":

Cinnamon ladies
in gingham bonnets
and white aprons
singing their *fleurs*,
calas or ginger cakes,
sitting on the banquettes
or walking under the eaves
of the Indian Market amid
Misu's, Herrmeisters, Chiefs,
and thieves, in their butter-soft
Créole language:
"*Calas, Tout chaud!*"
Or in Spanish:
"*Flores, Gardenias, Jasmines*"
or in French:
"*Petit gâteaux, Pralines,*"

whatever the visitor should please.

These *marchandes* would save
picayunes enough to one day

buy a sister or a son or
herself. Did Madam know
that every praline bought
meant a sweeter step to
liberty for one so hated?
That even under sun-boiled heat,
through days of rain and mud,
heavy fevered air that caught them
short of breath and sick-weary,
they remained?
That they became so fixed as
present day stuffed Mammy Dolls,
big as life and still the butt
of horrid jokes that belie what
dignity crowned that checkered
rag, that Créole kerchief, *tignon*,
mammy rag, nigger rag, dolls, play-
things, souvenirs?

Those earring hoops were made of
gold. Thick painted lips were
actually Senegalese small and
not rouged.
Bulging eyes were quite
proportioned, varied in color,
quick and clever.
And in that melodic speech
she was sure to answer your
vileness or evil and hurl curses
from old gods against you or
your progeny if you troubled her.

Oh, I would fear this caricature
despite her contorted face.
And do not mean her ill with backward glance or words. Her anger,
now more than two centuries old
could send a plague, a killer storm,
or something unexplained and in the
very air.[183]

"From the French Market" moves back and forth in space and time, as do many of Kein's poems, such as "The Diaspora and the Revolution" from *An American South*. The effect makes the past, particularly the long centuries of enslavement, live within the spaces of memory, language, and gesture of the present. The French Market, central to the commerce of the old city and the section known today as the Vieux Carré, is the place when the old and the new mingle, and it is the place in which the reality of Creole women of color from a mixture of cultures speak in multiple languages and belie the stereotype preserved in myths of their rotund bodies and grotesque laughter. The French Market functions as a sign and a place marker of the larger geography of race and gender in the old and new city.

In remarking the Senegalese features as a corrective to the prevailing images of the Mammy Dolls, Kein makes use of the historical scholarship of Gwendolyn Midlo Hall, who traced the transactions of slaves from Africa to Louisiana.[184] For over fifteen years, Hall researched the archives in Spain, France, and Texas and the courthouses in Louisiana in order to record available transactions relating to enslaved people. Locating the geographical origins and the group or tribal affiliations of the Africans brought to Louisiana was a monumental step forward in humanizing and individualizing their bodies, concretizing and marking them with the specific distinguishing features of their places of origins and their cultural matrices. Ultimately, this locational understanding allows for a reconsideration of the African diaspora and its impact on the shape of a Louisiana culture that signifies what might have been in other directions for U.S. life and culture. Kein's poem "The Diaspora and the Revolution," divided between part I, "Apartheid," naming Louisiana in 1895, and part II, with only the date 1995 but no place name, allows for a long-lens view of how legal segregationist practices, the apartheid of the 1980s, sent mixed-race people of African descent running across borders to find freedom.[185] Of those of fairer skin, the poet asks:

Where is Freedom?
in your soul? across that Mason
"Dixie" line? California?
Chicago? New York? Michigan?
Yes? And even in this south?

These are the ones who change the spelling of their names and pass into new spaces as new people without the baggage of the old race labels. The poet recognizes that even the dark-skinned passed out of Louisiana and into different identities: "Bid the darker ones go to Brazil, / Mexico, Cuba, anywhere;

Old French Market, Decatur St., New Orleans, Orleans County, Louisiana. For over two centuries, Creoles of Color vendors in the French Market of the Vieux Carré sold goods, fruit, vegetables, cooked food (such as calas and pralines), and hot coffee (from café au lait stands introduced by Rose Nicaud, free woman of color, in the early 1800s). (Frances Benjamin Johnston, photographer, 1937; Carnegie Survey of the Architecture of the South, Library of Congress Prints and Photographs Division, Washington, D.C.)

or bid them heartbreaking farewell forever." The idea of escape of people by the hundreds, those who "catch that/train, brothers and sisters and/*passé, passé, passé* on to freedom," is counterbalanced by the "millions with our schemes/and our plans and God-Help-Us/we shall overcome." These are the people of African descent who "Take up John Brown's sword of/Justice for that long tortuous/crusade." The poem makes clear the movement out of Louisiana and into the North and West, as well as to the nations of the old African diaspora that once sent its African-descended people to Louisiana and later welcomed them back during successive times of revolution and unrest.

The late twentieth-century poet from Louisiana whose poetry fits definitions of multicultural and transnational without depending upon Creole culture is Yusef Komunyakaa, a Bogalusa, Louisiana, native who has lived in New Orleans. His poem "Kosmos" from *Thieves of Paradise* owes much to Walt Whitman for the multiple spatial locations of the body, but also to a Louisiana landscape, historical and culture specific:

> Walt, you shanghaied me to this
> oak, as every blood-tipped leaf
> soliloquized "Strange Fruit"
>
> Who showed you how passion
> ignited dogwood, how it rose
> from inside the singing sap.
> You heard primordial notes
>
> murmur up from the Mississippi
> a clank of chains among the green
> ithyphallic totems, betting your heart
> could run vistas with Crazy Horse
>
> & runaway slaves. Sunset dock
> to whorehouse, temple to hovel,
> your lines traversed America's
> white space, driven by a train whistle.[186]

The second section of the poem begins "Believing you could be in three places/at once" and establishes the body in broad spatial terms, across cultures and places. In writing the body in the vein of Whitman's large sense of the enormity of the nation, Komunyakaa colors that body with all of the stripes of oppression, enslavement, and racism that made "America's white space." That space is aligned with Natasha Trethewey's "white space of forgetting" from *Bellocq's Ophelia*, but it is also linked to Whitman's own words that Trethewey used as an epigraph in the third and last section of *Native Guard*: "O magnet-South! O glistening perfumed South! my South! O quick mettle, rich blood, impulse and love! good and evil! / O all dear to me!"[187] To think of the white body and the white space of the continent as contingent spaces overlapping and drawn in geographic preciseness up from the Mississippi River into the regions of history and memory dramatically shifts perceptions of both what constitutes space and what makes "America."

chapter five

Parishes & Prisons

ERNEST GAINES'S LOUISIANA
& ITS NORTH CAROLINA KIN SPACE

I. PLANTATIONS AS REMEMBERED GEOGRAPHIES

If time unfolds as change then space unfolds as interaction. In that sense space is the social dimension. Not in the sense of exclusively human sociability, but in the sense of engagement within a multiplicity. It is the sphere of the continuous production and reconfiguration of heterogeneity in all its forms—diversity, subordination, conflicting interests.

—DOREEN MASSEY, *For Space* (2005)

"Ghosts," a Sybil Kein poem, asks the question that lingers in Louisiana memory:

> Who would embrace them
> even now, these *gens de*
> *couleur* of Louisiana?
> . . . .
> Despite the audacity of
> a third acronym, race,
> culture, African and European
> conjoined as bone, heart
> mind to produce this progeny.[1]

For Kein, there is little escape from the haunting legacy in Louisiana of "the perversion of color/as hoax, as cannon, as/dominion over the oneness/of all souls."[2] Creoles of Color "culled dignity/from a fragile freedom," she recalls, and generations later, after emancipation, after Reconstruction, after world wars to safeguard freedom, the question of color remains in a place that could have emerged with a progressive vision of race based on the fluid-

257

ity and mutability of available categories within Louisiana's spatial and social history.

While Kein's aesthetic and poetics are anchored in Louisiana as a historical construct with global reverberations in the Créolité of the present, Ernest Gaines's work is based on a conceptualization of Louisiana as a social geography whose localized configuration is interactive though not dynamic. Kein seeks racial and social equality for Louisiana's people of color, while Gaines seeks racial and social justice. Both stances are necessary given the state's history, and both utilize a spatial ground that follows from an understanding of racial constructions and residual contradictions from an earlier Louisiana. Gaines, not unlike Kein and other twentieth-century Louisiana writers, demonstrates a locational epistemology, shaped by a racial geography and an economic history that are still operational in the present. His repeated excavations of a specific Louisiana in his imagined Bayonne and St. Raphael Parish, however, have been more visible and have produced perhaps the major fiction to emerge from twentieth-century Louisiana. In it, Gaines engages the complexity of a racial hierarchy that is multitiered, and he explores the reality of a racial segregation that has been debilitating yet, from his standpoint, not debasing. Out of that reality, his narratives of a specific Louisiana space demonstrate why justice must be achieved. Modernist in their universalizing and humanistic discourses, his narratives foreground "becoming" as opposed to a static "being."

Gaines has articulated what may be called a geographical imagination. His readers have been unable to avoid the knowledge that he created Bayonne, Louisiana, and its surroundings to project that imagination and to preserve his memory of place. "I think one of the greatest things that has happened to me, as a writer and a human being, is that I was born in the South, that I was born in Louisiana," he has reflected in one of his many conversations about his birthplace.[3] Punctuating that early admission with additional descriptions of his particular South, he remembered his motivation for writing: "I wanted to smell that Louisiana earth, feel that Louisiana sun, sit under the shade of one of those Louisiana oaks, search for pecans in that Louisiana grass in one of those Louisiana yards next to one of those Louisiana bayous, not far from a Louisiana river."[4] He extrapolates the very name "Bayonne" from the French town in the Acquitaine, which sits where the rivers Adour and Nive meet. Bayonne is also the place that Roland Barthes identifies as "the perfect city."[5] Gaines's Bayonne, however, has more frequently been related to William Faulkner's Jefferson in Yoknapatawpha County, Mississippi.[6]

The site of memory for Gaines's space of narrative is Pointe Coupée, an oxbow cutoff of the Mississippi River; the oxbow forms False River, a lake of 3,212 acres that once was the region's main channel of the Mississippi River. The land forms Pointe Coupée Parish, which is bounded on three sides by water: on the east, the Mississippi River; on the north, Old River; and on the west, the Atchafalaya. On the south, Iberville and West Baton Rouge Parishes form the boundary. Within these borders are Lake Moreau, Raccouri Bend, False River, and the many bayous (Couteau, Moreau, Latanache, Cow Head). Waterways with bayous as prominent as the rivers they flow into are part of the physical and seductive beauty of the Louisiana landscape at False River that prompted Gaines to turn to writing as a way of making that Louisiana and its memory immutable.

Of all the major African American writers to emerge in the last half of the twentieth century, Ernest Gaines alone has repeatedly positioned his own autobiography with its place-based emphasis at the center of his articulation of both his literary objectives and his personal desires. For this reason, and far more than for any of his contemporaries, the spatial imaginary in Gaines almost demands an examination of place in his own background story and its figurative actualization in his fictive narratives. His writing recovers and preserves a culture and a place that is an exterior, realistic landscape but is also a representation of his own subjectively shaped interior life that is dependent on the space of the plantation as it existed in his youth.

Born on 15 January 1933, Gaines was a Depression-era child of a sugar plantation on False River in Pointe Coupée Parish, one of the thirteen alluvial land parishes where, after the Civil War, blacks outnumbered whites on an average of ten to one and where the plantation ordered the social system. His birthplace was in Cherie Quarters on River Lake Plantation, where African American plantation workers had lived during slavery and where for over 100 years five generations of his family had made their home while cultivating sugarcane, cotton, pecans, and corn on one of the historical plantations existing along False River since the late eighteenth century.[7] Like his parents and their ancestors who had known the intensity of labor and poverty under the plantation system, Gaines went as an eight-year-old to pick cotton, and a year later, he dug potatoes for fifty cents a day. The oldest of eight brothers and three sisters, Gaines has not romanticized growing up on a sugarcane plantation in the 1930s and 1940s, a time of individual and systemic hardship, but he has remained tied to the plantation as the spatial configuration and legible marking for his rendering of social interaction in his fiction. Yi-Fu Tuan

River Lake Plantation, New Roads vic. Point Coupee Parish, Louisiana. The "Big House" and the elaborate dovecote (pigeon house) on River Lake Plantation, the birthplace of Gaines, who was a resident of its Cherie Quarters when this photograph was made in 1938. (Frances Benjamin Johnston, photographer, 1938; Carnegie Survey of the Architecture of the South, Library of Congress Prints and Photographs Reading Room, Washington, D.C.)

has observed that "place is whatever stable object catches our attention."[8] For Gaines, the stability of the plantation renders it visceral and central to his visualizing of people and imagining of their daily activities.

Because Gaines's images of the land at Pointe Coupée are inextricably tied to the plantation and its ordering of life and society, they have led him not simply to descriptions of the physical landscape but to representations of the social and psychological region in which human beings act out tense dramas of individual, class, and caste struggles for survival. Michel de Certeau posits, "The kind of difference that defines every place is not on the order of a juxtaposition but rather takes the form of imbricated strata. The elements spread out on the same surface can be enumerated; they are available for analysis; they form a manageable surface."[9] However, given the logic of production,

River Lake Plantation, New Roads vic. Point Coupee Parish, Louisiana (interior view). Gaines's grandfather was the groundskeeper on River Lake Plantation and the gardener responsible for the flowers and plantings seen in this view of a yard and upper gallery. (Frances Benjamin Johnston, photographer, 1938; Carnegie Survey of the Architecture of the South, Library of Congress Prints and Photographs Reading Room, Washington, D.C.)

which engenders "its own discursive and practical space, on the basis of points of concentration," what may initially appear to be a legible, manageable surface morphs into opaque and layered places beneath. Gaines's Pointe Coupée Parish, with its small town of Oscar encompassing River Lake Plantation and its nearest larger town of New Roads, is a space formed by imbricated strata visible in the architectural structure of the plantation itself, with fields, quarters, big house, overseer house and store, church, and school all comprising the places in which at least three separate sets of people, from distinct but ancillary histories, function individually and collectively. Simultaneously, the complexity of the spatial difference in Gaines's Louisiana lies beneath a tense equilibrium of two complementary surfaces, the plantation and the quarters. "The revolutions of history, economic mutations, demographic mixtures," Certeau states, "lie in layers within . . . and remain there, hidden in customs, rites, and spatial practices. The legible discourses that formerly articulated them have disappeared, or left only fragments in language. This place, on its surface, seems to be a collage. In reality, in its depth it is ubiquitous. A piling up of heterogeneous places. Each one . . . refers to a different mode of territorial unity, of socioeconomic distribution, of political conflicts and of identifying symbolism."[10] The work that Gaines performs in his fiction, then, is that of articulating, translating, and practicing how the heterogeneous strata of Pointe Coupée function together.

Spatial awareness for Gaines coheres around the social relations shaped by the Louisiana environment—physical, material, and psychological. Gaines's articulation of his informing desire to write fits the concept of spatialization that Derek Gregory proposes among the four concepts—representation, articulation, spatialization, and authorization—central to his thesis in *Geographical Imaginations* (1994). Gregory states: "Spatialization refers to those ways in which social life literally 'takes place': to the opening and occupation of different sites of human action and to the difference and integrations that are socially inscribed through the production of place, space, and landscape."[11] For Gaines, the social life of his Louisiana familiars takes place in ways that are both unique and ordinary social inscriptions of the place, space, and landscape of Louisiana.

I coin the term "chaining" to come to terms with what is often unspoken about these aspects of Gaines's fiction, in a word, its pastness. Although critics make every effort to link Gaines's landscape, voices, people, events, and symbols to the "present" moment or to some contemporary corresponding scenarios as a way of understanding present-day life, for the most part these efforts seem remote and more valuable for thinking about individual conduct but not so easily translatable to the current known world. For many readers, the difference of the historical record reads like precisely that—historical record—although one crucial for understanding the past and the possibilities for human heroism under dire circumstances. This difference, then, does not deny the significance or the power of Gaines's fiction, but rather it suggests that his methodology is linked to an at-once closed system looped back around itself and also open in separate individualized spaces. It is also not to say that Gaines refuses to engage or to recognize events contemporary to his fictions; in *In My Father's House* (1978), for example, Vietnam, the Black Power movement, and the Black Muslim ascendency all figure alongside the nonviolent civil rights movement as led by Martin Luther King Jr. and as manifested in economic boycotts and protest marches. It is rather to suggest that the past as a space of narrative and personal engagement centrally informs Gaines's vision of human beings, their interactions, and their achievements or failures. Valuable for teaching lessons of life and conduct, Gaines's fictional landscape may be peeled back so that its layers can reveal points of connection to a communal ideal of human beings acting together for the "common" good or ultimately for their own individual well-being, even if that action goes against the norm. His strategy of representation and his articulation of human meaning conform to the best of modernist ideals regarding reading the past for the values that have sustained human beings through good and bad times.[12]

Chaining is a way of constructing the working of space in Gaines's imaginary. The links form connective tissue carrying ideas both forward and backward along a time-space continuum, and the open space within each link forms the contained and shaped ideas that are pushed or pulled along with the motion of the links or that remain static when the links are unmoving and stable. What destabilizes the links is any disruption of the formation anchoring the chain on either end. On the end farthest is the past, that is, the history of the people of Gaines's Louisiana place; but what constitutes the problematic for reading Gaines is that on the nearest end, there seems more or less to be a circling backward, as if to reencounter the past links, particularly those that emerge larger in size or magnitude from Gaines's own childhood and youth. He has, for example, spoken of a work in progress, "The Man Who Whipped Children," as a story stemming from the plantation disciplinarian he remembered from his youth in the quarters at River Lake Plantation, yet he has also admitted that while he has "five or six chapters . . . the energy is not there. The creative energy is not there."[13] The moving back into history and memory is a pattern that Gaines has successfully followed; however, it is not without the risk of reencountering the past in the same ways and without fresh insight, which Gaines himself recognized as a problem for his art when he abandoned projects such as "The House and the Field," which he began after his phenomenal achievement, *The Autobiography of Miss Jane Pittman* (1971), but which, he said, followed too closely the same direction of his writing about the plantation and his research into slave narratives for that novel.[14]

In conceiving "chaining," I want to suggest that the past is not merely a temporal sign in Gaines but a configuration of and platform for a black space that stems from the plantation as an architectural as well as imaginative structure with slavery and segregation shaping and influencing its boundaries and its interiority. Chaining is a means of addressing black space as the linkages Gaines demonstrates between place, particularly his Louisiana environment and landscape, and spatial locations in time, typically the past that manifests itself in the plantation, its culture, and its people. Within that space, open but linked, Gaines defines and interprets the past, but as he pointed out early in his career: "There is a difference between living in the past and trying to escape it. If you do nothing but worship the past you are quite dead. . . . But if you start running and trying to get away from the past, you will . . . eventually run yourself out of whatever it does to you. It will run you mad, or kill you in some way. . . . So you really don't get away. It's there, and you live it. That is especially true with the artist."[15] The past circulates in memory, and memory functions in the open space of chaining. While the interconnection offers a limitless space for the artist to produce his work, it is as well a defined set of connections as suggested by the trope of chaining as a process.

When the adult Gaines returned to his Louisiana homeplace in 1964, he understood the quarters and the fields, not merely as cultural spaces in which his people gather to talk or to work but as a closed microcosm of the larger economic society. The result was that he adopted the view of Louisiana that has remained dominant in his fiction. He began with the externalities: "Louisiana's probably the most romantic and interesting of all southern states," he has said in identifying "the land, the language, the colors, the bayous, the fields" as the dramatic pulls on his imagination.[16] His imaginative impulse, dependent upon the land and its actual and perceived meanings, and his writing, grounded in an initial consideration of place rather than character or incident, ranges beyond the romance of locality to the historical caste and class relationships to the land, to the stultifying effects of mandated social decorum, and to the contemporary upheaval of codified behavior and the disruption of traditional institutions.

The anomaly of being a twentieth-century black child on a nineteenth-century plantation is the unspoken conundrum in dispersal throughout Gaines's fiction. It references the place of contemporary individuals with an identity formation based on a platform of slavery—its legacies in sharecropping and tenancy—and of race—its hierarchies in white supremacy and black subordination. As Gaines has recalled: "I started to understand discrimination at a very early age. We were trained to understand those things. Blacks could not afford to forget. I had pressure on me to know and to remember. I felt the discrimination that any black Southern child would feel. New Roads was my little Bayonne. I couldn't eat or drink in certain places. I had to ride on the back of the bus and I couldn't go to the bathroom in certain places. I've been hurt and insulted and I've seen the same things happen to my mother, sisters and brothers."[17]

Gaines balances his evocation of a lush Louisiana rural landscape as muse for his writing with his recognition of Louisiana's history of segregation within its haunting geographical constructs, the plantation and the prison that drive his imagination. The plantation and the prison both attempt to exercise disciplinary control over bodies as well as over spaces, and this connective tissue repeatedly figures into the constructions of black life, remembered and memorialized, in Gaines's novels. The two form the competing heterotopias in Gaines's imaginary and share points of representation in the deviation from conventional norms of "ordinary" living, as Michel Foucault conceptualized in "Of Other Spaces."[18] The one, the plantation, becomes an economic system and a model of spatial organization that is often considered extinct or existing only in some residual formations. The other, the prison, having evolved rapidly since the nineteenth century as both a means of social control and a source of revenue, is one of the largest economic socioindustrial complexes within the United States. These two help to shape what may be read in Gaines as a black spatial aesthetic and a model for valuing black existence in the rural South.

Gaines's modern-day deployment of the plantation system follows the social organization and political economy of a racially segregated and class-bound population remembered in heightened intensity from his youth, when he observed the system at work on River Lake Plantation. The conjunction of memory and observance, or remembrance and surveillance, in Gaines's experience underscores the plantation and the prison as intersecting social structures and spatial systems. These twin aspects, surveillance and memory, combine in the way in which Gaines enters the materiality of the Louisiana that would emerge in his fiction. The combination enables him to find the language to represent his own place and past at Pointe Coupée. His process seems related to what Foucault suggests about the fundamental relationship between language and space: "Language gives the perpetual disruptions of time the continuity of space, and it is to the degree that it analyses, articulates, and patterns representation that it has the power to link our knowledge of things together across the dimension of time. With . . . language, the chaotic monotony of space is fragmented, while at the same time the diversity of temporal successions is unified."[19]

Gaines's work represents the plantation as a cultural space under surveillance and a cultural space being remembered in story by the author. In effect, the scrutiny of close, almost obsessive observation and the intense, detailed remembering lead to containment and entrapment within a space that, while imaginatively expansive, is already in the continuous process of imploding, folding in upon itself, and constantly in the process of disappearing or dying. Unlike Édouard Glissant's conception of the plantation as "collapsed everywhere, brutally or progressively, without generating its own way of superceding itself," Gaines's concept of the plantation encompasses ongoing processes that, while in a state of dying, retain the act of living concomitant with surviving and regenerating.[20] Charlotte, one of the older women Gaines portrays as still living on a plantation in *Catherine Carmier* (1964), understands as much when she looks out over the quarters on the Grover Plantation: "No one was anywhere in sight; no birds sang in any of the trees; no dogs barked anywhere in the quarters. . . . The grave is something like this, Charlotte thought; something just like this. Just 'while ago, they was all there, and now they all gone. The grave is something like this."[21] What Charlotte witnesses is not an evolution that breaks away from the past, but an analogous condition in which life has not ended but rather cannot be observed from the limited perspective that she has at that specific point in time.

By extension, at the logical end of Gaines's construction of the plantation with surveillance and memory central to the present moment is a necessary dying. Neither remembrance nor observance can revitalize the past, even if that past can be rendered in great detail. Neither process can emancipate the place or the people from the allowable and predictable limits of their animation. For this reason, Gaines admits that he cannot write directly about the present. As he revealed to Jeanie Blake, "I don't know if I could write about contemporary Louisiana."[22] He cannot reconfigure the past in new or unprecedented ways as Randall Kenan can in inventing the origin of Tims Creek that is at once rooted in historical possibility but made fantastically fictional, unrecognizable in any historical fact and unverifiable by all but invented record. Gaines's people and tropes, his places and practices, his concepts and symbols, though consistently powerful and affective, remain also consistent with a retreating toward the dying intermixed imaginatively with the already dead.

From Gaines's adult perspective, one sharpened by the multiculturalism of California and the political activism of the southern civil rights movement, the land at Pointe Coupée and its special characteristics shape the distinct groups of people living on it—Creole and Anglo planters, Cajun overseers and tenant farmers, Creoles of Color and black sharecroppers, all interacting within spatial boundaries, agrarian traditions, temporal suspensions, and racial identities. Yet the multiple groups are not equally progressive or mobile, as Gaines represents in his portraits of the twentieth-century plantation South in his fictional St. Raphael, dotted with family plantations all having their literal basis in his homeplace of River Lake Plantation on False River or the Parlange Plantation, the oldest in Pointe Coupée: the Grovers' in *Catherine Carmier*, the Heberts' in *Of Love and Dust*, the Samsons' in *The Autobiography of Miss Jane Pittman*, the Marshalls' in *A Gathering of Old Men*, the Pichots' in *A Lesson before Dying*. These imagined plantations function as a mythical space that is, in effect, "the spatial component of a world view, a conception of localized values within which people carry on their practical activities."[23] In this way of defining myth, order in the environment is paramount, so that "nature and society must show order and display a harmonious relationship."[24] It becomes a means of "placing" human beings in nature that is coherent and familiar. Mythical space is, nonetheless, constructed as a "response of feeling and imagination to fundamental human needs," so that as a construct, mythical space "ignores the logic of exclusion and contradiction."[25] In his version of the plantation as mythical space in his fiction, Gaines can emphasize order and harmony in the relationship between society and nature but also express the deeply felt experience of plantation slavery in the nineteenth century and sharecropping in the twentieth. Both pervasive economic systems have left their mark on Louisiana and have deposited a residual aspect that maintains Louisiana as irrevocably a site of memory manifested in the plantation and its social and economic system.

Beginning with Harriet Beecher Stowe's depiction of the Louisiana plantation of the vicious Simon Legree in *Uncle Tom's Cabin* (1852), there has been a persistent literary representation of Louisiana as the epitome of the worst of the brutal imprisonment of human beings in slavery. "Sold down the river" became synonymous with confinement so deep in a slave state that escape was nearly impossible. The Louisiana Purchase made that downriver area profitable for the expansion of new crops, especially for Virginia planters who by the beginning of the nineteenth century were losing money on tobacco crops despite their extraordinary wealth in slaves. New Orleans was soon to become the largest slave market in the united nation, as Walter Johnson details in *Soul by Soul: Life inside the Antebellum Slave Market* (1999).[26] Added to the financial motive for extending slavery was the dominant attitude toward slaves. Ned Sublette noticed in *The World That Made New Orleans* (2008) that Thomas Jefferson, in negotiating the Louisiana Purchase, enlarged not only the land mass of the United States but also "the vast expansion of the uniquely perverse institution of American slavery," and that Jefferson made quite plain that slaves meant capital in the emergent language of commerce: "I consider a woman who brings a child every two years as more profitable than the best man of the farm. What she produces is an addition to capital, while his labors disappear in mere consumption."[27]

The place at the end of the river was a plantation in Louisiana, the farthest-south state from the free states of the North. "The plantation landscape," Mike Crang states, "represents the coming together of a web of technologies and cultures to form a characteristic pattern based on highly unequal land control, matched with an orientation to export crops, embedded in a global system of extraction, and sustained by an impoverished and often enslaved workforce."[28] In a sense, Gaines inherits in the twentieth century that very landscape in Louisiana, the isolated and confined plantation and its economy and culture. His repeated explorations of modern plantation culture may be read in conjunction not merely with Stowe's mid-nineteenth-century iconic text, but also with the mid-twentieth century historical fictions of Frank Yerby, who was the only African American to turn his attention fully to plantation society from the perspectives of whites functioning across class lines, and sometimes across race lines.

Although Yerby's southern plantation novels were formulaic, they were not typical in their representation of whites.[29] His white southerners were people scrambling to rise in society, to accumulate wealth in the new market economy society, to use their capital—including their skin privilege—to obliterate their lower-class origins and to erase all traces of their past and the methods used to arrive at their present, as well as to disguise their ruthlessness from progeny. Beyond his representation of people, Yerby subverts all expectations for a black twentieth-century author in his appropriation of the plantation as "belonging" to or falling under the control, power, and literary purview of a black man with ties not to the elite white owners but rather to the slave property owned.

Gaines never mentions reading Yerby during his formative experience with writing, yet it would have been almost impossible to escape Yerby's highly visible popular novels in the period in which Gaines turns his attention to reading for evocations of spatial constructions reminiscent of his familiar Louisiana. The "plantation" genre adopted for mid-twentieth-century readability and financial success no doubt made Yerby visible to Gaines, whose first novel follows a version of Yerby's formula. I suggest that Yerby lurks in the background of Gaines's admitted dissatisfaction with his initial formative influences: European authors, such as Guy de Maupassant, who was an early favorite because of his storytelling ability marked by simple language and realistic portrayal of the young; and Russian novelists, particularly Chekhov, Tolstoy, Pushkin, Gogol, and Turgenev, who attracted Gaines because of their ties to the land and their skill in writing about peasantry without condescension. As a group, the nineteenth-century Russian novelists became Gaines's favorite authors for their mythmaking out of their familiar environment. In their texts, Gaines recognized what John Rennie Short has in connecting the environment to myth: "an intellectual construction which embodies beliefs, values, and information, and which can influence events, behavior, and perception." As Short explains, "Myths are (re)-presentations of reality which resonate across space and over time, which are widely used and reproduced, which are broad enough to encompass diverse experiences yet deep enough to anchor these experiences in a continuous medium of meaning."[30] Short's conception of environmental ideologies and myths stems from his analysis of environment in texts such as Tolstoy's, in which the Russian countryside figures prominently.

Although Yerby's fiction looks quite different from Tolstoy's, his repetitive attention to connecting a Deep South environment to myths is similar to the process Short describes. In addition, Yerby's work provided something the Russians could not. Gaines remarks that their icons—cabbage soup, kvass, verst, and steppes—were all foreign to him, and their religious worship, culinary habits, measurement practices, and naming customs were not similar enough to those of his native culture to appease his need for representations of his familiars. Gaines extrapolated: "The Russian steppes sounded interesting, but they were not the swamps of Louisiana. Siberia could be cruel, but it was not Angola State Prison."[31] One of the most visible aspects of Yerby's fiction about the Deep South is his careful attention not only to particular locations in Louisiana but also to the foods, dress, customs, and manners, which he made intrinsic to his representations; and this characteristic of his fiction, in conjunction with his focus on landscape and the myths produced out of space-time considerations, conveys a place much more accessible and familiar than any created by the Russians.

The Louisiana landscape was like the Russian one, however, in its system of peonage. In the middle of the twentieth century, segregated plantation culture still resembled what it had been decades before: devoid of educational opportunities for rural black children. Access to class mobility through education was only possible if a child could leave the homeplace and its system of modern peonage. Gaines himself left rural Louisiana in 1948 after finishing eighth grade because for African Americans there was no junior or senior high school near Oscar, the town closest to Cherie Quarters. That year becomes one of the primary temporal sites for much of his fiction.[32] His only viable option was migration elsewhere for the educational opportunity that his family believed would break the cycle of peonage in the sharecropping system.

Gaines's powerful longing for place combines with a political consciousness of the impact of racial segregation on the everyday lives of rural blacks to motivate his writing as a point of connection to the community he had left behind: "I wanted to see on paper those Louisiana black children walking to school on cold days while yellow Louisiana buses passed them by. I wanted to see on paper those black parents going to work before the sun came up and coming back home to look after their children after the sun went down. I wanted to see on paper the true reason why those black fathers left home— not because they were trifling or shiftless, but because they were tired of putting up with certain conditions."[33] Clear-eyed about the politics of place in a neoplantation society, Gaines understood segregation as creating the difficult educational conditions for black children and discrimination and economic conditions, including underpayment for labor, as constituting the inevitable lot of black men and women. Consciousness of the impact of racial segregation on the everyday lives of blacks in Louisiana was also a major aspect of Gaines's turning to write his narratives. His desire to record and capture the realities, the mixed positive and negative aspects of Louisiana, drew him back to his familiar place: "I wanted to see on paper the small country churches (schools during the week), and I wanted to hear those simple religious songs, those simple prayers—that true devotion. . . . And I wanted to hear that Louisiana dialect—that combination of English, Creole, Cajun, Black. . . . I wanted to read about the true relationship between whites and blacks—about the people I had known."[34] He had arrived at the ideological position constant in his career—that of a cultural artist predicating creative expression upon racial awareness and historical consciousness of a particular place.

The removal from Louisiana constituted the beginning of Gaines's "practicing" of place, to use Doreen Massey's term. Place, according to Massey, "does . . . change us, not through some visceral belonging (some barely changing rootedness . . .) but through the *practising* of place, the negotiation of intersecting trajectories; place as an arena where negotiation is forced upon us."[35] In the absence of the familiar Cherie Quarters and River Lake Plantation, Gaines began a process of realigning his spatial location with the remembered plantation past, producing a modern writer whose practice of place always is already in a time that was and in a place frozen in time-boundedness, an incarceral space. Much like Charles Dickens, Gaines sets his fiction in a time just slightly past but "remembered" vividly.

Gaines's experience is a version of one on which Linda McDowell has based her argument against accepting that "the consequences of increasing mobility have been a reduction of the extent to which women and men are members of relatively stable place-based communities and networks throughout their lives"; she does not deny mobility either of people or of money flows, but she argues that instead "places—local attachments—remain significant."[36] As McDowell contends of mobility and place attachment in general, in Gaines's case mobility did not reduce his sense of belonging to the community on River Lake Plantation. His residency in California, and all of its opportunities, including higher education, only increased his desire to maintain his relationship with the Louisiana of his childhood.

Gaines remembers his boyhood as enriched by a supportive extended family and community in the quarters on River Lake Plantation. He compresses much of what he remembers and memorializes about his Louisiana childhood into picturesque communal activity.[37] Such scenes of interconnection become comforting and educational in his telling, despite the condensed options they afford: "My movement was limited when I was a kid growing up. I mean I had the fields and things like that, but we were limited to the quarters as our living place. Just about everything we did was limited to the quarters . . . limited to that small area."[38] Gaines presents two aspects of his fictional craft as offsetting the limitations of life on a plantation. In one, he links his ability to represent place with his plantation upbringing: "My earlier teachers said I had that sense of place, using small areas and then a lot of dialogue, and that my whole scenes were place and then dialogue, place and dialogue."[39] In the other, he links his facility for accuracy in rendering voice and nuances of speech, storytelling, with his formative experience of listening to his elders on the plantation.

Gaines has often referred to his aunt Augusteen Jefferson, who provided him with access to talk and to the space in which the process of transmitting stories took place. It is his childhood role, however, in facilitating storytelling that addresses plantation life in the quarters as a public sphere and Gaines as an interlocutor within the public community. While Augusteen was from a family of storytellers, she was also a "recorder" who remembered events from the past.[40] Because of her disability, she could not easily visit the other residents of the Quarters, and so she received "company," female and male visitors from the community who came alone or in groups to spend time talking outside on the steps and gallery, the Louisiana term for a porch.[41]

Immersed in remembering his childhood position, Gaines also reveals the community under surveillance, under his watchful gaze. This aspect of surveillance is different from that in which the observation is used to keep individuals in their places by the threat of knowing any infractions of rules or regulations. Aunt Augusteen required Gaines, as the oldest child, to remain within hearing so that he could serve the visitors coffee, water, or homemade brew and retrieve whatever they needed from the cabin. The sound of talk and the practice of listening combined to make him attentive to voice and nuances of speech, particularly the Creole spoken by his aunt and other elders, and attentive as well to oral testimony and folk forms of storytelling. However, embedded in Gaines's recollection is the practice of observation and of intense focus on the movements, mannerisms, and gestures of the bodies of his relative and her visitors. The plantation community, then, comes under a redoubling of sensory apparatus.

Essentially, Gaines became the physical body connecting generations and functioning as "legs" for the older generation. His position is in between and, like the porch, it becomes liminal, a necessary mediation between oral performance and lived experience, between the past and the present, and between the natural outside world and the built environment of the cabin. His very body destabilizes distinctions between public and private spaces in the plantation quarters. These formative experiences infuse his thinking about performance so that his heritage of orality does not lead to a concentration on folkloric elements in his fiction, but rather to notions of inherent heroism within seemingly disabled or incapacitated or subjugated black bodies. The ability to "stand" that Gaines often observes as a marker of manhood is in effect also a way of making legible across gender, and sometimes race, boundaries the implication of his aunt and the larger meaning of both mobility and courage that he read into her active and unapologetic life.

Gaines's remembered communal activity with his aunt at the center of public conversation is not very different from what generations of black workers on Louisiana plantations experienced during the long centuries of enslavement. He has iterated this connection in numerous interviews, such as in his remarks to Ruth Laney: "Because I grew up on a plantation in the late thirties and the forties, I'm pretty sure it was not too much different from the way things could have been when my ancestors were in slavery. Oh, we could do a few things more. But that I went through that kind of experience—there's a direct connection between the past and what is happening today. I'm very fortunate to have had that kind of background."[42] Linking himself and his twentieth-century origins to those blacks enslaved and consigned to slave quarters is extraordinary. Gaines's sense of being fortunate functions inside a conjectural black space that is nourishing, communal, and educational. The abject bodies of black people in slavery and under segregation enter obliquely into the awareness Gaines represents of the way the past and his present conjoin in his plantation upbringing. The people who cannot control their environment are at the same time implicated in its production.[43] The plantation, then, is both a geographical space and a social configuration in Gaines's conception and in his fiction, which asserts the formative power of space- and race-specific experiences not unlike his own experiences growing up on River Lake Plantation. His biography, then, matters in situating readings of his literary production within discourses of space.

Because Gaines functioned in close proximity to both a beloved individual relative and an inclusive public community, he retained a sense of connection and commitment to Cherie Quarters as a space of belonging and intimacy. Every house was within sight of every other; every resident was known to every other in a shared small space, so that intimacy and observation functioned together. Grant Wiggins, a character in *A Lesson before Dying* who lives in the quarters on the Pichot Plantation, puts the spatial intimacy in simple terms: "I could look at the smoke rising from each chimney or I could look at the rusted tin roof of each house, and I could tell the lives that went on in each one of them."[44] Though the world outside of the quarters and beyond the boundaries of the plantation was hostile to the growth and education of a Louisiana black boy, Gaines did not have to experience that world on a daily basis.

If Richard Wright gives readers a secular landscape of economic greed, capitalist underpinnings, and social relationships impacted by economics, then Gaines renders nineteenth-century trappings for twentieth-century bodies and needs of Louisiana rural plantation blacks in whose lives pride and poverty collide. While Wright deploys the debilitating economics of race to bolster his desire for social equality, Gaines seeks social justice for a plantation population for whom he takes responsibility in representing. In reading Gaines's autobiographical reflections and reminiscences, one would be

Columbia Plantation Cabins, Louisiana. Cabins for blacks on Louisiana plantations in the 1930s were little changed from the old slave quarters. (Frances Benjamin Johnston, photographer, 1938; Carnegie Survey of the Architecture of the South, Library of Congress Prints and Photographs Online Catalog, Washington, D.C.)

hard-pressed to recognize his plantation culture in David Harvey's argument: "There has been a sea-change in cultural as well as in political-economic practices since around 1972. This sea-change is bound up with the emergence of new dominant ways in which we experience space and time."[45] Neither the newer modes of capital accumulation nor the different time-space compression in the organization of capitalism are resident within the social space Gaines recounts in his conversations about his Louisiana. Rather than using the history of the plantation in Louisiana as an entry into its relation to the present global marketplaces and the dispersal and dislocation of workers, Gaines maintains an older paradigm that, despite the conflict among competing black and Cajun workers and new farming technologies, represents the plantation as a macrocosm of human stories. In counterdistinction to those predominant memories of his communal plantation childhood, his rendering

Cabins for Sugarcane Workers, Bayou La Fourche, Louisiana.
The quarters on Louisiana sugarcane plantations conditioned both
separation and community. (Dorothea Lange, photographer, 1937; Farm
Security Administration/Office of War Information, Library of Congress
Prints and Photographs Online Catalog, Washington, D.C.)

of the rapacious economic system of the plantation in his first two novels, *Catherine Carmier* and *Of Love and Dust*, poses an opposition.

This modernist aspect of Gaines's fiction aligns with Jean-François Lyotard's reflection on the modernist aesthetic as "an aesthetic of the sublime, though a nostalgic one. It allows the unpresentable to be put forward only as the missing contents; but the form, because of its recognizable consistency, continues to offer to the reader or viewer matter for solace and pleasure. Yet these sentiments do not even constitute the real sublime sentiment, which is in an intrinsic combination of pleasure and pain: the pleasure that reason should exceed all presentation, the pain that imagination or sensibility should not be equal to the concept."[46] The nostalgia in Gaines's modernist leanings in his representation of plantation life is apparent not merely in his autobiographical statements but in his fictional formulations of the relations between blacks and the land they and their ancestors worked. Ned, for example, delivers a powerful sermon at the river in *The Autobiography of Miss Jane Pittman* that hastened his death because he is under surveillance by the Cajun deployed to murder him. He explains to the black plantation workers their present situation in the context of their history on the plantation: "'You don't own this earth, you're just here for a little while, but while you're here don't let no man tell you the best is for him and you take the scrap. No, your people plowed this earth, your people chopped down the trees, your people built the roads and built the levees.'"[47] Ned preaches a political consciousness about belonging to the plantation that is different from ownership and being owned: "'This earth is yours and don't let that man out there take it from you. . . . It's yours because your people's bones lays in it; it's yours because their sweat and their blood done drenched this earth. . . . But remember this . . . [y]our people's bones and their dust make this place yours more than anything else'" (107).

Gaines, then, does in fact observe the paralyzing effect of the changes on the quarters and the entrapment of its residents in a deteriorating economic structure, particularly in his fiction of the 1960s and 1970s. At the same time, he insists upon the inviolate relationship his plantation dwellers have with the land.[48] It is a manifestation of Gaines's own sense of ties to the land, to the ancestors buried on the land, and to the subjectivity formed through associations with the land. The chain of connection reverberates with messages of both strength and confinement. Ultimately, however, the message of strength, with its accompanying concept of an inviolate human dignity, prevails. It is evident in Gaines and his wife, Dianne, building a home on the very plantation at False River where he was born and where his ancestors had labored for generations in slavery and later in freedom. The message is an imaginative feat that understands and celebrates ties to the past and its favored or feared environment and at the same time reconfigures all linkages and access to that past by subverting and inverting the images and messages that have held sway over discourse. The Gaines house, *La maison entre les champs et la rivière*, on six acres of land once part of River Lake Plantation, functions in the space of a very differently imagined protest discourse.[49] That reiterated message of strength and dignity prevails in a 2010 *New York Times* story on Gaines that focused on his return to living on the land his family worked as sharecroppers and his rehabilitating the old graveyard where generations of his people are buried. Gaines's own words emphasize why he has returned and what he is restoring in caring for the burial ground: "They had nothing. . . . At least here they each have six foot of ground. . . . I'm going to do everything to keep up for them, in memory. That is my duty from now until I die."[50]

Gaines's first novel most graphically shows the dichotomy between the conditions of modern plantation life and the values inherent within the people living within the plantation system. Both the novel of modern plantation existence and his memory of the plantation function in relation to chaining, that process in which the idea of the land and its people pulls Gaines as author into a relationship with pastness. *Catherine Carmier*, with its consciousness of race, racial identity, and racist practices, provides a template for thinking about the plantation as a site of memory and surveillance and for reading the incarceral space central to so much of his fiction. It provides a mapped space for navigating his recurrent figures, tropes, and events, including, as he has humorously observed, a prefiguring of his marriage and return to False River.[51]

Gaines creates a network of social standpoints for interacting with this text. The narrative begins with the simultaneous sharing and contesting of space among the different racial and ethnic groups. Blacks represented by Brother, a Grover Plantation resident who has been displaced from working the land, and Cajuns represented by Paul and François Villon, who have been using new farming equipment to appropriate the land, meet in the plantation store, where Claude, the Anglo clerk, verbally assaults both. In response to a simple request for the mail, Claude says to Brother: "'Why the hell can't y'all come out here the same time? Look like the hotter it get the more you niggers want to bother people'" (4). Claude, according to François, had also "'[c]ussed out me and Paul the same way.'" In response to an ordinary pleasantry, "'How it go there, Claude?' He say, 'Cram it up your ass'" (4). The initial scene— with its references to awaiting new tractors, to people leaving the plantation and not returning, to waiting for the arrival of Jackson, Charlotte's nephew and Brother's friend from California, who is either a teacher or a demonstrator—establishes the ways in which the characters are carefully observing one another and establishes as well the tensions of the text that have to do with a diverse group in a contest for place. Almost immediately, the fourth group, the Creoles of Color, become entangled in the mix with the appearance of Catherine Carmier, who is also waiting there for the arrival of her sister Lillian from New Orleans. The watching of one another across race lines and the watching for the arrival of Jackson and Lillian, a black and a Creole, begin the surveillance of movement and interaction within the closed-off space of the plantation.

With the introduction of the Creoles of Color, the narrative shifts perspective and moves backwards in time to the story of Robert Carmier's arrival on the Grover Plantation to seek the long-vacant overseer house and with it to sharecrop on the land. The house, symbolic of the racial tensions and the economic changes on the plantation, was vacant because the white overseer moved when the Grovers began to use black sharecroppers. Thereafter, no white had sought it and no black was able to rent it from the Grovers. The issue of race is central to the history that emerges through the fateful transaction involving the overseer's house. Asked "What color are you?," Robert Carmier states his identity in terms of color and work: "'I'm a colored man' . . . 'but I can farm as well as the next one'" (8). After a negotiation that is an iteration and a reversal of the expected power hierarchy, Robert Carmier prevails in getting the house from Mack Grover; however, in farming sugarcane and in hauling the crop to the derrick, Robert displays the very same competitive behavior with the Cajuns that he initiated in his negotiation with Grover. It results in his disappearance and presumed death at the hands of the Cajuns.

This account of the Carmier family's history on the plantation sets the stage both for their difference from the blacks and their antagonism toward the Cajuns, despite the fact that all share the space of the plantation. The history of the Carmiers at once links the narrative to present tensions and closes it off in the past, so that Robert Carmier's life story on the plantation will circle outward and backward to enclose his son Raoul in a chaining process that Gaines conceptualized in this first novel.

In simply trying to make a living on the plantation, Raoul Carmier is the second generation of his family to situate himself in competition with the Cajuns and in counterdistinction to the blacks who are being forced off the land. The Cajuns have acquired almost all of the land: "'They have taken over the plantation. They have wrangled and wrangled until they have gotten everybody else to quit farming'" (73). The black farmers have quit because the Villon family of five cousins "kept asking for more land. Each year they showed Bud Grover where they needed more land. Bud Grover took the land from the Negroes and gave it to them" (73). The result is an ongoing destruction of the quarters as they once were. Houses are torn down to make way for more fields: "Houses don't sit between houses any more; now they sit between fields. It's all right at night. It's quiet at night. But in the day you might have a tractor running up to your fence any time" (77). The blacks are leaving the plantation for Baton Rouge and New Orleans and looking for whatever work they can find in the cities. Movement to the urban setting constitutes a step toward the annihilation of a way of life, which was actually occurring when Gaines wrote *Catherine Carmier* because the Major family, the owners of River Lake, sold the plantation in the 1960s, when mechanized farming had already displaced sharecroppers and dispersed Cherie Quarters.[52]

Despite the Cajuns being sharecroppers like the blacks, they have the advantage of skin privilege: "White is still white. . . . And white still sticks with white" (73). The economics of the situation with the Cajuns underlines and

An Old Tenant House with a Mud Chimney and Cotton Growing up to Its Door, Which Is Occupied by Mulattoes, Melrose, La. A family of mulatto tenant farmers occupied this house on a Louisiana plantation and grew cotton up to the door. (Marion Post Wolcott, photographer, 1940; Farm Security Administration/Office of War Information Color Photographs, Library of Congress Prints and Photographs Division, Washington, D.C.)

supports the race issue; the elderly schoolteacher Madame Bayonne translates the process in detail for an outsider:

> Cajuns have always made more crop for Bud Grover than the Negroes have. They've always had the best land—being white they got that from the start; and they have organization. That Villon bunch has always worked together. Having the best land and being able to work it all together, they grew twice as much. When you make twice as much, you can afford to buy more equipment, better equipment. Once they got the equipment, they wanted more land to work. So Bud Grover gave them the land—acre by acre until the Negro's farm was too small to support him. He quits, and the Cajuns get it all. The next year another one quits; the next year another one. Now, they've all quit. All but one. (74)

This description of an aggressive capitalism that is the plantation comes from the older schoolteacher who both belongs in and exists apart from the community in the quarters. Madame Bayonne is the earliest model not only of Gaines's male and female schoolteachers whose ironic vision of their social geography allows them to live within its contradictions, but also of Gaines's elderly black women whose strength and independence provide a potential model for living differently.

For blacks, sharecropping is part of the devolving world of the familiar, the plantation, in the quarters where they can remain even after they lose their work. In keeping with the legacy from slavery, no resident of the quarters pays rent. Madame Bayonne reveals: "You can stay here for free. As long as you keep your nose clean. You don't have your farm any more—no; the Cajuns have taken that. But you can stay here if you want to" (78). The staying in place or accepting a place, no matter how diminished, is the lot of the blacks in *Catherine Carmier,* and that becomes the choice frequently dogging Gaines's black men, whether or not it is framed and spoken. It is the dilemma that Gaines repeatedly dramatizes as a life-altering choice that is constituted as much out of the external environment as it is out of free will.

Jackson observes the worn and dilapidated houses in the quarters and the dispirited people living in them, and he concludes that he will not remain on the plantation, despite his elderly aunt Charlotte's desire. He cannot "bow," or accept the treatment of blacks in this Louisiana. At the same time, Jackson acknowledges that the constraints so visible in the quarters exist in the city, the place he has left: "They promised us, . . . they promised us. They beckoned and beckoned and beckoned. But when we went up there, we found it all a pile of lies. There was no truth in any of it. No truth at all" (80–81). The urban life in San Francisco is equally constricted, according to Jackson, even though he admits, "They don't come dressed in sheets with ropes" (81). This difference between Louisiana and California, between the rural and the urban, between the South and the West, is not sufficient to make Jackson believe that he can live in dignity and truth. From his experiences in California, Jackson understands his life as being surrounded by "a wall of bricks, of stones. A wall that had gotten so high by now that he had to stand on tiptoe to look over it" (94). He suggests that the incarceral space is not merely the southern Louisiana plantation but any place where race and class restrict individuals. He uses the examples of an Indian ("the red boy from New Mexico"), a Chinese ("the yellow boy from Hong Kong"), and an Anglo ("the white boy, born and raised in Dayton, Ohio") (94) to elevate his life in California as better than that in the South, but the strategy ultimately only forces him to the painful conclusion that he was not alone in his struggle against enclosure and entrapment behind the wall.

While a comparable walled space may be surrounding Raoul Carmier, he refuses to give up farming or to give in to the Cajuns. He may be "killing himself working, trying to keep up with them" (74), but because he sees himself as different from blacks, he resists "standing on a soapbox preaching against the treatment he's getting" (74). Raoul etches manhood into the narrative as the function of "standing" against all odds, which then surfaces as a signpost of masculinity in all of Gaines's novels. Raoul's position, comparable to the stance that Richard Wright takes toward black men in the South, is reducible to an unacceptable binary: stay and die or flee and live. His specific task is impossible not only because the Cajuns have tractors and technology on their side but because they also are white. Raoul's world of the neither black nor white is dying, or as his daughter Lillian observes, it is "over with": "That farming out there—one man trying to buck against that whole family of Cajuns—is outdated" (40). Lillian attempts to explain to her sister Catherine that, although she hates "black worse than the whites hate it," she hasn't opened her "heart to the white world either," but that she will pass into that white world because she knows what her father does not: "I must go somewhere. I can't stand in the middle of the road any longer. . . . Daddy and his sisters want us to be Creoles. Creoles. What a joke. Today you're one way or the other; you're white or you're black. There is no in-between" (48).

Not only does the Louisiana space create a cultural identity, but it also produces a racial identity. The very same quarters as a place that constructs individual and group identity also produces race. When Catherine is with her family in the quarters, she is Creole, but when she is with Jackson in the same space, she is black. When Lillian is with her New Orleans relatives, she is Creole, but when she is with her black friends in the city, she is black. The same configuration of place can shape a different racial designation for the same body. Lillian experiences added frustration with color and race codes in New Orleans because from the eighteenth century through the middle of the twentieth century, demographic patterns made the strictest physical segregation of the races difficult, as Shannon Lee Dawdy observed about the forming of racial identities in the colonial city: "Native-born (creole) New Orleanians of all colors grew up in more intimate and integrated quarters. . . . At the same time, they began to form more definite ideas about 'race.' Through these concepts, they chose a segregation of the mind rather than the body. French New Orleans was a place where people of different colors and legal statuses lived side by side, cheek by jowl."[53] The proximity of people of multiple hues and colors living in the twentieth-century city as white increased Lillian's sense of confinement within a racial segregation that was often built upon custom and perception rather than on any physical markers.

The inability of some individuals to sustain a single racial identity outside the living environment of the quarters is made clear in Lillian's case. While her father, Raoul, would keep both Lillian and Catherine within the domestic environment that he can control as personal and private, he cannot determine how his two daughters will be racialized outside of the structural space he controls. Lillian's residency in the city as opposed to the plantation makes her vulnerable to the racial designations that others apply to her but also to those she would choose for herself. External topographies map onto Lillian and Catherine, publicly and jointly, race traces that are specific and discontinuous. That is, the pluralization of racial identities that all Creoles of Color have inherited cannot be sustained over different place markers. Lillian and Catherine have to be only one thing at a time, only one race, only one racial identity at a time. Should Catherine leave the plantation with Jackson, she will become black. Lillian's resolution is to move to the North to consolidate her identity as white. The circulation of bodies that bear the markers of multiple races or multiple cultures has to be disallowed and those bodies policed so as not to disrupt the sense of social hegemony around issues of race and—in the earlier Louisiana context—language. That these ideas have continued to retain significance for Gaines since the 1960s is apparent in the several references he has made to them following the success of his last novel, *A Lesson before Dying*. Moreover, in his comments on the writing he plans to complete is a refrain that links that work to Catherine Carmier and her Creole of Color identity.[54]

In *Catherine Carmier*, however, Jackson and Catherine confront what it means to be raced black in a modern world colliding with history and roots, with place and tradition. They share a mutual dissatisfaction with the subject positions expected of them and frustration with the external restrictions determining their cultural and racial identities. Their reunion in a combined search for a place to exist outside of incarceral spaces is overshadowed by historical caste and class relationships and by the social decorum appropriate to those hierarchical relationships. In rendering their struggle for a kind of freedom from the tyranny of place, Gaines addresses the role of their childhood memory as a bond unifying them against the complexity of impending modernity on a time-bound society. From the standpoint of memory, they can engage their desire and their difference partly as a conflict between the past and the changing present.

Gaines speculates about the psychological position of the intellectual, Jackson, the thinking and reflective individual. Jackson has learned to analyze the various groups within the parameters of his vision and, as a result, becomes an archetype for subsequent introspective observers in Gaines's fiction. Jackson's contemplative surveying of the people and landscape surrounding him provides the psychological backdrop for his location outside of the expected place for blacks. In his immersion back into the practices of the plantation world, he becomes aware of the cultural responses to the otherness of blacks. Jackson's reflections and his watchful gaze mirror the questions about existence that the residents of the community—blacks, Creoles, or Cajuns in this multilayered, multicolored environment—intuit but cannot pose: who and what is the individual person under the strain of transition, how does the individual stand under the pressure of dislocation, where might the individual focus loyalties and find values as the old world passes and boundaries are being destroyed?

As Nancy Duncan suggests:

> Space is . . . subject to various territorializing and deterritorializing
> processes whereby local control is fixed, claimed, challenged, forfeited
> and privatized. In some cases this may have socially progressive results
> in terms of providing a safe base (site of resistance) from which previ-
> ously disempowered groups may become empowered. On the other
> hand, isolation in a private or quasi-private space or sphere may have
> an undesirable depoliticizing effect on a group, fortifying it against
> challenges from, and allowing it to inadvertently assume indepen-
> dence from, a wider public sphere.[55]

The plantation world of blacks that Jackson encounters is outside of the politics of competition and cooperation. These black sharecroppers understand themselves to have already been replaced, so that they have no way to compete. One of the problems, then, that Raoul Carmier faces is that he becomes more and more trapped in an obsolete way both of farming the land and of framing an identity. His stubborn and insular way of relating to plantation life is his only means of making sense of his world and himself. Linked irrevocably to the past and imprisoned by memory, his way of rendering his life meaningful requires a stifling of his wife, cutting her off from the blacks in the quarters, subjugating his daughter into a stranded quasi-filial position in the family, and even killing his own dark-skinned son.

Associated with the dying of the Creoles of Color as a distinct caste, Raoul is a man whose life revolves around the trap of his in betweenness and his containment within an institution that can no longer support him. He signifies the incarceral plantation space with its all-too-visible Louisiana race, caste, and ethnic particularities. Although he must recognize that his world is dying, Raoul maintains his private identity by denying that he is black and that his present condition has any connection to the racism inherent in the plantation system. He holds on to the prejudices of his father against other residents of the quarters: "the Carmiers had little use for dark-skinned people" (12). By ignoring his connections to all but the Creole world and his rented parcel of land, Raoul is destroying what is left of his family.

Despite his flawed psychology, Raoul ironically chains himself to life in the midst of dying and destruction. He holds on to his status as a man in a system that would deprive him of manhood. He becomes one lesson for Jackson in the meaning of living and of manhood in spite of his major failings, because as Jackson reluctantly admits, there is "something about the man, different from all the others around here. . . . He was still trying to stand when all the odds were against him. That was it, that was the only thing" (176). Standing itself signifies the heroic in Gaines's canon and is a referent back to Gaines's own plantation upbringing. The metaphor stems from his memories of his disabled great aunt, Augusteen Jefferson, who crawled to perform her work responsibilities. In so doing, she taught Gaines how to stand and to value that trait as most desirable because it encompasses exemplary strength of character and superlative moral values. Standing is a signification of power, especially a marker of positive black manhood and masculinity, persistent thematic and tropic inclusions characteristic of Gaines's fiction and often the subject of major critical assessments, such as those by Herman Beavers and Keith Clark.[56] As Suzanne Jones remarks: "Throughout his fiction, Gaines uses the physical act of standing as a symbolic representation of coming to manhood."[57] However, in the final scenes of *Catherine Carmier*, Raoul loses a fistfight to Jackson, who knocks him down, so that Catherine must urge him to stand: "It's not over with, Daddy. You have stood this long. You can keep on standing. I'll stand with you" (244). Raoul's standing, undermined by racial isolation and color prejudice, is powerless before the forces of change that will reconfigure his existence and reconstitute the plantation and alienate the quarters from their origins in slavery but retain the legacy of that past. It is a delicate balance, and one not typically represented in black imaginative space.

In observing the Cajuns, Creoles, and blacks on the Grover Plantation, Gaines dramatizes the conflict between a racial and cultural past and its configurations in the present that is fundamental to all of his writing. In that dramatization, however, he performs an insistent exploration of that past with an unrelenting representation of its stifling limitations and dying subjects. "There will always be men struggling to change," Gaines has told John

O'Brien, "and there will always be those who are controlled by the past. In many cases, those who are controlled by the past can be just as human and sometimes more human than those who try to change things. Yet, there must always be those who try to change conditions; there must always be those who try to break out of the trap the world keeps going in. Man must keep moving. . . . This is the kind of thing I am doing in all of my work."[58]

Yet as Joe Pittman puts it in *The Autobiography of Miss Jane Pittman*, human beings must try to do something, but they are put here to die: "'Now . . . man come here to die. . . . That's the contract he signed when he was born. . . . Now, all he can do while he's here is do something and do that thing good'" (89). This inevitability surfaces in all of Gaines's characters who try to break out of the traps by doing something; characters such as Marcus in *Of Love and Dust* and Robert X in *In My Father's House* affirm this concept with their deaths. Raoul in *Catherine Carmier* and Mathu in *A Gathering of Old Men* recognize the inevitable but persist in the unthinkable, resisting being made obsolete by the dominant power structure. In these cases of characters all impacted by the very real racial dynamics of plantation culture as well as in others in Gaines's fiction, those struggling to "do something," to effect change, are dying, literally or figuratively. The irony is, as Michel de Certeau observes, "the dying man *falls* outside the *thinkable*, which is identified with what one can *do*. . . . Nothing can be said in a place where nothing more can be done."[59]

The rebellions in word or deed that Gaines's characters would effect essentially render them outside of the cultural practices, beliefs, and values, and therefore outside of the living space of the culture. According to Certeau, "The dying are outcasts because they are deviants in an institution organized by and for the conservation of life. An 'anticipated mourning,' a phenomenon of institutional rejection, puts them away in advance in 'the dead man's room'; it surrounds them with silence or, worse yet, with lies that protect the living against the voice that would break out of this enclosure to cry: 'I am going to die.'"[60] Certeau suggests that the dying man is "intolerable in a society in which the disappearance of subjects is everywhere compensated for and camouflaged by the multiplication of the tasks to be performed."[61] In *Catherine Carmier*, not only Raoul and the Creoles, Catherine, Lillian, and Della, but also Jackson and the blacks, Brother, Charlotte, and Mary Louise, are all cast in the position of the dying in the manner in which they are imprisoned in a way of life that has proceeded from the plantation and has not allowed fully for their reconstitution as modern subjects.

Subsequent Gaines novels have comparable linkages to death and dying as part of the fabric of plantation life. *A Gathering of Old Men* represents an entire older generation of black men as plantation dwellers who unknowingly have been in the process of dying for much of their lives. In their moment of recognizing that they have been incarcerated by their own adherence to segregationist and racist ideology as much as by the power, dominance, and hegemony of whites in positions of authority, the eighteen men also accept the paradoxical relationship to dying that allows them to stand outside of all normative social constraints. In effect, that acceptance of death in moving away from all of their previous humiliating efforts to live, no matter how emasculated, frees them to perform an act of social rebellion, an uprising against their treatment and a revolt against the imprisoning life in the quarters.

Gaines's representation of the old men, like that of Raoul Carmier, suggests that his fiction is less about articulating stances of resistance than about forging oppositional space—essentially of articulating a third space, a space different from much of the history for people of color existing in Louisiana's plantation culture. The oppositional space corresponds to Gaines's desire for justice no matter how late in the coming, as evidenced in his own reclaiming and reversing the meanings of space on the plantation where he was born and now makes his home. The work Gaines performs with the elderly black men is the creation of an opposition that is spatially articulated and translated into an opportunity for facing death. It evokes what bell hooks calls a "radical standpoint" that forms a cultural practice in a counterhegemonic space.[62] While one reading might rightly be that of linking their actions to the centuries-long struggles of black people in the United States against an oppressive racial regime and economic system, another reading is that Gaines enunciates a new space, a third space, in keeping with the conceptions of hooks, Homi Bhabha, and Edward Soja, who argue for the formation of spaces of belonging in which identities are reconstituted as hybrids of individual and group identities.

In *A Gathering of Old Men*, the overt stance against racism with its debilitating personal costs is both individual and communal, private and shared. The resultant shared spatial ground reconstitutes the men into a group, a community that had not existed previously. Each one not only claims his responsibility for the killing but articulates his motive for the act. What they present is the reality of their figurative incarceration on the Marshall plantation. In no case is the murder unjustified, though in several the grievances are generations old. Uncle Billy tells of his son being beaten by the Cajuns, Fix's crowd, after he returned from World War II: "'They beat him till they beat him crazy, and we had to send him to Jackson. He don't even know me and his mama no more. We take him candy, we take him cake, he eat it like a hog eating corn.'"[63] Jacob's sister Tessie, "one of those great big pretty mulatto girls" who had chosen to live in the quarters with blacks, had been killed by white men on Mardi Gras day in 1947. Jacob joins the old men not merely because of what whites had done to his sister, but also because of his own weakness: he had adhered to his color-conscious mulatto family's refusal to accept Tessie's body back from the people of the quarters. Gabriel's shame is that his mentally challenged son, falsely accused of raping a white woman, died horribly in an electric chair that initially malfunctioned and extended the agony of the execution. Clatoo's sister cut Forest Boutan with a cane knife as he tried to rape her; as one of the plantation dwellers remembers: "She didn't kill him, but he was well marked for the rest of his days. And she was sent to the pen for the rest of hers, where after so many years she died insane" (25). Prison or penitentiary enters literally into the men's plantation narratives and is part of the secret they harbor in order to remain on the plantation. The grievances suffered in the past unite the group in one last chance to show that they can be men; that they can overcome their own internal caste and color prisons; that they can atone for the deaths of loved ones in the penitentiary and in the asylum, as well as in the quarters; that they can stand together against the powerful whites and create on the very plantation a new site. Here Gaines uses chaining to both connect the men to the past and free them into the open spaces between those links.

Unlike the beaten-down elders, Mathu has been strong, even rebellious in his years as a plantation worker, but he does not tell of his own past or of his version of the present. He becomes the powerful silence at the center of the drama and of the history of oppression voiced by a generation of submissive black males. He is an extension of the figure of Raoul Carmier, and his stance in relation to other blacks echoes Raoul's. While Mathu's representation foregrounds the viability of a courageous manhood and emergent identity in spite of brutalizing slavery and systematic suppression, it too encompasses the bitter toll of racism on the individual. As he explains his behavior over the years: "'I ain't nothing but a mean, bitter old man. . . . No hero. . . . Hating them out there on that river, hating y'all here in the quarters. Put myself above all—proud to be African. You know why proud to be African? 'Cause they won't let me be a citizen here in this country. Hate them 'cause they won't let me be a citizen, hated y'all 'cause you never tried'" (182). He thus reveals that what was taken for strength and healthy self-awareness was actually a spirit damaged and embittered by the exclusionary practices that function like the prison to isolate and punish blacks for their difference. In these revelations, Gaines articulates an ignored aspect of the politics of racial segregation: even the seemingly strong survivor can be scarred and in need of change, transformation, and justice.[64]

In one of the novel's most ambitious moves toward meaningful social transformation and racial justice, Gaines depicts Candy Marshall, a young white plantation owner who, though not overtly racist, has simply presumed white racial privilege and class authority over the black residents of the plantation. Her genuinely caring and protective relationship with Mathu is similar to that of many white southerners to the black women who nursed them as children, but in *A Gathering of Old Men*, Gaines reverses the more typical gender expectations of a male plantation owner and a female plantation worker. Going further in promulgating the necessity of change, Gaines uses the circumstances of Mathu's and the old men's independent stance to force Candy also to learn that change is necessary, and that with it the old racial dynamic and paternalistic hierarchy cannot be maintained. Candy discovers that, though she had conceived the plot to confuse the authorities, the old men do not need or want the paternalism and patronage of a white landowner. Her age, gender, and sympathies may make her a nontraditional landowner; nonetheless, her whiteness with her class locates her in the conventional order of systematic oppression. Within the space of the old men's new subjective positioning and determined self-actualization, Candy must relinquish her autocratic notions of leadership, protection, and control because they are rendered unnecessary and untenable. This projected reformulation of cross-racial relations on the Marshall Plantation and by extension in the larger southern community may be the most radical, because it would constitute the most profound unsettling of white normative behavior.

Although several of Gaines's more complex and innovative characters are women, whether relatively minor like Candy Marshall or impressively major like Miss Jane Pittman, his male characters primarily figure the unresolved tensions of place and memory in the continuation of the plantation as a social force in the lives of black people. Perhaps the most subtle and illusive of these figurations are the father and son in Gaines's *In My Father's House*, a novel that was not well received by critics and that Gaines admits was difficult to write.[65] Set in the civil rights era after the death of Martin Luther King Jr. in 1968, the novel is a discourse on absent space, the unfilled void between paternal responsibility and filial need. The absences, functioning similar to open spaces in a chain, are as much a part of the tether of connection as the more tangible and visible linkages. Black masculine subjectivity in the text develops somewhat opaquely out of modern-day plantation culture and its unrelenting pressures, the strata of economic, historical, and social forces.

The resolution depends on an understanding of the social and material history of black life on Reno Plantation and on the potential of a return to the space of the long-vacated plantation to effect a healing. Herman Beavers reads healing in *In My Father's House*, along with *Of Love and Dust*, in terms of self and communal censorship that mediates Reverend Phillip Martin's and James Kelly's "giving voice (or at least credence) to the painful aspects of their experience, of 'reading' society by using themselves as the starting point for analysis."[66] He links only Kelly and not Martin to the plantation, in that Kelly's storytelling constitutes "a transgressive act of voice" resisting the silence on the plantation that enables the status quo to maintain its authority and power.[67] Martin, as Beavers rightly concludes, engages in "the task of remembering," which "calls for an act of transgressive listening," which in turn will allow him to hear all that he has intentionally silenced in leaving his past behind.[68] That specific past, I would add, is not merely interpolated as a family left behind and their stories ignored, but it is articulated as the plantation itself that constitutes the shape and substance of Martin's past.

When confronted with the damage he has wrought, Martin blames his abandonment of his son and family on the legacy of slavery. His explanation is simplistic, because the larger systemic culture of the modern plantation is not just the legacy of slavery, but the extension and inculcating of exploitation and dependency in the face of alternative systems. It is the awareness of alternatives, even those that lead to dissipation and corruption, that enables the flight from the hardships of life as a plantation sharecropper. The rural and town spaces are contrapuntal to the dual existence of Martin and his son on the plantation and in the town. The public sphere collides with the private, both domestic and civic, in a suggested contest between the past and the present forms of black gender and social identity. In this narrative, the remembered psychic geography of Gaines's plantation childhood lurks hauntingly beneath a surface of Louisiana towns and cities in the early 1970s.[69]

Gaines constructs Reverend Phillip J. Martin in relational roles but figuratively as a dying man, similar to Raoul Carmier and the old men on the Marshall Plantation. Simultaneously, an individual black man confronting his failure to nurture his offspring and an objectification of black men generally abnegating paternal roles, Martin is a minister at Solid Rock Baptist Church who has transformed himself from youthful dissipation in the rural South to dedicated activism in the urban civil rights movement. He has become to the townspeople "King Martin," "our Martin Luther King."[70] He is a leader of "political and moral" character and courage. Religion saved him from drinking and gambling, which he blames on the legacies of slavery and the deprivations of Reno Plantation, where, he says, he "was an animal" (211). Martin's past returns, in the form of the illegitimate son he had abandoned, to challenge his self-righteous satisfaction with his public achievements.

In his role as a minister and an activist for social justice, Martin has succeeded in replacing the plantation with his church, his office, and his house, architectural structures that reconfigure his environment and his place within his community. He turns nonetheless away from his plan for new economic demonstrations that would extend the structures of his public responsibility as a community leader. He chooses instead to return to the plantation that structured his youth in order to confront his private responsibility as a father. Martin eventually comes to understand that he cannot absolve himself from the sins of his past, and that he cannot contain that past in shrouds of silence or public displays of courage. His explanation of his youth cannot repair the damage he has done: "I was paralyzed. Paralyzed. Yes, I had a mouth, but I didn't have a voice. I had legs, but I couldn't move. . . . It took a man to do these things, and I wasn't a man. I was just some other brutish animal who could cheat, steal, rob, kill—but not stand. Not be responsible. Not protect you or your mother. They had branded that in us from the time of slavery" (102). His self-serving version of black masculinity, as compromised by the negative conditioning of enslavement and subsequently eroded by the emasculating rules of plantation life, nonetheless articulates the desire for individual responsibility and familial protection. It locates Martin in his youth in an abject space similar to that occupied in the narrative present by his son Etienne, now Robert X. Martin cannot effect a reconciliation with his children; Justine, who was raped and beaten by her mother's lover, and Antoine, who took the eldest Etienne's place in killing the rapist, are both gone to a new life in New York, and Robert X, already psychologically dead, commits suicide, an act that completes the punishment of the father. Robert X jumps to his death into Big Man Bayou (203), and his death signifies Martin's destruction of his entire first family, Johanna and her three children, though they all commit acts of will. Martin's words in the conclusion, "I'm lost, Alma, I'm lost," posit his grief and despair against his wife Alma's comforting words of their beginning anew. The paralysis that he earlier evoked, however, may give way to an enunciated space in which the lost man can be found.

Although a powerful psychological drive is embedded in the narrative, *In My Father's House* is truncated in time and ultimately dependent upon a remembered plantation life that does not figure in the narrative line. Presenting the plantation directly in this text may have provided the narrative power that Gaines brings when he renders plantation life, customs, and talk in his fiction; however, he wanted to explore the psychology of the father and the absent father's impact on the son, both of which are areas he associated with plantation formations that differ from the more transparent aspects of that culture. The final encounters between Martin and Chippo Simon, his friend from Reno Plantation, provide the occasion for recounting indirectly a subject that borders on an unexplored aspect of Gaines's own autobiography. The chaining to the past and to the plantation is present, but the method depends upon Chippo's memories to reveal the social history of Johanna and her children after Martin abandoned them, and, importantly, for explicating the despair and pain of Robert X's life. Chippo functions not only as a storyteller but also as an agent of surveillance. He gathers information about the plantation and its residents, even those who, like Johanna, leave for California. Chippo presents the folk perspective on time and history, as Keith Byerman points out; the implication of his monologues is that "Martin must accept all of his history, both the past and the present, and himself in that history, as a man who must live with his guilt, his suffering, and his joy. His identity is not fixed as either the failed father of the plantation or the successful leader of the city; it is a process that contains both of those as well as whatever he makes of himself in the future."[71] Beverly Ricord, a teacher and civil rights activist, understands precisely what Phillip Martin and their movement signify when she says, "We work toward the future" (213). Her analysis is clear: "You wanted the past changed, Reverend Martin. . . . Even He can't do that. So that leaves nothing but the future" (213). Ultimately, futurity requires the work of unchaining oneself, yet that work may or may not be achieved, especially because the plantation past so haunts the memory of successive generations of blacks that it inhibits the necessary transition forward for both the men, who are in the foreground, and the women, whose lives are equally affected by plantation culture but whose presence in the text mainly serves to underscore the impact of the plantation on men.

II. LANDSCAPE AS PRISONSCAPE

This area of space is not firm ground on which to stand. In no way is it a surface.

This is space as the sphere of a dynamic simultaneity, constantly disconnected by new arrivals, constantly waiting to be determined (and therefore always undetermined) by the construction of new relations. —DOREEN MASSEY, *For Space*

The incarceral landscape and the imprisoning space of the plantation South inherited in the twentieth and twenty-first centuries are defining tropes in

Gaines's fiction. His prisonlike Louisiana forwards the metaphorical limits of incarceration as a psychic state associated with space. The parish, a Louisiana geographical and governing unit similar to a county, functions not only as a division of public space but also as a way of dividing resources and people. In Pointe Coupée, the parish is intricately connected with the plantation, because the elite landowners of the large plantations also controlled the parish. The connection between the plantation and the prison in Gaines's area of Louisiana is at once more metaphorical and more historical. The prison in his fiction becomes emblematical of the relegation of a cordoned-off, negative space for blacks, who in the physical constraints of their everyday experiential realities suffer the restraints of a color caste along with the race caste. At the same time, the prison is always also the material reality of Angola, the working plantation turned state penitentiary. Gaines's fiction, then, imagines an incarceral space that is persistently architecturally invested in spatial demarcations and the social distinctions stemming from the plantation and prison situated in a landscape at once beautiful and treacherous.

While Brenda Marie Osbey's architectonics of space is tied inextricably to the urban and its built environment, Gaines's incarceral fiction depends upon the principal rural social and economic structure, the working plantation, for its central spatial iconography. Developed and maintained by slave labor in the eighteenth and nineteenth centuries, the Louisiana plantation survived into the twentieth century, and it continues into the twenty-first not merely with sites named plantations but also with the state's largest prison, Angola, the site of the historic Angola plantation, which was a working plantation of over 18,000 acres formed in 1880 by joining four smaller plantations— Panola, Belle View, Killarney, and Angola—on land initially purchased in the 1830s with profits from a slave-trading firm. Even before Angola became the state penitentiary, the plantation used leased convicts to work the land. Still known as "The Farm" because its inmates continue to work field crops, Angola has since the 1950s been infamous for the brutal treatment of its mainly black inmates and their harsh work conditions. Highly publicized feature films, such as *Dead Man Walking* (1995), *The Green Mile* (1999), and *Monster's Ball* (2001), have utilized Angola for setting or story. The award-winning documentary *The Farm: Life inside Angola Prison* (1998) has shed light on the present and past conditions of inmates incarcerated at Angola, many for life or for long sentences that in effect mean life in prison without parole.

Gaines is not a "prison writer" in the vein either of the political type (for example, *Soledad Brother: The Prison Letters of George Jackson*) or the aesthetic type (such as Etheridge Knight's *Poems from Prison*). The intricate workings of Angola itself do not figure as such in his writing, despite the fact that Angola is a looming presence in Gaines's work as it is in Louisiana, and with the appearance of Wilbert Rideau's book, *In the Place of Justice: A Story of Punishment and Deliverance* (2010), much of the conditions at that prison during the forty-four years of Rideau's imprisonment are once again in the public eye. The book by Rideau, who spent a part of his incarceration as the editor of the prison magazine, *The Angolite*, the only prison organ in the nation that was not censored, adds another chapter to the place of Angola in public culture. In addition, Gaines has referred directly to his reading of *The Angolite* and to his contacting the warden at Angola specifically for accurate information while he was writing *A Lesson before Dying*.[72]

The unique situation of having one of the nation's largest and most infamous prisons linked to plantation culture and history a short distance away from the twentieth-century working plantation on which Gaines was born contributes to both the time-space compression and the incarceral trope noticeable in his fiction. Surveillance, an expected component of the prison, as Michel Foucault has explained, is in Gaines's Louisiana a necessary part of the functioning of Angola State Penitentiary, but inasmuch as the looming presence of Angola is also understood as a postslavery plantation, surveillance is as well integral to the plantation as a living work space in Gaines's fiction. That space is a material and metaphorical structure representing the enclosed, incarceral nature of life under legally sanctioned segregation. It is, in fact, "various prisons" whose operations must be infiltrated and subverted, as John Lowe has concluded in a richly detailed reading of surveillance in *A Lesson before Dying* using Foucault's *Discipline and Punish: The Birth of the Prison*.[73] Lowe applies Foucault's formulation of the "double foundation" of the prison, "juridico-economic" and "technico-disciplinary," to connect it to the "confinement and concealment of the poor," as in the plantation school that figures in Gaines's text. The interconnection between an understanding of incarceration as a prison house and a knowledge of confinement as a plantation space is constant in Gaines's representation of black life.

Whether in preemancipation or postslavery settings, Gaines connects the literal prison with the metaphorical incarceration manifested in his representation of the plantation and its force in the lives of its inhabitants. The prison structure and the plantation culture intertwined together become a more prominent and recognizable trope for the status of blacks in the American South. Throughout Gaines's canon, the spatial geography of the physical world utilizes the plantation and the social geography of first slavery and then segregation to constitute the incarceral for African Americans from the period prior to the Civil War through that of the civil rights movement. The implied connection between the plantation and the prison metamorphoses into the much more recognizable current-day prison complex in texts such as *A Lesson before Dying* or *Of Love and Dust*, in which an initial exchange between two characters leaves no doubt about how Gaines chains the two structures together. One character in *Of Love and Dust* states: "[T]hat pen [penitentiary] can kill a man," and the other responds, "That plantation can do the same to some people."[74] The only difference is "the open air" and "people who care about you" on the plantation. The linkages between prison and plantation are discernible in all of Gaines's novels because each one is never far from the reality of Louisiana's plantations and prisons, specifically Angola State Prison, which signified the fate of black men in his Louisiana as much as the literal plantation.

At the same time, however, Gaines does not write the narrative of the conjunction of plantation and prison as merely literal and material. The figurative projection is perhaps best embodied in the existential condition of Robert X, a.k.a. Etienne, in *In My Father's House*. He is the rootless son who searches for his father, ostensibly to confront him for ruining his life and that of his mother, Johanna, and his siblings, Antoine and Justine, but also to find meaning for his own existence. He appears not only ghostlike but occupies the subjective space of an ex-convict: "He was too thin, too hungry-looking. . . . He looked sick. His jaws were too sunken-in for someone his age. His deep-set bloodshot eyes wandered too much. He could have just been released from the state pen. He definitely looked like somebody who had been shut in. They probably had let him go because they figured they had punished him enough already and knew he would die soon" (3–4). Robert X has not been incarcerated in the state penitentiary, but he has been imprisoned by his life on Reno Plantation and the psychological toll of that life. Written on his body is the narrative of the conjoined carceral states in Gaines's fiction. Robert X's alienation and suffering are refracted in his casting off of his old Louisiana-inflected name and with it the traceable stigma of his illegitimacy and his plantation origins. What he is unable to disguise in a new political identity, however, is the personal mark of imprisonment, the existential confinement that wears down the body and the mind and that ultimately questions the efficacy of protest marches and simple idealism when the fundamental issues of human conduct go unaddressed.

Prison and plantation collide much more directly in *Of Love and Dust*, set on a False River plantation and centered on a young man sentenced to prison and bonded out to work on the Hebert plantation. Prison shadows the text and subverts the plantation into an incarceral space that blacks, whites, and Cajuns have learned to accept as the condition of their lives. Gaines has recalled that in *Of Love and Dust*, he wanted "to say something about my past, something of what I had left out of *Catherine Carmier*. I wanted to talk about the fields a little bit more, about the plantation story, the river, the church, the house fairs."[75] *Of Love and Dust* captures the ambivalence of the social fabric on a modern Louisiana plantation and unpacks the conventions of its social and economic system. The voice of the observant narrator, Frank James "Jim" Kelly, reverberates with the sounds of his community's storytelling traditions, and although detached and analytical, Jim has intimate knowledge of the social order. A plantation worker, Jim Kelly has in middle age gained trust and respect for his years of mediating between the black workers and the white managers (the Cajun overseer Sidney Bonbon and the landowner Marshall Hebert). Cautious in order to maintain his small stake in the economic hierarchy, Kelly has accepted his own victimization and that of the other blacks.

Kelly's promise to elderly Miss Julie Rand to look after her godson, Marcus Payne, who has been released from prison to work on the plantation, precipitates his involvement in events that will disrupt his existence. Miss Julie had been a cook on the Hebert plantation for forty years and knew how to extract a promise from Jim Kelly. Her extraction of a "favor," or in reality an obligation, is a familiar aspect of Gaines's fiction. In what may be labeled an archetypal moment in Gaines's representation of intergenerational interactions, an elderly black woman prevails upon a black man to step up in a moment of need or crisis in plantation society: "Miss Julie looked at me so long, I turned my head. . . . I just didn't feel comfortable with her looking at me like that. Old people look at you like that for two reasons. One, when you've done something wrong. The other is when they want you to do something for them. The thing they want you to do usually turns out to be a burden. The heavier the burden, the longer they look at you. And Miss Julie looked at me a long, long time" (11). The gaze bears the weight of the elderly woman's immediate close scrutiny but also of her long years of surveying the activities on the plantation.

Under the microscope, Jim discovers that although he has been living both within and just outside the boundaries of the plantation as a watchful country bluesman who plays guitar and sings songs of missed opportunities and lost loves, it is Marcus who is a true blues subject, the black "badman" in open defiance of and in conflict with conventional authority. Gaines's portrayal of Marcus as societal rebel challenging complacency in conduct and belief suggests that *Of Love and Dust* is a play upon Faulkner's *Intruder in the Dust*.[76] In

Cottage, Old Jail, Mix, False River, Point Coupee Parish, Louisiana. On False River, the old jail of the sort Gaines depicted was similar to the houses. (Frances Benjamin Johnston, photographer, 1938; Carnegie Survey of the Architecture of the South, Library of Congress Prints and Photographs Division, Washington, D.C.)

an inversion of the relationship between Faulkner's youthful narrator, Chick Mallison, and his elderly antagonist, Lucas Beauchamp, Gaines creates Jim Kelly as a mature narrative consciousness being educated by a young antagonist. Through Marcus, Kelly learns that the prevailing racial codes must be violated and that plantation life is not safe for the thinking man.

Marcus and Kelly on the plantation are versions of the characters jailed in "Three Men," a short story in *Bloodline* (1968), which initiated Gaines's discourses of black development within narrow spaces. Marcus appears to be a reconfiguration of the central subject of "Three Men," Proctor Lewis, a nineteen-year-old who turns himself in to the police for stabbing a black man, but who thinks: "Rodger Medlow would get me off like he had done once before. He owned the plantation where I lived."[77] Proctor's dilemma of self-definition revolves around his limited options: either accepting responsibility for his crime by remaining imprisoned and heading to the penitentiary at Angola, or becoming dependent upon whites and the system designed to emasculate him by choosing work release into field labor. Marcus's subjectivity begins with both a determination to take leased labor as a way out of prison and a conviction to live without bending to the system. Jim Kelly is an inversion of Munford Bazille, who has spent fifty years of his life in and out of jail for various acts of violence against other blacks, and who has deciphered how the social system and the racial structure in the plantation South depend upon subservient blacks who will kill or condition other blacks. Kelly, though imprisoned in his complacency with a racist social order, avoids at all costs the prospect of being jailed but, like Munford, plays his assigned role in the controlling system.

The third man in the story, Hattie Brown, is pivotal. He is a homosexual, whom Proctor dismisses as "the freak," effeminate, moving, acting, or gesturing "like a woman"; for example, "[t]he freak, Hattie, sat on his bunk, nibbling at his food. . . . All the time he was eating, he was looking at me like a sad woman would look at you" (134). Although Hattie consistently fills a positive affective function throughout "Three Men," he is excluded within the small cell and ignored for his difference. Munford states flatly that "Hattie is a woman" (127) by way of introduction, but he also articulates his and Hattie's connection within the social sphere of segregated southern life: "'What I mean is not one of them out there is a man. Not one. They think they men. They think they men 'cause they got me and him [Hattie] in here who ain't men. But I got news for them—cut them open; go 'head and cut one open— you see if you don't find Munford Bazille or Hattie Brown. Not a man one of them. 'Cause face don't make a man—black or white. Face don't make him and fucking don't make him and fighting don't make him—neither killing. None of this prove you a man. 'Cause animals can fuck, can kill, can fight" (138). By analogy, Hattie is, like the other two men in the cell, a figuration of the debased black male body and the symbolic materialized subject of the discourses on the emasculation of black men in the plantation, peonage, and prison interface. Hattie, "that thing over there" (137), represents one prong of what could happen to Proctor, and Munford is the other, "a beast . . . brutish" (140); either could become the material reality for Proctor if he lets Medlow get him out of jail so he can kill again.

Gaines makes neither viable in the negative representation and comparison of their actions and mannerisms. The masculinist conception of how to break the cycle of destructive homosocial behavior on the part of black men engages frank talk on sexuality and the usages of sex within the world black men inhabit. Proctor and Hattie separately attempt to comfort and aid a young boy of only fourteen who has been badly beaten for stealing and thrown untreated into the cell, but the boy's incarceration prompts Proctor to consider whether he can tolerate being in the penitentiary any more than he can being subjected to the humiliations of leased labor. Although "Three Men" concludes without Proctor's final decision, the direction of the narrative implies that he will remain in prison. "Three Men," then, ends within the close confinement of a jail cell in which black men willingly or unwillingly interact and confront themselves. It is an unresolved foray into examining incarceration and culture, but even its complexity turns upon the familiar concept of standing and a version of black manhood that cannot effect social change.[78] Read with In Love and Dust and Marcus, it underscores the complicated stance from which Gaines cannot move.

Unrepentant for stabbing a man and hostile to plantation life, Marcus is dangerous not because of his crime but because, in attitude and manner, he is a rebel, unwilling and unable to accept the narrow social space designated for black men. Bishop, the black manservant in Marshall Hebert's plantation big house, keeps the community under surveillance for his white employer, but he recoils in disbelief when Marcus enters the front door in violation of all racial custom and social convention: "He just pushed his foot in there. . . . The house his great grandparents built. The house slavery built" (215). Dramatically, in failing to protect the big house from a black interloper, Bishop feels both guilt and shame, and he asks "the old people who had died to forgive him for letting them down" (237). Marshall Hebert ignores Bishop's years of obedient service and summarily orders him to get out, even as Bishop cries: "'Your people say I can stay here. Your people liked me. They say as long as I was a good boy I could stay here. They say if I looked after y'all and I was a good boy, this house was my home till I died" (236). An old man chained to a racist hegemony, Bishop refers to himself as a boy, begs to stay on, but is repaid by being ordered to leave the big house. Marcus is a representation of the black man who figuratively brings the house down as he steps outside of the black communal acquiescence to racism and subservience to whites.

Sidney Bonbon's attempts to break Marcus by brutalizing him in the fields and Jim Kelly's efforts to regulate Marcus's behavior both fail. Bonbon only knows how to be "brutal because he had been brought up in a brute-taught world and in brute-taught times" (67). Jim only wishes to stay clear of Bonbon since his authorization came from the white plantation owners: "The big house had given him a horse and a whip" (67) and encouraged him to use the whip on black fieldworkers. Because of Marcus, Bonbon and Kelly reassess the role of the plantation in their lives and ultimately leave that now unfamiliar, unsafe place for the freedom of unknown space. Marcus effects revenge on the whites, particularly the overseer, by openly courting the black woman Pauline, who is Bonbon's mistress and the mother of his two children. When she rejects him, Marcus discovers what the rest of the quarters has always known and ignored about the interracial affair: Bonbon loves Pauline and she loves him. Marcus then turns his desire for revenge to Bonbon's wife, Louise, who has lived with the knowledge of her husband's infidelity and without his love. Selfishly and recklessly, Marcus enters a relationship with Louise, a relationship that develops into mutual love. He cares little about the certainty of a violent retaliation against him and the entire black community in the quarters because of his violation of the strict sexual codes prohibiting relationships between black men and white women.

Jim Kelly functions conservatively in listening to Aunt Margaret, who works in the overseer's house, keeps its occupants under her surveillance, and expresses the community's fears. Although he does warn Marcus about his behavior, Jim resents Marcus's disrespect in labeling him a traitor to his race, but precisely because he has cooperated with the whites and accepted their treatment of blacks, Jim is helpless to dissuade Marcus or prevent the tragedy. His own years of accommodation and submission become not only unnecessary but meaningless, except as strategies for cooperating in his own emasculation. His failure becomes clear when Hebert, under the pretense of arranging an escape for Marcus and Louise, deceives the lovers by betraying them to Bonbon, who kills Marcus. Louise retreats into madness and ends in the state asylum at Jackson. These events precipitate Jim's transformation: his recognition of Marcus's insistence on pride, dignity, and love as requisites for black manhood; and his realization that the landowner has underhandedly manipulated both the Cajun and the black to solve his own difficulties. As Jim reflects: "Bonbon had said, 'We is nothing but little people. They make us do what they want us to do and they don't tell us nothing.' So why blame Marcus? No, I didn't blame Marcus any more. I admired Marcus. I admired his great courage. . . . He was the bravest man I knew, the bravest man I had ever met" (270). Marcus's bravery has two positive results: Bonbon is believed to have fled to the North with Pauline; and Jim refuses a reference from Hebert and departs the plantation.

Jim Kelly leaves the plantation with the hope of reshaping his life and redeeming his manhood. In leaving, and in refusing to accept a recommendation from Marshall Hebert, he assumes the risks concomitant to any life worth living and accepts the message, if not the model, of Marcus's rejection of plantation ideology. While the plantation, no matter how debilitated, cannot transform itself, it can absorb the fact of dying into its social and economic system.

Gaines represents physical and spiritual incarceration in *A Lesson before Dying* (1993), which brings the ideology of imprisonment into full prominence. It makes plain one of his assessments of his rationale for writing: "I think one of the reasons I write is to try and catch . . . to catch some of the things that I think are important in my own America, the narrow little space that my people were allowed to move in and out of."[79] Set in the 1940s and in that "narrow little space," *A Lesson before Dying* recaptures a time when the criminal justice system in the South was still all white and the plantation communities were intact social entities. Within that temporal and spatial frame, a discourse on manhood, commitment, responsibility, and ultimately faith and belief unfolds. In examining a life struggling for meaning within the debilitating contexts of a racial and cultural past, the text signals Gaines's intellectual commitment to a particular spatial conception, a Louisiana that is still immured in its plantation history and a black community still suffering incarceration. In imagining both an illiterate death-row inmate and plantation schoolteacher connected by means of the process of constructing black manhood under the most adverse conditions, Gaines fuses the past with a present moment that, while different, has not undergone a complete transformation. He threads memory back through a chainlike structure in order to represent that past as interconnected links in a series. Chaining in application to *A Lesson before Dying* carries neither a positive nor a negative value but instead references that which restrains but also connects, or that which lifts but also pulls down, whether it is the youth in the penitentiary or the teacher on the plantation. In the resultant narrative, Gaines creates an incarceral world—segregated, polarized, and limited for its black residents.

The unmarked center of *A Lesson before Dying* is the plantation school. There, Grant Wiggins, a disillusioned teacher, discharges his duty knowing full well that the truncated and inferior education his pupils receive will not change their lives of racial subservience and economic subsistence. Grant's aunt, Tante Lou, enlists him to help Jefferson, a black youth slated for electrocution for a murder he did not commit. The twist is that the despairing Grant, who believes that nothing has or will change within their rural community, is to assist Jefferson not in obtaining a reprieve, but in facing his inevitable death in an electric chair with dignity and humanity. The novel takes the incarceration of blacks in a segregated society as its subject and with an ideology that had been implicit in Gaines's previous work. It demonstrates that the coming into manhood can only occur for Jefferson when he will be unable to live, when his life will be taken from him precisely because he is poor and black and uneducated and thus vulnerable to the racist institutions that devalue his very existence.

Jefferson's own defense attorney reduces him to racist stereotypes: "Look at the shape of this skull, this face as flat as the palm of my hand—look deeply into those eyes. Do you see a modicum of intelligence?"[80] The jury hears that Jefferson is "a cornered animal" who acts instinctively "out of fear, a trait inherited from his ancestors in the deepest jungle of blackest Africa" (7). He is a twentieth-century slave reduced to "a thing" lacking volition and intelligence and therefore deprived of personhood. He is reduced to "a thing" meant to act and labor only "on command": "A thing to hold the handle of the plow, a thing to load your bales of cotton, a thing to dig your ditches, to chop your wood, to pull your corn" (7–8). Incarceration is represented as redeeming the "thing-ness" of Jefferson; the redemption is brought about by the older black women who refuse the "thing-ness" assigned to blacks as objects without will, and who understand that in redeeming Jefferson as he goes to death in the electric chair, they are also redeeming Grant as he faces the realities of a debilitating, unsatisfactory, and constrained life teaching in the plantation school.

What Gaines attempts is an extraordinarily difficult move for a late twentieth-century writer. He aims to place a value on Jefferson's life in the space of imprisonment as a way of dying and not living. When Jefferson can no longer expect freedom in the material world of his restrictive Louisiana environment, he faces a choice, according to Gaines. He can die either like a man or like an animal. The defense attorney had closed his argument with the analogy: "I would just as soon put a hog in the electric chair as this" (8). The choice is by necessity unsatisfactory, because both options end in death. The question is how will Jefferson face death; it is not whether he will die. He is set to die in the electric chair, and that death is fixed, certain, determined. It is the fate of too many within the time-bound society that Gaines depicts. Black men are imprisoned and subject to death, whether within or without the prison. Grant himself, though unlike Jefferson in tangible ways, nonetheless is like the imprisoned youth sentenced to death by an unjust and racist system. Grant lives within that same system, is subject to its same insults and injustices. He occupies a space that is only marginally and nominally better than Jefferson's. His "death" is by degrees and comes with each new assault to his black body.

While there is a glimmer of hope for change at the end of the novel, the change is not systemic. It is rather from within individuals, who free themselves of their stereotypical ways of "placing" black people within the Louisiana social system. John Lowe concludes his insightful essay "Transcendence in the House of Death: The Subversive Gaze of *A Lesson before Dying*" with a powerful, optimistic, modernist reading: "*A Lesson before Dying* becomes a deeply instructive book for the ages to come, in its indelible presentation of the resilience of man's spirit."[81] It is the transcendent movement toward resilience and the afterlife of the body, spirit, or text that stymies any overt political or ideological struggle for justice in the here and now. The literal place that blacks occupy, that lower and less than positionality, in *A Lesson before Dying* does not change and is not transformed by justice being given to those who survive Jefferson's death. The lesson learned is applicable primarily in a society of subordination and deprivation, of incarceration and imprisonment that is accepted if not as just then as irrevocable.

Keith Byerman observes that Grant Wiggins does not believe in justice or God, but that in order to maintain his own manhood, he must believe in himself and in the possibility of transformation.[82] Black masculinity, a manhood based on the overcoming within one's self of the debilitating and dehumanizing aspects of racism, inequality, and injustice, is the objective that Grant attempts to maintain even while he tries to teach its outward signs to Jefferson, whose material legacy is a prison notebook claiming reconciliation and meaning. Grant signifies a black masculinity that is basically emasculated by the structures within which he must function if he is to function at all. He understands that the people on the plantation "must believe, if only to free the mind, if not the body. Only when the mind is free has the body a chance to be free. Yes, they must believe . . . [b]ecause I know what it means to be a slave. I am a slave" (251). He is a teacher, but the lessons he can best teach are those that have to do not with futurity and continuance but with presence and termination. Even his "lessons" to his pupils in the plantation school are exercises in place as present acceptance. The incarceral world goes on with its dividing lines, its racist segregationist codes, its systemic injustices.

Paul, the white sheriff's deputy, who witnessed Jefferson's death, travels to the quarters, where Grant is teaching his class. He brings both Jefferson's notebook and news of how he died. He reveals that Jefferson "'was the strongest man in that crowded room, Grant Wiggins'" (253). "'I'm not saying this to make you feel good; I'm not saying this to ease your pain. Ask that preacher, ask Harry Williams. He was the strongest man there. We all stood jammed together, no more than six, eight feet away from that chair. We all had each other to lean on. When Vincent asked him if he had any last words, he looked

PARISHES & PRISONS

at the preacher and said, 'Tell Nannan I walked.' And straight he walked, Grant Wiggins. Straight he walked. I'm a witness. Straight he walked'" (253–54).

In the final moments of the narrative, Paul comes to tell Grant that he is "a great teacher," and that he has seen "the transformation" in Jefferson (254). Grant, however, no longer believes, and in so many words he lets Paul know that race is at the bottom of the injustices and inequities in their society. For example, when Paul, who has never been in the quarters before, tries to make small talk about the end of school, Grant responds: "'We start a month later and get out two months earlier than the whites do'" (255). Grant emphasizes the difference between the races at the moment when Paul would like nothing better than to minimize race. Paul tries to compliment Grant regarding Vivian, the woman in his life: "'She's beautiful.' . . . 'You're a lucky fellow there, Grant Wiggins'" (255). Grant, however, insists on making the point of racial difference at this time of death: "'Yes, I'm lucky. . . . *Some of us* are'" (255; my italics). He refuses to allow Paul to turn him into an exceptional black man by separating him from the other blacks living in the quarters, or from the now-dead Jefferson. Paul's efforts end with his offer: "'Allow me to be your friend, Grant Wiggins. I don't ever want to forget this day. I don't ever want to forget him'" (255). A handshake ends with Paul taking both of Grant's hands in a gesture of friendship that encourages him to repeat his statement of Jefferson's bravery with the direction to give the children in the schoolroom that message. Grant's response is clearly another effort to restate the race difference in the society: "'Maybe one day you will come back and tell them so.'" Undeterred and perhaps unconscious of the implications, Paul answers: "'It would be an honor'" (256).

The exchange suggests the inherent possibility of societal transformation within the spatial ground that is the plantation quarters. The plantation is the place to which blacks like Jefferson have been consigned before being jailed. Jailing leads to the logical and almost inevitable extension of their incarceral society, the prison. Those blacks alienated and cursed with seeing the reality of black life too clearly, like Grant, return to the plantation quarters to make a small difference in the space itself, though possibly only in minute increments over long measures of time.

The children in Grant's class may be learning lessons in the classroom that would seem to be preparation for the future, but given the rigidity of the structures within which they must function if they are to live, and given their domination by power controlling their access to every part of the social order, they have a very limited future at best. Their prospects are only slightly better than Jefferson's because they may at least be able to read and to gain the knowledge of the wider world through books that literate individuals often use to escape from the entrapments and emplacements of their ordinary lives. In the conclusion, Grant returns to the church and the children: "Irene Cole told the class to rise, with their shoulders back. I went up to the desk and turned to face them. I was crying" (256). The moment duplicates one in Harper Lee's *To Kill a Mockingbird* when all the blacks in the gallery of the courthouse rise as Atticus Finch walks out, and one black man tells a kneeling Scout to stand up because her father is passing. In the correspondence, there is a recognition both of the place allotted to those who attempt to stand up with dignity in the face of brutalization and defeat and of the space within the community where the potential, no matter how slight, for change persists.

Gaines pulls off the very subversion of the power dynamic that Richard Wright imagined possible—subversion of the ideology of race by claiming and remembering the very space that would negate the human individual who is not white and therefore most frequently the object of domination and exclusion or confinement and imprisonment. Unlike Wright, Gaines has been accepted and supported in his native region. He was able to become a published writer, a professional man, and maintain a connection with the South and later a residency within the South, even though his publishing outlets have not been regional. Yet appearing in the decades after Wright, Gaines's representation of the literal and metaphorical prison in Louisiana, like his representation of Louisiana plantation culture, forwards the ideological limits of incarceration as a psychic state associated with space and extending over time.

In perhaps his best-known novel, *The Autobiography of Miss Jane Pittman*, for example, Gaines was able to connect the looming presence of imprisonment and Angola State Prison in black Louisiana life and the enduring memory of his youth on River Lake Plantation. He used that connected presence and memory to forecast not only one of the major social issues of the present moment (that is, the incarceration of black people, particularly black men, with a resultant circumvention of black progressivism), but also one of the primary ways of accessing that issue by means of the countervailing lives of black women. While incarceration would now immediately call up images of black men and women in prison and of the prison industrial complex's large omnipresence in the lives of so many black people, Gaines suggestively projected the term as symbol in 1971 with his narrative of Miss Jane. Two of the novel's four books, "The War Years" and "Reconstruction," position Miss Jane's life in temporal terms, while the other two, "The Plantation" and "The Quarters," use a spatial location to shape the events of that life. Gaines represents the spaces occupied by Ticey, Jane, Big Laura, and all of the enslaved people in the first part of the text as incarceral spaces. Imprisoned within the economic and social system that took their labor and the production of that labor (and reproduction in the form of literal black bodies), enslaved people are the incarcerated in Gaines's representation of history in *The Autobiography of Miss Jane Pittman*.

Typically, the temporal frame of the text is the most noticeable, the movement through time from 1962 of the introduction backward to "The War Years" of Book I, into "Reconstruction" of Book II. However, a fascinating shift occurs in the last two books—Book III, "The Plantation," and Book IV, "The Quarters." Almost imperceptibly, Gaines divides the books of the novel and thus the narrative between two primary points of attention, time and space, even though the two may not be inseparable in the telling of Miss Jane's story. Importantly, events occur in space as much as in time, despite formal attention most often being paid to the unfolding in chronology, in temporal terms, in time. That Gaines uses the spatial designation for the most recent temporal locations of his narrative points to the way in which I situate the plantation and the quarters as the incarceral spaces dominating the entire text. Clearly, in "The War Years" and "Reconstruction," the specter constricting the lives of Jane and her familiars is the place they occupy, the land that has been carved into plantations and the domiciles, the quarters, that have been allocated to blacks. Both contain, hold, and define the possibilities for movement, for living, for interacting. While they are both physical spaces mediating the activities of black people, they are also manifestations of the larger social structure—slavery and its aftermath—mandating inequitable division and unjust separation. Plantation and prison function inextricably together as an amalgam of public sphere and private domain, the collapsed space of living and dying for black people. The landscape of the plantation functions as prison and as the prism through which to ascertain the values of the people. Gaines's emphasis is on the constrictive nature of plantation culture and the relationships that form in opposition to its strictures. He represents the unequal power dynamic in terms of child-adult relations and youth-age, as well as male-female and the more obvious black-white.

What is almost unbearable to accept in the narrative is that the entrapment and imprisonment for blacks within the social geography of the Deep South cannot be overcome by escape through travel (for instance, Jane's iconic wandering in a failed attempt to reach Ohio) or through education (as in the case of both Ned and Jimmy). The enslavement defining the lives of Gaines's characters is permanent. What is, of course, problematical about a claim of permanence is that there is also the ultimate promise of change, which is held out in the narrative as a potential way out of the containment. The metaphor conveying this promise is that of "the one" or the desired, longed-for secular redeemer, the Moses of the people enslaved and imprisoned. But despite the promise of that discourse, and of "the one," that change never comes to the spatial world and never materializes within the social space. Instead, change is only a glimmer in the behavior of the people. Gaines deploys mobility and freedom in a reversal of the expected because the dual focus of the text is not merely on the short-circuiting of movement through spatial and legal terrains but also on the countervailing space that is atomized within Miss Jane herself. Thus time, the long 100-plus-year life span, serves as a space marking the interior movement that reconfigures the exterior stasis even while events of historic proportion are unfolding.

On closer examination, in all four books of *The Autobiography of Miss Jane Pittman*, the people, or at least some of them, have acted against the constrictions and displayed bravery and courage. Jane, Big Laura, Ned, and Joe Pittman are all examples. Their efforts, however, have not effected change within the environment, but rather the resultant action has most often been retreat and with it a defeat of the outward manifestations of change. That kind of retreat conflates the public with the private, in that what cannot be achieved in the public sphere also cannot be achieved within the private, whether that private is marked as a body or a building, a plantation or a town. This aspect is troubling because individual bravery does not make a dent in the social configurations holding the citizenry captive and imprisoned. And because the ideology does not change, the material circumstances of black people cannot change.

The imprisonment of the body is, therefore, a complex idea in *The Autobiography of Miss Jane Pittman* and in much of Gaines's fiction. It pertains on the most immediately observable level to the pervasive social and economic structures constraining black bodies in the modern plantation environment Gaines represents. That debilitating condition, then, obtains in less-accessible interior states because it deforms the psyche and destroys the spirit. It manifests itself as well in the complicated relationship rendered between spatial structures and human beings. However, Gaines also references the physical body itself as a prison, but one that can transcend its own limitations and carry positive thematic or symbolic value. In this representation, Gaines positions the body that is often considered the least desirable as a countervailing positive force. He identified early on in his fiction older black women whose actions and values contradicted not only the inhibiting segregationist mandates but also their own debilitating materiality. The archetype of such women is his Aunt Augusteen Jefferson, one of the three close relatives, including his grandmother and stepfather, to whom he dedicates *The Autobiography of Miss Jane Pittman*: "[T]o the memory of / My beloved aunt *Miss Augusteen Jefferson*, / who did not walk a day in her life / but who taught me the importance of standing" (Gaines's italics). His aunt Augusteen Jefferson was physically imprisoned in a body that did not have the use of legs, yet she emerges as the most agile of the family members Gaines recalls and the exemplar of the values of quiet heroism in ordinary life, genuine courage in surviving adversities, and sincere respect for commonplace activities, all of which have characterized Gaines's fiction. These values are evident as well in all of the older black women: Aunt Charlotte and Madame Bayonne in *Catherine Carmier*, Miss Julie and Aunt Margaret in *Of Love and Dust*, Aunt Fe in "Just Like a Tree," and Miss Jane in *The Autobiography of Miss Jane Pittman*, among others, who with dignity and strength overcome bodily limitations. These women may be the ones most imprisoned by their bodies, gendered and racial, and yet they are the ones who overcome the most if they attempt to break free of the social chains that oppress them, and who provide hope for subsequent generations.

In one of his earlier interviews about *The Autobiography of Miss Jane Pittman*, Gaines repeated his answer to a reader who wanted to know why Miss Jane was important:

> I said anyone who had lived 110 years in a country like this, under the conditions she lived, and could love God, could still love baseball and ice cream, was worth writing about. I went on to say that, if she could come out as a whole human being after living 110 years with the kind of life she had to live, she is worth writing about. Survival with sanity and love and a sense of responsibility, and getting up and trying all over again not only for one's self but for mankind—those achievements I find worth writing about. Miss Jane, not generals who had killed thousands of people . . . Miss Jane, who loved humankind so much she did not have to kill one person to continue life. . . . So when I mentioned the love in *Miss Jane Pittman*, this is the kind of thing I quite possibly could have been talking about.[83]

Jane, then, is positioned as countervailing to the dominant forces of destruction, despair, insanity, and hatred. She functions within a system of belief in love, God, ice cream, or baseball, all providing a not necessarily covalent sustenance or sustaining grace to the force that is basically the space of her bodily and spiritual being, living, and surviving as a whole human being. One interpretation, then, is that her very physical self participates in the material world as a site of struggle against the received hegemony and against the political meanings of the plantation world. She reorders the spaces she occupies, so that cabin and quarters in particular become regions for defining subjectivity and identity, for telling and shaping racial identity against the grain of racism and victimization. In making legible the spaces of plantation culture and black southern culture over time, Jane embodies both the folk and its vernacular culture and the educated, literate culture that is both Ned's and Jimmy's, as well as the African American teacher's who records and documents Miss Jane's narrative; however, in that embodiment, as rich as it may be in expressions of love that Gaines observes, the oppressive mistreatment of black people is neither obscured nor denied. Enacted as a force to compensate for the deprivations of ordinary black life, she provides an embodied material space on which may be read not merely age and survival but moral courage and heroic action neutralizing racist power and authority. Perhaps her forward motion at the end also signals a necessary break with the plantation as a default residency offering security and quasi safety in a space that nonetheless portends no future development for those blacks who remain there.

The observation Gaines made in 1976 fusing his memory of his aunt with his indomitable character Jane resonated on the night of 4 November 2008, when Barack Obama evoked Ann Nixon Cooper. In a brilliant move, Obama reviewed the history of the United States as a nation through the eyes of this 106-year-old black woman. He positioned her as the hallmark of history and of a historiography documented from her perspective. His message: "America can change. Our union can be perfected. And what we have already achieved gives us hope for what we can and must achieve tomorrow." Obama's chronicle of Ann Nixon Cooper's life telescopes the terrain covered by Ernest Gaines in his biography of Jane Pittman, except that Cooper was born in the generation after slavery, but as Obama said, in "a time when there were no cars on the road or planes in the air; when someone like her couldn't vote for two reasons—because she was a woman and because of the color of her skin." The body space Ann Nixon Cooper occupies in lived history and in Obama's rhetoric of "our union" functions very much like the countervailing force of Miss Jane in her experiential reality, the fictional American South.

The space that is the black woman's body transforms the expectations of the governed body and of the civil nation. That body space is as much a conduit as a materiality. The union of that body with "the one" creates the plausible and possible designation that can carry forward a future "more perfect union." Obama and Gaines before him articulate the implications of the arrival of "the one" in a new landscape by means of the constricted and divided landscape negating the black woman's body. Just as for Miss Jane, gender and race combined to prevent Ann Nixon Cooper from exercising her full rights as a citizen, and like Jane at the end of Gaines's narrative when she can place her body in a line of movement toward change, Cooper stood on line to cast her ballot for Obama in Atlanta, Georgia. Gaines allowed us to hear Jane's voice, and especially her propulsion into a new era with her last words and her gesture as she leaves behind Robert Samson, the white plantation owner who in the middle of the twentieth century continued to uphold a nineteenth-century ethos of social value and meaning that demanded subjugation and acquiescence. Miss Jane resolves to leave the plantation to travel to Bayonne after Jimmy has been killed: "Just a little piece of him is dead," Jane tells Samson. "The rest of him is waiting for us in Bayonne. And I will go with Alex" (245). Death is incomplete; the process of dying unleashes the potential for change. Jane has the will to go to Bayonne; her own strength and her love of the visionary one, Jimmy, propel her into what can only become a new era.

The novel concludes: "Me and Robert looked at each other there a long time, then I went by him" (246). Her words, her look, and her movement past Robert Samson situate her in the forward flow of history and the movement toward a new order and outside the confines of the plantation space, which is as much psychological as it is physical. The material condition of confinement signified by the plantation gives way to the potential of "going by" the fixity and rigidity of Robert Samson as person and proprietor, as well as all that he represents about the history and heritage of Jane and those blacks living on the Samson plantation.

When Barack Obama presents Ann Nixon Cooper's life, he very much echoes in a different format Gaines's interview statements about his aunt. Mr. Obama's words exemplify how spaces of opportunity and production diffuse inside the very boundaries established by exclusion to cordon off black experience and how those spaces can and do reverberate among and between other black writers. Mr. Obama said:

And tonight, I think about all that she's seen throughout her century in America—the heartache and the hope; the struggle and the progress; the times we were told that we can't and the people who press on with that American creed: Yes, we can.

At a time when women's voices were silenced and their hopes dismissed, she lived to see them stand up and speak out and reach for the ballot. Yes, we can.

When there was despair in the Dust Bowl and depression across the land, she saw a nation conquer fear itself with a New Deal, new jobs, and a new sense of common purpose. Yes, we can.

When the bombs fell on our harbor and tyranny threatened the world, she was there to witness a generation rise to greatness and a democracy was saved. Yes, we can.

She was there for the buses in Montgomery, the hoses in Birmingham, a bridge in Selma and a preacher from Atlanta who told people that "We Shall Overcome." Yes, we can.

A man touched down on the moon, a wall came down in Berlin, a world was connected by our own science and imagination. And this year, in this election, she touched her finger to a screen and cast her vote, because after 106 years in America, through the best of times and the darkest of hours, she knows how America can change. Yes, we can.[84]

Though Ann Nixon Cooper lived her 100-plus years in the climactic space of the late twentieth and early twenty-first centuries, she lived her life as a countervailing force in much the way that Gaines depicted Miss Jane Pittman. The result for both of these narrated lives is a reconsideration of the past, of history, but ultimately also of the present in that the unlikely virtual body of these black women becomes the nation and the configuration of progress and what Mr. Obama calls "the timeless creed that sums up the spirit of a people." Inscripted on the imprisoned body is the landscape that would be a prison, but that in the final analysis becomes the legible text perhaps to rewrite and reinvent black history itself as futurity.

Gaines, in understanding that segregated spaces are not merely sites of exclusion but also bounded areas of possibility, sites of diffusion in which blacks spread ideas and forms of knowledge and in which blacks also shape interactions that function against the grain—in opposition, as bell hooks would have it, and countervail to hegemonic power—may provide another way of thinking about the plantation. Moreover, within that space, which Elizabeth Alexander terms "the black interior," black people, whether artists like Gaines or extraordinary fictions like Miss Jane or ordinary folk like Mrs. Cooper, utilize the very structural barriers to develop and create modes of articulation, transferal, or translation, as Homi Bhabha suggests, that may not have been possible to envision or enact in other circumstances.

III. SPATIAL KIN AND
RANDALL KENAN'S NORTH CAROLINA

Spatialising the story of modernity (both in revealing its operational
spatialities and in opening it up to enable the presence of a multiplicity of
trajectories) has had effects—it has not left the story the same.
—DOREEN MASSEY, *For Space*

Two generations after Ernest Gaines initiated his rural Louisiana map, Randall Kenan has taken that model and applied it to a comparable space in North Carolina. Measured in miles, North Carolina is far from the plantation-bound Louisiana world depicted in Gaines's fiction. Yet the racial terrain central to the work of Randall Kenan is near kin to the spaces Gaines represents. The exclusions that segregate black writers have an oppositional inside, the interior black space that, while porous and conversant at the boundaries with diverse and multiple people, events, and cultures, retains a sense of awareness and connections among blacks, including black writers whose cultural productions spread and reverberate through that inside space. Gaines's presence has loomed large within that space, and for blacks who experience and write relations to modern black cultures of the land, the rural, and the folk, Gaines is unavoidable.

Kenan's fictive world evidences the diffusion within the associative creative space blacks occupy. While his specific ground is not the Louisiana Gaines imaged and wrote, it is similarly a rural black south, traditional and closed, contemporary and yet still segregated because of race, history, memory, and economics. In pointing to his formative environment in Chinquapin, North Carolina, Kenan has not only said, "I tote my fictional landscape around in my head," but he has elaborated:

> I was lucky enough to come from a very rural community in which I was
> literally raised up by people who were in their seventies and eighties
> and they were very loquacious. That was the world in which I moved, in
> which people told stories, in which people understood the world they
> lived in through talking about it, through relating not only events that
> happened to them, but to their forefathers. Literally, in the 1960s and
> 1970s, I could touch my great-great-grandaunt and reach back into the
> middle of the nineteenth century. Think about it: When she was a child,
> she had known people who were born at the turn of the century—the
> eighteenth century![85]

Like Gaines, Kenan relies on his memory in carrying his rural landscape around with him, and he depends on the voices from his elders for the oral storytelling and the folk and familial history.

Kenan, then, may be read as the literary heir of Gaines, even though he may initially seem to share much more with David Bradley or Toni Morrison in the African American tradition, or Caryl Phillips in the African diasporic tradition, because of his insistent creation of visionary narratives of slavery impinging upon a presentist narrative. Similar to Gaines, however, Kenan exhibits a determination to understand, by means of repetitive returns and reconsiderations, a particular place and its people, along with how a racial past continues to live in the present, even when that past is not represented. Kenan has created Tims Creek in rural North Carolina, which may be read as a metaphorical, incarceral plantation space, and he has explored the social spaces black people inhabit and the social relations they maintain during slavery and its aftermath in the segregated South. Originating in a nineteenth-century community of maroons, Tims Creek also has its beginning in rebellion from the chattel slavery of plantation culture. The unbounded world of the swamp that the founders first inhabit begins as a protective and subversive space, but ultimately it poses a threat that also delimits its maroons in a way similar to, if not as severe as, the plantations from which they escaped.

Like Gaines before him, Kenan has recognized the value of a specified geography and of engaging place that in both time past and time present carries with it restrictions on behavior and expectations. Just as Bayonne gave Gaines a microscope for his examinations of specified social geography, so Tims Creek allows Kenan to enter into and observe a relatively closed and isolated world. By means of his exploration of one place, with all of its problems of orthodoxy, narrowness, and rigidity that can result over time, Kenan also gestures toward a possible future. In texts teeming with the palpable residue and holds of the past, he grasps how futurity may be articulated within messages delivered in unexpected ways.

The concept of place is equally as complex in Kenan's fiction because even though he does not have the tripartite racial groupings in his North Carolina, he understands the legacy of race division. He accepts the role of slavery and subordination in the subsequent formation of a hegemonic black-white binary in southern relations, but similar to Gaines, he recognizes the more entangled threads of racial interactions and cultural appropriations that are also legible. When he turns to issues of race in the present, Kenan reveals: "Already I had rejected . . . race as a biological reality, but I could not ignore how the concept preyed on the modern mind—how the concept of race still

informed the way black folk and white folk interacted. So whether race existed or not, it was not a moot point."[86] In an extended commentary, he goes
on to paint the iconic details supporting his view:

> Culturally speaking blackness is both a chimera and an angel of change.
> It is hard to pin down because it is ever changing and belongs to every-
> one who has a back strong enough to seek it out and be true to it. An-
> thropologists can tell us what black Americans retain from the Ibo or
> from the Yoruba, but when my nieces dance to the music of Missy Elliot,
> it is not Ghana they dream of, but their present-day American Dream-
> scape: Wal-Marts and Chevy trucks, McDonald's value meals and Walt
> Disney, chicken fajitas and Eddie Bauer swimwear. Once that culture
> was defined by the church, the Bible, certain landscapes, and certain
> shared experiences of people segregated and physically excluded from
> the larger society. But that America vanished with World War II, the
> Civil Rights Act, radio, interstates, and Black Entertainment Television.[87]

These awarenesses situate Kenan on a continuum with Gaines, but they also
fast-forward him into a postmodern world that Gaines cannot approach in
his attention to the plantation and prison complexes of his young manhood.
In observing the near past that was defined by shared experiences of religion,
landscape, and segregation for black southerners, Kenan correctly evokes the
changes that new modes of communication and new practices of citizenship
have brought about. In this way, he can remark how in terms of postmodern
culture, blackness is not merely a binary opposite of whiteness but is itself a
product of the imagination and a model of change. These beliefs situate his
significant difference from Gaines and a reliance on ideologies of becoming.

Kenan's fiction encompasses what might be called an appreciation for
illusion (blackness as *chimera*) and for change (blackness as "an *angel* of
change"). Magical and mythical in both the secular and religious sense, then,
blackness holds powers that attract Kenan viscerally. He locates blackness
within the space of change, transformation, and transubstantiation. The realistic landscape that he appreciates from the past is simultaneously geographic
and chimeric. It is a mythical space of the kind Yi-Fu Tuan imagined that operates against "the logic of exclusion and contradiction" and is constituted
out of "feeling and imagination to fundamental human needs."[88] Not surprisingly, Kenan has identified Toni Morrison and Gabriel García Márquez, whom
he "twins," as influences that freed his imagination by giving him "a license to
go right on seeing the world the way I saw it."[89] In seeing the world his way,
Kenan exhibits and adheres to what may be called chimeric space.

Chimeric space manifests itself in all of Kenan's fiction. It is literal and historical as well as symbolic and mythical in its materiality. It is discursive, but also fantastic and speculative. It is at once identifiable with rural North Carolina and unimaginable as a specified place. The contradictory aspects of Kenan's chimeric space, however, do function at odds with one another.

Chimeric space is imbricated with Kenan's historical placement of slavery as both a site and a sign. Within his attention to the magnitude of the oppression under slavery and the immensity of survival in enslavement, Kenan enfolds the amazing and troubling ability of human beings to mistreat other human beings, particularly through the process of exclusion and expulsion from the ordinary context of the human. At the same time, Kenan engages the astonishing and mysterious capacity for human beings to defy dehumanizing forces and to make meaning out of the most incomprehensible conditions. The language of the chimerical occurs in the preface to *The Order of Things: An Archaeology of the Human Sciences* (1994) when Foucault takes up the "disconcerting effect of the proximity of extremes" in a passage by Borges that inspired him to think about categories of things and the limitations of systems of thought by distinguishing between types of disorder: the incongruous, which he defines as "the linking together of things that are inappropriate"; and the heteroclite, which is the "disorder in which fragments of a large number of possible orders glitter separately in the dimension, without law or geometry."[90] Foucault's consideration of the heteroclite, or the state in which "things are 'laid,' 'placed,' 'arranged' in sites so very different from one another that it is impossible to find a place of residence for them, to define a *common locus* beneath them all," leads to his formulation of heterotopia as opposed to the consolation offered by utopias. Heterotopias, accordingly, "are disturbing, probably because they secretly undermine language, because they make it impossible to name this *and* that, because they shatter or tangle common names, because they destroy 'syntax' in advance, and not only the syntax with which we construct sentences but also that less apparent syntax which causes words and things . . . to 'hold together.'"[91] Foucault's disturbing heterotopia suggests a comparison with Kenan's chimeric space, particularly as it is constructed out of his "messy" disordered narrative of the origins of Tims Creek.

In the contested history of Tims Creek, slavery as a process as much as a system produced some black individuals who were different and who, in not accepting enslavement as their lot, fled into a self-made society of maroons. Their difference would prove to be multifaceted, but the fact of their maroonage enabled Kenan's creation of a fictional people, place, and ideology in response to enslavement. His Tims Creek, North Carolina, came fully into existence in "Let the Dead Bury Their Dead," the title story of his 1992 collection of stories. I read this long narrative as the central construct of Kenan's fiction thus far, because it enacts and represents the chimeric as factual and fanciful, as vital and necessary. It creates the maroon community in a space appropriated from the plantation as a heterotopia and uses it as the background and backdrop for all of the stories emanating from the people of Tims Creek.

The last and longest of the amazing, fantastic narratives, "Let the Dead Bury Their Dead" began as a section of his 1989 novel *A Visitation of Spirits*. In an interview for *Book Page*, Kenan explains that the seemingly "found history" detailing the origins of Tims Creek "started inside *A Visitation of Spirits*, but got too out of hand," so that he began another strategy of "playing with the melding of fiction and fact which was not central to the story line of the novel."[92] What he arrived at in his composition of "Let the Dead Bury Their Dead" was an interweaving of fact and fiction that, he has suggested, "pulls together what I am trying to create in the book. It underscores how all fiction is lies and hopefully a lot more."[93] In the process, it foregrounds the magical elements found both in his novel and in his short stories. In allowing different spheres and realms of the imagination and reality to intertwine, Kenan produces a rural South that is simultaneously like multiple souths and unlike any other south.

"Let the Dead Bury Their Dead" may be read as central to the work of space in Kenan's fiction. In the narrative of Pharaoh and the maroons, Kenan moves to collapse the difference not only between fact and fiction, as he suggests, but between history and memory as well. It unfolds the history from 1854 to 1985 of the community of Tims Creek, or "the Former Maroon Society called Snatchit and then Tearshirt and later the Town of Tims Creek, North Carolina." Kenan effects a connection to the transnational narrative of maroons whose resistance to enslavement enabled them to constitute new social orders of blacks wherever they existed in the Atlantic world. The background for the narrative occurs in the introduction: "It is the record of a conversation with the Reverend's [James Malachai Greene] great-uncle, Ezekiel Thomas Cross [b. 1901], and great-aunt, Ruth Davis Cross [b. 1895], that took place on September 22, 1985, at the home of Mrs. Cross. It is in many ways emblematic of Greene's major preoccupations: the origins of Tims Creek; his family's slave past; the intermingling of the two Cross families, black and white; folklore and the supernatural; thanatology; issues of community leadership and decay."[94] All of these characters and their preoccupations appear in Kenan's novel as well.

The Reverend James Malachai Greene, who, according to the introduction, died in 1998, "seemed to have existed for Tims Creek" and left behind a large body of work that he collected and compiled on his birthplace (278). His complete works of over 500,000 words were purchased for the University of North Carolina, where they await cataloguing but from which "Let the Dead Bury Their Dead" was extracted for publication (279). In a stroke of ingenuous metafiction, Kenan creates a fictional town being historicized and written about by a fictional resident whose fictional date of death is prior to the actual publication of Kenan's literal book. In this playful making of historical myth and familial heritage, Kenan orders materials so that despite their coexisting in the foundational story, they stem from different imaginaries.

Kenan utilizes the concept of runaway slaves and the space they occupied to create the establishment of a maroon society, but it is a history that from the beginning is mixed with magic and the supernatural. The enslaved man Pharaoh was the founder of Snatchit, the original Tims Creek. Or perhaps he was not, and perhaps the town was never known as Snatchit. The doubts and inconclusiveness are built into the folkloric way of telling, and they connect to one epigraph from Zora Neale Hurston: "Now you are going to hear lies above suspicion" (276). Kenan sets up the narrative as an oral tale being told by Ezekiel Thomas Cross, whose story is constantly interrupted and challenged by Ruth Davis Cross, as well as by the footnotes with their running commentaries, real and imagined, that add documentation, authentic and fictional, to the oral tale. The author of the notes is Reginald Gregory Kain, who is listed as the editor of the publication and also the author of the introduction. Similar to the device of the black schoolteacher who records Miss Jane Pittman's narrative of her life, "RK," as he is listed after the full name on the title page, is educated but works with the folk history and recorded interviews from the Tims Creek residents that the Reverend James Greene collected. With initials duplicating Kenan's, RK performs the visible role of writer and editor and the metafictional role of signifying Kenan's hand in the creation and writing of the vernacular tale and the erudite notes.

Kenan takes up two trajectories of place in ascertaining the origins of the modern black community: place as a constructed challenge to external authority, such as the scholarly documentation in the footnotes intersecting with the oral folk representation in the voice of a male elder in the community, whose authority is itself challenged by the countermemory of a skeptical female elder from the same community; and place as an amalgamative location of solid earth and shape-shifting projections, whose opacity or transparency accommodate transformations of the people, animals, events, and properties of the living and the dead.

Ruth and Ezekiel argue over the accuracy of sites of memory precisely because of the different trajectories of place. Ezekiel, for example, accepts the implausible or fantastical that is the subject of myth and speculative exaggeration. He tells a story handed down to him about how the mound once at the center of the town has "no earthly explanation. Just is. Some folk say it was an Indian burial ground. Won't nothing grow on it cause it's a cursed people in the soil. Say they killed a whole tribe of folk and the medicine man damned em all. . . . Some say it was a church burned down with some runaway slave girls, girls running away from prostitution in New Orleans, burned up in spite by white folk. Say the earth is still mourning" (285–86). He delivers the several scenarios as a way to launch the story of origins handed down from his grandfather and other people in the area that the mound "had to do with that runaway town. . . . And if my recollection serves proper, it had a lot to do with a preacher-man. Least, that's what they tell me" (286). The notes to Ezekiel's telling of the story, both those corroborating and those doubting its accuracy, become so lengthy that they occupy more space than the text of his account. They demonstrate Kenan's conscious manipulation of the visual space of the story: "I was playing with academic history as opposed to oral history, and memory, and plain old gossip. And how at once they are all very different and disparate, and all very much alike."[95]

The fusion of form and space allows for an interactive narrative strategy, which invites the reader into the story. When Ezekiel pauses, Ruth launches her attack on his version of the story: "—Old man, who told you this lie? Ain't no such a thing" (286). Unlike RK's footnotes, Ruth's challenge is on the basis of the oral version she heard: "—I didn't grow up that far from here. I heard them lies you telling this boy. Boy, you wasting your time listening to this old fool" (286). But she is interrupted by Ezekiel: "—Woman, will you let me tell my story. . . . The boy asked me, and I'm gone tell him like it was told to me" (286). Ruth insists: "Ain't one bit of truth in it" (286). Throughout "Let the Dead Bury Their Dead," the pair constantly assess who is telling the truth and who, by virtue of lived experience and remembered storytelling, has the correct version of the founding of the town, but the chimeric holds the major place of attention in the narration. What the exchanges between Ezekiel and Ruth, as well as the interruptions in the story line interjected by RK's footnotes, accomplish is a reminder of the contested origins of Tims Creek and its possible fantastical connections "a long time ago" to decimated Native Americans, to persecuted slave girls, to an enslaved African, to a Preacher-man, to a number of recognizable aspects of African American history.

Memory is the cornerstone of the telling, even though memory is contested. The sites of memory are place based: the plantation, the maroon settlements, the Grave, and, in particular, the Mound, which is the site containing all of the possible interpretations of the past and circulating in living memory in the present. As a location of place, the mound is symbol and artifact, and it is the ground for the mystery surrounding Tims Creek. "Let the Dead Bury Their Dead" uses the mound as an existing artifact to document the fact-fantasy. The defiance of the natural in the explanations of the mound calls attention to the footnotes that project a not-to-be-doubted historical reality onto the page yet also convey the impossibility of that very reality. The notes grow in significance and supply as much text as the narrative itself, while also providing the texture of the real supporting the fantastic elements of the narrative.

Like the writers of neoslave narratives who engage maroon societies, those who as runaways reconstituted community and family in secret, hidden places that were difficult for outsiders to access, such as woods, forests, swamps, bayous, or mountains, Randall Kenan represents the place to which the slave Menes or Caesar or Pharaoh, as he is variously known, escapes and in which he creates a new community. The inaccessibility of the maroon community links it to the fifth principle Foucault outlined for heterotopias in "Of Other Spaces": "Heterotopias always presuppose a system of opening and closing that both isolates them and makes them penetrable. In general, the heterotopic site is not freely accessible like a public space. Either the entry is compulsory . . . or else the individual has to submit to rites and purifications. To get in one must have a certain permission and make certain gestures."[96]

In the forming of the slave community and in its interaction with the nearby plantations, Kenan explores questions of power that are not answered by pointing to the enslavement or imprisonment of black people by whites in positions of authority and control. In weaving a magical tale, he carefully establishes the fact of capture, forced migration, and slavery with the history of Pharaoh, but he also makes the constitutive elements of knowledge, agency, and motivation important to Pharaoh's story. Beginning with captured Africans in saltwater slavery, drifting through the international waters of the Atlantic, moving through various sites of New World enslavement and its slave markets, including New Orleans, Pharaoh ends in the upland of North Carolina. His journey is symbolic of the origins of the labor on New World plantations. The three Cross plantations become the places where Pharaoh, or Menes, is consigned to work for life, but because of Pharaoh's social history, the plantation is a vexed space from the moment of his arrival. Labor, then, on any one of the Cross plantations filters though the lens of the experience of the captured and enslaved African Pharaoh.

The plantation culture does not simply exert the will of the white owners on Pharaoh, who in Kenan's chimera space has acquired power. A runaway from places as diverse as Mississippi, South Carolina, and Virginia, Pharaoh has, by the time he arrives in North Carolina, lived a multiplicity of lives and learned how to survive in each. In his resistance to his condition and to the power his owners have over his physical body, Pharaoh uses what he can control to exert a counterforce, which is not merely a moral outrage at the violations done to his person but is also a utilization of all that he has learned of alternative ways of existing in the world. He has remembered modes for being from his African heritage, whether as a "chief or witch doctor or medicine man or wizard," and that heritage, according to Zaceus, a member of the community who tells Pharaoh's life story, meant that he "could work magic" (294). Pharaoh also has accumulated information about the native plants, herbs, waterways and landscape from the Waccamaw tribe, who also taught him their ways of healing. These skills all combine in Pharaoh's life and afterlife.

In the diary entries written by Rebecca Cross, the mistress of the plantation where Pharaoh was enslaved, the disturbing aspects of "bounding space" with its problem of distancing and misrepresentation come into focus. Canaan, the Cross plantation, is a designation in which the "intersection of space and people forms part of the routine for the reproduction of power relations in an advanced capitalist society."[97] Rebecca Cross understands that somehow the African slave, Pharaoh, whom her husband, Owen, won in a poker game and whom she describes as *"Huge & Black & has a Hoop in one Ear & has Frightening Scars about his Face of a most disturbing Nature"* (307; Kenan's italics), has used some horrible unnatural spell to ingratiate himself with and take control of her husband, who has renamed the African Menes and pronounces him "Genius" (308). Rebecca sees Menes as a cunning animal and fears his ability to undermine the life on the plantation as he slowly draws closer to the big house and obliterates the distinction between himself as a fieldworker and the house slaves. The racism in her writings (animalization and brutalization of Menes) links to David Sibley's identification of "a fear of mixing unlike things," which "often signifies a reluctance to give ground and relinquish power."[98]

Rebecca Cross desires to maintain the established social and spatial relationships by drawing increased hyperattention to Pharaoh's crossing of the boundaries in place on the Cross plantation. For her, the power that her husband exercises as state senator and plantation owner must manifest itself in protecting her with clearly delineated spatial boundaries, which also mark her psychic space of comfort and control. Without the exclusion of Pharaoh and those like him, Rebecca imagines herself living in uncertain and insecure spaces, both physical and psychic. She has accepted what she calls "*My Husband's long History of more conventional Fleshly Perversions & Shameful Self-Indulgences*[;] *I might think He has taken this Menes into Horrible Abomination, but My Husband, the Father of My Children, the Former Magistrate & now Senator is a Whole Man*" (308). However, she does allow herself to fear that Menes as "*the Devil Himself*" has corrupted her husband and will allow evil to reign in her house. Pharaoh as the object of Rebecca's obsessions is the sign of pollution and violation, of the invasive presence of evil and blackness: "*He is a Frightfull one, this Menes is. He has no place in a Fine House like Canaan*" (308; Kenan's italics and stress). Rebecca reports as well the negative responses to Pharaoh by the slaves working inside the house, who call him "*Big an Black an Hateful*" (308). Rebecca's dream about Menes is revealing: "*I dreamt that Menes had come into my room. Naked but for a white cloth about His Loins & Forced Himself upon me, but He did not Disturb My Virtue. He shackled me instead and Forced me to do labor as Phoebe & as Clem laughed!*" (310). The spatial defilement combines with the status violation to reduce Rebecca Cross's very body to an object of ridicule. In losing control of space, she loses power over the enslaved as well.

In locating Rebecca's thoughts within her diaries as both wildly paranoid and perceptively discerning, Kenan uses her words to reformulate an understanding of reality and fantasy. Menes/Pharaoh emerges as a mythical figure of great power. Pharaoh does deceive Owen Cross, and he does plot against the Cross house, which in fact he burns down before departing Canaan with the slaves he trusted to found his maroon community. Pharaoh succeeds in his plot not only to gain his freedom and that of eighteen blacks, but also to achieve revenge for their treatment. He kills five overseers and Cross's oldest son. He leaves behind a distraught Rebecca Cross, who rails against her god: "*I renounce such a Barbarous, Wicked God who would let inferior Blacks wreak such Terror on Good WHITE CHRISTIAN PEOPLE. . . . I have Cursed God, now just Let Me Die*" (311; Kenan's italics and stress).

Pharaoh emerges as subject rather than a polluting presence despite Rebecca's ranting; he is able through his abilities to move both himself and a group of blacks into their own space and to meld them into a community that itself is space controlled and protected from outsiders. This ability is confirmed by his trips back over a period of three years to rescue additional blacks from the Cross plantations, Canaan and its sister sites, Chinquapin and Charybdis. With each removal, Pharaoh builds his numbers, and only the Civil War and emancipation end his plan to free all the slaves in the area. In representing Pharaoh as a complex, powerful, but mysterious figure, Kenan explores boundaries separating zones of difference that are racial and historical and those that are metaphysical and exist in arenas between the natural and the supernatural.

One of the final images of Pharaoh in his maroon space occurs in a long letter the younger Cross son, the botanist Phineas Owen Cross, wrote to his lover, Nigel. The letter inserts both the reality of Pharaoh's maroon community and the extent of Pharaoh's power into a literal space that still belonged to the Cross family. It also asserts Pharaoh's humanity and his ability to distinguish and repay kindnesses from white slaveholders. After straying into the swampy land searching for *"Dionaea muscipula [Venus's-flytrap], that most amazing of God's insectivorous creations, beguiling, beautiful, and most deadly"* (321), Phineas finds one who might be similarly described. His accidental entry into a part of the Cross plantation, *"Imperial Owen's Land,"* that Pharaoh controls as his own maroon territory brings Phineas into contact with Pharaoh/Menes, *"the most awesome of Negroes I have ever beheld; I had always looked on him with more than a little fondness, having found him so bewitching, virile, and more than anything mysterious in that way that only Africans can be"* (324). Pharaoh allows Phineas to live because of his kindnesses to Pharaoh and others enslaved on the Cross plantation, but only on the condition that he not reveal the location of the maroon community. Pharaoh's words are direct and uncompromising: *"If you utter one word, one word about what you have seen this day, you shall die. You shall die before you speak the second word, and you shall die in great agony"* (235). Phineas realizes that he has already been struck with a kind of paralysis that renders him unable to do more than nod his agreement. Phineas terms the encounter "miraculous," and he later wonders whether it may all have been "a terrible dream," or perhaps "a mere phantasm" (326). He acquiesces, nonetheless, to Pharaoh's power over reality, and whether "African witchery" or not, he will not disclose the secret maroon space.

In the final segments of the narrative of the founding of Tims Creek, the dead Pharaoh is pitted against a living preacher, who is never named but whose sudden appearance in the community after Pharaoh's death fills a gap. The Preacher-man, a light-skinned mulatto with green eyes, fills the leadership vacuum with a presence that is different from Pharaoh's but equally as mysterious and powerful. His power begins with religious conversions but turns into magic and mystery, with sexuality, bestiality, and perversity transforming ordinary men, women, and especially children into unrecognizable deviants who must die to contain their abominations. In the representation of the preacher in his white clothing and his calls for purity, and his green eyes hypnotic with a sexual allure subsuming the place of Pharaoh, or being the new Pharaoh as the residents maintain, Kenan blurs subject identities and creates a postmodern unsettling body and space that is quite different from the African and the maroon community. The primary place becomes the grave where Pharaoh is buried with his book, since the preacher believes it is a map to treasures.

While digging up the grave provides humor, it also makes accessible the disturbing of the boundary between the living and the dead, between the natural and the supernatural—or, put another way, between the earth and other realms. Disturbing the grave disturbs the spirits and leads to an amazing battle that creates the next phase of the community and the mound where the Preacher rises up with "all them dead folk standing behind him like a army" (331). The story that Ezekiel tells of the moment is disturbing:

> Tell me they had all sort a evil creatures with em: wolves walking on they hind legs, buzzards eating people alive, red demons with bats' wings put bits in women's mouths and rode em, beating em with a thunderbush branch—you know, the kind with them thick thorns— raced them against one another like horses till they died. The dead folk shot at people's feet, make em dance till they could dance no more. The church was set afire. The general store. Three or four dead men would jump on a girl or a boy and have their way till the poor child could take no more. They said the Preacher-man held a baby in his arms, didn't know what he planned to do with it, and that's when ole Pharaoh come riding through. (331)

Pharaoh comes from his grave riding a bull to cut off the Preacher's head and save the baby, saying "Damnation and ruin. What began as good has ended in evil. We are not ready" (332). Pharaoh disappeared into the night with the baby, but "fire rained down from the sky just like the Lord sent to the cities of Sodom and Gomorrah and none of the wicked escaped. Said it burned for days like a furnace and didn't spread" (332). What was left was the mound, hot and smoking, and said to extend down into hell. This narrative of the battle at the mound pushes the founding of Tims Creek into the inexplicable that is very different from the plausible tale of maroons escaping enslave-

ment. The complicated myth of origins, nonetheless, depends upon difference and chimera.

While Gaines represents the imprisoning grip of place on his characters,
who in their racial difference struggle against tradition despite the certainty
of failure in the present, Kenan conjures a place founded to contain multiple
differences and to struggle with those differences. Tims Creek evolves out of
plantation land but becomes more than a realistic space from its founding. It
is linked throughout Kenan's fiction to identity and difference; subjectivity
and sexuality; communal expectations determined by history, memory, and
the culture; and individual dreams fueled by desires, commodities, and textuality. In *A Visitation of Spirits*, Kenan develops a concept to account by analogy
for the way humans develop in particular environments. Plant tropism is the
name Horace Cross gives the project on which he and Gideon Stone collaborate for their science project: "'It's the study of what makes plants grow the
way they do.'"[99] Plant tropism is defined so as to apply to Horace's own sexual
difference: "An orientation of an organism, usually by growth rather than by
movement, in response to an external stimulus" (155). External stimuli encourage internal development, and by extension interiority with the subject
formation. For Kenan, the external stimuli is bounded by Tims Creek as a
spatial configuration that has always already in its foundational discourses
contained the mythical and the chimeric.

These aspects reappear in the story of Horace Cross in *A Visitation of Spirits*
and in short stories such as "Clarence and the Dead," "Things of This World;
Or, Angels Unawares," "What Are Days?," and "Tell Me, Tell Me," in which
the dead in Tims Creek mingle freely with the living and voices speak from
the dead. In his stories, Kenan blends the impossible with the practical and
the known. Black subject formation is troubled and incomplete in the case
of obsessive individuals, such as Horace, and other characters, such as the
brother involved in an incestuous relationship in "Cornsilk" or the woman
who kills her husband's suspected love child in "The Strange and Tragic Ballad of Mabel Pearsall." Death and loss in individual human and communal
terms are reiterated in unusual ways in the novel and the stories: Horace
wanders in death among his family and residents of Tims Creek; an elderly
man socializes with an angel come to accompany him into death ("Things
of This World"); a grieving woman is brought out of her isolation by a short
affair with a phantom lover ("What Are Days?"); a poor white gay man is in
mourning after being used by a wealthy white to entrap a prominent black,
closeted gay mortician ("Run, Mourner, Run"); a remorseful Booker T. Washington, accompanied by a "crouching, mystery-shrouded doom" as compan-

ion, dedicates the new school of old friends in Tims Creek shortly before his death ("This Far; Or, A Body in Motion"). These characters are all heirs of the maroonage from "Let the Dead Bury Their Dead."

In challenging sexual and heterosexual social mandates by inscripting narratives of death and the affective spaces occupied by those left behind, Kenan revisits Pharaoh and the maroon community and its death-struggle with the Preacher-man and his perversions. In stories such as "The Foundations of the Earth," Kenan explores the conflict between a rigid religiosity and homosexuality. There a grandmother twice ignores a hypocritical minister who dictates beliefs in the most facile way; she chooses to come to terms with her dead grandson's life as a gay man when his lover, who is both from another region and of a different race, visits her. Kenan's take on male sexuality is complex and compassionate, but his reading of hypocritical religious ministers is sharply critical, especially as represented in "Ragnarök! The Day the Gods Die," when an adulterous minister preaches at his lover's funeral while remembering the details of their sexual encounters. As suggested by the phantasmagoric final scenes from "Let the Dead Bury Their Dead," Kenan displays a willingness to represent human sexuality in all of its manifestations.

Kenan's unflinching attention to same-sex relationships does not mean that he sees himself "as a voice for gay rights," but rather as connected to his perception of himself as a southern writer, one aware of the necessity of change: "David Leavitt's *Family Dancing* broke some important barriers in the early '80s for treating homosexual relations in fiction. I see myself trying to break some of those same barriers in the South in a way similar to writers like Rita Mae Brown."[100] In more detailed conversations about his writing, he has expressed the "powerful influence" that the Japanese writer Yukio Mishima had on him. According to Kenan, Mishima "was the first gay writer who wrote about his sexuality in a way that was totally unfettered."[101] Perhaps more significant is that Kenan understands how his writing functions to reshape power relations. His work as a black, southern writer challenges both racial hierarchies and racial dominance, so that a different power dynamic may result. The unusual and even bizarre events taking place in chimeric space function in relative freedom from the restrictions of ordinary southern life but may well encounter opposition based on conventional notions of proper behavior, heteronormative, and model subjectivities.

Place in Kenan's texts embodies transgression, the acting out of place. Tim Cresswell suggests that gays, lesbians, and bisexuals can be made to feel that they are "without place," that they are "out of place," when the concept of "place is used in the construction of ideas about who and what belongs where and when and thus in the construction of those seen as 'deviant' and outside of 'normal' society."[102] The body in Kenan, then, is connected to the sense of belonging or not belonging to place, particularly to Tims Creek and its strict moral views on sexuality and same-sex desire or relationships. In the introduction to *Sweet Tea: Black Gay Men of the South* (2008), E. Patrick Johnson comments on what the typical views of the South conceal: "[T]he sexual other who is implicated in both the region's guts and its glory, its horrific past and its present graciousness. . . . black gay southerners have coexisted in communities throughout the region for as long as there has been a 'South.' . . . [B]lack queers are a part of the patchwork quilt that is the diverse (and perverse) social fabric of southern living."[103] Johnson suggests that "the life histories of black gay men of the South provide not only different perspectives on the relationships between race and region, gender and geography, and sexuality and southernness, they also serve as an intervention in the prevailing histories of homosexuality in the South and in the nation."[104]

In his narrative of the thwarted maturation of youth racialized as black and gendered male, and marginalized by the customs and conventions of place or space as much as by race and gender, Kenan's *A Visitation of Spirits* speaks to the self/other enactment of power relations and interrogates a search, whether linear or circular, for identity that could have as the expected outcome an authentic, *essential* core that is hidden to consciousness. Such a project, however, Kenan rejects in his representation of Horace Thomas Cross, a protagonist struggling to understand why and how he has grown in a particular way, one at odds with his rural religious community but not so different from the pattern of growth implicit but suppressed in men and family members beloved in the community as the historical record shows. In this divergence, Kenan's text links back to the thematics of incarceration central to Gaines's representation of black masculinity within Bayonne and St. Raphael Parish.

Trinh T. Minh-ha, in "Not You/Like You: Postcolonial Women and the Interlocking Questions of Identity and Difference," states: "If identity refers to the whole pattern of sameness within a being, the style of a continuing me that permeates all the changes undergone, then difference remains within the boundary of that which distinguishes one identity from another."[105] Her point is that difference should not be excluded from the process of identity formation or of marking distinctiveness of identity. In *A Visitation of Spirits*, Kenan undertakes just such a project, one in which Horace's subjectivity is articulated through his seeking to understand his difference, his identity "as a by-product of a manhandling of life," to use Minh-ha's formulation of difference that very often lands an individual "in a hospital, a rehabilitation center, a concentration camp, or a reservation."[106] In Horace's case, the difference of race combined with sexuality produces madness and death.

With the five chapter titles, "White Sorcery," "Black Necromancy," "Holy Science," "Old Demonology," and "Old Gods, New Demons," Kenan represents the occult, black and white magic, and ancient properties articulated together and aligned with the contradictory sameness and otherness of Horace Cross and his cousin Jimmy, the theologian, preacher, teacher, first black principal of an integrated school in his county, and writer of sermons and playlike dialogues. James Malachai Greene's meditations form the historical and mnemonic backdrop for interrogating Horace's death: "It's as if I'm trying to write the sermon I want to hear, not the perfect sermon, but the perfect sermon for me. So I pore over the Bible, reading, taking notes, making tentative outlines. Banishing from my mind any thoughts of the present, of the recent past, of the uncertain future. Thinking only of God and his laws" (38). In many ways, Cousin Jimmy's meditative voice configures the contrapuntal access to interior space both of the Tims Creek community and of the demon complicating and truncating Horace's young life. He is the collector of the oral history of Tims Creek, and it is his recording of Ezekiel and Ruth that forms the basis of "Let the Dead Bury Their Dead." Zeke, speaking as a cultural insider, compares Horace and Jimmy: "Horace . . . Lord, he was like this here Jimmy. Quiet. Polite. There ain't nothing wrong with quiet. . . . But this was a difference" (55).

The text, however, while epigraphically playing off Charles Dickens's *A Christmas Carol* and Scrooge's question, "Are spirits' lives so short?," calls up and defines its demon against a second epigraph, William Gibson's observation in *Neuromancer*: "To call up a demon you must learn its name. Men dreamed that, once, but now it is real in another way." Noticeably, both epigraphs invoke spirits and demons, but importantly, they also evoke time and the imperative of the present, the moment of the immediate now: "'To-night at midnight. Hark! The time is drawing near'" (Dickens) and "Men dreamed that, once, but now it is real in another way" (Gibson). The conceptualization of time-space boundaries anticipate the scripture and biblical references to the House of the Lord as the challenged and contested site of knowledge and action within the present moment. Religion, myth, and demonology all intermingle in a James Baldwinesque (*Go Tell It on the Mountain*) fantasia of spiritual possession and homoerotics in Kenan's text.

A Visitation of Spirits is a "coming out" novel and a narrative of transfiguration, which takes into its realism about sexuality and same-sex desire a difference that incorporates the phantasmagoric to transform the possibilities for locating Horace within a southern site.[107] Although popular writers, such as the late E. Lynn Harris in particular, deal with gay and queer sexuality in the South, Kenan was in the vanguard of writers who took seriously their intersectional identities (racial, regional, classed, gendered, and sexuality) and, following Audre Lorde, the inseparability of their multiple ways of being themselves in the world.

One of Randall Kenan's contemporaries, the poet and psychologist Forrest Hamer, is also a North Carolinian who has responded directly in his creative work to the complexity of the South as a place and to being a gay man from the South even though he lives in California. In his "Goldsboro Narratives," a cycle of poems from the perspective of a child that appear throughout his two collections, *Call and Response* and *Middle Ear*, Hamer explores his North Carolina homeplace, because, he observes, "as I wrote more of the poems, they moved away from witness and into exploration of place, not only in terms of geography but what place means in terms of people's relationships with each other, in terms of being located somewhere psychologically . . . and located even in terms of a sense of identity. . . . [T]he poems became one way of maintaining a continuity between the place where I grew up and the places to where I have moved."[108] In a candid interview with Charles Rowell, Hamer confesses both his love for the South and his misgivings: "[T]he very thing we love can be the very thing that is in fact quite oppressive. That sense of familiarity, community, and connection can also be the same location . . . where people are silenced, where dissent is squelched, where people who are different in ways that are not prescribed can be sent away."[109]

Hamer observes the ambivalence in the black South toward gay people. He states:

> On the one hand, gays and lesbians . . . are quite valued as creators and maintainers of African-American culture. . . . [W]e see this is in terms of how many gays and lesbians are in the healing and care-giving roles in our communities. Yet another place we see it is how many are in fact involved in the black church in various roles, all roles, actually. At the same time, there is this condemnation of homosexuality and it's often driven by a kind of religiosity that is inconsistent with the very same acceptance that is implicit in the culture.[110]

These are the striking contradictions so evident in southern black attitudes toward black gays and lesbians who, as Hamer states, "have been 'othered,' especially those who assume public queer identities."[111] Speaking candidly about his own coming out, Hamer empathizes with his parents in that his being gay

> went against what they hoped would be my future not only in terms of specific things like giving them grandchildren (which was not, of course, precluded by being gay), but also some of the other things they expected like my returning to the South to live after college. . . . [I]t also disturbed them because they worried about the hostile judgments I (and they) would face from others, and . . . it represented a difference between us they were worried we wouldn't be able to bridge. To make it more complicated it was also a religious matter, especially for my mother. It was difficult for her to reconcile my homosexual identity with her religious beliefs.[112]

Apparent in his commentary is the locational identity that Hamer wishes to preserve, as someone from the South, the place to which he returned as the child of a military family with roots in North Carolina, and the place "you come back to, it's a place you come from": "It's where . . . my sense of music was born, my sense of aesthetics, my view of the world and of history was largely formed. . . . [I]t's also a place that connects me to Africa. . . . . But it's also where my language was formed and my voice, so it's important to me being a poet to speak from that."[113]

Hamer's effort to translate the complexity of his "southern" relational identity into accessible language is similar to Kenan's work through Horace Cross. In *A Visitation of Spirits*, it is as though the gender roles compelling a heterosexual erotics also constrict the fiction to fantasies of masculinity devoid of sex and imbued with character traits that ignore the physical body. Here Kenan takes to the next level the homoeroticism of late twentieth-century southern fiction. Kenan's text does break barriers and locates itself as a southern, black, queer fiction. It lays claims to the intersectionality of identity and is a fascinating corollary to E. Patrick Johnson's contention that the South is "a more complicated space in which to negotiate one's (homo) sexuality": "Because black queers experience their race and sexuality (and class and gender) in a southern context, their relationships and experiences also diverge from those of white southern queers."[114]

A Visitation of Spirits is elegant, daring, and sophisticated. Traditional storytelling techniques are absent and replaced by recognizable modernist techniques, such as stream-of-consciousness and fragmented narrative sequences. At the same time, the text is also a postmodernist exploration of black subjectivity with voices from the grave, spirits bound to remembering the past and to telling visions that produce tableaux of personal memory and communal history and transfiguration. It moves across time and space, living and dead, with an indulgent wonder at the possibilities and potential of freedom in form. It is a metafictional text in terms of orality (the writer can die before he can write his narrative but even in death can speak its truth) and playwriting (the performativity of the stylistic device of the play format).[115] It is narrative seeped in blood, killing, death, ghosts, and bodies; corporeal images that both transfix and transform. It is also an immense space constituted out of dreams and nightmares. Gaston Bachelard suggests that "immensity is a philosophical category of daydream": "Daydream undoubtedly feeds on all kinds of sights, but through a sort of natural inclination, it contemplates grandeur. And this contemplation produces an attitude that is so special, an inner state that is so unlike any other, that the daydream transports the dreamer outside the immediate world to a world that bears the mark of infinity."[116]

The first section, "White Sorcery," bears the epigraph: "The Lord is in his Holy Temple; / let all the earth keep silent before him. / I was glad when they said unto me, Let us go into the / House of the Lord." "White Sorcery" begins with time: "December 8, 1985 8:45 A.M." and the words of ninety-two-year-old Aunt Ruth, "Lord, Lord, Lord . . ." (3). Jimmy, her great-nephew, and Zeke (Ezekiel Cross, who is eighty-four) offer to help but are refused. References to hog killing, snow in December (red-tipped blackbirds swarming on the ground), and a car trip unite the three within a narrative space that is confined and cryptic. "Advent (or The Beginning of the End)" begins the brief subsegment of "December 8, 1985," and establishes the North Carolina space as rural farming country and emphasizes hog killing as a ritual of the area and its people, in particular the allowing of a boy to aim and fire a gun into the hog as part of an initiation into the local customs of masculinity and power.[117] The gun as a symbol of maturation, domination, and destruction recurs throughout the text as the naked boy Horace makes his way in a night world toward death, immensity, and infinity.

Horace Thomas Cross, "the Great Black Hope," is sixteen. His becoming is the transfiguration at the center of the text—a transfiguration resonant with the transformation of a sequence of animals: rabbit, fox, hawk, squirrels, mice and wood rats, snakes, dogs, butterflies, cats, and finally a bird. The transformation of humans into animals or vice versa marking fairy tales, folktales, and myths figures centrally in Horace's narrative. Horace concludes: "There are no moral laws that say: You must remain human. And he would not" (12). The tale that links transformation and vision is that of old Julia, who turns herself into an eel on the bottom of the ocean "to see what she could see" (12). Horace's own choice for his transfiguration is a red-tailed hawk (14–15). In seeking a way out of time and place, he links himself to Daniel, Isaac, and the woman at the well—all biblical seekers and believers (16).

Horace's room is papered with pictures of sorcerers, conjurers, magicians, Wonder Woman, and heroic action figures such as Batman (17). The space is an archive of popular print culture in which the human and superhuman collide. The iconography mixes time past, a mythic extended unmarked periodicity, with a temporal modernity of comic scripts and colored paper. The fluid bipolarity evident in the selection of pictures makes legible Horace's split between human and animal and between different fields of temporalities.[118] He is a changeling free floating through implausible dream spaces and narratives rendered in incompatible temporalities. The descriptions of his conjuring, burning the dead kitten, and incanting the demon; returning to the woods in the midnight hour and chanting; taking his grandfather's gun; and following a voice, one voice, the voice, all enact the power of the transformative. Descriptions of fornication and violence and danger taken together signify homoeroticism linked with dread and transfiguration.

The second dated section of "White Sorcery," "April 29, 1984 11:30 A.M.," a year earlier, is effectively backshadowing.[119] "White Sorcery" creates the subject by means of two archives: textuality—books, papers, pictures and images from books, reference texts, scientific books and ancient or invented and fictionalized rituals; and intertextuality—specifically with texts by Charles Chesnutt, who was from the same section of southeastern North Carolina as Kenan and who concerned himself with the transformative implicit in the fluidity of racial identity (his novels of passing, such as *The House behind the Cedars* [1900], and those early texts published posthumously only in recent years, *Paul Marchand, Free Man of Color* and *Mandy Oxendine*), and especially the transformative in his stories of transmigration and conjuring, *The Conjure Woman and Other Tales* (1899), with their racially and politically informed oppositional narrative stances, including black masculinity.

The second part, "Black Necromancy," bears the epigraph: "Whosoever will let him come . . ." and contains "James Malachai Greene Confessions," the Jimmy of the opening segment. He is a preacher-educator whose relationship with Philip Schnider, one of his professors at seminary, a Jew who converted to Christianity, centers on theology as a desire to know God (33). Schnider, like Jimmy's brother Franklin, a Howard law graduate, and his sister Isador, a Ph.D. student in architecture at the University of California, Berkeley, believes that Jimmy should leave the South. Jimmy's decision to remain is linked to his northern-born wife Anne's sense of mission to uplift in the South; however, after Anne's death, Jimmy remains unmovable. He links himself to Horace as having curiosity and begins the process of "contemplating the equation of eternal life. Why? How?" (36). A play scenario set on 30 April 1984, one day after Horace's death, and culminating with Jimmy's acknowledgment of the horror that his cousin Horace was possessed by a demon (43), provides access to the mystery of Jimmy's own existence and his relation with both his God and his family. His list of readings ("Augustine and Erasmus. Maybe Freud, or Jung, or Foucault. Black history: Franklin, Quarles. Fanon. Occasionally fiction") attests to the all-encompassing nature of his existence (44). With the inclusion of Jimmy's story, it becomes apparent that Kenan is thinking through what he calls "the emotional aspect of being black or white—a true ghost of the mind, the thing Americans will be trying to exorcize for a long time to come." Horace's possession, then, has as much to do with race as it does with sexuality and religion. As a young, gay, black youth, Horace has no models and no mentors to steer him away from schizophrenia and self-destruction. Jimmy, though linked to Horace in his unnamed "difference," is unable to provide a model.

"April 30, 1984 1:15 A.M." is the last part of "Black Necromancy" and returns to the late night–early morning of Horace's conjuring and his fight with the demon. It is his *Walpurgisnacht*, as in Goethe's *Faustus*. The question the Masai warrior asks, "Why didn't you kill it?" (67), begins to link the text to Alice Walker's civil rights novel *Meridian* in conflation of the ability to kill whites and to kill for a cause. In this case it is the voice compelling Horace to move, to walk, to act. The image of the crucifixion is akin both to Carl Van Vechten's homoerotic photographs of a black man in St. Sebastian-like poses and to that of a lynching, but the victim has wings and clearly is linked to the conception of angels and accounts of the struggles between the fallen angel Satan, the demon, and the good angels. The church of Tims Creek where Horace rings the bell leads back into his past, his grandmother, Aretha Davis Cross, his grandfather, chairman of the deacon board and a respected man in the community because he was "the center, the source of the church's memory, the link to the terrible past they all had to remember" (71). This segment is textually speaking back to and signifying on Dickens's *A Christmas Carol* and Scrooge's night journey into the heart of his own miserable life: "But how can these people be here? I mean . . . are they ghosts?" To which the demon responds, "Are you really as dumb as you look? . . . Ghosts? Yeah, you might call them ghosts. Ghosts of the past. The presence of the present. The very stuff of which the future is made. This is the effluvium of souls that surround men daily. All you have to do is take the scales off your eyes and look and see. You are seeing. I have removed the scales from your eyes" (73).

According to Bachelard:

> The two kinds of space, intimate space and exterior space, keep encouraging each other, as it were, in their growth. To designate space that has been experienced as affective space, which psychologists do very rightly, does not, however go to the root of space dreams. The poet goes deeper when he uncovers a poetic space that does not enclose us in affectivity. Indeed, whatever the affectivity that colors a given space, whether sad or ponderous, once it is poetically expressed, the sadness is diminished, the ponderousness lightened. Poetic space, because it is expressed, assumes values of expansion.[120]

For Bachelard, the movement in poetic spatiality is from "deep intimacy to infinite extent, united in an identical expansion" with "grandeur welling up."[121] The result is that "through their 'immensity' . . . these two kinds of space—the space of intimacy and world space—blend. When human solitude deepens, then the two immensities touch and become identical. . . . In the realm of images, there can be no contradiction, and two spirits that are identically sensitive can sensitize the dialectics of center and horizon in different ways."[122] In sharing intimate space and exterior space, Horace and Jimmy blend finally into one identity and one story of sexual and racial sensitivity to difference. The play scripts folded into the text allow the performative aspect of Horace's and Jimmy's sexuality to reverberate, particularly in Jimmy's fear of the dead, which mirrors his seeing himself in Horace.

The third part of "Old Demonology" is "April 30, 1984 4:45 A.M." with Horace Cross and the Crosstown theater (210), where Horace had worked the summer before his senior year. The poster advertising the play *Ride the Freedom Star*, and the play itself with its story of family history, become a textual reflection of the larger novel. The performances and the play noticeably misrepresent slavery and the past (213). The significance of the segment lies in Horace's description of the gay actors and his homoerotic attraction to their bodies, though he feels anger at the only black male actor, Everett Church Harrington IV, who falls downstairs and into Horace's arms at their first meeting but dismisses Horace and feels superior to him. With the emphasis on performativity of identity, Horace sees his own face as a harlequin and is stunned by the double image of a Horace in white face, a harlequin, clown face (220), and a Horace black, naked, and gun carrying. The shifting images fade into a discourse on the sexual relations among the actors. Horace's promiscuity with cast members is mentioned, but his affair with Antonio Santangelo is detailed, though their lovemaking leaves Horace fulfilled sexually but unfinished. A rehearsal of familial and race history does not resolve the tensions of identity. With a return to the destruction of "the fire next time" that echoes both the Bible and Baldwin (234), Horace shoots himself.

In the last part of the text, "Old Gods, New Demons," the epigraph is a definition of the subjunctive. It is made up of "Horace Thomas Cross Confessions," and his memories (with the repetition "I remember" [245–51]) and the final segment "April 30, 1984 7:05 A.M.," in which Horace commits suicide by shooting himself in the head (253). The intertextual allusions are specifically to Faulkner's Quentin Compson's suicide in *The Sound and the Fury* (1929) but also to Quentin's recurrence in intense male bonding with his roommate Shreve over reconstructing history and creating narrative in *Absalom, Absalom!* (1936).

After the horrific narrative of Horace Thomas Cross's confessions, the final section of the novel begins "A Requiem for Tobacco," a lament for that which is dead, times which are past: "You remember, though perhaps you don't, that once upon a time men harvested tobacco by hand. There was a time when folk were bound together in a community, as one, and helped one person this day and that day another. . . . But this was once upon a time" (254). As in Gaines, the nature of the rural and the farming communities is past, but it provides a space from which to understand the present. The emphasis on and the repetition of time in the context of storytelling, "once upon a time," "[t]here was a time," and "this was once upon a time," serve at once to mythologize the concept of harvest and to foreclose the narrative interrogation of harvest. The impulse is to hold on to the memory of harvesting tobacco by hand because too many have no memory, and yet the memory is itself curiously at odds with Horace's own subjective development and death, for it cannot contain the same-sex desire and consequences that charge the larger text. "It is good to remember, for too many forget" (257); the concluding words may speak to the now-lost tobacco culture, but they also evoke the Horace who is also lost to the terms, religious and sexual, of that culture. The site of memory, however, cannot be recuperated. The requiem in its largest implications also becomes a societal lament for a familiar but now vacant and lost southern rural culture, but there is no hint of nostalgia for its return. Neither Horace nor Jimmy nor any of the spirits within Kenan's text can survive in the world made out of the mound reaching down to hell. Like a postmodern master word sorcerer, Kenan succeeds in inventing a new image of the Upper South that links it to the direction of Alice Walker's fiction and to the space of the intimate in the everyday of black life, where persistence and revolution pose on the verge of becoming out of difference and confound the reductions of black people to limited typographies of being.

chapter six

Alice Walker Matters

THE FRUITS OF GENDERED SPACE

I. RECONSTRUCTION OF SOUTHERN RACIAL SPACE

How many maps, in the descriptive or geographical sense, might be needed to deal exhaustively with a given space, to code and decode all its meanings and contents? . . . It is not only the codes—the map's legend, the conventional signs of map-making and map-reading— that are liable to change, but also the objects represented, the lens through which they are viewed, and the scale used.—HENRI LEFEBVRE, *The Production of Space* (1991)

Alice Walker, that famous spirited Georgia native, certainly does not need a rehabilitation of her reputation. Yet, as I have been thinking about Southern Studies and scholarly production, I began to notice that Walker has slipped out of recent discourses and that her contribution to the ways in which we today think about the South, its literary and cultural production, has been occluded in part by her own adherence to what we might call New Age, non-heteronormative political spiritualism. With that notice, I began to think about how Alice Walker, an artist forged on the battleground of Mississippi during the height of civil rights activism, may have been one primary catalyst in naturalizing how so many scholars and artists approach the South today, and with that naturalizing a concomitant erasing of her very positionality in the process.

"The life of thought is a continuous story, like life itself," Yi-Fu Tuan observes in *Space and Place: The Perspective of Experience* (1977), "one book grows out of another as in the world of political commitment one action leads to another."[1] For me, in thinking about Walker, the concept of process intermingled with that of the continuous story and thus the necessity of following the thought backwards to pay closer attention to how the narrative came to be what it is. As a result, here I look backward over the multiple intersecting public and private spaces that constitute the material and theoretical contributions of Alice Walker to the multidimensional and multidisciplinary work today in the new Southern Studies.

Walker begins a postmodern stance toward both race and region in her deconstruction of arenas and hierarchies of power and in her transgression of the fixed and rigid notions of art, epistemologies of art, and production of art, as well as in her anticipation of the shifts in gender theory and with it cultural transformation in the very geographical matrix that was the South of her childhood and youth. When Walker brought together place and identity in her work, she destabilized both categories and began the process of the reformation of both. She invented her own "radically subjective politics" within a matrix of change, but she did not produce an identity that is fragmentary, conflicted, or contradictory despite its fluid boundaries. She produced texts, critical and creative and autobiographical, that defied the notion of clearly defined and readable meaning explicit in and based upon established transcendental precepts. She saw pluralism and relativism, rejected nostalgia and sentimentalism, and claimed political relevance for her transformative positions and subversive ideologies, all the while insisting on her own vision, certainly idiosyncratic and subjective but not fractured or paranoid. In beginning to write in the political and cultural upheaval of the 1960s, Walker envisioned both the importance of articulating her own new southern black woman identity and the necessity of new formations and new modalities—even while asserting the changing ground for all such formations and modalities. In particular, she was able to foreground the damaging impact of racism and patriarchal authority/power in her short fiction, poetry, and novels, as well as in her essays, and in the process, to create a space for the gendering of subjectivity and reassessing gendered racial hierarchies.

In the conjunction of her political and literary work, Walker examined gender and ideological formations under segregation and displayed an ability to map the postmodern at a time when among African American writers there was still a strong adherence to modernist aesthetic productions. Walker's emphasis on difference then becomes one of the primary ways of linking her to a postmodern aesthetic, especially by means of her collapsing the distinctions between genres and destabilizing the hierarchy of high and low culture, high and low art, and exploiting the class dynamics to challenge the hegemony of a white racialist society. In ascribing to Walker's work a revolutionizing southscape, I read her as personifying the political consciousness of location that bell hooks considers a "right to subjectivity" and one's own legitimacy and "a central location for the production of counter-hegemonic discourse that is not just found in words but in habits of being and the way one lives."[2]

Though William Faulkner, with his novel *Absalom, Absalom!*, is typically positioned currently as the southern writer used to configure a Global South, Alice Walker functions as the exemplar par excellence of the southern writer evolving over the course of an active career into a writer of the Global South in her fiction, poetry, and essays. Her late twentieth-century and early twenty-first-century writings, such as *By the Light of My Father's Smile: A Novel* (1998), *Absolute Trust in the Goodness of the Earth: New Poems* (2003), and *We Are the Ones We Have Been Waiting For: Inner Light in a Time of Darkness* (2006), with their hemispheric instantiations all move through enlarged global locations, all primarily part of the Global South, and they make their creative articulations not merely as a translation of uneven economic development. With each of her successive moves, Walker manifests the "global," as Henri Lefebvre defined it: "[T]he capacity to conceive of and deal with space on a wide scale, even on a world scale."[3] Her writing creates a space, a southscape, from which to make futurity critically and aesthetically visible in the raced and gendered body with its origins in the past of the twentieth-century segregated South. Her work, extending from the turbulent 1960s and now resolutely into the first decades of the twenty-first century, has made a critical intervention in the ways in which the South as a region can be represented and studied and provides a concluding southscape for meditating on the spatial-racial nexus in the construction of region.

Without denying the significance of Walker's generational precursors—for instance, the popular impact of Maya Angelou's personal writing or the methodological impact of Alex Haley's genealogical histories—I place Walker at a crossroads, like the bluesman Robert Johnson. Her crossroads position is the rethinking of how black people in the South from her grandmothers' and mother's generations to her own created and survived, and how they had managed to do so with an understanding of their intersectional identities and of the potential of power resident within some few spaces—ever expanding and never collapsing. Just by way of an initial example to help engage what I am attempting here, recall for a moment Minrose Gwin's brilliant essay "Her Shape, His Hand: The Spaces of African American Women in *Go Down, Moses*," in which she examines Faulkner's representation of black women, the "inscrutable face" of Tennie and the "blank spot" of the mulatta mistress's untold story. Gwin begins the section entitled "The Space of the Ledger" with the following: "It is this untold story that haunts Patricia Williams. Specifically, the erasure of her great-great-grandmother's life and narrative provides the vehicle for Williams's *The Alchemy of Race and Rights*, a brilliant study of the relations of race to individual and social contractual rights in this country. . . . Williams writes that she has tried 'to piece together what it must have been like to be my great-great-grandmother,' a girl purchased by a thirty-five-year old Tennessee lawyer."[4] The details of the documents that Williams uncovers reveal her eleven-year-old great-great-grandmother's purchase in a bill of sale and her being listed as the thirteen-year-old mother of an eight-month-old infant in a census record two years later.

For my purposes here, remember the words Gwin quotes from Williams, that she tried "to piece together what it must have been like to be my great-great-grandmother." Now move from Williams backward to the now-so-familiar words of Alice Walker in her brilliant essay "In Search of Our Mothers' Gardens": "Did you have a genius of a great-grandmother who died under some ignorant and depraved white overseer's lash? Or was she requested to bake biscuits for a lazy backwater tramp, when she cried out in her soul to paint watercolors of sunsets, or the rain falling on the green and peaceful pasture lands? Or was her body broken and forced to bear children (who were more often than not sold away from her) eight, ten, fifteen, twenty children— when her one joy was the thought of modeling figures of Rebellion in stone or clay?"[5] Walker's evoking of a racial ur-great-grandmother is, I argue, one of the root causes that gives permission to Patricia Williams in legal discourse to put herself in her enslaved great-great-grandmother's subjective place and enables Minrose Gwin in literary discourse to narrativize the blank spot in Faulkner's fiction. Gwin calls Williams's book "brilliant," and I call Gwin's essay "brilliant," and I suspect that many would call Walker's essay "brilliant." What I am after here is not the tracing of influence but rather a pointing out of the way in which Walker's "In Search of Our Mothers' Gardens" forms the interjection not merely into the way in which Williams can go after the concept of rights from the perspective of racial identity and social history, but also the way in which Gwin can construct an untold narrative in the deconstruction of a major text by perhaps the most famous of twentieth-century southern writers, William Faulkner.

This exercise, simply put, is what the work in this chapter is about: Alice Walker made ideological and narrative space possible for multiple blank spots. The work of Alice Walker from the 1970s and 1980s, in particular, informs a range of texts in a number of disciplines that have changed how we conceive of and practice Southern Studies, and so embedded and naturalized is her positionality in the process that we have lost track of the larger significance of her contribution to our work. Walker is a central figure in constructing a new spatial geography and in reconfiguring the landscape of the South and, with it, the geographies of race and region. Her accomplishment as a paradigm shifter is now often unrecognized because of the extent to which pervasive change has occurred following her seminal work. I am thinking here of work across genres and disciplines, from Shay Youngblood's *Big Mama Stories*, Dorothy Allison's *Bastard out of Carolina*, Patricia Yaeger's *Dirt and Desire: Reconstructing Southern Women's Writing, 1930–1990*, and John Lowe's *Bridging Southern Cultures: An Interdisciplinary Approach* to Judylyn Ryan's *Spirituality as Ideology in Black Women's Literature*, Grace Hale's *Making Whiteness: The Culture of Segregation in the South, 1890–1940*, and Houston Baker's *I Don't Hate the South: Reflections on Faulkner, Family, and the South*. Melvin Dixon, in *Ride out the Wilderness*, puts it another way. After considering that Walker's essay "In Search of Our Mothers' Gardens" "gives direction to the road imagery in Hurston's fiction and reinvents the woman's role as nurturer," he concludes: "Each group of writers expands the parameters of cultural mobility previously restricted by gender, race, sexual exploitation, or the artistic struggle to create meaning out of chaos."[6]

Walker's corpus of work unsettled the complacent acceptance of a high-culture critique and forced the turning to a broader spectrum of cultural practices in the analysis of the South as a space for the creation and production of art. Her writing has encouraged "the changed quality of practice that [theory] permits," as Charles Taylor has pointed out regarding the final judge of the merit of any theory.[7] Walker's perceptive attention to the practices of everyday black southerners, in particular to the domestic culture of women, resulted in her conceptualization of the possibilities for artistic creation and for regional identity within a subjectivity defining itself as racially black, ethnically southern, and gendered female.[8] Her novel *The Color Purple* (1982) made plain the devastating issues affecting black women *within* the family. Her clarity in exposing incest, rape, sexual abuse of young black girls, physical and psychological abuse of black women, alongside racial and gender oppression in the wider social and cultural arenas, initiated discourses that brought out openly the location of black writing and aesthetics within postmodernism. In particular, she was able to foreground the damaging impact not only of racism but of sexism and black and white southern patriarchal authority/ power in her short fiction, poetry, and novels, as well as in her essays. In the process, she managed to create a space for the gendering of subjectivity and reassessing gendered hierarchies. At stake throughout her work is the issue of justice, which makes politics a necessity.

Because of the popularity of black women writers in the 1980s and the emergence of Toni Morrison as the major figure, particularly after she received the Nobel Prize in 1993, it may now be difficult to recall that Alice Walker sparked a reconsideration of black writers and of the South within the paradigms of race, gender, class, and sexuality as categories of analysis. Walker's prominent activism and her global politics (her taking on issues of political prisoners in many nations, her expressing outrage at the continuation of female genital mutilation in Africa and the African diaspora, and her commenting publicly on other high-profile issues of pressing moral significance, including the environment) have in recent times obscured how deeply rooted she is in the American South and how much that geographical region, in culture, history, and mores, including the practice and ideology of segregation, has influenced her and impacted her work—and concomitantly how much she and her work have influenced late twentieth-century southern writing as well as thinking, particularly with her rediscovery of Zora Neale Hurston and her sparking the "womanist theology" movement. The obscuring of her contribution to discourses of southern contemporary writing, or critical approaches to it, is apparent, for instance, in Walker's absence from any mention or citation in Leigh Anne Duck's excellent study, *The Nation's Region: Southern Modernism, Segregation, and U.S. Nationalism* (2006), despite the fact that much of the underlying premise enabling her to reread Erskine Caldwell, Zora Neale Hurston, and William Faulkner depends, at least in part, upon reading backwards from the stances Walker took and made visible in the 1970s and 1980s.

Keith Cartwright rightly recalls that Walker's reclaiming of Hurston's texts and authority as a black southern voice meant "nothing less than a moving through the shame-barrier, a recovery of black cultural homelands." In recovering Hurston, Walker took back the folklore that had been usurped, stolen, and debased in the Uncle Remus tales of Joel Chandler Harris, which, as Cartwright puts it, had placed "a shameful barrier between black children and their removed, displaced folk culture."[9] Cartwright's reminder calls up Walker's own formulation of her early work in her essays "Saving the Life That Is Your Own" and "Looking for Zora," as well as her later reflection on reading Zora Neale Hurston: "I saw for the first time my own specific culture, and recognized it as such, with its humor always striving to be equal to its pain, and I felt as if, indeed, I had been given a map that led to the remains of my literary country. The old country, as it were."[10] It is perhaps no overstatement to suggest that Walker's cultural work constituted a reconstruction of southern racial space in which the specific geographies of black women's bodies could not be eclipsed.

Place as a powerful signifier of identity for a black person in the South cannot be overestimated. To reconsider place in relation to Walker's achievement is not a reactionary gesture. Place-identified writers have often served to foreground the characteristics of the South. The small town of Eatonton, Georgia, was Walker's childhood home, where she experienced mid-twentieth-century segregated southern life still closely linked to the social reality of the past. Born on 9 February 1944, she was the youngest child of Willie Lee and Minnie Tallulah Grant Walker's eight children, and like her parents and siblings, she entered a narrow world defined economically by sharecropping and legally by segregation. As a child of fieldworkers dependent upon the vicissitudes of a cotton crop, Walker spent her youth in rural poverty. Even with a good harvest, her father earned under $300 a year, and her mother's efforts to supplement the family's income with domestic work often netted only seventy-five cents a day. The material body and abstract capital inscribe the politics of race, place, and class into Walker's profile. The family's economic hardships magnified the inequities of segregated spaces for labor and domestic life. Their South with its specific history and sociology positioned Alice Walker and her family not only within a particularly rigid racial and social hierarchy but also within narrow spatial parameters and boundaries of experience. As Doreen Massey has observed, "It is not just that the spatial is socially constructed; the social is spatially constructed too."[11]

Segregation as both a spatial and a social construct functioned to enclose and contain as well as to shape and delineate identity for Walker. Because segregation in the South was a matter of official legislation and sanctioned custom, it impacted almost every part of Walker's formative years. The social conditions, poverty and its multiple manifestations, defining the public sphere for generations of black southerners were not without the personal, subjective constructions of space that functioned as a counterbalance to the official social narrative of black life. This South, while undoubtedly an inhibiting space, was nonetheless a landscape of desire and want that fed dreams, resistance, creativity, and revolution during the era of segregation. While Georgia was the place of Alice Walker's birth and upbringing, Mississippi was the space of her aesthetic, political, and racial formation. On the cusp of a sea change in identity politics, Walker spent an eventful part of her young womanhood and early career in the Deep South that was at once familiar and revelatory. She stated the meaning of the experience in direct terms: "I grew to adulthood in Mississippi."[12] Mississippi engendered a maturity of her radical vision and feminist voice. In 1967, following her marriage to Melvyn Leventhal, a civil rights lawyer and conscientious objector to the war in Vietnam, Walker moved to Mississippi and strengthened her resolve to write out of a social and moral consciousness, particularly because the interracial couple faced "disaffected parents, outraged friends," as she later put it, and because their relocation to an active battleground for the civil rights movement dramatized the realities of racial segregation. In Mississippi, Walker worked in voter registration while writing fiction along with poetry, teaching black studies, and collecting African American folklore. These activities brought her into close contact with older African American women, who, like her mother, had stories to tell. Listening to the stories and experiences of black Mississippi women inspired her to write her first novel. Mississippi functioned as a site of memory and inspiration. The signature work of Mississippi women in particular argued for a not-yet-depleted reservoir of creativity in that most controversial and historically brutal of Deep South spaces.

Walker envisioned the creative work of Mississippi women in ordinary activities such as gardening, quilting, and storytelling as emblematic of the often unrecognized creativity of black women past and present. The essays comprising *In Search of Our Mothers' Gardens* (1983) repeatedly return to the implications of Mississippi and the South as a locus of meaning for her writing and a way to reconceptualize spatial identities in relational terms.[13] She has said of herself: "Because I'm black and I'm a woman and because I was brought up poor and because I'm a Southerner, . . . the way I see the world is quite different from the way many people see it." This specific lens, intersectional and antiessentialist, has shaped her politics and her art, as she put it: "I could not help but have a radical vision of society. . . . [T]he way I see things can help other people see what needs to be changed."[14]

In a spatial identification with a geographical place heatedly contested and divided racially in the 1960s, Walker asserts her right as a black southerner and a black southern woman to claim that space as her own and to undo the ownership or domination of black bodies by a white-supremacist regime. She allows for difference and heterogeneity by understanding space as a sphere of possibility. Story or narrative, then, is not just the province of white men (a Faulkner perhaps) or white women (a Flannery O'Connor perhaps), but of blacks and black women who "tell" their stories differently and use different materials for legibility. Walker situates African American southerners within the spatial ground of a regional identification. That spatial ground is heterogeneous, as Michel Foucault has claimed of all the space in which individuals live and in which their history occurs. "We live," according to Foucault, "inside a set of relationships that delineates sites which are irreducible to one another and absolutely not superimposed on one another."[15] For Walker, it may well be that she asserts geographical claims in order to transgress regulatory boundaries and counter racial exclusion and to formulate a new politics.

Although she does not articulate the rationale behind her self-confident iteration of a spatial identification as empowering her "radical vision of society" and enabling others to "see what needs to be changed," Walker seems aware of the two spatial configurations inextricably linked to the projection of blackness in the United States and to the construction of black bodies as raced "black"; in *Meridian*, for example, she divides the setting equally between New York and Mississippi as the spaces for racing blacks. The first is the urban North, whose contextual orientation or place is always the city as center despite an understanding that urban is not synonymous with city and that any discourse on the city with attention to a racialized black body invariably becomes elided with "the ghetto" as a concept, or with the spatialization of race, as Douglas Massey and Nancy Denton have observed in *American Apartheid: Segregation and the Making of the Underclass* (1993). Massey and Denton describe segregation in terms of systemic attempts ("racist attitudes, private behaviors, and institutional practices") to isolate blacks within residential structures of "physical decay, crime, and social disorder."[16] Thomas Sugrue has labeled this process "racial geography," a form of racist ideology in which blackness takes on a spatial definition.[17]

The second spatial configuration linked to the construction of blackness is the rural South, where space reemerges as important in unyoking the new modern stereotypes of black from the ground on which the black body can be made visible. In the South, the rural has long been the dominant physical expression of the region as a spatial configuration. In renegotiating the significance of the rural in keeping with the global prominence of the urban, the cityscape, it becomes increasingly clear that the rural has not been completely undermined as a signifier of the South. The "in-placedness" of the black body is keyed into these two spaces, and while the two may indeed overlap, they also connote distinct ideas that resonate throughout Walker's texts.

Walker's conception of the South in the twentieth century as modern manifests itself in her acceptance of space as a controlling factor in social theory (also relationships). The South in the twenty-first century as postmodern can be configured with the shifting or transformation beginning to occur in the 1980s and continuing through the end of the century.

While Hazel Carby and, more recently, Madhu Dubey have implicated

Walker in the privileging of a southern folk aesthetic partially because of her rediscovery of Zora Neale Hurston, neither scholar seems fully aware that Walker, unlike the conservative Hurston, is far more radical in her criticism of the South and her rejection of sentimentality or romanticism in the representation of both the South and black folk. In addition, neither seems to recognize a particular geography of social relations, the stubborn refusal of the tradition-bound white southern literary and academic establishment to incorporate black writers into their work on the South. For example, Martyn Bone, in *The Postsouthern Sense of Place in Contemporary Fiction* (2005), reverts to the old pattern of excluding black writers, but in his case the exception is Toni Cade Bambara, whose novel on the Atlanta child murders fits into his discourse on the organization of Atlanta as a New South "nonplace."[18] Carby rightly calls attention to a tendency in late twentieth-century African American literature toward discursive displacement from the problems of the volatile urban to the romance of southern folklife.[19] Yet, she overlooks Walker's writing in the 1960s and 1970s as occurring during and out of a historical moment that was immediate at the time and not past. And neither Carby nor Dubey seems to comprehend fully the revolutionary agitation for visibility and space as black and southern that Walker's work signified. But both rightly recognize the significance of Hurston in Walker's development. Perhaps the central trope in Walker's relation to the South may be figured in her relation to Hurston—to her discovery of Hurston's writings, to her search for Hurston's grave, and to her eventual erection of a tombstone on that grave with the epitaph: "A Genius of the South." Dubey, following Carby, allows that Walker's "In Search of Our Mothers' Gardens" in fact "initiated the turn toward southern folk culture in African-American women's literature and criticism," but rather than exploring the particularities of Walker's work at that signal moment in 1974, Dubey focuses her attention on Toni Morrison's *Song of Solomon* (1977) and Gloria Naylor's *Mama Day* (1988) as evidence of an unfortunate elevation of an organic and magical southern folk culture that elides the complexities of modern black life.[20]

That Walker's writing has not become part of the analytical frame examining southern folk culture suggests that the cultural work she undertook in challenging the polarities of space and segregation in the 1960s and 1970s has not been fully understood. Unlike analyses that confine black culture in the South to a space that is specifically black, Walker insisted on constructing black culture as southern culture. Space, for Walker, is always in process and not closed, so that it is always outside of grand narratives of modernity. Similarly, unlike discourses on black writing engaging a sanitized, glorified,

ALICE WALKER MATTERS

and essentialist black community emanating from the South, Walker insisted on complicated, multifaceted, multidimensional, problematic communities of raced individuals within the South and on communities that change over time and rarely remain stable. Her South was not unilaterally rural or agrarian. She constructed Memphis and Atlanta and urban spaces as belonging equally to the lived South; moreover, she represented a commodity culture with its specific spaces of capitalism as inherent in the South. (The rise of Walmart as a global entity would not have surprised her and would have fitted into her cultural analysis.) She understood that the modern narratives of progress actually foreclose futurity which has to remain open and possible. As Doreen Massey reminds us: "Only if the future is open is there any ground for a politics which can make a difference."[21]

For Walker, in making a difference there was no retreat from the actualities of the victimization of blacks in the South and the appropriation of their labor, their art, and their lives. Without nostalgia, she writes of what was a twentieth-century South still entangled with the residue of past discrimination and the values of present-day white racial domination ("The Revenge of Hannah Kemhuff"). She shows the ways in which blacks suffer from the damaging impact of systemic racism ("Her Sweet Jerome") and paternalistic sexism ("Roselily" and "The Child Who Favored Daughter"), and she also writes of an Elvis Presley–like character who appropriates the music of a Big Mama Thornton–like blues singer in order to become a success ("1959"). But rather than a catalog of her accomplishments, perhaps the more important achievement to name is her demonstration that what constitutes art can be produced by a woman who is black and southern. Her understanding that the power to command space is vital and not resident only within those who command capital is suggestive of David Harvey's belief that preserving or constructing "a sense of place is . . . an active moment in the passage from memory to hope, from past to future."[22] In arguing for a recognition of the intersectionality of her identity as a writer, Walker claimed aspects of regional identity more typically disclaimed or denied or rejected.

In a wide-ranging 2004 interview for *Southern Cultures*, Walker spoke candidly about the continuing presence of her southern experience in her writing. "I will always draw on my background because it was so rich, and I always recognized it as being rich. I really have liked it," she confessed to William Ferris. In explaining her claim of the richness of her rural southern upbringing, she compared her response to that of Richard Wright, who "found little in his childhood to like and admire, and he often felt it was barren; I feel just the opposite. . . . When I go back to Eatonton, Georgia, I get these new reverberations of things, new enlightenment; I understand on a deeper level. That will probably always be there in the work."[23] The distinction she makes between herself and Wright is significant, because she so clearly accepts her evolution as a black woman writer from the rural South, who does not have to separate herself as distinct from her origins and therefore exceptional.

At the same time, however, Walker rejects the label of "southern writer": "I don't consider myself a southern writer. I think I'm dealing with regions inside people. The people are in the South, but I really just leave that up to other people to decide. If people can only understand the work by placing it in a context, that's fine. But I'm really trying to understand people and how they get to be the way they are. The region is the heart and the mind, not the section."[24] Her rationale for her position is revealing: "There are many reasons I am still not at ease with the southern label. Part of it is that any kind of label limits. . . . Also when you think of southern writers, you think of white southern writers. I don't really have any interest in integrating southern writers. On the other hand, how can I possibly ever not be considered a southern writer since I am a southerner and since I write?"[25] Walker's response displays the racial tension ever under the surface of the region-defined writing cadre.

In 1974, when "In Search of Our Mothers' Gardens" appeared, Walker already understood the concept of the everyday, and she articulated the practice of the everyday as crucial to a late twentieth-century understanding of the production of art and of artistic production and the art of living life fully and, as she insisted, whole. Understanding the commonplace, the ordinary, the everyday became possible as a direct result of reading the domestic landscape of quilts and gardens. The identification that Walker makes with the everyday is revolutionary, as she terms it: "*The real revolution is always concerned with the least glamorous stuff*. With raising a reading level from second grade to third. With simplifying history and writing it down (or reciting it) for the old folks. With helping illiterates fill out food-stamp forms. . . . The dull, frustrating work with our people is the work of the black revolutionary artist."[26]

Walker's identification and embracing of black women's space and the everyday, however, is not intended to bring a release from the indignity of the closed space of the segregated world of inequities for women workers. Neither does it suggest that access to the experience of the everyday in women's lives is adequate for comprehending the complexities of social and cultural relations. Walker, much like Etheridge Knight, refuses to find comfort in small victories over the containment imposed by the racial structures in place in Mississippi and the larger South. However, in her identifications that work against the grain of custom and convention, she undertakes the breaking down of oppositions, those that as Foucault suggests have "remain[ed] inviolable, that our institutions and practices have not yet dared to break down. These are oppositions that we regard as simple givens; for example, between private space and public space, between family space and social space, between cultural space and useful space, between space of leisure and that of work."[27]

What has not been sufficiently observed or credited to Walker is the geographical work of her fiction in the early 1970s. Quietly arguing against Ellison's trope of invisibility, she asserted that visibility itself is the problem. At issue, she pointed out, is the always visible, highly visible, magnified visible black body itself functioning in opposition to the naturalized white body. Her "ideological position stresses rebellion and liberation," as Elliott Butler-Evans states, and "her works address specific social and political issues," either "drawing on her involvement in the civil rights movement (an activity she views as 'revolutionary'), or arguing that her fiction must speak to the 'survival of the race,' or advancing her program for a 'womanist' ideology."[28] But rebellion and liberation come at a price both for Walker and the hypervisible, for any highly visible black body, but especially for one gendered female.

"I belong to a people so wounded by betrayal, so hurt by misplacing their trust, that to offer a gift of love is often to risk one's life," Alice Walker states in her preface to *The Same River Twice: Honoring the Difficult* (1996).[29] In positioning her own words within the context of a gift of love offered to her own black people, Walker acknowledges the several painful realities about race in America and about the role of the artist, a role she has insisted upon from the very start of her career in essays such as "The Black Writer and the Southern Experience," "'But Yet and Still the Cotton Gin Kept on Working . . .'" and "The Unglamorous but Worthwhile Duties of the Black Revolutionary Artist, or of the Black Writer Who Simply Works and Writes." She reiterates it again in *The Same River Twice*: "Art is the mirror, perhaps the only one, in which we can see our true collective face. We must honor its sacred function. We must let art help us."[30] Walker's conception of art and its place of honor within a matrix of nature and a matrilineal heritage is reflected in the titles of a number of her books: *Anything We Love Can be Saved: A Writer's Activism* (1997); *Sent by the Earth: A Message from the Grandmother Spirit* (2001); *Absolute Trust in the Goodness of the Earth: New Poems*; and *Now Is the Time to*

Open Your Heart: A Novel (2004). The spaces that Walker identifies are both natural and infused with spiritual values. My own reading is that they are all responses to the degraded sense of space emanating from a world distorted by the divisions of racial segregation and its visible inequities of material and human conservatorship, in horrific landscapes of lynching and brutality, in the injustice of extraordinary oppression rendered ordinary. This acknowledgment of a sanctification of space may function in relation to Foucault's claim that "certain desanctification of space (the one signaled by Galileo's work) has occurred, but we may still have not reached the point of a practical desanctification of space."[31]

The silencing of an oppressed group can occur, Walker reminds us, in everyday activities, in more ways than murder or lynching, which correctly or not has more often been associated with black men. Her brief sketch, "The Flowers," for example, owes much to Richard Wright's poem "Between the World and Me," in which after stumbling onto the site of a lynching replete with charred remains, white bones, scorched rope, tarred feathers, and tossed clothing, a surprised observer's perspective fuses with the lynch victim's experience of being lynched. As in Wright's visceral response to lynching, Walker introduces another layer of complexity to this recurrent horror in black experience.

Printed completely in italics, "The Flowers" locates the reality of oppression within the everyday of an innocent ten-year-old girl, who moves from the structures of rural life, *"hen house to pigpen to smokehouse"* and *"rusty boards of her family's sharecropper's cabin"* into the natural world of woods.[32] While collecting flowers in the woods, Myop discovers the remains of a lynching victim: *"It was then she stepped smack into his eyes. Her heel became lodged in the broken ridge between brow and nose, and she reached down quickly, unafraid, to free herself. It was only when she saw his naked grin that she gave a little yelp of surprise"* (120; Walker's italics). She enters the head of the lynch victim, becomes lodged there, and though she is able to disentangle her heel, she cannot free herself from the knowledge and the memory of that lynched black body. Walker concludes with the symbols of intertwined immediacy and memory: *"Myop gazed around the spot with interest. Very near where she'd stepped into the head was a wild pink rose. As she picked it up to add to her bundle, she noticed a raised mound, a ring, . . . the rotted remains of a noose, a bit of shredding plowline, now blending benignly into the soil. Around an overhanging limb of a great spreading oak clung another piece. Frayed, rotted, bleached, and frazzled—barely there—but spinning restlessly in the breeze. Myop laid down her flowers"* (120). The story ends: *"And the summer was over"* (120). With neither nostalgia nor bitterness, Walker collapses space and memory and imbricates into the idea of place the brutality with racial memory, with coming of age within a benign but horrific natural landscape, coming into knowledge of the forever present reality for the African American of the extraordinary oppression that was rendered ordinary.

At the same time, Walker suggests that spaces of exclusion, dislocation, and violence can be ameliorated in conjoining heart and earth, body to living body. In turning to a previously overlooked gendered aspect of work as oppression, Walker recounts her own mother's "working day," laboring in the fields, tending the household, raising many children: "But when, you will ask, did my overworked mother have time to know or care about feeding the creative spirit? The answer is so simple that many of us have spent years discovering it. We have constantly looked high, when we should have looked high—and low."[33] At once, Walker focuses attention on "overworked mother," "creative spirit," "discovering," "high—and low." In situating her overworked mother within the rhetorical and conceptual contexts of "creative spirit" and our "discovering" that creativity and spirit in "high" places (or art) and "low" places (also art), she positions her racialized mother within a space that redefines art as gendered and racial, but she also identifies oppressive work in terms of gender, the maternal duties and responsibilities taken for granted as fulfilling rather than oppressive.

The difference between the low place, where the creativity of those like Walker's mother manifests itself, and the high place, where the expected production of "art" resides, involves both gender stratification and racial arrangements. Spatial segregation, then, is both controlled separation and hierarchical compartmentalization. It is not merely about maintaining power but also about determining what constitutes power. As Daphne Spain points out, the division of labor in societies such as the one Walker depicts is simultaneously gendered and spatial: "By controlling access to knowledge and resources through the control of space, the dominant group's ability to retain and reinforce its position is enhanced. Thus, spatial boundaries contribute to the unequal status of women. For women to become more knowledgeable, they must change places."[34] This contextualization of change is, as well, the beginning of a proposition on how gender too is spatially constructed and how reading the domestic geography of quilts and gardens allows for a different construction of the southern racial space, one leveling the hierarchy of creative and artistic significance. Given her attentive gaze on the spaces occupied by earlier generations of women in her family, it is not surprising that on her fiftieth birthday in February 1994, Alice Malsenior Walker changed her middle name from that of one of her mother's sisters to "Tallulah-Kate" in honor of her mother, Minnie Tallulah Grant Walker, and her paternal grand-mother, Kate Nelson Walker.[35]

Contrary to race, space, and gender representation in the fiction of Ernest Gaines, who chose to make his fiction out of his racial and cultural memories of the past in a specified and contained space that is largely unchanged yet simultaneously dynamic and volatile, Walker refuses to ignore the presence of positive attributes of racial difference within a segregated society. Focusing on the social geography that makes exclusion and containment acceptable foregrounds the normalizing of restrictive social controls in order to produce a specific system of race-based identity and social relations in the South. If for Gaines the legal state construct, the parish, functions not only as a division of public space but as a way of dividing resources and people, then for Walker, it is the natural configurations of landscape itself, represented by gardens and growth, that signify what is enabling in the lives of oppressed people. While in Gaines's texts, prisons become emblematical of the relegation of a cordoned-off, negative space to blacks, who in the physical constraints of their everyday experiential realities suffer the restraints of a color caste along with the race caste, in Walker no human-made structures can imprison the spirit of individuals, particularly women, who connect their gifts of love and vision to creativity and reproduction, physical and aesthetic. Gaines's fiction is persistently architecturally invested in spatial demarcations and the social distinctions stemming from them; Walker moves in the direction early on of an ecology of space and race.

In her first book of short stories, *In Love and Trouble: Stories of Black Women* (1973), which ends with "To Hell with Dying," and in her first book of poems, *Once* (1968), Walker configures the emotional matrices and racial spaces that mark the public dimension of her vision: the American South, black women, Africa, and civil rights. But she also includes the main concerns of her personal life: love and suicide. The ironical story "The Diary of an African Nun" reconstitutes the emotional ambivalent tone of "Karamojans," a sequence of short poems set in an East Africa of Kenya and Uganda rife with cultural clashes and the incongruities between European and African ideology. The African name for Dee, the ambiguously figured daughter in the story "Everyday Use," is "Wangero Leewanika Kemanjo," comparable to "Wangari," the Kikuyu name given to the "I" narrator, a young African American college student, in "African Images: Glimpses from a Tiger's Back," the poetic sequence opening *Once* and questioning how to reclaim an alien heritage. From her earliest publications, Walker represented a fluidity as real and palpable between geographic spaces in the United States and Africa as well as bodily spaces of women of African descent in the diaspora.

The efforts by officials to brutalize and diminish the lives of blacks in Walker's fiction are never completely successful despite the legal reaches of Jim Crow. In "The Revenge of Hannah Kemhuff," two Depression-era black women counter the official denial of relief aid by reassessing their commodity holdings; the one with an excess of processed flour can exchange it for the other's abundant cornmeal. Not only does the value of the denied goods dissipate under the arrangement, but also the authority of the white relief worker over their lives diminishes. In breaking the hierarchical racial bonds signified by dependency, the exchange also levels the force of restriction and constraint and substitutes a horizontal gendered bonding marked by equity. Segregation has not been dismantled by the active cooperation of the women, but it has lost its ability to imprison the women within its economic structure.

"The Revenge of Hannah Kemhuff" repeats a story encoding dual spaces of memory: the collective one Walker's mother remembered about the Depression in Georgia and told to Alice during her childhood; and also the social one Zora Neale Hurston collected and represented as a curse from folk culture. The Depression in modern times functions as a heightened example of the economic deprivation and exploitation of African Americans that is one legacy of the unequal power relations evidenced during slavery, after emancipation, during Reconstruction, and during their aftermaths.

Walker values "art," whether oral stories or other aspects of expressive folk culture, as a metonym for the conversion of the private space into the public and for the assessment of value and worth out of a different set of measures. Her valuation would take more fully into account what Paula Gunn Allen has termed "background" in her interpretation of a Keres Indian tale:

> Westerners have for a long time discounted the importance of background. The earth herself, which is our most inclusive background, is dealt with summarily as a source of food, metals, water, and profit, while the fact that she is the fundamental agent of all planetary life is blithely ignored. . . . An antibackground bias is bound to have social costs that have so far remained unexplored, but elite attitudes toward workers, nonwhite races, and women are all part of the price we pay for overvaluing the foreground.
>
> In the Western mind, shadows highlight the foreground. In contrast, in the tribal view, the mutual relationships among shadows and light in all their varying degrees of intensity create a living web of definition

and depth, and significance arises from their interplay. Traditional and contemporary tribal arts and crafts testify powerfully to the importance of balance among all elements in tribal perspective, aesthetics, and social systems.[36]

Walker's quilt, then, may be read as balance between foreground and background, the relationship among shadows and light, "a living web of definition and depth," whose interconnection and interplay direct us at once toward and away from gender and race, traditional and nontraditional, high and low, as socially and culturally constructed distinctions or categories. Its pattern, technology, and production do not presuppose dominance from an external social or cultural reality. Its very existence is diversity creatively organized to make a textured, interdependent, and lasting whole.[37] Importantly, however, the quilt also becomes a map detailing that experience occurs within a place, and the reading of the map and its geographical accuracy will change over time with new boundaries and new demarcations but also with new readers who may well have a different spatial orientation, a different conception of their bearings, of where they are in relation to the marking on a map. It is as Audre Lorde suggested in an interview: "What you chart is already where you've been. But where we are going, there is no chart yet."[38]

Walker maps the black woman's body as one of the key spaces in reading postmodern space and global place, and she insists upon including her own body as the subject of geographical knowledge. The anonymous black woman artist from Alabama herself becomes the second part of the map that Walker outlines as part of her project of making a black woman's subjectivity central to thinking about both art and history. While assuming a locational epistemology based on changing geographical and historical specificity, she clearly has had this necessary dual reappropriation at the center of her work.

Walker's canon flows from the often dark interior, an internality that, once refracted, takes shape in the literal, the externality of physical places, people, voices, and institutions, all reflections of the visions conjured out of the night of a soul's deep struggle to actualize its existence concretely in discrete moments. Those moments transmuted become the action and events, the mythologies of multiple selves so prominent in her fiction. Central to the symbology of pain and struggle is the geography of the black female body, a geography mapped most vividly against the social and political realities of the American South.

II. GEOGRAPHIES OF THE BLACK FEMALE BODY

Any revolutionary "project" today, whether utopian or realistic, must, if it is to
avoid hopeless banality, make the reappropriation of the body, in association with
the reappropriation of space, into a non-negotiable part of its agenda.
—HENRI LEFEBVRE, *The Production of Space*

Mapping the black woman's body as the new geography of race and region may be one way of rethinking Walker's canon. Inscripted into Walker's fiction are the multiple geographies of identity and of the racial body, which repeatedly is the body of the woman. This positioning is suggestive of the fact that the black racial identity follows from the race of the mother and that women constitute a continuity of cultural identity, of futurity and possibility. Walker is invested in the ways of making the black woman's body visible within the polarities of race segregation and gender separation. One aspect of this investment is the prominence of the mother-woman as the space for reexamining not merely race or race relations, but cultural production and ultimately aesthetic relations as well. Walker inserts the black woman's body as one of the key spaces in postmodern readings of place.[39] The space of the body itself, then, is relationally understood, but not in the reductive way of defining women in terms of relational identities as wives, mothers, sisters, and so on. "If gender is defined as a construct that is congruent with the dominant discourses and practices of a particular location, rather than as a fixed or stale category," according to Linda McDowell, then "it prises [*sic*] open a space to examine not only the ways in which a particular heterosexual performance becomes hegemonic but also the prospect of resistance to it."[40]

While *The Third Life of Grange Copeland* (1970) or *The Color Purple* (1982) would serve equally well alongside her pathbreaking essays as illustrations of Walker's intervention in Southern Studies, I will here focus on *Meridian* (1976), which points both forward and backward in terms of the direction of segregation and the body and signals Walker's development of increasingly complex conceptions of race, gender, and location. "Meridian" is a geographical referent and a place name, the name of a town in the state of Mississippi. Meridian becomes not only the title of Walker's novel but also the name of the title character. Inscripted into Walker's fiction are the multiple geographies of identity and of the racial body, which repeatedly is the body of the woman in a life struggle for gender and cultural identity. Meridian Hill as black mother-woman emerges as the space for reexamining race and social relations, as well as political engagement and cultural production. Meridian as body and as space is the site in which new social arrangements can be formed and on which new political theory can be written.

Meridian, marking a philosophical turn in Walker's fiction, takes up the idea of protest and the forms of protest available to rights activists. Following The Third Life of Grange Copeland, in which Walker also takes up the civil rights activism of the 1960s, particularly the voting-rights campaigns in Mississippi and the rest of the Deep South, Meridian represents the human face of social change and transformation occurring after the Supreme Court's ruling in Brown v. Board of Education (1954) struck down the "separate but equal" ideology that had legalized segregation following Plessy v. Ferguson (1896). Meridian provides a personal narrative for the collective rights revolution and for what is at stake in the thinking about both mid-twentieth-century transformation in the interpretation of laws affecting rights and the regression in the interpretations at the end of the century. It recalls attention to the rationale and necessity of strategic bodies on the line during the marches, protests, and demonstrations, and the workings of capital in cultural contexts, by a recognition of the significance of commerce and financial units and by an understanding of the interconnectedness of business practices and social structures.

Meridian Hill lives through the segregation in the South, through northern migration, and through a return to the South to emerge as a new leader in the movement for social equality. Yet, in reading the novel through the lens of space, there are two interconnections, geographical power of location and the bodily condition of vigor, that emerge from the definitions of "meridian" delineated as a textual epigraph. Walker begins with the primary definition for "meridian" the noun, "pertaining to midday, or to the south," but quickly moves on to a list of six variant definitions. The second and the fifth are especially relevant here. The second is: "(a) the highest point of power, prosperity, splendor, etc.; zenith; apex; culmination; (b) the middle period of one's life, regarded as the highest point of health, vigor, etc.; prime." In calling attention to power and prosperity, and simultaneously health and vigor, Walker poses what will develop as an ironic commentary on the situation within her text, when the economics of power and cultures of wealth will be challenged by Meridian Hill who, as she enters her prime intellectually and spiritually in the recognition of rights and justice, is also devoid of health and vigor.

The fifth definition of "meridian" reads: "5. In geography, (a) a great circle of the earth passing through the geographical poles and any given point on the earth's surface; (b) the half of such a circle between the poles; (c) any of the lines of longitude running north and south on a globe or map, representing such a circle or half-circle." Geographical tropes, foreshadowed by the definitions of "meridian" Walker includes, connect the North and the South and occur throughout the text. For the circle of rights activists, their spatial location functions to define the beliefs and ideological conditions under which they function. These geographical tropes intersect with the idea of economic and political power poised against spiritual and moral power and economic justice. Whereas within both the civil rights movement and traditional political organizations, politics has generally focused on men and a masculinist enterprise, Walker turns the struggle for rights and power into a political realm that contains the domestic, the private or personal, and the physical body of a woman. The circular space she creates is in keeping with the new geographies of gender and of raced gender that were beginning to achieve prominence in the 1970s.

The protagonist, Meridian Hill, is no simplistic participant in civil rights activism. Instead, she is a woman akin to Fannie Lou Hamer who comes to terms with society's construction of gender roles, with the hegemony of social attitudes around race, with the deficiencies in the expectations for motherhood and maternity, with the burden of sexuality and heterosexual relations. In ever-widening spheres, Meridian becomes conscious of her rights as a woman, a citizen, and a black, and with the evolution of her thought, she moves to positions of greater isolation within the available communities. In isolation she reconnects to the geographies of rights that have reconfigured the history of the nation and its people. Walker ends the list of definitions of the noun and then the adjective, "meridian," with: "5. southern. [Rare.]." This definition is a way simultaneously of prefacing the construction of Meridian Hill herself and of locating the text itself in delineating the rights revolution. Here, keeping region as open to possibility and politically to difference, Walker allows specifically for both the southern context and for the rare appearance of Meridian, who at the very beginning of the novel stares down a tank purchased "during the sixties when the townspeople who were white felt under attack from 'outside agitators'—those members of the black community who thought that equal rights for all should extend to blacks."[41] Justice, conflated in this instance with Meridian's body and her action, is not an overarching, large, and opaque illusory pursuit, but rather it is immediate, personal, attainable, and transparent. But justice also becomes performative.[42]

The past, contextualized racially in the novel by seemingly digressive and metafictional narratives, has been fraught with pain and complicated by the legacies of the premodern period, in particular the Middle Passage, chattel slavery, failed Reconstruction, and Jim Crow segregation and justice. These social and historical realities have impacted family structure, gender roles, and self-actualization, naming, and subject formation. How to be a man or a woman given the social realities of enslavement and its detrimental political legacies? How to articulate gender construction and social roles for men and women within texts? They have raised questions about how to organize and perpetuate family given the destructive majority practices that would deny for nearly two centuries the existence of familial bonds among African Americans and the connections of African Americans to their white or Native American blood relatives. In one interrogation of race and color, Walker writes of one of the main white characters in *Meridian*: "By being white Lynne was guilty of whiteness. . . . Then the question was is it possible to be guilty of color? Of course, for years black people were 'guilty' of being black. Slavery was a punishment for their color" (149). How then to organize and perpetuate relationships or family within texts as well as in society? These are the questions African American writers continue to engage because at their root is the inescapable need to displace the simplistic objectification of black people and to establish the multifaceted subjectivity of individuals identifying with a group of people and a body of experience, not all of which is retrievable outside of a political and aesthetic construction of racial memory.

In *Meridian*, Walker describes African American life in spatial terms as a culture of embodied memory, of expressive, created, and creative racial memory that extends beyond cultural archeology, digging up the records, documents, myths, folklore, and stories of the past. It reaches beyond the reconstruction of history, changing the historical paradigms relegating African American lives to static oppositional and dominated rigidities. Walker's description instead frees and imagines the unimaginable always possible and always already free. Not surprising, then, Melissa Walker reads *Meridian* as "flashback documentary of the civil rights movement that presents raw history in a nonnarrative spatial structure" and as a "crazy quilt" but "more complex and intricate" because of its fragments and surreal stories and "pictures within pictures that the stories make."[43]

In situating the title character within a rural family, a southern black women's college, a northern city, and a civil rights movement, the text recombines the divergent dialogical and ideological strands of a contemporary African American woman's life into a modern parable of search for spiritual meaning and racial identity within the existing social and political structures and the educational and economic systems. In undoing an explicitly hegemonic and white racialized masculinist understanding of politics within the then-volatile context of the American South and African American life, Walker equates women's rights with the rights of "the people," as she repeatedly uses the term within the text. Political space gendered male then becomes as much her subject as racially segregated space. Meridian seeks a means of controlling space and of positioning herself bodily within a public sphere previously denied to people of color, particularly within the American South.

Similar to Richard Wright, Walker initiates a discourse on the problematical relationship between idealized desires for new space in public and complicated realities within redefined but shifting and migratory spaces. Whereas in writing the intersection between race and place, Wright sought to expose the exclusionary practices of the white South as rigid, often brutal enforcement of the segregation of races and a concomitant segregation of the professions, Walker draws the political and psychological space associated with the South/North axis and with the northern migration as less than liberating for Meridian, Truman Held, Lynne, or Anne-Marion, all of whom claim some form of art as their vocation.

The claim of art on the body is linked to one of the dominant discourses in Walker's poetry: the idea of "the too full self." She represents it as the spilling over into a reconciliation of self, the healing of the fractured physical body or mind, beautifying it to reflect the reality of an inner beauty or essence, the "soul" in both a black linguistic sense and a philosophical sense. As an erasure of a fractured and wounded self, reconciliation comes out of pain and despair, dark nights of the soul struggling with epistemological and existential questions. "Sometimes I feel so bad / I ask myself / Who in the world / Have I murdered?" This question, posed in "Family Of" from *Horses Make a Landscape Look More Beautiful* (1984), is not unlike the one Meridian's mother asks, "Have you stolen anything?" "Would you kill for freedom?" is another of the questions in *Revolutionary Petunias* (1973); it is the same question that culminates in Meridian Hill's ideological split with her radical friends. To release oneself from the physical prison that the body maimed by cultural, conditional, and social constructs can become requires self-examination, but also self-confrontation.

Walker constructs a countervailing black interiority in the title poem of *Revolutionary Petunias,*

Sammy Lou of Rue
sent to his reward
the exact creature who

murdered her husband,
using a cultivator's hoe
with verve and skill;
and laughed fit to kill
in disbelief
at the angry, militant
pictures of herself.[44]

On her way to the electric chair, Sammy Lou's last words are "'Always respect the word of God,'" and "'Don't yall forget to *water* / my purple petunias.'"[45] She prefigures Sofia in *The Color Purple*, the short sketch "Petunias" from *You Can't Keep a Good Woman Down* (1981), and the unnamed narrator of "How Did I Get Away with Killing One of the Biggest Lawyers in the State? It Was Easy" from the same collection of short stories. A racially defined avenger, Sammy Lou refuses the images projected onto her body. Having taken the life of a destroyer, she goes to her own death preserving beauty and affirming life.

In *Meridian*, Walker responds to the history of structural violence against black and native people within the United States and the South specifically. In contemplation of the human imprint on land, Walker presents the trope of the Indian burial mound and the trope of the Sojourner Tree. The burial mound in its roundness and the tree in the isolation that makes it round become figures of being. Each in a sense suggests what Gaston Bachelard remarks in *The Poetics of Space* as "being concentrated upon itself."[46] In the case of the immobile tree and mound, Walker contemplates how human beings attempt to shape the natural world to match their ideology and their thinking about hierarchy, about movement, and even about justice. Space divides as much as politics does. The Sojourner Tree, a giant magnolia that, according to legend, grew from the severed tongue of a slave woman named Louvinie, is isolated in an urban setting linking naturalized behavior (the Wild Child) with the desire for nature's empathetic existence (the tree itself). With these two tropes, Walker points to a displacement, a missing interdependence and an erasure of women's lives and an absence of ideology encompassing difference, both racial and gender difference. The Wild Child is run down by a car, the modern machine of individual mobility, and the tree is cut down by rampaging students rebelling against the repressive authority of Saxon College officials who had reprimanded the students for being activists against segregation.

The narrative strategy in part gestures toward realigning oneself with the past as a continuum and to understanding how economic structures lead

ALICE WALKER MATTERS

to the mistreatment and abuse of women and children, or those rendered helpless by the overdetermination and overexertion of patriarchal power. Segregation of the women into civilized and "primitive" (Saxon College and Wild Child) cannot be justified or maintained. The categories of separation in public spaces, whether by race, gender, or class, all come under attack.

Meridian's ancestor, Feather Mae, recognizes that what is hidden in the mound is akin to what is hidden within herself. Meridian also responds to the topology, to the secret graves, as part of herself. Feather Mae's story, like the digressive narratives flowing through the text, may be read as a recursive text, layering, as Karla Holloway has suggested in examining recursive structures in literature and language, "memory and discourse and mythic figures within language and culture until each is folded into the other."[47] The resultant body space is discursively and symbolically rich.

Walker connects poverty, racism, and sexism with economics. In particular, she examines the destruction of an Indian burial mound for a commercial park as part of the continuing commodification of culture and destruction of the spiritual. She constructs the feminist forerunner of Suzan-Lori Parks's *The America Play* (1994). Importantly, she constructs the female body and its female progeny as the site through which the politics must be viewed. In the representation of the burial mound, Walker juxtaposes the social configurations of segregated life in the South and the hierarchies of power inherent in physical spaces. The imaginative and political work Meridian Hill undertakes is an outgrowth of both nature and history and gender. The mound, feminized in Walker's rendering, foregrounds the visual work that connects the Sojourner Tree and burial mound.

Walker, however, locates the Indian burial mound as natural, primordial, but also constructed, built. It signifies the discursive and visual culture of images, metaphors, dreamscapes, and fantasies produced in her text as "southern" experience. Although she briefly incorporates paintings by black artists such as Romare Bearden into the domestic space of Truman's mother and also depicts Truman's own paintings in his New York art studio, Walker focuses greater attention on the burial mound. She concludes with the conception of the mound as an extension of the very body of Feather Mae, and with Feather Mae as the protector of the mound—a charge her descendants share. But given the mixture of fantasy and realism in the text, Meridian is ultimately powerless to stop the flow of "progress" or the commercialization of sacred and feminine space. Bachelard points out that "images of *full roundness* help us to collect ourselves, permit us to confer an initial constitution on ourselves, and to confirm our being intimately, inside. For when it is experienced from the inside, devoid of all exterior features, being cannot be otherwise than round."[48] He suggests that the "imagination of round being follows its own law. . . . The world is round around the round being."[49] That concept is one that Nikky Finney adheres to in creating the poems in *The World Is Round*.[50]

The importance of the southern Indian burial mound and Native American heritage to Walker's ideology became much more apparent at the end of the 1990s. In naming her passions for a *Ms. Magazine* interview, Walker mentioned the sovereignty movement in Hawaii and Hawaiian poet Haunani-Kay Trask's *From a Native Daughter* (1993) along with her desire to understand what it means to be black and Indian and her plan to initiate healing circles and women's and elders' councils on the land. She states: "These circles won't be designed to solve any problems, but for us to connect with each other and get grounded. Each circle will eventually connect with other circles around the globe so that, over time, we'll get a stronger sense of who we are, as just regular people, in the world. . . . . We will have to try to be present as loving, compassionate earthlings. . . . It's important to comfort and be with each other during this time because so many people are alone."[51] She links the idea of healing circles to her creation of the blended African and Native people, the Mundo, in *By the Light of My Father's Smile*.

In recent years, Walker has increasingly identified herself with a Native American ancestry. She has said, "My mother was Cherokee, and she had that real Indian belief that basically you let things live where they grow. When you grow them, you don't cut them, you just let them be. But my sister [Molly], who actually looks very much like my mother's grandmother, very Cherokee looking, had gone to school. She knew that there were people who actually cut flowers and brought them into the house. This was a different way of looking at things."[52] In the short stories of *The Way Forward Is with a Broken Heart* (2000), Walker presents an expanded version of the Native American heritage she discussed in her *Southern Cultures* interview and places the fictional characters within that lineage of mixed-race Native and African people:

> My sister who looks more Cherokee than me, and more European, tells me the Cherokee great-grandmother from whom we descend was herself mad. She was part African. What did that mean in a tribe that kept slaves and were as colorist . . . as the white settlers who drove them from their homes? I do feel I have had to wrestle with our great-grandmother's spirit and bring it to peace. . . . So that now when I participate in Indian ceremonies I do not feel strange, . . . but exactly who I am, an African-AmerIndian with a Native American in her soul.[53]

This narrative not only references the autobiographical Walker herself but the fictional Feather Mae as well.

In *Meridian*, the cost of the movement, of activity across race lines, the personal loss, including an alienation from family and community, and ultimately the potential for rejuvenation all play out in the body of Meridian Hill. Walker reads the interlocking structures of history in tracing the development of Meridian's associates in the movement, Truman Held and Anne-Marion. The missing, the erased, the absent, the lost all are written on Meridian's very body. As John Fiske has put it, "The body and its specific behavior is where the power system stops being abstract and becomes material. The body is where it succeeds or fails, where it is acceded to or struggled against. The struggle for control is top-down vs. bottom up, is waged on the material terrain of the body and its immediate context."[54] The trope of Meridian's undiagnosed debilitating illness with a concomitant hair loss destabilizes any notion of a clear-cut solution to the problem of conflicting ideology so highly visible in the text.

In the final section, Truman Held tells Meridian: "'[Y]our ambivalence will always be deplored by people who consider themselves revolutionists, and our unorthodox behavior will cause traditionalists to gnash their teeth'" (227). Meridian's response is clear: "'But that is my value. . . . Besides, all the people who are as alone as I am will one day gather at the river. We will watch the evening sun go down. And in the darkness maybe we will know the truth'" (227). Collective action remains Meridian's best hope for combating and resisting corrupt, false power. Two aspects of materiality conjoin—the body and the land (where land meets water in the flow of geographic reckoning). The "we," comprised of those who are not just women, black, and southern like Meridian but also men (like Truman) and white (like Lynne) and northern (like Anne-Marion), constitutes a new political entity engaged with the world as it is but charged to come together in a transformative process. Just as in the poems of *Revolutionary Petunias*, the civil rights movement becomes an agent for freeing individuals from a spiritually deadening lethargy that functioned as an escape from the racism circumscribing their lives. Freedom, however, burdens with isolation and loneliness and death; "we, cast out alone / to heal / and re-create / ourselves," Meridian Hill writes in her poem of "catharsis, redemption and hope," individual transcendence over suffering and confusion (219).

Years after writing those poetic lines for Meridian Hill in her novel, Walker expressed their substance once again in a context related to her own collection of poetry *Absolute Trust in the Goodness of the Earth*, written after "the attacks on the World Trade Towers and the Pentagon" when she recalls "feeling a deep sadness about the events and an incredible weariness that once again whatever questions had been raised were to be answered by war."[55] The poems came after a period in which, like Meridian, Walker said of herself: "I would like to become a wandering inspiration. . . . I had an image of myself showing up wherever people gathered to express their determination to have a future or to celebrate the present, speaking, reading, playing on my very simple musical instruments, and just being around."[56]

Walker replaces the fictional Meridian with her own wandering body. She further explores the connection between her own wanderings and those of the wandering woman character in the novel *Now Is the Time to Open Your Heart* (2003) by giving the wanderer-protagonist her grandmother's name, Kate Nelson, and investing her with facets of Walker's own autobiography, in addition to many of the concerns for the earth as Earth Mother evident in *Absolute Trust in the Goodness of the Earth* and some of the fusions of fiction and autobiography found in *The Way Forward Is with a Broken Heart*. Kate, like Walker herself and her fictional precursor, Meridian, travels through places as well as through spiritual realms in search of meaning and unity in her life. Kate dreams of rivers as the flow of life and sets out to find her own inner flow. She ultimately arrives in Hawaii, but she exists in a space where only love remains. Kate's discovery in the end echoes Meridian's return to spiritual and physical health and to a philosophy of love.

Some part of Meridian is, according to Truman, "exactly the same as she had always been," but a "new part had grown out of the old . . . new, sure and ready, even eager, for the world" (227). Her body, however, is not the same; it has not changed gender, but it has constructed a new, multiple-gendered identity. Meridian's preparedness for leadership moves her into a new reality of identity once associated with masculinity in the narrative, but her readiness for struggle and battle includes forgiveness and love, and with them an unwavering commitment to spiritual revolution as power within a very material world. Decidedly utopic in its final rendering of both the polarities of space and segregation and the body of a black woman, who perhaps may be read as transgendered, *Meridian* ultimately locates itself not merely in analogy to the American South but to all political spaces of society and as seminal in Walker's reading of her own heterotopic location both bodily and spatially today.

At the end of *The Third Life of Grange Copeland*, Walker depicts a carload of black and white youths driving Georgia's back roads to register black voters. She has one of them connect Grange Copeland's appearance to that of Bayard

Rustin, the brilliant organizer of the 1963 March on Washington. With that casual reference, Walker links a legendary hero of the civil rights movement and a gay rights activist with an uneducated, poor farmer in the segregated South. In so doing, she moves Grange, her first representation of the possibility for a transformative southern mentality and/or a changed configuration of southern rights and privileges, into a realm of political action for rights. That new realm is far beyond the sphere of suffrage and voter registration. It is situated in the arena of gender equity and in the space of sexualities heretofore unmarked in her texts. The iconography of the past melds into that of the future.

Walker's relocation away from Mississippi and the South would prove to be permanent. Since her departure in 1971, she has visited but not resided in the South. Yet, the South remained central to the work she produced throughout the 1970s and 1980s. When she moved to California in 1981, she located to a rural place "that [her] characters liked," as she put it: "And no wonder: it looked a lot like the town in Georgia most of them were from, only it was more beautiful and the local swimming hole was not segregated." She found in Northern California a peace in nature and a space for herself that issued in an even more productive literary career. There she completed the writing of *The Color Purple* (1982), her best-selling novel that won a Pulitzer Prize for Fiction and an American Book Award and made ignoring the cultural map that Walker drew impossible. She attended, as Deborah McDowell maintains in *"The Changing Same": Black Women's Literature, Criticism, and Theory* (1995), to family matters seldom discussed: physical and sexual abuse of black women by close kin. By entering into the most public of spaces with the book and the 1985 Steven Spielberg film, Walker focused attention not only on the South as subject but on ways of representing place and power. Minrose Gwin ably demonstrates how Walker's badly abused protagonist ultimately seizes control of all aspects of her material condition, her body, her sexuality, her letters, her self, and her "father's house and transforms it into felicitous space"—a term she draws from Judith Fryer's work in *Felicitous Space: The Imaginative Structures of Edith Wharton and Willa Cather* (1986).[57]

Though praised by many critics and feminists for unveiling the brutality of sexism within a racial community, the epistolary account of an abused, barely literate southern female offended other critics, who charged Walker with misrepresentation of African American males and promotion of negative racial images. Translated into twenty-two languages, the controversial book, coupled with Spielberg's even more controversial film, nonetheless made the author a celebrity.

From the mid-1980s on, however, African American male critics have attacked her vision in her writing. In "In the Closet of the Soul," she quotes at length from a review of her volume of poems *Horses Make a Landscape Look More Beautiful* in order to respond to a query from an African American woman who asked for her reaction to the criticism of her "negative" black male character, Mister, in *The Color Purple*. The reviewer, K. T. H. Cheatwood, wrote: "So as I receive Alice Walker's 11th book (she had edited an additional one as well) and her fourth volume of poetry, I face my usual decision: Given my disdain for what she and her work represent, in too large a part, should I assess her work? I know I can count on having to cut through her whimpering, half-balanced neurosis and wonder how on earth to avoid an exercise in negativity."[58]

Despite such hostile reviews of *The Color Purple*, Walker had the attention of southern critics and writers and black writers and critics. A "Black South" awareness became visible, and the space of race and identity within the southern context attracted notice from a variety of quarters, including Steven Spielberg and Hollywood. In just over a decade, Walker's revolutionizing southscape caused a major intervention in how southern identity and southern literature were conceived and written. In locating a spatial context that complements her sense of her self and her art, Walker produced visionary prose and poetry. She has become an active literary model for the gendered work of several succeeding generations of black southern women writers, including Gayl Jones, Elizabeth Brown-Guillory, Endesha Ida Mae Holland, Fatima Shaik, Shay Youngblood, Tina McElroy Ansa, Natasha Trethewey, Olympia Vernon, and Patricia Spears Jones, but she also became the inspiration for white writers as different as Dorothy Allison, Kaye Gibbons, and Jill McCorkle. At the same time, students and scholars of southern literature were hard-pressed to exclude black writers from their readings and analyses. The intervention that Walker made into a polarized and segregated area of study is remarkable both for the major break that it produced with past work and for the disappearance of her achievement from critical annals.

At the same time, however, her reputation as a major feminist essayist, earned initially with *In Search of Our Mothers' Gardens*, now reaches across racial and regional divisions. Cheryl Wall has maintained that "despite her reputation as a novelist, short story writer, and poet, [Walker] has done her best work in the essay, a genre that has at present little critical currency."[59] In fact, Walker's term "womanist" from her early volume has become a theoretical paradigm, one used in black feminist thinking and writing throughout the 1980s and that continues to hold currency now with ethicists, theologians, scholars, and preachers such as Renita Weems, Cheryl Townsend Gilkes, and Katie Cannon. Her second book of essays, *Living by the Word: Selected Essays, 1973–1987* (1988), confirmed her visionary faith in healing powers of the word and of human interconnection so admired by theologians. The final essay in the collection, "The Universe Responds: Or, How I Learned We Can Have Peace on Earth," has reiterated the message that is most prominent in her recent writings: "I know now [prayer] to be the active affirmation in the physical world of our inseparableness from the divine; and everything, *especially* the physical world is divine. War will stop when we no longer praise it. . . . Peace will come whenever it is sincerely invited. Love will overflow every sanctuary given it. Truth will grow where the fertilizer that nourishes it is also truth. Faith will be its own reward."[60]

Championing these values and beliefs, Walker has come to emphasize global peace and universal interconnection. *Horses Make a Landscape Look More Beautiful: Poems, Her Blue Body Everything We Know: Earthling Poems, 1965–1990* (1991), and *Hard Times Require Furious Dancing: New Poems* (2010) have demonstrated her commitment to poetic expression not only as "saving lives" but as healing hearts. *The Temple of My Familiar* (1989) expanded the range of creative concerns and historical parameters marking her previous novels and with *Possessing the Secret of Joy* (1992) in particular made the African diaspora center to her concerns with black women's bodies. The international geography apparent in her representations of France and Africa in her early writings has persisted, particularly because, with the loss of her immediate family members in Georgia, she has had fewer reasons to return to that region. The experimental *The Temple of My Familiar* affirmed her determination to push the limits of fictional forms beyond the expected or the safe. Each subsequent text has forwarded her visionary construction of herself and the world, and in turn each places her within the realm of global awareness marking new geographic demarcations at the center of recent scholarly interrogations.

Walker's prose and poetry reverberate with a cluster of themes recapitulated and modulated over the course of her career: spiritual survival, individual identity, familial heritage, community, freedom, power, and vision. Her social history as a southern child of poverty and segregation and her personal experiences as an African American female in a world of changing racial and gender dynamics contribute to her insistent discourses on human survival, on what she has termed "spiritual survival, the survival *whole* of my people." *Once*, and the poems that follow it, charts an emotive-responsive chronicle of autobiographical incidents and an emotionally ciphered exploration of formative ideas that are developed thematically in subsequent fictional texts, both short stories and novels. In her earliest fiction, she emphasized the survival of self in hostile environments.

The major restrictive environments were patterned after the American South and southern history, because as she has said, nothing is ever "a product of the immediate present." While history can become a prison locking African Americans into racial constructions based on societal figurations from the past, for Walker within the very polarities of segregation in the South of her youth is a space of futurity and liberation. In *The Third Life of Grange Copeland* and *In Love and Trouble*, she represented southern men and women who, oppressed because of their race and bondage to the land, suffered irreparable physical and psychological damage. Few of them, she concluded, survive whole. Victimized by racial and sexual oppression, dehumanized by economic exploitation, they often fail to recognize the forces distorting their lives, and as a result, they perpetuate the violence done to themselves. Yet, she has maintained that some of these individuals "persist in their beauty in spite of everything"; their whole stories demanded attention. In telling their stories, she returns to the possibility for transformation, for a rebirth and redemption. And in many ways, she rejuvenated racial writing in the South and forwarded a fresh awareness of gender within the literature of the South.

In her preface to *Absolute Trust in the Goodness of the Earth: New Poems*, Alice Walker renews the architectural imaginary that infused her early writing: "Most of these poems were written at Casa Madre, our ochre red house, my daughter's and mine, on the central coast in Mexico. I had moved out of the large white room with veranda looking toward the Pacific and into what is usually a guest bedroom. Smaller, darker, quieter; less yang, far, far more yin."[61] In the aftermath of September 11 and the attacks on the World Trade Center and the Pentagon, Walker believes that she "could not have written these poems in a bright sunny room where there were no shadows."[62] Even as she has moved into a wider and wider diasporic identity, leaving behind in time but not memory the South of her youth, Walker invests her rich present with the poverty of that past. In "New House Moves," she writes:

> I dreamed
> Last night
> That I had moved
> Into a roomy new house.
>
> How many new houses
> Have I moved into?

                And isn't there
        Something always
                        Behind
These new house
                        Moves?

        When I was a child
    We moved each year
                    My parents
            Working hard
        Making nothing
        For themselves
        Except decency
                    That went
            To the bone.

The poet dreams that she is always moving,

                    Finding shacks
                    & rundown
                    Houses
                Fixing them up
                & then moving
                    On.

But she realizes in a conclusion that returns to the image of her parents and
their South that dominated her childhood:

        Poverty never prepared me
                    For this wealth.

                    Or to live
            In the houses
                    My parents
                    Stubbornly
                    Dreamed.[63]

The dual focus on houses, domestic spaces connected to her own childhood
in Georgia, and on mobility, movement to other spatial locations and into
other class and wealth categories, mark much of the world poetry Walker has
produced in recent years. Repeatedly, there is a global focus emerging out of
the specifics of her southern roots and her regional acculturation as a share-

cropper's daughter from Georgia. In "My Ancestors' Earnings," for example, she writes: "For over a decade / My ancestors / Earned for me / Over a / Million dollars / A year." The irony, of course, is biting:

With our righteous loot
        We bought
                For me
        Every house
            We truly
            Loved
        Every car
              & work
Of art in earlier times
(Laboring, laboring
Over uncleared fields
      & kitchen floors
      That had no end)
           Drenched in
              Sweat
           We were
           Denied.[64]

The natural world that Walker values and the ecological awareness she champions now with a spiritual ferocity both emanate from her memory of the rural Georgia environment of her youth and flow from there through the many permeations of her experiences in Africa as a college student, in Mississippi as a young woman, and in California as a mature author. Casa Madre, the house in Mexico, is but another of the structures, pieces of the built environment, that she uses as a segue into the natural environment, the extension of the body itself—and the places marked by the contradictions of oppositional actions, the polarity harking back to the segregated world of her youth and the lessons learned there.

Walker has said that since the writing of her first book of poems, "it seems to me that all of my poems—and I write groups of poems rather than singles—are written when I have successfully pulled myself out of a completely numbing despair, and stand again in the sunlight. Writing poems is my way of celebrating with the world that I have not committed suicide the evening before."[65] A function of her poetry, then, is a psychological exploration of self, a mediating of the consciousness of one's very existence and an attending

ALICE WALKER MATTERS

to the emotional determinants of that existence, which is subsequently re-formulated and inscribed in her fiction. But for Walker, this function stems from a consideration of her physical body. The material body occupies the center of her ideology. Poetry becomes an experience of emotional purging, a release of emotion in expressions usually brief, but occasionally extended over several moods encapsulating one dominant idea, the development of which takes place in the longer fictional pieces. In "How Poems Are Made/A Discredited View," she writes:

Letting go
in order to hold on
I gradually understand how poems are made.

There is a place the fear must go.
There is a place the choice must go.
There is a place the loss must go.
The leftover love.
The love that spills out
of the too full cup
and runs and hides
its too full self
in shame.

.　.　.　.

I understand how poems are made.
They are the tears
that season the smile.[66]

"There is a place" signals two interconnected aspects. In one, the place locates the poem and its function as a container. In the other, place denotes the body from which the emotions and feelings flow. The emotive content of the body flows into the poem, the poetic container. Both places are marked by the contradiction of oppositional action.

In her poetry, Walker situates a self within familial and social constructs, just as she does in her prose. Though there is an active social consciousness, its manifestations are in a passive, reflexive unconsciousness tapped primarily in moments of poetic experiences that might loosely be termed out-of-body to evoke the spirituality embedded in the transforming or transformed self. The title poem ending the collection *Goodnight, Willie Lee, I'll See You in the Morning* (1979) argues resurrection and reunion both in the here and now and in the hereafter, where promised renewals and beginnings can occur:

Looking down into my father's
dead face
for the last time
my mother said without
tears, without smiles
without regrets
but with *civility*
"Good night, Willie Lee, I'll see you
in the morning."[67]

This tone, the civility of the mother's voice and the compassion of the daughter's thought, anticipates the conclusion of *The Color Purple*, published four years later, with a reformulated premise that healing, forgiveness, and return, literally from the dead in the novel, are the balm of familial misery and personal pain. The two faces, that of the grieving mother and that of the dead father, create a medium of exchange, a space that the daughter can read as inclusive and encompassing and into which she can articulate her own value. The exclusionary practices that segregate individuals, even those who are family members, are banished and reversed.

Hierarchies of power, whether they exist within the family or the state, oppress the powerless until, by miracle or verbal design, the powerless transform self by accessing, without naming, the resources that might otherwise be labeled liabilities. Walker's expressed particularities encompass southern segregation, American racism, family violence, macho expressionism, female reproduction, and more. "What is the point / of being artists / if we cannot save our lives?" Walker asks in "Songless" from *Horses Make a Landscape Look More Beautiful*:

That is the cry
that wakes us
in our sleep.
Being happy is not the only
happiness.

Midway in the poem, she turns to an archetype that has, in fact, guided her own aesthetics and politics:

They say in Nicaragua
the whole
government
writes,

makes music,
and paints, saving their own
and helping the people save
their own lives.[68]

The landscape of oppression and the potential of the artist to change it shift imperceptibly from the American South to Latin America, a shift most evident in *The Temple of My Familiar*, the 1989 novel of the transformative power of control over the ideality of self reflected in the physical world, and *By the Light of My Father's Smile*, a novel of migration from the United States to the Sierras in Mexico and alternative cultures and people, the mixed-race black and Indian Mundo people. It confirms that the world Walker sees currently in an unlimited sightedness is that same large encompassing world her daughter long ago observed in Walker's scarred bluish eye. The "I" consciousness, narrated voice as opposed to the eye, the seeing and sightless orb, the sense and the senseless must be supplanted by vision (inner) and visionary spirituality.

Yet it is not modern philosophy, politics, or science that most of her poems infuse into her fictional texts. It is a resident spirituality, a oneness and peace with the earth, growing and developing over the course of her career. She writes, for instance, in the poem "Despite the Hunger" included in *Absolute Trust in the Goodness of the Earth*:

> Despite
> the hunger
> we cannot
> possess
> more
> than
> this:
> Peace
> in a garden
> of
> our own.[69]

Or when she muses in "At First, It Is True, I Thought There Were Only Peaches & Wild Grapes": "To my delight / I have found myself / Born / Into a garden / of many fruits."[70] In "Bring Me the Heart of María Sabina," the long concluding poem to the volume *Absolute Trust in the Goodness of the Earth*, Walker writes of the gentle Mexican Indian spiritualist and healer:

This is the heart
That belongs
In us
We
Also
"The children"
Indigenous
Like
The mushroom
The tobacco &
The herb
Indigenous
To this
Continent
This hemisphere
We wish to take
Only
What the earth
Offers
& wants
Freely
To give
As it delights
Through every
Magic "child"
In reconnecting
Us to Itself.[71]

The end of the poem connects the heart of María Sabina to

Americans of all
The Americas
Both Mother
& Father

Grandmother
& Grandfather
Guiding Spirit
Of this
Place."[72]

The reconnection that Walker brought as an offering, a sacrifice and a gift, to southern literature in the 1970s and 1980s is what she taught us to comprehend and acknowledge when she focused so specifically on her own female body, on the bodies of black women in her writing. The contemporary global turn in southern literary studies is precisely the direction Walker began pointing toward with her creation of her ancestor Feather Mae in *Meridian*, her epigraph from the southern Cherokee writer Awiakta for *In Search of Our Mothers' Gardens*, and especially with her incorporations of Africa and the African diaspora, along with Mexico and South America, in so much of her fiction and poetry over the entire span of her career. Toward the end of *Absolute Trust in the Goodness of the Earth*, with its global vision and hemispheric architecture, Walker commingles Mississippi, where she spent so significant a part of her early adulthood under fire, and Bolivia, where Che Guevara was murdered.

If they come to shoot you
and because you lived in
Mississippi
where so many
died
you know
they might:
Ask them first
to let you find
your hidden
picture
of
Che Guevara.[73]

The regional space Mississippi fuses politically, intellectually, and emotionally with the death of the revolutionary in Bolivia, but also with the life of the Mexican mystic María Sabina, to whom the section is dedicated. In adding yet a third layer of geography and hemispheric reference, Walker forges ahead with the connections that are now inspiring the new Southern Studies to look beyond the borders of the traditional South and towards the Latin and South American nations for twenty-first-century comparative analysis. Charting the territory once again from her personal past and from the seedbed of Mississippi as foundational space, she envisions that for which "there is no chart yet." She moves toward a way of writing the experience of African Americans, and African American women in particular, into a global correspondence and hemispheric awareness that would once again change the old paradigms and race boundaries. Her continuing project is a southscape that has expanded both the region of the American South and the intellectual visions and paradigms informing critical studies of that region. This is the evolutionary path that *Southscapes* has charted out of the binaries of segregation and into the unbounded world.

Acknowledgments

This book has benefited from many generous friendships, old and new, professional and personal. In Nashville, Art and Helene Pellette, with Mary Elizabeth and Leah, enabled my work and dual residence with their care and commitment; Bill and Cecelia Tichi, David and Leah Marcus, and Sam and Scottie Girgus fed the body and the intellect; Bettye Harwell, Paulette Coleman, and Carol Cresswell Betsch infused art into the everyday. Elsewhere, Nell Painter painted me and *Southscapes* by way of visualizing the possible; Aishah Rahman brought unmatched wit and wisdom; Michael Harper sent poetic missives; Leslie Sanders held the Toronto–New York respite in place; Candida and Amerigo Ferreira made Portugal a reward; John and Christine Smith became the ideal audience; Barbara Savage read and imagined; Deborah McDowell offered laughter with reality checks; Sybil Kein kept the faith; and Ralph Singfield remained a safe harbor.

My library colleagues at the Huntington Library and the Center for Scholars and Writers of the New York Public Library gave me courage and models. My sister-professors in the Black Women's Intellectual History Working Group inspired perseverance, and Farah Jasmine Griffin gave superb advice; Janie King at the Vanderbilt University Library responded with professional skill and Delta sisterhood to my calls for help with citations. The computer wizards, Brian Kirk and Adam Podlaski, provided expert support and never laughed at my persistence with WordPerfect, even after a major computer crash.

I am especially grateful to colleagues for invitations to present keynote addresses derived from this book: Susan Donaldson, Randal Jelks, and the Southern Intellectual History Circle meeting at the University of Kansas, and Keith Cartwright, Maryemma Graham, and Minrose Gwin for their attentive responses to my talk; Barbara Ewell, Rebecca Mark, John W. Lowe, and the Society for the Study of Southern Literature meeting sponsored by Loyola University and Tulane University; Edith Frampton, Anne Donadey, Susan Stanford Friedman, and the Contemporary Women Writers International Meeting under the auspices of San Diego State University; Mike Hill, Marjorie Pryse, Joshua Bartlett, Erin Casey, and "Negotiating Land: New Readings" Graduate Student Association Conference, Department of English, University of Albany, State University of New York.

I am also thankful for having the opportunity to present several sections of this work during formative stages at conferences (American Studies Association and Modern Language Association) and at the University of Pennsylvania (Women's Studies Works-in-Progress and the Latitudes Group in the Department of English). Joni Adams (ASA) and Reggie Scott Young (MLA) included me on the stimulating panels they organized. Shannon Lundeen (Penn Women's Studies) took the time to send thoughtful feedback.

Sian Hunter believed in *Southscapes* for the University of North Carolina Press, and the readers she selected there pushed the envelope. In the final stages, Sarah Cockrum was an efficient angel in assisting with the bibliography. Research funding through the College of Arts and Sciences, the University of Pennsylvania, enabled my work, and the resources of the Van Pelt Library made it possible. The outstanding editorial, design, and production team of UNC Press made the book a better reality. I especially thank Kate Torrey and Jay Mazzocchi for their thoughtful efforts at crucial moments. Brenda Marie Osbey generously provided a much-needed education on poetry permissions, which led me to an even greater awed respect for each of the poets included in *Southscapes*, and to an expanded gratitude for all the real work they do.

My appreciation for so many kindnesses is heartfelt. My admiration is boundless for my family who, after the storm, inspires with a worldly, incomparable spirit of survival, and for my students, past and present, who continue to look back in wonder and thus encourage me to look forward in joy.

Notes

INTRODUCTION

1. Clifton, "Entering the South," in *The Terrible Stories*, 36.

2. In his chapter "The Word Itself," John Brinckerhoff Jackson uses the term "fact of the land" in order to distinguish it from the idea of landscape. See Jackson, *Discovering the Vernacular Landscape*, 3–8. His discussion is also reprinted in Horowitz, *Landscape in Sight*, 299–306.

3. Gillian Rose observes that landscape is a most resilient term in geography "because it refers to one of the discipline's most abiding interests: the relationship between the natural environment and human society." Gillian Rose, "Geography as a Science of Observation," 342.

4. Landscape, Mike Crang points out, "implies a collective shaping of the earth over time. Landscapes are not individual property; they reflect a society's—a culture's—beliefs, practices, and technologies." Crang, *Cultural Geography*, 15.

5. My term "southscape" responds to Edward W. Soja's challenge "to invent a different term to capture what [he was] trying to convey" with "Thirdspace" to make "both theoretical and practical sense of our contemporary life-worlds at all scales, from the most intimate to the most global." Soja, *Thirdspace*, 1–2.

6. Homi Bhabha initially articulated "Third Space" at the end of the 1980s. Operating from a provenance of postcolonial theory with India-Britain as his matrix and Frantz Fanon, Stuart Hall, Jacques Lacan, and Edward Said as his interlocutors, Bhabha identified Third Space as a "political strategy for empowerment and articulation" particularly useful in exploring questions of race and representation, as he explained in "The Other Question: Stereotype, Discrimination, and the Discourse of Colonialism," a 1992 essay reprinted in Bhabha, *The Location of Culture*, 66–84. See Gillian Rose and Steve Pile for the early acceptance of Bhabha's work as enabling new geographic paradigms. Edward Soja and Robert Young, among others, critique Bhabha for the somewhat abstract generalizations of his historical and geographical formulations.

7. Bhabha used "Third Space" in his 1989 essay "The Commitment to Theory" and in an interview with Jonathan Rutherford, "The Third Space: Interview with Homi Bhabha" (1990). He deployed the term to inscribe and articulate a culture of hybridity that could counter hegemonic colonial hierarchies. See Bhabha, "The Commitment to Theory" (1989), reprinted in *The Location of Culture*, 38ff., 25; and Rutherford, *Identity*, 207–21.

8. hooks, "Choosing the Margins as a Space of Radical Openness," in *Yearning*, 145, 146.

9. The Black Public Sphere Collective, *The Black Public Sphere*, 1, 3. The Collective responded to Habermas's *The Structural Transformation of the Public Sphere*.

10. Daphne Spain, for instance, has pointed out, "Space is essential to social science; spatial relations exist only because social processes exists. The spatial and social aspects of a phenomenon are inseparable." Spain, *Gendered Spaces*, 5. In recognizing the impact of people and social communities on landscape, cultural geographers have delineated forms such as communication networks, which demonstrate the inextricable interaction of the spatial and the social. One example that has had an impact across disciplinary boundaries is the work of social scientist Paul Gilroy, who in conceptualizing the "Black Atlantic" as a social space focused attention squarely on the interlocked social and spatial relations manifested in black migration and diasporic practices. See Gilroy, *The Black Atlantic*.

11. Certeau, *The Practice of Everyday Life*, 117.

12. Ibid. (Certeau's emphasis).

13. Ibid., 118.

14. Importantly, as David Harvey's interpretations have underscored, justice is as much a constitutive element of geography as is place and space. See Harvey, *Justice, Nature, and the Geography of Difference*. Harvey's chapter "City and Justice: Social Movements in the City," in his *Spaces of Capital*, links urban organization and environment with Marxism and the production of space and uneven geographical development.

15. Cresswell, *Place: A Short Introduction*, 11.

16. Certeau, *The Practice of Everyday Life*, 117.

17. Kathryn McKee and Annette Trefzer state in the forward to a 2006 special issue of *American Literature*: "As we plough new fields and chart new territories, we are certain in our knowledge of the South's metonymic relation to the nation and convinced of its centrality to American studies, but we are equally interested in the region's fascinating multiplicity and its participation in hemispheric and global contexts." McKee and Trefzer, "Preface: Global Contexts, Local Literatures," 677.

18. Greeson focuses on the role of the nineteenth-century South in the development of a national literature and concomitantly in the ascendancy of the United States as a world power. See Greeson, *Our South*.

19. In the early 1980s, for example, John Fraser Hart wrote in the *Annals of the Association of American Geographers* that regional geography is the highest form of the geographer's art. Hart, "The Highest Form of the Geographer's Art."

20. Gillian Rose, *Feminism and Geography*, 160.

21. Elizabeth Abel offers a salient point for the current "postracial" moment and its unstable political climate regarding race: "Segregation signs are prime examples of racial Americana. Having survived a century of refashioning in the hands of divergent producers and consumers, they seem ready neither to be discarded nor to be enclosed in a museum. Instead they have a social life that continues to propel them through changing scripts. Appalling and energizing, outrageous and absurd, they remind us that segregation was staged through representations that are still being written and still need to be read." Abel, "American Graffiti," 22.

22. Sibley, *Geographies of Exclusion*, 3.

23. Walton, *Mississippi: An American Journey*, excerpted in Kevin Young, *Giant Steps*, 252. Walton's 1996 book, composed of memoir, history, and poetry, engages the home state of his parents and the cultural space they left behind. In "Walkin' Blues," the last section of *Mississippi*, he joins his father in traveling through the state and his father's memories.

24. The experience of place has been increasingly mapped by scholars whose theoretical concerns range from postmodernism and global feminism to the body and prisons. See, for example, Lefebvre, *The Production of Space*; Doreen Massey, *Space, Place, and Gender*; and Harvey, *Spaces of Capital*.

25. See Adrienne Rich, "Notes toward a Politics of Location," which cited the body as a geography, in *Blood, Bread, and Poetry*. The concept of "the geography closest in" helped to foment theoretical interest in new geographies, including bodies, spatialities, and subjectivities, in feminist and women's studies. See the work of feminist geographers in Duncan, *BodySpace*.

26. See, for instance, Ainley, *New Frontiers of Space, Bodies, and Gender*; Blunt and Rose, *Writing Women and Space*; Higonnet and Templeton, *Reconfigured Spheres*; Columina, *Sexuality and Space*; Gloria Anzaldúa, *Borderlands, La Frontera*; and Fryer, *Felicitous Space*. Susan Stanford Friedman, in *Mappings: Feminism and the Cultural Geographies of Encounter*, assumes a locational epistemology based on changing geographical and historical specificities in her discourse on the future of feminism and incorporates attention to black women. See Friedman, *Mappings*, 3–13. See also Caren Kaplan's chapter "Postmodern Geographies: Feminist Politics of Location" in *Questions of Travel*.

27. See, for example, Soja, *Postmodern Geographies*.

28. In arguing that social theory is a way to read everyday life, Michael J. Dear defines the modern and presents characteristics of the postmodern in conjunction with an insistence on the importance of space as a concept in social thought. Dear, *The Postmodern Urban Condition*, 4.

29. Jameson, *Postmodernism, or, The Cultural Logic of Late Capitalism*, ix. See also Hutcheon, *The Politics of Postmodernism* and *The Poetics of Postmodernism*.

30. Lyotard, *The Postmodern Condition*, xxiii.

31. Ibid., xxiii–xxiv.

32. Dear, *The Postmodern Urban Condition*, 2, 4–5, 32.

33. Jarvis, *Postmodern Cartographies*, 7.

34. Yaeger, "Introduction: Narrating Space," 4.

35. Warf, "Derek Gregory," 145, 147.

36. Dubey, *Signs and Cities*, 2.

37. Mullen, "Black Nikes," 148–49. See also "Black Nikes" in Mullen, *Sleeping with the Dictionary*, 11. In her introduction to *Recyclopedia*, Mullen states of her work: "While some readers perceive *Muse & Drudge* as a more insistently 'black' text than the other two, I have written all of these works from my perspective as a black woman, which I believe is no less representative of humanity than any other point of view." Mullen, *Recyclopedia*, xi.

38. Following the integration of Torsten Hägerstrand's analysis of innovation diffusion, the Berkeley geographers pursued their study of diffusion as a process that enabled the tracking of various distributions of cultural elements. See "Diffusion" in Gregory, Johnston, Pratt, Watts, and Whitmore, *The Dictionary of Human Geography*, 160 (inclusive pages 160–62).

39. Leigh Anne Duck's temporal model of segregation, for example, works out of a consideration of segregation as separation of whites and blacks that was not merely a southern phenomenon but a national one, and that the modernist production of a central group of white writers had as one objective linking a supposedly southern condition to the larger nation-state, and incidentally that the work of several black writers—Ralph Ellison, Richard Wright, and Zora Hurston—contributed to this project. Duck situates her analysis as a temporal one in the 1920s and 1930s, with an investment in the formulation of a "national modernism" in the work of two white southern writers, Erskine Caldwell and William Faulkner, who are at the center of her reading. She places Hurston in a chapter between those on Caldwell and Faulkner as evidencing "temporal complexity" and "formal innovation." Her point, as stated, is that "the South's temporal multiplicity and, accordingly, its substantial ties to U.S. culture and governance challenged the idea that southern apartheid comprised an anomaly in an otherwise liberal nation." See Duck, *The Nation's Region*, 3, 7, 199, 210, 212.

40. Hale's concern is with how, in the period between 1890 and 1940, segregation created "modern whiteness" and how the South became "an essential part of the national whole." Two of her formulating statements illustrate the direction of her study and locate her fine book as a precursor of Duck's. She states: "My goal has been to illuminate who white southerners imagined they were and the stories and images that enabled them to make their collectiveness powerful and persuasive and true." In addition, Hale states: "The ways in which the South has served national imaginings have, after all, doubled the ways in which blackness has served American whiteness. The South has been, to use the language of our racial orderings, the darkness that has made the American nation lose its color." See Hale, *Making Whiteness*, xi, 3.

41. Mary Ellis Gibson makes a critical use of the southern colloquial term "homeplace" in her anthology, *Homeplaces: Stories of the South by Women Writers*. bell hooks repeatedly deploys the term as part of her analysis of home. See, for example, her chapter "Homeplace: A Site of Resistance" in *Yearning*, 41–50, as well as passing mentions in *Belonging*.

42. Alice Walker, *The Way Forward Is with a Broken Heart*, 199–200.

CHAPTER I

1. The photograph is part of the Farm Security Administration Office of War Information Photograph Collection, Library of Congress Prints and Photographs Division, Washington, D.C.

2. Certeau, *The Practice of Everyday Life*, 126.

3. Crang and Thrift, introduction to *Thinking Space*, 1. Crang and Thrift worry over the collapsing meanings of space and point out how different disciplines "do space differently."

4. Ibid.

5. Newton, "Publisher's Pushing Made Franklin Write Best-Selling History of Blacks," 2-B.

6. Doreen Massey, *Space, Place, and Gender*, 120

7. Newton, "Publisher's Pushing Made Franklin Write Best-Selling History of Blacks," 1.

8. See Fireside, *Separate and Unequal*, for an extended treatment of the case and its impact on the institutionalizing of racial segregation.

9. Chesnutt, "The Courts and the Negro," 151. Chesnutt's previously unpublished essay, written and revised between 1908 and 1911, attended to a series of court decisions that restricted the rights of people of African descent in the United States. See Chesnutt, "The Courts and the Negro," 151–60.

10. Sibley, "The Binary City," 244.

11. See, for example, Jessica Adams's review of *Look Away!* in the *Bryn Mawr Review of Comparative Literature*. *Look Away!* does include an essay by Richard King on Richard Wright's *Black Power* (1954), "Richard Wright: From the South to Africa—and Beyond" (227–50), and another by Jane Landers on African American and Native American resistance moves in colonial Florida, "Slave Resistance on the Southeastern Frontier: Fugitives, Maroons, and Banditti in the Age of Revolution" (80–93).

12. See Gray, *Writing the South*, xii. However, Gray was not alone in the lack of recognition or inattention to southern writers of color.

13. Ibid.

14. See ibid., 198, for a passing mention of Charles Chesnutt. See also Richard King, *A Southern Renaissance*, 8–9.

15. Frankenberg, *White Women, Race Matters*, 11–12.

16. Hale, *Making Whiteness*, xi.

17. Gray, *Writing the South*, 267. A decade later in 1998, Michael Kreyling would by means of inversion posit a different view of what or who constitutes the voice speaking in the margins. Kreyling, *Inventing Southern Literature*, xiv.

18. Barthes, *Roland Barthes by Roland Barthes*, 47.

19. Yaeger, *Dirt and Desire*, xii.

20. Holman, "No More Monoliths, Please," xviii.

21. Ibid., xix. Holman's listing of Ellison, Wright, Gaines, and Reed is a progressive step forward, but his inclusion of four black men recalls the ideology that inspired Gloria T. Hull, Barbara Smith, and Patricia Bell Scott to edit *All the Women Are White, All the Blacks Are Men, but Some of Us Are Brave*, which helped to initiate attention to black women writers and critics.

22. Kreyling's argument in *Inventing Southern Literature*, for example, overlooks Holman's reading of necessarily changing fixed conceptions and familiar paradigms with attention to new literatures by black writers.

23. Williamson, "The Soul Is Fled," 185.

24. Plumpp, "Heartbeat," in *Blues*, 128.

25. Cresswell, *Place: A Short Introduction*, 11.

26. See the publicity materials for Junebug Productions, Inc., Free Southern Theater Institute, Wednesday, 19 March 2008.

27. Morrison, *Playing in the Dark*, 63.

28. Morrison, "Epigraph from Nobel Lecture," v.

29. Natasha Trethewey, "Inscriptive Restorations," 1032. The interview provides substantive commentary from Trethewey on her writing.

30. Sherley Anne Williams, *Dessa Rose*, 236 (Williams's italics and open ellipsis).

31. Morrison, *Beloved*, 273.

32. Forrest, *Two Wings to Veil My Face*, 295ff.

33. Kreyling has written in defense of the publication of Randall's novel, against the Mitchell estate's claim of copyright infringement, and about Mitchell's various borrowings from southern fiction for her novel. Kreyling, "Real Gone for a Change," 37–38. See also Kreyling, "Parody, Memory, and Copyright," in *The South That Wasn't There*, 149–75.

34. Alice Walker, *The Color Purple*, 251.

35. Dear, *The Postmodern Urban Condition*, 8.

36. hooks, "Postmodern Blackness," in *Yearning*, 31.

37. Ibid.

38. Certeau, *The Practice of Everyday Life*, 116.

39. Alice Walker, "The Black Writer and the Southern Experience," 21. This revealing autobiographical piece was reprinted in Walker's first collection of essays, *In Search of Our Mothers' Gardens*.

40. Foucault, "The Eye of Power," 149. Originally published as a preface to Jeremy Bentham's *La Panoptique* (1977), Foucault's statement on space and power has become one of his most cited.

41. Bernice Johnson Reagon quoted as epigraph in Stack, *Call to Home*, vii.

42. Carol Stack provided a description of how she came to have Reagon's memorable statement and permission to use it. Carol Stack, e-mail to Thadious Davis, 6 June 2010.

43. While Margaret Walker Alexander's *Jubilee* (1966) and Ernest Gaines's *The Auto-biography of Miss Jane Pittman* (1971) may be read as the modern precursors, I locate Alex Haley's *Roots: The Saga of an American Family* (1976) and the televisual adaptation of the novel as foundational to changed and transformed relationships between African Americans and the South. As a result of a more widespread media exposure than was possible with the publication of *Jubilee* and *The Autobiography of Miss Jane Pittman* or the print version of *Roots*, the televised series enabled an expanded audience of viewers who were not necessarily prone to read massive novels to gain access to conceptions of history, heritage, and space. Public access to knowledge about the past, the roots in an Africa that was not a "Dark Continent," the realities of the Middle Passage, and the long night of enslavement made possible a different sense of personal and racial history that was further enhanced by the new recognition that it was pos-

sible to connect in tangible ways back to both the "assumed" generic African heritage and to a very specific African region with linguistic, tribal, and familial affiliations. I use "assumed" here because *Roots*, though claiming authentic and groundbreaking research, ultimately proved to be mainly a work of fiction. Not only were the claims of a specific African ancestor from a specific African village proven false, but some of the writing was lifted from other novels—Harold Courlander's *The African* (1968) and Margaret Walker's *Jubilee*. In 1978 Courlander received $650,000 from Haley in an out-of-court settlement, but Walker's suit, filed in 1988 and charging Haley with violating her copyright for *Jubilee*, was dismissed.

44. See Massaquoi, "Alex Haley's Hideaway."

45. McDowell, *Gender, Identity, and Place*, 4.

46. Dixon, "*Like an Eagle in the Air*: Toni Morrison," in *Ride Out the Wilderness*.

47. Patricia J. Williams, *Open House*, 8.

48. Ibid.

49. Mullen, *Sleeping with the Dictionary*, 27.

50. Painter, "'Slaves' with Volvos."

51. Redford quoted by Painter in "'Slaves' with Volvos."

52. Haley, introduction to *Somerset Homecoming*, xviii, xiv.

53. Redford, *Somerset Homecoming*, 220–21.

54. Ibid., 221.

55. Edward Ball, quoted in Bowman, "A Warrior in Scholar's Clothing."

56. Faust, "Skeletons in the Family Closet."

57. Kenan, "Dorothy Spruill Redford," 6. Kenan was the speaker at the 1998 Caldwell Award Banquet held on 24 October 1998 and honoring Dorothy Spruill Redford, who is now the manager of the Somerset Place Historic Site, where she continues to organize the biannual Somerset Homecomings.

58. Painter, "'Slaves' with Volvos."

59. Lester, *Do Lord Remember Me*, 3 (Lester's italics), 210.

60. Painter's list of black builders of Somerset Place in "'Slaves' with Volvos."

61. For discussions of this new tourism, see Adams, "Plantations without Slaves," 54–85; and Woolfork, "Slave Tourism and Rememory," 98–131.

62. Trethewey, "Pilgrimage, Vicksburg, Mississippi," in *Native Guard*, 20. Subsequent references to *Native Guard* appear parenthetically in the text.

63. Richard Wright to Paul Reynolds, 6 November 1958, quoted in Fabre, *The Unfinished Quest of Richard Wright*, 470. Wright wrote to Reynolds in response to the death of his editor at Harper, Edward Aswell, a southerner and friend, about whom Wright concluded in the letter: "There is no better Southerner than an honest one for he has a lot to face and accept. And Ed did that" (470).

64. Carl Van Vechten observed in counseling a black woman about contacts for her permanent relocation to Spain: "[Y]ou will be unlikely to run into him [Yerby] unless he is hungry for racial companionship which I doubt." Carl Van Vechten to Dorothy Peterson, 30 October 1959.

65. For a different but related version of this conclusion, see Avilez, "Housing the Black Body."

66. Ross, "Interview with Frank Yerby," in *Contemporary Authors New Revision Series*.

67. See "Frank Yerby: Seven Novels in Seven Years."

68. "The Golden Corn: He Writes to Please."

69. Ibid.

70. Stack, *Call to Home*, xiv. Stack's groundbreaking work forged a way of reassessing the migration of African Americans; as early as the 1970s, she had observed the then-unremarked movement of northern blacks, especially children and women, back to the South. Although she did not include those early observations in her 1974 book *All Our Kin*, on the kinship networks sustaining blacks in a midwestern city, they eventually led to her ethnographic research for *Call to Home*. See Stack, "Preface," *Call to Home*, xii–xiii.

71. Stack, "Preface," *Call to Home*, xv.

72. Jacquelyn Dowd Hall, "Open Secrets," 110.

73. Frey, "The New Great Migration," 1.

74. Michael Hayes, quoted by David Judson in "Links to the Past Draws Blacks Back to the South," *The Tennessean* (Nashville), 5 April 1998, A-8.

75. Frey, "The New Great Migration," 5 (table 2).

76. Mathis, "America's Race Picture Changing," *The Tennessean* (Nashville), 5 April 1998, A-8.

77. Frey, "The New Great Migration," 4, 11.

78. "Why Blacks Are Returning to the South," 15.

79. Bill Campbell, quoted in "Why Blacks Are Returning to the South," 15.

80. Frey, "The New Great Migration," 11.

81. Eula Grant, quoted in Stack, *Call to Home*, 199.

82. Stack, *Call to Home*, 199.

83. Marcia Gaudet and Reggie Young, introduction to Ernest Gaines, *Mozart and Leadbelly*, ix.

84. Reggie Scott Young, "Still Driven by That Louisiana Thing," 700.

85. Reggie Scott Young, in "Still Driven by That Louisiana Thing," describes Gaines's attachment to the land, to the church building, and to the grave sites (700–701) and includes a portfolio of River Lake Plantation images—including a reproduction of Gaines's letter of invitation to friends and relatives for the 2005 annual "Mt. Zion River Lake Cemetery Beautification in Cherie Quarters on All Saints Day" (708) and a photograph of the cemetery on Beautification Day 2001 (709).

86. Ibid., 700.

87. Knight, "Television Speaks," in *The Essential Etheridge Knight*, 59.

88. See Trethewey's revealing statement on her social history in "Inscriptive Restorations," 1032.

89. Trethewey, *Domestic Work*, 50–51. Subsequent references appear parenthetically in the text.

90. Rita Dove, introduction to Trethewey, *Domestic Work*, xii.

91. See Baker, *Modernism and the Harlem Renaissance*.

92. In reproducing circuits of culture, Trethewey makes intersectional gender, genre, and medium connections in the naming of her central figure Ophelia, whom she imagined from an anonymous woman photographed by Ernest J. Bellocq around 1912 in New Orleans and from John Everett Millais's painting *Ophelia* (1851–52, oil on canvas, 30 by 44 inches, Tate Gallery, London, based on the death of Ophelia from Shakespeare's *Hamlet*). Poetry, painting, and photography come together across space, time, and cultures as processes invested in the subjectivity and reverberation inherent within the creative process.

93. E. J. Bellocq (1873–1949), who photographed the women of Storyville, a red-light district that existed in New Orleans between 1897 and 1917, has himself become the subject of much critical attention because of his photographs of prostitutes and the unanswered questions concerning his motives and intentions. See Al Rose, *Storyville, New Orleans*; Rex Rose, "The Last Days of Ernest J. Bellocq"; and *Bellocq: Photographs from Storyville, the Red-Light District of New Orleans*, with an introduction by Susan Sontag (7–8). The large-size prints for this expanded edition of Bellocq's photographs were made by Lee Friedlander and revised in the 1970 *E. J. Bellocq: Storyville Portraits* exhibition at the Museum of Modern Art.

94. Trethewey, *Bellocq's Ophelia*, 24. Subsequent references appear parenthetically in the text.

95. hooks, *Yearning*, 147.

96. Ibid.

97. Adams, *Wounds of Returning*, 85. Adams concludes the chapter with an examination of vampires and the film adaptation of Anne Rice's 1994 novel, *Interview with the Vampire*. The "us" in the sentence ending Adams's chapter technically refers to Anne Rice's own comment included in the video version of the film: "Remember: It's not just about vampires. It's really about us" (Rice, quoted in Adams, *Wounds of Returning*, 84).

98. Trethewey, "Southern Gothic," in *Native Guard*, 40. Subsequent references to *Native Guard* appear parenthetically in the text.

99. Certeau, *The Practice of Everyday Life*, 108.

100. Barthes, *Camera Lucida*, 34.

101. Trethewey, "Inscriptive Restorations," 1028.

102. Barthes, *Camera Lucida*, 26.

103. Ibid., 27.

104. Trethewey, "Inscriptive Restorations," 1025.

105. Brooks, *Body Work*, xiii.

106. Patricia J. Williams, *Open House*, 13–14.

107. McDowell, *Gender, Identity, and Place*, 39.

108. Trethewey, "Inscriptive Restorations," 1027.

109. See Charles Wright, "Meditation on Form and Measure," in *Black Zodiac*.

110. Gwin, *The Woman in the Red Dress*, 60.

111. Trethewey, "Inscriptive Restorations," 1034, 1033.

112. Ibid., 1033.

113. Certeau, *The Practice of Everyday Life*, 108.

CHAPTER 2

1. Endesha Ida Mae Holland, prologue to *From the Mississippi Delta: A Memoir*, 9. Holland's words echo James C. Cobb's in *The Most Southern Place on Earth*. See also James Crespino, "Mississippi as Metaphor," 99–120.

2. Certeau, *The Practice of Everyday Life*, 129.

3. Ibid., 130.

4. Holland, *From the Mississippi Delta*, 9.

5. See Harry Watson's editor's essay, entitled "Front Porch," in each issue of *Southern Cultures*, a quarterly publication of the University of North Carolina's Center for the Study of the American South. See also Harris, *The Power of the Porch*; and Donlon, *Swinging in Place*. Donlon's images of porches are primarily from Louisiana; she does not show Mississippi porches.

6. Ernest Gaines to Marcia Gaudet and Carl Wooton, "Finding the Voice," in *Porch Talk with Ernest Gaines*, 37.

7. Ibid.

8. Ernest Gaines, "Miss Jane and I," *Callaloo* (1978); reprinted in Ernest Gaines, *Mozart and Leadbelly*, 5.

9. See Vlach, *Back of the Big House*. Interestingly, Vlach's conception is largely visual rather than spatial.

10. Gidley, introduction to *Modern American Landscape*, 1–16.

11. Ransby, *Ella Baker and the Black Freedom Movement*, 307.

12. Ibid.

13. Ibid.

14. Dittmer, *Local People*, 433.

15. The ephemera and photographs were initially exhibited at a New York gallery, and then at the New York Historical Society, once it became clear that large numbers of viewers were interested in seeing the exhibition. The collection is now permanently housed at Emory University in Atlanta.

16. Jacqueline Goldsby, for example, includes an extended analysis of Gwendolyn Brooks's poem "The Last Quatrain of the Ballad of Emmett Till" as the conclusion to her study *Spectacular Secret*, 294–307. Toni Morrison's play *Dreaming Emmett* (1986), Ishmael Reed's novel *Reckless Eyeballing* (1986), and Wanda Coleman's poem "Emmett Till" (1986) form only a sampling of the texts produced on Till's lynching. Langston Hughes, James Baldwin, James A. Emanuel, Audre Lorde, Bebe Moore Campbell, and Anthony Walton all composed work to remember Till, as did the celebrated Cuban poet Nicolas Guillén in "Elegiás a Emmett Till" (1977).

17. Although the initial name was Citizens Council, the addition of "White" made clear the segregationist and racist intent of the organization. See Howard Ball, *Murder in Mississippi*, 6.

18. For a discussion of Mamie Till Bradley's decision to make public images of her son's body and the resulting demands placed on her, see Goldsby, "The High and Low-Tech of It"; and Feldstein, "'I Wanted the Whole World to See.'"

19. See Bradley, the *Chicago Defender* interview with Ethel Payne, April-June 1956.

20. See Dora Apel's analysis, "The Lynching of Emmett Till and the Role of Photography," in *Imagery of Lynching: Black Men, White Women, and the Mob*, 178–88.

21. Huie, "The Shocking Story of Approved Killing in Mississippi." The article carried a headnote stating in part: "Disclosed here is the true account of the slaying in Mississippi of a Negro youth named Emmett Till."

22. Huie paid Roy Bryant and his half brother J. W. Milam ("Big Milam") to tell their story of the events, and the two complied, fully revealing the details of what happened that night and the following morning. See also Metress, *The Lynching of Emmett Till: A Documentary Narrative*.

23. See William Bradford Huie's follow-up article on Milam and Bryant, "What's Happened to the Emmett Till Killers?"

24. Elizabeth Alexander, "'Can You Be BLACK and Look at This?'"

25. Moody, *Coming of Age in Mississippi*, 103. Subsequent references appear parenthetically in the text.

26. Alice Walker, "Petunias," in *You Can't Keep a Good Woman Down*, 40.

27. Ibid.

28. Richard Wright, "The Man Who Killed a Shadow," *Eight Men*, 157.

29. Margaret Walker, "Natchez and Richard Wright in Southern American Literature," 120–21.

30. Margaret Walker, "Jackson, Mississippi," 62.

31. Walton, *Mississippi: An American Journey*, 4.

32. Plumpp, *Blues: The Story Always Untold*, 12. The long poem "Mississippi Griot" establishes the tone and the rhythm of the homage to Mississippi blues (see 11–15). Subsequent references to *Blues: The Story Always Untold* appear parenthetically in the text.

33. Richardson, *Black Masculinity and the U.S. South*, 215. See the final chapter, "Gangstas and Playas in the Dirty South" (197–227), in which Richardson also connects "dirty South" to the South of abjection and exclusion.

34. Knight, "The Last Words by 'Slick' (or a Self/Sung Eulogy)," in *The Essential Etheridge Knight*, 98.

35. Knight, "The Idea of Ancestry," in *The Essential Etheridge Knight*, 12.

36. Knight, *The Essential Etheridge Knight*, 13.

37. Ibid., 111.

38. Knight, "A Poem for Myself (Or Blues for a Mississippi Black Boy)," in *Belly Song and Other Poems*, 50. Subsequent references to *Belly Song and Other Poems* appear parenthetically in the text.

39. West, "Black Strivings in a Twilight Civilization," 87–118 (quotation from 105).

40. Adam Gussow, *Seems Like Murder Here*, 143 (Gussow's italics).

41. See Payne, *I've Got the Light of Freedom*.

42. Howard Ball, *Murder in Mississippi*, 5.

43. Hendrickson, *Sons of Mississippi*, 309, 313.

44. Thomas-Houston, *"Stony the Road" to Change*, 6.

45. Ibid., 10.

46. Ibid., 4.

47. Trethewey, "Miscegenation," in *Native Guard*, 36.

48. Walton, *Mississippi: An American Journey*, 163–64.

49. Lowenthal, "The Place of the Past in the American Landscape," 92; Tocqueville, *Democracy in America*, 2:104–6.

50. The outstanding cast of *Mississippi Masala* includes Denzel Washington as Demetrius, Sarita Choudbury as Mina, Tico Wells as Dexter (Demetrius's younger brother), and Rashan Seth as Jay, Mina's father.

51. John Young, review of *Mississippi Masala*, 64. Young observes: "Although the plot holds few surprises, other pleasures abound. Rich in detail, the film sketches affectionate portraits of the two closed societies, spoofing their absurdities without descending into cheap shots."

52. Written by Nina Simone, "Mississippi Goddam" appeared on the album *Nina Simone in Concert*, recorded in New York City in 1964. Robert Guillaume remembers going to hear Simone at the Village Gate: "[N]ight after night I'd wait for her to sing 'Mississippi Goddam.' 'Everybody knows about Mississippi—goddam!' she'd bellow as the audience went wild. I've never seen protest rendered so dramatically." Quoted in Kahn, "Civil Rights Diva." Natasha Trethewey uses only the line "Everybody knows about Mississippi" as an epigraph to one section of *Native Guard*.

53. Cowdrey, *This Land, This South*, 169.

54. Awiakta, *Abiding Appalachia*, 14.

55. Cowdrey, *This Land, This South*, 169.

56. Tuan, *Space and Place*, 149. Tuan observes of this cosmic view of home: "Such a conception of place ought to give it supreme value," so that "[s]hould destruction occur . . . the people would be thoroughly demoralized, since the ruin of their settlement [their home] implies the ruin of their cosmos" (149).

57. Holland, *From the Mississippi Delta*, 311–12.

58. Dove, "Mississippi," 23.

59. Walton, *Mississippi: An American Journey*, 4.

60. Ibid.

61. Ibid., 8.

62. Kane, *Natchez on the Mississippi*, 3.

63. Morris, "A Sense of Place and the Americanization of Mississippi," 3.

64. Federal Writers' Project of the Works Progress Administration, *Mississippi, A Guide to the Magnolia State*, 237, 254, 256, 208.

65. Richard Wright, "Blueprint for Negro Writing," 45.

66. Richard Wright, *Black Boy*, 14.

67. Ibid., 15.

68. Spirn, *The Language of Landscape*, 158.

69. Richard Wright, "Blueprint for Negro Writing," 48.

70. Richard Wright, "How 'Bigger' Was Born," vii.

71. Kavolis, "Literature and the Dialectics of Modernization," 99.

72. Richard Wright to Antonio Frasconi, November 1944, in Ellen Wright and Michel Fabre, *Richard Wright Reader*, 72–73. See the full exchange of letters in "Richard Wright to Antonio Frasconi: An Exchange of Letters."

73. Elizabeth Alexander, *The Black Interior*, 5.

74. Ibid.

75. See Madhu Dubey on Morrison and Naylor as "strain[ing] unsuccessfully to refigure reading as listening," and thus "betray[ing] the impossibilities of sustaining folk resolutions to postmodern crises of urban literary representation." Dubey, *Signs and Cities*, 15; and chapter 4, "Reading as Listening: The Southern Folk Aesthetic," 144–85.

76. Lyotard, *The Postmodern Condition*, xxv.

77. Dixon, *Ride out the Wilderness*, 2–3.

78. Vernon, "Finding Logic."

79. Ibid.

80. Vernon, *Logic*, 11. Subsequent references appear parenthetically in the text.

81. Doreen Massey, "Politics and Space/Time," 81.

82. Casey, "Cycle of Violence."

83. Komunyakaa, *Magic City*, 30.

84. Vernon, *A Killing in This Town*, 18. Subsequent references appear parenthetically in the text.

85. Febvre, *A Geographical Introduction to History*, 352.

86. Vernon, *Eden*, 3. Subsequent references appear parenthetically in the text.

CHAPTER 3

1. Hughes, speech to the Third Annual Writers' Congress.

2. Jessie Fauset was unsuccessful in finding employment related to writing and publishing in New York City, despite her offer to work at home. See Fauset, Letter to Joel Spingarn, 26 January 1926.

3. Richard Wright, *Black Boy*, 227. Subsequent references appear parenthetically in the text.

4. Ralph Ellison, "Remembering Richard Wright," 208.

5. Margaret Walker, "Richard Wright," 48.

6. Nelson Algren, quoted in Mangione, *The Dream and the Deal*, 121.

7. Richard Wright, "Blueprint for Negro Writing," 48. Subsequent references appear parenthetically in the text.

8. Hathaway, "Native Geography." Hathaway's essay is short (91–95), and the reprint from the Abraham Lincoln Presidential Library's Federal Writers' Project Collection of Wright's typescript "A Survey of the Amusement Facilities of District #35" makes up the remainder (96–108).

9. Richard Wright, *American Hunger*, 135.

10. Penkower, *The Federal Writers' Project*, 179.

11. Bontemps, "Why I Returned."

12. Cutler, *The Public Landscape of the New Deal*, 4.

13. Ibid., 19.

14. Margaret Walker, "Richard Wright," 48.

15. Ibid., 49.

16. Ibid., 48.

17. Gabbin, *Sterling A. Brown*, 70.

18. Certeau, *The Practice of Everyday Life*, 115.

19. Mangione, *The Dream and the Deal*, 259.

20. Ibid., 258, 259.

21. Ellison, "Remembering Richard Wright," 204.

22. Ibid., 204–5.

23. See Tidwell and Sanders, *Sterling A. Brown's "A Negro Looks at the South,"* 6–7.

24. Richard Wright, introduction to *Black Metropolis*.

25. Doreen Massey, *Space, Place, and Gender*, 11.

26. Ibid.

27. Fisher, "Introductory Note."

28. Richard Wright, *American Hunger*, 135. Subsequent references appear parenthetically in the text.

29. Edwards, *The Practice of Diaspora*, 11.

30. Ibid.

31. Stuart Hall, "Race, Articulation, and Societies Structured in Dominance," quoted in Edwards, *The Practice of Diaspora*, 12.

32. Edwards, *The Practice of Diaspora*, 12.

33. Tuan, *Space and Place*, 9.

34. Donald Gibson, "Richard Wright's *Black Boy* and the Trauma of Autobiographical Rebirth," 493.

35. See Tuan's definitions of place as security and space as freedom; "we are attached to the one and long for the other." Tuan, *Space and Place*, 3.

36. Tuan suggests that "mythical space" is a necessary part of complex systems of beliefs that hold on to a "terrestrial paradise" as part of a societal way of looking at the world. Wright's belief in a location wherein he could be the writer he desired is enmeshed in the unknown that is out there in "the North." Not surprisingly, Wright's encounter with the known that is Chicago meant that he could not sustain a belief in the North as paradise, but it also led him to transpose his idea of a "terrestrial" paradise to other places—New York and subsequently Paris, neither of which, much like Chicago, could hold up to his imagined space. On mythical space and place, see Tuan, *Space and Place*, 86.

37. Whitman, review of *American Hunger*.

38. Margarita Bowen coins the term "ecology of knowledge" in *Empiricism and Geographical Thought*, 272.

39. Du Bois, "Richard Wright Looks Back," 2.

40. Baker, *Blues, Ideology, and Afro-American Literature*, 145.

41. JanMohamed, *The Death-Bound Subject*, 146.

42. Hurston, "Stories of Conflict," 32.

43. Ellison, "Remembering Richard Wright," 216.

44. Dixon, *Ride out the Wilderness*, 56.

45. Ibid., 57.

46. Ibid., 58.

47. Ibid., 60.

48. Margolies, "The Letters of Richard Wright," 116.

49. A native of Columbus, Georgia, Shay Youngblood received a B.A. (1981) from Clark University (now Clark-Atlanta University) and an M.F.A. (1993) from Brown University. A playwright, screenplay writer, and novelist, she began her career as a writer with a distinctive, fearless voice exploring often-avoided family, gender, and race matters. In *The Big Mama Stories* (1989), sexual exploitation and sexual violence, rape, abortion, class antagonism, homophobia, black revolution, urban development and cityscapes, new familial configurations, kin by choice not blood, matriarchy and patriarchy, lesbianism, reproduction and reproductive rights, spirituality, dreams and dream makers, and love all came under her steady gaze and filtered through her visionary fiction into a consciousness of diversity in many manifestations. Not surprisingly, one of *The Big Mama Stories* won a Pushcart Prize. The decade of the 1990s was Shay Youngblood's decade of quiet fire: her plays *Shakin' the Mess Outta Misery*, adapted from her stories (1988), and *Talking Bones* were produced; she also wrote a screenplay of *Shakin'* for Columbia Pictures. Her play *Square Blues* was the Edward Albee Honoree at the 21st Century Playwrights Festival and was selected by Anna Deveare Smith to receive a playwriting award from the Paul Green Foundation.

50. McKittrick, *Demonic Grounds*, 61.

51. Grosz, "Bodies—Cities," 242.

52. Doreen Massey, *For Space*, 61.

53. Ibid., 119.

54. Youngblood, *Black Girl in Paris*, 1 (Youngblood's italics and boldface). Subsequent references appear parenthetically in the text.

55. Certeau, *The Practice of Everyday Life*, 121.

56. Ibid. (Certeau's italics).

57. See Polite, *The Flagellants* and *Sister X and the Victims of Foul Play*. Polite moved to France in 1964. *The Flagellants* was published in French, with an English version following in 1967. Her second novel, set in Paris, appeared after she had returned to the United States and begun teaching creative writing in 1971 at the University of Buffalo, where she taught until her retirement in 2000. Celebrated for her early treatment of black women and gender, Polite died at age seventy-seven on 7 December 2009.

58. See the gendered nature of labor, Leona and Ida as the primary workers, both waitresses, in Baldwin's *Another Country*; see also McDowell, "Spatializing Feminism."

59. McDowell, *Gender, Identity, and Place*, 131.

60. Certeau, *The Practice of Everyday Life*, 93.

61. Ibid., 97.

62. Stuart Hall, "Cultural Identity and Diaspora."

63. Certeau, *The Practice of Everyday Life*, 103.

64. McDowell, *Gender, Place, Identity*, 214.

65. Youngblood, *Soul Kiss*, 1–2.

66. See Tina McElroy Ansa's cover blurb for Youngblood, *Soul Kiss*.

67. Mondale, "Place-on-the-Move," 55.

68. Cosgrove, "Introduction: Mapping Meaning," 1.

69. Philip, "Dis Place—The Space Between."

70. Hammonds, "Black (W)holes and the Geometry of Black Female Sexuality," 494.

71. See her website (shayyoungblood.com) for illustrations of her paintings, many of which are untitled but have words contained within the painted space.

72. "Haiku by Richard Wright," 100–101. Ten of Wright's haiku poems appeared in this special issue, "The Life and Work of Richard Wright," edited by David Ray and guest coeditor Robert M. Farnsworth. Shortly after Wright's death, his haiku began to appear in print. The first appeared in Ollie Harrington's "The Last Days of Richard Wright," 93–94.

73. More haiku appear in Ellen Wright and Michel Fabre, *Richard Wright Reader*, 251–54. See also Rowley, *Richard Wright: The Life and Times*, 505–7.

74. Rowley, *Richard Wright: The Life and Times*, 505. Wright selected 817 haiku for publication, but the collection did not appear during his lifetime.

CHAPTER 4

1. See Douglas Massey and Nancy Denton, *American Apartheid: Segregation and the Making of the Underclass*, 13. Massey and Denton have identified the combination of behaviors and practices on the parts of individuals and institutions that result in segregated spaces and deteriorated residential structures.

2. In *The Origins of the Urban Crisis: Race and Inequality in Postwar Detroit*, Thomas Sugrue delineates the state, local, and federal laws, along with the private mechanisms (ideology, attitudes, and practices), that effectively confined urban blacks to less-desirable areas and then neglected those areas, blamed their impoverished conditions on the "raced" residents, and transferred a racial designation to those spaces. See Sugrue, *The Origins of the Urban Crisis*, 121.

3. See Haynes, *Red Lines, Black Space*, for an examination of the creation of racially defined residential space as the foundation for racializing American society and racially segregating educational, social, and religious institutional life, as well as for a discussion of how spatial conditions engendered racial consciousness that led to social solidarity and political mobilization as insulation from racism.

4. Houston Baker Jr., *Blues, Ideology, and Afro-American Literature*, 200, 202.

5. Rich, introduction to *My Mother's Dead Squirrel*, 14.

6. See Dyson, *Come Hell or High Water*; and Brinkley, *The Great Deluge*.

7. See, for example, Lowe, *Bridging Southern Cultures*. Houston Baker Jr., in *Turning South Again: Rethinking Modernism/Rereading Booker T.*, returns to a second consid-

eration of the South, modernism, autobiography, and the iconic Booker T. Washington. His *Critical Memory: Public Spheres, African American Writing, and Black Fathers and Sons in America* calls for "an energetic new southern studies." Baker and Dana D. Nelson, in editing "Violence, the Body, and the South," a special issue of *American Literature*, have forwarded the work of new southern studies.

8. Roach, *Cities of the Dead*, 179.

9. Hirsch and Logsdon, "Introduction to Part III: Franco-Africans and African-Americans," 189.

10. Ibid.

11. Marjorie R. Esman, in "About the Cajuns," a *Mississippi Quarterly* essay/review, observes, for example, that the recent proliferation of writings on Louisiana evidences a preoccupation with "Cajun culture to the exclusion of the cultures of other Louisiana groups" (113).

12. Brasseaux, Fontenot, and Oubre, *Creoles of Color in the Bayou Country*, 3.

13. Basing her work on contemporary accounts, Dunbar-Nelson provides a historical overview of free people of color from the earliest period to Reconstruction. Her text, written in English, appeared at a time when current histories, such as Charles Gayarré's *History of Louisiana* and Grace King's *New Orleans: The Place and the People*, made no effort to include people of color in their written records.

14. See Desdunes, *Our People and Our History*, 61–64. Desdunes identifies Joe Beaumont as the author of the Toucoutou song(s). According to Desdunes, Beaumont was a New Orleans native, born in 1820, who was an "ingenious and natural" poet; his songs especially displayed his "depth of thought" and his "teach[ing] of a moral based on life as it is" (61).

15. Bryan, "Marcus Christian's Treatment of *Les Gens de Couleur Libre*," 43.

16. Alejo Carpentier, quoted in Bongie, *Islands and Exiles*, 7.

17. Glissant, *Poétique de la Relation*, 46.

18. See, for example, Christopher L. Miller's *The French-Atlantic Triangle*, Ian Baucom's *Specters of the Atlantic*, Chris Bongie's *Islands and Exiles*, and Antonio Benítez-Rojo's *The Repeating Island*.

19. See Bernabé, Chamoiseau, and Confiant, *Éloge de la créolité/In Praise of Creoleness*, 87, 27–28.

20. Lewis, *Race, Culture, and Identity*, xvii.

21. See Glissant, *Poétique de la Relation*.

22. Mary Louise Pratt used the term "contact zones" to designate those areas in which different cultures come together. Benedict Anderson coined the phrase "imagined communities" to emphasize the formation of nationalism. See Pratt, *Imperial Eyes*; and Anderson, *Imagined Communities*. Carolyn Vellenga Berman used the metaphorical "crossings" to add to the vocabulary of colonial social formation. Berman, *Creole Crossings*, 4–7.

23. Bost, *Mulattas and Mestizas*, 89.

24. Ibid., 92.

25. Thernstrom, *Harvard Encyclopedia of American Ethnic Groups*, 247.

26. There has been a revisionist reading of de las Casas on African slavery to the extent that the Las Casas Centre for Human Rights has been established at Blackfriars Hall, Oxford University. Under the direction of Francis Davis, the new Las Casas Institute "aims to examine difficult questions in the spirit of dialogue, mutual respect, and friendship that is central to the Dominican intellectual tradition, enquiry, and disputation."

27. French, *Historical Collections of Louisiana*, part 3, 42. The first record of twenty Negro slaves arriving in the colony from Africa was made in 1713. See also Gayarré, *History of Louisiana*, 102.

28. Hanger, *Bounded Lives, Bounded Places*, 10. During the last two decades of the eighteenth century, the slave traffic increased so much that Gwendolyn Midlo Hall calls it the "re-Africanization" of Louisiana, with Africans being brought from Senegambia, the Bight of Benin, the Bight of Biafra, Central Africa, Cuba, and Saint-Domingue. See Gwendolyn Midlo Hall, *Africans in Colonial Louisiana*, 275–77.

29. Dunbar-Nelson, "People of Color in Louisiana," 5. Dunbar-Nelson uses the multivolume history of Charles Gayarré as her primary source of information on the changing population in the first decades of the eighteenth century.

30. Schafer, *Slavery, the Civil Law, and the Supreme Court of Louisiana*, 1.

31. Palmer, *The Louisiana Civilian Experience*, 101.

32. Dunbar-Nelson, "People of Color in Louisiana," 12.

33. Schafer, *Slavery, the Civil Law, and the Supreme Court of Louisiana*, 2–3. The French *Code Noir* prohibited self-purchase, and only masters over the age of twenty-five could, with the permission of the Conseil Supérieur and a legitimate reason, manumit a slave. See Schafer, *Slavery, the Civil Law, and the Supreme Court of Louisiana*, 1–2.

34. Hanger, *Bounded Lives, Bounded Places*, 3. By means of a study of the Spanish records of colonial New Orleans, Hanger traces the origins of Louisiana's large free-black population to the Spanish period and to Spanish law in particular.

35. Hanger labels the society in New Orleans, "hierarchical" and "patriarchal," but she suggests that it was also somewhat arbitrary in terms of racial formation, with decisions sometimes based solely on family connections or friendships or changing economic status. Hanger, *Bounded Lives, Bounded Places*, 15.

36. Schafer, *Slavery, the Civil Law, and the Supreme Court of Louisiana*, 3.

37. Ibid., 3–4.

38. Sibley, *Geographies of Exclusion*, 33.

39. Bell, *Revolution, Romanticism, and the Afro-Creole Protest Tradition in Louisiana, 1718–1868*, 11.

40. Sister Dorothea Olga McCants, foreword to *Our People and Our History*, by Desdunes, xi. She based her numbers on the 1810 census.

41. Bell, *Revolution, Romanticism, and the Afro-Creole Protest Tradition in Louisiana, 1718–1868*, 75.

42. Two Muller daughters survived the crossing in 1818 with their father and older brother, who died shortly after arriving from Europe. Their mother and baby brother

had died during the sea voyage. Left orphaned at under six years of age, Salomé and her sister Dorothea disappeared.

43. The Sally Miller case attracted George Washington Cable early on; see his account, "Salome Müller, The White Slave," in *Strange True Stories of Louisiana*. See also the contemporary texts: Wilson, *The Two Lives of Sally Miller*; and Bailey, *The Lost German Slave Girl*.

44. The declaration obtained in *Adéle v. Beauregard* in which Judge François-Xavier Martin considered that people of color could be descendants of Indians, whites, or free mulattoes and therefore presumed to be free. He underscored, however, that "Africans in slaveholding states" existed in the condition of slavery. Schafer, *Slavery, the Civil Law, and the Supreme Court of Louisiana*, 20.

45. Benítez-Rojo, *The Repeating Island*, 211.

46. Ibid.

47. Ibid., 211.

48. See Taylor, "New Orleans, 'America's European Masterpiece,'" chapter 4 of *Circling Dixie*, 9–128.

49. See the statement accompanying copyright of *Louisiana's Black Heritage*, ed. Macdonald, Kemp, and Haas. The project received a publication grant from the National Endowment for the Humanities.

50. Gruesz, *Ambassadors of Culture*, 109.

51. Ibid., 110.

52. Lowe, *Louisiana Culture from the Colonial Era to Katrina*, 20.

53. Ibid.

54. Hanger, *Bounded Lives, Bounded Places*, 15. Her conclusion is applicable to both Spanish and French New Orleans, though she draws her data primarily from the early Spanish records.

55. The discovery of the detailed records and the light they shed on the identities of enslaved people became major news stories at the start of the twenty-first century. See, for example, *New York Times*, national edition, July 30, 2000, 1, 13.

56. Bell, *Revolution, Romanticism, and the Afro-Creole Protest Tradition*, 65.

57. Desdunes especially praises Père Antoine for his tolerance of Creoles of Color and his support of their right to Catholic ritual. Bell details his part in various schisms within the colonial church and his advocacy of the rights of slaves and free blacks. Bell, *Revolution, Romanticism, and the Afro-Creole Protest Tradition*, 68–73.

58. Gross, "Litigating Whiteness," 176. See also Gross, *Slavery and Mastery in the Antebellum Southern Courtroom*.

59. See Archives of the Archdiocese of New Orleans, Louisiana. The records include the extant records of St. Louis Parish (church); of St. Louis Cathedral; and of baptisms, marriages, and burials of whites and nonwhites from 1772 to 1830. As is the case with the disappearance in 1966 of sixty-one bundles of civil records from Orleans Parish (government) that included petitions to establish purity of blood, emancipation suits, successions, and suits for breach of promise to marry and to collect money, there are St. Louis Parish records missing from the same period.

60. See Gilroy, *The Black Atlantic*.

61. Ibid., 15.

62. Ibid., 29.

63. See Cuevas, *African Mexicans and the Discourse of Modern Nation*; *The African Presence in Mexico*, an exhibition from the National Museum of Mexican Art cocurated by anthropologist Sagrario Cruz-Carrerto; and the film *The Third Root*, focusing on Veracruz, Acapulco, and La Costa Chica (which included Oaxaca and Guerrero).

64. Palmer, *The Louisiana Civilian Experience*, 3.

65. Ibid.

66. Blassingame, *Black New Orleans*, 10.

67. Ibid., 11.

68. Williamson, *New People*, xii. Two areas of the South, in particular, saw the most striking concentrations of mulattoes: the Charleston District in South Carolina and the lower Louisiana parishes, especially around New Orleans. As Williamson observed, "Over several decades after emancipation the distinctive mulatto elite disappeared, but it is virtually impossible to relate the history of Afro-America without appreciating the special role of these special people" (xiv). The U.S. Census from 1850 to 1920 designated "mulatto" to refer to any individuals of African descent in whom a mixture of white and black ancestry was visible.

69. New Orleans University actually was the oldest of the three, as it was formed out of three earlier institutions: Union Normal School (1868), Thompson's Biblical Institute, and Bayou Teche Academie. Straight University, which Alice Moore Dunbar-Nelson attended, survived the longest and became the most prestigious, especially in the 1870s and 1880s, when its student body was integrated. After the legal return to segregated education in 1877, the three universities provided black Louisiana with most of its teachers, doctors, and other professionals and contributed to the intellectual climate that indirectly helped to create a number of newspapers and journals that kept literary matters alive, if not flourishing, among blacks.

70. Sullivan also discusses Creoles of Color whose careers were local: Victor-Eugene McCarty, Samuel Snaër, Basile Barès (also Barrès), and the less-well-known Laurent Dubuclet. Neither Thomas J. Martin nor Frances Gotay, a Puerto Rican–born Holy Family nun (Sister Marie Seraphine), was a Louisiana Creole of Color, but both early twentieth-century composers illustrate the musical creativity within the communities of people of African descent in New Orleans.

71. See the liner notes from the compact discs for Lambert and Dédé.

72. See Sullivan, "Composers of Color of Nineteenth-Century New Orleans," 71. Sullivan includes an inventory of compositions by Creoles of Color included in New Orleans repositories (96–100). Sullivan's detailed essay for *Black Music Research Journal* 8.1 (1988): 51–82, provides the most substantial and careful archival work on the lives and careers of the nineteenth-century Creole musicians.

73. Sullivan, "Composers of Color of Nineteenth-Century New Orleans," 81.

74. Napoleon Bonaparte, quoted in *Daily Life in Louisiana, 1815–1930*, by Liliane Crété, 19.

75. Sullivan, "Composers of Color of Nineteenth-Century New Orleans," 55–56.

76. Ibid., 56.

77. To this day, members of the Dédé family in New Orleans—who still carry the name and to whom I am related by marriage—retell the story from generations past that he disappointed them by taking the money they had collected to send him abroad to study music but not returning to reside in New Orleans and by marrying outside to the Creole community. Dédé was a dark-skinned Creole of Color, and his marriage to a French woman might have been considered a move up by some, but to his New Orleans Creole family, it was a disappointment, whether for racial or provincial reasons.

78. Congo Square is now known as Louis Armstrong Park, named for the most famous of the New Orleans–born jazz musicians. By the mid-1990s, New Orleans began to receive more scholarly attention for it unique rituals, especially its carnival. See Mitchell, *All on Mardi Gras Day*; and Roach, *Cities of the Dead*.

79. See Martin, *"Plaçage* and the Louisiana *Gens de Couleur Libre*, 37–70.

80. Wilson, *The Two Lives of Sally Miller*, 59.

81. See Martin, *"Plaçage* and the Louisiana *Gens de Couleur Libre*." See also Guillory, "Under One Roof."

82. Dugué, "Memory of the Ball," 63.

83. Lanusse, "Epigram," 95. Lanusse also published a short story, *"Un Marriage de conscience,"* criticizing *plaçage*, in *Album littéraire: journal des jeunes gens, amateurs de littérature* (1843).

84. Schafer, *Brothels, Depravity, and Abandoned Women*, 31. Schafer's chapter "'Disgusting Depravity': Sex across the Color Line" uses court records and newspaper accounts to examine interracial sex (31–46).

85. Blassingame, *Black New Orleans*, 201.

86. Domínguez, *White by Definition*, 264.

87. Fabre, "New Orleans Creole Expatriates in France," 179. Fabre concludes his essay with a surprising generalization about the Creoles of Color in France: "They strove, with varying success, to maintain their families and earn comfortable livings as well as to build lasting reputations. They certainly enjoyed greater social freedom and professional opportunities in a country where they were largely exonerated from the burden of racial prejudice, and they fared well and felt at home in France. But they often found it difficult to carve out a territory for themselves, because competition was tough, because they lacked the supportive familial, social and professional network of Creole New Orleans, and because their French culture was too provincial for them to become part of the Paris elite." Fabre, "New Orleans Creole Expatriates in France," 195.

88. Charles Edwards O'Neill, Séjour's recent biographer, entitles his first chapter "Haiti, Louisiana, France" to signify the three nation-states associated with Séjour's early life. See O'Neill, *Séjour*, 1–19.

89. Blassingame, *Black New Orleans*, 11.

90. According to Auguste Viatte in *Histoire littéraire de l'Amérique française des origines à 1950*, 260, three of the contributors were white Creoles: J. L. Marciacq, Térence Rouquette, and Pierre Supervielle.

91. For a discussion of the contents of the four extant issues, all of which he located and read, see John Maxwell Jones Jr., *Slavery and Race in Nineteenth-Century Louisiana-French Literature*, 38ff.

92. Jarvis, *Postmodern Cartographies*, 7.

93. See Desdunes, *Our People and Our History*, 10; and Bell, *Revolution, Romanticism, and the Afro-Creole Protest Tradition in Louisiana*, 115.

94. Lanusse, introduction to *Les Cenelles: Choix de Poesies Indigenes*, 13.

95. Desdunes, *Our People and Our History*, 11.

96. Sollors, foreword to *Creole Echoes*, xvii.

97. Michel Séligny disgraced the family by his affair with a married white woman, with whom he eventually left Louisiana.

98. Thierry, "An Old Mulatress's Lament," 228–29.

99. Dalcour, *"Les Aeux"* ("Declaration"), 29. Desdunes refers to Dalcour's "quick, ready mind that made improvisation easy for him." Desdunes, *Our People and Our History*, 36.

100. Dalcour, *"Vers Ecrits sur L'Album de Mademoiselle***,"* in *Creole Echoes*, 29.

101. Sibley, *Geographies of Exclusion*, 33.

102. Desdunes, *Our People and Our History*, 40 (note 7).

103. Ibid., 26. Desdunes's brackets.

104. Desdunes, *Our People and Our History*, 39–40.

105. See Bell for a discussion of Constant Lépouzé, a white émigré from France who taught Creoles of Color and was himself a poet and a classical scholar. Bell, *Revolution, Romanticism, and the Afro-Creole Protest Tradition in Louisiana*, 118–20.

106. Latortue and Adams, *Les Cenelles: A Collection of Poems by Creole Writers of the Early Nineteenth Century*, xviii.

107. Valcour, *"L'Ouvrier Louisiannais,"* 10–11.

108. Edward Coleman, *Creole Voices*, xix.

109. Thompson, *Exiles at Home*, 116–17.

110. hooks, *Yearning*, 149ff.

111. Desdunes includes a memento from the New Orleans newspaper *L'Abeille* on the death of Madame Lamotte. Desdunes, *Our People and Our History*, 100–101.

112. Ibid., 101.

113. See Guillory, "Under One Roof," 67–92.

114. Desdunes, *Our People and Our History*, 141.

115. Ibid., 147.

116. Gloria Thompson Hull edited Alice Dunbar-Nelson's diaries, reclaiming Dunbar-Nelson's literary legacy for contemporary readers.

117. Bryan, *The Myth of New Orleans in Literature*, 70.

118. See Eleanor Alexander, *Lyrics of Sunshine and Shadow*, 44–73.

119. Dunbar-Nelson, "Brass Ankles," 311.

120. Dunbar-Nelson, "People of Color in Louisiana," 67–69.

121. See the chapter on her later life, "The Everyday Struggle and Contradictions of Uplift Ideology in the Life and Writings of Alice Dunbar-Nelson," in Kevin K. Gaines, *Uplifting the Race*, 209–33.

122. *Creole* appeared in 2000 from Louisiana State University Press under the editorship of Sybil Kein, poet, Creole of Color, and descendant of Alice Ruth Moore. Kein remembers her ancestor and asks for remembrance in her poem "Letter to Alice Ruth Moore, 14 April 1894": "With this I send to you a heartfelt plea—/ Be well and if you can, remember me." See Kein, *Creole Journal*, 50.

123. Latortue and Adams, *Les Cenelles*, xiv. Latortue and Adams find the poetry lacking the "subtexts of revolution and freedom which existed in the works of the best of the French Romantics" (xiii).

124. Senter, "Creole Poets on the Verge of a Nation," 181. Following the discourse on Creole ethnicity presented by Rodolphe Lucien Desdunes in *Our People and Our History*, Senter believes that "the mixed identity produced a syncretic and mercurial culture, one whose over expression could have only been possible during such a time of social transformation" (181).

125. Harvey, *Spaces of Capital*, 212.

126. Rodolphe Lucien Desdunes, the author of *Our People and Our History*, organized the committee in 1890 to challenge the new laws segregating railway cars by race. Arthur Esteves was president and Caesar Carpentier Antoine was vice president of the eighteen-member committee, which included prominent descendants of free people Numa E. Mansion (a journalist on the *Daily Crusader* newspaper), Lucien Mansion ("Lolo," a cigar manufacturer), and Louis A. Martinet (founder of the *Daily Crusader*). The Comité des Citoyens collected $2,767.25, which was designated especially for testing the constitutionality of Jim Crow car laws in what would become *Plessy v. Ferguson*, the famous case in which the Supreme Court ruled against Plessy, the challenger to segregated public train accommodations, and established the policy of "Separate but Equal," justifying segregation. See Rousseve, *The Negro in Louisiana*, 129.

127. Jay, *America the Scrivener*, ix.

128. Ibid.

129. Ibid., xi.

130. Ibid., 276.

131. Bhabha, *The Location of Culture*, 2. Using south-central Los Angeles as an example, Bhabha observes that histories of cultural difference within communities sharing histories of deprivation and discrimination have to be considered so as to avoid the expectation that "the exchange of values, meanings and priorities [will] always be collaborative and dialogical" within culturally diverse communities.

132. Ibid., 25.

133. "Trading on the Margin" was first titled "Good-bye Columbus" and presented at the 1990 American Studies Association meeting for the panel Firing the Canon. Gates, *Loose Canons*, 174.

134. Ibid.

135. Ibid., 175.

136. See Gates, "The Master Pieces: On Canon Formation and the African-American Tradition," in *Loose Canons*, 17–42.

137. Anzaldúa, *Borderlands*, 87.

138. Gilroy, *The Black Atlantic*, 3, 4. See also Spillers, "Who Cuts the Border?," 16.

139. Gates, *Loose Cannons*, 177.

140. Black Public Sphere Collective, *The Black Public Sphere*, 1. The Collective rethought the possibilities for understanding the public sphere from the perspective of race and political activism.

141. Black Public Sphere Collective, *The Black Public Sphere*, 3.

142. Takaki, *A Different Mirror*, 427. In a model of his premise of what it requires to "get along," Takaki completes his discussion with statements by Toni Morrison and Black Elk, both of which resonate with the notion of one made from many.

143. See Fireside, *Separate and Unequal*.

144. Domínquez, *White by Definition*, 37.

145. Ibid.

146. Ibid., 45.

147. Ibid.

148. See La. Rev., Stat. Ann. 42: 267—Supp. 23A of 1975.

149. Federal Writers' Project of the Works Progress Administration, *New Orleans City Guide*, 43.

150. Barthelemy, "Light, Bright, Damn *Near* White," 252–75.

151. See the most recent treatment of the Toucoutou case in Kein, "One Drop Rules," 136–46.

152. Domínquez, *White by Definition*, 2.

153. Foucault, "Of Other Spaces," 26.

154. Osbey, *All Saints*, 1.

155. Foucault, "Of Other Spaces," 22–27. Foucault discusses the cemetery as part of the second principle of heterotopias—that, as its history unfolds, a society "can make an existing heterotopia function in a very different fashion . . . according to the synchrony of the culture" (25).

156. Dixon, *Ride out the Wilderness*, 6. Dixon used the relationship between place and performance to advance African American language-based criticism promulgated in the groundbreaking work of Robert B. Stepto in *Behind the Veil*.

157. Osbey, "Desire and Private Griefs," in *All Saints*, 7.

158. Ibid., 10.

159. Osbey, "Faubourg," in *All Saints*, 37.

160. Osbey, "Elvena," in *All Saints*, 70.

161. Osbey, "Suicide City," in *All Saints*, 117.

162. Osbey, "I Want to Die in New Orleans," 246.

163. See the film by Logsdon and Elie, *Faubourg Treme: The Untold Story of Black New Orleans*.

164. Bryan, *The Myth of New Orleans in Literature*, 154.

165. Thomas, "Black Poetry in the '80s—Alive and Dancing," 12ff.

166. Osbey, "Ceremony for Minneconjoux," in *Ceremony for Minneconjoux*, 9.

167. Ibid., 21.

168. Osbey, "Geography," in *In These Houses*, 49.

169. Ibid., 48.

170. Osbey, "House of Bones, in *In These Houses*, 50.

171. Ibid., 51.

172. Lemmons, *Eve's Bayou*. The film was ranked as one of the best made in 1997.

173. See Hambly, *A Free Man of Color, Fever Season, Graveyard Dust, Wet Grave, Sold down the River*, and *Die upon a Kiss*. One of the later Benjamin January, *fmc*, mysteries, *Days of the Dead* (2003), is set in Mexico rather than in New Orleans.

174. See Kein, *Sérénade Créole: Rhythms of Love* (songs in Spanish, French, Creole, Kreyole, and English), *Creole Ballads & Zydeco*, and *Maw-Maw's Creole Lullaby*.

175. Morton, "Creole Culture in the Poetry of Sybil Kein," 317.

176. Kein, "The Use of Louisiana Creole in Southern Literature," 117–54.

177. Kein, *Gumbo People*, v.

178. Kein, "Contributions of the Gens de Couleur and Their Descendants to an American South," 131.

179. Kein, *Bonjour Créole!* The fifty-one-page manual includes Creole expressions, pronunciations, and English translations, along with a vocabulary section and a basic grammar.

180. Kein, *Maw-Maw's Creole ABC Book*.

181. Tuan, *Escapism*, 96.

182. Ibid., 97–98.

183. Kein, "From the French Market," *Creole Journal*, 51–52.

184. See Gwendolyn Midlo Hall, *Africans in Colonial Louisiana*.

185. Kein, *An American South*, 67–68.

186. Komunyakaa, *Thieves of Paradise*, 11.

187. Trethewey, *Native Guard*, 33.

CHAPTER 5

1. Kein, *Creole Journal*, 73.

2. Ibid.

3. Ernest Gaines, "A Conversation with Ernest Gaines," 68.

4. Ernest Gaines, "Miss Jane and I," 9.

5. Barthes, *Roland Barthes by Roland Barthes*, 6 (epigraph).

6. Gaines frequently mentions Faulkner in commenting on his influences, objectives, and style. See the multiple references in Lowe, *Conversations with Ernest Gaines*; and in Gaudet and Wooton, *Porch Talk with Ernest Gaines*.

7. Mary Ellen Doyle provides the most extensive biographical detail for Gaines's early life and family background in "Place, People, Personal Experience," 4–24.

8. Tuan, *Space and Place*, 161.

9. Certeau, *The Practice of Everyday Life*, 200.

10. Ibid., 201.

11. Gregory, *Geographical Imaginations*, 104.

12. Valerie Babb discusses Gaines as a modernist in "Old-Fashioned Modernism: 'The Changing Same' in *A Lesson Before Dying*," 250–64. See an early treatment of Gaines's modernism in Werner, *Paradoxical Resolutions*.

13. See Fuller, "Going Home: The Transcript." Reese's article is based on the interview that appeared in the *Times of Acadiana*, 5 March 2003.

14. Ibid. Gaines published the first chapter of "The House and the Field" in the *Iowa Review* in 1972.

15. Ernest Gaines, "This Louisiana Thing That Drives Me," 89.

16. Ernest Gaines, "A Conversation with Ernest Gaines," 68.

17. Ernest Gaines, "Interview with Ernest Gaines," 138.

18. Foucault, "Of Other Spaces," 22–27.

19. Foucault, *The Order of Things*, 113.

20. Glissant, *Poetics of Relation*, 63.

21. Ernest Gaines, *Catherine Carmier*, 36. Subsequent references appear parenthetically in the text.

22. Ernest Gaines, "Interview with Ernest Gaines," 146.

23. Tuan, *Space and Place*, 86.

24. Ibid., 88.

25. Ibid., 99.

26. According to Walter Johnson, New Orleans "throughout the antebellum period was unsurpassed in one respect. [It was] North America's largest slave market." Walter Johnson, *Soul by Soul*, 2.

27. Thomas Jefferson, letter to John Eppes, 30 June 1820, quoted in Sublette, *The World That Made New Orleans*, 219.

28. Crang, *Cultural Geography*, 24.

29. See James L. Hill, "The Anti-Heroic in Frank Yerby's Historical Novels"; Turner, "Frank Yerby as Debunker," 569–77; William W. Hill, "Behind the Magnolia Mask."

30. Short, *Imagined Country*, xvii. Short also cites the wilderness in classic American westerns and "bleak city scenes in Edward Hopper" along with his mention of Tolstoy as examples of environmental ideas used in texts (xvii).

31. Ernest Gaines, "Miss Jane and I," 9.

32. See Gaines's comments on the year 1948 in his fiction in "An Interview with Ernest Gaines," 306–7 (John Lowe, interviewer).

33. Ernest Gaines, "Miss Jane and I," 9–10.

34. Ibid., 10.

35. Doreen Massey, *For Space*, 154.

36. McDowell, *Gender, Identity, and Place*, 29.

37. See Ernest Gaines, "Finding the Voice," in *Porch Talk with Ernest Gaines*, ed. Gaudet and Wooton, 37.

38. Ibid.

39. Ibid.

40. Ernest Gaines, "A Conversation with Ernest Gaines," 58.

41. Ernest Gaines, "Miss Jane and I," 5.

42. Ernest Gaines, "A Conversation with Ernest Gaines," 68. Gaines also repeats almost verbatim his experience of growing up under conditions similar to his ancestors under slavery: "By the '30s, when I was born, conditions were not too much different from the times of slavery. We were attached to the place. . . . You couldn't move around and do whatever you wanted to do." Culpepper and Broussard, "Writer Draws on Pointe Coupee Childhood," 217.

43. Nancy Duncan points out that women and "others" become accustomed to "feelings of overwhelming immersion" in an environment they are less able than men to control, but that they "are more responsible for its production and reproduction." Duncan, *BodySpace*, 6.

44. Ernest Gaines, *A Lesson before Dying*, 38.

45. Harvey, *The Condition of Postmodernity*, viii.

46. Lyotard, *The Postmodern Condition*, 81.

47. Ernest Gaines, *The Autobiography of Miss Jane Pittman*, 108. Subsequent references appear parenthetically in the text.

48. See Gaines's extended discussions of Louisiana's people and customs that inform his fiction in Gaudet and Wooten, *Porch Talk with Ernest Gaines*. The sections "Family and Culture" and "Folklore and Ethnicity" take up the more complex issues of Louisiana Creoles of Color and Cajuns and blacks.

49. Tanya Brickley, Gaines's booking agent of many years, named the house. See Marcia Gaudet and Reggie Scott Young on the building of the Gaines house on False River in their introduction to Ernest Gaines, *Mozart and Leadbelly*, ix.

50. Ernest Gaines quoted in Seelye, "Writer Tends Land Where Ancestors Were Slaves."

51. Gaines has said: "I keep telling Dianne we've been married for thirty-three years, because this relationship is the one I dreamed of when I was writing *Catherine Carmier*." Ernest Gaines, "Bard from the Bayou," 281. Gaines extended his commentary by relating his marriage both to the relationship of Grant and Vivian in *A Lesson before Dying* and to that of Jackson and Catherine in *Catherine Carmier*: "Jackson is told that he must wait thirty years for his Catherine, and it's about thirty years between those two books—the first one came out in 1964. And I found my Dianne and married her thirty years after that! There's a close connection there. Someone met me the other day . . . and she said 'I am so exasperated with *Catherine Carmier*! . . . You have to write a sequel.' And I said 'the sequel is that Dianne and I got married!'" Ernest Gaines, "An Interview with Ernest Gaines," 302 (John Lowe, interviewer). References to *Catherine Carmier* appear parenthetically in the text.

52. See Berry, "The Haunting Voice of Ernest Gaines," 284.

53. Dawdy, *Building the Devil's Empire*, 175. Dawdy maintains that after the 1730s, "New Orleans became a multicolored place, both in neighborhoods and within individual households" (176).

54. Gaines gives the tentative title "The Girl Who Lived across the Fence" to a story he hoped to write "about a girl who grows up to be a young woman and eventually commits suicide. She's one of those girls who's nearly white, like Catherine Carmier,

and has problem after problem." Ernest Gaines, "An Interview with Ernest Gaines," 328 (John Lowe, interviewer).

55. See Duncan, "Sexuality in Public and Private Spaces," in *BodySpace*, 129.

56. See Beavers, *Wresting Angels into Song*; and Clark, *Black Manhood in James Baldwin, Ernest J. Gaines, and August Wilson*.

57. Suzanne W. Jones, "New Narratives of Southern Manhood," 47.

58. O'Brien, *Interviews with Black Writers*, 28.

59. Certeau, *The Practice of Everyday Life*, 190.

60. Ibid.

61. Ibid., 190–91.

62. hooks, *Yearning*, 146.

63. Ernest Gaines, *A Gathering of Old Men*, 80. Subsequent references appear parenthetically in the text.

64. Gaines's text not only demonstrates the transformation possible among black men, but it also portrays the changes taking place among the whites, perhaps most dramatically among the Cajuns, for whom masculinity has not accommodated racial difference. The brutality Sheriff Mapes has shown in dealing with all blacks ceases as he develops respect for the elders who would stand up to him and for themselves. Fix Boutan, aging no less than the black men, no longer demands vigilante action from his family and other Cajuns; he accepts that the law and courts can be responsible for justice. His son Gil, a student at Louisiana State University, is part of a new code of race relations; education has changed his inherited attitudes toward blacks, in part because of a general exposure to a wider world than the self-contained Cajun one and in part because of his individual association with a black teammate, who, with Gil, makes up the high-scoring football duo "Salt and Pepper."

65. Gaines repeatedly remarks that *In My Father's House* was difficult for him; he "just couldn't get it done." Ernest Gaines, "'I Heard the Voices . . . of my Louisiana People.'" See also Ernest Gaines, "This Louisiana Thing That Drives Me," 88–89; and Ernest Gaines, "A MELUS Interview: Ernest J. Gaines," 156.

66. Beavers, *Wresting Angels into Song*, 70.

67. Ibid., 71.

68. Ibid.

69. Perhaps the most intriguingly personal of Gaines's novels, *In My Father's House* contains scattered references to Gaines's social history at River Lake Plantation, to his absent biological father, and especially to his own mother, Adrienne Jefferson Colar—the town is St. Adrienne and a character's surname is Colar, even though women are mutable spaces within the text and suffer in the reconstructed stories men tell. Gaines admits his reticence in talking about his parents, especially his father: "My father went into—you know this is one of the things I'd rather not go deep into, family things—but my father went into the service during World War II. So he was not there." Gaudet and Wooten, *Porch Talk*, 68.

70. Ernest Gaines, *In My Father's House*, 30, 16. Subsequent references appear parenthetically in the text.

71. Byerman, *Fingering the Jagged Grain*, 97.

72. Ernest Gaines, "An Interview with Ernest Gaines," 306 (John Lowe, interviewer).

73. Lowe, "Transcendence in the House of Death," 148.

74. Ernest Gaines, *Of Love and Dust*, 11. Subsequent references appear parenthetically in the text.

75. Ernest Gaines, "Miss Jane and I," 16.

76. David Lionel Smith links Gaines's novel primarily to Faulkner's *Absalom, Absalom!* and to a lesser extent to *Light in August*. See David Lionel Smith, "Bloodlines and Patriarchs," 46–61.

77. Ernest Gaines, "Three Men," in *Bloodline*, 132. Subsequent references appear parenthetically in the text.

78. Keith Clark reaches a similar conclusion: "Gaines's dogged attempt to intervene upon the archetypal narrative of black southern male evisceration with his own revitalized portraitures is laudable but ultimately knotty." Clark, "Que(e)rying the Prison-House of Black Male Desire: Homosociality in Ernest Gaines's 'Three Men,'" 239.

79. Ernest Gaines, "Interview with Ernest Gaines," 144.

80. Ernest Gaines, *A Lesson before Dying*, 7. Subsequent references appear parenthetically in the text.

81. Lowe, "Transcendence in the House of Death," 162.

82. Byerman, *Remembering the Past in Contemporary African American Fiction*, 53.

83. Ernest Gaines, "This Louisiana Thing That Drives Me," 95–96.

84. Obama, "Victory Speech."

85. Kenan, "An Interview with Randall Kenan," 134.

86. Kenan, interview in *Brightleaf*.

87. Ibid.

88. Tuan, *Space and Place*, 99.

89. Kenan, "An Interview with Randall Kenan," 143.

90. Foucault, *The Order of Things*, xvii.

91. Ibid., xviii.

92. Kenan, "Meet Randall Kenan."

93. Ibid.

94. Kenan, *Let the Dead Bury Their Dead and Other Stories*, 279. Subsequent references appear parenthetically in the text.

95. Hunt, "A Conversation with Randall Kenan," 414.

96. Foucault, "Of Other Spaces," 26.

97. Sibley, *Geographies of Exclusion*, xiv.

98. Ibid., 183.

99. Kenan, *A Visitation of Spirits*, 151. Subsequent references appear parenthetically in the text.

100. Kenan in "Meet Randall Kenan," an interview with H. B. Grace. Kenan refers to Rita Mae Brown's 1973 novel *Rubyfruit Jungle*, a narrative tracing the coming out of Molly Bolt, a young southern feminist.

101. Hunt, "A Conversation with Randall Kenan," 415.

102. Cresswell, *Place: A Short History*, 13. See also Cresswell, *In Place/Out of Place*.

103. E. Patrick Johnson, *Sweet Tea*, 1.

104. Ibid., 6–7.

105. Minh-ha, "Not You/Like You," 415.

106. Ibid.

107. Truman Capote's exquisite *Other Voices, Other Rooms* left no immediate progeny. The subject is rarely something that African American literature before the late 1980s represented except in homoerotic-implicated situations and relational identities. The exception is James Baldwin in *Giovanni's Room* and *Another Country* and Ann Allen Shockley in *Loving Her*. Richard Wright in *Native Son* also laces exchanges between Bigger Thomas and his friends with homoerotic overtones. The attraction-repulsion between Trueblood and Norton in Ralph Ellison's *Invisible Man* may be figured as homoerotic as well as a voyeuristic exploration of desire and father-daughter incest, as Houston Baker Jr. has written of Trueblood in "To Move without Moving."

108. Hamer, "A Goldsboro Narrative," 1052. See also Hamer's two books of poetry, *Call and Response* and *Middle Ear*.

109. Hamer, "A Goldsboro Narrative," 1058.

110. Ibid.

111. Ibid.

112. Ibid., 1061.

113. Ibid., 1056.

114. E. Patrick Johnson, *Sweet Tea*, 5, 6.

115. See, for example, Kenan, *A Visitation of Spirits*, 40–43, 110–14, 181–88.

116. Bachelard, *The Poetics of Space*, 183.

117. Kenan, *A Visitation of Spirits*, 7–9; see also the final meditation on hogs and time past (9–10).

118. See Mikhail Bakhtin on Dostoevsky and chronotopes. Kenan uses an excerpt from Bakhtin's "Forms of Time and Chronotope in the Novel" (from *The Dialogic Imagination*) as an epigraph to "Let the Dead Bury Their Dead."

119. See Morson, *Narrative and Freedom*, 234, on the past as containing signs pointing to what happened later, or foreshadowing after the fact.

120. Bachelard, *The Poetics of Space*, 201.

121. Ibid., 202.

122. Ibid., 203.

CHAPTER 6

1. Tuan, *Space and Place*, v.

2. hooks, "Choosing the Margins as a Space of Radical Openness," in *Yearning*, 149.

3. Lefebvre, *The Production of Space*, 365.

4. Gwin, "Her Shape, His Hand," 84–85.

5. Alice Walker, *In Search of Our Mothers' Gardens*, 233.

6. Dixon, *Ride out the Wilderness*, 56. Walker persists in "creat[ing] meaning out of chaos" in her recent prose; see her *Overcoming Speechlessness*.

7. Michael Dear, in *The Postmodern Urban Condition*, 7, points out that such an imprecation applies equally to the political and scholarly worlds. He suggests: "De-centered individuals are obliged to invent their own radically subjective politics, and the production of identity (and place) becomes fragmentary, deeply conflicted, and frequently contradictory" (8).

8. It is no accident that Walker's story "Everyday Use" has become the standard-bearer for the politics of everyday life and the value of the everyday. The practical politics of the everyday is the forte that Walker explored and understood, perhaps in-tuitively, but understood nonetheless as always negotiated and contested, long before Michel de Certeau, Luce Giard, and Pierre Mayol published their study *The Practice of Everyday Life, Volume 2: Living and Cooking*, which has now called attention to the significance of the everyday as an object of analysis.

9. Cartwright, "Southern Polarities and Meridians of Alice Walker's 'Resident Spiritually.'"

10. Alice Walker, *Anything We Love Can Be Saved*, 46.

11. See Doreen Massey, "Introduction: Geography Matters," 1–11, for a consideration of how the social is also a spatial construction.

12. Alice Walker, "Recording the Seasons," in *In Search of Our Mothers' Gardens*, 231.

13. Walker returned to the North in 1971 and there completed a collection of short stories, *In Love and Trouble: Stories of Black Women* (1973), which articulated the stories of southern African American women and reflected the influence of several masters of short fiction, including Zora Neale Hurston, Flannery O'Connor, and Jean Toomer. *In Love and Trouble* won the Rosenthal Award of the National Institute of Arts and Letters in 1974; two stories from the collection, "Everyday Use" and "The Revenge of Hannah Kemhuff," appeared in the 1973 and 1974 editions of *Best American Short Stories* and have become her most frequently anthologized texts. Her second volume of poems, *Revolutionary Petunias and Other Poems* (1973), continued exploration of her social and historical relationship to the region of her birth. However, her father's death that same year prompted her reconsideration not only of his life, but also of her personal relationship to him and the family and community that she had left behind. Many of her essays collected in *In Search of Our Mothers' Gardens* (1983) and her poems in *Good Night, Willie Lee, I'll See You in the Morning* (1979) date from this period of self, familial, and communal reflection. The title poem, "Good Night, Willie Lee, I'll See You in the Morning," is a reflection on her father's life filtered through the words her mother spoke at his funeral.

14. Alice Walker, quoted in Krista Brewer, "Writing to Survive: An Interview with Alice Walker," 13.

15. Foucault, "Of Other Spaces," 23.

16. Douglas Massey and Nancy Denton, *American Apartheid*, 13. They also point to the social contexts that result from these spatial considerations.

17. Sugrue, *The Origins of the Urban Crisis*, 121. Sugrue traces the process by which law, practice, and custom confined blacks to the ghetto and then blamed them for the impoverished conditions existing there and transferred a racial designation to the space.

18. See Bone, *The Postsouthern Sense of Place in Contemporary Fiction*; and the discussion of Bambara's *These Bones Are Not My Child* that concludes Bone's study (219–40).

19. First published in 1991, Carby's "The Politics of Fiction, Anthropology, and the Folk: Zora Neale Hurston" attempts to collapse many historical moments into her indictment of an escapism into the romance of southern folk and community traceable to Hurston.

20. See Madhu Dubey's chapter "Reading as Listening: The Southern Folk Aesthetic" in *Signs and Cities*, 144–85. Dubey takes her title from Samuel Delany's *Neveryóna, or: The Tale of Signs and Cities*.

21. Doreen Massey, *For Space*, 11.

22. Harvey, *Justice, Nature, and the Geography of Difference*, 306.

23. Alice Walker, "I Know What the Earth Says," 12.

24. Ibid., 19.

25. Ibid. See also Rudolph P. Byrd's collection of Walker interviews, *The World Has Changed: Conversations with Alice Walker*, for similar comments.

26. Alice Walker, "The Unglamorous but Worthwhile Duties of the Black Revolutionary Artist, or of the Black Writer Who Simply Works and Writes," in *In Search of Our Mothers' Gardens*, 135 (Walker's italics).

27. Foucault, "Of Other Spaces," 23.

28. Butler-Evans, *Race, Gender, and Desire*, 123.

29. Alice Walker, preface to *The Same River Twice*, 13.

30. Ibid.

31. Foucault, "Of Other Spaces," 23.

32. Alice Walker, "The Flowers," in *In Love and Trouble*, 119–20. Subsequent references appear parenthetically in the text.

33. Alice Walker, *In Search of Our Mothers' Gardens*, 239.

34. Spain, *Gendered Spaces*, 14.

35. White, *Alice Walker: A Life*, 462–63. White quotes Walker as saying at the ceremony on 9 February 1994: "Whatever the word Tallulah means in itself, to me it means 'restored' in me. . . . The word Kate means 'remembered' in me" (462ff).

36. Allen, *The Sacred Hoop*, 243–44.

37. In "Patches: Quilts and Community in Alice Walker's [short story] 'Everyday Use,'" Houston Baker and Charlotte Pierce-Baker tell us: "A patch is a fragment. It is a vestige of wholeness that stands as a sign of loss and a challenge to creative design. As a remainder or remnant, the patch may symbolize rupture or impoverishment; it may be defined by the faded glory of the already gone. But as a fragment, it is also rife with explosive potential of the yet-to-be-discovered. . . . [I]t is a liminal element between wholes" (119).

38. See Lorde, "Interview with Pratibha Parmar and Jackie Kay."

39. See Duncan, *BodySpace*.

40. McDowell, *Gender, Identity, and Place*, 55.

41. Alice Walker, *Meridian*, 4. Subsequent references appear parenthetically in the text.

42. As John Kronik has observed of performance, "What was once an event, has become a critical category, now applied to everything from a play to a war to a meal. The performative . . . is a cultural act, a critical perspective, a political intervention." Kronik, "Editor's Note," 425.

43. Melissa Walker, *Down from the Mountaintop*, 171–72. Alice Walker herself deploys the terms "fragmented, surreal" (*Meridian*, 96) that Melissa Walker uses.

44. Alice Walker, "Revolutionary Petunias," in *Revolutionary Petunias*, 29.

45. Ibid.

46. Gaston Bachelard's explication of Rilke's *Poemes français* focuses on a lone walnut tree and its ability to command attention because of its location and its roundness, its function as a "document for a phenomenology of a being which is at once established in its roundness and developing it." See Bachelard, *The Poetics of Space*, 239, 240.

47. Holloway, *Moorings and Metaphors*, 37.

48. Bachelard, *The Poetics of Space*, 234.

49. Ibid., 240.

50. Finney, *The World Is Round*. The title poem is "The World Is Round: The Breast of the Garment Measured." Like the work of Walker's burial mound, Finney's poem focuses on the matrilineal connections and completions.

51. Alice Walker, "Alice Walker: On Finding Your Bliss," 42–50. Walker presents her ideas about isolation and loneliness in terms reminiscent of Meridian Hill. See the end of the interview: "life is about growth, struggle, and trying to expand your love of self and of other people. Also to really try hard to not cause harm—to cultivate a way of life that is harmless" (50).

52. Alice Walker, "I Know What the Earth Says," 17.

53. Alice Walker, *The Way Forward Is with a Broken Heart*, 36.

54. See Fiske, "Cultural Studies and the Culture of Everyday Life," 162.

55. Alice Walker, *Absolute Trust in the Goodness of the Earth*, xi.

56. Ibid.

57. Gwin, *The Woman in the Red Dress*, 95. Gwin titles her ambitious chapter on texts by Toni Morrison, Lee Smith, Alice Walker, Kaye Gibbons, Dorothy Allison, and Jane Smiley "Nonfelicitious Space and Survivor Discourse: Reading Father-Daughter Incest" (55–115). See Fryer, *Felicitous Space*.

58. K. T. H. Cheatwood, review of *Horses Make a Landscape Look More Beautiful*; quoted in Alice Walker, "In the Closet of My Soul," in *Living by the Word*, 86. Cheatwood's review appeared in the Richmond, Virginia, *News Leader* in 1984. Walker cites the review as an example of black male critics misinterpreting her work.

59. Wall, *Worrying the Line*, 211.

60. Alice Walker, *Living by the Word*, 192.

61. Alice Walker, *Absolute Trust in the Goodness of the Earth*, xi.

62. Ibid., xii. Not coincidentally, then, Walker incorporates a number of poems from *Absolute Trust* into *We Are the Ones We Have Been Waiting For: Inner Light in a Time of Darkness*.

63. Alice Walker, "New House Moves," in *Absolute Trust in the Goodness of the Earth*, 33–36.

64. Alice Walker, "My Ancestor's Earnings," in *Absolute Trust in the Goodness of the Earth*, 130.

65. Alice Walker, *In Search of Our Mothers' Gardens*, 249.

66. Alice Walker, "How Poems Are Made/A Discredited View," in *Horses Make a Landscape Look More Beautiful*, 17.

67. Alice Walker, "Goodnight, Willie Lee, I'll See You in the Morning," in *Goodnight, Willie Lee, I'll See You in the Morning*, 53.

68. Alice Walker, "Songless," in *Horses Make a Landscape Look More Beautiful*, 27–28.

69. Alice Walker, "Despite the Hunger," in *Absolute Trust in the Goodness of the Earth*, 20.

70. Alice Walker, "At First, It Is True, I Thought There Were Only Peaches & Wild Grapes," in *Absolute Trust in the Goodness of the Earth*, 59.

71. Alice Walker, "Bring Me the Heart of María Sabina," in *Absolute Trust in the Goodness of the Earth*, 227–28. Walker describes María Sabina as "Shaman, healer, priestess of the mushrooms . . . a legend in Mexico even while alive. Today she remains passionately revered, respected, loved, because she dedicated her life to the health and happiness of all humans." *Absolute Trust in the Goodness of the Earth*, xiv. "The children" in the poem refer to Sabina's mushrooms.

72. Ibid., 228–29.

73. Alice Walker, "If They Come to Shoot You," in *Absolute Trust in the Goodness of the Earth*, 211.

Bibliography

Abel, Elizabeth. "American Graffiti: The Social Life of Segregation Signs." *African American Review* 42, no. 1 (Spring 2008).

Adams, Jessica. "Plantations without Slaves." In *Wounds of Returning: Race, Memory, and Property on the Postslavery Plantation*, 54–85. Chapel Hill: University of North Carolina Press, 2007.

———. Review of *Look Away! The U.S. South in New World Studies*. *Bryn Mawr Review of Comparative Literature* 6, no. 2 (Fall 2007).

———. *Wounds of Returning: Race, Memory, and Property on the Postslavery Plantation*. Chapel Hill: University of North Carolina Press, 2007.

The African Presence in Mexico. Exhibition cocurated by Sagrario Cruz-Carrerto and Cesáreo Moreno. National Museum of Mexican Art, 2006.

Ainley, Rosa, ed. *New Frontiers of Space, Bodies, and Gender*. London: Routledge, 1998.

Alexander, Eleanor. *Lyrics of Sunshine and Shadow: The Tragic Courtship and Marriage of Paul Laurence Dunbar and Alice Ruth Moore*. New York: New York University Press, 2001.

Alexander, Elizabeth. *The Black Interior*. Minneapolis: Graywolf Press, 2004.

———. "Can You Be BLACK and Look at This? Reading the Rodney King Video." *Public Culture* 7 (1994): 77–94.

Allen, Paula Gunn. *The Sacred Hoop*. Boston: Beacon Press, 1992. Originally published 1986.

Anderson, Benedict. *Imagined Communities: Reflections on the Origin and Spread of Nationalism*. London: Verso, 1983.

Anzaldúa, Gloria. *Borderlands, La Frontera: The New Mestiza*. San Francisco: Aunt Lute, 1987.

Apel, Dora. *Imagery of Lynching: Black Men, White Women and the Mob*. New Brunswick: Rutgers University Press, 2004.

Archdiocese of New Orleans, Louisiana, Office of Archives. Sacramental Record Series, vols. 1–19 (1718–1831).

Avilez, GerShun. "Housing the Black Body: Value, Domestic Space, and Segregation Narratives." *African American Review* 42, no. 1 (Spring 2008): 135–47.

Awiakta, Marilou. *Abiding Appalachia: Where Mountain and Atom Meet*. Bell Buckle, Tenn.: Iris Press, 1994.

Babb, Valerie. "Old-Fashioned Modernism: 'The Changing Same' in *A Lesson before Dying*." In *Critical Reflections on the Fiction of Ernest J. Gaines*, edited by David C. Estes, 250–64. Athens: University of Georgia Press, 1994.

Bachelard, Gaston. *The Poetics of Space*. Translated by Maria Jolas. Boston: Beacon Press, 1969.

Bailey, John. *The Lost German Slave Girl*. Sydney, Australia: Macmillan, 2003.

Baker, Houston, Jr. *Blues, Ideology, and Afro-American Literature: A Vernacular Theory*. Chicago: University of Chicago Press, 1984.

———. *Critical Memory: Public Spheres, African American Writing, and Black Fathers and Sons in America*. Athens: University of Georgia Press, 2001.

———. *Modernism and the Harlem Renaissance*. Chicago: University of Chicago Press, 1987.

———. "To Move without Moving: An Analysis of Creativity and Commerce in Ralph Ellison's Trueblood Episode." *PMLA* 98, no. 5 (October 1983): 828–45.

———. *Turning South Again: Rethinking Modernism/Rereading Booker T.* Durham, N.C.: Duke University Press, 2001.

Baker, Houston Jr., and Dana D. Nelson, eds. "Violence, the Body, and the South." *American Literature* 73 (June 2001).

Baker, Houston, Jr., and Charlotte Pierce-Baker. "Patches: Quilts and Community in Alice Walker's 'Everyday Use.'" In *Afro-American Writing Today: An Anniversary Issue of the "Southern Review,"* edited by James Olney. Baton Rouge: Louisiana State University Press, 1989.

Bakhtin, Mikhail. *The Dialogic Imagination: Four Essays by M. M. Bakhtin*. Edited by Michael Holquist and translated by Caryl Emerson and Michael Holquist. Austin: University of Texas Press, 1981.

Baldwin, James. *Another Country*. New York: Dial Press, 1962.

Ball, Edward. *Slaves in the Family*. New York: Ballantine Books, 1999.

Ball, Howard. *Murder in Mississippi: United States v. Price and the Struggle for Civil Rights*. Lawrence: University Press of Kansas, 2004.

Barthelemy, Anthony. "Light, Bright, Damn *Near* White: Race, the Politics of Genealogy, and the Strange Case of Susie Guillory." In *Creole: The History and Legacy of Louisiana's Free People of Color*, edited by Sybil Kein. Baton Rouge: Louisiana State University Press, 2000.

Barthes, Roland. *Camera Lucida: Reflections on Photography*. Translated by Richard Howard. New York: Hill and Wang, 1981.

———. *Roland Barthes by Roland Barthes*. New York: Farrar, Straus and Giroux, 1977.

Baucom, Ian. *Specters of the Atlantic: Finance, Capital, Slavery, and the Philosophy of History*. Durham, N.C.: Duke University Press, 2005.

Beavers, Herman. *Wrestling Angels into Song: The Fictions of Ernest J. Gaines and James Alan McPherson*. Philadelphia: University of Pennsylvania Press, 1995.

Bell, Caryn Cossé. *Revolution, Romanticism, and the Afro-Creole Protest Tradition in Louisiana, 1718–1868*. Baton Rouge: Louisiana State University Press, 1997.

Bellocq, E. J. *Bellocq: Photographs from Storyville, the Red-Light District of New Orleans*. With an introduction by Susan Sontag. New York: Random House, 1996.

Benítez-Rojo, Antonio. *The Repeating Island: The Caribbean and the Postmodern Perspective*. Durham, N.C.: Duke University Press, 1992.

Berman, Carolyn Vellenga. *Creole Crossings: Domestic Fiction and the Reform of Colonial Slavery*. Ithaca, N.Y.: Cornell University Press, 2006.

Bernabé, Jean, Patrick Chamoiseau, and Raphaël Confiant. *Éloge de la créolité/ In Praise of Creoleness*. Paris: Gallimard, 1993. Originally published 1989.

Berry, Jason. "The Haunting Voice of Ernest Gaines." In *Conversations with Ernest Gaines*, edited by John Lowe, 282–86. Jackson: University Press of Mississippi, 1995.

Bhabha, Homi K. *The Location of Culture*. London: Routledge, 1994.

Black Public Sphere Collective, ed. *The Black Public Sphere: A Public Culture Book*. Chicago: University of Chicago Press, 1995.

Blassingame, John. *Black New Orleans, 1860–1880*. Chicago: University of Chicago Press, 1973.

Blunt, Alison, and Gillian Rose, eds. *Writing Women and Space: Colonial and Postcolonial Geographies*. New York: Guilford, 1994.

Bone, Martyn. *The Postsouthern Sense of Place in Contemporary Fiction*. Baton Rouge: Louisiana State University Press, 2005.

Bongie, Chris. *Islands and Exiles: The Creole Identities of Post/Colonial Literature*. Stanford: Stanford University Press, 1998.

Bontemps, Arna. "Why I Returned." In *Personals*. London: P. Breman, 1963; 1973.

Bost, Suzanne. *Mulattas and Mestizas: Representing Mixed Identities in the Americas, 1850–2000*. Athens: University of Georgia Press, 2003.

Bowen, Margarita. *Empiricism and Geographical Thought*. Cambridge: Cambridge University Press, 1981.

Bowman, Jayne L. "Edward Ball, A Warrior in Scholar's Clothing." In *Slaves in the Family*. CNN Interactive, 28 January 1999.

Bradley, Mamie T. "Blood on Their Hands," pt. 1. *Chicago Defender*, 1 October 1955.

Brasseaux, Carl A., Keith P. Fontenot, and Claude F. Oubre. *Creoles of Color in the Bayou Country*. Jackson: University Press of Mississippi, 1994.

Brewer, Krista. "Writing to Survive: An Interview with Alice Walker." *Southern Exposure* 9 (Summer 1981): 12–15.

Brinkley, Douglas. *The Great Deluge: Hurricane Katrina, New Orleans and the Mississippi Gulf Coast*. New York: William Morrow, 2006.

Brooks, Peter. *Body Work: Objects of Desire in Modern Narrative*. Cambridge, Mass.: Harvard University Press, 1993.

Bryan, Violet Harrington. "Marcus Christian's Treatment of *Les Gens de Couleur Libre*." In *Creole: The History and Legacy of Louisiana's Free People of Color*, edited by Sybil Kein. Baton Rouge: Louisiana State University Press, 2000.

———. *The Myth of New Orleans in Literature: Dialogues of Race and Gender*. Knoxville: University of Tennessee Press, 1993.

Butler-Evans, Elliott. *Race, Gender, and Desire: Narrative Strategies in the Fiction of Toni Cade Bambara, Toni Morrison, and Alice Walker*. Philadelphia: Temple University Press, 1989.

Byerman, Keith. *Fingering the Jagged Grain: Tradition and Form in Recent Black Fiction*. Athens: University of Georgia Press, 1985.

———. *Remembering the Past in Contemporary African American Fiction*. Chapel Hill: University of North Carolina Press, 2005.

Byrd, Rudolph P., ed. *The World Has Changed: Conversations with Alice Walker*. New York: The New Press, 2010.

Cable, George Washington. "Salome Muller, The White Slave." In *Strange True Stories of Louisiana*. 1889.

Capote, Truman. *Other Voices, Other Rooms*. New York: Random House, 1948.

Carby, Hazel V. "The Politics of Fiction, Anthropology, and the Folk: Zora Neale Hurston." In *New Essays on "Their Eyes Were Watching God*," edited by Michael Awkward, 71–94. New York: Oxford University Press, 1991.

Carpentier, Alejo. *Explosion in a Cathedral*. Translated by John Sturrock. London, 1963. Quoted in *Islands and Exiles: The Creole Identities of Post/Colonial Literature*, by Chris Bongie. Stanford: Stanford University Press, 1998.

Cartwright, Keith. "Southern Polarities and Meridians of Alice Walker's 'Resident Spiritually': A Response to Thadious Davis." Southern Intellectual History Circle Meeting, University of Kansas. 27 February 2009.

Casey, Maud. "Cycle of Violence: *A Killing in This Town* by Olympia Vernon." *New York Times Sunday Book Review*, 12 February 2006.

Certeau, Michel de. *The Practice of Everyday Life*. Translated by Steven Rendall. Berkeley: University of California Press, 1984.

Certeau, Michel de, Luce Giard, and Pierre Mayol. *The Practice of Everyday Life, Volume 2: Living and Cooking*. Translated by Timothy J. Tomasik. Minneapolis: University of Minnesota Press, 1998.

Cheatwood, K. T. H. Review of *Horses Make a Landscape Look More Beautiful*. *Richmond News Leader*, 1984.

Chesnutt, Charles W. "The Courts and the Negro." In *Plessy v. Ferguson: A Brief History with Documents*, edited by Brook Thomas. Boston: Bedford/St. Martin's, 1997.

Clark, Keith. *Black Manhood in James Baldwin, Ernest J. Gaines, and August Wilson*. Urbana: University of Illinois Press, 2002.

———. "Que(e)rying the Prison-House of Black Male Desire: Homosociality in Ernest Gaines's 'Three Men.'" *African American Review* 40 no. 2 (Summer 2006): 239–55.

Clifton, Lucille. "Entering the South." In *The Terrible Stories*. Rochester, N.Y.: BOA Editions, 1996.

Cobb, James C. *The Most Southern Place on Earth: The Mississippi Delta and the Roots of Regional Identity*. New York: Oxford University Press, 1992.

Coleman, Edward Maceo, ed. *Creole Voices: Poems in French by Free Men of Color, First Published in 1845*. Washington, D.C.: The Associated Publishers, 1945.

Coleman, Wanda. "Emmett Till." In *African Sleeping Sickness*, 204–8. Santa Rosa, Calif.: Black Sparrow Press, 1990.

Colomina, Beatriz, ed. *Sexuality and Space*. New York: Princeton Architectural, 1992.

Cosgrove, Denis. "Introduction: Mapping Meaning." In *Mappings*, edited by Denis Cosgrove. London: Reaktion Books, 1999.

Cowdrey, Albert. *This Land, This South: An Environmental History*. Lexington: University Press of Kentucky, 1983.

Crang, Mike. *Cultural Geography*. London: Routledge, 1998.

Crang, Mike, and Nigel Thrift. Introduction to *Thinking Space*, edited by Mike Crang and Nigel Thrift. London: Routledge, 2000.

Crespino, Joseph. "Mississippi as Metaphor: Civil Rights, the South, and the Nation in Historical Imagination." In *The Myth of Southern Exceptionalism*, edited by Matthew D. Lassiter and Joseph Crespino, 99–120. New York: Oxford University Press, 2010.

Cresswell, Tim. *In Place/Out of Place: Geography, Ideology, and Transgression*. Minneapolis: University of Minnesota Press, 1996.

———. *Place: A Short History*. Malden, Mass.: Blackwell Publishing, 1996.

———. *Place: A Short Introduction*. Malden, Mass.: Blackwell Publishing, 2004.

Crété, Liliane. *Daily Life in Louisiana, 1815–1930*. Translated by Patrick Gregory. Baton Rouge: Louisiana State University Press, 1981.

Cuevas, Marco Polo Hernández. *African Mexicans and the Discourse of Modern Nation*. Dallas: University Press of America, 2004.

Culpepper, Steve, and Mary Broussard. "Writer Draws on Pointe Coupee Childhood." *Baton Rouge Sunday Advocate*, 4 December 1988. Reprinted in *Conversations with Ernest Gaines*, edited by John Lowe, 217–20. Jackson: University Press of Mississippi, 1995.

Cutler, Phoebe. *The Public Landscape of the New Deal*. New Haven: Yale University Press, 1986.

Dalcour, Pierre. *"Les Aveux"* ("Declaration"). In *Creole Echoes: The Francophone Poetry of Nineteenth-Century Louisiana*, translated by Norman R. Shapiro, 29. Urbana: University of Illinois Press, 2004.

———. *"Vers Ecrits sur L'Album de Mademoiselle***"* ("Lines Written in the Album of Mademoiselle"). In *Creole Echoes: The Francophone Poetry of Nineteenth-Century Louisiana*, translated by Norman R. Shapiro, 29. Urbana: University of Illinois Press, 2004.

Dawdy, Shannon Lee. *Building the Devil's Empire: French Colonial New Orleans*. Chicago: University of Chicago Press, 2008.

Dear, Michael J. *The Postmodern Urban Condition*. Malden, Mass.: Blackwell, 2000.

Dédé, Edmond. *Mon Pauvre Coeur / Francoise et Tortillard / Mefisto masque*. Hot Springs Music Festival Symphony Orchestra, conducted by Richard Rosenberg. Naxos 8.559038, January 2000.

De Man, Paul. "Literary History and Literary Modernity." In *Blindness and Insight: Essays in the Rhetoric of Contemporary Criticism*. New York: Oxford University Press, 1971.

Desdunes, Rodolphe Lucien. *Our People and Our History: Fifty Creole Portraits*. Edited and translated by Sister Dorothea Olga McCants, Daughter of the Cross. Baton Rouge: Louisiana State University Press, 1973.

Dittmer, John. *Local People: The Struggle for Civil Rights in Mississippi*. Champaign: University of Illinois Press, 1994.

Dixon, Melvin. *Ride out the Wilderness: Geography and Identity in Afro-American Literature.* Urbana: University of Illinois Press, 1987.

Domínguez, Virginia R. *White by Definition: Social Classification in Creole Louisiana.* New Brunswick: Rutgers University Press, 1997.

Donlon, Joycelyn Hazelwood. *Swinging in Place: Porch Life in Southern Culture.* Chapel Hill: University of North Carolina Press, 2001.

Dove, Rita. Introduction to *Domestic Work*, by Natasha Trethewey. St. Paul, Minn.: Graywolf Press, 2000.

———. "Mississippi." In *Grace Notes: Poems.* New York: W. W. Norton, 1983.

Doyle, Mary Ellen, S.C.N. "Place, People, Personal Experience: 'This Louisiana Thing.'" In *Voices from the Quarter: The Fiction of Ernest J. Gaines*, 4–24. Baton Rouge: Louisiana State University Press, 2003.

Dubey, Madhu. *Signs and Cities: Black Literary Postmodernism.* Chicago: University of Chicago Press, 2003.

Du Bois, W. E. B. "Richard Wright Looks Back." *New York Herald Tribune Book Review*, 4 March 1945, 2.

Duck, Leigh Anne. *The Nation's Region: Southern Modernism, Segregation, and U.S. Nationalism.* Athens: University of Georgia Press, 2006.

Dugué, Charles-Oscar. "Memory of the Ball" ("Souvenir du Bal"). In *Creole Echoes: The Francophone Poetry of Nineteenth-Century Louisiana*, translated by Norman R. Shapiro. Urbana: University of Illinois Press, 2004.

Dunbar-Nelson, Alice. "Brass Ankles." In *The Works of Alice Dunbar-Nelson*, edited by Gloria T. Hull. Vol. 2. New York: Oxford University Press, 1988.

———. "People of Color in Louisiana." *Journal of Negro History* 2 (1917): 67–69. Reprinted in *Creole: The History and Legacy of Louisiana's Free People of Color*, edited by Sybil Kein. Baton Rouge: Louisiana State University Press, 2000.

Duncan, Nancy, ed. *BodySpace: Destabilizing Geographies of Gender and Sexuality.* London: Routledge, 1996.

Dyson, Michael Eric. *Come Hell or High Water: Hurricane Katrina and the Color of Disaster.* New York: Basic Books, 2006.

Edwards, Brent Hayes. *The Practice of Diaspora: Literature, Translation, and the Rise of Black Internationalism.* Cambridge, Mass.: Harvard University Press, 2003.

Ellison, Ralph. "Remembering Richard Wright." In *Going to the Territory.* New York: Random House, 1986.

Esman, Marjorie R. "About the Cajuns." *Mississippi Quarterly* 47 (Winter 1993–94).

Fabre, Michel. "New Orleans Creole Expatriates in France: Romance and Reality." In *Creole: The History and Legacy of Louisiana's Free People of Color*, edited by Sybil Kein, 179–207. Baton Rouge: Louisiana State University Press, 2000.

———. *The Unfinished Quest of Richard Wright.* Translated by Isabel Barzun. New York: William Morrow, 1973.

Fauset, Jessie. Letter to Joel Spingarn, 26 January 1926. Schomburg Center for Research in Black Culture, New York Public Library.

Faust, Drew G. "Skeletons in the Family Closet." *New York Times*, 1 March 1998.

Febvre, Lucien. *A Geographical Introduction to History*. New York: Alfred A. Knopf, 1925.

Federal Writers' Project of the Works Progress Administration. *Mississippi, A Guide to the Magnolia State*. 1938.

———. *New Orleans City Guide*. American Guide Series, revised by Robert Tallant. Boston: Houghton Mifflin, 1952. Originally published 1938.

Feldstein, Ruth. "I Wanted the Whole World to See": Race, Gender, and Constructions of Motherhood in the Death of Emmett Till" In *Not June Cleaver: Women and Gender in Postwar America, 1945–1990*, edited by Joanne Meyerowitz. Philadelphia: Temple University Press, 1994.

Finney, Nikky. *The World Is Round*. Atlanta: InterLight Publishing, 2003.

Fireside, Harvey. *Separate and Unequal: Homer Plessy and the Supreme Court Decision That Legalized Racism*. New York: Carroll and Graf, 2004.

Fisher, Dorothy Canfield. "Introductory Note." In *Black Boy: A Record of Childhood and Youth*, by Richard Wright. New York: Harper & Brothers, 1945.

Fiske, John. "Cultural Studies and the Culture of Everyday Life." In *Cultural Studies*, edited by Lawrence Grossberg, Cary Nelson, and Paula Treichler. New York: Routledge, 1992.

Forrest, Leon. *Two Wings to Veil My Face*. New York: Random House, 1983.

Foucault, Michel. "The Eye of Power." In *Power/Knowledge: Selected Interviews and Other Writings, 1972–1977*, edited by Colon Gordon, 149. Brighton: Harvester.

———. "Of Other Spaces." *Diacritics* 16 (Spring 1986): 22–27. Translated by Jay Miskowiec.

———. *The Order of Things: An Archaeology of the Human Sciences*. New York: Vintage Books, 1994.

Frankenberg, Ruth. *White Women, Race Matters: The Social Construction of Whiteness*. Minneapolis: University of Minnesota Press, 1993.

"Frank Yerby: Seven Novels in Seven Years." *Jet*. 21 February 1952.

French, B. F. *Historical Collections of Louisiana*. New York: A. Mason, 1875.

Frey, William H. "The New Great Migration: Black Americans' Return to the South, 1965–2000." Center for Urban and Metropolitan Policy, Living Cities Census Series. Washington, D.C.: Brookings Institute, May 2004.

Friedman, Susan Stanford. *Mappings: Feminism and the Cultural Geographies of Encounter*. Princeton: Princeton University Press, 1998.

Fryer, Judith. *Felicitous Space: The Imaginative Structures of Edith Wharton and Willa Cather*. Chapel Hill: University of North Carolina, 1986.

Gabbin, Joanne. *Sterling A. Brown: Building a Black Aesthetic Tradition*. Westport, Conn.: Greenwood Press, 1985.

Gaines, Ernest. *The Autobiography of Miss Jane Pittman*. New York: Bantam Books, 1971.

———. "Bard from the Bayou." Interview by Ruth Laney, 1993. Reprinted in *Conversations with Ernest Gaines*, edited by John Lowe, 276–81. Jackson: University Press of Mississippi, 1995.

———. *Bloodline*. New York: Norton Library, 1976. Originally published in 1968.

———. *Catherine Carmier*. San Francisco: North Point Press, 1981. Originally published 1964.

———. "A Conversation with Ernest Gaines." Interview by Ruth Laney. *Southern Review*. 1974. Reprinted in *Conversations with Ernest Gaines*, edited by John Lowe, 56–67 (Jackson: University Press of Mississippi, 1995).

———. "Finding the Voice." In *Porch Talk with Ernest Gaines: Conversations on the Writer's Craft*, edited by Marcia Gaudet and Carl Wooton. Baton Rouge: Louisiana State University Press, 1990.

———. *A Gathering of Old Men*. New York: Vintage, 1992. Originally published 1978.

———. "Going Home: The Transcript." Interview by R. Reese Fuller. http://www.reesefuller.com/articles/going-home/.

———. "I Heard the Voices . . . of My Louisiana People: A Conversation with Ernest Gaines." Interview by Bill Ferris. http://www.neh.gov/news/humanities/1998-07/gaines.html.

———. *In My Father's House*. New York: Norton, 1983. Originally published 1978.

———. "Interview with Ernest Gaines." *Xavier Review* 3 (1983): 1–3. Interview by Jeanie Blake. Reprinted in *Conversations with Ernest Gaines*, edited by John Lowe, 137–48. Jackson: University Press of Mississippi, 1995.

———. "An Interview with Ernest Gaines." Interview by John Lowe. In *Conversations with Ernest Gaines*, edited by John Lowe, 297–328. Jackson: University Press of Mississippi, 1995,

———. *A Lesson before Dying*. New York: Vintage Contemporaries, 1994.

———. "A MELUS Interview: Ernest J. Gaines." Interview by Mary Ellen Doyle, S.C.N. In *Conversations with Ernest Gaines*, edited by John Lowe, 149–71. Jackson: University Press of Mississippi, 1995

———. "Miss Jane and I." *Callaloo* (1978). Reprinted in *Mozart and Leadbelly: Stories and Essays*, edited by Marcia Gaudet and Reggie Young. New York: Alfred A. Knopf, 2005.

———. *Mozart and Leadbelly: Stories and Essays*. Edited by Marcia Gaudet and Reggie Young. New York: Alfred A. Knopf, 2005.

———. *Of Love and Dust*. New York: Dial Press, 1967.

———. "This Louisiana Thing That Drives Me: An Interview with Ernest J. Gaines." *Callaloo* 1 (May 1978): 39–51. Interview by Charles Rowell. Reprinted in *Conversations with Ernest Gaines*, edited by John Lowe, 86–98. Jackson: University Press of Mississippi, 1995.

Gaines, Kevin K. *Uplifting the Race: Black Leadership, Politics, and Culture in the Twentieth Century*. Chapel Hill: University of North Carolina Press, 1996.

Gates, Henry Louis, Jr. *Boston Globe*, 3 November 1998. Quoted by Alex Beam.

———. *Loose Canons: Notes on the Culture Wars*. New York: Oxford University Press, 1992.

Gaudet, Marcia, and Carl Wooton, eds. *Porch Talk with Ernest Gaines*. Baton Rouge: Louisiana State University Press, 1990.

Gayarré, Charles. *History of Louisiana*. 4th ed., pt. 1. New York: AMS, 1972. Originally published 1885.

Gibson, Donald B. "Richard Wright's *Black Boy* and the Trauma of Autobiographical Rebirth." *Callaloo* 9 (Summer 1986): 492–98.

Gibson, Mary Ellis, comp. *Homeplaces: Stories of the South by Women Writers*. Columbia, S.C.: University of South Carolina Press, 1991.

Gidley, Mick. Introduction to *Modern American Landscape*, edited by Mick Gidley and Robert Lawson-Peebles, 1–16. Amsterdam: VU University Press, 1995.

Gilroy, Paul. *The Black Atlantic: Modernity and Double Consciousness*. Cambridge, Mass.: Harvard University Press, 1993.

Glissant, Édouard. *Poetics of Relation*. Translated by Betsy Wing. Ann Arbor: University of Michigan Press, 1997.

———. *Poétique de la Relation*. Paris: Gallimard, 1990.

"The Golden Corn: He Writes to Please." *Time*, 29 November 1954.

Goldsby, Jacqueline. "The High and Low-Tech of It: The Meaning of Lynching and the Death of Emmett Till." *Yale Journal of Criticism* 9, no. 2 (Fall 1996).

———. *A Spectacular Secret: Lynching in American Life and Literature*. Chicago: University of Chicago Press, 2006.

Gray, Richard. *Writing the South: Ideas of an American Region*. Cambridge: Cambridge University Press, 1986.

Greeson, Jennifer Rae. *Our South: Geographic Fantasy and the Rise of National Literature*. Cambridge, Mass.: Harvard University Press, 2010.

Gregory, Derek. *Geographical Imaginations*. Cambridge, Mass.: Blackwell, 1994.

Gregory, Derek, Ron Johnston, Geraldine Pratt, Michael J. Watts, and Sarah Whitmore, eds. *The Dictionary of Human Geography*. Malden, Mass.: Wiley-Blackwell, 2009.

Gross, Ariela. "Litigating Whiteness: Trials of Racial Determination in the Nineteenth-Century South." *Yale Law Review* 108 (October 1998): 109–88.

———. *Slavery and Mastery in the Antebellum Southern Courtroom*. Princeton: Princeton University Press, 2000.

Grosz, Elizabeth. "Bodies—Cities." In *Sexuality and Space*, edited by Beatriz Colomina. Princeton: Princeton University Architectural Press, 1992.

Gruesz, Kirsten Silva. *Ambassadors of Culture: The Transamerican Origins of Latino Writing*. Princeton: Princeton University Press, 2002.

Guillén, Nicolas. "Elegías a Emmett Till." *La paloma de vuelo popular: Elegías* (1958). In *Man-Making Words: Selected Poems of Nicolas Guillén*, edited by David Márquez and Arthur McMurray, 87–90. Amherst: University of Massachusetts Press, 2003.

Guillory, Monique. "Under One Roof: The Sins and Sanctity of the New Orleans Quadroon Balls." In *Race Consciousness: African-American Studies for the New Century*, edited by Judith Jackson Fossett and Jeffrey A. Tucker. New York: New York University Press, 1997.

Gussow, Adam. *Seems Like Murder Here: Southern Violence and the Blues Tradition*. Chicago: University of Chicago Press, 2002.

Gwin, Minrose. "Her Shape, His Hand: The Spaces of African American Women in *Go Down, Moses*." In *New Essays on "Go Down, Moses,"* edited by Linda Wagner-Martin. Cambridge: Cambridge University Press, 1996.

———. *The Women in the Red Dress: Gender, Space, and Reading*. Urbana: University of Illinois Press, 2002.

Habermas, Jürgen. *The Structural Transformation of the Public Sphere: An Inquiry into a Category of Bourgeois Society*. Translated by Thomas Burger and Frederick Lawrence. Cambridge, Mass.: MIT Press, 1993.

Hale, Grace Elizabeth. *Making Whiteness: The Culture of Segregation in the South, 1890–1940*. New York: Vintage, 1999.

Haley, Alex. Introduction to *Somerset Homecoming: Recovering a Lost Heritage*, by Dorothy Spruill Redford with Michael D'Orso. New York: Doubleday, 1988.

Hall, Gwendolyn Midlo. *Africans in Colonial Louisiana: The Development of Afro-Creole Culture in the Eighteenth Century*. Baton Rouge: Louisiana State University Press, 1992.

Hall, Jacquelyn Dowd. "Open Secrets: Memory, Imagination, and the Refashioning of Southern Identity." *American Quarterly* 50, no. 1 (March 1998): 110.

Hall, Stuart. "Cultural Identity and Diaspora." In *Undoing Place*, edited by Linda McDowell. London: Arnold, 1997.

———. "Race, Articulation, and Societies Structured in Dominance." Quoted in *The Practice of Diaspora: Literature, Translation, and the Rise of Black Internationalism*, by Brent Hayes Edwards. Cambridge, Mass.: Harvard University Press, 2003.

Hambly, Barbara. *Days of the Dead*. New York: Bantam Books, 2003.

———. *Die upon a Kiss*. New York: Bantam Books, 2001.

———. *Fever Season*. New York: Bantam Books, 1998.

———. *A Free Man of Color*. New York: Bantam Books, 1997.

———. *Graveyard Dust*. New York: Bantam Books, 1999.

———. *Sold down the River*. New York: Bantam Books, 2000.

———. *Wet Grave*. New York: Bantam Books, 2002.

Hamer, Forrest. *Call and Response: Poems*. Farmington, Maine: Alice James Press, 1995.

———. "A Goldsboro Narrative: An Interview with Forrest Hamer." Interview by Charles H. Rowell. *Callaloo* 27, no. 4 (Fall 2004).

———. *Middle Ear*. Berkeley, Calif.: Roundhouse Press, 2000.

Hammonds, Evelyn. "Black (W)holes and the Geometry of Black Female Sexuality." *Differences: A Journal of Feminist Cultural Studies* 6, nos. 2–3 (1994): 126–45. Reprinted in *African American Theory: A Reader*, edited by Winston Napier. New York: New York University Press, 2000.

Hanger, Kimberly S. *Bounded Lives, Bounded Places: Free Black Society in Colonial New Orleans, 1769–1803*. Durham, N.C.: Duke University Press, 1997.

Harrington, Ollie. "The Last Days of Richard Wright." *Ebony*, 16 February 1961, 93–94.

Harris, Trudier. *The Power of the Porch: The Storyteller's Craft in Zora Neale Hurston, Gloria Naylor, and Randall Kenan*. Athens: University of Georgia Press, 1996.

Hart, John Fraser. "The Highest Form of the Geographer's Art." *Annals of the Association of American Geographers* 72, no. 1 (1982): 1–29.

Harvey, David. *The Condition of Postmodernity: An Enquiry into the Origins of Cultural Change*. Cambridge, Mass.: Blackwell, 1990.

———. *Justice, Nature, and the Geography of Difference*. Cambridge, Mass: Blackwell, 1996.

———. *Spaces of Capital: Towards a Critical Geography*. New York: Routledge, 2001.

Hathaway, Rosemary. "Native Geography: Richard Wright's Work for the Federal Writers' Project in Chicago." *African American Review* 41, no. 1 (Spring 2008): 91–108.

Haynes, Bruce. *Red Lines, Black Space: The Politics of Race and Space in a Black Middle-Class Suburb*. New Haven: Yale University Press, 2001.

Hendrickson, Paul. *Sons of Mississippi: A Story of Race and Its Legacy*. New York: Alfred A. Knopf, 2003.

Higonnet, Margaret R., and Joan Templeton, eds. *Reconfigured Spheres: Feminist Explorations of Literary Space*. Amherst: University of Massachusetts Press, 1994.

Hill, James L. "The Anti-Heroic in Frank Yerby's Historical Novels." In *Perspectives of Black Popular Culture*. Bowling Green, Ohio: Bowling Green State University Popular Press, 1990.

Hill, William W. "Behind the Magnolia Mask: Frank Yerby as Critic of the South." Master's thesis, Auburn University, 1968.

Hirsch, Arnold R., and Joseph Logsdon. "Introduction to Part III: Franco-Africans and African-Americans." In *Creole New Orleans: Race and Americanization*, edited by Arnold R. Hirsch and Joseph Logsdon. Baton Rouge: Louisiana State University Press, 1992.

Hobson, Fred C. *The Southern Writer in the Postmodern World*. Athens: University of Georgia Press, 1991.

Holland, Endesha Ida Mae. *From the Mississippi Delta: A Memoir*. New York: Simon & Schuster, 1997.

Holloway, Karla. *Moorings and Metaphors: Figures of Culture and Gender in Black Women's Literature*. New Brunswick: Rutgers University Press, 1992.

Holman, C. Hugh. "No More Monoliths, Please: Continuities in the Multi-Souths." In *Southern Literature in Transition: Heritage and Promise*, edited by Philip Castille and William Osborne. Memphis: Memphis State University Press, 1983.

hooks, bell. *Belonging: A Culture of Place*. New York: Routledge, 2009.

———. *Black Looks: Race and Representation*. Boston: South End Press, 1992.

———. *Yearning: Race, Gender, and Cultural Politics*. Boston: South End Press, 1990.

Horowitz, Helen Lefkowitz, ed. *Landscape in Sight: Looking at America*. New Haven: Yale University Press, 1997.

Hughes, Langston. Speech to the Third Annual Writers' Congress. 2 June 1939.

Huie, William Bradford. "The Shocking Story of Approved Killing in Mississippi." *Look* 20 (24 January 1956): 46–50.

———. "What's Happened to the Emmett Till Killers?" *Look* 22 (January 1957): 63–66.

Hull, Gloria T., Barbara Smith, and Patricia Bell Scott, eds. *All the Women Are White, All the Blacks Are Men, But Some of Us Are Brave.* New York: Feminist Press, 1982.

Hunt, V. "A Conversation with Randall Kenan." *African American Review* 29, no. 3 (Autumn 1995): 414.

Hurston, Zora Neale. "Stories of Conflict." Review of *Uncle Tom's Children. Saturday Review of Literature*, 2 April 1938.

———. *Their Eyes Were Watching God.* New York: Perennial Classics, 1998. Originally published 1937.

Hutcheon, Linda. *The Poetics of Postmodernism: History, Theory, Fiction.* New York: Routledge, 1988.

———. *The Politics of Postmodernism.* New York: Routledge, 1989.

Jackson, John Brinckerhoff. *Discovering the Vernacular Landscape.* New Haven: Yale University Press, 1984.

Jameson, Fredric. *Postmodernism, or, The Cultural Logic of Late Capitalism.* Durham, N.C.: Duke University Press, 1991.

JanMohamed, Abdul R. *The Death-Bound Subject: Richard Wright's Archeology of Death.* Durham, N.C.: Duke University Press, 2005.

Jarvis, Brian. *Postmodern Cartographies: The Geographical Imagination in Contemporary American Culture.* New York: St. Martin's, 1998.

Jay, Gregory S. *America the Scrivener: Deconstruction and the Subject of Literary History.* Ithaca: Cornell University Press, 1990.

Jefferson, Thomas. Letter to John Eppes, 30 June 1820. Quoted in *The World That Made New Orleans: From Spanish Silver to Congo Square,* by Ned Sublette, 219. Chicago: Lawrence Hill, 2008.

Johnson, E. Patrick. *Sweet Tea: Black Gay Men of the South.* Chapel Hill: University of North Carolina Press, 2008.

Johnson, Walter. *Soul by Soul: Life inside the Antebellum Slave Market.* Cambridge, Mass.: Harvard University Press, 1999.

Jones, Anne Goodwyn, and Susan Van D'Elden Donaldson. *Haunted Bodies: Gender and Southern Texts.* Charlottesville: University of Virginia Press, 1997.

Jones, John Maxwell, Jr. *Slavery and Race in Nineteenth-Century Louisiana-French Literature.* Self-published, 1978.

Jones, Suzanne W. "New Narratives of Southern Manhood: Race, Masculinity, and Closure in Ernest Gaines's Fiction." In *The World Is Our Home: Society and Culture in Contemporary Southern Writing,* edited by Jeffrey J. Folks and Nancy Summers Folks. Lexington: University Press of Kentucky, 2000.

Judson, David. "Links to the Past Draw Blacks Back to the South." *The Tennessean* (Nashville), 5 April 1998, A-8.

Junebug Productions, Inc. Free Southern Theater Institute. Publicity materials, 19 March 2008.

Kahn, Ashley. "Civil Rights Diva." *Four Women: The Nina Simone Philips Recordings.* Sound recording. The Verve Music Group, 2003.

Kane, Harnett. *Natchez on the Mississippi*. New York: William Morrow, 1945.

Kaplan, Caren. "Postmodern Geographies: Feminist Politics of Location." In *Questions of Travel: Postmodern Discourses of Displacement*. Durham, N.C.: Duke University Press, 1996.

Kavolis, Vytautas. "Literature and the Dialectics of Modernization." In *Literary Criticism and Sociology*, edited by Joseph P. Streika, 89–106. University Park: Penn State University Press, 1973.

Kein, Sybil. *An American South*. East Lansing: Michigan State University Press, 1996.

———. *Bonjour Créole! Éh La Bas! Learn to Speak Louisiana French Creole: An Introduction*. New Orleans: Gumbo People Products, July 2005.

———. "Contributions of the Gens de Couleur and Their Descendants to an American South." In *Gumbo People*, 131. New Orleans: Margaret Media, 1999.

———. *Creole Ballads & Zydeco*. Sound recording. 1996.

———. *Creole Classique*. Sound recording. 2000.

———. *Creole Journal: The Louisiana Poems*. Detroit: Lotus Press, 1999. This volume first appeared as *An American South* (East Lansing: Michigan State University Press, 1996).

———. *Gumbo People*. New Orleans: Margaret Media, 1999.

———. *Maw-Maw's Creole ABC Book*. Natchitoches, La.: Gumbo People Products, 2006.

———. *Maw-Maw's Creole Lullaby*. Sound recording. 1997.

———. "One Drop Rules: Self-Identity and the Woman in the Trial of Toucoutou." In *Louisiana Culture from the Colonial Era to Katrina*, edited by John Lowe, 136–46. Baton Rouge: Louisiana State University Press, 2008.

———. *Sérénade Créole: Rhythms of Love*. Songs in Spanish, French, Creole, Kreyole, and English. Sound recording. 1986.

———. "The Use of Louisiana Creole in Southern Literature." In *Creole: The History and Legacy of Louisiana's Free People of Color*, edited by Sybil Kein, 117–54. Baton Rouge: Louisiana State University Press, 2000.

———, ed. *Creole: The History and Legacy of Louisiana's Free People of Color*. Baton Rouge: Louisiana State University Press, 2000.

Kenan, Randall. "Dorothy Spruill Redford." In *North Carolina Humanities: Weaving Cultures and Communities* (Winter 1999): 6

———. Interview. *Brightleaf: A Southern Review of Books* (Fall 1998).

———. "An Interview with Randall Kenan." Interview by Charles Rowell. *Callaloo* 21, no. 1 (Winter 1998): 134.

———. *Let the Dead Bury Their Dead and Other Stories*. Orlando: Harvest Books, 1992.

———. "Meet Randall Kenan: 'Southern Writing Is Changing; It Has to Change.'" Interview by H. B. Grace in *Book Page*, April 1992. http://www.bookpage.com/BPinterviews/kenan492.html.

———. *A Visitation of Spirits*. New York: Anchor Books, 1990. Originally published 1989.

King, Grace Elizabeth. *New Orleans: The Place and the People*. New York: Macmillan and Co., 1895.

King, Richard. *A Southern Renaissance: The Cultural Awakening of the American South, 1935–1955*. New York: Oxford University Press, 1980.

Knight, Etheridge. *Belly Song and Other Poems*. Detroit: Broadside Press, 1973.

———. *The Essential Etheridge Knight*. Pittsburgh: University of Pittsburgh Press, 1986.

Komunyakaa, Yusef. *Magic City*. Middletown, Conn.: Wesleyan University Press, 1992.

———. *Thieves of Paradise*. Hanover, N.H.: University Press of New England for Wesleyan University Press, 1998.

Kreyling, Michael. *Inventing Southern Literature*. Jackson: University Press of Mississippi, 1998.

———. "Parody, Memory, and Copyright: The Southern Memory Market. In *The South That Wasn't There: Postmodern Memory and History*. Baton Rouge: Louisiana State University Press, 2010.

———. "Real Gone for a Change: If Margaret Mitchell Borrowed Plot Elements, Why Can't Nashville Author Alice Randall?" *Nashville Scene*, 26 April 2001, 37–38.

Kronik, John W. "Editor's Note." *PMLA* 107 (1992): 425.

Lambert, Charles Lucièn, Sr., and Lucièn-Léon Guillaume Lambert Jr. *Ouverture de Brodceliande and Other Works*. Hot Springs Music Festival Symphony Orchestra, conducted by Richard Rosenberg. Naxos 8.559037, January 2000.

Lanier, Parks, ed. *The Poetics of Appalachian Space*. Knoxville: University of Tennessee Press, 1991.

Lanusse, Armand. *Album littéraire: journal des jeunes gens, amateurs de littérature* (1843).

———. "Epigram." In *Creole Echoes: The Francophone Poetry of Nineteenth-Century Louisiana*, translated by Norman R. Shapiro, 95. Urbana: University of Illinois Press, 2004.

———. Introduction to *Les Cenelles: Choix de Poesies Indigenes*, edited by Armand Lanusse. Nouvelle Orleans: H. Lauve et Compagnie, 1845.

Latortue, Régine, and Gleason Rex Adams, trans. *Les Cenelles: A Collection of Poems by Creole Writers of the Early Nineteenth Century*. Boston: G. K. Hall, 1979.

Lefebvre, Henri. *The Production of Space*. Translated by Donald Nicholson-Smith. Cambridge, Mass.: Basil Blackwell, 1991.

Lemmons, Kasi (director). *Eve's Bayou*. Original release date 7 November 1997. DVD release date 23 January 2001 by Trimark Home Video.

Lester, Julius. *Do Lord Remember Me*. New York: Washington Square, 1984.

Lewis, Shireen K. *Race, Culture, and Identity: Francophone, West African, and Caribbean Literature and Theory from Negritude to Créolité*. Lanham, Md.: Lexington Books, 2006.

Lister, Rachel. *Alice Walker: The Color Purple*. Reader's Guide to Essential Criticism Series. New York: Palgrave Macmillan, 2010.

Logsdon, Dawn, and Lolis Eric Elie (directors). *Faubourg Treme: The Untold Story of Black New Orleans*. Serendipity Films, 2008. DVD distributed by California News Reel.

Lorde, Audre. "Interview with Jackie Kay and Pratibha Parmar." In *Charting the Journey: Writings by Black and Third World Women*, edited by Shabman Grewal, Jackie Kay, Lillian Landor, Gail Lewis, and Pratibha Parmar. London: Sheba Feminist Productions, 1988.

Lowe, John. "Transcendence in the House of Death: The Subversive Gaze of *A Lesson before Dying*." In *The World Is Our Home: Society and Culture in Contemporary Southern Writing*, edited by Jeffrey J. Folks and Nancy Summer Folks. Lexington: University Press of Kentucky, 2000.

————, ed. *Bridging Southern Cultures: An Interdisciplinary Approach*. Baton Rouge: Louisiana State University Press, 2005.

————. *Conversations with Ernest Gaines*. Jackson: University Press of Mississippi, 1995.

————. *Louisiana Culture from the Colonial Era to Katrina*. Baton Rouge: Louisiana State University Press, 2008.

Lowenthal, David. "The Place of the Past in the American Landscape." In *Geographies of the Mind: Essays in Historical Geosophy in Honor of John Kirtland Wright*, edited by David Lowenthal and Martyn J. Bowden with the assistance of Mary Alice Lamberty, 89–117. New York: Oxford University Press, 1976.

Lyotard, Jean-François. *The Postmodern Condition: A Report of Knowledge*. Translated by Geoff Bennington and Brian Massumi. Minneapolis: University of Minnesota Press, 1984.

MacDonald, Robert R., John R. Kemp, and Edward F. Haas, eds. *Louisiana's Black Heritage*. New Orleans: Louisiana State Museum, 1979.

Mallory, William E., and Paul Simpson-Housley. Preface to *Geography and Literature: A Meeting of the Disciplines*. Syracuse, N.Y.: Syracuse University Press, 1987.

Mangione, Jerre. *The Dream and the Deal: The Federal Writers Project, 1935–1943*. Boston: Little, Brown, 1973.

Margolies, Edward. "The Letters of Richard Wright." In *The Black Writer in Africa and the Americas*, edited by Lloyd W. Brown. Los Angeles: Hennessey & Ingales, 1973.

Martin, Joan M. "*Plaçage* and the Louisiana *Gens de Couleur Libre*: How Race and Sex Defined the Lifestyles of Free Women of Color." In *Creole: The History and Legacy of Louisiana's Free People of Color*, edited by Sybil Kein, 37–70. Baton Rouge: Louisiana State University Press, 2000.

Massaquoi, Hans J. "Alex Haley's Hideaway." *Ebony* 42 (September 1987): 52–60

Massey, Doreen B. *For Space*. Los Angeles: Sage Publications, 2005.

————. "Introduction: Geography Matters." In *Geography Matters!*, edited by John Allen and Doreen Massey. Cambridge: Cambridge University Press, 1984.

————. "Politics and Space/Time." *New Left Review* 196 (1992): 65–84.

————. *Space, Place, and Gender*. Minneapolis: University of Minnesota Press, 1994.

Massey, Douglas S., and Nancy Denton. *American Apartheid: Segregation and the Making of the Underclass*. Cambridge, Mass.: Harvard University Press, 1993.

Mathis, Deborah. "America's Race Picture Changing." *The Tennessean* (Nashville), 5 April 1998, A-8.

McDowell, Deborah. *"The Changing Same": Black Women's Literature, Criticism, and Theory*. Bloomington: Indiana University Press, 1995.

McDowell, Linda. *Gender, Identity, and Place: Understanding Feminist Geographies*. Minneapolis: University of Minnesota Press, 1999.

———. "Spatializing Feminism: Geographic Perspectives." In *BodySpace: Destabilizing Geographies of Gender and Sexuality*, edited by Nancy Duncan, 28–44. London: Routledge, 1996.

McKee, Kathryn, and Annette Trefzer. "Preface: Global Contexts, Local Literatures: The New Southern Studies." *American Literature* 78, no. 4 (December 2006): 677–90.

McKittrick, Katherine. *Demonic Grounds: Black Women and the Cartographies of Struggle*. Minneapolis: University of Minnesota Press, 2006.

Metress, Christopher, ed. *The Lynching of Emmett Till: A Documentary Narrative*. Charlottesville: University of Virginia Press, 2002.

Miller, Christopher L. *The French-Atlantic Triangle: Literature and Culture of the Slave Trade*. Durham, N.C.: Duke University Press, 2008.

Minh-ha, Trinh T. "Not You/Like You: Postcolonial Women and the Interlocking Questions of Identity and Difference." In *Dangerous Liaisons: Gender, Nation, and Postcolonial Perspectives*, edited by Anne McClintock, Aamire Mufti, and Ella Shohat. Minneapolis: University of Minnesota Press, 1997.

Mitchell, Reid. *All on Mardi Gras Day: Episodes in the History of New Orleans Carnival*. Cambridge, Mass.: Harvard University Press, 1995.

Mondale, Clarence. "Place-on-the-Move: Space and Place for the Migrant." In *Mapping American Culture*, edited by Wayne Franklin and Michael Steiner, 53–88. Iowa City: University of Iowa Press, 1992.

Moody, Anne. *Coming of Age in Mississippi*. New York: Dell, 1968.

Morris, Willie. "A Sense of Place and the Americanization of Mississippi." In *Sense of Place: Mississippi*, edited by Peggy W. Prenshaw and Jesse O. McKee, 3–13. Jackson: University Press of Mississippi, 1979.

Morrison, Toni. *Beloved*. New York: Alfred A. Knopf, 1987.

———. *Dreaming Emmett*. 1985. Produced in Albany by the Capital Repertory Company and directed by Gilbert Moses, 1986.

———. "Epigraph from Nobel Lecture." 1993. In *What Moves at the Margin: Selected Nonfiction*, edited Carolyn C. Denard. Jackson: University Press of Mississippi, 2008.

———. *Playing in the Dark: Whiteness and the Literary Imagination*. Cambridge, Mass.: Harvard University Press, 1992.

Morson, Gary Saul. *Narrative and Freedom: The Shadows of Time*. New Haven: Yale University Press, 1996.

Morton, Mary L. "Creole Culture in the Poetry of Sybil Kein." In *Creole: The History and Legacy of Louisiana's Free People of Color*, edited by Sybil Kein. Baton Rouge: Louisiana State University Press, 2000.

Mullen, Harryette. "Black Nikes." In *Giant Steps: The New Generation of African American Writers*, edited by Kevin Young. New York: Perennial, 2000.

———. *Recyclopedia: Trimmings, S*PeRm**K*T, and Muse & Drudge*. St. Paul, Minn.: Graywolf, 2006.

———. *Sleeping with the Dictionary*. Berkeley: University of California Press, 2002.

Nair, Mira (director). *Mississippi Masala*. Columbia Tri-Star, 1992.

Negro Going in Colored Entrance of a Movie House on Saturday Afternoon, Belzoni, Mississippi Delta, Mississippi. Farm Security Administration Office of War Information Photograph Collection, Library of Congress Prints and Photographs Division, Washington, D.C.

Newton, David. "Publisher's Pushing Made Franklin Write Best-Selling History of Blacks." *Durham Morning Herald*, 8 October 1987.

New York Times, national edition, 30 July 2000, 1, 13.

Nu, Camilo, and Reed Rickert (directors). *The Third Root/La Tercera Raíz*. 2010.

Obama, Barack. "Victory Speech." 4 November 2008. Transcript.

O'Brien, John. *Interviews with Black Writers*. New York: Liveright, 1973.

O'Neill, Charles Edwards. *Séjour: Parisian Playwright from Louisiana*. Lafayette: Center for Louisiana, University of Southwestern Louisiana, 1995.

Osbey, Brenda Marie. *All Saints: New and Selected Poems*. Baton Rouge: Louisiana State University Press, 1997.

———. *Ceremony for Minneconjoux*. Callaloo Poetry Series. Lexington: University Press of Kentucky, 1983.

———. *Desperate Circumstance, Dangerous Woman: A Narrative Poem*. Brownsville, Ore.: Story Line Press, 1991.

———. *In These Houses*. Middletown, Conn.: Wesleyan University Press, 1988.

———. "I Want to Die in New Orleans." In *Louisiana Culture from the Colonial Era to Katrina*, edited by John Lowe. Baton Rouge: Louisiana State University Press, 2008.

Painter, Nell Irvin. "'Slaves' with Volvos: Reflections on the Meaning of the Somerset Reunion." *North Carolina Independent*, 26 September–9 October 1986

Palmer, Vernon Valentine. *The Louisiana Civilian Experience: Critiques of Codification in a Mixed Jurisdiction*. Durham, N.C.: Carolina Academic Press, 2005.

Payne, Charles. *I've Got the Light of Freedom: The Organizing Tradition and the Mississippi Freedom Struggle*. Berkeley: University of California Press, 1995.

Penkower, Monty Noam. *The Federal Writers' Project: A Study in Government Patronage of the Arts*. Urbana: University of Illinois Press, 1977.

Philip, Marlene Nourbese. "Dis Place—-The Space Between." In *Genealogy of Resistance and Other Essays*. Toronto: Mercury Press, 1997.

Plumpp, Sterling D. *Blues: The Story Always Untold*. Chicago: Another Chicago Press, 1989.

Polite, Carlene Hatcher. *The Flagellants*. New York: Farrar, Straus and Giroux, 1966.

———. *Sister X and the Victims of Foul Play*. New York: Farrar, Straus and Giroux, 1975.

Pratt, Mary Louise. *Imperial Eyes: Travel Writing and Transculturation*. London: Routledge, 1992.

Ransby, Barbara. *Ella Baker and the Black Freedom Movement: A Radical Democratic Vision*. Chapel Hill: University of North Carolina Press, 2003.

Redford, Dorothy Spruill, with Michael D'Orso. *Somerset Homecoming: Recovering a Lost Heritage*. New York: Doubleday, 1988.

Reed, Ishmael. *Reckless Eyeballing*. New York: St. Martin's Press, 1986.

Rich, Adrienne. Introduction to *My Mother's Dead Squirrel: Lesbian Essays on Southern Culture*, by Mab Segrest. Ithaca, N.Y.: Firebrand, 1985.

———. "Notes toward a Politics of Location." In *Blood, Bread, and Poetry: Selected Prose, 1979–1985*. New York: Norton, 1986; reprinted Norton Paperback, 1994.

Richardson, Riche. *Black Masculinity and the U.S. South: From Uncle Tom to Gangsta*. Athens: University of Georgia Press, 2007.

"Richard Wright to Antonio Frasconi: An Exchange of Letters." *Twice a Year* 12–13 (1945): 256–61.

Rideau, Wilbert. *In the Place of Justice: A Story of Punishment and Deliverance*. New York: Borzoi Books, 2010.

Roach, Joseph. *Cities of the Dead: Circum-Atlantic Performance*. New York: Columbia University Press, 1996.

Roberts, Diane. *The Myth of Aunt Jemima: Representations of Race and Region*. London: Routledge, 1994.

Rose, Al. *Storyville, New Orleans: Being an Authentic, Illustrated Account of the Notorious Red-Light District*. University, Alabama: University of Alabama Press, 1974.

Rose, Gillian. *Feminism and Geography: The Limits of Geographical Knowledge*. Minneapolis: University of Minnesota Press, 1993.

———. "Geography as Science of Observation: The Landscape, the Gaze and Masculinity." In *Human Geography: An Essential Anthology*, edited by John A. Agnew, David N. Livingstone, and Alisdair Rogers, 341–50. Malden, Mass.: Blackwell, 1996.

Rose, Rex. "The Last Days of Ernest J. Bellocq." *Exquisite Corps; Journal of Letters and Life* 10 (Fall/Winter 2001–2).

Ross, Jean W. "Interview with Frank Yerby." In Contemporary Authors New Revision Series. Detroit: Gale Publishing, 1986.

Rousseve, Charles B. *The Negro in Louisiana*. New Orleans: Xavier University Press, 1931.

Rowley, Hazel. *Richard Wright: The Life and Times*. New York: Henry Holt, 2001.

Rubin, Louis D., and others, eds. *The History of Southern Literature*. Baton Rouge: Louisiana State University Press, 1985.

Rutherford, Jonathan, ed. *Identity: Community, Culture, Difference*. London: Lawrence & Wishart, 1990.

Schafer, Judith Kelleher. *Brothels, Depravity, and Abandoned Women: Illegal Sex in Antebellum New Orleans*. Baton Rouge: Louisiana State University Press, 2009.

———. *Slavery, the Civil Law, and the Supreme Court of Louisiana*. Baton Rouge: Louisiana State University Press, 1994.

Seelye, Katharine Q. "Writer Tends Land Where Ancestors Were Slaves." *New York Times*, 21 October 2010, A-18. Online version with images and a multimedia slide show available at http://www.nytimes.com/2010/10/21/us/21gaines.html.

Senter, Carolyn. "Creole Poets on the Verge of a Nation." In *Creole: The History and Legacy of Louisiana's Free People of Color*, edited by Sybil Kein. Baton Rouge: Louisiana State University Press, 2000.

Short, John Rennie. *Imagined Country: Society, Culture and Environment*. London: Routledge, 1991.

Sibley, David. "The Binary City." *Urban Studies* 38 (2001): 239–50.

———. *Geographies of Exclusion: Society and Difference in the West*. London: Routledge, 1995.

Simone, Nina. "Mississippi Goddam." *Nina Simone in Concert*. Sound recording. Nina Simone, 1964.

Smith, David Lionel. "Bloodlines and Patriarchs: *Of Love and Dust* and Its Revision of Faulkner." In *Critical Reflections on the Fiction of Ernest J. Gaines*, edited by David C. Estes, 41–61. Athens: University of Georgia Press, 1994.

Smith, Jon, and Deborah Cohn. *Look Away! The U.S. South in New World Studies*. Durham, N.C.: Duke University Press, 2004.

Soja, Edward W. *Postmodern Geographies: The Reassertion of Space in Critical Social Theory*. London: Verso, 1989.

———. *Thirdspace: Journeys to Los Angeles and Other Real-and-Imagined Places*. Malden, Mass.: Blackwell Publishing, 1996.

Sollors, Werner. Foreword to *Creole Echoes: The Francophone Poetry of Nineteenth-Century Louisiana*, translated by Norman R. Shapiro. Urbana: University of Illinois Press, 2004.

Sontag, Susan. Introduction to *Bellocq: Photographs from Storyville, the Red-Light District of New Orleans*, by E. J. Bellocq. New York: Random House, 1996.

Spain, Daphne. *Gendered Spaces*. Chapel Hill: University of North Carolina Press, 1992.

Spillers, Hortense J. "Who Cuts the Border? Some Readings of 'America.'" In *Comparative American Identities: Race, Sex, and Nationality*. New York: Routledge, 1991.

Spirn, Anne Whiston. *The Language of Landscape*. New Haven: Yale University Press, 2000.

Stack, Carol. *Call to Home: African Americans Reclaim the Rural South*. New York: Basic Books, 1996

———. E-mail message to Thadious Davis. 6 June 2010.

Stepto, Robert B. *Behind the Veil: A Study of Afro-American Narrative*. Urbana: University of Illinois Press, 1979.

Sublette, Ned. *The World That Made New Orleans: From Spanish Silver to Congo Square*. Chicago: Lawrence Hill Books, 2008.

Sugrue, Thomas. *The Origins of the Urban Crisis: Race and Inequality in Postwar Detroit*. Princeton: Princeton University Press, 1996.

Sullivan, Lester. "Composers of Color of Nineteenth-Century New Orleans: The History behind the Music." In *Creole: The History and Legacy of Louisiana's Free People of Color*, edited by Sybil Kein. Baton Rouge: Louisiana State University Press, 2000.

Takaki, Ronald. *A Different Mirror: A History of Multicultural America*. Boston: Little, Brown, 1993.

Tate, Linda. *A Southern Weave of Women: Fiction of the Contemporary South*. Athens: University of Georgia Press, 1994.

Taylor, Helen. *Circling Dixie: Contemporary Southern Culture through a Transatlantic Lens*. New Brunswick: Rutgers University Press, 2000.

Thernstrom, Stephan, ed. *Harvard Encyclopedia of American Ethnic Groups*. Cambridge, Mass.: Belknap Press of Harvard University, 1980.

Thierry, Camille. "An Old Mulatress's Lament; or, Sanite Fouéron's Despair." In *Creole Echoes: The Francophone Poetry of Nineteenth-Century Louisiana*, translated by Norman R. Shapiro. Urbana: University of Illinois Press, 2004.

Thomas, Lorenzo. "Black Poetry in the '80s—Alive and Dancing." *Houston Post*, Sunday Books, 5 February 1984, 12ff.

Thomas-Houston, Marilyn M. *"Stony the Road" to Change: Black Mississippians and the Culture of Social Relations*. New York: Cambridge University Press, 2005.

Thompson, Shirley Elizabeth. *Exiles at Home: The Struggle to Become American in Creole New Orleans*. Cambridge, Mass.: Harvard University Press, 2009.

Tidwell, John Edgar, and Mark A. Sanders, eds. *Sterling A. Brown's "A Negro Looks at the South"*. New York: Oxford University Press, 2007.

Tocqueville, Alexis de. *Democracy in America*. 2 vols. Translated by Henry Reeve. NewYork: Alfred A. Knopf, 1945.

Trethewey, Natasha. *Bellocq's Ophelia*. St. Paul, Minn.: Graywolf Press, 2002.

———. *Domestic Work*. St. Paul, Minn.: Graywolf Press, 2000.

———. "Inscriptive Restorations: An Interview with Natasha Trethewey." Interview by Charles Rowell. *Callaloo* 27, no. 4 (Fall 2004): 1022–34.

———. *Native Guard*. Boston: Mariner Books, 2007.

Tuan, Yi-Fu. *Escapism*. Baltimore: Johns Hopkins University Press, 1998.

———. *Space and Place: The Perspective of Experience*. Minneapolis: University of Minnesota Press, 1977.

Turner, Darwin T. "Frank Yerby as Debunker." *Massachusetts Review* 20 (Summer 1968): 569–77.

Valcour, B. *"L'Ouvrier Louisiannais." Les Cenelles*. Nendeln: Kraus Reprint, 1971.

Van Vechten, Carl. Letter to Dorothy Peterson. 30 October 1959. In the James Weldon Johnson Collection, Beinecke Rare Book and Manuscript Library, Yale University.

Vernon, Olympia. *Eden*. New York: Grove Press, 2004.

———. "Finding Logic: An Interview with Olympia Vernon." Interview by Dee Y. Steward. *African American Women Writers*, 24 July 2004.

———. *A Killing in This Town*. New York: Grove Press, 2006.

———. *Logic*. New York: Grove Press, 2004.

Viatte, Auguste. *Histoire littéraire de l'Amérique française des origines à 1950*. Paris: Presses Universitaires de France, 1954.

Vlach, John Michael. *Back of the Big House: The Architecture of Plantation Slavery*. Chapel Hill: University of North Carolina Press, 1993.

Walker, Alice. *Absolute Trust in the Goodness of the Earth: New Poems*. New York: Random House, 2003.

———. "Alice Walker: On Finding Your Bliss." Interview by Evelyn C. White. *Ms.* September/October 1998.

———. *Anything We Love Can Be Saved: A Writer's Activism*. New York: Random House, 1997.

———. "The Black Writer and the Southern Experience." In *In Search of Our Mothers' Gardens: Womanist Prose*, 15–21. New York: Harcourt Brace, 1983.

———. *The Color Purple*. New York: Harcourt Brace Jovanovich, 1982.

———. "Everyday Use." *Best American Short Stories*. 1973.

———. *Good Night, Willie Lee, I'll See You in the Morning: Poems*. New York: Dial Press, 1979.

———. *Hard Times Require Furious Dancing: New Poems*. Novato, Calif.: New World Library, 2010.

———. *Horses Make a Landscape Look More Beautiful: Poems*. San Diego: Harcourt Brace Jovanovich, 1984.

———. "I Know What the Earth Says." Interview by William Ferris. *Southern Cultures* 10, no. 1 (Spring 2004): 5–24.

———. *In Love and Trouble: Stories of Black Women*. New York: Harcourt Brace Jovanovich 1973.

———. *In Search of Our Mothers' Gardens: Womanist Prose*. San Diego: Harcourt Brace Jovanovich, 1983.

———. *Living by the Word: Selected Writings, 1973–1987*. San Diego: Harcourt Brace Jovanovich, 1988.

———. *Meridian*. New York: Harcourt Brace Jovanovich, 1976.

———. *Now Is the Time to Open Your Heart: A Novel*. New York: Ballentine Books, 2004.

———. *Overcoming Speechlessness: A Poet Encounters the Horror in Rwanda, Eastern Congo, and Palestine/Israel*. New York: Seven Stories Press, 2010.

———. *Possessing the Secret of Joy*. New York: Simon and Schuster, 1993.

———. "The Revenge of Hannah Kemhuff." *Best American Short Stories*. 1974.

———. *Revolutionary Petunias and Other Poems*. New York: Harcourt Brace Jovanovich, 1973.

———. *The Same River Twice: Honoring the Difficult*. New York: Scribner, 1996.

———. "The Unglamorous but Worthwhile Duties of the Black Revolutionary Artist, or, Of the Black Writer Who Simply Works and Writes." In *In Search of Our Mothers' Gardens: Womanist Prose*. San Diego: Harcourt Brace Jovanovich, 1983.

———. *The Way Forward Is with a Broken Heart*. New York: Random House, 2000.

———. *We Are the Ones We Have Been Waiting For: Inner Light in a Time of Darkness.* New York: The New Press, 2006.

———. *You Can't Keep a Good Woman Down: Stories.* New York: Harcourt Brace Jovanovich, 1981.

Walker, Margaret. "Jackson, Mississippi." In *This Is My Century: New and Collected Poems.* Athens: University of Georgia Press, 1989.

———. "Natchez and Richard Wright in Southern American Literature." In *On Being Female, Black, and Free: Essays by Margaret Walker, 1932–1992,* edited by Maryemma Graham. Knoxville: University of Tennessee Press, 1997.

———. "Richard Wright." In *Richard Wright: Impressions and Perspectives,* edited by Robert Fransworth and David Ray. Ann Arbor: University of Michigan Press, 1973.

———. *Richard Wright, Daemonic Genius: A Portrait of the Man, a Critical Look at His Work.* New York: Warner Books, 1988.

Walker, Melissa. *Down from the Mountaintop: Black Women's Novels in the Wake of the Civil Rights Movement, 1966–1986.* New Haven: Yale University Press, 1991.

Walker, Rebecca. *Black, White, and Jewish: Autobiography of a Shifting Self.* New York: Riverhead Books, 2001.

Wall, Cheryl. *Worrying the Line: Black Women Writers, Lineage, and Literary Tradition.* Chapel Hill: University of North Carolina Press, 2005.

Walton, Anthony. *Mississippi: An American Journey.* New York: Vintage Books, 1997.

Warf, Benny. "Derek Gregory." In *Key Thinkers on Space and Place,* edited by Phil Hubbard, Rob Kitchin, and Gill Valentine. London: Sage Publications, 2004.

Werner, Craig Hansen. *Paradoxical Resolutions: American Fiction since James Joyce.* Urbana: University of Illinois Press, 1982.

West, Cornel. "Black Strivings in a Twilight Civilization." In *The Cornel West Reader.* New York: Basic Civitas Book, 1999.

White, Evelyn C. *Alice Walker: A Life.* New York: W. W. Norton, 2004.

Whitman, Alden. Review of *American Hunger. Chicago Tribune Book World,* 22 May 1997, 7-1. Reprinted in *Richard Wright: The Critical Reception,* edited by John M. Reilly. New York: Burt Franklin and CS, 1978.

"Why Blacks Are Returning to the South." *Jet,* 6 April 1998, 15.

Williams, Patricia J. *Open House: Of Family, Friends, Food, Piano Lessons, and the Search for a Room of My Own.* New York: Farrar, Straus and Giroux, 2004.

Williams, Samm-Art. *Home.* New York: Dramatists Play Service, 1980.

Williams, Sherley Anne. *Dessa Rose.* New York: William Morrow, 1986.

Williamson, Joel. *New People: Miscegenation and Mulattoes in the United States.* New York: New York University Press, 1984.

———. "The Soul Is Fled." In *New Perspectives on Race and Slavery in America,* edited by Robert H. Abzug and Stephen E. Maizlish. Lexington: University Press of Kentucky, 1986.

Wilson, Carol. *The Two Lives of Sally Miller: A Case of Mistaken Racial Identity in Antebellum New Orleans.* New Brunswick: Rutgers University Press, 2007.

Woolfork, Lisa. "Slave Tourism and Rememory." In *Embodying American Slavery in Contemporary Culture*, 98–131. Urbana: University of Illinois Press, 2009.

Wright, Charles. "Meditation on Form and Measure." In *Black Zodiac*. New York: Farrar, Straus and Giroux, 1997.

Wright, Ellen, and Michel Fabre, eds. *Richard Wright Reader*. New York: Harper and Row, 1978.

Wright, Richard. *American Hunger*. New York: Harper & Row, 1977.

———. "Between the World and Me." *Partisan Review* 2 (July-August 1935): 18–19. Reprinted in *The Richard Wright Reader*, edited by Ellen Wright and Michael Fabre, 246–47. New York: Harper and Row, 1978.

———. *Black Boy: A Record of Childhood and Youth*. New York: Harper & Brothers, 1945.

———. "A Blueprint for Negro Writing." *New Challenge* 2 (Fall 1937): 53–65. Reprinted in *The Richard Wright Reader*, edited by Ellen Wright and Michael Fabre, 36–49. New York: Harper and Row, 1978.

———. "Haiku by Richard Wright." *New Letters* 36, no. 2 (Winter 1971): 100–101.

———. "How 'Bigger' Was Born." *Saturday Review* 22 (1 June 1940): 4–5, 17–20.

———. Introduction to *Black Metropolis: A Study of Negro Life in a Northern City*, by St. Clair Drake and Horace R. Cayton. New York: Harcourt, Brace and Company, 1945.

———. "The Man Who Killed a Shadow." In *Eight Men: Stories*. New York: HarperPerennial, 1996.

Yaeger, Patricia. *Dirt and Desire: Reconstructing Southern Women's Writing, 1930–1990*. Chicago: University of Chicago Press, 2000.

———. "Introduction: Narrating Space." In *The Geography of Identity*, edited by Patricia Yaeger. Ann Arbor: University of Michigan Press, 2001.

Young, John. Review of *Mississippi Masala*. *Video Magazine*, October 1992.

Young, Kevin, ed. *Giant Steps: The New Generation of African American Writers*. New York: Perennial, 2000.

Young, Reggie Scott. "Still Driven by That Louisiana Thing: On the Thirtieth Anniversary of *Callaloo*'s 1978 Special Issue on Ernest J. Gaines." *Callaloo* 30, no. 3 (2007): 699–701.

Youngblood, Shay. *Black Girl in Paris*. New York: Riverhead Books, 2000.

———. "Shay Youngblood." http://www.shayyoungblood.com/.

———. *Soul Kiss*. New York: Riverhead Books, 1997.

Index

Abel, Elizabeth, 378 (n. 21)

Abraham Lincoln Presidential Library, 147

Abused women, 58, 66, 68–70, 72, 78, 363

Acadians, 192, 196, 206, 207. *See also* Cajuns

Adams, Gleason R. W., *Les Cenelles* (translation), 220, 222, 228

Adams, Jessica, *Wounds of Returning*, 61

Adéle v. Beauregard (La., 1810), 395 (n. 44)

Africa, 19, 38, 40, 41, 110; black American heritage and, 382–83 (n. 43); genealogical searches in, 44, 47; as inspiration, 38; slave trade from, 47, 72–73, 196, 382; Walker and, 340, 350–51, 365, 368, 373. *See also* African diaspora

African American literature, 4, 5, 9–10, 15, 16–17, 34–39, 51; bridging and, 50, 62, 140, 150, 161, 163–64; Creole language and, 248; Creoles of Color and, 216–20; dream space and, 120; Federal Writers' Project and, 137, 139, 141, 143–46, 149, 151; gay identity and, 324–28; historical fiction genre and, 36–40, 48, 50–52, 268, 269; local color and, 226–28; narrative performance and, 239–40; 1930s and, 135–43; 1980s and, 32, 36–43, 50, 52, 77–82, 340; portrayals of Till's lynching and, 91–92, 96, 102, 386 (n. 16); postmodernism and, 16, 18, 19–20, 38, 40, 43, 59, 68, 120, 313, 316, 328–29, 339; recurring key spaces of, 15; return to southern home and, 36–38, 45, 56, 57, 167; southern folk culture and, 344; twenty-first century and, 9, 12, 32, 95, 119–21, 166–67; visibility of, 32, 347; women's writing and, 31, 339–40, 344, 345, 364, 381 (n. 21). *See also names of specific writers*

African Americans: divergent populations of, 40; family reunions of, 46–47, 48, 50; genealogical searches by, 44; as the Other, 27; post–civil rights era changed status of, 9–10, 12, 28, 31–32, 40, 41; regional identity and, 9–10, 19; return to New South of, 8, 18, 19, 34–35, 53–57;

southern cultural home of, 43, 55, 328, 344–46, 363. *See also* Black *headings*; Race; *specific issues*

African diaspora, 44, 45, 82, 193, 194; culture of, 82; Louisiana and, 200–201, 203–4, 206, 252–54; Walker's concerns with, 340, 351, 365, 373

Afro-Creole population. *See* Creoles of Color

Afro-French population, 190. *See also* Creoles of Color

Alabama, 5, 54, 81, 95; Birmingham church bombing, 172–73, 185

Album Littéraire, L', 216–17

Alexander, Elizabeth, 90, 120, 310

Alexander, Margaret Walker. *See* Walker, Margaret

Algren, Nelson, 137

Alienation, 14–15

Allen, James, *Without Sanctuary*, 86

Allen, Paula Gunn, 351–52

Allison, Dorothy, 364; *Bastard out of Carolina*, 339

Alsberg, Henry, 144, 145

Althusser, Louis, 150

American Hunger (Wright), 140, 149, 151–52, 153, 156–57, 158–59, 160–62, 163, 165

American Stuff, 139, 140, 145

Anastasie Desarzant v. Pierre Lablanc and Eglantine Desmazillier (1858), 191, 237, 400 (n. 150)

Anderson, Benedict, 194; *Imagined Communities*, 15, 194

Anderson, Sherwood, *Winesburg, Ohio*, 126

Andrews, William, *Sisters of the Spirit*, 42–43

Angelou, Maya, 337

Angola State Penitentiary (La.), 292–93, 304

Angolite, The, 293

Annals of the Association of American Geographers, 378 (n. 19)

Ansa, Tina McElroy, 167, 181, 364

"Antillanité" identity, 192–93

Black history, 38, 52–53, 57; Federal Writers' Project initiative and, 144–45, 146–48; physical monuments to, 45–46, 49; retrieval projects of, 42–48; as southern history, 25–26, 29, 47–48. *See also* Civil rights movement; Segregation; Slavery

Black masculinity, 21, 101, 330; *Color Purple* controversy and, 364; Gaines's signifiers of, 284, 288–91, 298, 300, 302–4, 325; gay identity and, 324–25; history of oppression of, 287; visibility and, 98–99

Black Metropolis (Cayton and Drake), Wright introduction, 148

"Blackness": representation of, 41, 313; slavery based on, 199–200. *See also* Black body; Race

Black Power movement, 38, 263

Black Public Sphere Collective, 3, 233

Black Studies, 32, 189; Federal Writers' Program research and, 144–45, 146–48

Black woman's body, 21, 42, 66, 72, 308–9; geographies of, 352, 353–54; memory and, 61; physical abuse of, 58, 68–70. *See also* Maternal body; Power; Sexuality; Women

Black Women's Studies, 32, 60, 336–37, 339–40, 346–49, 364

Blake, Jeanie, 266

Blassingame, John W.: *Black New Orleans*, 190, 207, 208, 215; *Slave Testimony*, 33

Block, Sam, 83–84

Blues, 29, 59, 78, 95–98, 101, 107, 111, 118; icons of, 97–98; southern violence and, 95–96, 102

Bluescape, 78, 102, 113

Bodenheim, Maxwell, 145

Body: belonging and, 325; damage to, 96, 102, 126, 133; environment and, 168; as prison, 306–7; as signifier, 58, 64, 66, 72, 133; as sociopolitical structure, 11, 66; space and, 14–15, 140, 308–9; as spatial and identity marker, 49, 79, 182, 308–9. *See also* Black masculinity; Black woman's body

Bogalusa, La., 119

Bolivia, 373

Bombings, 172–73, 176, 185

Bone, Martyn, *The Postsouthern Sense of Place in Contemporary Fiction*, 344

Bontemps, Arna, 39, 135, 137, 141, 143–44; *Black Thunder: Gabriel's Revolt, Virginia 1800*, 39; *Drums at Dusk*, 39; *The Poetry of the Negro* (ed.), 191

Book-of-the-Month Club, 139, 152

Border crossings, 232, 233

Border culture, 119–20, 232

Borderland, 201, 232

Border lives (Bhabha term), 231, 232

Borges, Jorge Luis, 314

Bost, Suzanne, 194

Boundaries: cultural, 201, 203; postmodern fiction and, 113; racial (*see* Segregation); social, 27, 140; spatial, 7–8, 27, 80, 140, 349

Bradley, David, 312; *The Chaneysville Incident*, 37

Bradley, Mamie Till, 87, 88

Brasseaux, Carl A., *Creoles of Color in the Bayou Country*, 190

Brazil, 204, 210, 211, 212

Brazilian National Institute of Music, 210

Bridging, 50, 62, 140, 150, 161, 163–64

Brookings Institution, Center on Urban and Metropolitan Policy, 53, 55

Brooks, Gwendolyn, "The Last Quatrain of the Ballad of Emmett Till," 386 (n. 16)

Brooks, Peter, 64

Brown, Linda Beatrice, 167

Brown, Rita Mae, 324

Brown, Sterling, 137, 140, 141, 143; Federal Writers' Project initiatives and, 144–45, 146–47; *Negro Caravan* (ed.), 148, 191; "Odyssey of Big Boy," 147; "Slim in Hell," 100; *Southern Road*, 147

Brown, William Wells, *Clotel*, 200

Brown-Guillory, Elizabeth, 167, 364

Brown v. Board of Education (1954), 87, 90, 229, 246, 354

Bryan, Violet Harrington, 191, 226, 243

Bryant, Roy, 89

Built environment, 80, 82

Bunche, Ralph, 144

Butler, Robert Olen, 19, 110

Butler-Evans, Elliott, 347

Byerman, Keith, 302

Byrd, James, 126

Cable, George Washington, 30, 227, 395 (n. 43)

Cajuns, 110, 192, 404 (n. 64); contemporary studies of, 189; definition of, 206; plantation system and, 267, 274, 278–79, 281, 283, 284, 295

Caldwell, Erskine, 340, 380 (n. 39)

California, 54, 67, 235, 271, 363, 368

Calinda, 212

Callaloo, 35

Calvino, Italo, 63

Campbell, Bebe Moore, 386 (n. 16)

Campbell, Bill, 54–55

Cannon, Katie, 365

Cao, Lan, 19

Capitalism, 13, 213, 274, 279–80, 345

Capote, Truman, *Other Voices, Other Rooms*, 406 (n. 107)

Carby, Hazel, 343–44

Caribbean islands, 8, 19, 110, 193–94, 203; African slavery and, 196; Louisiana migrations and, 195–96, 205, 206, 208, 211, 212, 238; model of race and, 192–93, 200–201; New Orleans influence of, 200–201, 202, 212

Carnival, 213

Carpentier, Alejo, 192, 205

Cartwright, Keith, 340

Casey, Maud, 125–26

Catherine Carmier (Gaines), 266, 267, 275, 276–88, 289, 295, 307, 403 (n. 51)

Catholic Church, 196, 204, 213, 224, 242

Cayton, Horace, *Black Metropolis*, 148

Cemetery, 238, 239, 241, 276

Cenelles, Les, 9, 23, 191, 214, 217–22, 223, 224, 228, 247; Adams and Latortue translation of, 220, 222, 228

Certeau, Michel de, 24, 42, 63, 74, 78, 144, 260, 262; definition of space, 5, 6; on dying man, 285; on map vs. itinerary, 171–72; *The Practice of Everyday Life*, 77, 112, 407 (n. 8); on walking, 177, 178

Césaire, Aimé, 193

Chaining, 62, 262–64, 265, 277, 300

Chamoiseau, Patrick, *Éloge de la Créolité*, 193, 194

Charlotte, N.C., 54

Chaumette, Alexandre, 216

Cheatwood, K. T. H., 364

Cheney, James, 103

Cherie Quarters, 56, 259, 270, 273, 278

Cherokee, the, 56, 110, 360–61, 373

Chesnutt, Charles W., 26–27, 30, 32, 226, 330; *The Conjure Woman and Other Tales*, 330; *Free Man of Color*, 330; *The House behind the Cedars*, 208, 330; *Mandy Oxendine*, 330; *Paul Marchand*, 330

Chicago, black writers in, 136–37, 138–39, 142, 143, 146–47, 157, 161, 163, 191

Chicago Defender, 87

Chicago Tribune Book World, 157

Child rape, 78, 85

Chimeric space, 313–14, 315, 319, 323

Chinquapin, N.C., 311–12

Choctaw, the, 214

Choi, Susan, 19

Chopin, Kate, 225

Choudbury, Sarita, 107

Christian, Marcus, 191–92; *High Ground*, 191; "History," 192

Civil Rights Act of 1964, 12, 90

Civil Rights Memorial (Montgomery, Ala.), 95

Civil rights movement, 13, 25, 38, 50, 78–79, 187, 263; Birmingham violence and, 172–73, 185; challenges of, 237; Creoles of Color and, 229, 235; current legal redress and, 103; legacy of, 230–31; memoirs of, 90–91; Mississippi and, 83–93, 95, 100, 102–5, 111, 187, 335, 354–56; Walker and, 335, 336, 342, 347, 354, 355, 356, 362–63

Civil War, 67, 70, 71, 73, 75, 83, 207

Clark, Keith, 284

Cleage, Pearl, 167

Clifton, Lucille, "Entering the South," 1–2

Code Noir, 196, 197

Cohn, Deborah, *Look Away!* (ed.), 29

Coleman, Edward Maceo, *Creole Voices*, 217, 220, 222

Coleman, Wanda, "Emmett Till," 386 (n. 16)

Collage, 170, 171, 177

Collins, Josiah, 48

Color line, crossing of, 235, 237, 252, 254, 330

Color Purple, The (Walker), 39–40, 41–42, 339, 358, 363, 370; controversy over, 41, 339, 363, 364; film adaptation of, 41, 363

Coming of Age in Mississippi (Moody), 77–78, 90–92

Comité de Citoyens (New Orleans), 229, 399 (n. 126)

Commodity culture, 345, 359
Communist Party, 139, 142, 147, 161, 163
Condé, Maryse, 194
Confiant, Raphaël, *Éloge de la Créolité*, 193, 194
Congo Square, 213
Congress of Racial Equality (CORE), 90, 91
Conservatoire de Musique, 211
Contact zones, 194
Cooper, Ann Nixon, 308, 309–10
Cooper, J. California, *The Wake of the Wind*, 37
Corps d'Afrique, 73–74
Cosgrove, Denis, 176–77
Cotton growing, 82–83, 110, 341
Courlander, Harold, *The African*, 383 (n. 43)
Cowdrey, Albert E., *This Land, This South*, 109–10, 111
Craft, William, 200
Crang, Mike, 25, 268, 377 (n. 4)
Creole (Kein, ed.), 227
Creole Ballads & Zydeco (CD recording), 247
Creole Classique (CD recording), 247
Creole Echoes (Shapiro, translation; Weiss, introduction and notes), 220
Creole language, 206, 218, 248, 249–52, 272, 282
Creole of Color (New Orleans newspaper), 228
Creole Romantic musicians, 209–12, 247
Creoles, 212, 213; definition of, 206, 228; ethnicity and, 203; Louisiana local color literature and, 225–26; male plaçage convention, 213–15
Creoles of Color (*gens de couleur libre*), 9, 20–21, 72–73, 186–87, 189–91, 194, 203–28, 237–38, 241–55, 267; background and colonial identities of, 195–96; broad definitions of, 195; cosmopolitan makeup of, 207–8, 228, 247; as creative inspiration, 241–55, 257–58; crossing of color line by, 235, 237, 252, 254; disappearance as distinct caste of, 283–84; as educated class, 216; *Eve's Bayou* film representation of, 246; as expatriates in France, 208–10, 211, 215–16, 218–19, 222–23, 224, 397 (n. 87); fluidity of, 208–23, 228; identity and, 208, 212, 215–16, 229, 277–78, 281–84; language fluency of, 212;

literary life of, 216–28, 247; literary representations of, 72–73, 225–23, 241–47; lost multicultural potential of, 247, 249; Louisiana court ruling on, 199–200; migration from South by, 216, 235, 249; as model for U.S. society, 234; music of, 203, 209–11, 246, 247; New Orleans population of, 198, 207–8; occupations of, 208; physical appearance of, 195, 212, 229, 235; plaçage and, 213–15, 224; post–Civil War loss of legal status of, 212, 225, 227, 228–29, 235; preservation of writings of, 191–92; property, wealth, and accomplishments of, 194, 208, 211, 213–15, rights encroachment challenge by, 228–29, 399 (n. 126) (see also *Plessy v. Ferguson*); women's acceptable activities and, 224–25
Creole Troubadours, 247
Créolité, 20, 188, 229, 246–47, 248, 258; definition of, 193–94
Creolization, 192, 194, 236
Cresswell, Tim, 6, 34–35, 324
Crews, Harry, "Mourns for Mules," 34
Crisis, The, 41, 87, 141
Cross-cultural formation, 188
Crossings, 194
Crozat, Anthony, 196
Cuba, 110, 201, 204, 205, 206, 212, 216; creolization and, 192
Cullen, Countee, 135, 141
Cultural flows, 164, 194, 198–238; borderlands and, 232; race and, 186, 199, 208–23, 228, 236–37, 330. *See also* Multiculturalism
Cultural geography, 20, 135, 138; diffusion studies and, 16–17; permeable boundaries and, 201, 203; southern changes in, 109–10
Cultural identity, 231, 313, 353; Creoles of Color and, 208, 212, 215–16, 229, 277–78, 281–84
Cutler, Phoebe, *The Public Landscape of the New Deal*, 142

Dalcour, Pierre, 218–19, 220; "*Les Aveux*," 219; "Lines Written in the Album of Mademoiselle," 219
Damas, Léon, 193
Danile, Rosemary, "The Southern Body," 34

Emanuel, James A., 386 (n. 16)

Embodiment. *See* Body

Emmett Till Unresolved Civil Rights Crime Act of 2008, 103

Enlightenment, 13

Equality, 28, 223, 235

Esman, Marjorie R., "About the Cajuns," 393 (n. 11)

Esteves, Arthur, 399 (n. 126)

Ethnicity, 28, 34, 107, 233; Louisiana and, 192, 203–4, 206. *See also* Multiculturalism

Evers, Medgar, 91, 103

Everyday, concept of, 77, 112, 334, 346, 407 (n. 8); domestic culture and, 339, 342; impact of segregation on, 270, 273

Eve's Bayou (film), 246

Exclusion, 18, 27–31, 37, 78, 186; black literary theme of, 36, 58, 80, 150; black professional writers and, 135; changes in southern practices of, 32–34; racial geography and, 140, 186, 343. *See also* Segregation

Expatriates: New Orleans Creoles of Color, 208, 208–10, 210, 211, 215–16, 218–19, 222–23, 224, 397 (n. 87); twentieth-century black writers, 20, 50–51, 52, 137, 148–49, 164–71, 176–80, 183–84, 185

Fabre, Michel: "New Orleans Creole Expatriates in France," 215–16; *The Unfinished Quest of Richard Wright*, 139, 153

False River, 56, 259, 267, 276, 277, 294

Fanon, Frantz, 377 (n. 6)

Farm, The: Life inside Angola Prison (film), 292

Faubourg Tremé (film), 243

Faulkner, William, 30, 105–6, 258, 337, 338, 340, 342, 380 (n. 39); *Absalom, Absalom!*, 74, 106, 205, 333, 337; *Intruder in the Dust*, 295–96; *Light in August*, 105; *The Sound and the Fury*, 333

Fauset, Jessie, 135, 141

Federal Arts Project, 136

Federal Theater Project, 136, 143

Federal Writers' Project, 136–37, 140–48; *American Stuff*, 139, 140, 145; black cultural research materials, 144–45, 146–48; development of professional black writers by, 137, 139, 141, 143, 144, 145,

146; Negro in Louisiana history project, 191–92; *New Orleans City Guide*, 236–37; state guidebooks, 114, 144

Female genital mutilation, 340

Feminism, 111, 364–65

Feminist Studies, 11, 32, 60

Fernández, Roberto G., 19

Ferris, William, 345

Fiehrer, Thomas Marc, "The African Presence in Colonial Louisiana," 200–201

Finney, Nikky, *The World Is Round*, 360

Fire!!!, 141

Fisher, Dorothy Canfield, 149–50

Fisher, Rudolph, 141

Fisk University, 51, 52

Flood of 1927, 70

Florida, 35, 81

Fluidity: racial, 186, 199, 208–23, 228, 236–37, 330. *See also* Cultural flows

Folk culture, 121, 146, 147, 312, 316, 342, 351–52; black women writers and, 340, 344. *See also* Storytelling

Fontenot, Keith P., *Creoles of Color in the Bayou Country*, 190

Forrest, Leon, 57; *Two Wings to Veil My Face*, 37

Forum, 141

Foucault, Michel, 266, 293; *Discipline and Punish*, 293; "Of Other Spaces," 185, 208, 234, 238, 239, 265, 318, 342–43, 347, 348; *The Order of Things*, 314; *Power/ Knowledge*, 42

Fourteenth Amendment, 235

Foxes of Harrow, The (Yerby), 51; film adaptation of, 51

France, 170, 365; black expatriates in, 50, 52, 148–49, 164, 166, 167, 176; Creoles of Color expatriates in, 208–10, 211, 215–16, 218–19, 222–23, 224, 397 (n. 87); Louisiana as colony of, 189, 190, 192, 196, 197, 203–4, 206, 212, 238; Louisiana's sale by (1803), 197, 198, 199, 203, 207, 210, 211, 267–68; overseas departments of, 193; twenty-first-century racial problems in, 176. *See also* Paris

Frankenberg, Ruth, 30

Franklin, John Hope, 25–26, 29; *From Slavery to Freedom*, 25

Frasconi, Antonio, 119

Freedom, 146, 151

Holman, C. Hugh, "No More Monoliths, Please," 32–33

Home, 15, 57–76, 113; exclusion from, 36, 37, 78; migratory experience and, 181; return to, 43, 45, 53, 55–56, 76, 102, 109, 111; simulacra of, 45, 49. *See also* Homeplace

Homelessness, 14–15, 212

Homeplace, 19, 48, 57, 70, 380 (n. 41)

Homesickness, 176

Homoeroticism, 326, 328, 330, 331, 406 (n. 107)

hooks, bell, 3, 12, 14, 40, 41, 223, 310; black feminist location and, 60; "homeplace" reference and, 380 (n. 41); on memory and forgetting, 60, 61; on "right to subjectivity," 336–37; Third Space and, 40, 286

Horton, James Oliver, *Free People of Color,* 189–90

Hughes, Langston, 135, 136, 141, 142, 143, 144, 166, 168, 170, 177, 386 (n. 16); *The Big Sea,* 140, 171

Hugo, Victor, 217

Huie, William Bradford, 89

Hull, Gloria Thompson, 225–26; *All the Women Are White, All the Blacks Are Men, but Some of Us Are Brave* (ed.), 381 (n. 21)

Hurricane Camille (1969), 75

Hurricane Katrina (2005), 194–95, 242; devastation of, 201; racial division and, 187, 195, 249

Hurston, Zora Neale, 31, 80–81, 135, 141, 164, 191, 205, 243, 316, 339, 380 (n. 39), 407 (n. 13), 408 (n. 19); review of *Uncle Tom's Children* by, 161; *Their Eyes Were Watching God,* 81; Walker's rediscovery of, 340–41, 344, 351

Hutcheon, Linda, 13

Hyperspace, 14

Identity, 8, 19, 35, 40, 43–45, 49, 171; difference and, 325–26; fluidity of, 192, 215–16, 330; formation of, 27; intersections of, 327; markers of, 28, 34, 49, 109, 172, 203, 235; narrative performance of, 240; place as signifier of, 6, 10, 37, 38, 43, 56, 58, 281, 328, 336, 341; self-awareness and, 231. *See also* Cultural identity; *specific identities*

Illinois Writers' Project, 136–37, 143–44, 146–47, 191

Incarceration, 18, 277, 285; as major black social issue, 304; metaphorical, 101, 286, 291–92, 293–99, 300–307, 325, 350. *See also* Prisons

Incest, 339

Indian burial mound, 358, 359, 360

In My Father's House (Gaines), 285, 288–91

Integration, 87, 89, 103, 171, 204, 233; Supreme Court school mandate (1954), 87, 90, 229, 246, 354; University of Mississippi and, 103, 104–5

Internationalism, 150, 167, 169

Interracial liaisons, 89, 107–9, 189, 207; plaçage and, 213–15

Interracial marriage, 148, 149, 204, 237, 342; Supreme Court ruling legalizing (1967), 12

Iton, Richard, *In Search of the Black Fantastic,* 195

Jackson, Miss., 93, 119, 120, 143

Jackson, George, *Soledad Brother,* 292

Jackson, John Brinckerhoff, 377 (n. 1)

Jackson, Samuel L., 246

Jacobs, Harriet, 31, 42

Jameson, Fredric, 13

JanMohamed, Abdul, *The Death-Bound Subject,* 161

Jarvis, Brian, *Postmodern Cartographies,* 14

Jay, Gregory, *America the Scrivener,* 229–30

Jazz, 29, 59, 209; musical roots of, 213

Jefferson, Augusteen, 271–72, 284, 307, 308, 309

Jefferson, Thomas, 49, 210, 268

Jet, 51, 87

Jim Crow. *See* Segregation

Joanni. *See* Questy, Joanni

Job, book of, 152–53

John F. Miller v. Sally Miller (1949), 199–200

John Reed Club, 136, 139, 142, 144, 163

Johnson, E. Patrick, *Sweet Tea,* 325, 328

Johnson, Georgia Douglas, 141, 142

Johnson, Jack, 159

Johnson, James Weldon, 52

Johnson, June, 84

Johnson, Robert, 97–98, 107, 118, 337

Johnson, Walter, *Soul by Soul,* 268

Prostitution, 60, 78, 85, 385 (n. 93); plaçage vs., 213, 214
Psychoanalytic theory, 8, 64
Public accommodations, 26–27, 88–89; "separate but equal" ruling and, 235, 399 (n. 126)
Public monuments, 45, 46, 49; black body and, 89, 95
Public space: black invisibility and, 80, 88, 89; multiculturalism and, 233–34; segregation signage and, 7, 12, 23, 80, 138; slave commemorations in, 49; visibility in, 80, 98–99
Puerto Ricans, 110
Punctum, 63–64

Queer, 20, 21, 166, 172, 180, 182, 325, 327, 328. See also Gay identity
Questy, Joanni, 216, 221

Race: American changing patterns of, 53–54; binaries of, 234–35; black-white genetic proportion and, 237; communal identity of, 42; contemporary France and, 176; contemporary South and, 6, 32; cultural changes and, 313; debate on portrayal in fiction of, 41; definitions of, 28, 199, 200, 203–4, 215, 237; diversification in Deep South of, 107–9; as essential marker, 6, 28–30; fictional representation of, 41; fluid designations of, 186, 199, 208–23, 228, 236–37, 330; geography of, 140, 186, 343; historical fiction and, 36–40, 51–63; Hurricane Katrina and, 187; justice and, 5, 26, 27–28, 89–90, 258, 286, 287, 339; memory and, 59, 60–61, 69–70, 71, 72, 112–13; modern concept of, 312–13; modernist/postmodernist theories of, 11–12; place intersection with, 137, 281, 341–42; pluralized identity of, 282; as power hierarchy basis, 5, 7–8, 13, 16, 20, 27–28, 29, 42, 80, 90, 100, 105, 125, 265; regional identity and, 41, 56, 57–76, 79; signifiers of, 198–200; social geography and, 12, 18, 305; space and (see Spatial-racial location); white appearance and, 235; whiteness as, 28–29, 30, 32. See also Mixed-race identity; Skin color
Racial prejudice, 234–35

Racism, 7–8, 12, 50, 78–79; ideology of, 90, 343; New Orleans Vital Statistics Bureau and, 236; persistence of, 104; psychic wound of, 93–95, 102, 117; publishing industry and, 135; "raced" space and, 186; traditional Western canon icons and, 231; visual representations of, 90, 96, 103; Walker and, 336, 339, 345, 359, 370; Wright's shifting environment and, 93–94, 95, 116, 148, 151, 164
Ragtime, 209
Railroad car segregation, 399 (n. 126)
Raleigh-Durham, N.C., 54
Randall, Alice, The Wind Done Gone, 39
Ransby, Barbara, Ella Baker and the Black Freedom Movement, 83
Rappers, 98
Reagon, Bernice Johnson, 43
Reconstruction, 226, 235
Redford, Dorothy Spruill, 46–48; Somerset Homecoming, 46
Reed, Ishmael, 32; Reckless Eyeballing, 386 (n. 16)
Region, 57–76; black historical fiction and, 39–40, 48; black writers and, 9–10, 36–38, 41, 42, 56, 339, 340, 342; as both space and place, 19, 38; definitions of, 24–25; public image of, 46; racial bonding with, 56; spatial-racial nexus and, 21, 24, 27–29, 34, 35, 48–49; studies of, 187
Reinders, Robert, 208
Religious schools, 224
Return migration, 8, 18, 19, 34–35, 43, 52–57; concept of, 43, 45; factors for, 53–57
Revue, 223
Rice, Anne, Interview with the Vampire, 385 (n. 97)
Rice, Anne P., Witnessing Lynching (ed.), 86
Rich, Adrienne, 11, 187
Richardson, Eudora Ramsay, 145
Richardson, Riché: Black Masculinity and the U.S. South, 98
Rideau, Wilbert, In the Place of Justice, 293
Rights, 27, 223, 229, 235
Rillieux, Victor, 215
River Lake plantation, 259–62, 263, 265, 267, 271, 278, 304; Gaines's return to, 56, 276
Roach, Joseph, 18; Cities of the Dead, 188

Sharecropping, 81, 83, 90–91, 117, 265, 267, 274, 278–79, 280, 283, 341
Ship Island, 75
Shockley, Ann Allen, *Loving Her*, 406 (n. 107)
Short, John Rennie, 269
Sibley, David, 16, 27; *Geographies of Exclusion*, 8; "zones of ambiguity" and, 197–98
Siete Partidas, Las, 196–97
Signage, 7, 12, 23, 80, 138
Simone, Nina, "Mississippi Goddam," 70, 100, 107
Skin color, 109, 198–200, 212; Creoles of Color and, 212, 219, 229, 235; passing and, 235, 252, 254, 330; privilege and, 278–79; as slavery basis, 199–200; social class and, 227; U.S. Census "mulatto" designation and, 396 (n. 68). *See also* Black body; Color line; Whiteness
Slave narratives, 32, 42–43, 200
Slave rebellions, 39, 198, 312
Slavery, 5, 6, 8, 25, 29, 30, 187, 192; black historical fiction and, 38–39, 50; black writers on, 44–45, 72, 252; as capital basis, 82, 268; contemporary family reunions and, 46–47, 50; emancipation (1863) from, 12, 82–83; escapes from, 312, 316, 319; familial bonds and, 356; as incarceration, 277, 285, 305; literary history and, 230; literary representations of, 267, 268, 305–9, 312, 314–15; living history sites of, 48; Louisiana colonial records and, 203–4; Louisiana legal codes and, 196–200; Louisiana cultural contribution and, 212–13, 267–68; miscegenation and, 207; monuments to, 45, 49; plantation life and, 46–49, 82, 267, 273; public impact of *Roots* TV portrayal of, 382–83 (n. 43); skin color basis of, 199–200; Spanish empire and, 196; structures built by labor of, 49
Slave trade, 13, 72–73, 355–56; Louisiana Territory and, 196; New Orleans market and, 268
Smith, Anna Deveare, 391 (n. 49)
Smith, Barbara, *All the Women Are White, All the Blacks Are Men, but Some of Us Are Brave* (ed.), 381 (n. 21)
Smith, Bessie, 97, 98
Smith, Jon, *Look Away!* (ed.), 29
SNCC. *See* Student Nonviolent Coordinating Committee
Social controls, 81, 140. *See also* Segregation
Social geography, 4, 6, 9, 10, 11; boundaries and, 27, 140; porch culture and, 80–81; race constructed by, 12, 18, 305; spatial geography's confluence with, 293–94. *See also* Segregation; Slavery
Social justice. *See* Justice
Social space, 4, 8, 16, 25–26, 378 (n. 10); African American claims to, 31–32; porch as, 81–82. *See also* Exclusion; Segregation
Social theory, 4, 11, 12, 25
Soeurs de la Sainte Famille, Les (Sisters of the Holy Family), 224
Soja, Edward W., 2–3, 40, 286, 377 (nn. 5, 6)
Sojourner Tree, 358
Sollors, Werner, 217
Somerset Homecoming, 46–48, 49
Song of Solomon, The (Morrison), 44, 45, 120, 121, 344
South: as black cultural home, 43, 55, 328, 344–46, 363; black migrations and (*See* Migration); black reclamation of, 8, 18–19, 23, 34–35, 43, 52–57, 66–67, 77–78, 167, 382–83 (n. 43); as both literal and symbolic space, 15; cultural transformation of, 336; deep context of, 118; dualities of, 75; expanded cultural definition of, 32; history of, 25–26, 29, 46–48, 75; images of, 6–7, 12–13, 20–21, 29–30; memory and, 29; modernity-to-postmodernity transition in, 12–13; multiple contexts of, 9, 12–13, 118; myth-making and, 7, 48; porch culture and, 80–82; post–civil rights era scholarship on, 29–30; postmodern configuration of, 343; racial markers of, 6, 18, 28–29; regional identity of, 21, 24, 27–29, 34, 35; as shared cultural space, 35–36; social theory and, 11; as spatial/ideological concept, 2, 4, 7, 10, 11, 24, 42, 80–82; time-space fabric of, 14–15. *See also* Deep South; Global South; New South; Rural South

South America, 8, 19, 110, 208, 211, 212, 238, 373

South Asians: Mississippi and, 107–9, 111; southern literature and, 19

South Carolina, 47, 54

Southern Agrarians, 12. *See also* Fugitive Poets

Southern Cultures, 345–46, 360–61

Southern literary culture, 2, 4, 5, 6, 9, 18, 30–34, 380 (n. 39); black former exclusion from, 30–31, 135, 342, 344, 364; black inclusion in canon of, 31, 32–34; contemporary changes in, 110; Creoles of Color and, 9, 23, 191, 214, 217–24; Louisiana and, 205, 225; minority inclusions in, 19, 110–11; Mississippi and, 10, 74, 105–6, 110, 113. *See also* African American literature; *specific writers*

Southern Magazine, 34

Southern rap, 98

Southern Studies, 6, 336, 338–39, 353, 373

"Southscape," concept of, 2–3, 11, 374, 377 (n. 5)

South Side Writers' Workshop, 136, 142, 143, 144, 163

Space: African American writers and, 15, 16, 20–21, 51; antagonisms of, 12; apertural, 57–76; black-defined, 78–79, 98–99; blackening of, 51; body's relationship to, 14–15, 49, 308–9; borders and, 232; boundaries of, 7–8, 27, 80, 140, 349; Certeau definition of, 5, 6; chaining and, 262–63; chimeric, 313–14, 315, 319, 323; contemporary analysis and, 25; contested, 185, 233; creolized, 82; cultural diffusion and, 16–17, 111; difference between real and imagined, 36; exclusion from (*see* Exclusion); freedom equated with, 146, 151; fugue, 113, 120, 121, 126, 133; gendered, 20, 21, 167, 335, 349; geography and, 25, 42, 136, 140, 262; global, 3, 140, 365, 367–68, 373–74; haiku as form of, 184; heterotopic, 238–39, 241, 265, 314, 318, 362; incarceral, 277, 291–92, 304, 350; institutional-geographical intersection in, 136; interior, 310, 311; interior-exterior bridging and, 50, 62, 140, 150, 151, 163–64; language and, 266, 314; literal vs. abstract, 23; literary narrative and, 14, 38–39; literary theory meaning of, 25; location and, 60; maps and, 176–77; modernist theorists of, 11–12, 25; movement in, 44–45, 118; mythical, 156–57, 177–78, 267, 313; narrative and, 14, 38, 49; object relations theory and, 8; oppositional (*see* Third Space); place and, 135, 149–50, 166; poetic, 332; porch culture and, 80–81; postmodern significance of, 11–12, 14, 16, 40, 168, 169; raced, 186 (*see also* Spatial-racial location); readings of, 11, 25; as representational strategy, 24–25; return as retrieval of, 45; "right" to define, 41; social significance of, 15; southern processes linked with, 4, 7, 10, 11, 42; subjective constructions of, 20, 27, 78; textual, 140; theoretical vs. actual, 25; violations of, 93. *See also* Public space; Segregation; Social space; Time-space continuum

Spain, 50, 52, 212; influence on New Orleans of, 189, 190, 200, 201; Louisiana as colony of, 195–97, 203–4, 206, 238

Spain, Daphne, 349, 378 (n. 10)

Spatialization, definition of, 262

Spatial-racial location, 2–4, 5, 10–11, 21, 42, 77, 88–89, 140, 185, 335–52; migration enabling, 151; public visibility and, 80; Trethewey's poetry and, 57–76; Walker and, 342–43

Spielberg, Steven, 41, 254, 363

Spillers, Hortense J., "Who Cuts the Border?," 232–33

Spirituals, 59

Spirn, Anne Whiston, 118

Stack, Carol, *Call to Home*, 43, 52–53, 55–56

State guidebooks, 114, 144

Sterkx, H. E., *The Free Negro in Antebellum Louisiana*, 190

Story magazine contest, 139, 163

Storytelling, 121, 271–72, 312, 351; porch talk and, 81, 272

Storyville, 385 (n. 93)

Stowe, Harriet Beecher, *Uncle Tom's Cabin*, 267, 268

Straight University (La.), 209, 225, 396 (n. 69)

Student Nonviolent Coordinating Committee (SNCC), 78, 83–84, 90, 91, 111

Everything We Know: Earthling Poems, 365; "Her Sweet Jerome," 345; *Horses Make a Landscape Look More Beautiful*, 357, 364, 365, 370–71; "How Did I Get Away with Killing One of the Biggest Lawyers in the State? It Was Easy," 358; "How Poems Are Made/A Discredited View," 369; *In Love and Trouble: Stories of Black Women*, 350, 366, 407 (n. 13); "In Search of Our Mothers' Gardens," 42, 338, 339, 344, 346; *In Search of Our Mothers' Gardens*, 111, 342, 364, 373, 407 (n. 13); "In the Closet of the Soul," 364; "Karamojans," 350; *Living by the Word*, 365; "Looking for Zora," 340; *Meridian*, 42, 331, 343, 353–57, 358–59, 361, 362, 373; "My American Earnings," 368; "New House Moves," 366–67; *Now Is the Time to Open Your Heart: A Novel*, 347–48, 362; *Once*, 350, 365–66; "Petunias," 93, 358; *Possessing the Secret of Joy*, 365; "The Revenge of Hannah Kemhuff," 345, 351, 407 (n. 13); "Revolutionary Petunias," 357–58; *Revolutionary Petunias and Other Poems*, 357–58, 407 (n. 13); "Roselily," 345; *The Same River Twice*, 41, 347; "Saving the Life That Is Your Own," 340; *Sent by the Earth: A Message from the Grand-mother Spirit*, 347; "Songless," 370–71; *The Temple of My Familiar*, 365, 371; *The Third Life of Grange Copeland*, 42, 353, 354, 362–63, 366; "To Hell with Dying," 350; "Tranquil, Mississippi," 93; "The Unglamorous but Worthwhile Duties of the Black Revolutionary Artist, or of the Black Writer Who Simply Works and Writes," 347; "The Universe Responds," 365; *The Way Forward Is with a Broken Heart*, 21, 360–61, 362; *We Are the Ones We Have Been Waiting For*, 337; *You Can't Keep a Good Woman Down*, 93, 358
Walker, Kate Nelson, 350, 362
Walker, Margaret (Margaret Walker Alexander), 57, 93, 95; Federal Writers' Project and, 136–37, 141, 143–44; "Jackson, Mississippi," 94; *Jubilee*, 39, 382–83 (n. 43); *This Is My Century*, 94
Walker, Melissa, 356
Walker, Minnie Tallulah Grant, 341, 350, 351, 360

Walker, Willie Lee, 341, 407 (n. 13)
Wall, Cheryl, 364
Walton, Anthony, 9, 95, 106, 113–14, 115, 117, 120, 386 (n. 16)
Ward, Theodore, 137, 141, 143–44
Warren, Robert Penn, 74
Washington, Booker T., 323
Washington, Denzel, 107
Washington, Mary Helen, *Invented Lives* (ed.), 43
Weatherby, William J., *The Negro in New York*, 148
Weaver, Robert, 144
Weems, Renita, 365
Weiss, M. Lynn, *Creole Echoes* (introduction and notes), 221
Welty, Eudora, 110
West, Cornel, 12, 102
West Indies. *See* Caribbean islands
White, Deborah Gray, *Ar'n't I a Woman*, 33
White, Walter, 144
White Citizens Council, 87
White Knights of the Mississippi Ku Klux Klan, 103
Whiteness, 7, 12; Creoles of Color and, 212, 235; guilt of, 356; legal claim to, 237; Louisiana five-generation test for, 237; meaning of, 28–29, 30, 32, 380 (n. 40); new southern Sunbelt and, 28, 35, 36; physical appearance and, 235; plantation culture and, 278–79; recognition of slavery and, 47, 199
Whitfield, Lynn, 246
Whitman, Alden, 157
Whitman, Walt, 74, 254, 255
Williams, John A., 95
Williams, Myrlie Evers, 103
Williams, Patricia A., 64–65; *The Alchemy of Race and Rights*, 337–38; *Open House*, 44–45, 49
Williams, Samm-Art, *Home*, 34
Williams, Sherley Anne, *Dessa Rose*, 37
Williamson, Joel, 208; *Crucible of Race*, 33
Winfrey, Oprah, 85
Wirth, Louis, 143
Witnessing Lynching (Rice, ed.), 86
Wolcott, Marion Post, 23–24, 25
Womanist theology, 340, 347, 364–65
Women: artistic production of, 342, 346; black historical narratives of, 42–43;

Creole plaçage and, 213–15, 224, 247; Creoles of Color acceptable activities for, 224–25; enslavement conditions of, 304–5; Gaines's portrayal of, 304–9; new southern identity of, 336; plaçage as wealth accumulation by, 213–15; plantation culture and, 288; return to South by, 55–56; sexual abuse of, 58, 66, 68–70, 72, 78, 363; southern domestic culture of, 339, 342, 346, 349, 367; Walker's concerns and, 335–74. *See also* Black woman's body; Gender; Sexism

Women's rights, 357

Women's Studies, 32

Works Progress Administration (WPA), 137, 140, 142, 145; accomplishments of, 148; founding of, 136. *See also* Federal Writers' Project

World poetry, 367–68

Wright, Charles, "Meditation on Form and Measure," 68

Wright, Richard, 9–10, 20, 32, 50, 101, 113, 115–19, 120, 133, 136–65, 170, 172, 175, 176–80, 185, 357, 380 (n. 39)
— life and career of: acceptance as American author of, 140, 149; autobiographical work of, 140, 149, 150, 151–58, 160–62, 164; biographers of, 139, 153; black inspirations for, 159; bridging and, 50, 62, 140, 150, 151, 163–64; Communist Party and, 139–40, 142, 147, 161, 163; early ambitions of, 136, 137, 142; expatriate life of, 148–49, 164–68, 177, 180; Federal Writers' Project and, 136–37, 139–43, 145, 146–47, 148, 191; final period of, 183–84; Gaines contrasted with, 273, 304; haiku of, 183–84; literary authenticity of, 153; literary models for, 159–60, 163; literary scope of, 162; mobility of, 148–49, 151–54, 164–65; modernist narrative of, 118, 150, 151, 153, 168; move to North of, 136–37; as professional writer, 137, 143, 144, 145, 149, 158, 162–63, 165, 167; publishing success of, 139–40, 148; southern racism and, 93–94, 95; view of South of, 117, 345, 346
— works of: *American Hunger*, 140, 149, 151–52, 153, 156–57, 158–59, 160–62, 163, 165; "Between the World and Me,"

164–65, 348; "Big Boy Leaves Home," 143, 147; *Black Boy*, 115–16, 140, 149, 151–56, 157–58, 160, 161–62, 163, 164, 165, 172, 180; *Black Metropolis* (introduction), 148; *Black Power*, 381 (n. 11); "Blueprint for Negro Writing," 115–19, 137, 147; "Bright and Morning Star," 140; "The Ethics of Living Jim Crow," 140; "Fire and Cloud," 139, 145; "Hell's Voodoo Half Acre," 138; "How 'Bigger' Was Born," 118; *Lawd Today*, 137; *The Long Dream*, 50; "The Man Who Killed a Shadow," 93; *Native Son*, 139–40, 147, 406 (n. 107); *Uncle Tom's Children*, 137, 139, 140, 147, 161, 163

Writers' Congress (1939), 135, 139, 166

Yaeger, Patricia, 14; *Dirt and Desire*, 31, 339

Yellin, Jean Fagin, *Incidents in the Life of a Slave Girl* (ed.), 42

Yerby, Frank, 50–52, 268–69; *Benton's Row*, 51; *The Dahomean*, 50; *A Darkness at Ingraham's Crest*, 50; evocation of place by, 269; expatriate life of, 50–51; Federal Writers' Project and, 137, 141, 143–44; *The Foxes of Harrow*, 51; *The Girl from Storyville*, 51; *The Saracen Blade*, 51; *The Serpent and the Staff*, 51; success of, 51–52; *The Vixens*, 51; white plantation romances of, 50, 51–52, 268–69

Yoknapatawpha County, 258

Young, John, 107

Young, Kevin, 167; *Giant Steps*, 9

Young, Reggie Scott, 56

Young, Robert, 377 (n. 6)

Young, Stark, *So Red the Rose*, 51

Youngblood, Shay, 10, 11, 20, 166–83, 185, 364; background and career of, 391 (n. 49); *Big Mama Stories*, 339, 391 (n. 49); *Black Girl in Paris*, 166, 167–80, 182, 185–86; effect of 9/11 on, 167, 182, 183, 184; "In a House of Wooden Monkeys," 166; pictorial method of, 168, 169–70, 177; *Shakin' the Mess Outta Misery*, 391 (n. 49); *Soul Kiss*, 172, 180–82; *Square Blues*, 391 (n. 49); *Talking Bones*, 391 (n. 49)

Zydeco, 247

www.ingramcontent.com/pod-product-compliance
Lightning Source LLC
Chambersburg PA
CBHW020648110726
47901CB00001B/94